40

£ 20-00
β2

Disability in Twentieth-Century German Culture

CoRPORealities: Discourses of Disability

David T. Mitchell and Sharon L. Snyder, editors

Disability in Twentieth-Century German Culture

Carol Poore

THE UNIVERSITY OF MICHIGAN PRESS   Ann Arbor

Copyright © by the University of Michigan 2007
All rights reserved
Published in the United States of America by
The University of Michigan Press
Manufactured in the United States of America
⊗ Printed on acid-free paper

2010   2009   2008   2007   4   3   2   1

A CIP catalog record for this book is available from the British Library.

Library of Congress Cataloging-in-Publication Data

Poore, Carol.
    Disability in twentieth-century German culture / Carol Poore.
        p.   cm. — (Corporealities : discourses of disability)
    Includes bibliographical references and index.
    ISBN-13: 978-0-472-11595-2 (cloth : alk. paper)
    ISBN-10: 0-472-11595-2 (cloth : alk. paper)
        1. People with disabilities—Germany (West)—History—20th
century.   2. People with disabilities—Germany (East)—History—20th
century.   3. People with disabilities—Germany (West)—Public
opinion.   4. People with disabilities—Germany (East)—Public
opinion.   5. Public opinion—Germany (West)   6. Public opinion—
Germany (East)   7. People with disabilities—Nazi persecution.
8. People with disabilities—United States—Case studies.   I. Title.

HV1559.G3P66   2007
305.9'08509430904—dc22   2007010657

Acknowledgments

In many ways, this book is a product of my entire personal and scholarly life, and it is deeply rewarding to thank everyone who has given me such extraordinary help and support along the way. My heartfelt appreciation goes to LeAnn Fields, senior executive editor at the University of Michigan Press, for guiding this book to publication. David Mitchell and Sharon Snyder honored me by including my book in their disability studies series, Corporealities. Rebecca Mostov and Anna M. Szymanski fielded my many technical questions with skill and patience, and Marcia LaBrenz and Jan Opdyke provided meticulous copyediting. A fellowship from the George A. and Eliza Gardner Howard Foundation and a sabbatical from Brown University gave me time for writing.

Grateful acknowledgment is made for permission to reprint portions of my articles: "'But Roosevelt Could Walk': Envisioning Disability in Germany and the United States," *Michigan Quarterly Review* 37:2 (spring 1998); "From Problem Child to Human Being: Positive Representations of Physical Disability in Germany," in *Heroes and Heroines in German Culture,* ed. Stephen Brockmann and James Steakley (Amsterdam: Rodopi, 2001); "'No Friend of the Third Reich': Disability as the Basis for Antifascist Resistance in Arnold Zweig's *Das Beil von Wandsbek,*" in *Disability Studies: Enabling the Humanities,* ed. Sharon Snyder et al. (New York: Modern Language Association, 2002); "The (Im)Perfect Human Being and the Beginning of Disability Studies in Germany," *New German Critique* 86 (spring-summer 2002); "Who Belongs? Disability and the German Nation in Postwar Literature and Film," *German Studies Review* 26:1 (February 2003); and "Recovering Disability Rights in Weimar Germany," *Radical History Review* 94 (winter 2006).

I conducted most of my research at the University of Wisconsin-Madison, including the Memorial Library and Special Collections, Kohler Art Library, Steenbock Agricultural Library, Law School Library, and Middleton Health Sciences Library. The outstanding collections there on national socialism and the German Democratic Republic proved especially useful. I also thank the Brown University interlibrary loan office, the Staatsbibliothek Preußischer Kulturbesitz (Berlin), and the libraries of the Humboldt University, the Free University, the Universität-Gesamthochschule Essen, and the Evangelische Fachhochschule Bochum. At Harvard University I used the Widener Library and the Botany Library of the Arnold Arboretum.

Colleagues and friends in Germany who carried on long conversations with me and supplied invaluable information about disability include Uschi Aurien, Theresia Degener, Ulrike Gottschalk, Gerda Jun, Rebecca Maskos, Erika Richter, Birgit Rothenberg, Ilja Seifert, Gusti Steiner (deceased), and Matthias Vernaldi. Friends and colleagues in the United States who supported me in similar ways include Richard Baker, Jan Cal, Bill and Lo Crossgrove, Jim Ferris, Milan Hauner, Keri Hickey, Dennis Hogan, Robert Holub, Simi Linton, Fred and Ursula Love, David Mitchell, Brigitte Palmer, Sharon Snyder, Jim Steakley, John and Connie Susa, and Rosemarie Garland-Thomson. Thanks to Katharina Gerstenberger and the graduate students at Cornell University, Jürgen Schaupp and the graduate students at the University of Wisconsin-Madison, Stephen Brockmann, and Jim Steakley for inviting me to give lectures that eventually became book chapters.

At Brown, I have learned a great deal from the students in my disability studies courses, especially Dominika Bednarska and Alina Engelman. Thanks to Susan Pliner, Elyse Chaplin, and Catherine Axe, successive disability support services coordinators at Brown, who gave me opportunities to reach the wider university community and worked tirelessly to create a more accessible university. Many facilities management employees, especially Alice Chin, Robert La Vigne, and Michael McCormick, constructed and maintained the safe, accessible environments that are the necessary basis for my research and teaching.

I am grateful to colleagues who read and critiqued my manuscript, including Sally Chivers, Bill Crossgrove, Ulrike Gottschalk, Vicki Hill, Nicole Markotic, Diethelm Prowe, Marc Silberman, Roberto Simanowski, Duncan Smith, Anne Waldschmidt, and the anonymous readers. Of course, any errors remaining in the book are mine alone. Special thanks go to David Bathrick for being the first to encourage me to write about disability in Germany during a conversation many years ago on Rutledge Street. He published my first article on this topic, and Helen Fehervary wrote a long, serious critique of it. I greatly appreciate Sander Gilman's interest in my work over the years. As so many times before, Jost Hermand was my first and most engaged reader.

Throughout my life, I have been unusually fortunate to encounter many people who gave me opportunities often unavailable to disabled people, and I thank them all. At the beginning was Mrs. Hampton Rowland, principal of Chase Street Elementary School in Athens, Georgia, who allowed me to attend kindergarten at my local public school in 1954 long before children with disabilities had the legal right to an appropriate education. I would also like to recognize my colleagues in the Brown University Department of German Studies who hired me in 1982: Dagmar Barnouw, Bill Crossgrove, Kay Goodman, Fred Love, Albert Schmitt, Duncan Smith, and Bob Warnock—a unique group of genuine intellectuals. The medical treatment I received at the Georgia Warm Springs Foundation in the 1950s and 1960s was always premised on the belief that people who had had polio would go on to live full lives. More recently, Dr. Julie Silver and her staff at the Spaulding Rehabilitation Center introduced me to the pleasures of scootering, which has given me more energy for intellectual pursuits.

For all kinds of personal support, I am indebted to my friends Pat Desnoyers, Vicki, Dennis, Emily and Lucas Hill, Kathy McElroy, David Newby, and Wit Ylitalo. I was lucky to grow up in a loving family that was always a source of strength and fun among my aunts, uncles, and cousins Hugh and Laura Poore, Drayton and Jan Poore, Edna and Hale Bradley, Ann Gurley, James Poore, Douglas Bradley, Wayne Bradley, Marie Dawkins, and Hope Beasley.

This book is dedicated to the memory of my father, Charles Lee Poore (1917–97), who was always there; and to my mother, Lillian Jasa Poore, who has survived a lifetime of mental illness with great fortitude and dignity.

Contents

Illustrations

Abbreviations

ABM	Arbeitsgemeinschaft Behinderte in den Medien (Project Group on Disabled People in the Media)
ABiD	Allgemeiner Behindertenverband in Deutschland (General Association of the Disabled in Germany)
ADA	Americans with Disabilities Act
BDM	Bund deutscher Mädel (League of German Girls)
BSV	Blinden- und Sehschwachenverband (Association for the Blind and Visually Impaired)
CDU	Christlich-Demokratische Union (Christian Democratic Union)
CeBeeF	Bundesarbeitsgemeinschaft der Clubs Behinderter und ihrer Freunde (National Coalition of Clubs of the Handicapped and Their Friends)
DKOV	*Deutsche Kriegsopferversorgung*
DKP	Deutsche Kommunistische Partei (German Communist Party)
FDP	Freie Demokratische Partei (Free Democratic Party)
FRG	Federal Republic of Germany (West Germany)
GDR	German Democratic Republic (East Germany)
GSV	Gehörlosen- und Schwerhörigenverband (Association for the Deaf and Hard of Hearing)
HJ	Hitler Jugend (Hitler Youth)
ISL	Interessenvertretung Selbstbestimmt Leben in Deutschland (Independent Living Movement in Germany)
KLV	Kinderlandverschickung (Nazi program for evacuating children during World War II)
KPD	Kommunistische Partei Deutschlands (Communist Party of Germany)
NSDAP	Nationalsozialistische Deutsche Arbeiterpartei (National Socialist German Workers Party/Nazi Party)
NSKOV	Nationalsozialistische Kriegsopferversorgung (National Socialist War Victims Association)

NSV   Nationalsozialistische Volkswohlfahrt (National Socialist People's Welfare Office)

ORP   Rassenpolitisches Amt (Office of Racial Politics)

PDS   Partei des demokratischen Sozialismus (Party of Democratic Socialism)

POW   Prisoner of war

RBK   Reichsbund der Körperbehinderten (Reich League of the Physically Handicapped)

RBV   Reichsdeutscher Blindenverband (German Association of the Blind)

REGEDE   Reichsverband der Gehörlosen Deutschlands (Reich Union of the Deaf of Germany)

RWU   Reichsanstalt für Film und Bild in Wissenschaft und Unterricht (Reich Institute for Films and Images in Science and Education)

SA   Sturmabteilung (Nazi brown-shirt storm troopers)

SBK   Selbsthilfebund der Körperbehinderten (Self-Help League of the Physically Handicapped)

SBZ   Sowjetische Besatzungszone (Soviet Occupation Zone)

SED   Sozialistische Einheitspartei Deutschlands (Socialist Unity Party of Germany)

SMAD   Soviet Military Administration in Germany

SPD   Sozialdemokratische Partei Deutschlands (Social Democratic Party of Germany)

SS   Schutzstaffel (Nazi black-shirt storm troopers)

UCLA   University of California at Los Angeles

UN   United Nations

VdK   Verband der Kriegsbeschädigten, Kriegshinterbliebenen, und Sozialrentner (Association of War-Disabled, War Survivors, and Social Pensioners)

Preface

The goal of this book is to write disability into a central place in the German cultural history of the twentieth century. It is actually surprising that this has not been done before. After all, many leading artists, writers, filmmakers, and others have taken disability as one of their most significant themes. Intense debates have occurred in many sociopolitical contexts over how to interpret and evaluate particular kinds of variations in human bodies. In these controversies, disability has often been a focal point for clashes between more inclusive, democratic visions of citizenship and intolerant, authoritarian standpoints. And fundamental ethical questions about the value and quality of human life have frequently revolved around issues related to disability.

Even a cursory survey can easily show that both cultural representations of disability and debates about the proper places for disabled people in German society have often been central to major controversies about aesthetics, normality, individuality, citizenship, and morality. Yet, with a few notable exceptions, disability has remained outside the focus of most cultural historians in German studies.[1] This is so for a number of reasons. First, until recently most scholars have considered disability mainly from a medical rather than a minority perspective. That is, they have viewed disability primarily as a problem of individual impairment and thus as a subject for experts in medicine, rehabilitation, or education rather than as a cultural, political, and social phenomenon having to do with the meanings given to particular kinds of bodies. Second, when historians have dealt with disability, they have usually defined their research according to its cause. For example, there are historical studies about disabled veterans, the social welfare system for disabled workers, and the development of eugenics. Monographs recount the history of treating and educating various groups such as people who are mentally ill, blind, or deaf. And there are even a few analyses of how members of some of these groups have been represented in the cultural sphere. The main drawback of such partial approaches, however, is that they do not tie these phenomena together as comprising general discourses about disability and disabled people. Third, it is still a relatively new idea to most cultural historians that ubiquitous one-sided representations of disability have real consequences for people who are disabled—in contrast to more generally accepted views about the harmfulness of, say, anti-Semitic, racial, or gender stereotypes. It is all the more surprising that German cultural historians have neglected to focus on disability because struggles over definitions of *normality*—which has often been held up as the antithesis of *disability*—had such grave consequences in twentieth-century Germany.

Scholars who are themselves members of previously excluded groups—such as women, racial and ethnic minorities, gays and lesbians, and sometimes even working-class people—have generally taken the lead in challenging and transforming outmoded interpretive paradigms rooted in paternalism or prejudice. Linked to the disability rights movement that began in the United States in the late 1960s, disabled scholars have been hired as American university faculty in somewhat more significant numbers in recent decades. Some of these colleagues, along with nondisabled researchers who share their perspectives, have been engaged in developing disability studies in the humanities, though more so in areas such as English and American cultural studies and history than in German studies. Scholars in this rapidly growing interdisciplinary field consider disability not in terms of medical issues but with regard to far-reaching questions about how bodies are represented in culture. Viewed like this, disability becomes a category of human variation to be studied in the complex ways accorded to race, ethnicity, class, gender, or sexual orientation. Informed by this perspective, my book has two main trajectories. In political terms, I focus on the struggles among advocates of charity, rehabilitation experts, and proponents of segregation or elimination, on the one hand, and the increasingly successful efforts of disabled people and their allies to create more democratic models of inclusion on the other. In cultural terms, I trace a development from the traditional use of disability as a negative metaphor to more realistic depictions of disabled people as ordinary human beings and to the growing participation of disabled people in creating cultural texts. My book shows how disabled people in Germany have moved from being relatively passive objects to more active subjects and from being represented mainly by others to telling their own stories.

I have found it easier to bring disability into focus as a cultural phenomenon by keeping in mind two problems of definition. First, and more specifically, it is often useful for purposes of interpretation to distinguish among disabled veterans, people with disabilities considered to be hereditary who were the main targets of eugenics, and other civilians whose disabilities resulted from illnesses or accidents. It is just as important, however, to be attuned to the links among these three groups such as representations that blur the borders between them or fears of falling from a relatively unproblematic status to a more stigmatized position. Second, I have attempted to employ the most expansive definition of *disability* possible. At first, I planned to focus on cultural representations of physical disability, but I soon found this to be an untenable limitation. For one thing, I learned that the dividing lines between physical and mental disabilities were often not all that clear. For another, since people with mental disabilities have always been the most stigmatized group and they were the main disabled victims of Nazism, I soon saw that the subject of mental disability was essential to my project. Consequently, the range of embodied characteristics that I associate with disability includes physical, sensory, cognitive, and mental impairments along with all those familiar cultural figures such as freaks, invalids, monsters, cripples, idiots, and the insane. I am well aware that this approach leads to impreciseness at points. I hope, however, that it also illuminates unexpected connections and opens up thought-provoking problems that other scholars will refine in the future. Here a note about the language used in this book is necessary. I do not place quotation marks around pejoratives such as *cripple* or *idiot* when it is obvious that they are other people's words used in the context of earlier times. I do set them off whenever it seems necessary to indicate clearly that the terms are not my own.

Intensively studying disability in German culture opened up rich perspectives and a host of fascinating questions that I had not imagined before. This means that the main organizational problem in writing this book was not contending with a dearth of material but having to select from an enormous amount of potential sources. Some readers may take issue with the topics I chose to emphasize. I hope they will go on to research other areas in this field. Rich projects await colleagues interested in writing about the cultural history of disability in Germany before World War I. Topics that immediately come to mind include representations of disability understood as broadly as possible in art, literature, and the public sphere; the cultural history of monstrosities and freaks; the meanings of ugliness and beauty in classical aesthetics; automatons and prostheses in romanticism; cultural discourses about degeneracy and heredity in the late nineteenth century; gendered portrayals of disability and illness; and so forth.[2]

My book can be described as an extended exercise in seeing disability where its broader significance as an important cultural phenomenon has previously been overlooked. To accomplish this, I follow two strategies. First, awareness of disability as an important sociocultural category makes it possible to reinterpret many well-known art and literary works, films, and media depictions as texts that are also about disability, although scholars have generally not emphasized this before. Second, I also focus on points where intense debates erupted over the proper places for disabled people in the public sphere. These controversies were often flash points of struggles over such things as the meaning of "Germanness," the makeup of the nation, the emancipatory possibilities of socialism, or the inclusiveness of democracy. Where appropriate, I also include comparisons with the United States in order to critique assumptions about normality more effectively. Throughout, I have been concerned with trying to recover the lost or suppressed voices of disabled Germans themselves.

Against the background of the two main prewar discourses about disability—the integrative approach of rehabilitation and the antidemocratic perspectives of eugenics—chapter 1 analyzes the flood of images of disability after World War I found in visual art (especially that of Grosz, Dix, Beckmann, and Hoerle), literature (Leonhard Frank, Toller, and Remarque), and other kinds of texts such as autobiographies, films, political statements, and rehabilitation manuals. Diverging perspectives on disability were integral to debates over the meaning of democracy in the Weimar Republic. Many progressive artists and writers depicted disabled veterans using disability as a metaphor through which to critique social injustice. Others, influenced by dadaism and constructivism, explored the new connections between human bodies and prosthetic technologies, linking the figures of the disabled veteran and the factory worker. Advocates of eugenics used negative images of disability both to attack modern art as degenerate and to argue that people with hereditary disabilities should be eliminated. And in a democratic spirit some disabled Germans rebutted stereotypical views of disability and founded their first self-advocacy organizations.

Chapter 2 explores how central disability was to Nazi culture and politics by drawing together material about disabled veterans, people considered to have hereditary diseases, and other disabled civilians. Since national socialists always stressed the effectiveness of "pictures" for indoctrinating the population, this chapter highlights how important visual images of disability were during the Third Reich with respect to both propaganda and the appearance of disabled people in public. First, I discuss how national socialists claimed to honor disabled veterans as the "leading citizens of the nation" and orchestrated gatherings of these men on official occasions. Next I review the laws and practices that excluded people viewed as having hereditary diseases from the national community as background for a detailed overview of Nazi propaganda directed against this group of disabled people. In the following section, about the disabled victims of sterilization and "euthanasia," I try to retrieve the voices of these individuals as much as possible. Then I examine how the official Nazi organizations for disabled civilians presented images of disability to the public and attempted to negotiate between collaboration and self-advocacy. The most difficult aspect of writing about disability during the Third Reich is to try to imagine how disabled people themselves experienced Nazi propaganda about them and Nazi policies whose purposes ran the gamut from rehabilitation to elimination. In many ways this is an impossible task, for indifference, neglect, censorship, or murder silenced their voices. Creative use of sources, however, enables the historian to uncover indications of how some disabled people reacted to Nazi propaganda and policies and even some noteworthy stirrings of resistance to stigmatization and exclusion.

From 1933 to 1945, it was only in exile that Germans could publicly continue to profess a commitment to universal human equality and advocate adequate support for poor, disabled, and ill people. Chapter 3 investigates several texts written in exile by opponents of Nazism. The philosopher Ernst Bloch critiqued rigid eugenic norms of health and insisted instead on remedying social injustices that were rooted in class inequalities. And in literary works published in exile a few authors (Bertolt Brecht, Maria Leitner, and Arnold Zweig) depicted disabled characters in ways that challenged exclusionary norms. These writers created utopian visions that conceived of disabled people as ordinary human beings, portrayed their social exclusion as caused by oppressive environments rather than inherent individual flaws, and even imagined them as positive heroes.

During the Third Reich, images of disability and illness constantly circulated as the Nazis attempted to define whom they considered to be inferior outsiders. Therefore, studying images of disability in postwar culture, as well as how disabled people appeared in the public sphere, is a crucial part of debates about continuities and transformations of Nazi ideology. The first part of chapter 4 analyzes disability in the art, literature, and films of the immediate postwar period. I compare representations of disability in several works of postwar literature and then contrast the first postwar German film, *Die Mörder sind unter uns* (The Murderers Are among Us, 1946), with the American film *The Best Years of Our Lives* (1946), using this as a case study for representations of disabled veterans in both countries. I then reinterpret the most scandalous postwar film, *Die Sünderin* (The Sinner, 1951) as a film about disability and a remake of the Nazi "euthanasia" film *Ich klage an* (I Accuse, 1941).

The second part of the chapter focuses on public controversies over cultural representations of disability, including sections on disabled veterans as victims or activists, rehabilitation rhetoric and early self-help efforts of physically disabled civilians, and the growing efforts to treat and represent people with mental impairments as individuals with human dignity rather than as "lives unworthy of life."

Chapter 5 presents three transitional representations of physical disability in (West) German film, literature, and media since the late 1960s. These illustrate how old representations of disability as nothing but negative metaphors began to break down and be replaced by more complex depictions. The film director Rainer Werner Fassbinder set out to break taboos but ended up re-creating stereotypes of disability in his film *Chinese Roulette* (1976). The dramatist Franz Xaver Kroetz rejected metaphors of disability in favor of depicting disabled characters who are simply ordinary human beings searching for happiness. Finally, in the debates over whether Wolfgang Schäuble could be chancellor while using a wheelchair and whether Franklin D. Roosevelt should be shown as disabled, the old view of disability as standing for shameful incompetence and weakness clashed with a newer perception that visibly disabled people could also be competent and powerful in a positive sense.

The relationship of socialist theory and practice to the body, and specifically to the disabled body, is a long, complex story. Chapter 6 investigates disability and socialist images of the human being in the culture of the German Democratic Republic (GDR) from two angles. Against the background of the difficult postwar years, early hopes for constructing a better Germany, and growing disillusionment with really existing socialism, I first show how many authors began to represent disability and illness in order to challenge the claim within socialist realism that collective and individual interests are identical. Using sources such as laws, official policy statements, and biographies and autobiographies of disabled GDR citizens, I then focus on locations assigned to disability in the socialist state in light of the importance attached to performance and the development of the "socialist personality." The socialist state provided many benefits to disabled people. Nevertheless, their experience of marginalization made many of them ready to participate in the popular movements of 1989, which demanded more democratic rights. Consequently, a specific, unresolved problem of disability within socialism was that of reconciling equality (based in economics) with freedom (based in human variation).

In chapter 7, I survey the emergence of disability rights, disability culture, and disability studies since the early 1970s in West Germany and reunified Germany. I highlight the efforts of disabled West Germans to claim their civil rights, and I assess the state of disability rights in Germany up to the passage of the General Law on Equal Treatment in 2006. I give an overview of the multitude of disability culture projects in Germany, such as autobiographies, women's groups, theater and dance organizations, films, art, exhibitions, and so forth, which are all concerned with developing new forms of self-expression for embodied experience. Finally, I consider the similarities and differences between disability studies in Germany and the United States today. Just as disabled Germans have been increasingly successful in gaining civil rights, disabled scholars there are beginning to have a greater impact on setting the terms of debates about disability.

Chapter 8 shows how concepts of the "German" and the "American" appear as national subtexts in major biocultural and bioethical debates related to disability today. First, I discuss briefly how these debates in the United States refer to Germany almost solely through the negative example of the Nazi past. To illustrate the different ways in which knowledge about this past shapes these discussions, I then contrast the reactions in each country to the controversial philosopher and bioethicist Peter Singer. In German debates about bioethics, the United States frequently appears as a source of technological and scientific innovation, which some view as desirable and others criticize for neglecting ethical issues in favor of economic profits. I show how these conflicting views emerged in the so-called Philosophers' Debate of 1999–2000 over Peter Sloterdijk's speech "Rules for the Human Zoo," which considered the ethical limits of gene technology. Finally, in contrast to these mostly negative or ambivalent views of the United States, I discuss the current efforts in Germany to pass an antidiscrimination law as a biocultural debate that draws on a positive conception of the United States as a model for civil rights. In conclusion, I reflect on some of the lessons that Germans and Americans might learn from each other's histories in these areas.

Narratives about disability have the potential to illuminate the strength of norms within particular societies, for if told in the right way they must always reflect on both the individual and the societal responses to someone who disrupts assumptions about how the human body should function and thus about what it means to be a human being. Keeping this framework in mind, the brief memoir that serves as the concluding chapter has two main emphases. The first part recounts how I experienced West Germany during my first stay there in 1970–71 as a visibly disabled young American woman. I know of no other autobiographical text by a disabled American traveler to Germany. In the second part, I reflect on what it has been like for me as a disabled person to become a university professor of German studies in the United States, to return to Germany over the years, and to develop a professional interest in disability studies. This approach hopefully connects my personal story with larger developments. One of these is the enormous transformation in Germany since 1945 from the Nazi view of many disabled people as "lives unworthy of life" to the current efforts to pass an anti-discrimination law. Another is the ongoing debate over the meanings of *access* and *diversity* in the United States. I finished this chapter some time ago, before writing the greater part of this book, and laid it aside. Upon rereading it, I found that it complements many of the issues addressed in the preceding chapters, and so I decided to take it out of the drawer and put it in the book. I hope the reader will view my story as a small building block in the much larger comparative cultural history of Germany and the United States.

CHAPTER 1 • Disability in the Culture of the Weimar Republic

How did disabled people fit into the era of war and revolution, cultural experimentation, economic turmoil, and political crisis that was the Weimar Republic? What was old and what was new about the options open to them? On the one hand, many remained objects of charity or social outcasts. Some lived their lives as invalids hidden away by their ashamed families, and about seventy thousand starved to death in psychiatric institutions in the hunger years during and after World War I.[1] The presence of "crippled beggars" on the streets still recalled medieval scenes at times. Others appeared in freak shows at fairs such as Uncle Pelle's Rummelplatz in the working-class Berlin district of Wedding, where the artist Christian Schad painted *Agosta, der Flügelmensch und Rasha, die schwarze Taube* (Agosta, the Winged Man, and Rasha, the Black Dove, 1929). But, by contrast, many other disabled people received competent medical care, rehabilitation for work, and education in regular schools or institutions for "crippled children" to become as self-supporting as possible. They lived conventional lives or more audacious ones as it suited them, finding circles of friends, acquaintances, workmates, colleagues, and comrades in which they moved and were accepted with relative ease. In a society struggling to make the transition from authoritarian empire to democracy, the life possibilities open to disabled people oscillated between limited forms of stigmatized existence and more expansive choices shaped by commitments to solidarity.

In the unstable Weimar Republic, disability became a focal point for sociopolitical and cultural controversies in newly intense ways, and ascertaining the positions of disabled people in society was a means of measuring the success of the new democracy. The Weimar constitution proclaimed the ideal of equality, but who would actually enjoy all the privileges of being a citizen in the German nation? Were people with certain types of bodies going to have fewer rights than others?[2] And who would decide? The masses of disabled veterans returning from World War I presented a new challenge to goals of social inclusiveness. Before the war, the problem of disability had seemed bound up to a great extent

Fig. 1. Christian Schad, *Agosta, the Winged Man, and Rasha, the Black Dove,* 1929. Oil on canvas, 120 × 80 cm. Private Collection. (Photo courtesy of Kunsthaus Zürich. © 2007 Christian Schad Stiftung Aschaffenburg/Artists Rights Society [ARS], New York, VG Bild-Kunst, Bonn.)

in the social question. At that time, disabled people were disproportionately poor children and adults or workers injured in industrial accidents, and the churches had taken the lead in caring for them before government welfare programs began.[3] While the relationship between disability and class background never ceased to be significant, the war created large numbers of disabled veterans from all social classes. This meant that providing for disabled people could no longer be viewed as primarily a charitable endeavor for the poor. Rather, since healthy young men from all across the socioeconomic spectrum had suddenly become disabled in the service of the fatherland, they seemed to have an unquestionably legitimate claim to the moral and financial support necessary for reintegrating them into society. Consequently, rehabilitation professionals who had previously worked mainly with "crippled children" began to apply their expertise to the needs of disabled veterans. Furthermore, plans to rehabilitate veterans often intersected with new sorts of discourses about rehabilitating disabled workers. Improvements in prosthetic technologies, along with increasing emphasis on efficiency and modern production methods, meant that a wider range of occupations opened up to many persons with functional impairments. These transformed interrelationships between human bodies and machines had both liberating and oppressive aspects that were constant sources of political and cultural tensions.

Competing with discourses that called for rehabilitating and reintegrating disabled veterans, workers, and young people were various types of stigmatizing, eliminationist discourses that challenged the right of some disabled people to a place as equal citizens and even their right to exist. The "cult of health and beauty" associated with the life reform movement since the late nineteenth century still flourished after the war, serving in many ways to create a hostile atmosphere toward those viewed as ill, disabled, or ugly.[4] Similarly, the discourses of degeneracy and eugenics had also begun in the late nineteenth century. The perception that the war had killed or disabled many of the healthiest young German men, however, gave a strong impetus both to postwar advocates of eugenics, who opposed squandering the nation's resources on the "unfit" and thus wanted to limit their reproduction, and to proponents of outright "euthanasia" such as Karl Binding and Alfred Hoche, who entitled their influential pamphlet of 1920 *Die Freigabe der Vernichtung lebensunwerten Lebens* (Permission for the Annihilation of Lives Unworthy of Life). These eliminationist discourses became even stronger after the onset of the world economic crisis in 1929.

All of these debates—whether well intentioned or hostile—about the proper place for disabled people in society were carried out largely by rehabilitation and medical experts, government officials, and cultural critics. That is, they were for the most part opinions of people who were not disabled about what should be done with those who were. But in the new democracy some disabled people began to assess their own situations and assert their rights in a number of ways. Disabled veterans formed large self-advocacy organizations, and disabled civilians created self-help groups that were small but significant exercises in democracy. Struggles occurred over hierarchies of disability having to do with cause (military or civilian, acquired or hereditary) and type (physical or mental). Yet for the first time some disabled people united to define their own needs, claim their civil rights, and oppose those who wanted to curtail their opportunities. In this manner, they challenged many opinions of the self-proclaimed experts.

Just as significant sociopolitical controversies were occurring over the place of disabled people in the German nation, the question of representing disability took on new dimensions in the Weimar Republic. Representations of disability were plentiful and conspicuous throughout the cultural sphere—from popular culture to high culture, from events designed for the masses to the most sophisticated works of art. Interpretations of the bodies of disabled veterans intersected with depictions of other disabled people in multitudes of ways. Large fairs and exhibitions brought disability and illness to the attention of mass audiences. For example, a Reichstag exhibition in Berlin entitled "The Wartime Care of Sick and Wounded Soldiers" drew up to 100,000 spectators in the winter of 1914–15.[5] Later the "Gesolei" hygiene exhibition ("Gesundheit, Sozialfürsorge, Leibesübungen" or Health, Social Welfare, Exercise), which emphasized eugenics, attracted 7.5 million visitors in Düsseldorf in 1926.[6] Popular magazines, films, and lectures interpreted the bodies of disabled veterans for a wide public.[7] Rehabilitation manuals presented photographs of men (rarely of women) enabled to work again through the wonders of medicine and prosthetic technology. Progressive and leftist artists, photographers, and writers created a flood of images of impoverished "war cripples" and horribly wounded soldiers in order to critique militarism and social injustice. In their copious publications, advocates of eugenics attacked some disabled people as "useless eaters" and aesthetically repellent. And for the first time significant numbers of disabled people undertook to represent themselves in a variety of ways. Disabled veterans' organizations challenged outdated stereotypes of invalidism and dependency, creating forums for dialogue and information sharing in their publications. Tens of thousands of these men participated in carefully choreographed mass demonstrations throughout Germany, confronting the public with their disabled bodies in an attempt to voice their grievances effectively. And a few better-educated disabled people wrote autobiographical texts, historical analyses, or scholarly articles, giving their own views of their lives and the world around them.

As in the sociopolitical arena, all of these cultural representations of disability oscillated between the old and the new, between depictions of disabled people as pitiful, ill, ugly, repellent, or uncanny and those that began to imagine them as more capable, healthy, and ordinary, particularly with regard to the sphere of work. Yet the tensions between these two ways of looking at disability were not simple contrasts in black and white. In texts drawing on older iconographies of disabled people as pathetic victims, strange creatures, or human monstrosities, even these traditional figures often resonated with new meanings in the rapidly changing society that was Weimar Germany. And in innovative depictions linking disabled people and the working world—whether in photography or art—a new trend toward inclusiveness frequently seemed to come at the price of molding the compliant human body to fit into rigidly Taylorized production.

In controversies over how disability should be represented in the cultural sphere, conservative nationalists were often pitted against progressives and leftists. Believing that art should uphold the "ideal," specifically the ideal of a strong, healthy, authoritarian nation, the conservative camp generally wanted to eliminate representations of disability, along with all other extreme images of misery, from the cultural sphere. These circles still agreed with Emperor Wilhelm II, who had condemned modern art in a speech on December 18, 1901 as follows: "If art does nothing but portray misery as even more disgusting than it actually is (which frequently happens now), art commits a sin against the German people. The cultivation of ideals is the greatest cultural task."[8] By contrast, progressive and leftist artists and writers did not want to blot out images of disability but rather made it into one of their most significant themes. Intensifying culturally familiar discourses about disabled people as pitiful or grotesque, they created shocking representations of disabled and wounded veterans in order to confront the public with the hollowness of nationalistic, militaristic ideals. And with their portrayals of disabled workers as functional assemblages of mechanical, prosthetic parts they created unforgettable anticapitalist images.

As is characteristic of most eras in which those creating the memorable images generally do not belong to the group they are representing, it was the ways in which disability appeared to constitute some kind of pressing social problem that caught the attention of artists, writers, critics, and other intellectuals. This means, however, that the most famous images of disability from Weimar culture should not be misconstrued as giving a true picture of the range of experiences open to disabled citizens at this time. The bodies of disabled veterans could be infused with symbolic meanings to make statements about the German nation. The bodies of disabled workers could be depicted to make statements about the promises and perils of technology in a time of rapid social change. The bodies of those with congenital or hereditary impairments could be presented in eugenic terms as threats to the health and even the survival of the German people. But in general these well-known cultural discourses about disability were quite selective and hardly made room for other types of stories that might have shown disabled people simply as ordinary human beings. In a unique survey of a group of physically disabled people carried out by a disabled teacher in Berlin in 1932, for example, along with sad and difficult experiences, many respondents told of being accepted and supported by family and friends, finding satisfying work, and living rather contented, happy lives.[9] Much more historical research that makes creative use of documents is needed if we are to understand how such positive experiences came about and how typical they were. Any discussion of disability in Weimar culture, however, needs to complement canonical representations by taking into account as much as possible how disabled people themselves viewed their lives and the world around them. No group of representations yields the one truth about disability, but taken together they create multilayered interweavings of embodied relationships.

This chapter focuses on the major ways in which disabled people appeared in the public sphere, were represented by others, and represented themselves during the Weimar Republic. First, I discuss the significance of disabled veterans as a large, new social group, the goals of the German rehabilitation system for them, and some culturally important reactions of these veterans to becoming disabled. Then, after briefly describing how disability and illness appear in prewar expressionism, I analyze depictions of disabled veterans in Weimar art and literature that show these figures in a socially critical manner as impoverished, pitiful, or grotesque. Next I explore the intersections between such portrayals of disabled veterans and those of workers, including photography, rehabilitation manuals, and other texts. Here the main tendency was to reflect from several perspectives on how these figures were connected through their prostheses with the technological world of machines and industry. The following sections focus on disabled civilians, particularly those groups that eugenicists targeted for elimination. Here I bring out the major ways in which the advocates of eugenics conceived of disabled people as defective and, linked to this, held much of

Weimar art to be degenerate. Finally, I present some significant examples of how disabled people formed self-advocacy organizations and wrote about their own lives and perceptions of the world around them during this period.

The Disabled Veterans Return

Organ Grinders or Respectable Citizens?

With the 2.7 million disabled or permanently ill veterans who returned from the battlefields of World War I, disability came into view in the public sphere in Germany in a different way and to a greater extent than ever before.[10] Fifty years earlier, during the Franco-Prussian War, 80 to 90 percent of seriously wounded soldiers had died of infections and other complications,[11] and only about 70,000 "war invalids" lived through that conflict.[12] Receiving insufficient government pensions, many of these men had no alternative but begging—traditionally the only means of survival for many disabled people throughout history[13]— and so the sight of disabled veterans playing their barrel organs for a handout or selling matches and other sundries became common throughout Germany in the late nineteenth century.[14] By World War I, however, medical advances enabled many more soldiers to survive previously mortal wounds, and advances in rehabilitation technology made it easier for more disabled veterans to return to work. Yet in the economic and social turmoil of the postwar years the government struggled to provide the substantial resources necessary to reintegrate these men into society. In spite of great efforts to meet their needs, both economic exigencies and problematic welfare policies increasingly alienated these men from the Republic, often making them susceptible to Nazi recruitment in the later Weimar years.[15]

Accordingly, the sudden presence of masses of newly disabled men was one of the most pressing tests facing the new Weimar democracy. Could men with these multiple kinds of disabilities be reintegrated into the defeated nation and, if so, how? Were men with such bodies to be viewed as heroes, pitiful victims, or ordinary citizens? What was the relationship going to be between the "war disabled" and those whose disabilities had other causes (the "civilian disabled" or "peacetime disabled")? The barrel organ became an icon of the controversies over these questions. In the tradition of the nineteenth century, hundreds of these instruments were produced in Germany as soon as the war began in 1914, indicating the widespread assumption that newly disabled veterans would soon need to be playing them on the streets for alms.[16] An older artist, Heinrich Zille, drew disabled organ grinders and other "crippled beggars" in their Berlin milieu in a naturalistic style that demonstrated his sympathy for these poor outcasts. An expressionist artist, Max Beckmann, however, in his *Leierkastenmann* from the *Berliner Reise* ("Organ Grinder" from the "Berlin Journey," 1922), heightened the feelings of social fragmentation and physical grotesqueness through elongations and distortions of the disabled figures. From many quarters, voices were heard rejecting the barrel organ as an unworthy, humiliating fate, including trade union activists, rehabilitation experts, and many disabled veterans themselves. These persons argued that it would be advantageous for both individuals and society in general if these men would become self-supporting again. Social outcast or respectable citizen—these were the poles between which attitudes toward disabled veterans—and other disabled people as well—moved in the new democracy.

Rehabilitation between Conformity and Empowerment

In 1915, the orthopedic surgeon Konrad Biesalski (1868–1930) published an influential pamphlet entitled *Kriegskrüppelfürsorge: Ein Aufklärungswort zum Troste und zur Mahnung* (The Care of War Cripples: A Word of Enlightenment to Console and Admonish). Biesalski was the director of a large institution for crippled children called the Oskar-Helene Home in Berlin-Zehlendorf (today the Orthopedic Clinic of the Free University) and one of the leading rehabilitation experts in Germany. In his pamphlet, he summed up the goal of rehabilitation with the rallying cry that he wanted to create "taxpayers rather than charity recipients!" While he applied that slogan to all disabled people, he made a special point about disabled veterans: "The numerous war cripples should merge into the masses of the people as if nothing had happened to them."[17] This statement captures the contradictory tendencies in rehabilitation theory and practice at the time. On the one hand, an expert such as Biesalski viewed disabled people, and veterans in particular, as having the right to be integrated into society rather than stigmatized and as capable in almost all instances of returning to gainful employment. On the other hand, he characterized rehabilitation as a practice of forgetting the injuries of war. Consequently, this was a field in which the experts were to set the terms and which thus might be quite at odds with the actual experiences of veterans in adjusting to their disabilities. Or, to put this contradiction another way, rehabilitation could have a democratic thrust in terms of helping disabled people regain the possibility of living full lives, but it could also have an authoritarian, repressive effect by reintegrating soldiers into the military apparatus and workers into a rigidly controlled industrial system.

Influenced by portrayals of grotesque cripples and robotic, prosthesis-wearing workers in Weimar art, cultural historians have generally emphasized the latter view of rehabilitation as having mainly the function of propping up German industrial capacity and keeping the military machine supplied with human fodder.[18] If one keeps in mind the entire spectrum of the goals and effects of rehabilitation for all disabled people, however, its complexity as a cultural phenomenon becomes clearer, as some social and medical historians have demonstrated.[19] The German rehabilitation system as it developed during and after World War I was not merely a terroristic system for enforcing oppressive norms, as some Foucauldians assert, even though it certainly did tend in this direction to some extent.[20] Beyond this, it was also known as the most advanced and best-organized rehabilitation system in the world with its mixture of church-run and state-sponsored institutions and clinics. For example, two laws passed in 1920 were models of progressive policy in this area. Broadly debated within rehabilitation, legal, and political circles, the Prussian Law on Cripples' Welfare (Krüppelfürsorgegesetz) was the first German law to guarantee medical treatment, education, and vocational training to young people with physical disabilities.[21] A prominent Düsseldorf pediatrician who advocated this law described its purpose as follows: "No one in Prussia should become a cripple if this can be avoided. No cripple who can be healed or improved should have to do without the possibility of healing or improvement. No cripple who can learn an occupation should remain unemployed. No cripple should have to live in the future without love, care, and attention."[22] Furthermore, promoted by social democrats, trade unions, and other groups, the Prussian Law for the Employment of the Severely Disabled (Gesetz über die Beschäftigung Schwerbeschädigter) established quotas for employing disabled veterans and job protections for them.[23] Consequently, in order to understand the context of artistic depictions of the entire complex of disabled veterans, rehabilitation, and prosthetic technology, it is necessary first to explicate briefly the tensions within rehabilitation theory and practice over goals and methods as well as these experts' underlying assumptions about disabled people.

The roots of the rehabilitation system for disabled veterans in Germany go back to the orthopedic treatment of "crippled" children in the nineteenth century, and this development can be followed in the career of Konrad Biesalski. As soon as the war began, he proposed that his own children's clinic and others like it should admit disabled veterans for rehabilitation and prepare them to return not only to the army but also to their families, workplaces, and social environments.[24] Biesalski then applied his experiences rehabilitating disabled veterans after the war to "crippled" children and played an important role in securing the passage of the Law on Cripples' Welfare of 1920, which promised substantial improvements in the lives of disabled young people.[25] He began his pamphlet of 1915 by asserting that "today many thousands of our severely wounded brothers are looking fearfully with their families into the future, . . . wondering how they are to find work and bread again" (3). He thus addressed his pamphlet to disabled veterans, whom he exhorted to overcome their disabilities by following their treatment plans with steadfast willpower. Significantly, he also wanted to transform the negative attitudes of the general public toward cripples. He admonished his readers to overcome feelings of pity and revulsion and to accept these men back into their midst as valuable, capable citizens. In this connection, he declared that "the undignified sight of the war cripple as organ grinder or peddler should never be seen on our streets again" (20), and he proclaimed that "the cripple is not a repulsive picture of misery but my brother who is closer to me than ever before" (4).

Biesalski cast his own role in this process as that of the indispensable expert whose knowledge of wound management, physical therapy, and above all of prosthetic technology was crucial for rehabilitating these men. To illustrate his remarks more vividly, the pamphlet contains eighty-five photographs of successfully rehabilitated veterans, many working at various occupations while wearing prostheses. Frequently reprinted in newspapers and magazines, these photographs were part of a large visual discourse that sought to demonstrate the accomplishments of prosthetic technology. Similar images could often be seen in medical journals, advertisements of the orthopedic industry, information brochures of war cripples relief organizations, slide shows, and lectures. Furthermore, contemporary reports tell of groups taking tours through institutions for cripples in order to see for themselves what the patients could do with the help of new technologies and orthopedic appliances.[26]

A few examples serve to illustrate how Biesalski presented the varied purposes of rehabilitation. After ten weeks of treatment, an officer with a shattered arm and shoulder was "fully healed and returned to the front" (11). Outfitted with a lightweight prosthesis nine weeks after the amputation of his left leg, a captain was able to mount a horse again (23). In other photographs, the rehabilitation process could apply to any dis-

Fig. 2. "Master craftsman with no hands or feet working at the lathe, where he earns his bread like a healthy man." (From Konrad Biesalski, *Kriegskrüppelfürsorge: Ein Aufklärungswort zum Troste und zur Mahnung* [Hamburg: Voss, 1915], 30. Courtesy of Auburn University Libraries.)

abled person, although most of the men shown were undoubtedly veterans. Wearing prostheses, men with missing limbs, including some with neither hands nor feet, are shown working at various manual occupations such as operating a drill press or lathe. As was typical for the time, disability is presented here almost solely as a male problem because of the emphasis on veterans and workers, but two photographs show a young woman born with only one hand sewing without a prosthesis and knitting while wearing one. Obviously, Biesalski wanted rehabilitation to serve the goals of the military, but he also had a much more comprehensive conception of its goals, as he expressed in this statement: "The most important principle is that to the greatest possible extent the wounded man should return to his former workplace and live at home. No confinement in institutions or special settlements, but dispersal among the working population! No undignified welfare or charity, but work and return to his previous surroundings!" (28). Deinstitutionalization, independence, self-reliance, acceptance by others as an equal—all this had a strong democratic thrust.

By indicating the complexities of how the rehabilitation system developed in Germany in connection with World War I, it is possible to bring out some of the contradictory results for disabled people, as well as to indicate how attitudes toward them changed as a result of these developments. As a positive consequence, the public became more accustomed to the idea that disabled veterans were frequently capable of working and living more or less "normal" lives. Contrary to what happened in the aftermath of earlier wars and also to the images handed down in the best-known works of art from this period, with the backing of the new laws the vast majority of disabled veterans did return to work, though frequently as unskilled laborers in industry. As a result, leaving aside the disabled veterans whose injuries were so severe that they were not able to work at all, the unemployment rate for disabled veterans was lower than average during the Weimar Republic. In 1927, the unemployment rate in Germany was 12 percent but 8 percent for the disabled, and in March 1931 the corresponding figures were 21 versus 11 percent.[27]

This measure of social integration of disabled veterans necessarily also had a certain positive effect on attitudes toward the practicality of integrating disabled civilians into society rather than consigning them to live as isolated, dependent invalids. For example, because so many Gymnasium graduates were blinded in the war, the Blindenstudienanstalt was founded in Marburg in 1916 in order to prepare blind people for university study. This did not mean that they easily found appropriate work after completing their studies, but it was an indispensable first step in opening up more possibilities for them.[28] In many instances, various rehabilitation experts defended their patients—whether disabled children, adults, or veterans—against racial hygienists who labeled those with certain types of disabilities as inferior, burdensome, and undeserving of the state's financial assistance. Biesalski had maintained in his pamphlet of 1915, for example, that even those with the most severe disabilities could almost always be rehabilitated, and he showed

the photographs to prove it. At the Fourth German Congress for Cripples' Welfare, held in Cologne in 1916, one speaker stated pointedly that
orthopedists and specialists in the care of cripples could and should
help even children with congenital deformities (a main target of the
racial hygienists) to work, marry, and raise children.[29] And another
commentator rejected the idea in 1920 that the physically handicapped
were inferior, stating that they were equal to other people and deserved
the same access to treatment and care as anyone else.[30]

Victims or Heroes? Disabled Veterans Present
Themselves in the Public Sphere

During and immediately after the war, the nationalistically minded public gave extremely generous financial and moral support to disabled veterans. Furthermore, rehabilitation and legal measures sought to promote
their social integration according to the terms of the experts. By the time
the economic crisis began in 1929, however, the hostility of these veterans toward the Republic was a widely acknowledged fact, as was the
conspicuous antagonism between them and their fellow citizens, who
frequently characterized these men as a burden on the nation. In an
effort to centralize government control over the provision of welfare
benefits and rehabilitation, laws had been passed that strictly regulated
charities and philanthropy, thus eliminating most citizens' initiatives to
assist these men.[31] At the same time, as the economic situation worsened, many people became resentful of veterans' demands for still more
benefits in a time of growing crisis. It appears that the Weimar welfare
state staked its reputation on the care of disabled veterans, but problematic expectations and assumptions about disabled people often undermined these efforts. With regard to pensions, the legal system placed
veterans on the same level as poor people, accident victims, and
invalids. Disabled veterans complained repeatedly about being viewed
by other citizens and treated by the bureaucracy as "welfare cases," that
is, as inferior people on the same level as the "civilian disabled." Many
veterans were insulted and angered by this loss of status. As a result of
all these factors, even though German disabled veterans received relatively generous benefits—in contrast to, say, British veterans—they
often felt that their fellow citizens did not honor or respect them enough
for their sacrifices. This increased their alienation from the Republic and
made them likely candidates for Nazi recruitment.

When disabled veterans presented themselves in the public sphere,
powerful discourses of disability became evident. This large group of
men had recently marched off to war in nationalistic fervor with the

overwhelming support of the populace. Now, because of their newly disabled bodies, they found themselves lowered to the position of some of the most stigmatized groups in society. How did this affect their self-conceptions, and how did they deal with the fact that others suddenly viewed them differently than before? They immediately became politically active, forming large war victims' organizations to represent their interests. The journals of these organizations, along with material from pension cases and newspaper reports, tell about veterans' efforts to interpret their disabilities for themselves and to the public. The nature of these sources as highlighting abuses or complaints necessarily means that it is almost impossible to find out about disabled veterans from this time who were satisfied with the rehabilitation and medical treatment they received, those who went on to live contented family lives and find acceptable work—although this would also be an important story about disability in Germany between the world wars. In any event, the structure of the rehabilitation and legal systems meant that disabled veterans were often placed in situations in which they had to present themselves either as victims or as heroes in order to try to gain both the material support they needed to survive and the honor and recognition they craved.

From the perspective of the rehabilitation system, the reconstruction of the bodies of disabled veterans was a highly successful example of modern technological progress. Experts such as Biesalski urged these men to overcome their disabilities by reestablishing normative ways of physical functioning. Many of the veterans themselves, however, interpreted their disabilities as terrible diminishments of their lives that were extremely difficult, if not impossible, to overcome. Biesalski and his colleagues often expressed a one-sidedly cheerful, can-do attitude that came across as a lack of empathy for the enormous losses these veterans had experienced. In 1918, one of the major war victims' organizations, the Reichsbund der Kriegs- und Zivilbeschädigten, Sozialrentner und Hinterbliebenen, for example, criticized a rehabilitation exhibition of photographs that showed how easy it supposedly was for disabled veterans wearing prostheses to take up their former work and hobbies again. The Reichsbund took the exhibition to task for creating the false impression that it was a "pleasure to have to go through life with just one leg!"[32] Or in his diary, Victor Klemperer expressed outrage at a rehabilitation exhibition in Leipzig for the "tactless" way it displayed blind war veterans performing various kinds of work, comparing the scene to watching animals in a zoo.[33]

To promote the approach of the rehabilitation experts, an aristocrat with one arm named Freiherr Eberhard von Künssberg wrote a frequently republished self-help manual entitled *Einarm-Fibel: Ein Lehr-, Lese- und Bilderbuch für Einarmer* (One-Arm Primer: A Book of Instruction, with Text and Pictures, for the One-Armed, 1915). Featuring a drawing of Götz von Berlichingen's "iron hand" on the cover, the pamphlet exhorted these veterans to take pride in their war injuries and master the use of their new prostheses in order to continue serving the fatherland through work. By contrast, however, the autobiography of Carl Herrmann Unthan, entitled *Das Pediskript: Aufzeichungen aus dem Leben eines Armlosen* (Pediscript: Notes from the Life of an Armless Man, 1925), furnishes a significant counternarrative to that of the rehabilitation experts. Unthan was born without arms in 1848 in East Prussia to a loving family that encouraged him as much as possible. As an adult, he traveled with various impresarios and fairs throughout Europe, the United States, Mexico, Cuba, and Russia, displaying to the public what he could do with his feet. He wrote that he chose this life because he could find no other way to make as much money as he wanted. In the concluding section, illustrated with photographs, Unthan explained how he performed activities of daily life such as washing, dressing, eating, writing, playing chess, and so forth, hoping that this information would be useful to both children born without arms and newly disabled adults. He recounted going to military hospitals and speaking to veterans whose arms had been amputated, stating that he had met with quite an unenthusiastic reception from officials when he proposed this initiative. Probably this coolness was partly due to Unthan's success in living independently without prostheses and his strong skepticism toward the rehabilitation system for its emphasis on prosthetic technology. For example, he mentioned the veteran known as the "Hoeftmansche Mann," whose legs and arms had been amputated and who had been displayed at rehabilitation conferences working with his prostheses as a machinist. Unthan claimed that in fact this man never went back to work at his trade but made his living appearing at such conferences.[34] The thrust of Unthan's remarks was to argue that nonnormative ways of using one's body might in fact be more satisfying and successful for the individual. On the other hand, he said little about how disabled veterans received his message. It is easy to imagine that many of them—sharing the prejudices of their time—would not have wanted to be associated too closely with such a "freak."

In their desperation over their newly acquired disabilities, some veterans turned to what had frequently been the only option open to poor disabled people throughout history. They became beggars, presenting themselves as victims rather than heroes. In turn, rejecting this public image, the war victims' organizations often participated in official government efforts to eradicate begging.[35] The sight of disabled men begging in the streets while wearing their uniforms and Iron Crosses was so conspicuous and disturbing that it drew comments from all sides. In a diary entry from December 1918, for example, Evelyn Blücher made this observation about the striking street scenes she witnessed in Berlin: "All the blind, the halt, and the lame of Prussia seem to have collected here."[36] Immediately after the war, the press was full of articles about the "plague of beggars." Journalists often criticized these veterans from an aesthetic standpoint for offensively confronting the postwar public. On November 26, 1919, for example, the *Deutsche Tageszeitung* took men to task "who take to begging while insistently emphasizing their suffering and present an ugly sight in the streets and squares of the big cities."[37] This entire phenomenon, however, was more complex than it appeared on the surface. For, when welfare officials investigated the "mass epidemic" of military beggars in 1919–20, they found that many were either disabled civilians or nondisabled people feigning ailments who found that they received larger handouts when they put on a uniform.[38] In turn, this "comedy of misery" fueled major ongoing controversies over malingering (*Simulantentum*) and pension psychosis (*Rentenpsychose*) throughout the Weimar era, particularly with regard to psychiatrists' doubts about veterans' claims of mental illness—the so-called war neurotics or *Kriegszitterer* (war shiverers).[39] It also furnished plentiful material for a writer such as Bertolt Brecht, whose *Dreigroschenoper* (Threepenny Opera, 1928) took up the theme of begging to point out in an entertaining way how ludicrous it was to expect human sympathy in a capitalist society based solely on profit.

If some disabled veterans took the individual step of presenting themselves as beggars, the demonstrations of disabled veterans that took place in the economic chaos of the early and late Weimar years were self-presentations on a massive scale. Usually organized by the local branches of the war victims' associations, these demonstrations were concerted efforts of disabled veterans to make themselves visible to the public and interpret the meaning of their bodies for the nation. They demanded material assistance from the state, such as improved pensions, but they also wanted moral support and recognition for their sacrifices from the public. Often bitter at feeling cast aside, these veterans frequently marched carrying banners with the slogan "Is this the thanks of the fatherland?" The demonstrations were carefully choreographed in order to create the most provocative visual effect.[40] They were usually led by men with the worst injuries: amputees in wheelchairs or on open carts and blind men led by family members or guide dogs. Widows and orphans accompanied the men. The press com-

Fig. 3. Disabled veteran begging in Berlin after World War I. (Photo: akg-images.)

mented on these spectacles as bitter parodies of the enthusiastic columns that had marched off to war in 1914. For example, the largest such rally of the Reichsbund took place on December 22, 1918, in Berlin, when ten thousand war victims marched to the War Ministry demanding better care and greater honor.[41] These parades became a subject for a socially critical artist such as Otto Dix, as well as for Weimar authors such as Leonhard Frank and Erich Maria Remarque.

In these self-presentations, disabled veterans offensively stylized themselves as victims, but, on the other hand, they were frequently shocked when others treated them as outcasts, supplicants, and second-class people. With all their might, they resisted the humiliations that many other disabled people had always experienced. Suddenly, rather than being unquestionably accepted in their nation and communities, they were set apart as objects of curiosity. For example, a journalist described the public that gathered to watch hospital trains unloading the wounded as gossiping and nearly twisting their heads off staring, "as if monkeys and camels were coming."[42] Some veterans complained that young people mocked them, for example, by imitating the way amputees walked.[43] Others were enraged over finding themselves the object of revulsion. One amputee angrily reported a comment made by a woman who was staring at him during a theater performance: "God, isn't that disgusting! They could have left that one behind!"[44] Along with such difficult interactions in daily life, the structure of the pension system often forced disabled veterans to present themselves as invalids in order to obtain financial support—an impossible contradiction to the rehabilitation experts' demand that they should "overcome" their disabilities through heroic willpower. A typical complaint of such veterans went: "The war-disabled are men and not dogs, as so many people unfortunately think today."[45] The Nazi Party capitalized on this alienation of many disabled veterans from the Republic, establishing a special section for war victims in its directorate in September 1930. The party began to recruit disabled veterans with the slogan "Even a poor fatherland can be grateful," and this opportunistic promise of recognition fell on fertile soil among this disaffected group. After Hitler came to power in 1933, while the financial situation of disabled veterans did not improve significantly, they were repeatedly honored in mass ceremonies as the "first citizens of the nation."[46] Even as the Nazis began planning for the compulsory sterilization and "euthanasia" of people with certain hereditary disabilities, they praised disabled veterans for their sacrifices to the nation on the battlefield.

Disabled Veterans and Workers in Weimar Art and Literature

Illness and Disability in Prewar Expressionism

In the sphere of high culture, expressionism marks the transition between old prewar and new postwar ways of representing disability, of suffusing particular kinds of bodies with meanings. To an extent not found since romanticism, expressionist artists and writers made human suffering their theme, and from about 1910 to 1915 in particular they created innumerable depictions of illness—that is, disease. At this time, they were particularly fascinated with insanity and altered psychic states but depicted physical disabilities relatively infrequently.[47] In general, the interest of the expressionists in these themes arose from their concern with extreme human experiences located outside respectable bourgeois social conventions and aesthetic norms. Within this common basis, however, they took many different approaches. Accordingly, some represented the suffering person as mute, cast down, and destroyed by illness, whereby the individual often symbolizes the existential pain of all creatures. On the other hand, for many expressionists it was precisely the extremity of illness that could lead to spiritual or religious renewal, emotional refinement, and emancipatory, redemptive, or utopian moments. Illness in their works can thus be an overpowering, destructive force or a catalyst for breaking through claustrophobic restrictions.

On the whole, prewar expressionist depictions of illness, insanity, and disability aimed to make general statements about the human condition rather than situating these experiences in any specific, readily identifiable social context. A good illustration of this approach in art is the numerous portrayals of ill people—children, women, and men—by artists such as Erich Heckel, Ernst Ludwig Kirchner, and Karl Schmidt-Rottluff, which strive to capture inner emotional states rather than being painted in the style of representative individual portraits.[48] In literature, for example, Georg Heym's poems and short stories on the theme of insanity written in 1910–11 demonstrate a typical expressionist fascination with the hell of the insane asylum and with the exaggerated emotional intensity of abnormal mental states.[49] In his short story "Der Irre" (The Insane Man, 1911), a mentally ill man depicted as psychotic, paranoid, megalomaniacal, and apelike goes on a murderous rampage until he is finally shot and dies in ecstasy.[50] Similarly, the disabled figures in Heym's poems, including "Der Bucklige" (The Hunchback), "Der Blinde" (The Blind Man), "Der Bettler" (The Beggar), "Die blinden Frauen" (The Blind Women), "Die Tauben" (The Deaf People), and "Ganz dicht aufeinander . . ." (Very Close atop Each Other), are all shown in an abstract, timeless way, symbolizing deep isolation and sadness, bitter resentment and envy, or frantic, sometimes grotesque efforts to move from darkness to light.[51] Similar examples may be found in works by authors such as Ernst Barlach, Johannes R. Becher, Kasimir Edschmid, Walter Hasenclever, Jakob van Hoddis, Klabund, Georg Trakl, and Franz Werfel.[52] In this manner, these expressionist artists and writers achieved a new, antibourgeois intensity while continuing to employ old, familiar metaphors of illness and disability.

"Those in the Darkness No One Sees": The Threat of Disability Made Visible

Visual artists took up the subject of disability more often during the Weimar era than at any other time in German cultural history except perhaps for the frequent depictions of crippled beggars in medieval religious art. As soon as disabled and wounded veterans began returning from the front, the bodies of these men became major themes for the visual arts and to a lesser extent for literature as well. Gendering disability as masculine, artists frequently linked the figures of the disabled veteran and the misshapen, syphilitic prostitute as casualties of war and postwar metropolitan life. In formal terms, depictions of the shattered bodies of disabled and wounded veterans correspond to the dismembered female bodies in the Lustmord (sexual murder) paintings of these artists around 1918.[53] In contrast to the later devastation of Germany in World War II, World War I had not been fought inside German borders, and so the bodies of disabled veterans were the most visible reminders of that war. This was surely a fundamental reason why the mutilated, amputated bodies of some of these men became sites of intense struggle over cultural representation and national memory. In the chaotic immediate postwar years, progressive and leftist artists and writers turned to depictions of disability in their search for convincing ways to denounce German militarism and capitalism.

The selectiveness of Weimar artists and writers in choosing to depict certain types of disabilities shows how they made disability into a discourse with specific goals in mind. The majority of disabled veterans did not have obvious injuries or severe wounds but rather, for example, stomach disorders or less conspicuous mobility difficulties. Yet the disabled veterans depicted in art and literature are generally shown as horribly disfigured, with their amputated limbs, grotesque facial wounds, or bodies trembling from nervous shock. In particular, the veteran using crutches with one or both legs amputated became an iconic figure in Weimar art, surely because this seemed to be a particularly helpless figure. Furthermore, although the majority of disabled veterans were provided for by the state, at least to some extent, artists often chose to depict veteran amputees as beggars, as relegated to the lowest possible socioeconomic status, in order to attack the militaristic system that had created such misery. These artists selected the most visually striking features to lend their works socially critical force. They associated disability with the ugly, pitiful, and grotesque, seeking to shock the public by portraying veterans as reduced to the level of other disabled people who had so frequently been social and aesthetic outcasts.

As soon as disabled veterans began returning from the front, many artists moving in the orbit of expressionism began to shift from timeless depictions of suffering and illness to concrete social references to the war. They now portrayed wounded, mutilated, insane soldiers who contrasted starkly with all official efforts to promote patriotism by presenting these men as strong, virile heroes. Ernst Ludwig Kirchner, who had suffered a nervous collapse while in the military, painted himself in uniform in his well-known *Selbstporträt als Soldat* (Self-Portrait as a Soldier, 1915), in which his right arm with the hand used for painting appears as a bloody stump. A similar perspective comes through in Max

Pechstein's drawing of an amputee entitled *Der Gärtner, Somme IX* (The Gardener, Somme IX) and especially in works by Erich Heckel such as the etching *Straße in Ostende* (Street in Ostende, which shows an amputee using crutches) from 1915; the woodcuts *Im Lazarett* (In the Military Hospital), *Zwei Verwundete* (Two Wounded Men), and *Verwundeter Matrose* (Wounded Sailor) from 1915; and the lithographs *Irrer Soldat* (Insane Soldier) and *Krüppel am Meer* (Cripple at the Sea) from 1916.

It was at the end of the war, however, when masses of disabled veterans appeared as an easily identifiable group in a society torn by violent political conflict and economic chaos, that a flood of depictions of these men began to appear in the visual arts, most notably in works by Max Beckmann, George Grosz, Otto Dix, and Heinrich Hoerle. With the turn of most artists to a more "objective" style after relative economic stabilization in 1923, such images dwindled to a large extent, although a few of the most memorable depictions of disabled veterans were created by artists and writers in the middle and later years of the Weimar Republic.

In his autobiography of 1946, George Grosz recalled what struck him the most upon returning to Berlin in 1916 after being discharged from the army. He described the sights that he immediately took as subjects for his antimilitaristic, satirical drawings and paintings: "The Berlin to which I returned was cold and gray. . . . The same soldiers who were seen in the cafés and wine cellars singing, dancing, and clinging drunkenly to the arms of prostitutes, were to be seen later dirty and unkempt, dragging their weary way from station to station. . . . My drawings expressed my despair, hate and disillusionment. I had utter contempt for mankind in general. . . . I drew soldiers without noses; war cripples with crustacean-like steel arms; two medical soldiers putting a violent infantryman into a strait-jacket made of a horse blanket; a one-armed soldier saluting a lady decorated with medals who was putting a cookie on his bed; a colonel, his fly open, embracing a nurse; a medical orderly emptying into a pit a pail filled with various parts of the human body."[54] This passage may be used as a guide through the portrayals of disability in Weimar art and literature. First, Grosz did not turn his gaze away from any sight—no matter how horrible—in postwar Germany. He was determined to face everything. Like many other artists of the time, he linked the soldier/disabled veteran and the prostitute as conspicuous male and female counterparts in the gray postwar chaos of the metropolis. Second, while he of course viewed disabled veterans as impoverished, pitiful victims in certain ways, he also emphasized that many of them had learned nothing from their terrible experiences and were still willing cogs in a militaristic, authoritarian system. Finally, as an artist he was fascinated with the new forms on display: the shape of wounds, the prostheses that created grotesque intersections between technology and the body, and the disposable nature of the human being.

Max Beckmann used disabled figures in his portfolio of ten lithographs entitled *Die Hölle* (Hell, 1919) in order to bring out one of its main themes: the commitment to seeing rather than turning away from the violence of war and the misery it causes. Like a circus barker, the artist beckons his audience on the title page to draw near and see for itself the brutal reality of postwar Germany. In the first plate, *Nachhauseweg* (The Way Home), two figures face each other beneath a street lamp. One is a veteran whose face has been largely blown away; he is without a nose and almost eyeless. The stump of his arm protrudes from his sleeve, which the other figure, Beckmann himself, grips with one hand while pointing "the way home" with the other. In the background, two crippled veterans hobble along on crutches behind a prostitute. It is not clear whether the wounded veteran can see where Beckmann's finger is pointing. But Beckmann is looking intently at the veteran's terribly disfigured head, to which the lithograph draws the viewer's gaze. The second plate, *Die Straße* (The Street), includes a disabled veteran using a clumsy wheelchair along with a blind beggar in the chaotic clinch of bodies on the street during the November Revolution. Disability becomes a formal organizing principle in this fragmented, compressed jumble of limbs. The viewer must look closely to discern where one body ends and another begins; where body and inanimate object merge. If these lithographs employ images of disability to insist on acknowledging the horrible results of war, Beckmann references disability in another way in plate 6, *Die Nacht* (Night), which duplicates a famous painting of the same name that he completed just before beginning the *Hölle* portfolio. The head of a vicious intruder holding a child under his arm is taken from a portrayal of a blind beggar in the fresco *The Triumph of Death* (1355) in the Camposanto in Pisa, possibly by Francesco Traini.[55] In the fresco, the crippled beggars longing for release are ignored by Death, who is felling the young, beautiful, and wealthy. This reference intensifies the allegory in Beckmann's painting of "blind" violence raging among human beings who have no hope of salvation.

These Weimar artists were determined to depict disability caused by the war so disturbingly that viewers could not turn their gaze away. In their works portraying disabled veterans mainly as impoverished, pitiful, grotesque victims, Weimar artists generally aimed to attack militaristic authoritarianism and the heartlessness of a capitalist society based only on profit and later, after the economic situation had become

Fig. 4. Max Beckmann, *Hell: The Way Home,* 1919. Lithograph, 87 × 61 cm. Scottish National Gallery of Modern Art. (© 2007 Artists Rights Society [ARS], New York/VG Bild-Kunst, Bonn.)

more stable, the superficiality of a materialistic society. Numerous works by George Grosz and Otto Dix take this approach. In 1921, for example, Grosz illustrated a pamphlet by Willi Schuster with the title *Der Dank des Vaterlandes* (The Thanks of the Fatherland). The Communist Party of Germany (KPD) used this phrase and Grosz's cover drawing in 1924 on its election posters, thus illustrating how central discourses about disability were in the sphere of politics.[56] Schuster's vignettes of street scenes in Berlin contrasted ostentatious rich people with miserable disabled veterans begging for a handout. Describing his times as "the era of war cripples, the blind, the mutilated, the lost," he called for these men to unite with the proletariat and overthrow capitalism.[57] Grosz's accompanying drawings show a sad amputee selling matches with his little daughter, pitiful amputees begging from fat, well-to-do members of the bourgeoisie, and men on crutches holding out their caps for alms. One of Grosz's best-known paintings from the same year, *Grauer Tag* (Gray Day, 1921), which was exhibited at the Mannheim Neue Sachlichkeit (New Objectivity) exhibition in 1925 under the title *Magistratsbeamter für Kriegsbeschädigtenfürsorge* (State Functionary for the Welfare of the War Disabled), takes the same approach. Here a satirically portrayed, well-dressed official turns his back on a faceless worker carrying a shovel and on a downcast veteran with an amputated right arm who is walking with the help of a crude stick. The wall separating the official from these two figures indicates the state's indifference toward those on the bottom rungs of the social ladder.

In his portfolio of fifty etchings entitled *Der Krieg* (War, 1924), Otto Dix created one of the most memorable graphic cycles condemning war and documenting its victims. About these works, Dix stated that, in contrast to the expressionists, he wanted "no ecstatic exaggerations" but rather wanted to portray "objectively" the consequences of war.[58] It was precisely this commitment to almost documentary truthfulness that caused these works to attract an enormous amount of notice. The war victims portrayed in this cycle include the subjects of Dix's *Verwundeter* (Wounded Man), which features a man lying in a twisted position with terrified eyes; *Nächtliche Begegnung mit einem Irrsinnigen* (Nocturnal Encounter with a Lunatic), in which a figure stands before the war-ravaged landscape of the front; *Die Irrsinnige von Sainte-Marie-à-Py* (The Madwoman of Sainte-Marie-à-Py), an infrequent depiction of an insane *woman* in front of a destroyed house; and *Transplantation* (Skin Graft), which portrays a soldier with a huge facial wound. In *Appell der Zurückgekehrten* (Roll Call of the Returning Troops), an officer faces a line of six ragged men who are blind, mutilated, crippled, or dazed. This image recalls with bitter irony the huge, nationalistic parades of healthy young soldiers who had marched off enthusiastically into war ten years earlier. Accordingly, Dix's portrayals of the devastation caused by armed conflict provoked controversies between those who did not want to see these disabled and wounded victims made visible in the cultural sphere and those who accepted these sights as necessary shocks that might promote antiwar positions.

The depiction of facial wounds in art and photography provides a particularly clear instance of the form some of these controversies took over whether and why certain types of disabled war victims should be shown in public. That those with such wounds (one source estimates that three hundred thousand veterans had head injuries) were considered to be disabled was made clear by one commentator in 1916, who stated: "The special characteristic of this type of invalidism . . . is loss in an aesthetic sense, that is, inferiority in outward appearance."[59] One railroad worker poignantly described the effects of his facial injury in a letter protesting the government's denial of pension benefits to him, saying that he did not dare to go out in public because people took such offense at his disfigurement, that he was afraid he would never be able to marry, and that as a result he felt he was no longer a "full-valued member of human society."[60] Medical science frequently documented these wounds with photographs and wax images, and in 1916 a journal of popular science called *Die Umschau* (The Review) published medical photographs of some of these men. Later on, however, these images disappeared from public view, just as some of the most badly disfigured men remained hidden away in military hospitals, not daring to go out in public or even allow relatives to see them. Artists such as Grosz, Dix, and Beckmann created a few images of veterans with facial wounds, but they much preferred to depict veterans as crippled beggars and amputees with grotesque prostheses. They did this in order to emphasize how the war had rendered these formerly virile men helpless and to denounce militaristic atrocities and Taylorist applications of technology.

In 1924, however, the year in which Dix created *Der Krieg* and antiwar commemorations took place all over Germany, the pacifist Ernst Friedrich published a book, *Krieg dem Kriege!* (War on War!), which included photographs of veterans with gruesome facial wounds. Intending to shock the public into antimilitarist opposition, Friedrich also displayed some of these photographs in the storefront window of his Antiwar Museum in Berlin. The Berlin police immediately prohibited the display and confiscated the photographs. While a few pacifist and social democratic groups exhibited some of the photographs in other places, nationalist organizations protested the book and even attempted to have it banned, calling it "an incredible, insidious calumny against the old army."[61] The controversy revolved around the fact that showing men with such extreme disfigurements to the public undermined the rhetoric of heroism and honor necessary to link them with the German nation. The documentary photographs in Friedrich's book elicited a stronger reaction than a work of art such as Dix's etching *Transplantation,* which—while certainly not aestheticizing the facial wound—is less

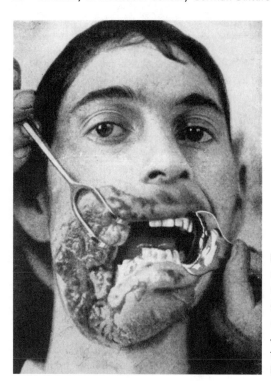

Fig. 5. " 'War agrees with me like a stay at a health resort.' (Hindenburg)." (From Ernst Friedrich, *Krieg dem Kriege!* [Berlin: Freie Jugend, 1924]. Courtesy of the Dartmouth College Library.)

shocking than a photograph due to the artistic fascination with form and composition. As the *Süddeutsche Zeitung* wrote in 1924 about Dix's cycle, "The content of these visions would be unbearable if not for the fact that a great creative talent has shaped the horror into artistic forms."[62] Accordingly, Dix's etchings of disabled and wounded war victims were successfully exhibited, whereas the photographs of these men in Friedrich's book were banned from public view.

Dix painted one more major work depicting the disabled veteran as victim: the triptych *Großstadt* (Metropolis), which he created in 1927–28 in the style of the late medieval masters. The central panel depicts with grotesque irony a stylish group of men and women dancing to a jazz band. This scene from the so-called Roaring Twenties resonates with many layers of meaning due to its juxtaposition with the two side panels, where Dix's iconic figures of the prostitute and the war cripple appear. In the right panel, high-class prostitutes parade past lavish theater scenery, ignoring a drably clothed war cripple sitting on the ground. He displays the naked stumps of his amputated legs, wears a small black patch over his missing nose and facial wound, and holds his hat in his lap to beg for alms. Stigmatized and outcast because of his disability and disfigurement, he looks down in shame rather than at the nude or extravagantly dressed women. In contrast to the pompous architecture of the right panel, the left panel shows a desolate cobblestone street under an elevated railroad track. Cheaply dressed prostitutes point the way to a brothel, and a drunken man lies on the street. Standing over him is a war cripple, the dominant figure in the panel. He wears an old uniform, and both of his legs have been amputated. Unlike the beggar in the right panel, however, his stumps fit into medieval-looking wooden peg legs, and he supports himself on a primitive wooden crutch. A dog barks at him, marking him as an intruder. This man is not ashamed but rather is looking intently at the prostitutes, whom he undoubtedly wants but cannot afford.

On the one hand, the most obvious meaning here is that these disabled veterans and others like them are victims, excluded from the erotic, materialistic swirl of life around them. On the other hand, though, Dix gave the disabled veteran on the left his own features, and the veteran's gaze extends across all three panels. This identification of the artist with the disabled veteran's perspective makes him the central figure of the painting as he observes what has been termed "this modern dance of death."[63] Because of his disabled, stigmatized body he sees through the empty materialism and pleasure seeking of a society that would like nothing better than to forget the horrors of the past. He longs for the temptations and forgetfulness that he sees, and at the same time his distance from them serves to bring out their superficiality. This validation of the war cripple's perspective indicates the complex relationship between disability and truth, for his disability serves to both exclude him and enable him to see beneath the surface of things.

In the same year in which Dix completed his triptych, the author Bertolt Brecht and the composer Kurt Weill created the biggest hit of the 1928 Berlin theater season, *Die Dreigroschenoper* (The Threepenny Opera). In this musical drama featuring criminals, prostitutes, and corrupt officials, Brecht employed his entertaining, thought-provoking theatrical techniques of alienation to displace current German discourses about disability into the London underworld. There are two main ways in which the play takes up the themes of disabled people as victims and explores what happens when disability becomes visible in the public sphere. First, Peachum's scenes as the beggar king clearly reference issues having to do with disabled veterans in Weimar Germany: the sight of veterans as beggars; the question of malingering; and the connections among cripples, begging, and poverty.[64] Peachum provides prospective beggars with costumes that he characterizes as the "basic types of misery," including the victims of war and technological progress (industrial and traffic accidents). He describes the disguise of a traumatized veteran as follows: "The annoying shiverer, harasses the passers-by, [and] evokes disgust that is lessened by his medals."[65] Peachum's business is to defraud members of the public by putting them in an unnatural state in which they feel compassion and are willing to part with their money. Here Brecht refunctioned the traditional image of the crippled beggar. Whereas earlier Christian iconography portrayed this pitiful figure as an opportunity for others to do good works by giving alms, Brecht used these likable malingerers in a comic yet serious way to poke fun at a capitalist society in which everyone is out for himself and money rules the world.

In these scenes, the disabled victims are not what they seem to be, but when the sheriff is about to arrest Peachum he threatens to unleash a huge "demonstration of misery" in order to disrupt the queen's coronation. In a scene that recalls the mass demonstrations of disabled veterans in Weimar Germany, Peachum has his beggars set about painting signs with slogans such as "I gave my eye for the king." Having observed that the propertied classes can create misery but cannot bear to see it, he describes how unpleasant it would be for the queen to confront hundreds of people with mutilations and facial sores. He muses to the sheriff: "What will it look like if six hundred poor cripples have to be beaten down with clubs at the coronation? It would look bad. Disgusting is how it would look" (466). The threat that the poorest of the poor, the cripples, might invade the sphere of the wealthy and powerful is too much for the sheriff, who abandons his plan to arrest Peachum. The version of the final song that closes the film adaptation of the play, *Dreigroschenfilm* (Threepenny Film, 1930), captures ironically the stigmatized, invisible position not only of the poor in capitalist society but of people who are disabled and ill, outcasts of all sorts: "For some are in the dark / And the others are in the light. / And one sees those in the light. / Those in the darkness no one sees" (497).

"Four of These Don't Add up to a Whole Man": Disabled Veterans as Holdovers of Militarism

While the works discussed up to this point portray disabled veterans largely as victims, Weimar artists—whether in the phases of experimental dadaism, socially critical verism, or new objectivity—presented social misery in a very different way from the older naturalists, who sought to inspire sympathy for such figures, or the prewar expressionists with their evocations of human pathos. Frequently, these artists depicted such victims in a merciless way, showing them as grotesque, repellent men who had learned nothing from their war experiences. Consequently, they hardly seemed any different from the militarists, industrialists, and representatives of the bourgeoisie who had brought about the war and the ensuing social chaos. Grosz's illustrations for Schuster's book, for example, show begging disabled officers still proudly wearing their medals and Iron Crosses and one even blaring out "Deutschland über alles" on his portable gramophone. Taking the approach of total satire, Grosz made his disabled veterans appear just as unsavory as the piggish capitalists or the brutal, steel-helmeted, military men he frequently excoriated.

In such works of art, the prosthesis—marking the juncture between technology and human flesh—became an organizing principle.[66] Grosz heightened the grotesqueness of these figures by drawing jumbles of their leg and arm prostheses, crutches, and canes. As an artist, he was horrified by yet fascinated with the new forms on display: the shapes of wounds, the inventive new prosthetic technologies. In a similar manner, in *Früchte im Baum der Ebert-Republik* (Fruits in the Tree of the Ebert Republic, 1921) Heinrich Hoerle drew all kinds of fantastic prostheses hanging from the limbs of a tree. Such artists interpreted prostheses critically, as symbols of the disposable nature of the human being in the militaristic, nationalistic war machine and in the mechanized, industrial capitalist system. Angered by the seemingly unstoppable momentum of this destructive process, they portrayed wounded and disabled veterans with grotesque prostheses as complicit in this oppressive system, as part of an uninterrupted cycle of repetitive slaughter.

Otto Dix's four paintings of 1920, which have been termed his "prosthesis-wearers' series," are the most substantial, multilayered artistic reflections on the meaning of prosthesis in this sense.[67] An influential forerunner of these works is Brueghel's famous painting *The Cripples* (1568), in which the grotesque, crutch-using, amputated figures appear both as bitter social caricatures and as suffering outcasts. Depicting prostheses as a way to reflect on nationalism and technology, Dix was responding not only to the war but also to the reactionary Kapp Putsch of March 1920. The theme of corporeal fragmentation enters into the physical composition of these works through the use of collage: Dix pasted elements such as newspapers, hair, photographs, and pamphlets into the paintings. From impossibly mutilated survivors to men with the most fanciful prostheses, the figures in these four paintings present exaggeratedly grotesque views of disability in order to intensify symbolic meanings.

In *Der Streichholzhändler I* (Match Seller I), a man identifiable as a veteran by his old uniform cap sits on the pavement. Black glasses indicate his blindness, he has lost both arms, and his two leg stumps fit into short wooden peg legs. His amputated legs are made even more conspicuous in contrast to the elongated legs of three passersby, who want to avoid him and are striding away from him. As a final indignity, a dachshund lifts its leg to urinate on him. This painting leaves somewhat more room for empathy with the disabled veteran than the other three in the cycle do since he appears isolated and poor and is not identified as an officer or medal wearer. His prostheses simply underscore his helplessness and vulnerability.

The three remaining paintings focus in varying ways on the political implications of the artificial body or body parts. Two war cripples appear in *Prager Straße (Meinen Zeitgenossen gewidmet)* (Prague Street, Dedicated to My Contemporaries). In the background of this main shopping street in Dresden are two store windows: one a beauty salon (women's sphere) with manikin heads and the other an orthopedic appliance shop with artificial limbs for sale (to men). This juxtaposition indicates the feminized, passive position of disabled veterans. One man sits on the ground in front of the windows. Wearing impossible prostheses, his legs appear as two sticks, and his left arm is a strange mechanical apparatus. His right hand is held out for alms. The other veteran, wearing a medal, is missing the entire lower half of his body. Seated on a rolling platform, he propels himself along with two sticks. (Photographs of disabled veterans in Germany after both world wars show that such makeshift conveyances were in fact used at times.) Whereas the first veteran has a forlorn expression, the pompous military bearing of the second half man wearing a bowler hat heightens the grotesque effect.

Dix employed a similar style in *Die Skatspieler* (Skat Players, also known as Crippled War Veterans Playing Cards), which has been termed the most important antiwar picture ever produced by a German artist.[68] Here three disabled veterans identified as officers by their posture and medals are playing cards at a coffeehouse table. Each man has injuries that could not possibly be survived and wears fantastic prostheses. The veteran on the left is the only man who still has one leg. He holds his cards in his one remaining foot while resting his sticklike hand prosthesis on the table. He is blind and wounded in the face, and he has a long, snakelike ear trumpet. The central figure, missing all four limbs, plays cards with his teeth while his head is filled with pornographic fantasies of women. The wearer of the Iron Cross on the right, an officer with smartly parted hair, holds a card before his missing nose with his robotic arm. To underscore the cynicism of trying to put such destroyed men

Fig. 6. Otto Dix, *The Skat Players (Crippled War Veterans Playing Cards),* 1920. Oil and collage on canvas, 110 × 87 cm. Nationalgalerie, Staatliche Museen zu Berlin. (Photo by Bildarchiv Preussischer Kulturbesitz/Art Resource, New York. © 2007 Artists Rights Society [ARS], New York/VG Bild-Kunst, Bonn.)

back together again, this last figure is wearing a special prosthesis for his missing jaw. It has Dix's photograph on it along with the label "Lower jaw: prosthesis brand: Dix. Only genuine with the photograph of the inventor."

One art critic has stated that perhaps no other painting portrays the mutilated human being so pitilessly.[69] Through the intertwining of prostheses with chair and table legs and the impossible contortions of limbs and various apparatuses, the composition of the painting causes the viewer to look closely, with cold or perhaps amused curiosity, in order to discern how everything functions together, to determine what is human and what is inanimate matter. That is, the painting creates a freak show effect, an ambivalent fascination with the three war cripples, who are also presented in a radically negative manner as representatives of the war machine. The grotesqueness of their prostheses marks them with bitter irony as monstrous holdovers of an authoritarian system. They are still dyed-in-the-wool militarists, and they keep on playing their game the way they have always played it.

The fourth painting, *Kriegskrüppel* (War Cripples), also known as *45% erwerbsfähig* (45% Work Capacity, referring to how pension benefits were determined), was first exhibited in June 1920 at the First International Dada Fair in Berlin. The Dresden Stadtmuseum purchased it but removed it from view in 1924 because it was so controversial and stored it in what was known as its "chamber of horrors."[70] Subsequently the Nazis exhibited it as one of the prime examples of degenerate art, singled it out as an image for a propaganda poster condemning the "painted military sabotage" of the modernist avant-garde, and finally burned it.[71] It is likely that Dix was familiar with postwar mass demonstrations of war victims and took these sights as material for this painting. Here four grotesque war cripples wearing medals parade down the street in front of a shoemaker's shop led by a noncommissioned officer. As in the other three paintings, they are wearing primitive or fantastic prostheses except for the third man, who is a torso being pushed along in a wheelchair by the fourth. The wavy lines and blurred image of the second man mark him as a "shiverer." This is a rare image in Weimar art of one of the psychically traumatized veterans whom many contemporary commentators noticed on the streets. In the background of the painting a hand points to Dix's own profile with crosshairs over it, perhaps indicating that it was only by chance that he escaped a similar fate during his military service. The subtitle of the painting, *Vier geben noch keinen ganzen Menschen* (Four of These Don't Add up to a Whole Man),[72] makes explicit Dix's passionate critique of the inhuman uses of technology. At the same time, the pomposity of the shattered figures and their absurd effort to maintain a military bearing and keep marching in step mark them as contemptible, ridiculous remnants of Prussian militarism. The machinery of war produced these human wrecks, but Dix's depiction of their grotesque prostheses shows that peacetime technology is not able to put these men back together again.

"Prosthetic Economy Instead of Soviet Dictatorship": Artists Critique the Medical-Industrial Complex

Shortly after the Kapp Putsch in 1920, the dadaist Raoul Hausmann published a brief, ironic prose piece in the journal *Die Aktion* entitled "Prothesenwirtschaft: Gedanken eines Kapp-Offiziers" (Prosthetic Economy: Thoughts of a Kapp Officer). Here the reactionary narrator blusters that Germany needs workers with prostheses because artificial limbs never tire and the proletarians could then work twenty-five hours per day. Accordingly, the officer's solution for rebuilding Germany is "a prosthetic economy instead of a Soviet dictatorship," referring to the failed German revolution of 1918–19.[73] This article was not mere dadaist silliness but rather a concrete satire that referred to the peppy discourse in rehabilitation circles about getting disabled veterans back to work as soon as possible. Along these lines, for example, an Institute for Psychotechnics in Berlin had advocated redesigning industrial machinery in order to fit prosthetic limbs better and had claimed that companies might actually become more efficient by integrating technologically enhanced workers' bodies into their systems of production.[74]

Hausmann was not the only Weimar artist to perceive the social trend toward functionalizing the bodies of workers in the service of industry and capitalist profits rather than transforming alienated working conditions so that workers would be treated like human beings rather than machines. Fritz Lang's film *Metropolis* (1926), for example, employs a multilayered discourse of prosthesis extending from mythological references to futuristic technology. The inventor Rotwang, who is creating "machine men," inhabits a realm of disability in his strange, ancient house. For an instant, the film shows his hunchbacked servant, a fairy-tale character, and Rotwang himself has a black prosthetic hand. When he introduces Fredersen, the ruler of Metropolis, to the robot he has created, he waves his prosthetic hand before Fredersen's face and exclaims, "Isn't it worth the loss of a hand to have created the man of the future, the machine-man?" This image recalls the Greek god Hephaistos, who was lame (and thus disabled) and, as the blacksmith of the gods, ruled the creative fire and made marvelous inventions. Rotwang's artificial hand connects him to this realm of uncanny, premodern powers, on which he draws in order to create his robot, a total prosthesis embodying the most modern technology, which is to replace the living workers.[75] In other words, Rotwang is busy creating the "prosthetic economy" of Hausmann's Kapp officer for Metropolis. That the robot is destroyed in the end by no means situates the film on the side of the

"Soviet dictatorship," however, for its ultimate message is that of a rapprochement between capital and labor.

More radical artists sharply critiqued the tendencies in the Republic toward a "prosthetic economy." If an artist such as Dix had used prosthetic imagery in his dadaist *Kriegskrüppel* painting to denounce militarism, other artists—particularly George Grosz, Rudolf Schlichter, and Heinrich Hoerle—drew on prosthetic imagery in related ways that added further dimensions to their political statements. First, in dadaist images of artificial limbs, machine men, and marionettes, the prosthesis became a negative metaphor for the artificiality and hollowness of the bureaucratic state, for the weak foundations of democracy. Second, the Cologne progressivist Heinrich Hoerle was unique among Weimar artists in linking figures of disabled veterans and workers wearing prostheses in order to bring out the alienation of the worker in an industrial world of rigidly mechanized labor.

Around 1920 many German artists came into contact with the Italian metaphysical paintings of Giorgio de Chirico and Carlo Carrà. Combining this approach with Vladimir Tatlin's "machine art," dadaists such as Grosz and Schlichter immediately began to create their own paintings in this style, situating marionettes, puppets, and figures wearing prostheses in uncanny, often empty cityscapes. Examples include Grosz's *Ohne Titel* (Untitled, 1920), in which a faceless, handless torso is positioned on a cube in the middle of a city street; his *Diabolospieler* (Diabolo Player, 1920), an automaton with sticklike prostheses; and Schlichter's *Dada-Dachatelier* (Dada Rooftop Studio, ca. 1920), which shows an uncanny collection of prosthesis-wearing marionettes, figures wearing gas masks, and the torso of a "glass man" with the inner organs exposed. While such paintings depict mechanical figures without any overtly political references, Grosz's *Republikanische Automaten* (Republican Automatons, 1920) situates this discourse of prosthesis firmly within the political arena of the Republic. Two faceless, prosthesis-wearing automatons with cylindrical, machinelike limbs appear here against a background of rectangular buildings and empty streets. The one on the right is a disabled veteran with amputated arms who is still a stalwart militarist, as his Iron Cross and the slogan "1 2 3 Hurra" emanating from his hollow head indicate. The clothes of the figure on the left mark him as middle class, and his peg leg and functional arm prosthesis mark him as a disabled veteran. With his metal claw, he holds the black, red, and gold flag of the Republic, which seems to be on very shaky footing, indeed, if such mechanical men spouting empty slogans constitute its foundation.

Grosz's brief metaphysical phase influenced many artists in the following years, particularly Heinrich Hoerle (1895–1936), who continued to paint prosthesis-wearing figures with references to this style as late as 1930. Preoccupied with the theme of the cripple, as were so many Weimar artists, Hoerle had first turned his attention to this subject in quite a different way. In 1920, he created a controversial collection of twelve lithographs entitled *Die Krüppelmappe* (The Cripple Portfolio), which can hardly be called dadaist but rather has strongly verist tendencies. Depicting veterans with various types of disabilities, the lithographs emphasize the isolation, suffering, and helplessness of these cripples. Men with no legs beg for a handout or drag themselves along the sidewalk while being stared at; a man with no hands, wearing an Iron Cross, simply stands with his eyes closed in despair; and a downcast man wearing two hooks tries to embrace a woman. Other images attempt to capture the cripple's emotional state in more surrealistic ways: helpless, impotent men see their missing limbs growing from flowerpots or dream of glorious erections. Contemporary reviewers compared the intensity of Hoerle's images to Goya's *Horrors of War*. They also understood these works as denunciations of the military-industrial complex, as did Hoerle's fellow artist, Franz Seiwert, in an article entitled "Krupp-Krüppel" (Krupp Cripples) in 1920. Here Seiwert described Hoerle's cripples with expressionistic pathos as monuments to the guilt of all those still producing armaments. He urged the public to face these "terrible sights" and be moved to oppose war.[76]

Hoerle and his colleagues in the Cologne Group of Progressive Artists did not continue to paint in this verist style for long, however. Coming into contact with various left-radical communist groups, they soon developed a new style in which they sought to imbue strict geometrical constructions with an anonymous collective consciousness beyond all concern with individual psychology. Of all the artists discussed here, Hoerle is the only one who returned repeatedly to what has been termed "the synthesis of man and machine, commonly called a cripple," throughout the Weimar era.[77] Along with the sociopolitical implications of this figure, Hoerle seems simply to have been fascinated with the formal aspects of prostheses as junctures between machines and the body. He is the only artist of this time who experimented with drawing women as prosthesis wearers, as he did in *Schreitende mit Gelenk für eine Armprothese* (Striding Woman with Joint for an Arm Prosthesis, 1920).

If Hoerle's *Krüppelmappe* was a passionate moral protest against the brutality of war, his new constructivist style linked representations of veterans and workers in order to show, in an often ironic way, the reintegration of their prosthetically rehabilitated bodies "into the postwar industrial infrastructure."[78] Hoerle took this approach in numerous paintings, drawings, and linoleum cuts that feature strict geometric constructions, including *Krüppel, bettelnd,* also known as *Kriegskrüppel, bettelnd* ([War] Cripple, Begging, 1921); *Krüppel mit Frau* (Cripple with Woman, ca. 1921); *Fabrikarbeiter* (Factory Worker, 1922); *Frau mit Krüppel* (Woman with Cripple, ca. 1922); *Krüppel, gehend* (Cripple, Walking, 1923); *Arbeiter, 2. Zustand* (Worker, 2nd Version, 1923); *Der Europäer* (The European, 1923); *Kopfprothese* (Head Prosthesis, 1923); *Sitzender Krüppel raucht* (Seated Cripple Smoking, 1923); *Krüppel* (Cripple, ca. 1925); *Melancholie* (Melancholy, 1928, an unusual depiction of a woman with an amputated hand and a machine man); and *Feierabend* (Quitting Time, 1930).[79] One of these paintings has been called by various titles that underscore the technological project of transforming disabled veterans into efficient workers by means of prostheses: *Drei Invaliden, Arbeitsmänner, Maschinenmänner, Die Heimkehrer,* and *Prothesenträger* (Three Invalids, Workmen, Machine Men, The Returnees, and Prosthesis Wearers, 1930). Hoerle's best-known painting on this subject is *Denkmal der unbekannten Prothesen* (Monument to the Unknown Prostheses, 1930) with its overtones of the "unknown soldier." Here two machinelike male figures face each other wearing functional arm prostheses reminiscent of the work arms developed by the rehabilitation industry.[80] A small figure is seated in the background with holes in its amputated limbs where prostheses could be inserted. All the works mentioned here feature (war) cripples with removable or interchangeable body parts, artificial limbs similar to factory machinery, or even entire bodies that appear to be mechanisms. In this manner, Hoerle left behind the emotional concern with the individual expressed in his *Krüppelmappe* and sought to depict the complete alienation of the rehabilitated veteran, now the worker, as the "cripple" of the inhumanly mechanized industrial system, the "prosthetic economy."

"Your Medicine Will Not Cure Humanity": Disability in Weimar Literature

Disability was one of the most significant themes in Weimar visual art. There were few major representations of disability in literature during this period, however, for two main reasons. First, the conspicuous presence of disabled veterans and to a lesser extent of disabled workers

Fig. 7. Heinrich Hoerle, *Monument to the Unknown Prostheses* (1930). Oil on cardboard, 66.5 × 82.5 cm. Von der Heydt-Museum, Wuppertal. (© 2007 Artists Rights Society [ARS], New York/VG Bild-Kunst, Bonn.)

could be captured more strikingly in visual art. More generally speaking, until the rise of disability rights movements in the late twentieth century, disability has functioned as such a strongly marked category that it has almost always obliterated other dimensions of individuals from view in the cultural sphere. Thus, visual artists created major works that focused solely on a few very selective aspects of disability, but until fairly recently writers seldom conceived of disabled people as living the multifaceted lives necessary for depicting them as compelling main characters in literature.[81] The one exception in this regard around the time of World War I and during the Weimar Republic is literature and films that portray the complexity of insanity or altered mental states, usually in an expressionistic, intense style.[82] There are, however, a few important literary works from this period that deal significantly with disabled veterans, and as for visual art a central theme here is the place of these disabled men in postwar German society. While the works written in the closing months of the war call for all the oppressed—even including the disabled—to carry out a revolutionary transformation of society, those written somewhat later no longer express a belief in this possibility, and so their disabled characters appear as resigned, embittered outcasts.

Leonhard Frank's collection of five novellas, *Der Mensch ist gut* (Man Is Good, 1918), depicts the effects of war throughout society, building to a climax in the last novella, "Die Kriegskrüppel" (The War Cripples). In contrast to the statement "Der Mensch ist ein Vieh" (man is an animal) by a more aggressively radical artist such as Grosz, Frank voiced with expressionistic pathos the hope that mankind would renounce the brutality of war and create a better world. The loosely connected sections of "Die Kriegskrüppel" are linked by the character of the military surgeon, a rare positive depiction of a physician in expressionist literature. In the first section, he is trying heroically to save wounded soldiers at the front, performing amputations in a makeshift operating room where a huge container full of limbs is emptied daily. The rescued cripples wonder how they can go on living with their damaged bodies, and the doctor hallucinates that he is amputating millions of limbs for all of Europe. The scene then shifts to a hospital train carrying the doctor and all the wounded men back to Germany. Their shattered bodies cause the men to question nationalistic ideology while the doctor intends to oppose the warmongers. He even imagines new words for the German national anthem: "The massive armies of cripples / Break into the light / Of the great, profound vision: / All men will be brothers."[83] The third section portrays disabled veterans being rejected for employment because they are viewed either as too weak or too disfigured for it. Having no alternative, "hundreds of thousands" become beggars. Recalling the mass demonstrations of disabled veterans that began toward the end of the war, the final section begins with a "cripples' march" of twenty thousand soldiers that swells to fifty thousand when workers, hospital patients, and spectators join it. The march is headed by a flatbed truck carrying a corpse, a soldier "without a face," men with amputations, and a man who is only a "torso," who is described as the "naked symbol of the war" (137). The Spartacist leader Karl Liebknecht appears, and the narrator imagines disabled veterans and workers uniting in a revolutionary spirit of love and brotherhood. Frank thus depicts disabled veterans as passive sufferers who embody the pitiful consequences of war, but he also imagines them becoming active participants in the revolutionary struggle for love and freedom. In this ecstatic expressionist vision, nationalism is overcome, and cripples, moving from the darkness to the light, become part of humanity.

Writing in 1931, Erich Maria Remarque portrayed a similar demonstration but came to very different conclusions in his novel *Der Weg zurück* (The Way Back). This is a sentimental story of the Lost Generation of young veterans who are disillusioned with politics and alienated from everyday life after returning from service at the front. At one point, the main characters see a demonstration of disabled veterans taking place during the period of inflation.[84] Carrying banners with slogans such as "Where is the thanks of the fatherland?" and "The war cripples are starving," the participants appear sequentially in groups: one-armed men, blind men led by guide dogs ("with the mute plea that those who can still see should really look"), one-eyed men, those with facial wounds, the long rows of men with amputated legs, the shiverers, and those who can still walk pushing men in wheelchairs and one "torso" on a handcart. In contrast to Frank's invocations of brotherhood, Remarque's narrator—in this book written after the economic crisis was in full swing—imagines that these men will remain nothing but victims, brushed aside by politicians with a few glib speeches.

This move from optimism to pessimism is illustrated especially strikingly by the contrasts between two of Ernst Toller's plays. Internationally the best-known dramatist of this period, Toller came from a middle-class family and volunteered for service at the front in 1915. After thirteen months at Verdun, he suffered a nervous and physical breakdown, was hospitalized, and then began to study in Munich, write plays, and become involved with the growing revolutionary movement of workers and soldiers. Believing that only insanity would cause someone from such a middle-class background to ally himself with working people, his worried mother had him committed for a few days in 1918 to the Munich university psychiatric clinic, where the famous professor Emil Kraepelin examined him. In his autobiography, Toller wrote sympathetically about the other patients he met and critically about the psychiatrist, stating that the former were harmless sick people locked up by the latter, whom he described as a truly dangerous advocate of nationalism as a cure for all ills.[85] Toller's extensive experiences at the front, along with his brief, involuntary stay in the mental institution, gave him firsthand exposure to disabled people and medical professionals, which he worked into material for his plays.

Toller began to write *Die Wandlung: Das Ringen eines Menschen* (The Transformation: The Struggle of a Human Being) in 1917, and it premiered in Berlin on September 30, 1919. In January of 1918, however, he had already distributed the scenes about war cripples on leaflets to striking munitions workers in Munich. One of the best-known expressionist dramas, this play written in free verse traces the transformation of Friedrich—who is loosely modeled on Toller himself—from an enthusiastic army volunteer and nationalistic patriot to a revolutionary advocate of brotherhood. Throughout the play, confrontation with disability is an essential impetus to Friedrich's transformation. First, a brief scene at the front shows wounded, insane soldiers who are beginning to question why they had to sacrifice their health while Friedrich still tries to defend war for the fatherland. The sixth scene presents two opposing views of disability. Here there appears an elegant doctor dressed in black whose head is a skull with glowing eyes. He displays to his medical students—one of whom has Friedrich's face—"seven naked cripples" who are wearing prostheses and whose faces all look alike. The doctor boasts that as fast as the armaments industry is creating new patients, the medical system is transforming them into machines that are again useful to the state. In this spirit, he declaims, "We are armored against all horrors. / We could call ourselves the positive branch; / The negative branch is the armaments industry."[86] The doctor's functionalist interpretation of these men's bodies is undercut when other cripples begin to speak from their beds. A blind man asks if it is already night, a man with no arms pleads for help relieving himself, and a paralyzed man begs for death. Rejecting all consolation, these men ask why no one resisted the war that brought them such misery. They thus refuse to be reintegrated again into the well-oiled military-industrial machine that the doctor is charged with maintaining. When the play was performed, nationalist circles were outraged at this bitter medical satire, taking it as mocking war victims, whom they preferred to view as heroes.[87]

With his figure of the sinister physician, Toller tapped perceptively into a fundamental shift in the social role of doctors and the social function of medicine. Throughout most of the nineteenth century, physicians were primarily family doctors for the middle and upper classes, while the lower classes generally took care of themselves as best they could with home remedies. When mass insurance programs were established in the latter part of the century, however, the role of doctors changed significantly. Suddenly they were charged with speedily treating huge numbers of patients, acting as gatekeepers for the pension system, and determining fitness for military service. In short, the *Hausarzt* (family doctor) became a *Halbgott* (demigod or god in a white coat).[88] These social changes were reflected in cultural representations. With the notable exception of the unfeeling physician who torments the soldier Woyzeck in Georg Büchner's play (written in 1836–37 and published 1877), doctors generally appear as fatherly, kind figures in nineteenth-century German literature. In expressionist literature, however, the physician becomes a much more negative type, depicted as an authoritarian bureaucrat who is devoid of human empathy and even aggressively hostile toward his wounded or disabled patients.[89] Toller returned to such a figure one more time in his play *Hoppla, wir leben!* (Hoppla, Such Is Life! 1927). Here a social Darwinist psychiatrist rants using eugenic terminology that revolutionaries who want to improve life for the masses should be "sterilized and eradicated."[90] Consequently, with his evil doctor characters Toller joined all those Weimar writers and artists who portrayed medicine and the rehabilitation system as serving militaristic, nationalistic, and even racist interests.

After the hospital scene, another confrontation with disability provokes Friedrich's final transformation. He now appears as a sculptor trying unsuccessfully to create a statue of a nude man, which is described as a muscular, brutal symbol of the victorious fatherland. Suddenly he hears an organ grinder, and a war-disabled, syphilitic woman enters with her traumatized, insane husband, Friedrich's former comrade. Upon seeing the disabled couple and learning from the woman that only the wealthy benefit from the war, Friedrich destroys his monumental, heroic statue. This action recalls Beckmann's lithograph, *Nachhauseweg,* for Friedrich realizes that a representation of the perfect body can no longer stand for the fatherland in view of the overwhelming misery caused by the war. After this decisive turning point, Friedrich casts aside his bourgeois past. In a final exchange with the doctor, he proclaims, "Your medicine will not cure humanity" (281) and calls instead with expressionist intensity for universal brotherhood. Rejecting the prosthetic economy of the doctor's technocratic cures, Friedrich allies himself with the revolution of the poor and the oppressed.

Disability is one of several important themes in *Die Wandlung,* but in *Hinkemann* (translated as Brokenbrow, 1921–22) Toller made a disabled veteran the main character and created the most substantial literary depiction of disability penned in the Weimar era. Written while Toller was in prison after the failed revolution of 1918–19, this tragedy mourns dashed hopes for radical social change and voices the hopelessness of a veteran stigmatized because of his disability. In contrast to visual art, literature can of course more easily depict invisible or hidden conditions, which Toller did here by portraying Hinkemann as castrated by a war injury. Bringing this further dimension to Weimar representations of disability, the play revolves around the ways in which Hinkemann, his wife, and his former friends react to this type of demasculinization, exploring what social positions were open to such a man in German society.

Many men in fact suffered from such wounds, and one historian has uncovered an article from 1934 that deals with 310 cases of castrated veterans based on patients' records.[91] The experiences of these men were written down because they were asking to be classified as disabled and thus entitled to pensions. They told, for example, of being denied employment because of feminizing hormonal changes that made them blush inappropriately or caused their voices to rise. In doctors' notes, these patients also reported that when their condition became known some people laughed at them, called them names such as *Karlchen ohne* (Carlie without), and made fun of them for being childless. In short, as one farmer lamented, they were viewed as "despised cripples." Some veterans agreed that their wives should have children by other men so they would not be mocked, while one woman wrote a letter demonstrating her touchingly naive belief in the omnipotence of prosthetic medicine, pleading, "Wouldn't it be better, esteemed welfare office, since you give out so many spare parts, if you could also provide a spare part for my husband? He doesn't even dare to go out in public any more. . . . Isn't this really hurtful for someone who fought for his fatherland? . . . Please, I want a child so very much" (76). Whereas the rehabilitation system could attempt to remasculinize veterans with some other types of disabilities, such as amputations, by outfitting them with prostheses and putting them back to work, the castrated veterans presented an insuperable challenge to traditional concepts of masculinity in the postwar situation, and this is precisely the theme of Toller's tragedy.

In his autobiography, Toller described the guiding thought behind his play as follows: "How would someone look at life who has been castrated in the war? Aren't healthy people really the blind ones?"[92] This statement speaks on several levels simultaneously that indicate why the play is such a fascinating, contradictory cultural representation of disability. First, Toller was making a unique, genuine effort to write from the perspective of a veteran disabled in this way and to validate his views of life. The metaphor of "healthy" people as "blind," however, points to a pervasive use of disability as negative metaphor throughout the play. This technique undermines the sympathy created for Hinkemann since it serves to assign disability to a realm of grotesqueness that Toller employs for political allegory.

Living in a working-class milieu, Hinkemann is worried about whether his wife still loves him and afraid that others will find out he is a cripple and laugh at him. His wife finally breaks down and tells his best friend how ashamed she is that Hinkemann is "not a man" any longer. She sleeps with the friend and becomes pregnant. Meanwhile, wanting to provide for his wife and finding no other decent-paying job, Hinkemann agrees to perform in a freak show at a fair, biting off the heads of live rats. The barker allegorizes his performance as follows: "*The* German hero! *The* representative of German culture! *The* German strong man! *The* favorite of all the elegant women!"[93] His wife and friend happen to pass by and overhear this, and the friend immediately laughs at the sham, exclaiming, "So that's what the German hero looks like! Somebody without. . . . A eunuch. . . . Hahahahaha! So that's what the German defender of the homeland looked like!" (20). After this scene, Hinkemann talks with his friends at a pub about what will happen to all the war cripples, and in a sharply ironic exchange they cheerfully assure him that society will provide rehabilitation and loving care for these men. In a hallucination similar to Dix's *Kriegskrüppel,* Hinkemann sees amputees with barrel organs who are ready and willing to march off to war again. Finally, his remorseful wife commits suicide, leaving him alone to describe himself as "colossal and ridiculous"—a monstrous figure.

Throughout the play, Hinkemann tells how becoming a cripple has made him see the world in a different way. He calls the castrating gunshot a "fruit from the tree of knowledge" that opened his eyes to all the pointless suffering around him (52). In tones echoing those of Büchner's Woyzeck, he observes how people are caught up in a vicious circle of brutality and do not want to transform themselves, even though they could be so much happier. In such passages, Hinkemann is the figure of identification in the play whose disability has given him deeper insights into reality in a manner similar to the disabled veteran Dix painted with his own features in his *Großstadt.* On another level, however, Hinkemann's disability stands for the castrated, demasculinized German nation. Consequently, this character also functions as a grotesque, provocative allegory of defeated Germany and the impotence of the front generation, as indicated by the play's original title, *Der deutsche Hinkemann* (The German Hinkemann).

Nationalistic circles quickly zeroed in on this meaning of disability in Toller's play. Because of his leadership in the Munich Soviet Republic and subsequent imprisonment, his Jewishness, and his provocative works, he had become known as the most controversial author of the early Weimar Republic. The scandals involving his plays climaxed at performances of *Hinkemann* in 1923 and 1924 in Leipzig, Dresden, Vienna, and Berlin, where hostile nationalists, national socialists, and volkish students disrupted performances and even provoked street fights. These anti-Bolshevist, anti-Semitic groups attacked "Hinkemann Toller" for allegedly insulting war victims by putting a castrated veteran onstage for the public to see. The fracas at the Dresden Staatstheater even led to a debate in the Saxon parliament on January 24, 1924. One right-wing representative claimed that the play "mocks Christianity and the German people, ridicules our wounded war heroes, and is the worst filth imaginable." This politician moralized that "the theater is not a whorehouse where physical or mental eunuchs, toilet-bowl artists, or criminals can celebrate their orgies—without being punished."[94] By contrast, in a review of the Berlin production of *Hinkemann* on April 15, 1924, Joseph Roth praised the play as "the beginning of a new literature" about the proletariat. Noting that Hinkemann was castrated "on the field of dubious honor, of 'male' honor," he pointed out that it was precisely this ironic view of "German heroism" and "German manliness" that the nationalists could not abide (154). Nationalists wanted disabilities caused by war to remain hidden outside the public sphere, but a leftist such as Toller insisted on showing the terrible aspects of war disabilities as provocatively as possible. In this respect, the scandal over *Hinkemann* is an early instance of a culture war about who would set the terms for interpreting the meaning of disability for the German nation.

Disabled Civilians, Eugenics, and Rehabilitation Psychology

While the best-known representations of disability in Weimar art and literature are those of disabled veterans and workers, various types of discourses about other groups of disabled people were also central to cultural, social, medical, economic, and political controversies during this period. The discourse of rehabilitation advocated helping disabled people, including crippled children, become self-supporting, but it was also based on problematic assumptions about abnormal psychology and the need for social control. Furthermore, the discourse of eugenics, known in Germany as racial hygiene, expanded exponentially during the Weimar period.[95] Coined in 1881 by the British naturalist and mathematician Francis Galton, the term *eugenics* was defined by a leading U.S. advocate, Charles B. Davenport, as "the science of the improvement of the human race by better breeding."[96] Accordingly, eugenicists stressed both "positive" approaches (encouraging "superior" people to have more children) and "negative" approaches (advocating sterilization to prevent the "inferior" from reproducing). The eugenicists hardly supported outright euthanasia, for they generally believed that sterilizing the "unfit" was the best way to achieve their goals.[97]

Having developed within the larger context of social Darwinism in the late nineteenth century, eugenics became a widespread discourse and practice in many countries, including the United States and Great Britain. In particular, the majority of U.S. states passed involuntary sterilization laws that were applied mostly to patients in mental institutions and to prison inmates.[98] In Germany after the end of World War I, however, shocked by the large numbers of healthy soldiers who had been killed or disabled and by the socioeconomic crisis, voices from across much of the political spectrum, from conservatives to social democrats, began to advocate eugenic policies more strongly.[99] In what one historian has termed a "genetic allegory of the stab-in-the-back legend," these circles argued that while healthy, productive Germans had died on the battlefield, the unfit and unproductive had survived and procreated at home, frequently living off the meager resources of the state.[100]

Any analysis of disability in Weimar culture and society must deal with how disabled people were targeted by the racial hygienists and those moving in their orbit in the cultural sphere. No single study can accomplish this task, but it is possible at least to explicate some of the most significant tendencies in this area. In the following sections, I describe briefly who disabled civilians were and discuss how rehabilitation theories demonstrated supportive attitudes but also sometimes a eugenic mind-set. Next I show how circles on the right extended their attacks on disabled people they viewed as degenerate into the realm of culture by declaring much of the avant-garde art discussed here to be degenerate also. This pervasive discourse about degeneracy paved the way for Nazi cultural policies that attacked modern art by comparing it to artworks created by people who were mentally ill. As was the case for debates about disabled veterans, many of the controversies about other groups of disabled people also focused on their proper place in German society, the meaning of their bodies for the German nation, and how they were to be represented in culture.

Although disabled veterans had many types of impairments, the civilian disabled population was even more heterogeneous. People of both sexes and all ages were affected by a much greater variety of physical, sensory, cognitive, and mental impairments, including conditions that were hereditary or congenital. Large numbers of civilians—especially children—had also become disabled as a result of wartime conditions, above all due to the malnourishment and poor hygiene that caused an explosion in diseases such as rickets and (spinal) tuberculosis. As one welfare group wrote in 1926, "Never before have our wards been so crowded with dying tubercular children. Never before have we seen so many extreme manifestations of bone deformities."[101] Since disability is always a fluid rather than a sharply delineated category, it is useful to summarize briefly the most factually comprehensive effort to characterize the disabled population during the Weimar period. This was the national government survey of disabled people undertaken in

1925–26, which is to date the only survey of its kind ever carried out in Germany. Published by the Statistisches Reichsamt and entitled *Die Gebrechlichen im Deutschen Reich nach der Zählung von 1925–26* (The Infirm in the German Reich according to the Survey of 1925–26), the survey defined the "infirm" as encompassing the blind, deaf and dumb (those who were born deaf or lost hearing before age seven), deaf (those who lost hearing after age seven), physically infirm (divided into severely and slightly infirm), and mentally infirm (including the mentally ill, epileptic, and hereditarily or congenitally feebleminded and noting that 39.5 percent were born with their condition).[102] The purpose of the survey was to collect useful facts for providing treatment and welfare benefits. It included questions about medical condition, age, residence, living conditions and marital status, income and occupation, and education.

The survey's organizers admitted that there were significant methodological problems with their data collection, including undercounting, misinterpretation of questions, and the reluctance of many respondents to provide information about income and employment due to fear of losing benefits. Keeping these limitations in mind, however, the survey provides a fascinating glimpse into some central aspects of disabled people's lives at this time. These statistics tell us nothing about subjective experiences of acceptance or rejection. Nevertheless, the numbers still indicate something about the extent to which various groups of disabled people had opportunities to live in their communities and to fulfill age-appropriate social roles. Accordingly, the survey's findings about residence and marital status, education, and employment are especially significant. In view of what was to come, residence is important because it was above all placement in institutions that would later make many disabled people vulnerable to Nazi "euthanasia." Education is significant as preparation for work, and employment is significant both because of the stress put on it by the rehabilitation experts and because ability to work would later be a way of escaping Nazi eugenic policies to some extent.

For those with sensory and physical disabilities, residence in an institution was connected in most cases with rehabilitation and education, and only small numbers of people from these groups were permanently institutionalized. Although 17.5 percent of blind people lived in institutions, the vast majority were children and young people being educated in schools for the blind. Blind people living in their own households, with relatives, or in unreported circumstances accounted for another 80.4 percent. A total of 59 percent of young deaf and dumb people aged seven to fifteen were being educated in institutions, whereas very few older people from this group were institutionalized. Of the severely physically disabled, about 4.5 percent of males and 9.2 percent of females resided in a cripples' home or other institution such as an old age home. Of those aged fifteen to twenty, about 80 percent lived with parents or other relatives, while 13 percent of boys and 7.9 percent of girls were in cripples' homes where they were receiving treatment and vocational training. Marital status differed greatly among this group by gender. Among men, 63 percent were married and 31.7 percent were single, whereas these numbers were reversed among severely physically disabled women, with 21.3 percent being married and 60.4 percent single. The survey explained this by stating that women were frequently willing to care for a disabled husband, whereas it was only "natural" that few men would marry a disabled woman. Institutionalization was highest among the "mentally infirm" with about 63.3 percent of this group living in state hospitals and nursing homes (Heil- und Pflegeanstalten), institutions for epileptics or the feebleminded, or other types of institutions. In terms of absolute numbers, other sources indicate a rise in institutionalization over the course of the Weimar period. Thus, there were 185,397 psychiatric patients in 1924 and over 300,000 in 1929,[103] and cripples' homes had expanded their number of beds from 3,400 in 1906 to 12,500 in 1931.[104] In a related area, the number of pupils in Hilfsschulen (special schools for the "educable feebleminded") increased from 43,000 in 1914 to 72,000 in 1928 (173). A complex mixture of humanitarian and disciplinary factors influenced these developments. After the Great Depression began, however, racial hygienists cited such numbers as disturbing illustrations of the economic overextension of the Weimar welfare state and called for drastic solutions to curtail spending on such "degenerates."

The questions about education and training elicited information that reveals significant efforts to provide at least some schooling to those with sensory and physical disabilities, while these questions were not even asked about the mentally infirm. Of blind people, only 1.7 percent of men and 2.3 percent of women had no formal school education while about 70 percent had only finished elementary school (Volksschule). Of the deaf and dumb, about 8 percent had received no formal schooling, and the majority were educated in an institution. Of the severely physically disabled, 1.4 percent of men and 3.4 percent of women had no formal schooling while 84.8 percent of men and 86 percent of women had only finished elementary school. Almost all of those with slight physical disabilities attended regular schools.

In 1925, for the German population as a whole, 68 percent of men and 35.6 percent of women were employed outside the home. Among blind people, however, 38 percent of men and 13.5 percent of women were employed, most frequently in the stereotypical occupations of basket maker and brush maker. Of the deaf and dumb, 63.8 percent of men and 29.8 percent of women worked, the majority in factories and the trades. Of the severely physically disabled, 64 percent of men were employed, most frequently as tailors, shoemakers, carpenters, basket makers, mechanics, peddlers, and so forth, while 15 percent of women worked, especially in occupations having to do with sewing, knitting, and so forth. Of the mentally infirm, only about 13.1 percent of men and 3.5 percent of women worked, generally performing simple farm tasks or manual labor. This fact made it all the easier for racial hygienists to write these people off as "ballast existences" who were supposedly draining the nation's resources and to advocate their elimination.

When historians have dealt with disabled civilians during this era, they have generally focused on the theory and practice of medicine, rehabilitation, and special education; on institutions such as cripples' homes and mental hospitals; and on the history of racial hygiene. This large body of research is essential to understanding many aspects of disabled people's lives and to exploring the origins of Nazi eugenic policies. What the survey of 1925–26 indicates, however, is that historical research focusing on institutionalized disabled people leaves the lives of many others outside its purview. As can be seen from these statistics, the vast majority of people with sensory and physical disabilities did not live in institutions, and a significant number of the mentally disabled (about one-third) lived in their own communities. The group of physically disabled children and young people is a case in point. Since the Prussian Law on Cripples' Welfare of 1920 only applied to children from poor families, it was generally these children who were institutionalized in state cripples' homes.[105] Almost nothing is known about the lives of disabled people who lived outside institutions, those from families with the means and the will to care for children at home and with the persistence to insist that their children attend regular schools and receive vocational training or higher education. Accordingly, the results of the survey indicate the relevance of social class in shaping the diverging experiences of large groups of disabled people and in veiling many of their lives from the historian.

Keeping these limitations on knowledge in mind, much may still be said about how the theory and practice of rehabilitation during this period both supported and marginalized particular groups of people with disabilities. The earlier discussion of disabled veterans gains further dimensions by linking it to how some influential rehabilitation experts viewed the disabled children under their care in institutions. Once again the orthopedist Konrad Biesalski and his colleagues at the Oskar-Helene Home in Berlin may serve as examples. On the one hand, their institution was a model for its time that provided not only medical and rehabilitation facilities but also schooling, opportunities for play and recreation, and time outdoors in the sun and fresh air to the young patients. Guided in many ways by enlightened principles, these experts wanted to provide the comprehensive treatment and vocational training that would enable their charges to become self-supporting members of society, independent citizens rather than charity recipients.

In spite of this goal of social integration, Biesalski and his colleague Hans Würtz (1875–1958), the education director at the Oskar-Helene Home, were influenced by physiognomic theories and thus believed that the deformed bodies of cripples necessarily shaped the development of their emotional makeup. Biesalski claimed, for example, that a soldier who had lost a leg, a worker whose hand had been torn away by a machine, or a child who suddenly became paralyzed were not only physically impaired but also in danger of acquiring negative emotional qualities, of becoming "withdrawn, suspicious, envious, easily offended, bitter, and arrogant."[106] In turn, they argued that disabled people—particularly the young—should be treated and educated in institutions rather than remaining at home or attending regular schools. They asserted that the expertise of physicians (particularly orthopedists) and educators like themselves was necessary in order to straighten both the bodies of cripples and their sick souls, to instill in them the iron will to overcome their impairments, and to make them into productive workers. Würtz was especially prolific in writing about what he termed "cripples' souls," as the titles of some of his books attest: *Der Wille siegt* (The Will Conquers All, 1915); *Sieghafte Lebenskämpfer* (Victors in the Struggle for Life, 1919); *Das Seelenleben des Krüppels* (The Soul Life of the Cripple, 1921); and, last but not least, *Zerbrecht die Krücken: Krüppelprobleme der Menschheit—Schicksalsstiefkinder aller Zeiten und Völker in Wort und Bild* (Break the Crutches: The Problems of Cripples for Humanity—Stepchildren of Fate from All Times and Peoples in Words and Pictures, 1932). This last book is an obsessive—though useful—compilation of lists of cripples in history and depictions of cripples in art, literature, and proverbs. Proceeding from undoubtedly humanitarian intentions, Würtz's "cripple pedagogy" ultimately provided a rationale for segregating disabled people and contributed to the further stigmatization of people with orthopedic impairments.[107]

The most problematic aspect of theories such as those of Biesalski

Fig. 8. Children with spinal tuberculosis enjoying the fresh air at the Oskar-Helene Home in Berlin. (From Konrad Biesalski, *Grundriss der Krüppelfürsorge* [Leipzig: Voss, 1926], 13. Courtesy of the Library of the University of Kentucky.)

and Würtz was the overbearing emphasis they placed on work in connection with their construction of an abnormal psychology of disabled people. Partly to legitimate their own field, these experts insisted that most disabled people could learn or relearn to work—a guiding principle that of course had many positive, empowering aspects. They applied this principle in an extremely inflexible manner, however, viewing those who would not work as having weak wills or other negative psychological characteristics. Furthermore, the result of this approach for those who truly could not work or care for themselves—the most severely physically disabled people and the majority of those with mental illnesses or cognitive disabilities—was the conclusion that they should be consigned to the margins of society and frequently to institutions. Already during the period of astronomic inflation in the early Weimar years, voices had been raised calling for money to be spent only on rehabilitating those cripples who could be trained to work, and these proposals became more widespread after the economic crisis began in 1929.[108] In 1932, in *Zerbrecht die Krücken,* for example, Würtz declared that "modern orthopedics separates the curable cripple from the incurable invalid: modern cripple pedagogy separates the morally healthy cripple who is open to becoming autonomous from the feebleminded, who remain morally immature and dependent."[109]

Although Biesalski and Würtz did not explicitly use the term *degenerate,* their positing of an abnormal "cripple soul" and their methodology of ranking disabled people as acceptable or inferior according to their tractability and work capacity participated in the eugenic discourse of degeneracy that was so pervasive at the time. Psychiatrists and government officials frequently applied similar ideas to veterans with mental problems caused by the war—those who might be described today as affected by post-traumatic stress disorder.[110] Over the course of the Weimar period, it became more difficult for such veterans—called "war neurotics" or "pension psychotics"—to receive financial compensation for war-related psychological suffering. The psychiatrists who were gatekeepers to the pension system increasingly opposed such compensation, often categorizing these men as constitutionally deficient and prescribing hard work as the only cure for their maladies. Furthermore, the accusations of malingering frequently directed against these men mirrored the rehabilitation experts' view of the inferior "cripple soul" as work shy. These psychiatric casualties were often linked with the revolutionaries of 1918–19 in that both groups were condemned as psychopathic and unpatriotic.[111] In this manner, the right-wing discourse of degeneracy combined attacks on disabled people (especially the mentally ill), Marxists, and Jews as threats to the racial makeup and political stability of the German nation.

Affronts to the Healthy Eye: The Aesthetic Discourse of Degeneracy

With their methods for treating disabled children and adults, the rehabilitation experts rigidly upheld the social expectation that citizens should engage in productive work, thus fueling debates over what should be done with "unproductive" groups of people. In such controversies, social norms were frequently intertwined in complex ways with aesthetic norms that extolled the healthy and beautiful while condemning the sick, disabled, and ugly. These pervasive discourses about disability are evident in clashes over the actual presence of disabled people in public, cultural representations of disability, and the labeling of modern art as degenerate. With regard to the perceptions of the public, on the one hand there were certainly many who supported efforts to help disabled people, but many also did not want to be confronted directly with such "unfortunates" in daily life. The frequent citizens' protests against plans to locate cripples' homes in their proximity are revealing instances of this mentality. Of course, economic considerations and fears of decreased property values were an important factor, but aesthetic considerations also played a significant role. For example, an article published in the *Nationalzeitung* on May 24, 1910, assailed a proposal to build such an institution on the North Sea island of Norderney as follows: "Norderney is a world-class spa with a rather small beach. Should droves of unhappy crippled children be led around and allowed to swim there among the elegant, cheerful visitors to the spa? People would constantly be looking at these children with curiosity, pity, or disgust. Is that good for the poor cripples? And is it good for those who want to refresh themselves for a few weeks and recover from their responsibilities and from their work in pleasant surroundings at the seaside!"[112] Similarly, in 1912 plans to build an institution in Wiesbaden were canceled after residents protested that they could not be expected to put up with the sight of "Siamese twins" and children with "water on the brain" in their beautiful parks (222). Furthermore, in Berlin well-to-do residents living near the Oskar-Helene Home prevailed upon its directors to omit the word *Krüppelheim* (cripples' home) from its official name and demanded reassurances that the sight of the young patients would not be "repulsive" (251). If curiosity, exemplified in the freak show, was one extreme reaction to bodily deviation from the norm, such protests exemplified its opposite. Feeling disgust and aversion, these citizens, who had no doubts about their own health and normality, wanted to banish visibly disabled people from their sight. It was not a very big step from such hostility toward disabled people in daily life to eugenic thinking that wanted to eliminate them altogether.

Whether consciously or not, such efforts to remove disabled people from the public sphere of respectable citizens coincided with the broader discourse about degeneracy that had received its quintessential statement in Max Nordau's *Entartung* (Degeneration, 1892–93). It is an irony of history that with this book, Nordau—a physician, writer, son of a rabbi, and later a leading Zionist—provided the method of using medical concepts to attack modern literature that the national socialists were to employ in their attacks on aesthetic modernism. Nordau characterized degeneracy as deviance from the aesthetic and social norms and sensibilities of the educated middle classes (Bildungsbürgertum). For him, degeneracy in culture was shown by qualities such as dissonance, artificiality, agitation, strangeness, obscurity, excessive sensuality, and irrationality; while its opposite, health, was indicated by harmony, naturalness, calm, familiarity, clarity, self-control, and rationality. Furthermore, he made the fatal leap from characterizing cultural trends as degenerate to labeling certain people as degenerate. These were disabled people who manifested anatomical deformations he termed "stigmata" but also modern artists, whom he described as "spiritual eunuchs, cripples, vermin."[113] Accordingly, he wrote, "The normal person with a clear mind, logical thinking, sober judgment, and a strong will concedes at the most, out of scornful pity, the shelter of the hospital, the insane asylum, or the prison to the helpless degenerate" (45). Influenced by social Darwinism, Nordau thus argued that the healthy should forcibly expel the degenerate, who were not only inferior but also harmful to respectable society.[114]

Voices across much of the political spectrum proposed various types of eugenic measures to achieve this goal of eliminating the degenerate during the Weimar Republic. It was only right-wing nationalists, however, who linked discourses about disability and degeneracy with cultural criticism of modern art. Through comparisons with the appearance of visibly disabled people, these ideologues declared much of modern art to be degenerate, also, because of its characteristic deviations from "nature." Of course, since about 1890 there had been many volkish nationalists who typically attacked modernism as "un-German." But the Militant League for German Culture (Kampfbund für deutsche Kultur), founded by Alfred Rosenberg in 1928, was the first organization to channel these older nationalist views in an explicitly national socialist direction. Its adherents employed fascist vocabulary to label modern art as degenerate, subhuman, subversively Jewish, or culturally Bolshevist.

The publication emanating from these circles that had the most fatal consequences was Paul Schultze-Naumburg's *Kunst und Rasse* (Art and Race, 1928). Schultze-Naumburg was a well-known nationalist architect whose traditional aesthetic, founded on an environmentalist culture of the homeland, was displaced increasingly by the internationalism of the Bauhaus school after 1918. This declining professional success may have provoked him to denounce the coldness of the Bauhaus as un-German and claim that aesthetics had a racial basis, as he did in a 1926 altercation with the leading Bauhaus architect, Walter Gropius.[115] Two years later, in *Kunst und Rasse,* Schultze-Naumburg extended this criticism to much of modern art, including expressionist and verist works, which he defamed as degenerate by comparing them to photographs of disabled people.

Schultze-Naumburg left no doubts about his revulsion toward the

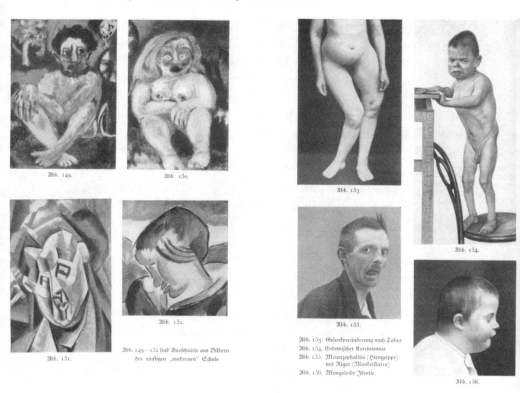

Fig. 9. Juxtaposition of modern art with photographs of disabled people. (From Paul Schultze-Naumburg, *Kunst und Rasse* [Munich: Lehmann, 1928], 98–99. Courtesy of the University of Wisconsin-Madison Libraries.)

people shown in these photographs, which he acquired from Dr. Wilhelm Weygandt, the director of the Friedrichsberg state mental hospital and head psychiatrist at the university clinic in Hamburg. Schultze-Naumburg's display of these medical photographs blotted out the individuality of these patients and reduced them to objects used for a purpose counter to their real interests. The patients are identified by their medical diagnoses, including paralysis, Mongoloid idiocy, paralysis of eye muscles, microcephaly, idiocy, elephantiasis, rickets, anencephaly, acromegaly of hands and lower face, severe harelip, chondrodystrophy, obesity, cretinism, nervous disorder of late-stage syphilis, and encephalitis. Significantly, not all of these conditions are hereditary or mental illnesses. Rather, the photographs Schultze-Naumburg selected are of people whose appearance deviated greatly from his aesthetic ideal of the "healthy, Nordic man."[116] Writing that it was only in the "deepest depths of human misery and human scum," in the "idiot asylums, psychiatric clinics, cripples' homes, lepers' colonies, and hideouts of the most debased" that such "material" might be seen, he praised charitable welfare services for endeavoring to keep such "creatures" out of "public view."[117] In the preface to the second edition of his book (1934), along with praising the national socialists for expelling Jews from influential positions, he welcomed their involuntary sterilization law, stating, "The eradication of the inferior is no longer an ideology out of touch with life, but rather it has been anchored in legislation and thus in reality. After the timid attempts we have observed in individual states in North America, Germany has become the first country to organize its entire state apparatus around this new volkish principle."[118] This train of thought demonstrates especially clearly how an aestheticization of health served to stigmatize many disabled or ill people and abet forcible efforts to eliminate them from the body politic.

Schultze-Naumburg juxtaposed these photographs to works by both German and foreign avant-garde artists, including, though he did not name them, Picasso, Kokoschka, Modigliani, Hofer, Nolde, and Schmidt-Rottluff. Using racial terms, he assailed Weimar art for rarely portraying "Nordic man" and for preferring "exotic, primitive" types that showed all the signs of degeneracy found among the "ill and the physically deformed." In contrast to the purity of art in antiquity and the early Renaissance, which "enriches us and makes us happy," he attacked Weimar artists for creating a "hell of the subhuman."[119] Accordingly, he labeled these avant-garde art works degenerate. This perspective resonated among broad sectors of the public, whose members had little understanding of modernistic distortions in art and preferred more realistic images.[120] It also resonated among those who believed art should glorify national ideals rather than subverting them as Beckmann, Dix, Grosz, Hoerle and others had done with their depictions of disabled veterans. The right-wing nationalists who wanted to see strong, heroic representations of military men instead of Toller's Hinkemann came from precisely the circles that were most receptive to Schultze-Naumburg's arguments. These debates about traditionalism or modernism, in which attitudes toward the social and aesthetic positions of disabled people played a central role, foreshadowed the Nazis' campaign against degenerate art. In the preface to the third edition of his book, published in 1938 after the Degenerate Art exhibition of 1937, Schultze-Naumburg praised the cultural politics of the Nazis. Here, just as he had greeted efforts to keep disabled people out of sight or eliminate them, he stated that many of his hopes had been realized for the "remnants of the degenerate art of the Republic had almost totally disappeared."[121]

Disabled People Tell Their Own Stories

Self-Advocacy Organizations

Discourses about medical treatment, rehabilitation, degeneracy, and eugenics were for the most part discourses of nondisabled people about what should be done to help, train, control, or eliminate disabled people. Furthermore, nondisabled Weimar artists and authors only created narrowly circumscribed representations of disabled veterans or workers that fit their political agendas and almost never depicted other areas of disabled people's lives or people with other types of disabilities. But how did disabled people themselves respond to these varying discourses? How did they perceive and organize themselves to represent their interests in the Weimar Republic? The heterogeneity of the disabled population would require complex historical answers to these questions, but several significant trends and examples may be indicated here. In the majority of instances, however, the life stories of disabled people were not deemed worth recording or taking seriously, and so they have been lost forever. Little is known about the subjective experiences of children, young people, and women with disabilities—whether in medical or rehabilitation settings or in daily life. Similarly, almost nothing is known about how people with cognitive disabilities and mental illnesses—a prime target of the racial hygienists and always the most stigmatized group—experienced their lives inside or outside institutions.

Nevertheless, there were significant efforts by disabled people during the Weimar Republic to expand their rights in the new German democracy, critique the negative ways others perceived them, and tell their own stories. Disabled veterans were a massive group of adult men who had all acquired their disabilities in the war and thus claimed the nation's support. Their war victims' associations, which had affiliations across the political spectrum from the Communist Party to the German Nationalists, were the first large, influential organizations of disabled people.[122] In turn, some groups of disabled civilians also began to organize for the first time to demand treatment under the law equal to that accorded to disabled veterans. The Reich Association of the Blind (Reichsdeutscher Blindenverband), for example, founded in 1912, had fourteen thousand members by the end of the Weimar Republic. In 1920 and 1922, groups of the so-called peace blind demonstrated successfully in Berlin to be covered by the social welfare laws passed for the "war blind." And smaller, more specialized organizations, from the German Association of Blind Academics (Verein der blinden Akademiker Deutschlands) to the Association of Blind Industrial Workers (Verein blinder Industriearbeiter), worked to further the interests of their members.[123]

Deaf Germans had been especially active since the nineteenth century in organizing their own clubs and associations.[124] The first newspaper for deaf people, *Der Taubstummenfreund* (The Deaf-Mute's Friend), was founded in 1872, and others included *Die Stimme* (The Voice) and *Der deutsche Gehörlose* (The Deaf German). Political, social, and athletic associations of deaf people flourished in Weimar Germany, with about twenty-five existing in Berlin alone in 1932. The political groups there mirrored those among the hearing population, including the Deaf Labor Union Group of the Workers' Alliance, the Deaf Labor Union Group in the Social Democratic Party, the German Nationalist Group, the Deaf Section of the Nazi Party, and the largest one, the Greater Berlin Deaf Section of the Communist Party. Deaf people also organized around issues of specific relevance to them, and in 1927 they combined their regional associations into the Reich Union of the Deaf of Germany (Reichsverband der Gehörlosen Deutschlands or REGEDE).

One of the main goals of REGEDE was to create more positive perceptions among members of the public about the capabilities of deaf people. To further this aim, the organization produced an hour-long film, *Verkannte Menschen* (Misjudged People, 1932). Directed and with a script by Wilhelm Ballier, who was both deaf and a Nazi sympathizer, the film is an important document about the German deaf community in the final years of the Weimar Republic.[125] The first part concentrates on education. In contrast to the past, when deaf people had to depend on charity, the film shows the advances made in contemporary Germany. There is compulsory education for all deaf children, who learn to speak, read, and write; acquire work skills; and grow up to participate in the electoral process. The second part emphasizes all the ways in which deaf people are good German citizens even though they are often misjudged and rejected. They are shown leading productive, useful lives at work in factories, laboratories, and dental offices, at home, or on the farm. When they are not working, they participate in community activities such as sports. The film challenged eugenic trends by showing a deaf married couple communicating orally with their hearing child and by reminding its viewers that 90 percent of the children of deaf parents could hear. In the closing image of the film, a stereotypical blond, muscular, "Aryan"-looking man holds a work implement over his shoulder while the voice-over admonishes the spectator, "Don't pity, give them their rights: work and bread." The film portrays deaf people as capable, normal, and happy and only seeking an end to the discriminatory employment practices of the hearing world. The Nazis did not want to promote this positive image of the deaf community, however, and so the Reich minister of propaganda, Joseph Goebbels, banned the film in 1934.

Physically disabled Germans founded their first self-advocacy organization in 1919 in Berlin. It was called the Self-Help League of the Physically Handicapped (Selbsthilfebund der Körperbehinderten or SBK), and it changed its name to the Reichsbund der Körperbehinderten (RBK) in 1931. The life stories of the individuals involved in this organization, as well as their ideas about the proper place for physically disabled people in society, present very different pictures from those promulgated by the rehabilitation experts. The SBK was also known as the Perl League (Perl-Bund) after Otto Perl (1882–1951), one of its most active founders.[126] Perl's story reveals an independent thinker who worked to benefit others in spite of his extremely limited circumstances. Born on a farm close to Torgau in Saxony, Perl contracted a joint inflammation at the age of thirteen that left his limbs stiff and largely immobilized. His mother cared for him until her death in 1898, and then he lived in various invalid homes (Siechenhäuser) for the next ten years. These were institutions for the poor that provided the bare necessities to people of all ages and with all types of physical and mental disabilities, the sick and dying, alcoholics, and so forth. In 1908, Perl moved to the Oberlinhaus in Nowawes, close to Potsdam, an institution for crippled children run by the Inner Mission of the Protestant Church. He had never attended school but always read and studied on his own, and in 1918, encouraged by a teacher, he passed his Abitur examination. By then, he had learned to walk short distances with crutches, and in 1922, probably helped by an assistant or friend, he began to study at the Humboldt University in Berlin while living in an old-age home there. He studied for four semesters before moving to another institution in Nuremberg in 1926. In that year, he published a book, *Krüppeltum und Gesellschaft im Wandel der Zeit* (The Crippled and Society throughout the Ages), the first history of disabled people in Germany by a disabled writer. Against his will, he was transferred in 1934 to an invalid home in Magdeburg. Nothing is known about his life for the next nine years, but in an autobiographical sketch of 1946 he recalled the Nazi "terror" in the institution, saying that patients had to refrain from insisting on their rights. He specifically mentioned being a witness to "euthanasia," stating, "Many a person from my surroundings was forced to take the path to the lethal injection."[127] In 1943, he went to live with his brother, then back to an invalid home in Wittenberg, where he died in 1951. Throughout his life, in spite of his severe disability, Perl resisted oppressive circumstances and asserted his humanity and his rights.

Perl frequently described how he suffered as an intelligent, young, physically disabled man confined in institutions with—in his words—idiots, epileptics, morphine addicts, and people with all types of illnesses, including tuberculosis and venereal diseases.[128] This negative personal experience of being equated in life-defining situations with "worthless cripples" led him and his fellow activists in the SBK to emphasize that they were merely physically disabled and frequently to support eugenic measures directed against the mentally impaired. Accordingly, the name they gave their organization is revealing with respect to their self-conception and goals. They coined the word *körperbehindert* (physically handicapped) in order to set themselves above the "inferior" feebleminded or mentally ill. By using this term, they wanted to emphasize that their minds were sound and also that many of them were capable of working and being productive citizens in contrast to mentally infirm cripples. In a similar manner, many disabled veterans had also distanced themselves from the word *cripple* with its connotations of helplessness, burdensomeness, and incompetence. As early as February 1915, high-ranking military officials had declared that soldiers injured in war should not be referred to as war cripples since this was an "unsuitable, ugly, unpleasant" word.[129] Rather, they preferred the terms *war invalid* (Kriegsinvalider) or *war injured* (Kriegsbeschädigter or Kriegsversehrter).

The SBK defined itself as an organization for people who were physically disabled from birth or childhood rather than for disabled veterans or workers. In 1929, ten years after its founding, it had fifty local chapters with about six thousand members.[130] It participated in conferences and exhibitions, created its own work-training centers, and published a newsletter that became a full-fledged journal called *Der Körperbehinderte* (The Physically Handicapped). In many ways, the goals of the SBK for physically disabled people hardly differed from those of the rehabilitation experts: medical treatment, educational and vocational training, appropriate work, and financial independence rather than charity. However, these activists insisted on determining for themselves the best ways to achieve these goals, which put them fundamentally at odds with all paternalistic approaches. Along these lines, Perl's book provides an eloquent early rejection of the medical model of disability in favor of the social model with its declaration, "The subject here is not a medical or scientific question, but a legal principle: namely, the right to self-determination, which welfare law has always denied to welfare recipients!"[131] It was this insistence on self-determination that caused some care providers to feel quite threatened by the activities of the SBK, as did one pastor from the Protestant Inner Mission, who called "the Perl League members the Spartacists among the cripples receiving welfare support."[132]

In contrast to the physiognomic views of experts such as Biesalski and Würtz, members of the SBK argued that there was no such thing as an abnormal "cripple soul" that necessitated the segregation of physically disabled people and the special education of disabled children in institutions. Rather, they argued that remaining part of the family and normal daily life was the basis for healthy individual development. In particular, the women members of the SBK advocated educating disabled children in regular schools with their nondisabled peers, asserting that this would benefit all the children concerned. One of the most active proponents of this mainstreaming was Marie Gruhl (1881–1929), the only woman among the founders of the SBK.[133] Born without feet into a middle-class family (her father was a school inspector), she used prostheses and a wheelchair. With the loving support of her parents, she attended a regular school and became a secondary school teacher in Berlin. Gruhl acknowledged both the medical treatment she received and her integration into the world around her, writing, "Everything imaginable was done to improve my physical ability and make me as self-reliant as possible. But aside from this I was brought up like a normal, healthy child. I grew up in the sunshine of my parents' home; I was allowed to attend public school; I was allowed to get an education that followed my inclinations; and today I am allowed to assume my place in life as a public schoolteacher together with healthy people." Hoping to provide more disabled children with these advantages, Gruhl traveled to institutions for crippled children throughout Germany, where she urged both staff and parents to send these children to public schools. At the national congress on cripples' welfare held in Leipzig in 1920, she summed up her convictions by stating that a crippled child could not be prepared for life in an institutional environment that was not free but rather should be completely integrated into the "community of the healthy."

The efforts of the SBK to promote self-determination and resist the methods of the experts generally concentrated on concrete areas such as education and work. In one instance, however, a member of the SBK undertook a unique project intended to refute the theoretical underpinnings of contemporary rehabilitation psychology. Little is known about the life of Irma Dresdner.[134] Disabled since childhood, she was a Jewish teacher at the Philanthropin, the school of the Israelite Community (Israelitische Gemeinde) in Frankfurt am Main. She was involved with the bourgeois women's movement as well as SBK and RBK groups in

Frankfurt and Berlin. When the RBK became a Nazi organization, it expelled Dresdner along with all its Jewish members, and all further traces of her life are lost. In April 1933, Dresdner managed to publish an article entitled "Über Körperbehinderung und seelische Entwicklung" (On Physical Handicap and Emotional Development). There she reproached rehabilitation experts such as Biesalski, Würtz, and others for developing their theories without taking the perspectives of disabled people themselves into account. In particular, quoting Biesalski, she criticized their concept of the "cripple soul" as characterized by abnormalities such as oversensitivity, irritability, resentment, vengefulness, envy, distrust, rigidity, arrogance, self-centeredness, and delusions of grandeur.[135] By contrast, Dresdner asserted that in her lifetime of experience as a disabled person and in the company of disabled people she had rarely observed such characteristics among them. She noted, however, that there were almost no readily available autobiographical accounts by disabled people that might challenge the unfounded opinions of these experts.

Consequently, Dresdner distributed a list of eighteen questions, along with a request for life stories, to members of the RBK in 1932, asking them how they would describe themselves.[136] She received responses from people in Frankfurt, Berlin, and other cities, which she collected and analyzed. A number of the questions explicitly referred to the assumptions of Würtz's "cripple psychology," and in their answers the respondents almost always denied having unusual feelings of resentment, vengefulness, envy, inferiority, disadvantage, self-centeredness, and so forth. Some made a point of saying that they only felt hostile, sad, or frightened when healthy people stared or laughed at them, thus turning the tables and showing that these negative feelings were caused by the behavior of the nondisabled rather than the supposedly inherent inadequacies of the disabled. Many noted that they were accepted by relatives and friends, had playmates as children, attended school in a wheelchair, and so forth, and some were proud to be self-supporting. Frequently, they stated that they did not dwell on their disabilities but rather had a wide variety of interests such as hobbies, music, swimming, reading, listening to the radio, and religion. Love and marriage seemed to be the most problematic area since almost all the respondents were single and felt that potential partners had rejected them because of their disabilities.

Dresdner selected the life story of one woman, a seamstress of forty-four, as deserving of particular attention (410–11). Born in a small village in northern Germany, this woman had contracted polio at the age of three and been left with a paralyzed leg. Her family neglected her, kept her apart from her siblings, and did not send her to school. She learned how to read on her own. Finally, at the age of fifteen, with the help of the village minister, she received medical treatment, some schooling, and vocational training. When she wrote to Dresdner, she was supporting both herself and her mother. Dresdner emphasized how respectable, responsible, generous, and forgiving this woman was in contrast to the experts' ideas about the negative characteristics of the "cripple soul." In general, the responses of physically disabled people to Dresdner's survey totally contradicted the stigmatizing views that were typical of contemporary rehabilitation psychology. No greater contrast to Hans Würtz's deterministic linking of physical disability with emotional abnormality can be imagined than this declaration by one of the respondents: "Today I can truthfully say that my handicap made me more free. It made me into an independent, thinking, active person" (425). It goes without saying that because Dresdner's article was published in 1933 these significant findings could have no resonance. Consequently, it is all the more important to remember her project as one of the first instances in which physically disabled Germans tried in a coherent way to define their own identities and present themselves as human beings rather than as institutionalized cases.

Portrait of the Writer Max Herrmann-Neiße

Aside from members of such organized groups, the stigmatized position of disabled people and their lack of access to higher education meant that almost no other disabled individuals wrote explicitly at this time about how they experienced disability. One notable exception is the author and lyric poet Max Herrmann-Neiße, who became part of the avant-garde artistic scene in Berlin and reflected at numerous points in his writings on how his disability had affected his life. Herrmann-Neiße, the son of a tavern owner, was born in 1886 in the Silesian town of Neiße, as his name indicates. He was apparently always frail, and he developed a spinal curvature after a fall from a small bridge as a child. Others described him as dwarfish, disproportioned, hunchbacked, and ugly, thus defining his disability as much in aesthetic terms as with regard to functional impairments. Herrmann-Neiße recalled growing up in a loving, protective family and feeling relatively at ease in elementary school. However, when he entered the Gymnasium at the age of nine, his new classmates constantly bullied and humiliated him because of his appearance. As he entered adulthood, he suffered keenly from rejection by women until he became engaged to the beautiful Leni Gebeck in 1912. To escape the hostile, stifling atmosphere in Neiße, where provin-

Fig. 10. George Grosz, *Portrait of the Writer Max Herrmann-Neiße,* 1925. Oil on canvas, 100 × 101 cm. Städtische Kunsthalle Mannheim. (Art © Estate of George Grosz, licensed by Visual Artists and Galleries Association, Inc. [VAGA], New York.)

cial gossips dubbed Leni the "cripple's whore," the two moved to Berlin in 1917 and married.[137]

In an essay written in the late 1920s, Herrmann-Neiße reflected on why he had become a writer. He remembered an early interest in litera-ture and theater but also stated that he developed intellectual interests partly as compensation for his disability, explaining, "The fundamen-tally hard, violent, terrible impetus that—so to say—caused my wound to bleed, the first really intense suffering that turned me into a poet, was my experience of physical deformity, of being malformed."[138] Having experienced so much mistreatment and exclusion because of his "ugli-ness," he began to play off his "intellectual superiority" against those who were "stupidly healthy." He recounted, for example, writing one of his earliest short prose pieces, "Groteske" (Grotesque), after his more robust classmates had bullied him mercilessly. In this text, a man armed with a revolver appears in school, planning to shoot all the "healthy, strong, beautiful" boys, the "empty-headed elite" who have not been "poisoned by the destructive spirit of the Enlightenment." The man intends to spare "cripples and geniuses," however.[139] Herrmann-Neiße's earliest poems frequently express fury as well as sadness and resignation, but he soon stopped referring explicitly to his disability in his lyric poetry, turning to more traditional subjects such as love, landscape, and moods. This does not mean, however, that he felt more accepted as an adult than he had been when he was younger, as he explained in this statement about his works: "If the truth be told, only the form of my works became more mature. With respect to experiences, the same things can still happen to me today that happened to me earlier. I am no safer from tactless insults now than I was in the past."[140]

Herrmann-Neiße by no means thought of himself as a victim, however, but rather he tried to develop his talents and live life to the fullest. In Berlin, he wrote theater reviews, published prize-winning poetry, and even acted onstage in his own play, *Albine und Aujust* (Albine and Aujust). Using the current vocabulary of degeneracy, a review in the *Berliner Tageblatt* critiqued his performance, observing that he "appears on stage, looking sickly, a degenerate sight, but uninhibited. He makes jokes at his own expense and is suffused with cutting irony. But he also intimates that he has risen far above his own problems."[141] Enjoying nightlife wherever he lived, Herrmann-Neiße spent much of his time in Berlin artists' cafes, theaters, cabarets, and brothels. He cultivated contacts with many of the best-known artists and writers of his day, including George Grosz, who became his friend and painted the well-known *Portrait of the Writer Max Herrmann-Neiße*. Shown at the Mannheim Neue Sachlichkeit Exhibition in 1925, this painting was later displayed by the Nazis as a prime example of degenerate art both because of its formal distortions and because it portrayed a deformed person. Herrmann-Neiße's bohemian lifestyle meant that he was never self-supporting. Rather, he and Leni lived in a ménage à trois with Leni's lover, a well-to-do jeweler named Alphonse Sondheimer, who supported the three of them. This arrangement lasted until Herrmann-Neiße's death in London exile in 1941. Leni then married Sondheimer and committed suicide when he died in 1961. It would be fascinating to know more about the life of this woman, who dared to break with social conventions in so many ways.

Immediately after the Reichstag fire on February 27, 1933, the three left Germany for as yet undetermined reasons in March 1933, first going to Switzerland and then settling in London. Herrmann-Neiße became a member of the London PEN Club, moved in circles of exiled writers, and corresponded with some of the most prominent exiled intellectuals, including Thomas and Heinrich Mann. While in exile, he continued to write poetry and also wrote drafts of several long novels that were never published in his lifetime. One of these, *Die Bernert-Paula* (Paula Bernert), contains an especially revealing depiction of disability. The main character is a hunchbacked girl from a poor family. The outsider's perspective resulting from her physical difference enables her to see through hypocrisy and lies and to perceive reality more accurately than others. Since her disability liberates her from constricting social and gender roles, Paula is amoral and independent. It is easy to imagine that the exiled author was drawing on his own life experiences when he had his narrator describe Paula as follows: "In any event such a creature is annoying to every sort of crowd, because she cannot be used for their purposes. The crowd immediately perceives: here is someone who doesn't want to do what we have to do."[142] This passage hints at Herrmann-Neiße's anti-Nazi convictions, which he expressed more explicitly in his published poetry.

In a letter to Hermann Kesten on January 17, 1934, Herrmann-Neiße explained that, although he was neither Jewish nor a leftist, he opposed fascism as a believer in freedom and democracy who did not want to live "in the atmosphere of lies, torture, and robbery that prevails in Germany today."[143] Beyond this, however, unlike the disabled Nazi party members and sympathizers in organizations such as REGEDE and the RBK, his experiences as a disabled person obviously contributed to his antifascism. He rejected trends in mass culture that Nazism would incorporate, particularly the anti-intellectualism that overvalued uniform physical beauty and health. Along these lines, he wrote already in the late 1920s that "overestimation of unearned physical beauty and contempt for intellectual and artistic achievements are enjoying scandalous triumphs in an age obsessed with athletics" (437). More specifically, the abuse he endured also sensitized him to threatening developments. As early as 1912, he wrote to Leni that "everything rigidly male, warlike, and arrogantly correct is a hostile principle to me" (26). Later, in an essay probably written in exile, he linked his school experiences with contemporary events in Nazi Germany as follows: "For the first time in my life I was exposed to the brutal reality of a human community in which the weak were totally at the mercy of the physically strong. For the first time I experienced for myself what brute force is and what it can do. . . . This early suffering already contained everything that violent people with no inhibitions are doing to defenseless victims in Germany today" (16). Herrmann-Neiße's experiences as a disabled person were painful, but they also opened his eyes to the violence underlying Nazi propaganda about racial purity, health, and beauty. His insights into this reality led him to identify himself as an antifascist and to flee Nazi barbarism. As a result, the Nazi government revoked his citizenship in 1938, thus condemning his hope for preserving the democratic traditions of Germany to the void of exile.

CHAPTER 2 • Disability and Nazi Culture

During the Third Reich, cultural representations of disability and, in a broader sense, of illness constantly circulated. Along with anticommunist and anti-Semitic propaganda, national socialists created countless images of disabled people as the third major prong of their efforts to define the racial goals of their violent political movement. Their attacks on communism frequently presented "Bolsheviks" as subhuman, animalistic types and employed visual images recalling insane people or criminals.[1] They condemned Jews as "parasites" or "viruses" who threatened the purity of the "German race." And, according to their eugenic racism, the existence of large numbers of degenerate "Aryan" Germans endangered the hereditary health of the body politic (Volkskörper) from within. Nazi requirements for creating family trees illustrate how their racism intermingled these three groups. In many situations, citizens had to produce family genealogies that indicated the presence of Jewish ancestors or relatives with hereditary diseases. Furthermore, Nazi eugenicists frequently included Communist Party membership in family trees as an undesirable trait. In the most general sense, then, the main thrust of Nazi racist propaganda was to label some people as valuable, superior Germans and others as undesirable, inferior, and even subhuman outsiders.

Three broad groups of disabled people were central in very different ways to national socialist politics and propaganda. First, Nazi ideologues inveighed against the alleged neglect of disabled veterans during the Weimar Republic, promised to respect and honor them, and created heroic, sanitized images of disabled and wounded soldiers in contrast to the helpless, grotesque war cripples found in Weimar art and literature. By contrast, Nazi propaganda presented another group as an unacceptable drain on national resources and a dangerous threat to the hereditary health of the national community. These were the people who fell under the provisions of the Law for the Prevention of Offspring with Hereditary Diseases, especially all those institutionalized patients who were unable to work. Occupying a middle ground between these two poles were the official Nazi organizations for blind, deaf, and physically hand-icapped civilians. If disabled veterans had already made an incompara-bly great sacrifice for the good of the nation, many disabled civilians could contribute their labor power in smaller ways. Accordingly, repre-sentations of these groups of disabled people generally highlight their potential for rehabilitation and above all for a productive working life in the service of the national community.

Obsessed with creating rigid norms for what it meant to be a racially acceptable German of full value, Nazi propagandists generally sought to draw clearly hierarchical demarcation lines between these three groups of disabled people. For example, playing on the resentments of many former soldiers, in 1933 the head of the section in the Nazi Party's direc-torate for disabled veterans, Hanns Oberlindober, attacked the social policies of the Weimar Republic for placing the defenders of the nation on the same level as worthless "invalids."[2] In other statements, Nazi racial hygienists sought to reassure the public that their sterilization law applied only to people with hereditary disabilities and not to those whose disabilities had resulted from military service or workplace acci-dents. In yet another line of argument, Nazi publications often empha-sized that through the iron application of willpower, many disabled people could be rehabilitated to contribute their labor to the national cause. Nazi jargon often contrasted these potentially valuable disabled people with the unproductive insane and idiots who were languishing in institutions, the "useless eaters" who were nothing but a "burden to themselves and others" and should be "released from their misery."

Historians have generally studied these three groups of disabled people separately with respect to various aspects of Nazi propaganda and policies. Above all, much meticulous historical scholarship is avail-able in English about the Nazi sterilization and "euthanasia" programs directed against people viewed as having hereditary diseases. Outstand-ing research is also available in English about disabled veterans during the Third Reich. In Germany, of course, much more research has been published about all three of these groups, including local studies of how psychiatric institutions and other hospitals were involved in steriliza-tion and "euthanasia," as well as studies about various organizations of disabled people during the Third Reich.[3] There are also exhaustive his-tories of racial hygiene in Germany in both German and English.[4]

It is unnecessary to duplicate this scholarship here. Rather, this chapter explores how central disability was to Nazi culture and politics by drawing together material about all three groups of disabled people. Since the Nazis always stressed the effectiveness of "pictures" for indoc-trinating the public, this chapter highlights how important visual images of disability were during the Third Reich with respect to both propaganda and the appearance of disabled people in public. The broad masses were exposed to these images in many different contexts whether or not they were inclined to sympathize with eugenics. First, I discuss how national socialists sought to honor disabled veterans as the "leading citizens of the nation" and orchestrated the appearance of these men in public on official occasions. Next I review the laws and practices that excluded people thought to have hereditary diseases from the national community as background for a detailed overview of Nazi propaganda directed against this group. In the following section, which deals with the disabled victims of sterilization and "euthanasia," I try to retrieve the voices of these individuals as much as possible. After this, I examine how the official Nazi organizations for disabled civilians presented images of disability to the public and attempted to negotiate between collaboration and self-advocacy. The most difficult aspect of writing about disability during the Third Reich is to try to imagine how disabled people themselves experienced Nazi propaganda about them and Nazi policies whose purposes ran the gamut from rehabilitation to elimination. In many ways, this is an impossible task, for indifference, neglect, censorship, or murder silenced their voices. The creative use of sources, however, enables the historian to uncover indications of how some disabled people reacted to Nazi propaganda and policies and even some noteworthy stirrings of resistance to stigmatization and exclusion.

The Disabled Soldier as Hero

Even before 1933, national socialists had attacked the Weimar government for not recognizing the sacrifices of disabled veterans appropriately and for treating them as second-class citizens and welfare recipients. Therefore, hoping to win over this large bloc of men and their families, the Nazis vowed to treat disabled veterans as heroes and the "first citizens of the Reich." The war victims' associations of varying political affiliations were subjected to Gleichschaltung in July 1933 when the National Socialist War Victims Association (National-Sozialistische Kriegsopferversorgung or NSKOV), directed by Hanns Oberlindober, was declared to be the official unified organization of German war victims. By the end of the year, it had more than a million members, and all disabled veterans were dependent on it to represent their interests.

As is true of so many areas of Nazi social policy, in fact disabled veterans were treated in contradictory ways that resulted from the party's inconsistent ideological premises. On the one hand, national socialism idealized the front soldier, "glorified war, and promised to reward military sacrifice."[5] In a typical statement, Oberlindober declared that disabled veterans wanted honor and respect, not merely pensions. Accordingly, at the 1933 Nuremberg Party Congress he proposed a twelve-point program that included granting them a special medal, reserved seats at public functions, preferential treatment in government offices, reduced rates for transportation and cultural events, and preferential hiring with quotas in public service jobs (37). Such policies undoubtedly gave disabled veterans a psychological boost by providing them with the public recognition they had not received during the Weimar era. On the other hand, national socialism also placed a heavy emphasis on efficient production (Leistung) and continued work capacity. It was a pillar of Nazi ideology to prefer the strong to the weak and to reduce state support to people viewed as unproductive, for "ultimately continued utility, not past sacrifice, was paramount for the Nazi state" (45).

Consequently, in spite of all the propaganda to the contrary, the basic structure of the pre-1933 pension system remained more or less the same with respect to veterans' benefits under national socialism. Most disabled veterans received little more than they had under the "pacifist" Weimar Republic, and some actually lost out. For example, about sixteen thousand men were dropped from the pension rolls, mainly those receiving pensions for nonorganic mental illnesses (39–41). This practice undoubtedly reflected the prevalent eugenic thinking that opposed giving state financial support to a group of people viewed as inferior. When the war began, men who suffered the same wounds that their fathers had received in World War I found that their benefits were less, and this became a source of complaints among the populace (50). As it became evident that Germany was in danger of losing the war, the hollowness of propagandistic slogans about honoring disabled veterans became more and more obvious. In July 1943, the NSKOV began to form Marschabteilungen, paramilitary groups composed of disabled and discharged soldiers, in order to wring the last bit of military utility out of them. In the end, the Nazi strategy of total war and fighting to the bitter end created more disabled veterans than ever before. After the unconditional surrender in 1945, these men experienced greater dishonor and impoverishment than would have been imaginable during the Weimar Republic.

Representations of disabled and wounded soldiers in Nazi culture also had somewhat contradictory tendencies. In general, however, they were all characterized by a sanitized, idealized approach, whether in the ways disabled veterans were presented in public or in visual images such as photographs and artworks. The main vehicles for propaganda about disabled veterans under national socialism were NSKOV-spon-sored rallies and demonstrations; the organization's monthly magazine, *Deutsche Kriegsopferversorgung* (DKOV); and works by approved pho-tographers, artists, and filmmakers. On the one hand, Nazi ideologues were well aware that the broken bodies of disabled veterans had great propaganda value. Accordingly, in the early years of the Third Reich, NSKOV members were mobilized regularly to display their disabled bodies to the public in support of the regime's policies, especially those that were portrayed as righting the wrongs of the Treaty of Versailles. The first major mobilization took place in connection with the Reichstag elections of November 12, 1933, and the referendum in support of Ger-many's withdrawal from the League of Nations (47). On election day, NSKOV rallies were held throughout the country, featuring long parades of uniformed, disabled veterans, many in wheelchairs and carrying plac-ards with the inscription "German, have you voted yet? If not, then my sacrifice was in vain." In the following years, the NSKOV held many similar events, including ones in border areas where the sacrifice of dis-abled veterans was used to justify demands for territorial expansion.[6] These rallies contrasted sharply with the mass demonstrations disabled veterans had organized during the early Weimar years, when they dis-played their disabilities, wounds, and poverty as drastically as possible in order to lend force to their demands for better care and benefits. At the NSKOV events, disabled veterans were well dressed in uniforms and lined up in orderly rows rather than parading in ragtag fashion. Also, photographs show a conscious effort to hide some of the most severe dis-abilities, for example, with blankets covering the legs of amputees in wheelchairs. Rather than displaying the bodies of disabled veterans in a pitiful or gruesome way that would remind the public of the inevitable effects of combat, care was taken to disguise and aestheticize them in order to promote the policies of the Nazi state and ready the populace for war.

Nazi propagandists frequently presented disabled veterans as hav-ing sacrificed their health and bodily wholeness for the good of the nation, but, on the other hand, the Nazi regime sought to blunt their memories of pain and loss by portraying them as heroes. This cultural tradition of depicting wounded warriors or soldiers extends far back in time to the heroic epics and is by no means typical only of Nazi propa-ganda. It includes all those figures throughout history who have been shown as persevering in spite of pain and disability or as having acquired their disabilities and wounds through bravery and honorable self-sacrifice.[7] Such representations of disabled veterans as heroes became extremely problematic, however, when they were put in the ser-

Fig. 11. Hitler greeting disabled veterans in Berlin, March 12, 1939. (Photo: akg-images.)

vice of nationalistic, chauvinistic tendencies. This can be seen especially clearly in the ways Nazi ideologues intensified prefascist tendencies in this direction. Once in power, Nazi propagandists foregrounded images of the heroic disabled soldier in order to insist on unquestioning self-sacrifice for the sake of the fatherland and on fighting to the bitter end without surrendering no matter what the losses might be. Millions of Germans attended local and national celebrations in honor of disabled veterans, along with all members of the armed forces, as the Nazis carried out their campaign to militarize German society. The DKOV journal published frequent photographs of these events, showing Hitler and many top Nazi leaders greeting disabled veterans, frequently men sitting in wheelchairs. Photographs of national NSKOV celebrations in Berlin show the grandiose scale of these events, which recognized thousands of men. National holidays honoring the armed forces, such as the Heldengedenktag and the Reichskriegertag, became elaborate pieces of Nazi pageantry and gave disabled veterans a public prominence and official recognition they had not enjoyed during the Weimar Republic.[8]

If disabled veterans were to be represented heroically, a vocabulary was needed that would set them apart from those whose disabilities were acquired in less "honorable" ways. The insistence of military officials since World War I that disabled veterans should not be referred to as cripples but with less pejorative terms such as *war injured* became a matter of life and death during the Third Reich, when being labeled a cripple could mean that one was a likely candidate for Nazi sterilization or "euthanasia." The following example reveals how sensitive Nazi authorities were to these questions of terminology regarding disability. In 1941, the NSKOV received a complaint about a short novel published that year entitled *Der Vergessene* (The Forgotten Man), by Kurt Ziesel, a minor Nazi author. This work depicted a disabled veteran as a begging organ grinder, referred to the character as a cripple, and included an illustration of this passage. The complaint lambasted Ziesel for describing a front soldier in this manner, as well as for the book's illustration, saying that this ran counter to national socialist principles, overlooked the efforts of the NSKOV to provide for disabled veterans, and was likely to undermine the morale of young soldiers. Consequently, in the next edition of the novel, in 1942, the illustration was omitted and the character was described as a "wounded man."[9] Concern about drawing a clear dividing line between heroic soldiers and "inferior," undeserving, disabled people went so far that one standard biology textbook of the time, Otto Schmeil's *Der Mensch* (The Human Being, 1938), made a point of countering popular misconceptions by stressing that it was impossible for the children of "our frontline soldiers" to inherit their fathers' acquired scars or amputated limbs.[10] In general, then, negative images of disability during the Third Reich were reserved for those labeled as hereditarily diseased, degenerate cripples while disabled veterans were presented in a heroic light and exhorted to continue contributing to the fatherland through work if they were able.[11]

The pre-1933 German rehabilitation system had a strongly nationalistic thrust, aiming to get soldiers back into the field and workers back to the production front as quickly as possible. In this context, self-help and rehabilitation manuals often referred to the cultural tradition of the heroic disabled warrior as a model, but their chauvinistic, racialized tendencies became more pronounced during the Third Reich. Two books for soldiers on how to cope with losing an arm, one written during World War I and the other during World War II, provide particularly apt illustrations of this development. The first, Freiherr Eberhard von Künssberg's *Einarm-Fibel: Ein Lehr-, Lese- und Bilderbuch für Einarmer* (One-Arm Primer: A Book of Instruction, with Text and Pictures, for the One Armed), had to be reprinted within a month of its publication in 1915 due to the large demand.[12] Künssberg appropriated the literary tradition of heroic epics for his purposes, stating, "The oldest German heroic epic, the epic of Waltharius, relates the duel of the hero with Hagen in which Walter loses his right hand. He binds it, inserts the stump into the straps of his shield, and simply fights on with his left hand."[13] Giving examples of German soldiers who kept on fighting in spite of similar wounds, Künssberg claimed that "such a sense of heroism is still alive today in our armies." His message to one-armed veterans was that they should be "proud" of having incurred their injuries in a "holy struggle." Accordingly, he exhorted them to master their fates as amputees and continue serving their fatherland by returning to work.

Similarly, Carlo von Kügelgen's memoir *Aus eigener Kraft: Gedanken und Erfahrungen eines Einarmigen* (I Did It by Myself: Thoughts and Experiences of a One Armer, 1943) is dedicated to the "German war disabled and injured workers," but it employs a more consciously eugenic terminology than Künssberg's pamphlet does. Prefaced by endorsements from a high-ranking Schutzstaffel (SS) officer and a physician in the military high command, Kügelgen's book admonishes its readers not to despair but to "fight and overcome." In contrast to the "infirm and sick," soldiers who had limbs amputated were advised to take pride in their wounds as heroic badges of honor.[14] Like Künssberg, Kügelgen summoned up earlier representations of heroic figures in order to urge his contemporaries to follow their example and focus on regaining lives "worth living." (The term *lebenswert* carries with it the unspoken yet unmistakable reference to those disabled people whom racial hygienists called "lebensunwertes Leben," that is, "lives not worthy of life.") In this vein, Kügelgen described Lessing's Major von Tellheim as overcoming the stigma of his paralyzed arm after Minna von Barnhelm, his bride to be, appeals to his strength and manliness.[15] As another example, he cited the wearer of the most famous prosthesis in German history, the brave knight Götz von Berlichingen with his iron hand, who appears in Goethe's play as the essence of everything healthy, upright, strong, and heroic. Finally, he referred back to Germanic times, when terrible scars and missing limbs were "honored as signs of having resisted mortal dangers." He also recalled the ominous passage from Waltharius in which the maimed warriors joke together after wounding each other, stating, "This is not a portrayal of invalids who evoke or even lay claim to pity. Rather, these men are ideals of victorious strength, men who will proudly carry their marks of unconquerable heroism into future battles."[16] Needless to say, all such glorifications of the cultural tradition of the disabled war hero in Germany ended abruptly in 1945 with the unconditional surrender and the revelations of war crimes and the Holocaust.

Exclusionary Laws, Murderous Practices

If the national socialists sought to break with Weimar policies regarding disabled veterans, they also aimed, by contrast, to radicalize the racial hygiene movement that had been winning more adherents since the beginning of the world economic crisis. Immediately after coming to power, the Nazis began to pass eugenic laws aimed at excluding certain groups of disabled people from the national community. In late June 1933, Interior Minister Wilhelm Frick convened a panel of experts, set forth his ideas about population and racial policies directed against disabled "Aryans," and presented his draft of the involuntary sterilization law.[17] In his speech to the panel, which was typical of the eugenic discourse of the time, he recalled how Germany had lost enormous numbers of its "best men" in World War I. By contrast, he claimed that up to 20 percent of the German population was hereditarily defective and thus should not be allowed to procreate. He went on to say that, because these inferior people (especially the feebleminded) tended to have more children than the racially superior, the quality of the German people was declining dangerously. Linking criminals and outsiders of various types to mentally and physically disabled people, Frick also declared that the state was paying far too much to take care of "the inferior, asocials, the sick, the feebleminded, the insane, cripples, and criminals." An anti-Semitic stab-in-the-back legend is discernible in Frick's statements that the "humanistic" and "liberal" social policies of the Weimar Republic had created this situation. With these justifications for evaluating the population according to its "hereditary value," he presented the Law for the Prevention of Offspring with Hereditary Diseases (the Sterilization Law) to the panel, describing its purpose as "selection and eradication." In addition to this negative eugenic measure, citing Germany's declining birthrate in contrast to those of Eastern European countries, Frick also called for positive measures to encourage "valuable" Germans with no hereditary defects to have more children.

The Sterilization Law was enacted on July 14, 1933, and went into effect on January 1, 1934.[18] It specified congenital feeblemindedness, schizophrenia, manic-depressive psychosis, hereditary epilepsy, St. Vitus's dance (Huntington's chorea), hereditary blindness and deafness, severe hereditary physical malformation, and severe alcoholism as reasons for sterilization. Even within the framework of the law, it is important to note the limits of diagnostic precision at the time as well as the overbearing influence of ideological biases on medical decisions. Such factors permeate the official commentary on the Sterilization Law written by Arthur Gütt (a physician, SS brigade leader and director of the Public Health Division in the Ministry of the Interior), Ernst Rüdin (a professor of psychiatry at the University of Munich and cofounder of the German Society for Racial Hygiene), and Falk Ruttke (a lawyer and managing director of the Reich Committee for the Public Health Division). The authors characterized "severe hereditary physical deformities," for example, as those that had fatal consequences for the continuation of the race and that "made the individual in question incapable of carrying out remarkable things in life, for example, the things that are necessary in war or for overcoming dangers."[19] In general, the commentary defined the conditions specified in the law as those falling outside a narrow range of acceptable biological variation of the human species. Official commentaries on the law were generally careful to state that it only applied to people with hereditary diseases and not to those whose disabilities had resulted from accidents or illnesses. Eugenic discourse was so pervasive, however, that even these acquired disabilities were sometimes viewed as evidence of a hereditary taint. For example, in an article published in a leading medical journal in 1938, Dr. Kurt Hofmeier of the children's hospital in Berlin-Charlottenburg asserted that paralyzation due to polio was evidence of hereditary weakness. The proof he offered was that among the relatives of twins he had treated for polio, he had found "a weak nervous system, an abundance of allergies, and a suicide case."[20] Because of such inexactness and speculation, individuals were undoubtedly sterilized who did not fall under the provisions of the law. Writing in his diary in January 1935, for example, Victor Klemperer made the following note about a physician friend who had helped hide his manuscripts in Dresden: "She spoke with special bitterness about the involuntary sterilizations that were often carried out in cases where they were unnecessary and inappropriate."[21] Furthermore, the law served to create an intimidating atmosphere of suspicion and hostility directed against people whose physical and mental conditions— whether disabilities, illnesses, or unusual appearance—fell outside narrowly defined norms.

Sterilization could be applied for by the person to be sterilized or a legal representative, by physicians, or by directors of medical institutions or prisons. The law created a system of Hereditary Health Courts charged with evaluating applications for sterilization. It made the procedure involuntary by specifying that a court-approved sterilization could be carried out against an individual's will, and it empowered the police to bring unwilling individuals to the operating room by force. To determine whether sterilization was necessary, doctors worked up family trees showing the presence of disabilities and diseases in their patients' backgrounds. These exercises in genealogy were often highly ideological and included not only medical but also moral labels such as lazy, asocial, or criminal. As early as 1925, in *Mein Kampf* (My Struggle), Hitler had declared sterilization of the "hereditarily defective" to be one of the central goals of the volkish state.[22] Consequently, in a speech delivered to the Reichstag about the Sterilization Law on January 30, 1934, Hitler praised it as a "revolutionary measure" that would prevent "millions of healthy people from having the most necessary things in life taken away from them in order to keep millions of unhealthy people alive artificially." He went on to declare the law part of the biological "foundation" of national socialism and to rank it first among the "laws about blood and soil"—assertions that were constantly repeated in the press and by racial hygienists.[23]

Nazi Germany was, of course, not the only or even the first country to pass a sterilization law. In particular, Nazi racial hygienists referred approvingly to sterilization laws passed in many U.S. states and a number of other countries. The physician Walter Gross, head of the Office of Racial Politics, was one of the many German racial hygienists who participated in world congresses of demographers and eugenicists. He praised involuntary sterilization programs along with antimiscegenation laws and Jim Crow practices in the United States.[24] There were, however, crucial differences between the Nazi law and those passed in other countries.[25] In Nazi Germany, the Sterilization Law was an inflexible national law applied both within German borders and in occupied countries, in contrast to U.S. state laws, which were unevenly applied and sometimes hardly applied at all. Furthermore, sterilization laws in the United States applied only to people in institutions. By contrast, the German law potentially applied to the entire population with physicians of the public health service responsible for reporting candidates for sterilization to the authorities. In fact, all health care professionals in Germany, including doctors, dentists, nurses, masseurs, midwives, and practitioners of alternative medicine (Heilpraktiker), were required to report individuals whose conditions might fall under the provisions of the Sterilization Law. This meant that whenever a person visited one of these professionals for any cause—no matter how trivial—a sterilization investigation might be initiated (265).

It is impossible to know precisely how many people were sterilized under the terms of the German Sterilization Law. Nazi statistics, which were published only through mid-1937, indicate that a minimum of 197,419 people had been sterilized up to that time (233). It seems that public support was greater at the beginning, when people with the most severe disabilities were proposed for sterilization. By 1937, however, as a wide range of people with less severe disabilities began to be threatened, hostility began to grow among the population. The authorities took note of this and slowed the pace of sterilizations. On the one hand, in view of the mobilization for war, government officials did not want to antagonize the population unnecessarily. On the other hand, however, as soon as the war commenced "euthanasia" began to replace sterilization as a way to eliminate the "inferior." In any event, according to the most recent historical research, about 400,000 Germans and citizens of occupied countries were sterilized during the twelve years of the Third Reich (238). By comparison, about 64,000 eugenic sterilizations were performed in the United States over the course of the twentieth century up to the early 1960s.[26]

Once an application was made for sterilization, it was extremely likely to be carried out. Statistics show that 93 percent of the applications to the Hereditary Health Courts for sterilizations were approved in 1934, 89 percent in 1935, and 85 percent in 1936.[27] The law included an appeals process, but no matter how stubbornly an individual resisted, it was improbable that a sterilization decision would be overturned. By far the largest number of people sterilized had cognitive disabilities or mental illnesses. As was typical of so many physicians, State Secretary Arthur Gütt welcomed sterilization by stating enthusiastically, "We are longing with all our hearts for the day to come soon when there will be no more insane or feebleminded in the world, either inside or outside institutions. It will certainly be splendid to live in such a world, in which everything else is also sure to be perfect."[28] Accordingly, in 1934, 52.9 percent of the sterilizations were for congenital feeblemindedness, 25.4 percent for schizophrenia, 14 percent for hereditary epilepsy, 3.2 percent for manic-depressive psychosis, 2.4 percent for severe alcoholism, 1 percent for hereditary deafness, 0.6 percent for hereditary blindness, 0.3 percent for severe hereditary physical malformation, and 0.2 percent for Huntington's chorea.[29] This breakdown seems typical for the sterilization statistics as a whole. Because of the comprehensiveness of the sterilization program and because it was so widely discussed among the population, however, it was undoubtedly a cause of anxiety and fear among an extremely wide range of disabled people who worried about whether they might be threatened by the law, as well as among their relatives, friends, and potential marriage partners.

Insight into how widely medical professionals involved with sterilization cast their net can be gained from the journal *Der Erbarzt* (an *Erbarzt* is a physician who diagnoses hereditary diseases), which was a supplement to the *Deutsches Ärzteblatt* (German Medical Journal) received by all doctors.[30] The journal published frequent questions from doctors about whether their patients fell under the Sterilization Law or other eugenic laws, along with answers from experts. Most frequently, the responses were given by the physician Otmar von Verschuer, who became the director of the Institute for Hereditary Biology at the University of Frankfurt in 1935. He subsequently trained key SS medical personnel, including Josef Mengele, who conducted gruesome medical experiments on prisoners in Auschwitz and directed selections for the gas chamber there. These cases are particularly revealing since they were all instances in which physicians were uncertain about whether a condition fell under the law. That is, they indicate how broadly the law could be applied. In one case, a doctor inquired about a patient who had a harelip and cleft palate, and Verschuer replied that this was cause for sterilization.[31] Another doctor doubted that rickets could be hereditary. Verschuer answered that, even though the disease had environmental causes, there could sometimes be a hereditary disposition to contract it, and so it could be considered a cause for sterilization.[32] One woman went to the state registry office to be married, and the registrar noticed that she was wearing special eyeglasses for cataracts. He requested that she be examined for sterilization.[33] In another instance, Verschuer decided that a boy with deformed hands and feet was suffering from a hereditary condition and should be sterilized, while a girl born with only one hand did not have to be sterilized because her condition was not hereditary.[34] There were also numerous cases in which individuals did not technically fall under the provisions of the law but Verschuer still advised their doctors to caution them strongly against marrying. A class bias also runs through the cases. For example, a "healthy, intelligent" academic couple wrote that they had one child with clubfeet and one "healthy" child and inquired whether they should have more children. Even though a severe clubfoot could be cause for sterilization, Verschuer encouraged the couple to have another child, saying that he was reluctant to advise "highly gifted families" not to procreate.[35]

Nazi Germany enacted many other eugenic laws and decrees designed to reduce the numbers of the "inferior" and prevent them from receiving state financial support. Accordingly, groups of disabled people were excluded from all state-financed measures intended to support procreation, as well as welfare measures such as child subsidies, education grants, housing assistance, and the Nazis' program for evacuating children during World War II (Kinderlandverschickung or KLV).[36] On June 1, 1933, a program to provide marriage loans (Ehestandsdarlehen) to men was established in an effort to raise the birthrate by enabling couples to marry earlier and have more children. One-fourth of the loan was canceled for each birth in a family of up to four children. Probably at the initiation of Arthur Gütt, these loans were only given for marriages that were "in the interest of the national community." Jews (including Mischlinge [people defined as part Jewish] after 1937), people with hereditary diseases, people with infectious diseases (mainly prostitutes and people with venereal diseases), and people of the "wrong" political persuasions were not eligible (147).

Yet, for the Nazi racial hygienists, marriage loans were not nearly effective enough as a negative eugenic measure, and so they soon instituted much more exclusionary policies. On September 15, 1935, the Law for the Protection of German Blood and German Honor (the so-called Nuremberg Laws) was enacted, which prohibited marriages and all sexual contact between Jews and Germans. One month later, on October 18, 1935, a similar law directed against disabled people was enacted, the Law for the Protection of the Hereditary Health of the German Volk (the Marriage Health Law). A passage from Hitler's *Mein Kampf* was frequently cited as justification for this law: "The volkish state has the duty of restoring marriage as a revered institution that has the mission of begetting humans in the image of the Lord rather than monstrosities that are a mixture of humans and apes."[37] The law prohibited marriage if either one of the partners had an infectious disease that might harm the other partner or the children, had a mental impairment that made the marriage undesirable for the national community, was under guardianship, or had a hereditary disease that fell under the Sterilization Law. This last condition was not enforced if one of the partners was sterile, if the male was a foreign national, or if the woman was over forty-five years old.[38]

In order to receive marriage loans and be allowed to marry, couples had to be examined by a public health doctor and secure a marriage fitness certificate (Ehetauglichkeitszeugnis) stating that they were hereditarily healthy and possessed none of the impediments mentioned earlier. This procedure became a way for the authorities to search out candidates for sterilization and also to discriminate economically against people who were "unwanted" for eugenic or racial reasons.[39] A report about the first three months of 1934 stated that during this period there had been 77,869 applications for marriage loans, of which 2,205 (2.84 percent) had been rejected for eugenic reasons.[40] Historians have not yet uncovered further statistics about the percentages of marriage loans denied or marriage certificates refused. However, even if these percentages were small, the fact that all couples had to undergo this screening shows the comprehensive way in which eugenic goals were being introduced into the awareness of the masses. Furthermore, even when the partners did not technically fall under the provisions of the eugenic laws, doctors frequently advised individuals not to marry if their family trees indicated the presence of hereditary defects or "undesirable" moral and social qualities.[41] Several cases from Der Erbarzt illustrate the decisions doctors made with respect to certifying couples as fit for marriage and marriage loans. In one, a man and woman who had both recovered from tuberculosis were advised not to marry. If they went ahead with the marriage, the doctor would refuse to certify them for a marriage loan since he thought they had a hereditary disposition toward tuberculosis.[42] In another case, a doctor inquired early in 1935 if there was anything he could do to prevent a young epileptic man from marrying a healthy woman. Verschuer replied that unfortunately this marriage could not yet be prevented (the Marriage Health Law had not yet been passed) but that the man should be reported for sterilization.[43] Another doctor wrote that he would be inclined to grant a marriage loan to a man with a cleft palate because this defect could be repaired through surgery. Verschuer answered that this man should not be encouraged to procreate by receiving a marriage loan.[44] A doctor inquired whether a young woman who had multiple sclerosis should marry since the disease was not specifically mentioned in the eugenic laws. The answer noted that it was unclear whether the disease was hereditary but decreed that the marriage should not be allowed because of the negative prognosis for the woman.[45] A woman worker had been reported for sterilization as feebleminded. In this instance, the Hereditary Health Court decided against sterilization because witnesses described the woman as industrious, practical, and self-supporting. Her application for a marriage loan was rejected, however.[46]

In another group of cases, after consulting with Der Erbarzt, doctors advised individuals to go ahead with plans for marriage and children. These borderline cases are significant because they give an impression of the extent to which worries about hereditary disabilities were circulating in the population. Typical examples include the case of a man who was about to marry into a family with "deaf and dumb" members. He was ready to dissolve his engagement because he did not want his children to have this condition. He presented the family tree of his fiancée, and Verschuer replied that since the deaf and dumb relatives were quite distant, the man should marry as long as there were no cases in his own family.[47] In another instance, a woman was worried about marrying a man whose sister had epilepsy, and she was prepared to break her engagement if her children might have the disease. She was advised that this was not very likely and she should go ahead with the marriage.[48] In a related type of case, the sister of a man's wife became schizophrenic and was institutionalized. The man wanted to know if his wife and children were now considered hereditarily diseased and if he should divorce his wife in order to have healthy children. The answer was that his children might be more likely to become mentally ill, but grounds for divorce would exist only if his wife became schizophrenic.[49] In such cases, "healthy" members of the public had absorbed the teachings of the racial hygienists and were prepared to break off relations with people thought to be hereditarily tainted, thus indicating growing unease about disability and a readiness to stigmatize disabled people.

Eugenic laws and decrees discriminated against groups of people with disabilities and particular health conditions in many other areas of life, placing them under economic and psychological pressure by withholding state financial support and threatening them with sterilization. On September 29, 1933, the Reichserbhofgesetz (Reich Hereditary Farm Law) was passed, which created more farms that could be inherited in perpetuity. This law, rooted in prefascist concepts of settlement policy that became more widespread during the world economic crisis, made land available to the younger sons of peasants who did not have inheritance rights. Also an anti-Polish measure, the law invited men to apply to become new peasants with permanent rights of inheritance in the eastern areas of Germany. Only those men were eligible who proved to be "healthy and unobjectionable with respect to race and heredity."[50] This meant that Jews, people with "colored blood," and those with hereditary and other undesirable diseases were excluded from this government program.[51] As was the case for marriage loans and certificates, a public health doctor had to approve each application to become an Erbhof peasant. In 1934 in Prussia, for example, doctors examined 13,345 applicants—quite a large number—and found 632 or 4.7 percent to be unfit.[52] Reasons for rejection included illness or hereditary disease and the unsuitability of family members, particularly wives. In a case reported in 1938, a man lost the privilege of having his farm registered as an Erbhof and was classified as "unfit to be a peasant" because he "was a carrier of a hereditary disease and also because he did not have the appearance of a healthy person."[53]

Education was another major area permeated by exclusionary eugenic practices directed against groups of disabled people—in this instance, against children and young people with particular disabilities. In this connection, Martin Staemmler, a professor of medical ethics at the University of Breslau, characterized the goal of Nazi selection as follows: "It is above all the healthy person. . . . We have no use for feeble-minded athletes, astute weaklings and cripples, or rogues with great physical and mental gifts."[54] Along these lines, on March 23, 1935, Reich Education Minister Bernard Rust issued a decree stating that, in contrast to the previous "liberalistic age," the volkish state intended to take not only intellectual ability but also physical ability and character into account when considering whether to allow pupils to receive more than an elementary school education (i.e., to continue attending school past the age of fourteen). In particular, with respect to "physical selection," the decree stated, "Institutions of higher education will not accept young people with severe ailments, whose vitality is seriously weakened and whose condition cannot be expected to improve, or carriers of hereditary diseases, for they are unsuitable."[55]

The Reichsbund der Körperbehinderten (RBK, the official Nazi organization for the physically handicapped) protested immediately to Rust, complaining that the decree was causing great unrest among the organization's members and especially among parents of physically handicapped children. A year later the RBK reported that the physically handicapped were only to be excluded from education beyond elementary school under certain conditions and that—as for other eugenic measures—public health doctors would be responsible for certifying whether they qualified.[56] Conditions that made a pupil definitely unfit included chronic kidney disease, organic nervous or brain diseases, mental impairments in addition to physical ones, deafness, or being deaf and dumb. Pupils could possibly be classified as unfit if they had physical impairments that might prevent them from working. (The RBK still disagreed emphatically with this provision, noting that many young people were seriously disabled from polio, for example, but were still able to do quite well in school.) Conditions that did not disqualify a pupil included spinal and joint deformities, clubfoot, harelip, and cross-eyes. Historians have not yet determined how many young people with disabilities were forced to end their education much too early because of this measure, but it is yet another example of an effort to limit state spending on disabled people viewed as inferior and thus to limit their possibilities for living full lives.

Pupils attending special schools, including those for blind, deaf, crippled, and above all feebleminded pupils (Hilfsschulen), were especially vulnerable targets for the Nazi eugenicists. The Brüning Emergency Decrees of 1932 had already eliminated some of the Hilfsschulen as a cost-cutting measure. Soon after 1933, the Office of Racial Politics criticized policies that permitted spending money on "inferior" pupils rather than hereditarily healthy ones and suggested dissolving these schools altogether.[57] This drastic step was not taken, probably because national socialists viewed these schools as convenient collection points for the "unfit," who could then be subjected to eugenic measures, and also because they thought these pupils could be useful to the nation if they learned to perform "mechanical, soulless" work that people of normal intelligence would reject.[58] Accordingly, the Reichsschulpflichtgesetz (Reich Compulsory School Law) of November 1, 1938, was the first German law to mandate segregation of the feebleminded in special schools, stating that children who "could not follow along" in regular elementary school had to be placed in Hilfsschulen.[59] Furthermore, this law labeled the "weaker" Hilfsschule pupils "uneducable" and excluded them from attending school altogether (107). National socialists viewed these exclusionary measures as benefiting pupils in normal schools who would no longer be burdened by attending classes with "inferior" children, stating, for example, that "viewed from the volkish perspective, the special school is not only for the special pupils, but it also serves the interests of the normal ones" (132). The Nazis cut the budgets of Hilfsschulen, closed sheltered workshops for the feebleminded, and stopped training special education teachers. Pupils in the Hilfsschulen did not receive free school meals and were not included in the KLV. At first, young people who had attended Hilfsschulen were excluded from the compulsory Labor Service, but in the course of rearmament after 1935 they began to be viewed as potential workers. Many were then called up for Labor Service and drafted into the military as "useful Hilfsschule pupils."[60] This trend was part of the increased emphasis national socialists placed on rehabilitation after 1937, which largely aimed at wringing the last bit of utility out of people who were chronically ill and disabled.[61]

When the existence of the special schools was threatened in 1933, many special education teachers saved their positions by becoming outspoken advocates of eugenic measures directed against their pupils. Although some teachers were opposed to sterilization and coached their pupils to pass intelligence tests, they appear to have been in the minority. Many special education teachers reported their pupils for sterilization and sought to convince pupils' relatives that this measure was necessary and in the best interest of the national community.[62] One of the most explicit expressions of this mind-set among special education teachers is the handbook *Erbe und Schicksal: Von geschädigten Menschen, Erbkrankheiten und deren Bekämpfung* (Heredity and Fate: On Disabled People, Hereditary Diseases, and the Fight against Them, 1942) by Karl Tornow and Herbert Weinert. Probably the most influential Hilfsschule teacher during the Third Reich, Tornow was editor in chief of the professional journal *Die deutsche Sonderschule* (The German Special School) and a member of the national directorate of the Office of Racial Politics (Rassenpolitisches Amt or ORP). Weinert, a teacher of deaf students from Dresden, was also a fervent advocate of sterilization and affiliated with the ORP. Written in simple language, their book was intended for use in schools to teach about hereditary diseases and the necessity of sterilizing the hereditarily unfit. The writers employed a hostile, aggressive vocabulary, especially to describe the feebleminded and mentally ill. They also included discussion questions—such as "Why would it be better if this child had never been born?" and "Why is it good that this child died at a young age?"—for which they supplied an answer key in the back of the book.[63] It will never be known exactly how many pupils were sterilized as a result of denunciations by their teachers, but historians have been able to compile some partial statistics on the basis of local studies. Horst Biesold has shown that in some institutions and schools for the deaf, teachers reported over 50 percent of their pupils for sterilization.[64] Less research has been done on the history of blind people during the Third Reich, but it appears that between 2,400 and 2,800 were sterilized, and some of these were pupils reported by teachers in schools for the blind.[65] Furthermore, it is likely that at least 50 percent of the pupils in Hilfsschulen were sterilized.[66]

As these examples show, doctors played the key role in determining whether these eugenic measures would be applied to individuals. By and large the majority of nonsocialist and non-Jewish German doctors welcomed Hitler in 1933 and were willing to take on the task of evaluating people for their hereditary fitness. In the process of Gleichschaltung, doctors joined the Nazi organizations to a degree twice as high as members of any other profession: 45 percent joined the Nazi Party; 26.5 percent joined the Sturmabteilung (SA, Nazi brown-shirt storm troopers) (compared to 11 percent of teachers); and 7.3 percent became SS officers (compared to 0.4 percent of teachers).[67] The professional medical journals relevant to the treatment of disabled people, such as those in the fields of psychiatry and orthopedics, show how quickly these doctors jumped on the bandwagon of national socialism. The typical view was that doctors were no longer responsible only for treating the individual but also for assessing the value of the hereditarily diseased person to the national community. As the Reich Medical Regulations of December 13,

1935, decreed, "The German medical profession is called to work for
. . . the preservation and improvement of the health, heredity, and race
of the German Volk."[68] The family doctor indeed became a god in a
white coat or a black SS uniform, as Nazi physicians evaluated candidates for sterilization and selected patients in institutions and inmates
in concentration camps for death.

The eugenics movement was international, but it was only in Nazi
Germany that it led to the mass killing of disabled people. As the historian Christopher Browning has written, "In comparison to the 'twisted
road' that led to the mass killing of Jews and 'Gypsies,' the path to the
killing of the handicapped was extraordinarily straight."[69] As early as
1920, Binding and Hoche had conflated arguments for voluntary
euthanasia with the state-authorized killing of disabled people they
viewed as inferior degenerates, the "horrible counterpart of real
humans," and "ballast existences" who were unable to work and thus
placed an unnecessary economic burden on the national community.[70]
In *Mein Kampf,* Hitler had used a similar vocabulary to express his
hatred of disabled people, and as early as 1935 he had revealed his
intention to implement "euthanasia" in the event of war. Consequently,
as the war became imminent, preparations for "euthanasia" began. In
May 1939, Hitler told his accompanying physician, Dr. Karl Brandt, to
prepare for the killing of children with mental impairments. At some
undetermined point, Brandt brought Hitler a petition from the parents of
a severely disabled child (Gerhard Herbert Kretschmar, the so-called
Knauer child) asking that the child be put to death. Hitler told Brandt to
investigate the case and, if warranted, to authorize euthanasia.[71] The
child was killed on July 25, 1939, the first murder in the Nazis' biological war against disabled people. On August 18, 1939, the Interior Ministry, headed by Wilhelm Frick, circulated a decree ordering physicians
and midwives to report all newborns and children below the age of three
with the following conditions: idiocy, Mongolism, blindness, deafness,
microcephaly, hydrocephalus, all deformities (missing limbs, severely
defective closure of the head and spine, and so on), and paralysis,
including Little's disease (spastic diplegia).[72] During the summer of
1939, plans for adult "euthanasia" also took shape.[73]

The killings began in the last ten days of September 1939, when
patients in mental institutions on Germany's eastern borders were shot
in a succession of local actions in both Poland and Germany. About
7,700 mentally ill people were killed there, the first group of victims in
the Nazi "euthanasia" program that was now getting under way. As
Christopher Browning has explained, "In the first two years of the war,
the systematic, countrywide 'euthanasia' program that emerged had four

distinguishable but overlapping procedures with four distinct sets of victims: infants [and later children up to age sixteen], adults, institutionalized Jews, and concentration camp prisoners." By the end of the war, about 5,000 children had been murdered, usually by means of an overdose of medication but sometimes by starvation. The adult "euthanasia" program, known as Operation T4 because its headquarters was located at 4 Tiergartenstraße in Berlin, was much larger and more centralized. Similar to the reporting procedure for children with disabilities, the Interior Ministry circulated a decree on September 21, 1939, requiring all hospitals and institutions to fill out questionnaires on all patients "who had been institutionalized for more than five years or committed as criminally insane, were of non-Aryan race, or had one of a long list of specific conditions and were unable to work" (190–91). The conditions included schizophrenia, epilepsy, senile diseases, therapy-resistant paralysis and other forms of syphilis, encephalitis, Huntington's disease and other terminal neurological diseases, and every type of feeblemindedness. A patient's ability to perform economically productive work was paramount for the T4 physicians, who decided which patients would live or die.[74] Those selected for death were murdered by gassing beginning in January 1940 at one of six "euthanasia" killing centers. German adults with disabilities were thus the first group of victims to be systematically gassed by the Nazi regime. By August 1941, at least 70,273 had been murdered in this manner.[75] Jewish patients with mental and physical disabilities were initially evaluated the same way as others, but this situation did not last long. Soon all Jewish patients, no matter why they were institutionalized, were selected for "euthanasia" and sent to the killing centers. Finally, in the spring of 1941, T4 personnel began to cooperate with the SS to kill prisoners in concentration camps in what was known as Operation 14f13.

Just as eugenic sterilization was widely discussed among the German population, by the late summer of 1940 the "euthanasia" killings had become public knowledge and were known about in neutral countries as well as in countries fighting against Germany. On June 23, 1941, the British Royal Air Force even dropped fliers over Hamburg reporting the "euthanasia" crimes.[76] The killings could not be kept secret for many reasons. The sudden deaths of large numbers of disabled people at a few specific institutions could not be explained satisfactorily. Relatives became suspicious when patients died shortly after their secret transfer to the killing centers, and bureaucratic blunders were made in notifying relatives about fictitious reasons for the deaths. Furthermore, local inhabitants observed bus transports of disabled people entering the killing centers and soon afterward saw and smelled the smoke rising from the crematoriums.[77] Rumors spread fast in these areas to the point that even children living close to the killing center in Hadamar knew what was happening there. When they saw a bus transport, they were reported to have said, "Here comes the murder crate again," and they were overheard making remarks to each other along the lines of "You're not very smart. You're going to the oven in Hadamar."[78] Many other documents indicate that knowledge about the killings was widespread throughout the population. On October 31, 1940, for example, Rudolf Kraemer, a blind scholar and opponent of eugenics in Heidelberg, wrote a Braille letter to an acquaintance that read, "You have probably heard that the mentally impaired are paying a lot of attention to Saint Euthanasius nowadays."[79] In his diary, Victor Klemperer noted on August 22, 1941, that the killing of mentally ill people at the Sonnenstein institution was a frequent topic of conversation in Dresden.[80] And the historian Joachim Fest recalled that his teachers in Freiburg im Breisgau, liberals and self-assured Catholics, spoke openly in religion class about the "euthanasia murders."[81]

Nazi propaganda tried to distinguish sharply among disabled veterans who deserved support and honor, disabled civilians who were potentially useful to the national community, and useless, hereditarily unfit people who were unable to work. Yet the tendency of Nazi practices was to create a constantly expanding circle of those viewed as burdensome and harmful to the Volk and thus as fair game for elimination. The best-known warning about this dangerous "slippery slope" came from Clemens August Count von Galen, the bishop of Münster, who denounced the killings of mental patients as murder in a sermon of August 3, 1941. He preached that if it was permissible to kill these "unproductive" people, whom he termed "our fellow human beings," then everyone was a potential victim, including those who became old and frail, who lost their health through workplace accidents, or who returned crippled from the battlefield.[82] Well aware that such a statement could provoke dangerous public unrest, the Nazi leadership issued guidelines for responding to Galen's declaration that disabled veterans might be candidates for "euthanasia." The press was instructed to refer to these men as "honored citizens of the German people" or "honored pensioners of the nation" and to stress that they always received vocational rehabilitation or good care in dignified rest homes.[83] Church opposition to the "euthanasia" program reflected the widespread public knowledge about the killings and the complaints of many citizens about the deaths of close relatives.[84] As a result, concerned with maintaining calm on the home front, Hitler ordered an end to the first phase of adult "euthanasia," that is, to the gassings in the killing centers, on August 24, 1941.[85]

This so-called stop order did not mean that the Nazi "euthanasia" program had ended. Rather, the killing operations became more decentralized and hidden. The order did not apply to children's "euthanasia," and physicians and nurses continued to kill disabled adults by means other than gassing, including tablets, injections, and starvation. There were still a few courageous voices that spoke out against "euthanasia," as a pathology professor, Franz Büchner, did in a lecture about the Hippocratic oath at Freiburg University on November 18, 1941. There he attacked Binding, Hoche, and all advocates of eliminating "lives unworthy of life," declaring, "Life is the only master whom the physician must serve. From a medical viewpoint, death is the great opponent of life and of the physician. If the physician would be expected to initiate and carry out the killing of the incurably ill, however, this would mean forcing him to make a pact with death. But if he makes a pact with death, he stops being a physician."[86] In fact, though, more disabled people were murdered after the stop order than before. Bishop von Galen's fears of a slippery slope were well founded, for after 1943 victims of the late phases of the "euthanasia" program included residents of old-age homes, people suffering from traumatic shock after the bombings of German cities, soldiers with psychic disturbances caused by war experiences, and tubercular and mentally ill forced laborers from Poland and the Soviet Union.[87] The number of "euthanasia" victims can never be precisely known. According to the most recent historical research, however, in addition to the approximately 70,000 victims of Operation T4, about 117,000 patients in state hospitals and nursing homes in the German Reich and the annexed areas were killed. Furthermore, approximately 20,000 patients were murdered in Polish institutions and 20,000 in Soviet institutions. In France, 40,000 institutionalized patients starved to death as a result of the national socialist war of aggression. Therefore, Nazi "euthanasia" claimed at least 267,000 disabled victims.[88]

Eugenic Propaganda: Like This or Like That?

Degenerate Art and Disability

Just as certain groups of disabled people were to be eliminated from the national community in order to create a healthier and more beautiful German race, art considered to be degenerate was to be excluded from Nazi culture in favor of a healthy, beautiful art depicting ideals of phys-

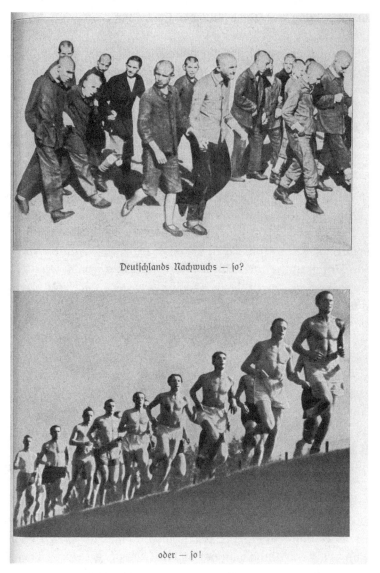

Deutſchlands Nachwuchs — ſo?

oder — ſo!

Fig. 12. Illustration from a high school biology textbook captioned "Should Germany's future generations look like this or like that?" (From Otto Schmeil, *Der Mensch,* revised by Paul Eichler, 97th ed. [Leipzig: Quelle und Meyer, 1938], 152. Courtesy of the Department of Special Collections, Memorial Library, University of Wisconsin-Madison.)

ical and racial perfection. For example, a eugenics reader by Georg Ebert and the physician Fritz Heinsius entitled *Sonne und Schatten im Erbe des Volkes: Angewandte Erb- und Rassenpflege im Dritten Reich* (Sun and Shadow in the Heredity of the Volk: The Applied Science of Heredity and Race in the Third Reich, 1935) made a particularly explicit connection between eliminating certain groups of people and certain types of art. In order to create a more "ideal" Germany, the authors wrote, necessary measures included not only "the prevention of the existence of physically and mentally ill people and the removal of foreign racial elements from the German body politic, but also the elimination of everything in the intellectual and artistic spheres that is racially foreign and unhealthy."[89] In this vein, Nazi ideologues condemned modern art as degenerate by associating its forms and themes with disability and disabled people along with Jews and communists. On June 30, 1937, propaganda minister Joseph Goebbels issued a decree defining works of degenerate art as those that "insult German feeling, or destroy or confuse natural form, or simply reveal an absence of adequate manual and artistic skill."[90] On the basis of this decree, works were selected for inclusion in the Degenerate Art exhibition, which opened in Munich on July 19, 1937. By the time the exhibition closed four months later, according to Nazi propaganda, over two million visitors had seen it, and nearly one million more people viewed it when it traveled throughout Germany and Austria over the next three years.

Goebbels's stress on including artworks that distorted realistic forms provided the link to eugenic thinking about disability. This means that a programmatic Nazi standpoint about cultural representations of disability emerges especially clearly in the campaign against degenerate art and for the alternative of a truly "German" art. The presentation of disability in the Degenerate Art exhibition was derived from Paul Schultze-Naumburg's *Kunst und Rasse,* which had denigrated modern art by comparing its distorted human forms to photographs of disabled people.[91] In the exhibition, however, works of modern art were compared to artworks created by institutionalized mental patients. The source of these images was a book by a Heidelberg psychiatrist, Hans Prinzhorn, *Bildnerei der Geisteskranken* (Artistry of the Mentally Ill, 1922). Prinzhorn had collected and studied more than five thousand works by 450 patients, and his book influenced many artists, including Arp, Klee, Ernst, Dali, and Picasso.[92] He himself was skeptical about concepts of decadence and degeneration, and he rejected efforts to draw simplistic parallels between contemporary art and these images as specious. In his book, he mocked such thinking as follows: "To draw the conclusion: This painter paints like that mentally ill person, therefore he is mentally ill, is no more convincing or intelligent than to say: Pechstein, Heckel, and others make wooden statues like Cameroon Negroes, therefore they are Cameroon Negroes" (36). Prinzhorn's collection of these works was kept at the Heidelberg University Psychiatric Clinic. His work had begun under Karl Wilmanns, who fled the Nazis, and shortly after Prinzhorn's death in 1933, the directorship of the clinic was taken over by Carl Schneider, who became one of the head evaluators of patients for Nazi "euthanasia." Schneider used the collection to support his theories about degeneration and inferiority. He made the collection available for Nazi propaganda, and, ironically, this is why these artworks by mentally ill people were not destroyed during the Third Reich (30).

Through contacts with Schneider, several works from the Prinzhorn collection were displayed in the Degenerate Art exhibition next to works by well-known artists. One pair of works, labeled "Two 'Saints,'" juxtaposed a painting by Klee with one by a "schizophrenic from a lunatic asylum." A grouping of drawings, including two by Kokoschka, was captioned "Which of these three drawings is the work of an inmate of a lunatic asylum?" Other pairings juxtaposed sculptures by "incurable lunatics" with those of modern artists.[93] Through such comparisons with artworks by mentally ill people viewed as degenerate, the exhibition defamed contemporary artists as degenerate also. With respect to disability, the strategy of the exhibition was similar to one of the important functions of freak shows, where viewers could enjoy feeling part of a normal group while viewing stigmatized monstrosities. By displaying human forms considered to be unnatural, deformed, or repulsive, the exhibition sought to appeal to an audience of normal, healthy Germans who probably considered most modern art to be incomprehensible or elitist.[94]

The exhibition did not attack only the small number of artworks juxtaposed with works from the Prinzhorn collection, however. In a more general sense, almost all the works labeled degenerate art were condemned by being associated with disability because of their fragmentation, distortion, and ugliness. Along these lines, according to the exhibition guide, the intellectual ideal of the modern artist was "the idiot, the cretin, and the paralytic." As a result, the text continued, portraits by these artists appeared to be of "cretin-like faces and figures."[95] Pejorative references to disability occurred frequently in publicity about the exhibition. For example, George Grosz's *Portrait of the Writer Max Herrmann-Neiße* was displayed as a prime example of degenerate art both because of its formal distortions and because of the "degenerate loathsomeness of the subject," as one reviewer put it (245). Another review attacked Grosz's etching *Maul halten und weiter dienen* (Shut Up and Do Your Duty, 1927), claiming that it mocked Christ on the cross "as a disgusting cripple with goggle eyes and epileptic features."[96] Furthermore, Hitler's statements in the exhibition brochure used eugenic terminology to denounce all the art on display by relating it to disability. About these artists, he stated, "And what do they fabricate? Deformed cripples and cretins, women who provoke nothing but repulsion, men who are more like animals than human beings, children who—if they lived like this—would have to be thought of as a curse of God!"[97] All these types of images were undesirable in the art of the new Reich, and so after the Degenerate Art exhibitions concluded, Nazi functionaries set about removing these artworks associated with disability from museums and galleries along with art associated with Jews and communists. As a result, most of these works were sold abroad, hidden away, or destroyed, which was the fate of Dix's *Kriegskrüppel.*

Nazi diatribes against degenerate art revolved to a significant extent around rejecting negative images of disability and calling for heroic images to be substituted for them, above all with regard to soldiers. Along these lines, the exhibition brochure featured a section entitled "Art in the Service of Marxist Propaganda for Refusing Military Service," which attacked the "caricatures of war cripples" in modern art. Included in the exhibition were some of the best-known works created during World War I and the Weimar Republic that portrayed disabled veterans: Kirchner's *Selbstbildnis als Soldat,* Beckmann's *Leierkastenmann* (called *Die Bettler* [The Beggars] in the exhibition), and Dix's series *Der Krieg.* The guide singled out Dix's *Kriegskrüppel* for special condemnation, labeling it "painted sabotage of national defense" (370). Recalling the right-wing attacks on Toller's indictment of war in *Hinkemann,* the brochure characterized these artworks as "disgusting" insults to veterans and thus as one of the main manifestations of degenerate art that was to be removed from public view.

Instead of such portrayals of disabled veterans as grotesque or pitiful, the exhibition guide called for representations of soldiers that would highlight military virtues of courage and combat readiness. Along these lines, in their own works Nazi artists and filmmakers took the approach of aestheticizing the wounds of war (if they depicted this subject at all). This meant that they almost always confined themselves to depicting injured soldiers with bandaged foreheads or arms in slings who were often striking heroic poses to indicate their will to keep on fighting or soldiers with indiscernible wounds being supported by others to emphasize the bonds of comradeship. For example, Elk Eber's painting *So war SA* (The SA Was Like This) features a man with a bandaged forehead marching in the midst of his SA unit.[98] Franz Eichhorst's *Erinnerung an Stalingrad* (Memory of Stalingrad, 1943) is an aestheticized depiction of dead and wounded men in trenches that contrasts starkly with Dix's paintings of trench warfare (226). In Reinhold Launer's *Kameraden* (Comrades), two soldiers support a third with his arm in a sling (782). A linoleum print in an old-fashioned style by Georg Slyuterman von Langeweyde, entitled *Ein Pfui dem Mann, der sich nicht wehren kann* (Shame on the Man Who Cannot Defend Himself, 1939), depicts a fighter with a bandaged head wearing knightly armor (1280). The representative Nazi sculptor Arno Breker created statues of several of these types, including *Verwundeter* (Wounded Man, a seated nude with a bandage around his head) and *Kameraden* (Comrades, 1940, a relief sculpture of a nude hero holding up a fallen comrade in a graceful pose) (1643). Adolf Reich's painting *Das größere Opfer* (The Greater Sacrifice, 1943) was an exception with its relatively stark portrayal of a veteran on crutches with an amputated leg.[99] Even this painting, however, was exhibited in the House of German Art in Munich in 1943 and was clearly intended by the artist to stimulate its viewers to make sacrifices for the national community. Similarly, Nazi newsreels, documentaries, and feature films such as *Wunschkonzert* (Request Concert, 1940) show wounded and disabled soldiers receiving good care, lying comfortably in clean hospital beds, or back on their feet wearing crisp uniforms.[100] All these artworks and films blot out the bloody destructiveness of war by never depicting the wounded, shattered, dismembered, disabled body. Instead of the war cripples that were such a frequent theme in Weimar culture, Nazi culture displayed soldiers' bodies that appeared hardly damaged at all. If alive, they are still hard, muscular bodies functioning smoothly in the military machine or if dead they are idealized in noble poses.

In a broader sense, national socialists rejected depicting any hint of illness, disability, or deformity in their art in favor of promoting ideals of health, normality, beauty, and racial purity. As the Nazi painter Wolfgang Willrich, the author of *Die Säuberung des Kunsttempels* (Purging the Temple of Art, 1937), asserted in an article about the "great task of German art," the main requirement for how artists should depict the "model Germanic man of full value" was "health" while everything "sick" was to be eliminated: "The nation is served well only by simple, unselfconscious art from the hearts and hands of perfectly healthy masters without broken souls or crushed spirits."[101] Along these lines, in order to show the public positive alternatives to degenerate art, the Nazis presented the First Great German Art Exhibition to inaugurate the new House of German Art in Munich in 1937.[102] Running concurrently with the Degenerate Art exhibition, this show presented art that the Nazis viewed as healthy, decent, and in accord with the taste of the broad masses. Along these lines, in his speech at the opening of this exhibition, Hitler attacked images created by "stuttering artists" and called instead for the creation in both life and art of a new type of human being, one who would be healthier, stronger, and more beautiful. As an example drawn from life, he declared that the recently concluded Berlin Olympic Games furnished the best model for this physical ideal rooted in the aesthetics of antiquity.[103] Leni Riefenstahl's film *Olympia* (1938) also belongs in this context of upholding aesthetic ideals of classical physical perfection in contrast to the distortions of expressionist cinema, just as "Gypsies" were removed from the streets of Berlin while the Olympics were in progress.[104]

The 884 works included in the First Great German Art Exhibition were meant to provide a representative survey of the new spirit in the arts. Popular themes selected to appeal to the "healthy" taste of the broad public dominated rather than heroic or Nordic ones that the masses would have rejected as too exaggerated. Consequently, the main emphasis of the exhibition was on idyllic, preindustrial landscapes and genre scenes that had been popular in the nineteenth century. Other numerically significant themes were placid scenes of peasant life (20 percent), portraits (15 percent), and depictions of animals (10 percent). Works with explicitly national socialist themes, that is, SA paintings and portraits of Nazi functionaries, made up less than 5 percent of the exhibition. As time passed and the Nazi leaders felt more securely ensconced, their artistic tastes became more luxurious, as can be seen in their growing preference for nudes painted in the style of the salon art of the late nineteenth century (e.g., by Adolf Ziegler) and for sculptures of nudes by Arno Breker, Georg Kolbe, Josef Thorak, and others. The gendered vision of beauty in such works emphasizes fitness for either struggle or procreation since the male nudes are exaggeratedly muscular and athletic while the female nudes display broad hips and full breasts.[105]

In contrast to previous expressionist or leftist art, which had stressed the alienated aspects of life, Nazi art satisfied a longing in broad sectors of German society for something higher and more beautiful, but it did this in a false way by channeling such yearnings to serve the goals of the party (221). Consequently, Nazi art "inevitably culminates in a one-sided beatification of 'militarism' and 'racial soundness' based on the struggle against and even liquidation of all things not beautiful, i.e., non-German, non-Aryan. National socialist art is thus not unproblematically 'beautiful,' not merely devoted to perfect forms and empty content; it is also eminently brutal, an art based on convictions which, when realized, literally left corpses in their wake" (233). And many of these corpses were those of disabled people whose bodies did not conform to national socialist ideals of health, productivity, and beauty.

The Institution as Freak Show

National socialists regulated how disabled people appeared in public, as can be seen from their strictly organized veterans' rallies, which hid severe disabilities and wounds from view. Similarly, Nazi propagandists also kept tight control over how disability was represented in the cultural sphere, calling for high art to portray beautiful, healthy physical types. This emphasis on biological, racial, and aesthetic ideals in Nazi culture does not mean, however, that cultural representations of disability disappeared during the Third Reich. On the contrary, Nazi propagandists produced a flood of written texts and drastic visual images of people considered to be hereditarily diseased. Their goals were to convince the public that it was necessary to decrease the numbers of these disabled people through involuntary sterilization and other eugenic measures, as well as to introduce the idea of euthanasia of the unfit into the public consciousness.

The link between efforts to eliminate disability from public view and eugenic propaganda about disability is revealed especially clearly in Nazi policies that banned freak shows and replaced them with another kind of staring at disabled people. Writing in 1936, the physician Wilhelm Weygandt, who had furnished photographs of disabled people to Paul Schultze-Naumburg for inclusion in *Kunst und Rasse,* described another way in which disabled people were frequently put on display: the freak show. He furnished medical diagnoses of some types of freaks that could commonly be seen at fairs, including "troupes of Lilliputians, who are mostly endocrine cases; 'Last Aztecs,' for which microcephalics with receding foreheads are used; chondrodystrophic dwarf clowns; and so forth." Specifically, he mentioned a woman known as Zitronenjette, who was a popular attraction at a Hamburg fair and whom he diagnosed as "a feebleminded dwarf who is a cretin." According to Weygandt, she was finally placed in a psychiatric institution.[106]

The life course of Zitronenjette was undoubtedly not unique among disabled people in similar situations for early in 1938 Heinrich Himmler, head of the SS and chief of the German police, issued a decree banning freak shows. An article in the *Berliner 8-Uhr-Blatt* summarized this decree as follows: "People speculate on the desire of fairgoers for sensations and try to make money from human misery, from pitiful, deformed beings. And steps have now been taken against this. The police have been directed to take severe measures against such excesses in the sideshows. This action is thoroughly welcome. Therefore, sideshows are prohibited that run counter to healthy popular sentiment or to the goals of the national socialist state. The police directive lists specifically what will not be allowed in the future. This includes displays of disgusting human abnormalities and hereditarily diseased cripples, for example, fish people, crab people, bird people, paralyzed people, animal people (hay eaters), and so forth. As far as their mental and physical condition requires, these people displayed in the sideshows will be placed in state hospitals and nursing homes according to the relevant regulations."[107] What might have appeared on the surface as a humane effort to prevent the exploitation of helpless people was in fact evidence of a lethal intent. For in these state hospitals and nursing homes, Nazi "euthanasia" would begin the following year, undoubtedly claiming the lives of some disabled people removed from freak shows.

Yet, just because it was forbidden to display freaks at fairs and circuses, this did not mean that patients in the state hospitals and nursing homes were to be removed from the gaze of the public. Rather, what this transfer from the fair to the institution signified was that Nazi eugenicists intended to transform the type of gaze directed at this group of disabled people. Previously fairs had been places where a largely working- and lower-class public could go to stare in amazement, wonder, and perhaps titillated disgust at disabled people whose appearance went far beyond the boundaries of the "normate."[108] Furthermore, even though these freaks were largely under the control of caretakers and fair owners, a few managed to express themselves in the public sphere before 1933, most notably Carl Unthan in his autobiography *Das Pediskript.* Furthermore, in his painting *Agosta, der Flügelmensch und Rasha, die schwarze Taube,* the Weimar artist Christian Schad had even imagined the possibility that a freak might look back contemptuously at those people who had come to marvel at him. Now, however, in the context of Nazi eugenic policies, institutionalized disabled people were to be stared at with a pathologizing, omnipotent, exterminating gaze. Furthermore, the circles of those instructed to stare at disabled people in this way were to be extended far beyond the traditional fairgoing public.

In an educational pamphlet entitled *Was muss der Nationalsozialist von der Vererbung wissen?* (What Must the National Socialist Know about Heredity? 1933), which was recommended reading for all Nazi party organizations, including the SA, SS, and Hitler Youth, Albert Friehe of the Office of Racial Politics explained that institutions for inferior people had two important tasks. First, they should sterilize their inmates for the good of the healthy Volk. And, second, he stated that these institutions "must become a school of visual instruction for the healthy. The anonymity of these institutions must cease. Every young person, and especially every Volk comrade of either sex who desires to get married, must be led once through the wretchedness and unspeakable misery of an insane asylum, an idiot asylum, a cripples' home, or a similar institution."[109] The immediate purpose of such tours was to teach healthy people not to bring such children into the world. An equally important goal, however, was to stir up popular resentment against these institutionalized "useless eaters" and plant the idea among the public that both these miserable disabled people and the national community would be better off if they were dead. Thus, these institutions were to be used to display "lives unworthy of life" and demonstrate the necessity of negative eugenic policies, first of sterilization and then of "euthanasia."

These proposals did not remain in the realm of ideology for long but soon became common practice. Statistics indicate the extent of such tours through institutions as well as who the participants were. In 1935, a report stated that over two thousand people had toured one of the asylums in the Rhineland, including members of the SA and SS, leaders of the Hitler Youth and League of German Girls, the Nazi Women's Organization, doctors, midwives, nurses, lawyers, and teachers.[110] In 1937, a doctor reported that between thirty and fifty thousand visitors per year from party organizations and schools had been brought through the large institution in Bethel in order to view "the hereditarily inferior."[111] In 1938, high school pupils were taken through the asylum in Emmendingen, close to Freiburg in the Black Forest, and assigned to write essays about their impressions. Obviously repeating what they had learned from their teachers, they all mentioned saving money for the state as the chief argument for instituting "euthanasia."[112] From 1934 onward, groups of over one hundred people were regularly conducted through the asylum at Eglfing-Haar close to Munich. After a press tour in February 1934, Munich journalists wrote lurid accounts of the disabled people they saw there, describing them, for example, as "grinning grotesques, who bear scarcely any resemblance to human beings." From 1933 to 1939, over twenty-one thousand people toured this asylum, and nearly six thousand of these were members of the SS.[113] About 90 percent of the participants in these tours were men (SS, SA, political leaders of the NSDAP, and civil servants), indicating that what they were being taught there had nothing to do with the traditionally female caregiving areas of nursing and social work.[114] Each tour ended with a lecture using human subjects to demonstrate the symptoms of various mental illnesses. In a retrospective account, one visitor recalled a tour through Eglfing-Haar in the fall of 1939 during which the director, Hermann Pfannmüller, brutally displayed both disabled children and nondisabled Jewish children who were being starved to death.[115] If the participants in these tours asked at the end why such people were even being kept alive, the purpose of this political instruction in negative eugenics had been achieved.

One can only try to imagine how the patients in these institutions felt about being displayed to the public in such a brutal manner by doctors and other medical personnel who were to become their murderers in many instances. On this matter, the historical record is silent. But the awareness of having been at the mercy of this malevolent, medicalized gaze cast a long shadow over the lives of disabled people in Germany in the postwar period, as the following chapters will discuss. For now, it must suffice to mention that in 1938, the same year Himmler issued his decree consigning freaks to institutions, a baby with muscular dystrophy named Gusti Steiner was born who later became one of the main initiators of the disability rights movement in West Germany. Steiner wrote that he probably survived the Third Reich because his mother kept him hidden away from view, believing that it was better "not to leave the physically handicapped to the mercy of the public." For years after the war, Steiner's mother continued to keep him largely confined to their apartment and prevented him from getting a wheelchair, which would have made it easier for him to go out in public.[116] The persistence of this behavior pattern indicates how intense the fear of being seen in a hostile way must have been for some disabled people, along with their relatives and friends, during the Third Reich.

"A School of Visual Instruction for the Healthy"

Just as the Nazis contrasted "sick" degenerate art with the "healthy" art displayed in their Great German Art Exhibition, the approach they took in all their propaganda was based on a binary aesthetics that contrasted the ugly with the beautiful, the weak with the strong, the abnormal with the normal, the chaotic with the orderly, the asocial with the respectable, the non-German with the German, and so forth. Accordingly, the basic technique in their eugenic propaganda was to juxtapose images from these opposing spheres in order to stigmatize inferior disabled people—above all those with mental impairments—and promote superior Germans of full value to the national community. It is beyond the scope of this chapter to indicate more than cursorily that there are obvious similarities between eugenic images of this group of disabled people in Nazi Germany and such imagery in other countries. Consequently, it would be an important task for future comparative research to explore what, if anything, is specifically national socialist about these images.[117] Perhaps their distinguishing feature is not so much their substance as their frequency. Since they were produced and promoted by the dictatorial state, they were undoubtedly much more pervasive in Nazi Germany than in countries where eugenics did not become a centralized, state-sponsored policy.

Eugenic propaganda about disabled people in Nazi Germany relied on crass binary distinctions between health and degeneracy that are tiresomely predictable. Once you have seen a few of these images, you have truly seen them all. Therefore, it is unnecessary to try to document all of them—an impossible and boring task in any event. It is more important to show how these images of disabled people permeated Nazi culture on many different levels and in many different contexts beginning in 1933 and 1934 with the widespread propaganda campaign that accompanied the announcement of the Sterilization Law. No matter if one was a Nazi supporter or not, one could hardly escape being exposed to propagandistic images of this group of disabled Germans—images intended to be "a school of visual instruction for the healthy." And it is important to remember that many disabled people, along with their relatives and friends, were also frequently confronted with these widespread, stigmatizing images. For those who were disabled themselves or felt emotional solidarity with disabled people, this situation undoubtedly gave rise to feelings of stress, anxiety, or fear.

The central government office in charge of creating eugenic propaganda directed against disabled people was the Office of Racial Politics. Created in the spring of 1934, it evolved out of the Office for Enlightenment on Population Policy and Racial Welfare, which had been founded in 1933. It was headed by a young physician named Walter Gross, who praised Hitler as having discovered the "great Truth," the "eternal genetic inequality of all men."[118] The task of the ORP was "to promote ethnic thinking in every aspect of public life" and to "infuse public culture with knowledge about the supposedly superior Volk and the undesirable 'others': Jews, the 'genetically damaged,' African Germans, gypsies, homosexuals, and asocial elements such as sex criminals, hoboes, and others" (112, 105). The extent of ORP activities is indicated by its subdivisions: education, propaganda, foreign relations, counseling, applied demography, public relations, science, and programs for women and girls. It worked closely with the Propaganda Ministry and Education Ministry, as well as the Office of Agriculture (Reichsnährstand) and the Racial and Settlement Office of the SS (Rasse- und Siedlungsamt der SS). It played a central role in introducing instruction about racial politics and eugenics throughout the school system. Gross's office trained and certified medical school professors and more than three thousand racial political educators (114). It collaborated with Nazi associations such as the Labor Front and the National Socialist Women's Association to develop racial and eugenic education projects, and it held a huge number of meetings around the country "to popularize knowledge about ethnic health and racial damage" (122). In 1937, for example, the ORP estimated that its programs had reached more than three million people.[119] Along with other leading Nazi propagandists, Gross emphasized that vivid, easily comprehensible visual experiences were key to winning the masses over to the regime's eugenic policies.[120] Therefore, the ORP, along with other Nazi offices and organizations, exposed the German public to innumerable negative images of "the hereditarily diseased" in photographs in the print media, slides for group presentations, posters shown at huge exhibitions and placed in government offices, plays, and films.[121] And in most instances these images of "inferior" disabled people were contrasted with "positive" images depicting "healthy Aryans."

Countless journals, magazines, calendars, pamphlets, and books carefully calibrated for all sectors of the population spread the teachings of racial hygiene.[122] Each year, for example, the ORP published a calendar with images of racially ideal Germans that sold between 150,000 and 500,000 copies.[123] By contrast, journals and magazines also focused on negative images of disability in many contexts. Two of the most characteristic periodicals in terms of the visual presentation of disabled people were *Volk und Rasse* (Volk and Race) and *Neues Volk* (New Volk). *Volk und Rasse,* founded in February 1926, was the official journal of the Reich Committee for the Public Health Service (Reichsausschuss für Volksgesundheitsdienst) and the German Society for Racial Hygiene (Deutsche Gesellschaft für Rassenhygiene). Its first issues concentrated mainly on topics such as peasant folklore and settlements, Nordic sagas, and Germanic peoples and book reviews about eugenics. After the beginning of the world economic crisis in 1929, however, its tone became much more explicitly negative toward disabled people. The entire issue of June 1931 was devoted to negative eugenics and particularly to the need for sterilizing the insane, describing them as an unacceptable economic burden on the nation. From 1933 onward, the racial hygienists writing for the journal knew that the state backed their efforts to put theory into practice. Aimed at a readership of medical professionals, political leaders, cultural activists, and well-educated laypersons, the journal included medically oriented articles featuring family trees about heredity, photographs of the hereditarily diseased, reports about racial hygiene exhibitions, articles on art and culture, and information about the countrywide activities of the ORP.

In 1933, the journal reprinted illustrations from Otto Helmut's widely distributed pamphlet *Volk in Gefahr: Der Geburtenrückgang und seine Folgen für Deutschlands Zukunft* (Volk in Danger: The Declining Birthrate and Its Consequences for Germany's Future, 1933). These drawings of "the physically and mentally impaired, deaf and dumb, and blind," as well as criminals and parents of Hilfsschule pupils, emphasized the misshapenness, strangeness, and slovenliness—that is, the degenerate appearance and the asocial tendencies—of all these groups. In a typical line of argument constantly repeated in all Nazi eugenic propaganda, Helmut stated that these inferior people were procreating at a much faster rate than healthy Germans and that as a result huge sums of money were being spent to care for them while "German workers" were forced to forgo life's basic necessities.[124] Such images were common in the pages of *Volk und Rasse* until the beginning of the war. Then they became less frequent as the emphasis in negative eugenic policy began to shift from involuntary sterilization to "euthanasia."

The mass-market illustrated magazine *Neues Volk,* with a layout resembling *Life* and *Look,* was aimed at more middlebrow readers. Launched in 1933 by Walter Gross, it was an official publication of the ORP and, like *Der Erbarzt,* was a supplement to the *Deutsches Ärzteblatt.* Its chief editor was the ophthalmologist and author Hellmuth Unger, head of the ORP's Division of Press Politics.[125] The magazine had a circulation of seventy-five thousand in 1933 and over three hundred thousand in the late 1930s and was delivered to all doctors, dentists, and pharmacists as reading material for waiting rooms. It could be found in schools and public libraries as well as in private homes. Emphasizing positive images, the magazine was filled with photographs and articles about "physically fit and racially ideal Aryans," but graphics and photographic essays about "undesirables" (Jews, blacks, criminals, asocial types, leftists such as members of the International Brigades in Spain, and the hereditarily diseased) were also included regularly.[126] As was true for *Volk und Rasse,* most of the images of disabled people in *Neues Volk* appeared in the first few years of the magazine's publication, when the sterilization program was at its most intense, and became less frequent after the war began. These were among the best-known visual images created by Nazi eugenicists. They were frequently reprinted in other publications and were also enlarged to poster size for display in various exhibitions.

The images of disability in *Neues Volk* were almost solely of people identified as feebleminded, idiotic, or insane. Using the most unam-

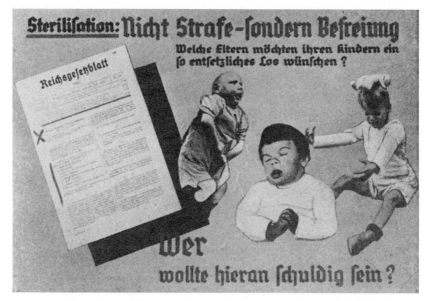

Fig. 13. "Sterilization: not punishment, but liberation. What parents would wish such a horrible fate for their children? Who would want to be guilty of this?" (From *Neues Volk* 4:2 [February 1936]. Courtesy of the University of Wisconsin-Madison Libraries.)

biguous propaganda technique, these images were generally juxtaposed with positive ones in order to steer readers toward inescapable conclusions. Photographs captioned "Who might live here?" contrasted a comfortable institution for feebleminded women with the run-down housing of working families in order to make the point that more money was being spent on the disabled than on healthy Germans.[127] A photograph of a "criminal, hereditarily diseased Negro" was juxtaposed with "the splendid young men in the Labor Service," thus contrasting unproductive "degenerates" with productive workers.[128] Similarly, a reproduction of a poster used in large eugenics exhibitions was entitled "You are helping to carry this burden." It depicted a strong, tall, blond man bent under the weight of a barbell with two apelike, hereditarily diseased men perched on it and included a caption about how much they cost the state. These images generally condemned hereditarily diseased adults morally by associating them with "inferiority, maliciousness, and depravity" while the healthy were linked with "joy, contentment, and therefore success in life."[129]

The images of feebleminded, idiotic children in *Neues Volk* were presented in a somewhat different way. They were also shown as ugly and grotesque in contrast to beautiful, healthy children, but they were not linked to criminals and asocial types. Rather, the magazine attacked hereditarily unfit parents who had not been sterilized for bringing such pitiful creatures into the world. Accordingly, the images of children contrasted the joyless lives of the disabled with the happy lives of the healthy. A particularly revealing example of this propagandistic technique is a juxtaposition of photographs contrasting a little girl living in an institution with a healthy girl described as the joy of her parents. The institutionalized child was characterized as follows: "This pitiful creature, who was brought into life by inferior parents and quickly forgotten, is growing up in a state hospital, a joy to no one and merely wasting away rather than living. In order to prevent her from scratching herself, her little arms must be protected with cardboard cuffs. She runs around with a doll on her head, plays with it in the sand, and goes to sleep with it. Should Germany's future generations look like this?" The answer, of course, was "No! We need healthy children who are the joy of their parents, children who guarantee our nation a secure future."[130] The photographs and text aimed to show that this child's misery was caused solely by her disability and not by her surroundings. Therefore, from this eugenic perspective, the only solution was to prevent such children from coming into the world where a sad life inevitably awaited them.

Of course, one wonders whether any of the readers of *Neues Volk* looked at these photographs in a different way. Some may have thought that the child was unhappy not only because of her disability but because of the way others were treating her. She was dressed in dirty clothes, restricted in her movements, and placed uncomfortably on the ground. She appeared thin and malnourished with a strange doll obviously attached by someone else to her head, and she was being photographed alone rather than held and comforted. In any event, however, the contributors to *Neues Volk* did not intend for readers to question how disabled people were being cared for in Nazi Germany. They expressed pity for the "terrible fate" of these children, concluding that they never should have been born. And, by contrast, they viewed the ability to experience joy in life as possible only for those Germans who conformed to accepted norms of appearance, health, racial makeup, and behavior.

In addition to visual images about eugenics in the print media, the ORP created many series of slide lectures in editions of thousands— some also available as large wall posters—which were circulated throughout the national school system and local party organizations.[131] Topics included racial politics, the laws of heredity, and hereditary physical and mental impairments.[132] In a memoir about his schooldays during the Third Reich, for example, the author Hans Bender recalled,

"The biology teacher showed slides that were supposed to prove to us the differences among races, and of course the Semitic race was the most despicable. The same biology teacher took us through the institution for incurables, the 'Hub,' where the raving, slobbering sick people—poor creatures condemned to death—were supposed to convince us pupils how justified it was to perform 'euthanasia.'"[133] A Hitler Youth slide show produced by the ORP included photographs such as one labeled "A crippled idiot. Bound forever to his bed." Such images were not intended to arouse sympathy but rather to provoke revulsion at useless people.[134] In May 1934, *Neues Volk* advertised another slide show entitled *Erbnot und Aufartung: Bild und Gegenbild aus dem Leben* (Hereditary Misery and Regeneration: Images and Counterimages from Life), put together by Rudolf Frercks, a physician who was head of the ORP foreign relations subdivision, and Arthur Hoffmann. Intended for racial hygiene instruction, the slides included photographs of "shocking scenes from insane asylums, Negro children from the Rhineland, and prominent Jewish bastards." In particular, the hereditarily diseased were contrasted to "a glowing display of new, strong, healthy humanity, i.e. the 'new Volk.'" The compilers asserted that these vivid images and counterimages—presented without complicated explanations—would convince viewers that the Sterilization Law was necessary and beneficial.[135]

Together with other government offices, the ORP sponsored exhibitions about eugenics, population policy, and public health that were seen by hundreds of thousands of Germans.[136] These exhibitions were presented throughout the country from the smallest villages to the largest cities.[137] They featured sections about eliminating the hereditarily unfit, using images of disabled people similar or identical to the ones in the journals discussed earlier. In early 1934, the Reich Committee for the Public Health Division, the publisher of *Volk und Rasse*, organized a traveling exhibition entitled "Erbgesund—Erbkrank" (Hereditarily Healthy—Hereditarily Diseased).[138] Later that year the Reich Committee, together with the ORP, organized a similar exhibition in Berlin called "Wunder des Lebens" (Wonders of Life). The entrance to the exhibition was flanked by Wolfgang Willrich's four large paintings depicting ideal racial types: a workman, a young female athlete, a physician, and a teacher wearing a Nazi uniform.[139] In 1936, the Reich Committee presented a public health exhibition entitled "Das Leben" (Life) in Essen. Also in 1936 the German Hygiene Museum in Dresden, which played a leading role in creating and distributing eugenic propaganda, put together six traveling exhibitions that were shown in eighty-two domestic and foreign cities and were visited by 1.2 million people.[140] In 1938, a national exhibition called "Gesundes Leben—frohes Schaffen"

(Healthy Life—Cheerful Work) was presented in Berlin.[141] According to reports in the Nazi press, these exhibitions all impressed the public with the way they "worked out the contrast between hereditarily healthy and hereditarily diseased families and their offspring."[142]

The national exhibitions sponsored by the Reichsnährstand (the organization responsible for Nazi agricultural policies) deserve special mention because, as Walter Gross pointed out, this division of the government was especially active in spreading propaganda about racial and eugenic policies.[143] Founded in September 1933, the Reichsnährstand synchronized all aspects of agriculture that had formerly been dealt with by separate organizations. It had three subdivisions: Der Mensch (Man, i.e., propaganda directed toward peasants), Der Hof (The Farm), and Der Markt (The Market).[144] The ideology of the Reichsnährstand was influenced mainly by prefascist beliefs in "blood and soil," above all those propagated by the Artam League, founded in 1923, which championed a cult of the peasant and worked to establish homesteads on Germany's eastern borders. Heinrich Himmler, who had a degree in agricultural science and worked as a chicken breeder, joined the Artam League in 1928 and ordered the SS to wear the "peasant black" of the Artamans when he became head of that organization in 1929. The head of the Reichsnährstand, Reich Peasant Leader Walther Darré, also a "former agricultural specialist who had concentrated on questions of animal breeding," held similar ideas.[145]

The Reichsnährstand sponsored huge national agricultural exhibitions in various cities that attracted tens of thousands of visitors. They featured livestock and crop exhibitions, programs about the latest farming techniques and machinery, and sections of particular interest to women and children along with food and entertainment, which made them enjoyable family outings. These exhibitions also contained sections about racial politics and eugenics that were geared to appeal to peasants. Typically, the displays drew direct parallels between breeding better plants and animals and breeding better people in order to try to convince the rural population that the regime's eugenic measures were justified.[146] The first Reichsnährstand exhibition was held in Erfurt in May and June of 1934 and included a special section devoted to "questions of blood for the peasantry," which attacked Jews as a "foreign race," criticized the "liberalistic age" for allowing the hereditarily diseased to thrive, and called for the hereditarily healthy to have more children.[147] In 1937, an article in *Volk und Rasse* summarized the efforts of the Reichsnährstand over the past four years to educate peasants about racial and eugenic policies.[148] The organization had spon-

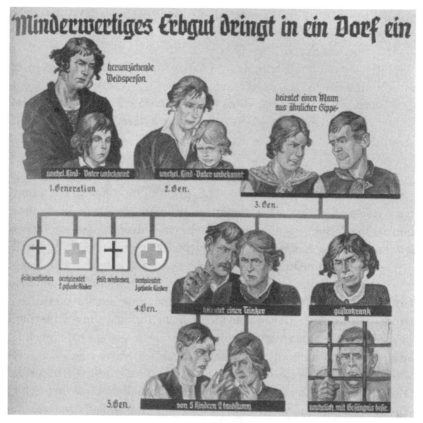

Fig. 14. "Inferior hereditary material penetrates a village." Exhibition poster of the Reichsnährstand. (From *Volk und Rasse* 11 [1936]: 337. Courtesy of Department of Special Collections, Memorial Library, University of Wisconsin-Madison.)

sored eight national exhibitions that included sections about the Germanic races, the "dangers of Jewish influence," the necessity of the Sterilization Law, and how to bring up healthy children. It created 380 large-format posters on these topics, some by well-known artists such as Wolfgang Willrich. Exhibition posters depicting the "hereditarily diseased" included "The Consequences of a Rash Marriage,"[149] "The Terrible Legacy of a Female Alcoholic" (334), "The Consequences of Marriage among Relatives Carrying Hereditary Diseases" (336), and "Inferior Hereditary Material Penetrates a Village" (337). All of these posters emphasized the cost of caring for the unfit, their high reproduction rate in contrast to that of the healthy, and the link between hereditary disease and asocial or criminal behavior. These images were frequently reproduced in the press, and so the special exhibitions of the Reichsnährstand about racial and eugenic policy were important educational tools in both the cities and the countryside.

Film was another central way in which Nazi propagandists exposed mass audiences to images of disability and illness. On the one hand, newsreels and documentaries about wounded and disabled veterans sought to create the impression that these men were well cared for in hospitals and were receiving excellent rehabilitation so that they would not have to live as "cripples."[150] By contrast, however, other films were produced to spread concepts of eugenics, to promote the Sterilization Law, and to insinuate ideas about "euthanasia" into public consciousness. Genres included educational, medical, and scientific films, short documentary films, and a feature film. They were meant for various audiences: party functionaries, officials and medical personnel, those carrying out "euthanasia," and the public.

From the creation of the new medium of film, Germans had been leaders in its development. During the Weimar Republic, more than five hundred films had been produced for medical training and research and to acquaint the public with principles of social hygiene, sex education, and eugenics. The first German film with an explicitly eugenic agenda was entitled *The Curse of Heredity: Those Who Shouldn't Be Mothers* (1927). It focused on hemophilia, alcoholism, and epilepsy as reasons to prevent childbearing.[151] By contrast, another educational film made in 1928–29 illustrated the progress made in treating mentally ill people by contrasting their brutal treatment in the past to the more humane treatment they were now receiving in modern, comfortable institutions. As a contemporary source described this film, "We recognize how all the multifaceted efforts of physicians, nurses, and orderlies serve the sole purpose of healing the sick, of awakening and reinforcing in them new courage and joy in life, as well as a sense of community."[152] This approach was exactly the opposite of that taken in all genres of Nazi films about disabled people, especially people with mental impairments.

The Nazi organization responsible for making scientific films was the Reich Office for Educational Films (Reichsstelle für den Unterrichtsfilm), called after 1940 the Reich Institute for Films and Images in Science and Education (Reichsanstalt für Film und Bild in Wissenschaft und Unterricht or RWU). Between 1933 and 1945, it produced approximately 900 films, of which about 480 were meant for research and teaching at universities and 270 for use in schools. Its director, Kurt Gauger, was an enthusiastic supporter of the Sterilization Law, having declared about the people who were its targets, "We have neither time nor room for such creatures." Its films and slide series were important teaching tools for instructing university students and school pupils about eugenics and the necessity for sterilization, and some of the scientists who produced RWU medical films were involved in the "euthanasia" program.[153] The films about patients with various mental impairments provided anything but authentic, objective representations of their symptoms. Rather, doctors constantly manipulated, staged, and directed images. For example, bright lighting and jerky camera movements were used to stigmatize the patients by intensifying their strange appearance. Patients with tremors were placed in uncomfortable positions and filmed while undressing or holding a glass of water in order to increase their shaking movements. A four-year-old boy who was unable to stand, sit, or talk was filmed naked on the floor from above to show him as an "underdeveloped animal." Most patients in these RWU productions were filmed naked in front of bare walls even when nakedness was not necessary for diagnosis.[154] One producer asserted that these techniques were employed in order to make films "that medical students would not forget."[155]

The RWU film *Eine 4 1/2-jährige Mikrozephalin* (A 4 1/2-Year-Old Microcephalic Girl, 1936–37) is "an exemplary source reflecting German medical conduct in the 1930s and the particular attitude towards the mentally ill."[156] The film was made by the psychiatrist Gerhard Kujath under the supervision of Karl Bonhoeffer at the psychiatric department of the Charité Hospital in Berlin.[157] The child shown in the film, Valentina Z., was born in Nottingham, England. Her parents were traveling circus performers with no permanent residence. Valentina's mother had left her with her grandmother in Berlin, and when the film was made her parents were in Chicago. Her aunt and grandmother had brought her to the Charité because she had an abnormally small head. She could not talk, walk, or stand, and it is likely that she was also blind. Nurses described her as sweet and cheerful, happily recognizing people she knew and enjoying particular foods. From the beginning of her hospital stay, doctors at the Charité regarded Valentina as an interesting case for scientific research. They subjected her to painful, frightening experiments such as loud noises and bright lights, pinpricks, cold, and drinks of salty, sour, and bitter solutions in order to test her reactions. The film shows some of these procedures, including scenes of Kujath demonstrating Valentina's underdeveloped reflexes by holding her upside down by her feet, hurling her through the air, and placing her in other terrifying, uncomfortable positions. The child cries, screams, and tries to push Kujath's hands away, but neither Kujath nor a nurse gives her any comfort. Valentina died on October 28, 1941, in the Special Pediatric Ward in Berlin-Wittenau, and it must be assumed that she was killed with an overdose of Luminal in the children's "euthanasia" program. Research pathologists immediately dissected her corpse, and Kujath later dissected her brain. As a document showing the torture of a mentally impaired child, the film reveals the cruel attitude of these German medical professionals toward those they considered unworthy of life.

Films about the hereditarily unfit were not just for circles of experts, however. Nazi propagandists believed that because films "encompass the body and the soul simultaneously," as Walter Gross wrote, they could make a powerful impression on large audiences.[158] Therefore, as soon as the Sterilization Law went into effect on January 1, 1934, the first newsreel promoting it appeared in German movie theaters. The following month Hellmuth Unger thanked the UFA film company for helping produce a large number of such educational newsreels. He described one that began with a speech by Gross about the Sterilization Law and then contrasted "shocking scenes of hopeless, feebleminded children in institutions" with "the powerful bodies of our Olympic athletes."[159] Soon the ORP, together with other offices, began larger film projects and created a number of documentary films to promote sterilization: *Sünden der Väter* (Sins of the Fathers, 1935), *Abseits vom Wege* (Off the Beaten Path, 1935), *Das Erbe* (The Inheritance, 1935), *Erbkrank* (Hereditarily Diseased, 1936), *Alles Leben ist Kampf* (All Life Is Struggle, 1937), *Opfer der Vergangenheit* (Victims of the Past, 1937), and *Was du ererbt* (What You Have Inherited, 1939).[160] All the films were silent except for *Opfer der Vergangenheit*. The ORP was allowed to photograph and film patients in state hospitals and nursing homes, as well as inmates of prisons, and it appears that the majority of the films were shot in and around Berlin.[161] For some scenes in *Opfer der Vergangenheit*, asylum inmates were filmed without their knowledge, a technique praised in the *Deutsches Ärzteblatt* as skillful filmmaking.[162] A report in 1936 noted that five hundred copies of each ORP film were being shown in movie theaters, in factories, at exhibitions, and to party members throughout the Reich. Some of the films were also approved for screening to high school pupils. In addition, the author of the report thought it worth mentioning that the American eugenicist Harry Laughlin had obtained a copy of *Erbkrank* from the ORP for showing in the United States.[163] *Opfer der Vergangenheit*, which was made at Hitler's express wish with a script by Frercks, was ordered to be screened in all 5,300 German movie theaters.[164] It is also known that ORP films were shown to people involved in the "euthanasia" actions. Before being deployed at the Hadamar killing center, for example, a building worker recalled having to watch a film showing psychiatric patients "who could scarcely be described as human."[165] Every year a total of about twenty million people viewed at least one ORP film.[166]

The ORP sterilization films all employ similar principles of propaganda. In general, they rely on a freak show aesthetic intensified by juxtaposing disabled with healthy people. Reports about the films show that they were meant to play to the curiosity of the public about sensationalistic things that were normally hidden from view. For example, the voice-over for a sequence of seven "idiot faces" in *Opfer der Vergangenheit* states, "The German people . . . know nothing about the oppressive spirit in those institutions where thousands of the babbling feebleminded, who are lower than any animal, have to be fed artificially and cared for. . . . Anyone who has seen such creatures cannot continue to maintain that it would not be humane to prevent the creation of such creatures."[167] This stigmatizing vocabulary incited thoughts of exterminating these patients even though these films did not explicitly address "euthanasia." In order to make the greatest possible impression on the spectators, patients were selected for filming who were visually most conspicuous, those who were the ugliest, most bizarre, or most helpless (73). In this sense, these films continued the tradition of displaying "monsters" in freak shows. Attempting to stoke popular resentments, the films emphasized the financial burden of caring for these disabled people, who were linked repeatedly with violent criminals and all manner of asocial types. Some of the films were also anti-Semitic, claiming either that excessive efforts to care for the ill had resulted from Jewish liberalism or that a high number of Jews were hereditarily diseased.[168] Generally the films closed with positive sequences showing large, happy families, athletes, groups of marching workers and soldiers, and so forth. These symbols of health were intended to offer viewers a norm with which they could identify and thus enable them to feel part of the national community that was eliminating its sick and diseased elements through involuntary sterilization.[169]

Opfer der Vergangenheit was the last of the sterilization documentary films to be shown widely, for after about three hundred thousand sterilizations had been carried out, as the yearly report of the German Hygiene Museum stated in 1938, the propaganda for sterilization was generally viewed as more or less successful and complete (47). On another level, though, the public opposition that began in the fall of 1940 to the "euthanasia" program made officials hesitate to produce more crassly simplistic documentary films for mass audiences since they wanted to avoid provoking more hostility.[170] Historians know of two documentary films about "euthanasia" made by Hermann

Schweninger on the instructions of Viktor Brack, the manager of the "euthanasia" program in the Chancellery of the Führer, and Paul Nitsche, the medical director of Operation T4, but these were never shown to the public (195ff.). Schweninger was commissioned to visit institutions throughout the Reich, selecting patients for filming who presented particularly extreme cases.[171] The first of these films, *Dasein ohne Leben* (Existence without Life), was probably completed in 1941 and was shown to a group of military doctors in Berlin on December 22, 1942. Their reaction was quite mixed, especially in view of the unfolding catastrophe at Stalingrad. Some suggested that in order to counter rumors among the troops and the population at large, it was crucial to emphasize that disabled veterans were not threatened by "euthanasia" measures.[172] The second of Schweninger's documentaries, *Geisteskrank* (Mentally Ill), survives in two versions, one for a lay and one for an academic audience. This film was to show an actual gassing of patients, which was to be presented as "releasing them from their misery." This part of the film has never been found, but in 1970 Schweninger admitted that he had filmed patients being gassed at the Sonnenstein killing center.[173] According to the film scholar Gertrud Koch, in *Dasein ohne Leben* the unintended contradiction comes out especially clearly between the fascinated, mortified gaze of the camera and the patients who are looking back into the camera and not begging at all for "deliverance."[174] For example, the camera voyeuristically shows a baby with no arms or legs, and then a nurse touches it on its arm stump, causing it to smile happily. This image could just as well be used to argue for preserving the lives of disabled people, but the Nazis intended it as an unimpeachable argument for their deaths.

In a letter written on December 19, 1940, to Viktor Brack, Himmler ordered a stop to the killings in the Grafeneck institution because of public unrest and suggested that educational films about "the hereditarily and mentally ill" might be shown in that region of the country. Himmler had the ORP sterilization documentaries in mind, but the "euthanasia" coordinators already had much more ambitious plans under way to make feature films that would be subtler and thus, they hoped, more effective.[175] Goebbels's famous speech of February 15, 1941, to the Reich Film Chamber on the nature of propaganda advocated this strategy, although it did not refer specifically to "euthanasia." He stated, "The best propaganda is not that in which the actual elements of propaganda are always clearly revealed. Rather, the best propaganda is that which works in an invisible way, so to speak. The best propaganda pervades the entire public, without the public becoming aware at all of the initiative of propaganda" (138). Along these lines, in the fall of 1940 the "euthanasia" planners had begun to develop a feature film based on Hellmuth Unger's novel *Sendung und Gewissen* (Vocation and Conscience, written in 1935, published in 1941).[176]

After many film script treatments and an exhaustive censorship process, including interventions by the Operation T4 planners Viktor Brack and Philipp Bouhler, the film *Ich klage an* (I Accuse) premiered in Berlin on August 19, 1941, less than a month after Bishop Galen's sermon of August 3 (209). Directed by the well-known Wolfgang Liebeneiner, it was praised by Goebbels in his diary as a film "for euthanasia. A film to be discussed. Splendidly made and entirely national socialist."[177] *Ich klage an* is constructed with a main plot and a subplot that propagandistically conflate the issues of euthanasia in the sense of assisting a person to die who supposedly wants to die and "euthanasia" in the sense of killing "lives unworthy of life."[178] The two plots feature two types of doctors: the scientific, rational bringer of death who wants to serve the national community is juxtaposed with the family doctor pledged to treat and comfort the individual. The main plot tells the story of Hanna, a radiant, energetic young woman who is happily married to a medical professor named Thomas. She contracts multiple sclerosis, and the disease progresses rapidly. Hanna expresses her fears of becoming "deaf, blind, and idiotic" and her wish to be "released" before that happens. When her symptoms worsen, Thomas gives her a lethal dose of medicine in order to "release her from her misery," and Hanna dies peacefully in her husband's arms. Subsequently Thomas is put on trial for murder, and the issue of killing by request is raised in the courtroom scenes.

The subplot features Thomas's friend Bernhard, who is portrayed as a kind doctor of the old school who initially views Thomas as a murderer. Bernhard has taken extreme measures to save the life of a sick child. Later he learns that the child has become "deaf, blind, and idiotic" (exactly what Hanna fears for herself) and has been committed to an institution. In a significant contrast to the ORP documentaries, when Bernhard goes to see the child, the hospital door closes before the camera. The child's condition is left to the imagination of the spectator in an unusually long shot of the closed door lasting fifteen seconds. This technique has several possible effects: it avoids provoking reactions of sympathy for the child, but it also relies on the fact that imagination is often worse than reality. Bernhard emerges from the ward looking shaken, and after an exchange with a professor that implies the child would be better off dead, he hurries to the courtroom to testify in defense of Thomas. Bernhard has thus been converted into a supporter of both killing by request and state-sponsored killing measures. The jury weighs the argu-

Fig. 15. Publicity poster for the film *Ich klage an* (I Accuse, 1941). (From Landeswohlfahrtsverband Hessen, ed., *"Verlegt nach Hadamar": Die Geschichte einer NS-"Euthanasie"-Anstalt* [Kassel: Eigenverlag des LWV Hessen, 1991], 121. Courtesy of the Princeton University Libraries.)

ments and appears ready to acquit Thomas. But in the final scene he delivers his own accusations against "laws that prevent physicians and judges from serving the Volk." He states, "I have released my wife, who was incurably ill, from her sufferings at her request" and asks the court to pronounce its verdict. With this, the film ends, technically leaving Thomas's fate open. This strategy makes the film all the more insidious as propaganda since the development of the plot steers the spectator toward viewing him as innocent.

By the end of the war, 15.3 million people in Germany had seen *Ich klage an,* and it also played in numerous other European countries. A well-made melodrama with competent actors, it received a prestigious prize at the Venice Biennale in September 1941. Special showings were arranged for doctors and medical students throughout Nazi Germany.[179] The film clearly caught the attention of the public, provoking intense discussions, as well as worries, in many sectors of the population. One doctor who belonged to an antifascist circle in Berlin stated, for example, that many of his women patients had suddenly expressed unfounded fears of contracting multiple sclerosis and that husbands whose spouses actually had the disease had wondered if it would be better to "put their wives to sleep."[180] In January 1942, the Security Service of the SS (Sicherheitsdienst) produced a summary of audience responses to the film.[181] The report claimed that, with some reservations, the majority of the population supported the film's arguments in favor of killing by request. Whereas the Catholic Church rejected the film and even warned parishioners not to see it, the Protestant Church was somewhat more ambivalent. Younger doctors were said to be generally in favor of euthanasia as it was presented in the film, while older doctors were more cautious. Some members of the public had been heard to say that doctors could make mistakes and everyone knew of cases in which sick people had recovered even when doctors had predicted they would soon die. Others commented that the situation in the film was just like that in institutions where the insane were being killed. Some expressed fears of a slippery slope, that if euthanasia were legalized, the state could manipulate such a law to eliminate anyone held to be undesirable. The report claimed, however, that the working-class viewers were favorably inclined toward the film for the pragmatic reason that they did not have the money to pay for prolonged medical care. It is impossible, of course, to reach a definitive conclusion about the effect of *Ich klage an* on German audiences. In contrast to the heavy-handed sterilization documentaries, however, this feature film skillfully steered the spectator toward considering that euthanasia might be a welcome deliverance from disability and illness. Accordingly, the mass screenings of the film gave rise for the first time to a broad discussion slanted in favor of euthanasia of disabled and ill people throughout the German Reich, which is exactly what Goebbels and the "euthanasia" planners had wanted.[182]

The Disabled Victims

Reactions and Resistance to Sterilization

Almost nothing is known about what disabled people or their relatives, friends, and allies thought about this barrage of propaganda calling for their elimination and death. Much is known, however, about how they sometimes tried to resist exclusionary laws, particularly the Sterilization and Marriage Health Laws, and in the process voiced self-conceptions that were quite at odds with eugenic propaganda. On the one hand, as postwar documents show, those subjected to eugenic sterilization were often plagued by intense feelings of shame along with physical pain and the emotional anguish of loneliness and unfulfilling family lives. In this vein, one deaf man who had been sterilized wrote in 1960, "Sterilization makes a body worthless. I no longer feel like a real person."[183] Having been told repeatedly that they were inferior and having been warned by Nazi authorities not to talk about sterilization, many of these victims remained silent for the rest of their lives. Forty years after the end of the war, for example, a West German organization of blind people issued a statement that read, "Most of the blind who were sterilized at that time and who are still alive today met their fate in their youth. They were usually not at home but in an institution for the blind, where no one supported them and where they often had to endure the scorn and contempt of others. That affected them so deeply that they are still ashamed to talk about their sterilization today."[184] On the other hand, as the historian Gisela Bock has shown in her analysis of more than one thousand trials in the Nazi sterilization courts, when ordered to present themselves for sterilization many people appealed, resisted, protested, quickly got pregnant in order to have a longed-for child, ran away, or even left Germany.[185] The documents from these cases are a highly significant source of self-representations by disabled people whom Nazi eugenicists viewed as hereditarily diseased and thus candidates for elimination.

In general, the greatest number of protests against sterilization came from Catholic and rural areas. In 1934, for example, 24 percent of the candidates for sterilization in Bamberg and Munich appealed to the courts, in contrast to 5 percent in Kiel and 9 percent in Berlin, with a national average of 15 percent. In 1936, police had to bring 9.4 percent of the sterilization candidates to an operation clinic by force, with some people fighting and struggling against being taken away. Again this percentage was higher in Catholic and rural areas (281). Those who contested their sterilization in court used a wide variety of arguments. Many remained within the prevailing value system, arguing that perhaps other people (especially the mentally impaired) deserved to be sterilized but they themselves were not affected by a hereditary disease and thus were not inferior. Men felt that their honor was being impugned, while women expressed fears that not being able to bear children would destroy their deepest female identity. Some people claimed that they had no intention to marry or have children in the first place. Others worried that the stigma of being sterilized would carry over to the children they already had, who would suffer discrimination as hereditarily tainted. Some complained about being excluded from all the economic benefits given to the hereditarily valuable. A head doctor reported that in his state hospital and nursing home it was difficult to prevent patients threatened with sterilization from "revolting, rebelling, and running away" (284). Parents sometimes supported their disabled children by declaring that since they had never received any state financial support, sterilization was not appropriate. Occasionally some called sterilization into question in a more fundamental way, saying either that it was against God's will or that it was unconstitutional. And some of the protesters rejected the accusation of being a burden on the Volk by turning the tables and asserting that sterilization was actually a policy directed against the poor. Along these lines, one woman wrote, "I want to make it clear to you that I am not feebleminded, but just poor. I do not have no [sic] hereditary disease, but I'm just depressed and pushed around. . . . Why not just go ahead and drown poor people's children right away?" (287). On the whole, then, these were incisive protests against the involuntary nature of the sterilization procedure as well as against the eugenic doctrine of human value.

As was discussed earlier, the vast majority of sterilization applications were finally approved and carried out, no matter how tenacious the protesters were. Accordingly, it is all the more important to emphasize that in their appeals to the courts sterilization candidates loosed a flood of complaints against doctors, judges, the Nazi Party, and the government. A few examples give a sense of the tone and arguments used in these protests. In January 1935, a public health doctor applied for the sterilization of two siblings from a peasant family because of hereditary blindness. They and their parents fought the decision bitterly, with their father stating to the court, "In no case will my children hand themselves over for this, and as their father I am also most strongly opposed" (221). The sterilizations were carried out in fall 1936. In June 1940 a welfare office requested the sterilization of a young woman factory worker. Her mother wrote to the court: "But my daughter does not consent at all to this, and we don't, either, my husband and I, because in the first place she isn't feebleminded, but indifferent, and that is no grounds for sterilization. The children that she has are all healthy and normal; none of them are idiotic" (222). The sterilization was carried out in June 1941. Occasionally people went so far as to threaten some unspecified revenge, as did a woman farm worker who told the court, "If this decision should be upheld, it is an injustice and a crime and a disgrace . . . and then there will be consequences and I will have my revenge. I . . . won't hand myself over to be sterilized" (285).

The eugenicist and teacher of the deaf Herbert Weinert wrote that it was necessary to counter deaf people's "subversive agitation" against sterilization. He complained that they could relay "rumors" quickly through sign language, avoiding conventional avenues of communication that were more easily monitored.[186] During the early 1980s, Horst Biesold interviewed 1,215 deaf people who had been sterilized, and of these only 17 stated that their sterilization was voluntary. About one-third said they had ignored the written summons to come to a clinic for sterilization and that they were brought in forcibly by the police. A deaf man named Karl Wacker, who was a social democrat and an activist in organizations for the deaf in Baden-Württemberg, engaged himself on behalf of deaf people prosecuted under the Sterilization Law. In 1938, he wrote a letter to the Superior Hereditary Health Court in Stuttgart in which he refused to spread propaganda promoting sterilization. He stated, "In the past months, objections and complaints have been lodged by numerous deaf persons implicated under the law. These are just normal deaf people pursuing their livelihood. They are capable of earning their own living and are in no way a burden to the state. Why have they, nonetheless, been made to suffer such great pain through sterilization? A decent person could never understand this. . . . These people are not inferiors as your explanatory pamphlet sets out. . . . As a defender of the deaf, I urgently request that you take into consideration their capacity for work and do not implicate them under the law. For my part, I will engage my efforts so that the implementation of this inhuman law may be impeded as far as possible" (118). The court responded to this brave challenge to its authority by placing Wacker under Gestapo surveillance, but he continued to support deaf people threatened with sterilization.

The life story of Gertrud Jacob is one of unusually courageous resistance by a deaf person to eugenic sterilization in Nazi Germany (121 ff.). Born in 1904 in Gotha, Jacob could hear and had begun to speak when she was struck on the head with a soccer ball at the age of two years and nine months. The resulting ear inflammation left her almost totally deaf. Jacob came to the attention of the authorities in 1936 when she attempted to secure a marriage fitness certificate. Public health doctors, as well as Herbert Weinert, did not believe that she was born a hearing child and pressed for her sterilization even though she collected numerous supportive statements from relatives, friends, doctors, and teachers. She repeatedly appealed to the Hereditary Health Court in Jena and even in desperation to Hitler himself (187). Finally, she discovered that the Sterilization Law did not apply to a couple if the man was a foreign citizen. This loophole was her salvation, for her fiancé was a deaf man from Prague whom she had met at the World Games for the Deaf in London in 1935. They married and settled in Prague, where they had two hearing children. Jacob preferred going into exile rather than succumbing to sterilization and devaluation as an inferior person in Nazi Germany. As Gisela Bock has stated, all such efforts by disabled people and their allies to challenge eugenic policies present "exceptional documents of resistance against the theory and practice of national socialist racism."[187]

All of these protests were noticeable enough that Nazi officials became concerned about their potential to provoke unrest. Consequently, the media published numerous statements to the effect that people who had been sterilized deserved gratitude for making a great personal sacrifice in the interest of the national community (281). Just like the castrated war veterans, sterilized people feared being teased and ridiculed, and there were even a few press reports about successful lawsuits being brought against people for slandering someone who had been sterilized. In 1935 in Gießen, for example, a sterilized man brought such a suit because the defendant had publicly stated, "Now he's castrated. Now he'll get fat from eating dry bread and drinking black coffee." The sterilized man won his lawsuit, with the court holding that since he had made a great sacrifice for the common good, the state had a duty to protect him against mockery.[188] In a similar case in 1937, one Albert O. was also found guilty of slander and sentenced to two months in jail for making a hateful remark to a sterilized man who wanted to sit at his table in the local pub. The court found that it was a crime to insult someone who had made a sacrifice for the health of the nation.[189]

Given the massive flood of propaganda directed against the hereditarily diseased, however, these rare instances of state intervention on behalf of those who had been sterilized come across as mere window dressing. Generally sterilized people were left alone to deal with their worries, anxieties, and shame as best they could. Even though sterilization was supposed to be kept secret, it became a common topic of conversation among the population, and especially in rural areas it often became known that someone had been sterilized.[190] Sterilized women (especially the cognitively disabled) were sometimes viewed as fair game for rape. One man reported, for example, "There was a girl in our town who had been sterilized. Whenever she went out in the evening, twelve fellows went along." A peasant requested that a local institution send him a "sterilized girl" to work on his farm with the obvious intention of sexually abusing her. One eugenicist complained, "I'm sorry from the bottom of my heart for the poor sterilized feebleminded girls who are sent back to the village and become the whores of all the local fellows." He suggested, however, that perhaps these young women needed to be locked up in an institution (393–94). In such instances, the persecution of people viewed as hereditarily diseased by no means ended with the sterilization procedure itself.

The Victims of "Euthanasia"

The people murdered in the "euthanasia" program are among the most invisible victims of national socialism, and historians have unearthed only a few statements by those who were threatened with "euthanasia" but somehow survived.[191] Existing documents and postwar trial records, however, along with some published case histories of victims and private letters of relatives, furnish much information about how both patients and their relatives reacted when confronted with state-sponsored murder.[192] In contrast to propaganda that portrayed institutionalized patients, particularly the mentally impaired, as animalistic idiots and cripples incapable of any understanding, accounts often mention that many patients were quite aware that they were threatened with death. For example, one patient who was turned back at the entrance to the gas chamber in Grafeneck because he was a veteran stated that the killings were a common topic of conversation among his fellow patients in the Reichenau institution.[193] A woman patient wrote to her parents and siblings from the Stetten institution that she was afraid for her life because the buses that transported patients had been there again. She remarked perceptively, "The government doesn't want so many institutions, so they want to get rid of us" (185). Reports noted that patients were pale and trembled in fear as they were put on the buses to go to the killing centers and that some took leave forever of those who remained behind (186). A patient who was a Catholic nun said upon getting into the bus, "Now we're getting in, we who have been sentenced to death," and another woman screamed, "We will die, yes, but the devil will get Hitler" (187). In contrast to propaganda that cast euthanasia as a form of deliverance from the "misery" of disability and illness, these patients clearly did not want to die.

Of course, many patients were too weak and helpless to struggle against being murdered, but at times they tried to resist being sent to the killing centers in various ways. Some wrote letters to their relatives in which they expressed their fear of being taken away and begged to be taken home before they were killed. A woman wrote to her sister, "Yesterday the cars were there again, and a week ago, too. They took away a lot of people again, where you wouldn't have expected it. It was so hard for us that we all cried, and it was especially hard for me when I didn't see M.S. anymore. . . . Now I would like to ask you if you would vouch for me so that I will be allowed to come and live with you because we don't know if they will come back next week" (185). When the transport buses arrived, terrible scenes occurred when patients tried to hide or run away. Some patients pleaded for their lives and struggled against being forcibly loaded onto the buses. A nurse recounted that when she told a schizophrenic woman she would be taken away, the patient "flung her arms around my neck in tears and cried that she was going to be killed. She asked if I couldn't help her because she had to die and wanted so much to live. The patient had an illegitimate child and wailed that she couldn't take it with her" (187). A worker in the Niedernhart institution, where patients were kept before being sent to the Hartheim killing center, testified, "Most sensed what was to come. Some knelt down with raised hands before the director of the institution, Dr. Lonauer, and begged him not to send them away. Nothing helped them." A nineteen-year-old woman patient at Stetten, described as "severely feeble-minded," tried to run away. When the transport personnel caught her and dragged her to the bus, she struggled and screamed to the nurses, "Miss Sophie, stay here, I stay with Miss Anna" (188). A doctor from the Austrian institution Mauer-Öhling reported that the patients there were terrified at the sight of the transports and stated, "I was violently attacked by the sick. [They] threatened revenge and so forth" (189). Such documents bring out the humanity of these patients—their fear of death, their feelings of attachment to others, their love of life—in contrast to eugenic propaganda, which portrayed them as abnormal persons unworthy of life.

With respect to the way relatives and others responded to the killings, the surviving documents necessarily tell a slanted story. We know quite a lot about the complaints that left a paper trail but very little about those who might have supported "euthanasia" for their disabled and ill relatives. Nazi eugenicists frequently referred to a study conducted in 1925 by Ewald Meltzer, the director of an asylum in Saxony, who was actually an opponent of Binding and Hoche.[194] He had conducted a survey of 162 parents of mentally impaired children in his asylum and was surprised to find that 73 percent said they would agree to the "painless curtailment" of the life of their child "if experts established that it was suffering from incurable idiocy." Of course, this was merely a hypothetical question, but it indicates a sizable reservoir of sentiment in favor of euthanasia even before 1933. When the killings began, there were some reports of relatives being indifferent, feeling relieved that they no longer had to make payments to institutions, or even welcoming the deaths of family members with whom they no longer had contact (143). In a few cases, relatives asked doctors to kill patients, as one woman did who wanted to remarry without having to get divorced. She asked a doctor in Zwiefalten "to act in step with the times" and kill her schizophrenic husband by injection.[195]

Historians generally contend that such cases were exceptions and that even committed Nazis seldom wanted to see their relatives killed and sometimes used their connections to protect them (308). Doctors reported that institutions were admitting fewer new patients because of relatives' anxieties. Victor Klemperer made a diary entry on August 22, 1941, for example, about an acquaintance who did not want to take her senile mother to a hospital in Dresden for fear she would be killed. He wrote that the killing of the mentally ill was a topic of general discussion.[196] Some relatives tried to take patients home or have them transferred to another institution where they might be in less danger. Karl Wacker, the director of the Home for the Aged Deaf in Stuttgart-Botnang, notified the brother of a patient that his sister was being sought by the Department of Public Health and urged him to remove her to a safer place. The man put her in a convent in Augsburg, thus saving her life.[197] One woman took her son, aged twenty-six, home to her village in the Allgäu, though after a while she brought him back to the institution, explaining that the villagers supported the idea of killing the mentally ill and refused to tolerate him in their midst. The man was transported to his death in 1940.[198] In that same year, a secretary working for the SS in Munich became worried about her brother, whose legs were paralyzed due to polio and who had been confined to an institution close to Dachau since the age of fifteen because of his physical disability (316–17). Although her brother was "completely intact mentally," he was about to be transferred to the insane asylum in Kaufbeuren. The secretary appealed to Rudolf Hess, asking him to intervene, pointing out that anyone could get polio, and expressing her fears that asylum inmates were dying sudden deaths. A week later her supervisor, a professor, wrote a letter supporting her request and stating that if everyone who had polio were locked up in an insane asylum, then two of his colleagues at the university in Königsberg would have to be taken away. Soon a vague response came from Berlin to the effect that nothing could be done. Relatives also frequently protested to doctors, institution directors, and other officials about not being notified when patients were transported from one institution to another, a place they later learned was a killing center. A mother wrote to a nurse in Gallneukirchen, for example, stating, "I'm flabbergasted. That's really the limit, to transfer the child to another institution without informing the mother. . . . Even if she's mentally inferior, she is and always will be my child, and I worry about her just as much as about my other children."[199] And relatives often undertook desperate efforts to ascertain the whereabouts of their loved ones when officials tried to obfuscate.

The documents tell many stories about relatives who responded with sadness, shock, disbelief, and outrage after family members were killed. Many reacted angrily to the lies told in falsified letters of condolence from officials, as did the sister of a murdered man who wrote to an institution director, "After all we are talking about a poor, sick, *helpless* human being and not an *animal!*" (311). A woman whose daughter was murdered declared in a letter to a trusted nurse, "Everything the Sonnenstein institution wrote is nothing but lies that I cannot believe" (138). Many relatives referred openly to the murder of patients and talked about the "executioners." Soldiers who returned from the war accused doctors of killing their mothers.[200] A mother inquiring about the fate of her son at Sonnenstein wrote, "Now I would like to ask if this was the first transport or if some were already taken away earlier (like animals going to the slaughter!)."[201] The sister of another patient killed at Sonnenstein expressed deep sadness, as well as anger, because she would never be able to get over her brother's death: "The poor, good fellow, who never hurt anyone, and whose biggest pleasure was giving presents to others, couldn't even end his humble existence with a natural death. . . . Today they poison the rest of life for healthy people, too, because I can't get this act out of my mind, and in Albert's case I can't accept the rationalizations that highhanded people throw at me" (24–26).

Some relatives—still hoping that the rule of law prevailed—tried to bring charges for murder, but, needless to say, these went unheeded. A lawyer notified the district court in Sangerhausen/Thuringia that his mother "did *not* die a natural death in the Brandenburg state hospital."[202] A woman teacher from Berlin whose mother had been killed at Hartheim was determined to press charges for murder but gave up after her lawyer advised her that the courts would never hear such a case and her mouth would be shut in a concentration camp (316). In his sermon condemning "euthanasia," Bishop Galen proclaimed that he had done his duty as a citizen by reporting the murders of patients—whom he called "our fellow human beings"—to the police and district court in Münster.[203] Furthermore, judges acting as guardians for patients or in other capacities complained many times to the Reich Ministry of Justice when they discovered that their wards had disappeared. The first of these complaints was brought on July 8, 1940, by Lothar Kreyssig, a judge in Brandenburg. He stated that "numerous wards of his court had died suddenly after transfer to certain institutions, that he had concluded that they were killed there as part of an ongoing program, and that as a Christian he must object."[204] Kreyssig filed a murder complaint with the state attorney in Potsdam, and when he insisted on pressing charges, Reich minister of justice Franz Gürtner forced him into early retirement.

Nazi eugenicists and the killers in Operation T4 had assumed that the majority of the population would welcome the "euthanasia" program, and they were surprised by the strength of public opposition (188). The effort to draw a sharp, unbridgeable dividing line between the healthy and the diseased was at the foundation of all eugenic propaganda and practices. But these eugenicists had not reckoned with the fact that many relatives and others still felt emotionally attached to disabled and ill people in institutions (and in the community, too). In contrast to propaganda calling for the elimination of inferior subhumans, they still viewed these disabled people as loved ones, friends, and neighbors, as people who had rights and needed help, support, and good care. It was reported, for example, that in one south German village peasant women refused to sell cherries to nurses from the local state hospital, telling them, "You don't get cherries here, just move on. We will not sell you anything, because you treat our neighbors in such a terrible way, simply transporting them away and shooting them" (189). It was close relationships with disabled victims that led many to view their deaths as murder rather than in ideological terms as release from suffering or as a desirable improvement to the hereditary health of the national community. And, as discussed earlier, this public opposition was strong enough that it eventually brought an end to the gassing, though decentralized, "wild" euthanasia continued in deeper secrecy until the end of the war.

Collaborators or Self-Advocates?

Organizations of Disabled Civilians under National Socialism

There were no organized groups that represented the interests of cognitively disabled and mentally ill people—the prime targets of the eugenicists—until much later in the twentieth century. But, as was the case with all social organizations, including those of disabled veterans, the self-advocacy associations of blind, deaf, and physically disabled civilians were subjected to Gleichschaltung as soon as the Nazis took power in 1933. These organizations were placed under the control of the National Socialist People's Welfare Office (Nationalsozialistische Volkswohlfahrt or NSV) and soon expelled their Jewish members. Those among their leaders who opposed Nazi policies were removed from their positions and replaced with disabled people who were Nazi Party members or sympathizers. With respect to the images of disability these organizations projected in their journals and public activities, they generally tried to negotiate a middle position between the heroic representations of disabled veterans and the negative characterizations of the hereditarily diseased in Nazi propaganda. Intensifying a familiar argument from Weimar rehabilitation psychology, they emphasized overcoming disability and conforming as closely as possible to rigid norms of health. They insisted that through willpower disabled Aryan citizens could become productive workers in the service of the national community and the war effort. In this respect, they always tried to distinguish their members from "degenerate cripples and idiots" who were unwilling or unable to work and posed a threat to the hereditary health of the nation. That is, they tried to claim a position for themselves as Germans of full value in contrast to those whom they stigmatized as inferior.

Since we know almost nothing about the daily lives of blind, deaf, and physically disabled civilians during the Third Reich, it is impossible to arrive at any general conclusions about what their attitudes toward these organizations were. Careful reading of the sources, however, gives glimpses of how complex the relationship was between the organizations and disabled people as a whole. For one thing, although the organizations' official journals were heavily censored, at times there are hints of differing opinions about how to interpret disability that are somewhat more complex than might be expected. For another, the life stories of a few exceptional disabled individuals from this time shed some light on how they tried outside the official organizations to continue self-help projects that they had begun during the Weimar Republic.

The synchronization of organizations of blind people under national socialism is shown most clearly by their support for the Sterilization Law. On December 23, 1933, for example, the German Association of Blind Academics sent a statement to the Propaganda Ministry agreeing with the provisions of the law but criticizing the way in which blind people were portrayed in eugenic propaganda.[205] They urged their members whose blindness was hereditary to make the great sacrifice of volunteering to be sterilized for the good of the German people rather than waiting to be forced. The statement went on to note, however, that in contrast to earlier decades, when blind people had received sympathy and help, the prevailing one-sided eugenic view of them as inferior was provoking dislike and even contempt for them among the public. These prejudices, the statement declared, were undeserved since blind people—even the hereditarily blind—were not to blame for their fate. Obviously the Propaganda Ministry paid no attention to this appeal for more tolerance.

A few instances are known that indicate the distance between some blind people and the synchronized organizations for the blind. In September 1933 in the journal *Blindenwelt* (Blind World), for example, an anonymous writer urged readers not to join these organizations, fearing that if they identified themselves as blind in this way they would be in greater danger of sterilization (28). The blind scholar and activist Rudolf Kraemer, who will be discussed in greater detail in the following pages, published a critique of eugenics that led to his expulsion from a leading position in the German Association of the Blind. Max Schöffler, a blind member of the Communist Party, had secured many benefits for blind people in Dresden during the Weimar Republic and was removed from his position in the Bavarian Association of the Blind in March 1933.[206] Max Telschow, who had founded the Association of Blind Industrial Workers in 1919, was removed from his post in 1933 because he opposed Gleichschaltung (169). Betty Hirsch, a blind Jewish teacher who ran a private vocational school for blind people in Berlin, went into exile in England in 1934 and escaped the fate of her relatives, who died in concentration camps (175). All these individuals advocated concepts of self-help and social integration that were totally at odds with the synchronized organizations, which lined up with Nazi ideology to accept eugenic measures and the curtailing of life possibilities for blind people.

Similarly, the Reich Union of the Deaf of Germany (REGEDE), which had been chaired from its founding in 1927 by Fritz Albreghs, a member of the Nazi Party, became the official Nazi organization for deaf Germans within the NSV. The REGEDE played a central role in implementing contradictory Nazi policies that assumed deaf people were educable and

Fig. 16. Blind girls playing music at a meeting of the Nazi Winter Aid Charity. (From Karl Tornow and Herbert Weinert, *Erbe und Schicksal* [Berlin: Metzner, 1942], 99. Courtesy of the Yale University Medical Library.)

employable but also inferior. On the one hand, there were units of deaf young people known as the Bann G (Unit D; G=Gehörlose or "Deaf") in the Hitler Youth (Hitler Jugend or HJ) and the League of German Girls (Bund deutscher Mädel or BDM). The Bann G organized summer camps for its members along with other typical Hitler Youth activities.[207] In 1933, Albreghs assembled a deaf SA unit that had 296 members. The Nazi Party outlawed it in the fall of that year, presumably because it clashed with the image of the Nazi fighter as a perfectly sound physical specimen, but as late as 1937 there were photos of deaf SA men (84). Nazi Germany sent deaf athletic teams to London in 1935 and Stockholm in 1939 to compete in the International Games for the Deaf.[208]

On the other hand, as in the organizations for the blind, REGEDE leaders were strong proponents of eugenic sterilization, sometimes denouncing their members to the authorities. As one REGEDE district leader was said to have stated, "The hearing must sacrifice their lives as soldiers. The deaf do not need to be soldiers. But sterilization is a sacrifice like soldiering. We must make this sacrifice!"[209] The organization had 3,900 members in 1934 and 11,588 in 1937. If some people stayed away from the synchronized organizations because they worried that membership would make them more vulnerable to sterilization, this fear may have motivated other deaf people to join REGEDE and the Nazi

Party. As one deaf man recalled, "It was not inner conviction that prompted me to this step, but rather the hope that as a party member I would be protected from the sterilization law" (98). This strategy did not work for the man for he was sterilized anyway. For long after the war, altercations continued among deaf Germans over REGEDE's role in enforcing involuntary sterilization.

The Reich League of the Physically Handicapped (RBK), now under the leadership of a Nazi Party member, Hellmut Neubert, was also incorporated into the NSV in 1933. It issued a statement that the physically handicapped were proud to belong to the "new Germany" and emphasized that they—along with the blind and deaf—were just as much a part of the Volk as were disabled veterans and workers.[210] The RBK specifically excluded the mentally abnormal from membership even if they had physical handicaps, continuing its practice of distinguishing between the physically handicapped of full value and the mentally ill who were unproductive.[211] Statistics the RBK published about its activities indicate an effort to make the organization appear more effective than it really was. The RBK claimed that it had undertaken 510,387 "consultations" in 1939, its highest annual total, although this figure undoubtedly includes individuals who turned to the RBK for advice or participated in its sports courses more than once.[212] Of these, 223,014 were unspecified consultations about welfare matters, 99,356 had to do with questions about vocational training, 96,482 were for participation in local RBK sports courses, 50,681 dealt with procuring assistive devices, 6,023 were for assistance in getting a job, and the rest were for a variety of reasons. These consultations dropped off precipitously after the war began, with only 163,078 occurring in 1943.[213] Generally the statistics show that the RBK was most active in giving advice about welfare matters and organizing sports courses. In spite of its insistence that the physically handicapped could and should work, it appears to have aided only a relatively small number in finding appropriate employment.

The standpoint of the RBK toward the Sterilization Law went through three phases, whose development can be followed in the organization's official journal, Der Körperbehinderte (The Physically Handicapped).[214] At first, the members of the RBK decisively rejected the law and engaged in intense discussions about how it was to be applied. Frick's speech of June 28, 1933, caused a great deal of anxiety among physically disabled people, who thought he had connected them too closely with the mentally impaired and criminals and had strengthened the popular misconception that most physical disabilities were inherited. Accordingly, the RBK stated in September 1933 that, while it agreed with the basic eugenic premises of both the Sterilization Law and the program for marriage loans, the effect of these policies should not be overestimated since most physical handicaps were not hereditary. Continuing in what can only be described as an astonishingly liberal tone, the statement declared that the RBK wanted to prevent crippling not only through sterilization but above all through adequate prenatal precautions, good care for infants and children, and the elimination of disease and accidents. The RBK went on to emphasize that the physically handicapped did not deserve to be marginalized but rather should have the best possible medical treatment, education, and employment for "the cripple, too, has a German soul."[215] When the Sterilization Law went into effect on January 1, 1934, the RBK tried even harder to portray the "hereditarily sound" handicapped as Volk comrades of full value in contrast to the mentally impaired and those with hereditary physical handicaps. Finally, the RBK began to attempt to convince its members with hereditary conditions that they should volunteer to be sterilized, thus spreading eugenic propaganda and conducting surveillance within its own ranks.

During the Weimar Republic, the SBK and RBK had emphasized that many physically handicapped people were able to work, but the independent organization had taken the limitations of individuals into account and had also viewed paid employment as only one among many ways to give life meaning. For a short time after 1933, the RBK still tried to follow this line, continuing to support adequate care for the most severely disabled people as well as measures to enable their participation in the community.[216] Soon, however, this humane concept of self-help was displaced by a Nazi-oriented concept: the demand that the physically handicapped should work to support themselves and their families and give up all claims to financial support from the state.[217] Over and over again, the publications of the RBK upheld work, performance, and total economic independence as the only honorable goals for the physically handicapped. At the first national conference of the RBK, held in Berlin in 1935, for example, the ORP head Walter Gross called for replacing "pity" with "increased performance" and then went on to defend the Sterilization Law as being in the national interest while noting that most physical defects were not hereditary. He concluded that the physically handicapped who "gave their all" and accepted eugenic measures earned a place in the "hard, proud" national community, proclaiming, "Today, my friends, you are fully entitled to stand alongside each one of us."[218] Under these conditions, national socialism made room in its ideology and politics for an affirmative image of certain disabled people.

Following Gross's line, the RBK continued to point out that anyone could become handicapped and to insist in contradictory ways that the physically handicapped could be independent and make valuable contributions to the nation. This one-sided emphasis on overcoming disability and on performance intensified the male-oriented character of the RBK as women who had played leading roles in the organization during the Weimar Republic were increasingly displaced by male Nazi Party members. In turn, this gender constellation shaped the way the RBK presented the physically handicapped to the public. For example, male members of the RBK participated in a festival in the Berlin district of Steglitz in 1935, demonstrating various trades (carpentry, painting, tailoring, and gardening) while riding on a wagon draped with a banner reading, "Not welfare, but work!"[219] The photographs in *Der Körperbehinderte* are mostly images of men working at various occupations or engaging in strenuous sports (mainly for amputees) while Hitler and other Nazi high officials sometimes watch. A few photographs from local chapters show men and women—some using crutches, canes, or wheelchairs—participating in leisure activities such as going for a boat ride, to the zoo, or for a walk, and one photo is pointedly captioned "Healthy children of the physically handicapped." An article by a male author about the "woman question" asserted that physically handicapped women could marry and have children if they had no hereditary illnesses, that they should work and do gymnastics, and that they should dress so as to hide their handicaps.[220] These images of physically disabled Germans highlight their efforts to conform as closely as possible to norms of health and appearance.

Beginning in 1937, *Der Körperbehinderte* published accounts of cases in which the RBK had helped a physically handicapped person obtain work for the first time or retraining after becoming disabled. Using the slogan "Handicaps do not handicap!" the journal reported on two men with polio who had become a master shoemaker and a tailor, men with amputated hands or arms who had become factory workers or orthopedic technicians, and so forth.[221] A few accounts were about women, including one who had learned to do all her housework from her wheelchair and another who used a wheelchair due to polio and was now an office worker. After the war began, the emphasis shifted to those described as "fighters on the home front," who were sent to work in the armaments industry.[222] There were even several reports about the physically handicapped serving in the military, including one about a soldier with a 60 percent disability caused by an accident who was proud of his service in Poland.[223] In 2000, I spoke with an elderly woman in Berlin who had always used a wheelchair due to polio and had worked as a bookkeeper during the Nazi era. That interview corroborated the impres-

Fig. 17. High jump performed by a member of the RBK. (From *Der Körperbehinderte* 6:3 [March 1936], 1. Courtesy of the Humboldt University Library, Berlin.)

sion conveyed by RBK publications that some of the handicapped led relatively normal daily lives at that time. The woman was not a member of the RBK, but she told me that friendly women colleagues had always helped push her wheelchair to work and she had never been made to feel excluded or inferior.

These cases followed the predictable pattern of overcoming disability and claiming normality, but others were more complex. For two years or so, beginning in April 1940, the RBK asserted rather pointedly that it wanted to help even the most severely handicapped—including some with congenital or hereditary disabilities—find work. This is precisely the period when many Germans gradually found out about the "euthanasia" program, and so these statements appear to express veiled opposition to Operation T4 at least insofar as the RBK believed some physically disabled people to be threatened by it. For example, the RBK claimed to have helped a man with muscular dystrophy to become an inspector in a factory, a man born with no hands and no left leg to get an office job in an armaments factory, and an innkeeper with multiple sclerosis to get an easy factory job and a used car for commuting to work. Of course, there is no way of knowing whether these individuals really felt they were better off after the intervention of the RBK. At least, however, the organization claimed "success in difficult cases," perhaps implying that in addition to removing such severely disabled individuals from the welfare rolls, these people were worth helping and had something to contribute to society.[224]

The RBK tried to convince physically handicapped Germans to join it by declaring that it was furthering their equality, presenting them not as suffering invalids but as strong members of society, and urging all Germans to overcome their prejudices toward the handicapped.[225] Membership statistics, however, show that the majority of physically disabled people kept their distance from the RBK. In early 1933, it had about six thousand members, and a statistic from 1940 claimed thirty-four thousand.[226] Since the RBK estimated that there were a total of four hundred thousand physically handicapped Germans, its small number of members indicates an obvious unwillingness within this large group to join it. It is likely that some were afraid of being identified irrevocably as inferior if they became members, while others objected that the RBK was too much of a clique and they wanted to forget about their disabilities rather than emphasizing them.[227] Still others disagreed with the ideology of the RBK. In 1946, the SBK cofounder Otto Perl, who had always supported eugenic sterilization for the mentally impaired, could finally air his real opinions.[228] He harshly criticized the policies of the RBK toward the physically handicapped, saying that it—along with the NSV—was to blame for "our total loss of rights in the 'Third Reich,' the suppression of our economic and cultural efforts in 1933, the theft of our hard-earned money by the Nazis, and the brutal exploitation of our fellow unfortunates in the armaments factories and offices of the Naziocracy. Thousands of these miserable impaired people were ruined by overwork and malnourishment."[229]

Some physically disabled people obviously hoped that they would be safer and perhaps even preserve some limited possibilities for action if they remained inconspicuous. Consequently, following a strategy of inner emigration, they stayed away from the RBK. The social worker and youth welfare worker Hilde Wulff (1898–1972) is a case in point. The daughter of a wealthy factory owner, Wulff had polio and was active in the SBK during the Weimar Republic. Recognizing the dangers of national socialism for disabled people, she wrote in 1932 that it aimed to replace mutual assistance with the "principle of power and the survival of the fittest." In 1933, Wulff left the RBK and founded an institution for disabled and nondisabled children in Berlin, which she relocated to an isolated village near Hamburg in 1935 in order to be "free of all national socialist influences." By living in obscurity and with the help of doctors and other welfare workers, she was able to bring all the children safely through the Third Reich.[230]

Just as there were units in the Hitler Youth and League of German Girls for the blind and deaf (known as Bann B and Bann G), units for the physically handicapped (known as Bann K) were founded beginning on August 14, 1935, both outside and inside institutions for crippled children.[231] Nazi Party member Sepp Held, who directed handicapped sports in the RBK, was placed in charge of Bann K. A decree issued by Reich Youth Leader Baldur von Schirach specified that Aryan boys aged ten to eighteen and girls aged ten to twenty-one could join if their handicaps were covered by the guidelines of the RBK, if they were "hereditarily healthy," and if a doctor certified they were "fit for service in a limited way."[232] It was estimated that seventy-five thousand handicapped youths met these conditions, but certainly only a tiny fraction of that number joined the Bann K. Organizers envisioned that its members would participate above all in physical exercise, sports, and vocational training, calling for them to reject pity and join the ranks of the productive. In this vein, Held addressed handicapped youths as follows: "You, my dear boys, are not 'cripples,' as people call you. It depends mostly on your active participation in the HJ whether you can hold your own through your deeds. You must only become hard."[233] In spite of such pep talks about equality, however, Bann K members were not allowed to wear their uniforms in public without approval from the district office. This policy was obviously meant to preserve the healthy, strong image of the HJ and BDM by preventing young people with obvious disabilities from appearing in their ranks (111).

The ideology of the Bann K reflected that of the RBK, as is shown in a revealing article entitled "Das körperbehinderte Kind im neuen Deutschland" (The Physically Handicapped Child in the New Germany, 1935) published in *Unsere HJ* (Our HJ), the official newsletter of the

Bann K.[234] The writer criticized Weimar liberalism for trying to provide everything for the weak rather than encouraging them to take care of themselves. By contrast, every physically handicapped child capable of achievement could expect a bright future under National Socialism for "those capable of even the smallest effort must act for the benefit of the whole." It appears that with some accommodations for their impairments, members of the Bann K participated in most of the same activities as the regular HJ: excursions, camps, crafts, singing, ideological indoctrination, and above all exercise and sports.[235] For example, Bann K units frequently hiked for several kilometers through the countryside. Photographs show that most participants seemed to have no or only slight mobility impairments, although a few were using wheelchairs and apparently exerting themselves far beyond their strength. Since some young people had been transferred from regular units of the HJ into the Bann K, this raises the question of whether the Bann K actually included many members with more severe disabilities.[236] In any event, the Bann K was dissolved on February 5, 1937, for as yet undetermined reasons, less than two years after its founding.[237]

No memoirs exist describing what young disabled people really thought of the Bann K, Bann B, or Bann G: whether they viewed these special units as abusive or humane, segregating and stigmatizing, or providing new opportunities. Yet a thoughtful memoir by the prominent cultural historian Jost Hermand yields much insight into the contradictions between the Nazi ideology of comradeship and actual experiences in the Hitler Youth with respect to disability. A highly intelligent yet frail boy with a severe speech impediment, Hermand spent much of the war in five different HJ camps that were part of the Nazis' program for evacuating children from large cities threatened by bombing (the Kinderlandverschickung or KLV). At times, the adults in charge treated the children well, but generally an atmosphere of brutality prevailed based on the survival of the fittest. In the adolescent pecking order that developed, the weaker boys suffered from the inordinate emphasis placed on sports and paramilitary drills. They were often abused and even raped by the stronger boys. Hermand's memoir exposes how contempt for the weak was central to all Nazi indoctrination in contrast to any enlightened, peaceful concepts based on solidarity that would nurture "sensitive and handicapped children" and give them the "proper prerequisites for a happy adult life."[238] Without a doubt, the special units of the HJ and BDM also upheld this hierarchy, as can be inferred from their emphasis on performance and sports and from their silence about the place of more severely disabled young people in the new Germany.

Critic of Eugenics: The Blind Scholar and Activist Rudolf Kraemer

In April 1933—at the last possible moment—the blind scholar and activist Rudolf Kraemer (1885–1945) published a pamphlet entitled *Kritik der Eugenik: Vom Standpunkt des Betroffenen* (Critique of Eugenics: From the Standpoint of One Affected by It). Among all the contemporary writings by opponents of eugenics, this is a unique document, for it is the only well-founded, critical publication against eugenic measures written by a disabled person who was directly threatened by them.[239] Kraemer was born in Heilbronn into a wealthy family that owned several newspapers. He was blind in one eye at birth and gradually lost the very weak sight in his other eye due to glaucoma. He also had a severe speech impediment, which he never overcame completely. Kraemer's parents loved him and could afford to pay for the best education, medical treatment, and speech therapy. He attended regular schools, sitting in the last row of his high school class surrounded by sound-dampening boards so his Braille typewriter would not distract the other pupils. An absolute exception for someone blind from birth, he attended universities in Tübingen and Heidelberg, receiving doctorates in both economics and law for his dissertations on legal matters affecting blind people. Kraemer was happily married to a woman who had been his private secretary and reader during his student days. From the beginning, he planned on becoming a "lawyer for the blind."[240] He played an important role in founding the Reich Association of the Blind (Reichsdeutscher Blindenverband or RBV) in 1912, was active in the German Association of Blind Academics and numerous other self-advocacy groups, and became the legal adviser to the RBV in 1929, working tirelessly to secure more civil rights and improve financial benefits for blind civilians.

During the Weimar Republic, Kraemer also began to speak and write against the dangers of eugenics. His first article on this subject, "Die Austilgung der Minderwertigen" (The Eradication of the Inferior, 1927), appeared in the journal *Blindenfreund* (Friend of the Blind) and argued that no one but the person concerned could ever decide whether or not a life was worth living (177). Two years later the RBV published both print and Braille versions of Kraemer's pamphlet *Blindheitsleid und Glücksgefühl* (Suffering from Blindness and the Feeling of Happiness), which has been described as the most substantial self-characterization from the Weimar era by a person who was blind from birth (168). Kraemer explained that he had written his pamphlet to counteract the common belief that blind people were always unhappy. He soberly enumerated the limitations caused by blindness such as difficulties in finding employment, restricted enjoyment of nature, sports, and certain hobbies, the impossibility of studying certain fields, and problems in finding a marriage partner, which were much greater for blind women than blind men. He also distinguished between the experiences of people born blind and those of persons who had acquired their blindness later in life, noting that of course the process of going blind was traumatic. On the other hand, he also listed many things that blind people were able to enjoy just as fully as the sighted: physical pleasures such as sex and good food, love and positive emotional connections with others, intellectual pursuits, satisfying work, leisure activities such as music and games, political and community involvement, and so forth. Declaring that blindness was worst when it led to poverty, Kraemer urged welfare services to help blind people find appropriate employment. As long as their material needs were satisfied, he viewed blind individuals as no more or less happy than anyone else. In the context of the ongoing upswing in eugenic thinking, Kraemer's pamphlet opposed the idea that disabled people needed to be released from their suffering.

On the eve of the Nazi takeover of power, Kraemer published a satirical piece against eugenics in the 1932–33 New Year's edition of *Blindenwelt* (Blind World) entitled "Das Blindenpferd, der Triumph der angewandten Vererbungswissenschaft" (The Seeing-Eye Horse, the Triumph of the Applied Science of Heredity). Intended to ridicule the leading German eugenicists Fritz Lenz, Hermann Muckermann, Erwin Baur, and Eugen Fischer, the text tells of three professors named Lenzmann, Mucker, and Fischbauer. This trio successfully crosses a gentle mare with a German shepherd guide dog to produce a seeing-eye horse, *Typhlohippus eugenicus,* which blind people enjoy riding through the Tiergarten park in Berlin (180). Three months later, writing in the most serious scholarly vein, Kraemer published *Kritik der Eugenik* in which he argued against unscientific conceptions of inferiority and attempted to expose their subjective, ideological nature. He proposed that blind people had an obligation to engage seriously with eugenics since it promised to reduce the numbers of the blind through sterilization. Making careful use of statistics from the 1925 survey of the impaired, he claimed that for many reasons blind people rarely had blind children. Consequently, he argued that blindness could be prevented much more effectively by improving ophthalmology and general medical care rather than sterilizing large numbers of the blind. He specified that he had nothing against voluntary sterilization. He warned against the involuntary sterilization law proposed by the national socialists, however, saying with uncanny foresight that it would be outrageous to imagine the police dragging citizens into the operating room (363). Kraemer also asserted that eugenics showed its most repulsive side in proposals by the likes of Alfred Ploetz, Ernst Mann, Karl Binding, and Alfred Hoche for the euthanizing of useless persons. By contrast, he argued that it was necessary to distinguish between the value of a life for the person concerned—which depended solely on an individual's subjective feelings—and the value of that life for others. He critiqued the euthanasia advocates for falsely claiming that impairments necessarily made people miserable, for their vastly exaggerated cost estimates of caring for the impaired, and for their utilitarian emphasis on productivity and military fitness. In conclusion, Kraemer argued incisively that instead of sterilization a much better way to reduce the number of the impaired would be to renounce war.

The RBV was courageous enough to publish Kraemer's pamphlet, but the organization also distanced itself from his critique of eugenics and invited the eugenicist Otmar von Verschuer to write a response. In his *Blindheit und Eugenik* (Blindness and Eugenics), also published by the RBV in 1933, Verschuer attacked Kraemer for supposedly misunderstanding the science of heredity and maintained that eugenic measures could significantly reduce the numbers of blind people. As soon as the Sterilization Law was passed in July, the synchronized organizations of the blind began to attack Kraemer because of his opposition to eugenics. Finally, the RBV discharged him from his position as legal adviser in September 1934, over his protests, thus expelling one of the most effective self-advocates for blind people from its ranks. Afterward Kraemer made a diary entry in which he described the fate of all self-help efforts under national socialism: "Furthermore, in the new welfare organizations the blind have again become what they were in the nineteenth century: the object of welfare organized from above by the sighted. The chronicler [i.e., Kraemer] had helped found the so-called 'movement of the blind' and had led it intellectually with the goal of making the blind the organizers and administrators of their own welfare work. All of that is now completely over" (162).

An activist intellectual such as Kraemer could not bear to withdraw totally into private life, however, even under the Nazis' oppressive regime. Rather, beginning in 1935, he began to offer speech therapy courses to try to help other people with speech impediments by teaching them what he termed his autosuggestive method for overcoming stuttering (298). As early as 1901, he had described his speech impediment as "my mortal enemy, which brings me countless times daily ridicule, deathly embarrassment, insults, despair verging on melancholy, and disadvantages and unpleasantness of all kinds" (36). He stated on numerous occasions that he suffered much less from his blindness than from the fear, embarrassment, and isolation caused by his stuttering (37). Consequently, he planned a program of lectures and courses on how to overcome speech problems, although they never attracted many participants. After this last self-help endeavor failed, Kraemer survived the war years by managing concerts by blind musicians, which were charitable fund-raisers with a long tradition in Germany. In an essay written immediately after the war and shortly before he died in 1945, he pointed out with his typical incisiveness that in spite of all their brutal efforts to eliminate the unfit and create a perfectly healthy master race, the Nazis had actually produced more disability, illness, and suffering than any regime in German history. It seems fitting to quote Rudolf Kraemer at the conclusion of this chapter on disability and Nazi culture: "The number of the impaired was supposed to have been reduced through involuntary sterilization. In fact, however, because of the millions of new war cripples, it has risen to a height that even a thousand years of natural selection could probably not have brought about" (296).

CHAPTER 3 • No Friends of the Third Reich: Different Views of Disability from Exile

During the twelve years of the Third Reich, it was only in exile that Germans could publicly continue to profess a commitment to universal human equality and advocate adequate support for poor, disabled, and ill people. Since eugenics had found supporters across the political spectrum before 1933, however, very few exiled Germans opposed to national socialism were concerned with protesting against Nazi eugenic measures.[1] In fact, some German Jewish exiles, such as the psychiatrist Franz Kallmann, continued to advocate eugenic sterilizations in the United States and exerted a strong influence on American psychiatry in this regard. Accordingly, it is all the more important to remember those other exiles who expressed convictions that the lives of "weak" people had inherent value, that disabled people deserved compassionate care, and that such people might even make worthwhile contributions to society if given the opportunity.

In his major work, *Das Prinzip Hoffnung* (The Principle of Hope), which was written in 1938–47 in exile in Boston and published in 1954, the philosopher Ernst Bloch furnished a framework for critiquing rigid eugenic norms of health as well as national socialist eugenic policies of "selection and eradication." In the section entitled "The Struggle for Health: Medical Utopias," Bloch cut through the obfuscation of all solely biologistic perspectives, arguing incisively that health is not only a medical category but also a social concept based on particular norms. Looking back over the centuries, he postulated, for example, that health meant the ability to enjoy life for the ancient Greeks, the ability to believe in God during the Middle Ages (thus the view that illness is a sign of sin), and the capacity for gainful employment in the capitalist era. Consequently, Bloch saw the role of the physician as frequently manifesting a reactionary tendency for in restoring the type of health validated by respective societies the physician typically acted to enforce such social norms.

At the same time, however, Bloch also perceived not only restorative goals in medical practice but also longings for renewal that were potentially just as problematic. Utopian thinkers had frequently imagined eliminating hereditary defects, enhancing the human body, selecting for sex and other characteristics, increasing the life span, and so forth. All such plans generally had a reactionary thrust as well, according to Bloch, because they advocated solving social problems by means of biological intervention in the "hereditary substance" of individuals. Specifically, Bloch described the Nazis' efforts to regulate marriage and procreation according to eugenic criteria as aiming to create a standardized race that was more easily manipulated. And, if such selective breeding was being attempted before birth, afterward—in a clear reference to Nazi "euthanasia"—Bloch knew that violent methods of elimination were being employed. As he declared, in Nazi Germany "all those who fall outside the norm" were threatened with "murder," and "for the Nazis the only norm is to have the ass below and the beast above."[2]

Bloch's alternative to this reactionary racial hygiene was a progressive "social hygiene" that would strive to transform all the ways in which society itself was sick (532). Rather than a solely medical approach to rectifying ills, he insisted on the necessity of remedying fundamental injustices arising out of class inequality. Stating that by far the greatest number of goldfish had always swum in the depths, that people from the lower classes had rarely had the chance to develop their talents, he called for creating social and economic justice rather than focusing on questions of individual biology. Consequently, just as some socialist physicians had done in Germany before 1933,[3] Bloch asserted that the best eugenics "presumably consists of good food and living quarters, of an untroubled childhood. These things promote growing up well and make it superfluous to carry out selection according to the strange tincture that has been called pure blood" (532). By following this line of argument, Bloch turned the philosophical question of norms from its head to its feet. Rather than advocating the elimination of those who fell outside narrow eugenic norms of health, he advocated a materialist critique of the genesis of these norms that exposed whose interests they actually served. Although Bloch was writing about health in a general sense rather than specifically about disability, his argument is not unlike that of today's disability studies theorists, who contrast the medical category of impairment with disability as a socially constructed category.

In a few isolated works published in exile after 1933, nondisabled German authors first represented disabled civilians in more realistic or even positive ways that challenged exclusionary norms from a perspective similar to Bloch's. In opposition to the overwhelmingly negative cultural tradition of stigmatizing disability, these writers created different, even utopian visions that conceived of disabled people as ordinary human beings, portrayed their social exclusion as caused by oppressive environments rather than inherent individual flaws, and even imagined them as positive heroes. One writer I will discuss here took a more documentary approach, whereas two others created disabled characters who were obviously intended as metaphors for weakness, helplessness, and insufficiency. Even in these instances, though, as is so often the case with truly great authors, the texts know more than the authors did. By exploring how these characters break through the limitations of traditional discourses about disability, it becomes apparent that they are much more than merely negative metaphors. In fact, these disabled characters are less one-sided and more realistic than any we have encountered so far in German culture.

In accordance with the principles of his epic theater, the dramatist Bertolt Brecht distanced the themes of war, violence, and profiteering from his contemporary audience by setting his play *Mutter Courage und ihre Kinder* (Mother Courage and Her Children) at the time of the Thirty Years' War. Written in Scandinavian exile in 1938–39, this chronicle tells the story of the camp follower Mother Courage and her three children, who make a living selling goods to the opposing armies. Among other things, Brecht intended his play to demonstrate thought-provoking examples of false and real heroism. Mother Courage's oldest son, Eilif, is characterized as "brave and smart" and exemplifies the virtues of the traditional war hero. After a short-lived peace is declared, however, he "performs one heroic deed too many," robbing a peasant and killing his wife.[4] Even though he was rewarded for precisely this kind of heroism during the war, he is now led away in disgrace to be executed. That Brecht's play was understood after 1945 as a critique of just such destructive violence is shown by an article published in the communist newspaper *Neues Deutschland* (New Germany) on January 13, 1949, two days after the play opened in Berlin. The reviewer wrote that Brecht's masterpiece of the epic theater poses the question "Who still dares to speak of 'heroes' . . . in view of the battlefields spread out like a scourge across the continent?" And yet, the reviewer went on to assert, the play does in fact have a dramatic heroine, "Courage's mute daughter, Kattrin."[5]

In contrast to Eilif, her brave brother, Kattrin's heroism is rooted in her empathy and good heart. This virtue manifests itself especially in her deep love of children, which enables her to overcome fears for her own safety. In this sense, Kattrin is not an unusual figure but one in the series of Brecht's many female characters who exemplify stereotypical virtues of motherliness, empathy, and selflessness. Kattrin is also a disabled young woman, however, and this makes her a unique figure, not

only among Brecht's female characters but also among earlier representations of disabled women in general. Throughout the play, others
explicitly identify Kattrin in terms of her disabilities: first, her muteness,
caused by a soldier who stuffed something into her mouth when she was
a child; and later a disfiguring facial scar, the result of an attack by soldiers. When Mother Courage introduces Kattrin, she says, "My daughter's nothing. At least she can't talk; that's something" (23). Kattrin is the
"poor animal" who cannot express herself, the helpless "cripple" whom
her mother tries to protect by keeping her inconspicuous (42–43). In
spite of Mother Courage's coarse language and rough manner, she is
attached to Kattrin and feels responsible for her. At one point, an army
cook asks Mother Courage to give up her wandering life and help him
run an inn he has inherited in Holland. She feels inclined to accept until
the cook refuses to let Kattrin come along. Moved by economic considerations, the cook fears that Kattrin's presence would drive away his
customers. He declares, "The customers don't want to have to look at
something like that all the time. And you can't blame them" (93). On
hearing this, Mother Courage rejects the cook's offer and leaves him
behind, remaining loyal to her disabled daughter.

In contrast to cultural stereotypes of nondisabled women that frequently portray their actions as motivated by their sexuality or motherliness, disabled women have rarely been represented as also possessing
these attributes. Brecht's Kattrin, however, embodies these ordinary
female characteristics, and this is precisely what makes her an unusual
figure with certain utopian qualities. She is the one character in the play
who does not think about profiting from the war but only wants peace to
come so she can marry and have a family of her own. In contrast to the
prostitute, Yvette, who sells her body to soldiers, Kattrin "wants to do it
for nothing, for pleasure," as her mother complains (42). In contrast to
those who are only thinking of their own safety, Kattrin saves an infant
from a burning farmhouse. Mother Courage unwittingly evokes a
utopian moment of peace with her exasperated description of her
daughter cradling a stranger's baby in her arms and humming a lullaby:
"There she sits, happy in the midst of all this misery" (63). And, in contrast to the members of a peasant family who are intent only on saving
themselves, Kattrin beats her drum from their barn roof in order to alert
the sleeping city of Halle to the imminent attack of Catholic troops. Dis-
regarding the peasant's shouts to "stop beating, you cripple," she is shot
down by soldiers at the moment when she successfully awakens the city
and saves the children in it (102).

When Mother Courage and her friend the cook are reduced to begging, they sing the "Solomon Song," which enumerates the "worthless"

virtues embodied by her three children. Evocatively reversing the old cultural tradition of depicting cripples as beggars, the song compares Kattrin's selflessness to that of Saint Martin, who is customarily shown giving a crippled beggar half of his coat. In the song's cynical text, this self-sacrifice is ultimately useless, for both Saint Martin and the poor man freeze to death. But the figure of Kattrin has another message. On the one hand, she is able to save others but not herself, being too weak and isolated to prevail against the war's overwhelming destruction. On the other hand, as the most dramatic character in the play, she is the one who provides a legitimate point for audience identification, the one who demonstrates that "the most helpless person is ready to help," as Brecht put it.[6] With his Kattrin, Brecht thus created a unique portrayal of a disabled young woman who is loved by her mother, longs for an ordinary life, acts as a subject in the world, and performs the only good deeds in the play. As the representative of peace, Kattrin is the martyred positive heroine who takes worthwhile action for others. At the same time, true to Brecht's efforts to activate his audience, the play leads the spectator to think that there *should* be a world in which a young woman like Kattrin would be happy rather than victimized.

Two further works of German exile literature, situated during the Third Reich, employ disabled characters specifically to critique Nazi eugenic practices among other things. The first of these, Maria Leitner's *Elisabeth, ein Hitlermädchen: Roman der deutschen Jugend* (Elisabeth, a Hitler Girl: A Novel of German Youth), published in the *Pariser Tageszeitung* in 1937, employs a basically documentary approach. Leitner was born in 1892 into a German-speaking Jewish family in Varazdin (then part of Austro-Hungary, today in Croatia).[7] A member of the Communist Party of Hungary, she fled to Vienna after the fall of the Hungarian Soviet Republic in 1919, lived in Berlin for several years, and traveled widely in the United States, South America, and the Caribbean, taking working-class jobs and writing numerous reportages about the lives of working people in these areas. Because her novel *Hotel Amerika* (1930) was on the first list of books banned by the Nazis, Leitner went into hiding in 1933 and then lived in exile in Paris from 1934 to 1940. She undertook several illegal trips back into Nazi Germany and reported in the exile press on preparations for war and daily life in the Third Reich. After two months in the French internment camp of Gurs, Leitner escaped and was last seen by several exiled German writers in Marseilles in the spring of 1941. It seems likely that she died of illness and starvation there.

In her novel *Elisabeth, ein Hitlermädchen*, Leitner depicted the experience of young women in the Nazi Labor Service.[8] Spanning a narrative time of one year beginning in 1933, this novel centers on the character of Elisabeth, a young department store clerk and enthusiastic member of the Nazi League of German Girls (BDM) who is sent to a Labor Service camp. There young women from all class backgrounds have been brought together to work for the national community under the supervision of a tyrannical female squad leader, a ruthlessly committed Nazi who lectures the girls about eugenics. Leitner highlighted the conflicts between the girls' physical, mental, and emotional integrity, on the one hand, and the requirements of a brutal system on the other. Obviously familiar with Nazi eugenic propaganda and practices, Leitner introduced the character of a girl who has been sterilized in an institution for wayward children because she was labeled feebleminded and asocial. Although she is supposed to keep this a secret, she frightens the other girls deeply by telling them her story. Finally a girl named Gilda discovers that the squad leader has been taking notes about the girls' health, heredity, and parents. The leader, who is entitled to make sterilization applications, has classified Gilda as having severely defective heredity because her father, a psychically traumatized veteran, died in a mental institution. Afraid that she will be sterilized, Gilda commits suicide. After this tragic event, the rest of the girls rebel and burn the squad leader's records, only to be punished and sent away to work on distant farms. Elisabeth, who is taken to be a leader of the revolt, is expelled from the BDM and left to wonder whether she will ever find a secure sense of belonging anywhere again.

Leitner's effort to imagine how awareness of the Sterilization Law might have affected a group of young women is—to my knowledge—unique in German exile literature.[9] To be sure, the novel has some flaws in its conception and aesthetic technique. Even though it is critical of eugenic sterilization, it glosses over the question of disability by attributing health problems of the younger generation mainly to difficulties in coping with the war injuries of their fathers. This reductionist approach makes the novel less convincing as a documentary work. As the historian Gisela Bock's research has shown, however, many people threatened with sterilization did in fact try to resist it in various ways. Leitner's novel is thus quite realistic in showing how young women's fear of physical mutilation may have worked against forcible efforts to establish a national community based on eugenic norms where those whose bodies were judged to be inferior were to be excluded or eradicated.

The other major work of German exile literature with disability as a central theme is Arnold Zweig's *Das Beil von Wandsbek* (The Axe of Wandsbek), published in 1943 in Hebrew translation and in 1947 in German.[10] This novel furnishes a unique example of what an alternative portrayal of a disabled character could entail at a time when Nazi eugenic propaganda had been in full swing for a decade and the most intense repression was being directed against groups of disabled people through the Nazis' involuntary sterilization and "euthanasia" campaigns. What makes this novel even more interesting as an example of disability imagery is that Zweig, according to his own statements, intended to use his character's disability in a traditional way, but in fact he created a character who turned out to be a genuinely utopian figure.

Arnold Zweig (1887–1968) is one of Germany's best-known twentieth-century novelists of the realist tradition. After the mid-1920s, an increasingly serious visual impairment made it necessary for him to dictate almost all his novels and other works to a secretary. Having become internationally famous for his antiwar novel *Der Streit um den Sergeanten Grischa* (The Case of Sergeant Grischa) in 1927, Zweig was intensely engaged in speaking out against fascism in the last years of the Weimar Republic. Immediately after the Nazis came to power in 1933, he and his family went into exile, settling in Palestine. They remained there until 1948, when Zweig was invited to return to the Soviet Occupation Zone. Until his death twenty years later, he remained an active and much honored writer in the German Democratic Republic (East Germany) while he was more or less ignored in the former Federal Republic of Germany (West Germany) due to his leftist politics.[11]

Das Beil von Wandsbek has been called "the most convincing depiction of German fascism in the exile novel."[12] The setting is Hamburg in the years 1937 and 1938, a time when national socialism appeared to be invincible. Yet Zweig stated he had found a plot that enabled him to portray the "rising Third Reich as containing its own downfall."[13] Similar to Brecht's *Mutter Courage,* Zweig's novel is also, among many other things, an extended meditation on false and genuine heroism that juxtaposes a strong, militaristic character with a weaker, disabled figure. The butcher Albert Teetjen is a small shopkeeper, war veteran, and SS member who is gradually being squeezed out of business by larger grocery stores. When a prison in Hamburg searches for an executioner to behead four communists, Albert takes the job because it pays well and he believes in the Nazis' political mission. For a time, things seem to go well for Albert and his wife Stine. However, although Albert carried out the execution while wearing a mask, rumors surface among his Wandsbek neighbors that he killed the four prisoners with his butcher's ax. For a variety of reasons, they boycott his shop, and in the end he and Stine commit suicide. Zweig wove a number of subplots into this narrative, thereby creating a complex depiction of fascism among all social classes in Hamburg.

In this novel, which probes deeply into psychic entanglements between humane and cruel impulses, the only major character who remains untainted and points most positively toward a better future is the young "cripple" Tom Barfey, the son of a washerwoman. It is Tom who, as a committed antifascist, unleashes the boycott that finally destroys Albert. In an epilogue to the 1951 edition of his novel, Zweig described what he intended with this character: "It was one of the underlying thoughts in my novel that the German resistance to Nazism was crippled like my Tom Barfey, and was just as brave as he was" (598). In other words, Zweig meant this disabled character to serve as a metaphor for the courageous effort to overcome weakness, a stereotypical attribute often employed in well-intentioned depictions of disability. Closer scrutiny, however, shows that Zweig actually created a much more interesting portrayal, one so unusual, in fact, that critics have hardly known what to say about Tom Barfey because he confounds their assumptions about disability.[14]

It is possible to ascertain the functions of this disabled character by exploring the nature and significance of Tom's antifascism, specifically, how it is linked to Albert, the executioner. This focus shows that the portrayal of Tom's disability is central in two main ways to Zweig's far-reaching critique of national socialism. These are a depiction of the hostility and cruelty directed against Tom because of his disability, which Zweig used to expose the violent underpinnings of the Nazis' national racial community (Volksgemeinschaft), and an affirmative portrayal of Tom as an ordinary young man who desires to lead an active, full life in every respect. This focus presents an alternative both to Nazi policies, which sought to exclude and eliminate people like Tom, and to the entire overbearing cultural tradition of defining disabled people solely in terms of their "defects."

Albert's downfall is caused mainly by his desire to belong to what the novel shows as the wrong kind of community, the national racial community based on the violent exclusion of outsiders. As a small shopkeeper, Albert fears he will sink to the level of factory workers dependent on wages, and so he is ready to go to any length to maintain his status. At numerous points when things appear to be going well for them, both Albert and Stine remark on how wonderful it is "to belong," to be secure among people just like themselves (39).[15] Albert feels that he fits in because he has carried out the execution as the higher-ups wanted. On another level, he is proud of his manly strength and feels that his well-functioning body also entitles him to be accepted into this type of community. As Zweig wrote in a note about his novel in 1955, reflecting on Nazi eugenics, "Health [was] the precondition for becoming a tool of the ruling class" (604).

Tom Barfey first appears in close conjunction with Albert and Stine, who desire to belong to the national racial community from which Tom is excluded. Tom and his mother live in a dilapidated gable room across the street from Albert and Stine's apartment in the working-class neighborhood of Wandsbek. When the couple looks up in his direction, they can see him moving around in front of the stars, a small, almost otherworldly figure. Throughout the novel, Albert's relationship to Tom is one of benevolent distance while Stine's is more complex. The narrator introduces Tom as a boy who came into the world "crippled," with legs that were much too small and weak, and contrasts how he was treated during the relatively progressive Weimar Republic and after 1933. As a child, Tom received free, adequate medical care and was more or less integrated into his surroundings. Having learned to propel himself through the streets like a small disabled veteran on a low, homemade, wheeled platform, he attended school, had enlightened, humane teachers, and delighted his neighborhood when he did well.

After 1933, however, these protective, kind attitudes toward Tom gradually change as the Nazis begin to proclaim a "cult of youth, beauty, and health" and to inveigh against "coddling the sick and disadvantaged" (48). Soon Tom hardly dares to go out on the street anymore, let alone to school, for fear of being attacked by storm trooper toughs, and he withdraws to the world of the rooftops. The narrator describes what Tom has lost in the Nazis' exclusionary national racial community as follows: "With the disappearance of the Republic and its government, its humanitarian and democratic institutions, he had been robbed of his youth, and indeed, of life itself. He was young; he saw things clearly; since he couldn't use his legs, he used his mind. Albert Teetjen was right enough when he suspected that Tom Barfey was no friend of the Third Reich" (48). From the outset, then, Tom is depicted as a young man with much potential whose opportunities have been drastically curtailed by the cruel propaganda and policies of the Nazis. The novel thus shows Tom's growing isolation as caused by this oppressive system of enforcing racial and eugenic norms rather than by his own supposed physical or moral defects.

Tom's antifascism is motivated by his well-founded fear of violence and, more generally, by the increasing hostility directed against him because of his conspicuously nonconforming body. In the first passage in which Tom appears, a sympathetic physician, Käte Neumeier, is explaining to his mother what to do if the authorities want to "castrate" him—that is, how to prevent him from being sterilized under the Nazis' Law for the Prevention of Hereditarily Diseased Offspring. Her advice is to claim that Tom's disability resulted from his mother's overwork rather than from "some sort of degeneration" and to point out that sterilizing him would destroy the "hereditary substance" of his father, a brave, healthy soldier who died in the war. The Nazis' plans to eradicate people like him make Tom into their implacable enemy. The narrator states: "This explained the deadly hatred with which Tom followed every move of the new state. . . . Anyone associated with this state or anyone who acted enthusiastically on its behalf was in his eyes damned. On the day of reckoning, that person must be removed" (50).

Tom has to stop attending school and is threatened with sterilization, but the violence directed against him is shown as having a further dimension. With rare insight, Zweig captured one of the most intense yet indirect ways in which exclusion of people with visible disabilities has been practiced over the centuries. Tom is depicted as sensing that there is a growing danger behind the way people look at him when he is out in public. Their staring at his conspicuous body is a first step toward objectification and indicates the propensity to violence against him that is seething just below the surface. This theme is particularly explicit in a passage in which Dr. Neumeier offers to take Tom along on a trip to the Hamburg zoo. The prospect delights him since he has never been there: "Earlier he had been too small to propel himself out there, and now he didn't dare to attract people's attention." Tom even feels that he has to exercise caution and avoid his formerly friendly neighbors. He says to his mother and Dr. Neumeier: "I won't put them to the test and lead them into temptation, but I'll deliver them from the evil of my appearance, unless they care to visit me themselves." Having been forced to withdraw into isolation, Tom experiences his excursion to the zoo as liberation from his "voluntary-involuntary citadel." The gatekeepers put up some argument when they see Tom approaching on his wheeled platform, but Dr. Neumeier persuades them to admit him. They finally agree because "there weren't so many visitors on this Sunday afternoon, visitors who would have made the appearance of the cripple into a sensation by staring and turning around to gape at him" (166–70). In the novel's depiction of Nazi Germany, Tom is surrounded by people with normatively functioning bodies whose self-preservation depends increasingly on being able to fit smoothly into the social organism. Therefore, he is constantly being seen as a disturbance in the synchronized visual field of the national racial community.

The ways in which Tom is shown as directly and indirectly marginalized are obvious motivations for his antifascism. But the antifascist significance of this character also comes out in a more unusual way—paradoxically, because he is depicted as a rather ordinary young man. In spite of Zweig's express intention to use Tom as a metaphor for the brave will to overcome adversity, such bravery is not the ultimate message of the novel. Rather, the narrative more or less takes for granted that Tom wants to lead an active life through work and to express love and sexuality. Since the Nazis and their sympathizers want to prevent him from doing these things, his very existence is a challenge to national socialist ideology and policies.

Tom's desire to develop himself as much as possible is thwarted when he has to stop attending school. Confined to his room, he helps his mother by earning a little money through secretarial work, copying letters, leaflets, and advertisements. While many contemporary readers probably would have viewed this occupation as adequate for a disabled person, Zweig shows the job as far below Tom's intellectual capabilities. Of more significance for the plot is the portrayal of Tom's political commitment, specifically his involvement in the neighborhood boycott of Albert. After Dr. Neumeier realizes that Albert executed the four communists, she conceives the boycott plan. Wondering how many Germans are ready to carry out such orders, she decides that it is her duty to render this one harmless. Accordingly, she asks Tom to start spreading the rumor that Albert beheaded the four communists with his butcher's ax, the same one he is using to cut up meat.

Despite his involuntary confinement to his attic room, Tom is still entwined in a working-class milieu through his mother and other visitors. He is not a communist, but he has read Marx and sees the deleterious effects of wage labor on his mother and most of the people around him. As a result, both his solidarity with the four executed communists and his own oppressive situation make him eager to bring the truth to light by unleashing the boycott against Albert. He tells his mother the rumor and instructs her to gossip about it in the households where she washes clothes. Once the story begins to spread, Albert gradually loses customers. Some boycott him because of their antifascist sympathies, others because of reservations about the hygiene in his shop, and still others, his SS comrades, because he did not share his executioner's pay with them. Albert becomes furious and then desperate, feeling that he, a "real man," is powerless against the "invisible dwarfs" who are weaving their net around him (359).

Several aspects make this portrayal of a disabled character extremely unusual for its time. First, instead of drawing on stereotypes of passivity, the narrative invests Tom with subjective agency, showing that his political commitment and his embeddedness in the working-class milieu enable him to become the antifascist catalyst for the executioner's downfall. Second, the narrative does not highlight Tom's bravery in taking on an active, oppositional stance. Rather, it strikes the reader as self-evident that Tom acts according to his life experiences and interests. Finally, although his options are severely circumscribed, he is described as an "opponent to be reckoned with" (544). That is, instead of using the stereotypical technique of associating disability with power to represent evil or danger, the novel portrays a disabled character whose resisting actions are directed toward a positive end: the over-throw of an oppressive system.

A similar approach is evident in the passages in which Tom expresses feelings of love and begins to live out his sexuality. In the European cultural heritage, disabled people have almost always been represented either as sexless (and therefore either angelic or embittered) or weirdly perverse. Tom is neither. Zweig not only depicted his dis-abled character as capable of intense desires and emotions but also imagined Tom as inspiring similar feelings in women. Such interper-sonal relationships are absolutely ordinary, the kind of clichéd material commonly found in romance novels. Because Tom is disabled, however, they take on a utopian quality.

As most young working-class men would have done, Tom has trysts with some of the young women in his neighborhood. They seem to enjoy meeting him in his attic hideaway although they are faced with the typ-ical problem of having to avoid his mother (322). These are only diver-sions, however, compared to Tom's real love, which is for Stine, Albert's wife. Zweig constructed this strand of the plot in such a way that Stine is placed between her husband, whom she cares for deeply, and Tom, to whom she is increasingly drawn as the boycott against Albert pro-gresses. In this sense, the novel is the story of a typical love triangle.

Stine visits Tom and his mother frequently to bring them leftover cuts of meat and plan her washing day. In the first passage in which Tom appears, she asks Albert whether she should put up her hair before going up to the roof, and he replies that no one is going to fall in love with her on the stairs. It does not occur to Albert that someone like Tom could possibly be his rival in love. When Stine's head emerges through the roof's trapdoor, however, Tom takes advantage of the opportunity to kiss her and bury his face in her loose hair. She pushes him away, saying that she could really like him if he weren't so impertinent. The most striking thing about this passage is that Stine responds to Tom in a very natural way, neither patronizing nor repulsed. She reacts as a married woman might to any other likable but fresh young man. His disability is shown as a fact, but it is not presented as the defining factor that overshadows all his other qualities.

In the context of Stine's unease about the execution and the couple's growing awareness that they are being boycotted by their neighbors, her feelings gradually turn more toward Tom: "Stine did not tell [Albert] that Tom had been becoming more demanding recently, and that she had great difficulty 'putting him in his place,' as people say" (344). After experiencing economic ruin, Stine's ultimate decision to commit suicide is intertwined with her thoughts about Tom. When Stine goes up to visit Tom for the last time, she finally allows herself to think of him as a lover who has displaced Albert: "She realized with pleasure what strong arms he had, and that now she had a lover whose mustache felt very different from Albert's familiar one" (524). Thinking of her impending death, Stine regrets that she will not be alive to see what will become of Tom, musing to herself, "A lad with such a bright mind and with so much love to give—and instead of normal legs, the legs of a child, pitiful sausages. When he got older and had children, would their limbs be straight and would they be all right? The Nazis didn't think so, but what did *they* know!" (506). Stine simply assumes that Tom will find a partner and father children someday and that there is no reason to prevent him from doing this. Here the reader sees Tom from Stine's perspective, which is not one of cold curiosity or medicalized brutality but that of a loving woman. Thus, Tom appears not as a dehumanized object of Nazi eugenic policies but as a desiring and desirable man. The positive portrayal of his ability to love is a direct challenge to all fascist efforts to exclude and eliminate people like him from the synchronized national racial community.

How was it possible for Zweig to create such an unusual disabled character, one who is unique in German literature from this period? Perhaps his own disability, a severe visual impairment, gave him an understanding of some of the complexities of living as a disabled man in Germany at this time.[16] Another factor can be deduced from the novel itself: the depth of Zweig's approach to realistic narrative, which sought to create both psychologically believable characters and social types. Zweig was not content to rely on the fallacious, physiognomic stereotypes that often made a direct link between disability and moral flaws. Rather, even though he knew well the dangers of being an outsider, he also saw that affirming such a position could entail the possibility of representing a more profound liberation. Therefore, Zweig not only explored how an ordinary man such as Albert could become an executioner under the extreme, murderous conditions of Nazism.[17] He also created in his Tom Barfey a great utopian image: a character whose antifascism is rooted in his disability and who is simultaneously, in the best sense of the word, an ordinary man.[18]

CHAPTER 4 • Disability in the Defeated Nation: The Federal Republic

People with disabilities were the group on whom the national socialists attempted most intensely to enforce their distinctions between the sick and the healthy with the ultimate aim of eliminating the sick from the body of the German nation. Consequently, studying both the lives of disabled people and significant images of disability in postwar German culture would seem to be a crucially important part of debates about continuities and transformations of Nazi ideology in the postwar period. Yet cultural historians have hardly explored this topic. The historians who have dealt in some way with disability in the postwar period have generally defined their research topics according to the cause of the disability, focusing particularly on disabled veterans or disabled people who were the objects of Nazi eugenics. They have hardly looked at disability as an overarching phenomenon or at the organizational and representational links among various groups of disabled people. Furthermore, it is still a relatively new idea to most cultural historians that ubiquitous one-sided representations of disability have real consequences for people who are disabled—in contrast to more generally accepted views about the harmfulness of, say, anti-Semitic or racial stereotypes. As a result, while a large body of research exists on representations of Jews or blacks (specifically, the Afro-German children of African American soldiers) in postwar German culture, scholars have thus far paid little attention to representations of disability in the same period. Yet, as is true for all victims of national socialism, the place of people with disabilities in postwar German society and culture is an important indicator of the lack or growth of democratic consciousness. By this, I mean the realization that disabled people are entitled to equal rights as German citizens.

Considering how central disability was in so many different ways to both Weimar culture and Nazi propaganda, it might seem at first as though this entire thematic complex suddenly became a more or less taboo subject in German culture after 1945. There were many more disabled veterans after World War II than after World War I, but, in contrast to the ubiquitous images of these men in Weimar culture, they were depicted only infrequently in any substantial way in German art or literature after 1945. With respect to those disabled people whom Nazi propaganda had labeled lives unworthy of life, defamatory eugenic imagery disappeared immediately in 1945 as the Allied authorities instituted strict censorship in all four occupation zones and as German perpetrators of involuntary sterilization, and especially of "euthanasia," began to cover up evidence of their actions. And, with respect to other disabled people who had long been considered worthy of rehabilitation, the large number of civilians injured in bombings and the collapse of the economic infrastructure meant that efforts to help these people remained soberly practical. After 1945, rehabilitation experts did not indulge in the high-flown ideological speculations about placing technology in the service of the nation that often ran through Weimar rehabilitation debates.

Discourses about the place of disabled people in German society and culture were thus structured differently after 1945 than after 1918, but in spite of these silences and taboos disability was still a major concern in many ways in defeated Germany. In the following pages, I will begin to bring the discursive phenomenon of disability in the postwar period into focus by employing two approaches to interpretation. First, a consciousness of disability as a sociocultural category makes it possible to reinterpret some well-known postwar literature and films as texts that are about disability although they have hardly been viewed this way before. Here I am not limiting my examples to works that reflect a legal definition of disability as the diminished capacity for employment. Rather, I will explore from various comparative angles how three categories of disability—disabled veterans, disabled people who were the objects of Nazi eugenics, and other disabled civilians—were maintained, mingled, challenged, or transformed. In this context, the lens of gender is especially significant because of the compromised masculinity of defeated, disabled veterans. Second, in order to explore the complex intersections between discourses of disability and national narratives in the postwar period, it is also necessary to consider how these groups of disabled people appeared in the public sphere by looking at other kinds of texts besides art, literature, and film. To do this, I will focus for each of these three groups on an analysis of selected cultural representations and on several public debates about the place of disabled people in occupied Germany (1945–49) and the Federal Republic of Germany (West Germany) into the early 1970s.

Disability in the Art, Literature, and Film of the Immediate Postwar Period

Disability in Rubble Literature and Art

Disabled women hardly seem to figure in postwar German cultural texts. At first thought, the reason for this appears obvious: there were many disabled veterans and returning prisoners of war, and it was the task of women to care for their men. For example, statistics from 1956 break down as follows according to gender and cause for those with an officially recognized physical disability that reduced their earning power by more than 50 percent: disability related to military service, 634,866 men and 6,024 women; civilian war-related disability, 18,443 men and 15,771 women; disability caused by illness or accident, 195,518 men and 91,727 women; congenital disability, 27,765 men and 29,097 women; for a total of 876,612 men and 142,619 women.[1] Yet the much greater number of disabled men did not translate into frequent attention to them in literature and art. Thus, it is necessary to look beyond mere statistics to explain the striking absence of the theme of disability in high culture. To be sure, various postwar sources attempted to establish a connection between men's more obvious physical disabilities and women's emotional suffering after the war. For example, a sociologist claimed in 1955 that, whereas most disabled veterans had been able to return by then to respectable positions, women were sometimes even worse off for they were still living in isolation and mental anguish.[2] More specifically, similar comparisons emerged in discussions about mass rapes at the end of the war. An Austrian woman, for example, who was raped by Soviet soldiers and whose husband lost his arm in the war, identified herself as a "war-disabled person," explaining, "My husband became a cripple, and I was ruined emotionally."[3] Consequently, in her controversial film about these mass rapes, *BeFreier und Befreite* (Liberators Take Liberties, 1992), the director Helke Sander went so far as to state that these women should also be given "the status of disabled veterans (Kriegsbeschädigte) under federal pension law."[4] While recognizing rape victims in this way may well be justified, viewing all those who suffered some kind of generalized trauma in the aftermath of war would expand the concept of disability so much that it would become meaningless. Nevertheless, the postwar discourse of disability in Germany frequently linked men's officially recognized war disabilities and women's psychic suffering. At the same time, however, hardly any cultural models existed for showing the reintegration into society of women whose minds or bodies functioned in "abnormal" ways.

The case of the author Inge Müller of the German Democratic Republic (East Germany) illustrates these problems. For three days at the end of the war in Berlin, she was buried under a bombed building that had collapsed. She was not physically disabled, and she went on to become a writer and collaborate with her husband, the dramatist Heiner Müller. She never recovered emotionally from her traumatic encounter with death, however, and committed suicide in 1966. Beginning in the early 1950s, her writings portray women's experiences in a broad context of disability in the immediate aftermath of the war. The story fragment "Weiße Hyazinthen" (White Hyacinths), for example, tells of a man who lost a leg in the war and gets drunk because he is a cripple and of his daughter, who is "not quite right in the head" because her husband was shot before her eyes.[5] Müller's highly autobiographical poems manifest an enormous effort to deal with the psychic trauma of her own experiences. The poem "Trümmer 45" (Rubble 45) may serve to illustrate this. It reads: "There I found myself / And wrapped myself in a cloth: / A bone for mama / A bone for papa / One for the book" (34). Here it is only the act of writing that seems to provide any stability amid pervasive agony and destruction. As Müller wrote in another poem: "How can one make poems / Louder than the screams of the wounded / . . . / How can one not make poems?" (228). This lyric voice appears isolated, unable to find a sense of belonging anywhere in the postwar psychic landscape. The example of Inge Müller reflects the absence of any reliable cultural patterns for integrating disabled or emotionally traumatized women into the couple, the family, the workplace, or society as a whole. Lacking such models, it seemed almost impossible to imagine how to write these experiences into postwar narratives of national reconstruction.

There are also some works of art and literature created shortly after the end of the war in which abandonment and isolation are shown as the fate of disabled men, especially of the most severely wounded soldiers. Just as after 1918 these artists focused on the figure of the amputee to drastic visual effect, but now the disabled veterans they depicted were often identified as returning prisoners of war (Heimkehrer). Karl Hubbuch created a series of drawings entitled *Vergessen?—Niemals!* (Forget?—Never!) in 1945–46, which included one called *Es gibt auch Menschen, an denen die Schrecken des Krieges spurlos vorübergingen* (There Are Also People Untouched by the Horrors of War). Here satiated members of the bourgeoisie look out the window of their comfortable house at miserable people walking by, including expellees, men with canes and crutches, and an amputee. In a drawing published in the satirical magazine *Ulenspiegel* on October 5, 1946, Rudolf Schlichter portrayed an exchange between three people and a veteran amputee: "What do you want, a cigarette?" "No, more than that. Understanding." Also in 1946 the artist Albert Heinziger drew *Der Heimkehrer* (The Returning Prisoner of War), which depicted an amputee carrying his boot in his backpack. And in that same year Erwin Oehl painted *Fraternisierung,* which shows an American soldier embracing a German woman in a landscape of ruins. She is kicking aside a pitiful German veteran, an amputee with a crutch. In 1947, Oskar Nerlinger painted *Der letzte Soldat* (The Last Soldier), which depicts death as a wounded, ragged soldier pointing the way to a disabled veteran with a cane. Otto Dix returned to the subject of disability in 1948, painting both *Invalide in Trümmern* (War Invalid in Ruins) and a unique depiction of a disabled girl, *Blindes Mädchen in Trümmern* (Blind Girl in Ruins). And in 1950 A. Paul Weber drew *Die Heimkehrer* (The Returnees), which shows a disconsolate man with amputated legs sitting on a low, wheeled platform and a woman kneeling beside him. Except for these few examples from the immediate postwar period, however, German visual art hardly depicted the massive disability and suffering caused by the war, and this subject matter remained the province of photography. Rather, abstract art soon became the prevailing trend in West Germany as a sign of individuality under reconstructed capitalism.

The best-known literary depiction of severe disability from the immediate postwar period is Heinrich Böll's short story "Wanderer, kommst du nach Spa . . ." (Stranger, Bear Word to the Spartans We . . . , 1950), in which a young soldier who has lost both arms and one leg is brought back to his former school, now a makeshift military hospital. Betrayed by his nationalistic teachers and Germany's leaders, he is now helpless and abandoned to his fate. For this severely disabled young man, there is no way to reestablish connections with others, no way back to "Germany." The hopelessness here contrasts starkly with a story such as Leonhard Frank's *Die Kriegskrüppel* (The War Cripples) of 1918, which depicts an even more severely disabled veteran but ends with a flaming appeal for revolution and brotherly love. This thematic complex is taken to another level in Bertolt Brecht's poem "Der Einarmige im Gehölz" (The One-Armed Man in the Thicket) from his *Buckower Elegien* (Buckow Elegies, 1953). The first lines of the poem evoke sympathy for a man struggling to gather wood with one arm who then lifts his hand to feel whether it is raining. But the last line forces the reader to problematize this sympathy: "His hand raised / The dreaded SS man."[6] The tension in this impressive short poem is concentrated in the single image of disabled man and Nazi, victim and perpetrator. This perspective can go far toward explaining why there are so few images of physical disability in postwar German culture, as I will discuss with regard to postwar film.

A transitional work that captures conflicting ways of writing about disability at this time is Wolfgang Borchert's play *Draußen vor der Tür* (The Man Outside, 1947). Here a returning veteran, Beckmann, who is both psychologically traumatized and limping from a leg wound, wants to commit suicide because he discovers his wife has been unfaithful and because, as he says, "I couldn't stand it any more. All this hobbling and limping."[7] Beckmann cannot bear to be in the position of a disabled veteran who is not regarded as a hero. Recalling Nazi categories of disability, he is suddenly in the position of those who had been regarded as worthless cripples. The guilt Beckmann feels over his role as a commanding officer is manifested in his hallucinations of legions of dead soldiers surrounding him, whom he describes as "one-eyed, toothless, one-armed, legless, without hands, blind" (124). Here Germany appears as a nation of crippled and psychically damaged soldiers who are haunted by guilt. The only fleeting ray of light in this nightmarish postwar landscape comes when a young woman takes Beckmann to her warm home. This scene hints at an available pattern for the reintegration of disabled veterans into civilian life through acceptance by women back into love and family relationships.

In these examples from early postwar literature, the disabled people that are missing, of course, are those the Nazis categorized as lives unworthy of life. The only way these texts even hint at their existence is through vague expressions of fear that a disabled veteran might be cast down to their inferior level. A work that offers a unique perspective in this regard, is Wolfgang Borchert's early short story "Schischyphusch oder der Kellner meines Onkels" (Schischyphusch or My Uncle's Waiter). Told from the perspective of a young nephew, a confrontation ensues between the uncle, a war veteran with a speech impediment caused by a facial wound, and a waiter who has the same speech impediment caused by a "birth defect." Because their speech impediments have different causes, their lives have taken extremely different courses. The uncle still feels very much a part of society, "laughing the loudest himself when people laughed at him."[8] The waiter, by contrast, is described as "cast out, ground down by the fate of his tongue. . . . A thousand times a day he was mocked; at every table people smiled, laughed, grinned, pitied him, yelled at him" (288). When the uncle and the waiter begin talking to each other, each believes at first that the other is making fun of him. They almost come to blows before they realize that they have the same speech impediment. But then comes an insight that is unique in postwar German literature. The uncle exclaims, "Poor little raschcal!

Have they been hounding you like that ever schince you were born?"
(291). The disabled veteran not only expresses empathy but also
denounces those who have persecuted the waiter all his life. This text
thus exposes the cruel majority with their exclusionary practices and
offers an unusual vision of solidarity between disabled people. Here the
category of German citizen is expanded to include both of these men
regardless of the cause of their disability.

By focusing on discourses of disability, new dimensions may be
revealed in well-known postwar texts. Admittedly, however, most of
these examples are so brief that they provide mainly tantalizing hints of
how earlier perspectives on disability were continued or transformed in
the postwar period. To explore in a more complex fashion the intermingling of these discourses, as well as the evidence for emerging democratic perspectives, I will turn now to two more extensive examples
from postwar film.

Disabled Veterans in German and American Films

Comparative perspectives on disability across cultures and historical
time periods can shed light on the ways in which disability is a socially
constructed category, thus demystifying disability as a phenomenon
that is often held to be merely natural and not in need of interpretation.
In this regard, representations of disability in American and German
films are particularly intriguing. Martin Norden's standard work, *The
Cinema of Isolation: A History of Physical Disability in the Movies*
(1994), lists approximately five hundred American feature films with
major or minor characters who have some type of visible physical disability. Throughout the history of German cinema, however, physically
disabled characters whose bodies do not conform to socially approved
norms of appearance have rarely been shown. This striking difference in
the cinematic traditions of these two countries would warrant an in-
depth study, but a specific way to focus on the place of visibly disabled
bodies in these two national narratives is to consider how disabled veterans appear in film. There were many more disabled veterans in Germany than in the United States after World War II. Furthermore, in Germany at this time, 80 percent of severely disabled people were veterans
whereas the corresponding statistic in the United States was 5 percent.[9]
Yet in the United States a minigenre of films was produced about visibly
disabled American veterans returning home after the war.[10] In Germany,
however, with only a few exceptions, images of obviously disabled veterans hardly appear in the films of the "rubble years."[11] The American
film *The Best Years of Our Lives* and the German film *Die Mörder sind*

unter uns (The Murderers Are among Us), both released in 1946, can be used to work out important differences and similarities in the cultural responses to disability in the two countries at this time.

William Wyler's *The Best Years of Our Lives* is undoubtedly the best-known American film about a World War II veteran who has a physical disability. It actually recounts the stories of three veterans who are returning to their hometown, but the one named Homer has lost both hands in a Navy ship explosion and now uses hooks. Played by the veteran Harold Russell, who had in fact lost both of his hands in a military training accident, the film has been described as breaking new ground "in its use of a severely disabled actor and in its realistic visualization of severe disability."[12] The stories of the three men receive relatively equal attention, and Homer's story is not sensationalized. Worried about how his girlfriend Wilma will receive him, he has to construct a new life as a severely disabled civilian. (This plot element is similar to that in *The Men* [1951], another film about a physically disabled veteran, which featured Marlon Brando in his first starring role.) In spite of Wyler's interest in making a realistic film, his indebtedness to the Hollywood system is shown by the film's sentimental, happy ending.

The depiction of Homer's physical disability is closely connected to the film's structuring of gender relations. As long as Homer is only with veterans or other men, he is quite at ease with his disability. He has learned how to function comfortably in daily life, and the bonding of male comradeship appears to nullify any feelings of strangeness or tendencies toward voyeurism that his physical difference might provoke in others. Homer cannot imagine, however, that his girlfriend will continue to love him in his maimed condition. Proudly rejecting what he takes to be her pity, he urges her to leave him. In a spirit of self-renunciation, he believes at first that he would be nothing but a burden to her if they married. In this respect, the film's limited conception of the way disability discourses function is that it locates Homer's problems with adjustment solely within himself rather than also pointing to social prejudices.

This romantic, melodramatic strand of the plot, which revolves around Homer's wounded masculinity, is resolved in two parallel ways. First, in contrast to scenes with his buddies, in which Homer seems quite mild-mannered, other scenes show him finally asserting himself aggressively. After this, with his masculine self-confidence somewhat restored, he guides his relationship with Wilma toward a decisive moment of truth. Taking her to his bedroom, he removes his hooks and tells her that he is now as "helpless as a baby." The moment when the spectator sees Russell's handless stumps has nothing of the voyeuristic freak show about it but rather is impressive and dramatic. This is because, as the film constructs the American national narrative in 1946, Homer has sacrificed his hands for his nation's good cause. Consequently, the moral message suggested here is that he should not be rejected but welcomed and loved. And so Wilma is not frightened or repulsed by Homer's hooks or his helplessness. Rather, she assures him of her love, and Homer is finally able to believe that she accepts him as he is. The marriage scene at the end of the film, with its close-ups of Wilma's hands and Homer's hooks interlocking at their wedding ceremony, shows the unit of the American couple restored.

This film shows the path to reintegration—that is, remasculinization—of a physically disabled veteran as taking place on several levels. First, Homer's male comrades comfortably accept his disability. Their relationship is presented as one of respectful equality based on shared war experiences. Second, Homer is shown as regaining an ability to express anger, even though many may tend to view him as weak or helpless. Finally, Homer's woman partner has the function of restoring his masculinity through her unconditional, even motherly love. Thus, on the one hand the film challenges stereotypes of disabled men as weak, passive, and asexual. But it resists these stereotypes of disability by insisting on the necessity of reestablishing traditional gender roles in order to enable the smooth reintegration of demobilized soldiers into peacetime America.

Directed by Wolfgang Staudte, *Die Mörder sind unter uns* was the first film to be released in occupied Germany after the war. It depends less obviously but just as centrally on discourses of disability to construct its statements about the condition of the German nation at the time of unconditional surrender. In order to bring out the significance of disability for this film, it is crucial to focus on both how bodies appear and how minds and emotions function in it. The film begins with three brief scenes of three people returning to bombed-out Berlin. First, a man later identified as Mertens is walking through the rubble, looking lost and dazed. Next, on a train overflowing with refugees, a young woman arrives. We soon learn that this is Susanna (played by Hildegard Knef in her first starring role) and that the time she has spent in a concentration camp has had no effect on her beauty or her optimism. Finally, in the one scene in the film in which physical disability is shown, a man using crutches laboriously makes his way through a crowd of refugees on a Berlin street. A large PW (meaning prisoner of war) is lettered in white on the back of his shabby overcoat. He sits down wearily in front of what appears to be a travel poster of a romantic castle with the word *Deutschland* on it, a poster hanging askew on a crumbling wall. This scene could have been taken directly out of a painting from the early Weimar Republic in which physical disability symbolizes the collapse of Germany. The film then continues with the stories of Susanna and Mertens, a returning veteran who is not physically disabled but is emotionally traumatized.

Susanna finds Mertens quartered in her old apartment and moves back in over his protests. Wanting to remain alone, he drinks, has emotional outbursts, and disappears without explanation at times. Susanna, a pillar of strength and hope, cleans up the apartment and begins to do her artwork again, drawings with the theme of "saving the children." As she begins to fall in love with Mertens, she also takes care of him. Mertens, by contrast, suffers intensely from flashbacks of wartime atrocities and is not able to work or love. Discovering that the officer who ordered a mass murder in Poland that Mertens witnessed is still alive, he visits this Captain Bruckner, only to find him living happily with his family and successfully reestablishing his large business. Outraged over this state of affairs, Mertens decides to shoot Bruckner, but Susanna prevents this at the last moment. Relieved that he has not become a murderer himself, Mertens delivers the film's closing message, a demand that war criminals be brought to justice.

Two types of experiences in the immediate aftermath of the war make it possible for Mertens to find his way back to civilian life—that is, to overcome the psychic disability that prevents him from working and loving. Early in the film, he tells Susanna that he is a surgeon by profession. Emotionally immobilized by his traumatic experiences, he now believes cynically that mankind is no longer worth curing. The turning point in this regard comes when he encounters a woman whose daughter is about to die and saves the girl's life. After all the wartime deaths and murders Mertens has witnessed, this positive action helps him overcome his psychic trauma.

If Mertens finds his way back to useful work through regaining his ability to heal others, he is healed of his own emotional numbness by Susanna's selfless, motherly love for him. In this context, the film's script explicitly compares his psychic disability to a physical disability. Speaking to her fatherly old neighbor, Susanna asks, "Would you refuse to help someone; would you reject him only because he had the misfortune of coming home from a war with terrible wounds? And if he depends on you in his helplessness, would you reject him?" The implication here is a humane one: that physically disabled veterans should be accepted and not treated like outcasts. Susanna continues, "There are wounds that are invisible, and much insight, patience, and love are necessary to heal them." The film shows that Susanna's unconditional love gradually heals Mertens's invisible but severe psychic disability. After

Mertens saves the girl's life, he returns to Susanna and can finally say that he loves her.

Both *The Best Years of Our Lives* and *Die Mörder sind unter uns* are about what it takes for a disabled veteran to "overcome" his disability, that is, to be reintegrated into civilian life. Their approaches to telling these stories are strikingly different in major respects yet similar in others. In the American film about veterans returning from fighting on the honorable, winning side of the war, male comradeship can remain a source of support for both disabled and nondisabled veterans. Because this male comradeship is still intact, the physical disability of one man does not have to become the dominant story. In the German film, by contrast, male comradeship appears as totally compromised and shattered for it is at the root of the Holocaust and other wartime atrocities. Therefore, the story of Mertens's psychic disability threatens to become overwhelming for he cannot be shown as finding a refuge with other German war veterans. He is totally isolated at first, left alone to be tormented by his memories and his guilt.

Furthermore, the American film can tell the story of a visibly disabled veteran in a relatively matter-of-fact way because Homer can be invested with an aura of heroism. The film thus carries a moral message with regard to physical disability. By advocating integration of this newly disabled veteran into peacetime society, it claims a public place for at least this group of disabled men.[13] The German film, however, shows a physically disabled veteran for only a few brief seconds. It could not carry on the perspective of Weimar artists, who often wanted to evoke sympathy for such broken figures, because in 1945 German disabled veterans were returning from a war in which Germany was responsible for committing terrible crimes against humanity. Obviously, these veterans could not be presented heroically, as the Nazis would have done.[14] As a result, the stories of physically disabled veterans remained ones that film generally did not tell in the political, moral, and emotional landscape of postwar Germany. Rather, this film concentrates on recounting the story of Mertens's psychic disability, which is rooted in his experience of his nation's war crimes, his nation's guilt, and his own bad conscience. In order to overcome this disability, that is, to regain his psychic balance, he must find ways to participate in a new German national narrative based on justice and the repudiation of violence.

Yet, regardless of whether their disabilities are physical or emotional, whether they are heroes or lost souls, and whether their nations helped defeat fascism or brought about the Holocaust, in the end both of these disabled veterans find their way back into civilian life with the same kind of help from their female partners. It is the function of both

Wilma and Susanna to restore the disabled men to a normal life by loving them unconditionally. This cross-cultural similarity in the depiction of disabled veterans from countries with such different wartime experiences indicates how important it was to reestablish traditional gender roles in order to reintegrate disabled veterans into the national experience. In cultural texts from many times and places, this way back to normalcy is a life course that frequently seems open to disabled men but hardly ever to disabled women, as the discussion of Inge Müller indicated. Consequently, the greatest similarity of these two films is their ultimately humane message of acceptance and love directed toward both physically and psychically disabled men. But this message is limited in both instances because it relies on stereotypes of gender that have never made room for similar stories about the integration of disabled women into the national experience in Germany or the United States.

Euthanasia in a Postwar Film

Released in January 1951, Willi Forst's *Die Sünderin* (The Sinner), starring Hildegard Knef, became the most popular film of that year in the Federal Republic and also gave rise to the biggest film scandal of the postwar period. By the end of the year, 6.5 million people had flocked to see it, drawn in part by curiosity over the efforts of the Protestant and Catholic churches and various conservative groups to ban it. Those outraged by the film did not complain about the brief scene in which Knef appears in the nude—the first such scene in postwar German cinema. Rather, they attacked the film for a number of other reasons as a threat to the moral reconstruction of West German society and culture. They used *Die Sünderin* as an occasion to criticize the film industry's self-supervision of its releases and to demand more state censorship of films for their immoral content and potential to harm youths. Calls for Christians to boycott the film and organized demonstrations against it at movie theaters led police to shut it down in a number of locations. Subsequently, the film's distributor, Herzog-Film GmbH, brought several lawsuits in administrative courts against these police actions. Finally, the Federal Administrative Court ruled in 1954 that it had been illegal to ban the film because it was a work of art protected by the constitutionally guaranteed freedom of expression. Thus, the scandal about *Die Sünderin* was ultimately a case that tested attitudes toward federal regulation of the media in the years shortly after the Nazi dictatorship.[15]

To date, historians have interpreted the heated conservative opposition to this film as having to do mainly with the way it portrays postwar gender relations. Heide Fehrenbach, for example, in her insightful analysis of the controversies surrounding the film, claims that most of its critics focused primarily on Hildegard Knef's character, Marina, a glamorous postwar woman who prostitutes herself for material gain.[16] Following Fehrenbach, it can be said that conservative Christians took this film as an occasion to vilify women's loose behavior as representing a general postwar moral decline, which they associated with everything bad about modernity. This analysis is quite convincing as far as it goes. However, the film's critics did not attack it only for its portrayal of gender relations and prostitution. They also denounced it for its depiction of another theme, which they described using the words *suicide, voluntary death, assisted suicide, killing on request,* and *murder.* This aspect of the controversy shows that the film's portrayal of postwar gender relations needs to be viewed in a much more complex way, for the film is just as much about disability—specifically, about euthanasia in the sense of assisting a disabled person to commit suicide. This can be seen not only from the contemporary reception of the film but also by interpreting it as to some extent a postwar remake of the one feature film the Nazis made to promote their "euthanasia" program, Wolfgang Liebeneiner's *Ich klage an* (I Accuse, 1941).

Die Sünderin is constructed as a sentimental narrative of a love affair between the prostitute Marina and a painter, Alexander, whose eyesight is being slowly but inexorably destroyed by a brain tumor. The first scene immediately recalls the death scene in *Ich klage an* in which Thomas gives his wife, Hanna, a lethal dose of medicine to drink. Marina and Alexander drink champagne containing a lethal dose of sleeping pills, and she thinks to herself, "I've killed you. Did I do the right thing?" The main body of the film is then an extended flashback told mostly from Marina's perspective. The function of her recollections is for Marina to assure herself and the spectator that she has done the right thing by helping Alexander die. The narrative progresses to the point of Marina's opening monologue and moves on to conclude with Alexander's death and Marina's suicide.

How does this film portray Alexander's disability and illness, and why does he want to die? After Marina finds sleeping pills in his pocket, he tells her he has a brain tumor that will inevitably blind him and cause him a painful death. As a painter, he cannot imagine losing his eyesight, and it is fear of this disability, along with fear of suffering, that makes him want to "determine the hour of death himself." He allows Marina to keep the sleeping pills, and she tries desperately to save his eyesight and his life. But suddenly she comes home one day to find him sitting in the darkness, and she realizes he has become blind. This is the beginning of the death scene. Both the dialogue and the mise-en-scène recall the death scene in *Ich klage an.* The atmosphere is peaceful and relaxed. Like Hanna, Alexander says he feels no pain but is "so strangely light-headed. So clear." But then, echoing Hanna's fears and using the vocabulary of euthanasia, which always preyed on fears of losing self-control, he asks Marina to help him "before I start to scream and have fits, before I lose my mind." Marina puts sleeping pills into Alexander's champagne glass, and the film has now returned to its opening scene. As he lies dying, Marina puts pills into her own glass and drinks, saying that life has no meaning for her without him. In another pose reminiscent of *Ich klage an,* she lies down with her head on his chest. Both die with blissful expressions on their faces. The film thus depicts suicide and euthanasia in the sense of mercy killing in a totally positive way.

Unlike *Ich klage an, Die Sünderin* does not refer directly to "euthanasia" in the sense of killing patients in institutions, although such a reference was removed from the final script. In one of the flashbacks to Marina's girlhood, her stepfather beats up her stepbrother upon discovering that he and Marina have been having sex. In the original script, Marina recalls, "My so-called stepbrother remained a cripple for the rest of his life. Later, as an idiot, he was put into an institution. He died there during the war or he was caused to die."[17] This is just a small indication of a subliminal consciousness of Nazi "euthanasia" in the associations made by the film. However, the main differences and parallels between the two films are to be found in the ways they deal with the entire question of disability and killing on request. In this regard, the most significant difference between the two films is that the gender roles are reversed. In *Ich klage an,* a strong, decisive, male scientist decides to kill his wife in order to put an end to her suffering, thus exercising his authority to dispose of the woman's body. In *Die Sünderin,* an energetic woman helps a man die who becomes progressively more disabled and ill, and this is one of the main things that led conservative critics to attack the film so vehemently. However, even here traditional gender roles are upheld to some extent. After all, Alexander still controls the time and manner of his death and only asks Marina to help him. She does this and more by dying for love. In this sense, in spite of its portrayal of the independent, materialistic prostitute, the film is also infused with quite traditional, sentimental notions about gender relations.

The main similarity between the two films lies in their perspective on disability, illness, and euthanasia in the sense of helping a person die who has expressed a wish to die. Neither film suggests that life with a disability—whether multiple sclerosis or blindness—could be bearable or preferable to death. Neither film suggests that it might be possible to relieve pain rather than dying before pain begins. Rather, both films suggest that the only alternative is either for the disabled person to be totally cured or for that person to ask to be put out of her or his misery. The only difference between the two films in this regard is that in the Nazi film the embedding of Hanna's death into her husband's trial for murder and his final speech about allowing doctors to serve the Volk makes a not so subtle plea for state-sanctioned "euthanasia" in the sense of killing the inferior. In postwar Germany, where knowledge about the crimes of Nazi "euthanasia" was widespread, though generally unacknowledged, a film such as *Die Sünderin* illustrates the individualizing and privatizing of an eliminationist mentality. Marina is not put on trial for helping Alexander die. Rather, the film is constructed around her trying to justify her actions to herself as having been selfless and in his best interest. No matter what the justification, though, the consequences for the two disabled characters are the same. Hanna, the disabled woman, and Alexander, the disabled man, are both dead in the end, and each film presents this as inevitable and humane. In both films, Germany appears as a country embodying Hanna's longing for "a land where there are no illnesses."

Any discussion of the reception of *Die Sünderin* and the scandal it provoked should take into account how those who attacked the film responded to its themes of disability and euthanasia. Attention to this aspect necessarily complicates historians' dismissal of these critics as nothing but reactionary Christian moralists.[18] Fehrenbach, for example, who bases her assessment of the film's critics on their resistance to cultural representations that they saw as corrupting the national project of normalizing gender relations, states that their ideology "would have seemed comfortably familiar to Adolf Hitler."[19] However, the aspect of their ideology that was at odds with Nazism, and, indeed, the one historians view as an act of antifascist resistance when writing about Bishop Clemens von Galen's condemnation of Nazi "euthanasia," was the perception that the film glorified euthanasia and suicide. Thus, when the film censorship body (Freiwillige Selbstkontrolle, or FSK) approved the film for release, the Protestant Church representative resigned in protest, stating that the film "glorified killing by request and suicide as the only possible way out of human misery."[20] Likewise, the archbishop of Bamberg attacked the film as a "reprehensible portrayal of killing a seriously ill person and of suicide as a self-evident way to escape guilt and suffering." Many others drew similar conclusions (357).

Most significantly for postwar views of disability, such statements criticizing the film viewed Alexander's assisted suicide as insulting to disabled veterans. Reacting to Alexander's death, for example, a Protestant Men's Club stated, "We also know from firsthand experience of disabled ex-servicemen, who, with quiet valor, accept and bear their fate given by God."[21] Furthermore, the court decisions upholding the banning of the film prominently made such references, for which a statement by the Landesverwaltungsgericht Hannover of January 31, 1952, may serve as an example: "Thousands of German men, the war-blind and war-disabled, who bear their sufferings bravely and do not steal out of life through suicide, are being told by this film that the Christian prohibition of suicide is wrong."[22] Two conflicting attitudes toward disability underlie such statements. On the one hand, these were important voices in the postwar landscape that insisted on the sanctity of human life and protested against any suggestion that it is morally acceptable to kill people who are weak, disabled, or ill. In this sense, these voices represented a positive, democratic point of view after the eugenics of the Nazi period. On the other hand, however, the far-fetched association of Alexander with disabled veterans (his brain tumor is not a war injury) brings out a more problematic aspect of these attitudes toward disability. For, after all, these critics did not take the film as an occasion to reflect on the disabled people who were the real victims of the Nazis' "euthanasia" program, which would have been much more obvious. Rather, they seemed to object to the idea that after the war disabled veterans could be viewed, and might even think of themselves, as having sunk to the level of those disabled people who had in fact been the objects of the Nazis' eliminationist practices. In this sense, then, even when the film's critics attacked its portrayal of euthanasia, they continued to distinguish between disabled veterans who had served their country and disabled people who were considered inferior.

Given the facts that Nazi eugenic propaganda had permeated German society and that 15.3 million Germans had seen *Ich klage an,* one wonders, of course, how the audiences who saw *Die Sünderin* viewed its theme of killing on request and suicide. There are no sources that can answer this question directly, but in 1950 the popular illustrated magazine *Kristall* (Crystal) ran a substantial series of articles and readers' letters expressing opinions about euthanasia in the sense of whether doctors should be allowed to "put people out of their misery."[23] This series gives one indication of the range of public opinion about this matter at the time *Die Sünderin* was released. The introductory article by the editor and former Nazi journalist Ivar Lissner describes a case in New Hampshire in which a doctor was on trial for murdering a terminally ill cancer patient who had expressed a wish to die. Seeking expressly to distance the American doctor's actions from the portrayal of euthanasia in *Ich klage an,* Lissner stated, "This film was an irresponsible act. There are more completely spontaneous cures that occur with this illness [multiple sclerosis] than with any other!" (6:4). Reporting that the American doctor was acquitted because the jury believed the woman was dead before he administered the lethal injection, the article then invited the magazine's readers to express their opinions about the issues raised in the case.

In subsequent issues, readers' letters revealed a range of attitudes toward disability, illness, the several meanings of euthanasia, and Nazi crimes against people with disabilities. The majority agreed with the doctor's action and called for killing on request to be legalized. Echoing eugenic perspectives and Nazi propaganda, they expressed two main arguments. First, they spoke of a "gentle death" as a merciful deliverance (Erlösung) from suffering for ill or disabled persons. Second, some readers claimed that caring for the sick and retarded cost too much money while the healthy did not have enough resources at their disposal. The magazine claimed that it only wanted its readers to debate the question of killing on request and not the question of "killing the incurably ill who are unable to give their consent" (10:8). But it steered the debate in this direction by printing two long statements by parents of cognitively disabled children who wished that doctors were allowed to end their children's lives (11:10–11). All these statements indicate a reservoir of pro-euthanasia attitudes in Germany at this time, regardless of whether euthanasia is understood in the sense of killing on request or of killing people too disabled or ill to give their consent. It is certainly not going too far to maintain that *Die Sünderin* tapped into these beliefs. Many, and perhaps even the majority, of its viewers may have believed that Alexander's death was quite in order, that life with a disability or an illness is not worth living.

Other statements in *Kristall* condemned the American doctor's action as murder, and these are particularly interesting with respect to the attitudes toward disability that they manifest. One doctor expressed this point of view as follows: "Every violation of the fundamental requirement to protect human life has serious consequences. The Nazi state began with involuntary sterilization. Then came forced abortions performed on foreign women as a way station on the path toward killing 'lives unworthy of life.' These acts culminated in the gas chambers and the scientific experiments on concentration camp inmates that resulted in mutilation and death. All this happened after the inviolability of human life was revoked in one single instance" (10:5). In this view, allowing any kind of killing on request necessarily entailed the danger of misusing state power and the likelihood that disabled people would be murdered. Furthermore, several people wrote about experiences in which doctors had given up all hope of curing patients but the patients still wanted to live and eventually recovered. A couple wrote about their love for their retarded daughter and stated that killing her would be murder. It is likely that these letter writers would have been quite critical of the way *Die Sünderin* portrayed Alexander's death. In any event, in both the controversies about *Die Sünderin* and the euthanasia discussion in *Kristall,* the main place where an alternative to Nazi attitudes toward disability emerged was in those voices that spoke out, however hesitantly, for valuing the lives of all people equally regardless of whether these voices came from the churches or democratically inclined members of the public.

These examples from postwar art, literature, and film demonstrate that focusing on discourses of disability yields new interpretations of well-known postwar texts. Additional examples could be cited such as the Swiss author Friedrich Dürrenmatt's play *Der Besuch der alten Dame* (The Visit, 1956), whose main character is a grotesque total prosthesis, or the significance of the Radio Play Prize of the War Blinded for the development of West German radio plays in the 1950s. On the whole, however, disability did not become a central theme in West Germany in the same way it did in Weimar culture or post-1945 American film. It is necessary to turn to other types of discourses about disability in the postwar period to get a better idea of how disabled people appeared in the public sphere after the ravages of national socialism and of how disability entered into public debates about reconstructing West Germany as a democracy.

Public Controversies and Cultural Representations

Disabled Veterans as Victims or Activists

Statistics on the numbers of disabled veterans after World War II are imprecise and difficult to analyze for many reasons, but one fact is indisputable. There were many more disabled veterans after 1945 than after 1918, by some accounts up to three times as many.[24] The only available statistics are for those men officially recognized as war disabled who received pensions. According to one source, after World War I there were 663,700 disabled veterans whose earning capacity was reduced by at least 30 percent, whereas after World War II there were 1,472,100 with a reduced work capacity of at least 50 percent in West Germany and West Berlin alone.[25] In 1950, those war victims entitled to a pension included 1,537,192 disabled veterans (generally requiring at least a 50 percent reduction in earning capacity), 998,468 widows (out of a total of about 2.5 million) and widowers, 1,337,881 half orphans, and 41,212 orphans.[26] In West Germany, there were 207,000 amputees, 56,000 brain-injured men, 34,000 with artificial eyes, and 6,600 blind veterans.[27] Such official statistics, however, give only a partial picture of the extent of disability, illness, trauma, and suffering following Germany's war of aggression and the Holocaust. While more than 3 million Germans were prisoners of war (POWs) in the Soviet Union, only 2 million returned, and many of these never recovered from the aftereffects of harsh treatment. In contrast to World War I, air raids had killed 600,000 civilians, 900,000 were wounded, and 7.5 million were homeless. Between April and September 1945, Soviet troops raped nearly 110,000 women in Berlin, about 7 percent of the city's female population. By 1950, 11 million Germans from eastern areas (Heimatvertriebene) had fled to the West, and an additional 2 million had died on the way. A survey of young men in 1952 stated that 19 percent had a disabled family member. Some scholars have concluded that up to half the adult German population had some firsthand experience with a threat to life, the death of a relative, or rape.[28] The commonality of these traumatic experiences meant that the public was constantly confronted with the physical and mental suffering of all those who had experienced the war.

As the cultural historian Svenja Goltermann has stated, "after the destruction of the body politic in 1945, the metaphor of the healthy 'body of the people' (Volkskörper) also disappeared."[29] This meant that other metaphors appeared to fill the void. In particular, the physically and psychically wounded bodies of disabled veterans could be read as signs of the damaged collective body of the nation. Veterans were by far the most numerous, conspicuous group of disabled people in postwar landscapes—the streets and squares of the bombed-out cities—and their presence was captured in a multitude of photographs and ephemera such as caricatures and posters. These cultural representations should be interpreted in the context of intense debates over the place of these men in the reconstructed German state. Many photographs emphasize the helplessness of these men, who in some instances almost recall depictions of cripples from medieval times with regard to the severity of their disabilities and their poverty. These images show men with no legs dragging themselves along the ground with their hands, traumatized men staring into emptiness, and exhausted men on crutches begging for a handout. Yet the responses to the reality captured in these photographs were complex. Of course, many felt sympathy, but on the other hand contemporary observers such as Karl Bonhoeffer surmised that since civilians had suffered so much themselves they were less ready to pity and support these men than they had been after World War I (90).

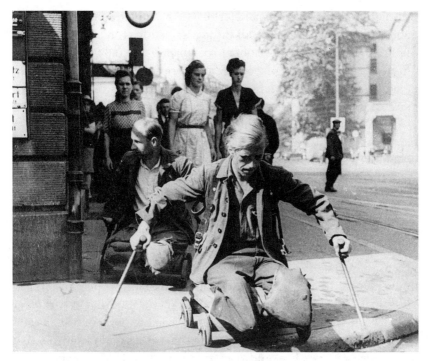

Fig. 18. Two disabled veterans with amputated legs on homemade wheeled platforms, 1947. (Photo: akg-images.)

Rehabilitation professionals went to work immediately on the practical problems facing disabled veterans, frequently drawing on Weimar models of therapy and legislation.[30] The Allies had prohibited military pensions, believing that the favored treatment of war victims had encouraged militaristic sentiments in the Weimar era. As a U.S. military government report stated, "The objective of abolishing war pensions is to discredit the military class in Germany, to reduce their influence in society and to impress upon the public that a military career bears neither honor, profit, nor security."[31] In 1950, however, the Federal Republic repudiated this Allied policy by enacting the Federal War Victims' Benefits Law (Bundesversorgungsgesetz) as the country's first major piece of social legislation. Because resources were limited, this law set strict—and, many thought, unacceptably narrow—standards for awarding pensions to disabled veterans, requiring a disability of at least 50 percent and thus excluding those who had lost, for example, a hand, foot, or eye (109, 127). The Prussian Law for the Employment of the Severely Disabled of 1920 had already set hiring quotas. It was used as a model for the Law on Employing the Severely Disabled (Gesetz über die

Beschäftigung Schwerbeschädigter) of 1953, which established hiring quotas for disabled veterans, all those disabled in workplace accidents, the blind, and victims of national socialism.[32] By 1962, 89 percent of physically disabled men of working age were employed in the FRG compared to 99 percent of nondisabled men. This statistic shows that these laws were quite successful at integrating physically disabled men, and veterans in particular, into the workplace. This was not the case for many other civilians with disabilities, including women and the young.[33]

Rehabilitation professionals and legal experts, as well as war victims' organizations, also referred to Weimar models that emphasized returning disabled veterans to work in order to make them self-sufficient breadwinners. They noted that disabled veterans often tried hard to resume a normal working and family life, but they also found it necessary to counteract the preconceived notions of some veterans about the limited possibilities open to them as newly disabled people. They urged these men not to yield to weakness and demoralization and in particular tried to convince them that there was no need to beg. An article published in 1953, for example, maintained that it was unimaginable that the English or French would degrade themselves in this manner and chastised German disabled veterans who resorted to begging, writing, "Of course these men can be seen sitting in all the streets of Europe, but they are seen more frequently in Germany than anyplace else. In no other country have so many proud men ended up in the gutter."[34] Thus, the press frequently published stories about severely disabled veterans who had been successfully rehabilitated. One told, for example, about a man who was a double amputee and used a wheelchair. He was married with three children, received a pension, worked part time at home, and was proud to be taking care of his family. He declared he would never resort to begging.[35] Photographs reflecting this point of view show disabled veterans becoming reintegrated into society by returning to work and participating in increasingly popular adapted sports such as skiing. In all of these discussions, the main departure from Weimar rehabilitation rhetoric was that after 1945 these voices assumed a decidedly less nationalistic tone, stressing instead the importance of work for individual self-esteem and enjoyment of life.

A more ideologically charged discourse developed around the group of veterans called the Heimkehrer, two million men who had returned from POW camps in the Soviet Union, many disabled in some way. In her diaries, Ruth Andreas-Friedrich gave her impressions of these returnees in Berlin: "Are these the glorious victors whom Adolf Hitler years ago had sent into the war so well equipped? They shamble around like walking ruins. Limbless, invalid, ill, deserted, and lost. A gray-bearded man in a tattered uniform leans against a wall. With his arms around his head he is quietly weeping. People pass by, stop and shyly form a circle around him. He does not see them."[36] Photographs of these men show them leaning on crutches, collapsed in despair, or dazed and staring vacantly into space. All over Germany, the presence of these men constantly confronted the German public with visible reminders of their country's defeat. In his novel *Landnahme* (Land Takeover, 2004), for example, Christoph Hein described a disabled Heimkehrer who was expelled from Poland and settled in an East German village: "Haber was the only war cripple in Guldenberg, and his lost arm reminded all the villagers of their defeat and the humiliation of being at the mercy of the Allies. His missing arm was the obelisk that Guldenberg had not erected for the lost war and the seven dead soldiers of the village."[37]

Until the late 1950s, West German doctors and psychiatrists debated the condition of these men and even created a special label for it: "dystrophy." The invention of this diagnosis is a prime example for the social construction of a disability and also illustrates the interweaving of postwar psychiatry and discourses about victimization. One could say that these psychiatrists were diagnosing post-traumatic stress disorder, a term that came into use after the Vietnam War. But both the symptoms and diagnoses of this condition after both world wars took very different forms. Shell shock or war neurosis was the specific trauma of World War I. Its symptoms included shaking; stuttering; tics; disorders of sight, hearing, or walking; insomnia; emotional outbursts; and nervous exhaustion.[38] When psychiatrists described dystrophy (also labeled Heimkehrer neurosis or barbed-wire neurosis) after World War II, they included some of these symptoms but also discovered more stomach problems, rheumatism, deafness, muteness, exhaustion, anxiety, depression, and withdrawal, which they characterized as hysterical reactions.[39] If shell shock meant a loss of control, dystrophy signified the reduction or even extinction of bodily functions, that is, complete demoralization.

The dystrophy discussion evidences complex continuities and breaks with eugenic perspectives on disability and illness. On the one hand, given the continuity in personnel within the medical and psychiatric professions, it is not surprising that many of these physicians characterized mentally and physically ill Heimkehrer as having hereditarily weak constitutions and portrayed them as the inferior losers of a "racial war of extermination in which defeat was always associated with racial or moral inferiority."[40] On the other hand, the term *dystrophy* was only applied to German soldiers who returned from Soviet POW camps, and not to any other veterans. This discourse presented these suffering Heimkehrer as victims of totalitarianism in an effort to provide a counterweight to Nazi crimes in the concentration camps. Accordingly, the Heimkehrer were also thought worthy of rehabilitation as postwar citizens, and they were given the same preferential treatment in employment as disabled veterans and victims of fascism. Dystrophy had signified the "breakdown of the Nazi ideal of the racially superior warrior on the Eastern front," and this was now to be replaced with a civilian ideal of masculinity that emphasized the family roles of Heimkehrer as husbands and fathers (62, 72). In this process, the difficult transitions of these men were often privatized into the sphere of the family. One wife of a Heimkehrer described the task facing her in 1952: "I want to make my husband feel that Heimkehrer from Russia are still human beings."[41] That is, German women had to carry out the generally unrecognized work of helping disabled and ill veterans adjust. This fact, along with the booming West German economy, which led to full employment by the end of the 1950s, meant that disabled veterans were not positioned at the flash points of destabilizing social conflicts as they were during the Weimar era.

Veterans were the first disabled citizens to organize themselves after the war although, since the Allies prohibited associations consisting solely of war victims, they were compelled to include other disabled people in their groups. The largest of these, with 1.5 million members, was the Association of War Disabled, War Survivors, and Social Pensioners (Verband der Kriegsbeschädigten, Kriegshinterbliebenen, und Sozialrentner or VdK). Both through their organizations and as individuals, disabled veterans presented themselves in public debates in a wide range of ways that reflect all the characterizations discussed earlier. In one additional way, however, some took the initiative to break with Germany's militaristic past. Initially this activity took the form of protests against the inadequacy of their pensions, but by the early 1950s their mass demonstrations often took on a decidedly antiwar character in the context of the controversy over rearmament. These were the events in the postwar period in which visibly disabled men appeared in public in the greatest numbers to voice their interests.

Heinrich Böll's short story "Mein teures Bein" (My Expensive Leg, 1948) picks up on the precarious economic situation of many disabled veterans at this time. In it, an official tells a veteran with an amputated leg that a job shining shoes in a public toilet is all he can expect. The man protests and demands a higher pension, which he does not receive. He rescues his self-esteem, however, by turning down the demeaning job. The year 1950 saw the first large protests of disabled veterans against delays in passing the Federal War Victims' Benefits Law and its limitations on pensions. On March 26, several thousand disabled veterans organized by the VdK assembled in Munich to demand higher pensions and sufficient employment. Such demonstrations continued until at least 1959, when Federal Labor Minister Theodor Blank of the Christian Democratic Union (Christlich-Demokratische Union or CDU) proposed reforming the pension structure. Fearing cuts in their benefits, disabled veterans immediately turned out in force all over the FRG, including twelve thousand in Passau on February 28, twenty thousand in Stuttgart marching behind a banner demanding "Justice, Not Pity" on May 3, and twenty-five thousand in Düsseldorf on June 20.[42]

If the earliest demonstrations focused primarily on economic issues, they soon began to feature slogans against war and proposals to reinstitute conscription as the rearmament debate got under way in 1951–52. In this context, discourses of disability functioned in two ways: as a deterrent but also as proof that disabled veterans were capable of activism. Thus, at a rally in Frankfurt on April 26, 1953, over 50,000 war victims demanded more economic security but also carried banners reading "Never again war" (2:769). On December 11, 1954, the VdK organized a silent march of 5,000 war victims in Bonn, including many amputees and men using wheelchairs, who demanded "sufficient pensions instead of new soldiers" (2:1083). By 1955, the Social Democratic Party (Sozialdemokratische Partei Deutschlands or SPD) and the trade unions decided to mount a campaign of more than 6,000 events throughout the FRG against rearmament, many featuring disabled veterans as speakers or marchers. The poster used in this campaign depicted a ruin in the shape of an amputee using crutches and the slogan "Never again! Negotiate!" Later many disabled veterans continued to be active in protests against the threat of nuclear war. At a demonstration of 150,000 organized by the group Kampf dem Atomtod (Fight the Nuclear Menace) in Hamburg on April 17, 1958, for example, a speaker representing disabled veterans called for his generation to be "the last war victims of all times" while banners proclaimed "We want healthy children, not nuclear cripples" (3:1849). And in 1959, in the course of nationwide protests against registering the cohort of 1922 for the draft (the Stalingrad cohort), groups of disabled veterans demonstrated not only against this but also against rearmament and nuclear war (3:2255). Speeches and visual images at all these events presented disabled people as victims, thus employing the rhetoric of disability as a frightening deterrent to war. On the other hand, these groups of disabled veterans also appeared in public as much more than pitiful, stigmatized victims. They

Fig. 19. "Sorry, but I have to supply both of these things together." Cartoon against rearmament published by the Verband der Kriegs-beschädigten, March 26, 1950. (From Wolfgang Kraushaar, *Die Protest-Chronik, 1949–1959* [Hamburg: Rogner und Bernhard, 1996], 1:202. Courtesy of the Sozialverband VdK Deutschland.)

appeared as men who were developing a critical consciousness, as opponents to militarism and nuclear war, and as activists taking the first steps toward creating a culture of peace.

Rehabilitation Rhetoric and Early Self-Help Efforts of Physically Disabled Civilians

Although veterans were the most conspicuous group of disabled people in postwar Germany, various types of disabilities also affected large groups of civilians. Enormous numbers suffered war-related injuries, and of course many continued to be affected by workplace accidents. In addition, the hunger years after 1945 led to an increase in disabilities due to malnourishment, tuberculosis, and spinal tuberculosis, often among young people. The two German states were spared the huge polio epidemics that occurred in the United States through the early 1950s. Nevertheless, smaller epidemics broke out there in the late 1940s, and thirty-four thousand West Germans contracted polio between 1952 and 1961 before the oral vaccine was introduced there in 1962.[43] These groups of disabled civilians were so heterogeneous, however, that they

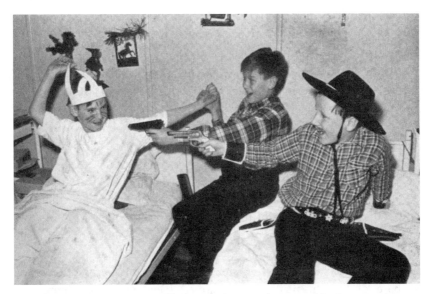

Fig. 20. Young polio patients playing cowboys and Indians at the Oskar-Helene Home in Berlin. (From Wolfgang Albert, *Lösung des Schwerbeschädigtenproblems durch Arbeit* [Berlin: Duncker und Humblot, 1956], 64. Photo by Oskar-Helene-Heim, Berlin. Courtesy of Duncker und Humblot, Berlin.)

did not attract public notice in the same way that the well-defined group of disabled veterans did. Consequently, photographs or other visual images of these disabled people rarely circulated in the press or other public situations. In order to unearth visual representations that would shed light on daily life in this period, it would be necessary to search through collections of family photographs and the archives of hospitals, rehabilitation centers, and institutions for the disabled.

Nevertheless, rehabilitation professionals, physicians, and other experts also debated the proper ways to care for these disabled civilians and the larger question of their roles as German citizens. It is striking that in all these discussions there was almost never any reflection on the fate of disabled people under national socialism or the involvement of professionals and special education teachers in carrying out the policies of racial hygiene. Accordingly, a typical approach was to recall that Germany had been a world leader in rehabilitation in the years after World War I, pass in silence over the twelve years of the Third Reich, and point out that Germany had now fallen behind in this field and needed to learn from other Western countries.[44] A good example of this process is the debate over whether to refer to physically disabled civilians as cripples (Krüppel) or the physically handicapped (Körperbehinderte) and also over exactly which disabled people could be integrated into German society through rehabilitation.[45] The stages in this debate can be followed through the name changes in the professional organizations that were refounded after the war. The most important one called itself the German Society for Cripples' Welfare (Deutsche Gesellschaft für Krüppelfürsorge) when it was reestablished in 1947. Some members of the society, as well as many physically disabled Germans, protested against this derogatory term. At the national conference of this organization in 1953, for example, Eugen Glombig stated, "We, the physically handicapped, don't want . . . to be 'cripples' anymore. We are the *physically handicapped*. And so it's incomprehensible to me that there are still some people who want to continue using the old term, 'cripple,' even though they surely know that this provokes the unanimous resistance of the physically handicapped" (265). Consequently, in 1957 a new name was chosen, the German Association for the Promotion of the Welfare of the Physically Handicapped (Deutsche Vereinigung zur Förderung der Körperbehindertenfürsorge). Yet this name implied that only the physically handicapped could benefit from intervention, whereas the mentally handicapped were still viewed as inferior, uneducable, and so forth. Under the influence of Anglo-American developments, more voices began to be heard in the Federal Republic calling for replacement of the term *Fürsorge* (welfare) with *Rehabilitation,* for the latter was understood to encompass the effort to integrate all disabled people into work and society regardless of the type or cause of their disability. Consequently, in 1962 the organization changed its name yet again to the German Association for Rehabilitation of the Handicapped (Deutsche Vereinigung für die Rehabilitation Behinderter). These changes in terminology reflect changing attitudes about the value of human lives and demonstrate a slowly expanding consciousness of equal rights for people with disabilities.

These struggles over terminology reflected concrete economic and social policies toward disabled people. In a book commissioned by the Labor Ministry, *Der Beschädigte und Körperbehinderte im Daseinskampf einst und jetzt* (The Disabled and Physically Handicapped in the Struggle for Existence in Former Times and Today, 1956), Helmut Ziem defined the disabled as war or workplace victims whose health had been harmed in the service of society while the physically handicapped were those formerly called cripples with all other types of acquired or congenital impairments.[46] Other contemporaries categorized these two groups as the genuine (*echt*) and non-genuine (*unecht*) disabled.[47] The former were entitled to pensions and the protection of hiring quotas and welfare laws whereas the latter were taken care of mostly by their families and charitable and church-run organizations rather than the state. Throughout the 1950s, most rehabilitation professionals recognized that care for physically disabled Germans was inadequate and needed to be improved, but most seem to have concurred that it was proper for the state to invest its limited resources first in caring for those who had sacrificed for society.[48] Although some advocates, particularly from the trade unions, had called since 1949 for hiring quotas to apply to all disabled people regardless of the cause of their disability, this goal was achieved only in 1974 with the reform of disability legislation.[49]

Approaches to rehabilitating these groups were filled with contradictions, which disabled people themselves would later critique. On the one hand, many policymakers and rehabilitation professionals made humane statements about their overall goals. In another book commissioned by the Labor Ministry in 1956, the physician Wolfgang Albert described rehabilitation as encompassing medical treatment, psychological healing, and the return to a normal life of work and leisure for all the physically handicapped.[50] He made a point of stating that the impaired person must be taken seriously as a human being. By this, he meant that parents of handicapped children should be respected and not pitied, that handicapped children should be treated positively, that help should be offered only when wanted, that the handicapped should not be avoided, and that they should have appropriate work (213). Albert also criticized prevailing negative attitudes of "pity and contempt" toward the handicapped, attributing these to the still widespread belief that disability was somehow a punishment from God. Consequently, he proposed that rehabilitation had the pedagogical task of counteracting these prejudices among the parents and relatives of the handicapped as well as the general public (109–10).

The limitations of these progressive ideas lay in the assumption that most disabled people needed to be segregated in some way for rehabilitation, education, and even to some extent work. As was typical of his time, Albert stressed that treatment for reintegration into society had to take place in various institutions for the handicapped and that parents should agree to place their children in these facilities (106). Although he advocated higher education for handicapped young people if they were qualified, he also argued strongly for placing them in special schools or at least in special classes in regular schools, maintaining both that they would be strongly stigmatized in regular classes and that it would be impossible for any teacher to cope with such mixed classes (144–46). He summarized a number of cases compiled by a doctor at a Berlin employment office that illustrate the limited capacity of such professionals to imagine the true capabilities of disabled people. One case, for example, was that of a twenty-year-old woman described as having severe cerebral palsy and above-average intelligence. She would have been qualified to learn a trade, but this was not allowed because of her "conspicuous symptoms." Rather, it was recommended that she become an office assistant, preferably in an institution for the severely disabled (42).

The effect of this approach to rehabilitation was to keep many disabled people segregated, and thus it failed to challenge widespread prejudices against them. In a West German study conducted in 1963, for example, 66 percent of the respondents said they believed that physically handicapped children should not attend the same schools as nonhandicapped children.[51] In an EMNID Institute survey comparing attitudes toward epilepsy in the FRG in 1967 to the United States in 1959, twice as many Germans as Americans would not allow their children to play with children who had epilepsy and three times as many Germans as Americans believed that people with epilepsy should not be employed.[52] A majority of the population continued to believe that few disabled people were capable of regular work and considered suitable jobs for them to be office assistant, elevator operator, brush maker, and basket weaver.[53] Especially regarding more severely disabled people who could not conform to norms of performance and appearance, it seems that many thought it was sufficient to provide for their financial needs through welfare rather than taking steps to integrate them into society.

These statistical surveys of attitudes correspond to typical reactions disabled people often encountered in everyday life. Although there are few autobiographies by disabled Germans that cover the two decades after the war, there are still certain ways of imagining what daily life was like for people with disabilities in postwar Germany. It is revealing, for example, to consider a few rare statements by disabled Germans who traveled to the United States. Born in 1946 with cerebral palsy, Regina Schier traveled to Iowa in 1961 to visit an American family who had sent her family CARE packages during the 1950s. In an interview conducted in 1980, she recalled that summer as the first time she had ever felt accepted by others in contrast to the intrusive curiosity and even hostility from strangers that she and her parents had experienced in the FRG.[54] And in 1966 Eugen Glombig, a physically disabled Bundestag representative who had long advocated improving the West German rehabilitation system, described a trip to the United States and Canada for the Eighth World Conference for Rehabilitation of the Handicapped. In Germany, he claimed, disabled people were often viewed as objects of fear or curiosity and burdens to society. By contrast, in his opinion, "the American people interact with the handicapped in all areas of life in a more understanding way than can be observed in Germany." He also maintained that it was easier for disabled people to find appropriate employment in the United States. Praising the American media for extensively covering issues facing disabled people, he claimed this was still unthinkable in Germany. He concluded by criticizing the FRG for segregating rather than integrating disabled people and urged his country's rehabilitation system to modernize.[55] The similar perspectives of these two disabled Germans—a young woman and an older man—hint at a fascinating, as yet untold story about the difficult daily lives of those viewed as having bodies that did not conform to rigid norms. Indeed, how could it have been otherwise? Old prejudices rooted in religion, along with the value judgments of racial hygiene, did not disappear overnight when Germany surrendered unconditionally on May 8, 1945. Yet due to this continuity of ideology, stories about disability and disabled people were hardly deemed worth telling and preserving. Before it is too late, researchers should collect oral histories of disabled people about their lives in postwar Germany.

By the early 1960s, the FRG had established a well-functioning social welfare system, but disabled people continued to experience severe segregation in many areas of life—whether in living arrangements, education, employment, or personal interactions. Books published in the FRG in the 1970s and early 1980s, as disability rights organizing got under way, indicate the extent to which many disabled people had been suffering from this exclusion.[56] The negative reactions many disabled people often encountered in daily life ranged from fleeting unpleasantness to outright discrimination directed against them because they violated norms of performance, behavior, or appearance. They wrote of being stared at frequently, of being addressed by strangers with the familiar *du* rather than the polite *Sie,* of being asked tactless questions or offered money by strangers, and of being ignored as incompetent. They told of being ordered about; of being refused help when they needed it or having help pressed on them when they did not want it; of being denied admission to theaters, restaurants, and so forth; of being rejected for employment; of being ridiculed or threatened; and of various other kinds of discrimination and hostile treatment. They also challenged experts in medical and policy-making fields who viewed disabled people solely in terms of deficits that were to be normalized rather than in terms of their human dignity and real capabilities.

The pervasiveness of such prejudices led some physically disabled civilians to organize against discrimination. As early as 1952, the Reich League of the Physically Impaired: Self-Help League (Reichsbund der Körperbeschädigten: Selbsthilfebund) had split off from the larger Reichsbund for disabled veterans and civilians because these civilians felt that their interests were not being taken seriously.[57] Similarly, in 1955 people who had had polio and others with paraplegia founded an organization called Welfare/Self-Help of the Physically Handicapped (Sozialhilfe-Selbsthilfe Körperbehinderter). Beginning in the early 1960s, parents of "spastics" and physically handicapped children founded various self-help groups that grew over the years into established service organizations.[58] A decade later, as the postwar generation of disabled people grew into adulthood, its members began to rebel against these parents' organizations and founded their own self-help groups, the Clubs for the Disabled and Their Friends (Clubs Behinderter und ihrer Freunde). Influenced by the worldwide student movement and particularly the African American civil rights movement, these disabled West Germans began to take their first steps toward developing a positive self-image, asserting their rights, and challenging all forms of exclusion. And so the disability rights movement was born in the FRG.

Between 1957 and 1961, about 5,000 children were born in the FRG whose mothers had taken the drug thalidomide, called contergan in that country and marketed as a harmless sleeping pill. About 2,200 of these infants died shortly after birth, often without the cause of death being registered, which of course gave rise to suspicions of passive or active "euthanasia."[59] The 2,800 who survived have various disabilities, including shortened or missing limbs, blindness, deafness, or incompletely formed inner organs. Historians have devoted quite a bit of attention to the 3,000 Afro-German children fathered by African American servicemen in postwar Germany, viewing this as a test case for the inclusiveness of postwar German democracy.[60] Similarly, a historical and cultural study of German attitudes toward the children affected by thalidomide would be an important way to analyze continuities and breaks with the eugenic racism of national socialism for, after all, children with similar impairments had been prime candidates for Nazi "euthanasia." The births of these children led to greatly increased media reporting about physical and mental disabilities.[61] While some of this journalism was sensationalistic and produced images that recalled monsters in freak shows, there were many more serious efforts to deal with issues of medical treatment, rehabilitation, and education for these children.[62] Most recently, Andreas Fischer directed an impressive television documentary film entitled *Contergan: Die Eltern* (Thalidomide: The Parents, 2003), and he is planning a second part called *Contergan: Die Kinder* (Thalidomide: The Children). Furthermore, some people affected by thalidomide have written memoirs or other autobiographical statements about the difficulties they have encountered and their efforts to resist discrimination and lead full lives. In *Der Kampf mit dem Honigbrot:*

Lebenserinnerungen einer Contergangeschädigten (The Struggle with the Honeycake: Memoirs of a Woman Disabled by Thalidomide, 1997), Franziska Heller told a heartrending story of rejection and poverty. By contrast, the well-known professor and human rights lawyer Theresia Degener has recounted her involvement in self-help groups of disabled women and in the West German disability rights movement.[63] Most recently, the internationally renowned classical music singer Thomas Quasthoff published *Die Stimme* (The Voice, 2004), a fascinating autobiography of an unusually talented and successful disabled person.

The changing public reactions to the children affected by thalidomide as they grew into adulthood provide a particularly salient illustration of how disabled people have resisted prejudice and insisted on self-help, respect, and equal rights. This transformation can be seen particularly clearly in the development of Aktion Sorgenkind (Campaign Problem Child), the largest and best-known German charitable organization. It was founded in 1964 by public television (ZDF) and leading welfare organizations, initially in order to raise money for children affected by thalidomide. Later it extended its benefits to disabled adults. This organization has always enjoyed the strong support of the public and has raised more than three billion marks through its lotteries to support a host of projects. As disability rights consciousness began to take hold in the FRG, however, Germans with disabilities increasingly rejected being labeled as "problem children." They criticized Aktion Sorgenkind for investing most of its donations in facilities such as sheltered workshops that in effect segregate disabled people and relegate them to the status of second-class citizens. Like American critics of Jerry Lewis's annual muscular dystrophy telethons,[64] German disabled activists pointed out that such media campaigns raise funds by propagating an image of disabled people as pitiful charity recipients.[65] Consequently, these activists successfully pressured Aktion Sorgenkind to change its focus, and it now supports integrated day care centers, kindergartens, and schools as well as services such as improved transportation and employment counseling for disabled people. Furthermore, in 1997–99, together with 104 organizations representing various groups of disabled people, Aktion Sorgenkind coordinated an extensive publicity campaign called Aktion Grundgesetz (Campaign Basic Law). Its purpose was to inform the public about the prohibition against discrimination on the basis of disability that has been part of the federal constitution since 1994. Finally, under strong pressure from many self-advocacy groups, Aktion Sorgenkind changed its name to Aktion Mensch (Campaign Human Being) in 2000. Ottmar Miles-Paul, the head of the Independent Living Movement in Germany (Interessenvertretung

Selbstbestimmt Leben in Deutschland or ISL), welcomed this as an important symbolic step toward a fundamental rethinking of the place of people with disabilities in German society.[66]

From "Lives Unworthy of Life" to Individuals with Human Dignity

On November 6, 1946, Rudolf Amelunxen, whom the British had appointed governor (Ministerpräsident) of North Rhine-Westphalia, delivered a speech to the assembled students and professors at Cologne University in which he declared, "I call upon the medical students among you to learn from your professors as much as possible about the biologistic worldview of the past, so that later, when you are researchers and physicians, you will be able to uproot and remove the damage done by unfortunate population policies. . . . Euthanasia [is] a disgrace to a civilized nation. . . . As Christians of the deed, we view it as the solemn duty of the state and of every ethical community to be able to support and protect even weak individuals."[67] Amelunxen's noble, compassionate statement was hardly heeded for many years in postwar Germany, however. Rather, in the hunger years immediately after the war, many people who had been threatened by Nazi "euthanasia" continued to suffer and die in institutions. Those who survived, along with disabled people living in the community, including those who had been forcibly sterilized, had to cope with continuing prejudice directed especially against those viewed as having hereditary disabilities. The disabled people who had been the objects of Nazi eugenic policies were not recognized as victims of fascism and did not receive any monetary compensation until decades later. And in most instances the medical personnel and other Nazi officials who had carried out involuntary sterilizations or "euthanasia" either remained in their positions or were eventually restored to them as if nothing had happened.[68] Except for a few isolated voices, many years passed before a younger generation of historians and medical professionals began to critique Nazi racial hygiene and its aftermath in a spirit that reflected the task Amelunxen had outlined.

Although almost nothing is known yet about how those disabled people who had been the targets of the racial hygienists and lived outside of institutions experienced the immediate postwar period, quite a bit is known about the catastrophic conditions in institutions at the end of the war. Historians estimate that about twenty thousand patients died in state hospitals and nursing homes during the four years of the occupation period up to the founding of the two German states in 1949.

While almost all these deaths were from starvation, in at least one institution, the state hospital in Kaufbeuren, patients were still murdered after the war ended.[69] As the availability and distribution of food gradually improved, the death rates slowly declined, but almost thirty years would pass before a fundamental reform in psychiatric treatment got under way in the Federal Republic.

One can only try to imagine the suffering of starving patients during these years. Sometimes they were even abandoned by medical personnel, as happened in Ueckermünde in Pomerania in April 1945. After the staff there fled from the approaching Soviet army, witnesses surmised that many patients died on the street or in the forest (677). Thanks to one doctor, however, unique documents exist regarding the starvation in Eichberg/Hesse, which had been one of the T4 killing centers. A doctor named Hinsen had directed this institution until 1938, when he was replaced by the T4 official Friedrich Mennecke. Hinsen was reinstated in December 1945 and immediately began trying to get more food for his patients. He documented their terrible physical condition and also described their emotional reactions, stating that while those with acute psychoses or severe idiocy showed no change all who still interacted with their environment complained of hunger. Hinsen reported, "One hears heartbreaking complaints and pleas; one encounters threats and rebelliousness. Everyone tries to get whatever food he can. There are frequent break-ins into the kitchen or cellar, often with the help of useful instruments. For example, patients had attached a nail to a long pole, which they put through an open cellar window to skewer potatoes and get them out. . . . It is impossible to have potatoes peeled in the kitchen without half of them being eaten or disappearing into pockets that the women have sewn under their skirts." In sum, he concluded that "everything from complaints to hunger revolts are the order of the day." Here a glimpse appears of patients who were not totally passive and were trying to survive as best they could. After Hinsen's many complaints to German and American officials, the mentally ill patients in Eichberg were given the same rations as sick people in other hospitals in mid-1947. As a result, the death rate declined there from 646 in 1946 to 117 in 1948 (691–94).

The historian Heinz Faulstich attributes these mass deaths to a number of causes, placing them in the context of the general malnourishment and starvation among the German population as a whole during these years. The percentages of deaths in institutions differed locally and according to occupation zones and were thus partially influenced by policies of the occupation authorities. They were responsible only for the total amount of food available in their respective zones, however, and even though they sometimes ordered that patients should be given higher rations than the average citizen, they generally left it to German officials to distribute food. Many Germans did not follow occupation directives, and even if they tried there was frequently not enough food available. In addition, only a few directors of institutions were removed from their positions, and so there was a great deal of continuity in personnel who had observed or participated in Nazi "euthanasia." Faulstich concludes that, with only a few exceptions, the staff in institutions seems to have taken the starvation deaths of patients in stride. For example, a German official responsible for distributing food in the Pfalz area made a characteristic statement: "We don't have enough for the healthy, so the fools really don't need anything!" (661). In some instances, thinking of their own survival in these desperate times, personnel or the local population stole food meant for patients (674, 699, 717). Furthermore, it is striking that none of the newly founded psychiatric journals contain any articles about the starvation deaths. That is, most psychiatrists seem to have thought that these deaths deserved no comment. In a rare expression of criticism, the new director of Zwiefalten (previously the Grafeneck killing center) called attention in 1945 to the low ethical standards of the personnel, whom he faulted for "neglecting everything that has to do in any way with general humane care for the ill" (698). It appears, then, as Faulstich concludes, that the responsibility for the starvation deaths lay significantly, and perhaps mainly, with German medical personnel and officials (716).

The fate of the institutionalized disabled people who died after 1945, as well as those who survived the Nazi period, was hardly a topic of spontaneous public interest, just as a veil of silence and repression lay over the entire subject of Nazi "euthanasia." Yet there was one way in which the crime of "euthanasia" came up repeatedly in the public sphere: the postwar trials of "euthanasia" perpetrators. In all of these trials, the prosecution and defense presented opposing views of disabled people, the former viewing them as individuals with human dignity and the latter viewing them according to the eugenic paradigm as inferior, useless ballast. As early as the Nuremberg Medical Trial of 1946–47, U.S. occupation authorities had accused twenty-three high-ranking national socialists of war crimes and crimes against humanity. While the prosecution focused chiefly on medical experiments the Nazis had conducted on concentration camp prisoners, it also put Viktor Brack and Karl Brandt on trial for planning and carrying out the "euthanasia" program.[70] The two men were sentenced to death and executed on June 1, 1948. The earliest postwar publications dealing with Nazi "euthanasia" were reports on this trial, but they attracted little notice: Alexander

Mitscherlich and Fred Mielke's *Das Diktat der Menschenverachtung* (The Dictate of Contempt for Humanity, 1947, reprinted in 1960 as *Medizin ohne Menschlichkeit: Dokumente des Nürnberger Ärzteprozesses* [Medicine without Humanity: Documents of the Nuremberg Medical Trial]); and Alice Platen-Hallermund's *Die Tötung Geisteskranker in Deutschland: Aus der deutschen Ärztekommission beim amerikanischen Militärgericht* (The Killing of the Mentally Ill in Germany: From the German Medical Commission at the American Military Court, 1948). Another early description of the "euthanasia" program that included shocking interviews with witnesses was completed in 1945, but no German publisher was willing to bring it out until twenty years later: Gerhard Schmidt's *Selektion in der Heilanstalt, 1939–1945* (Selection in the State Hospital, 1939–1945, 1965).

The Nuremberg Medical Trial emphasized crimes committed by Germans against members of the Allied armed forces and citizens of other nations. After late 1945, however, the Allied occupation authorities began to return limited sovereignty to German courts over crimes that Germans had committed against Germans and later against stateless persons. On November 13, 1945, the *Frankfurter Rundschau* editorialized about a trial in Wiesbaden in which Allied authorities had convicted the staff at the Hadamar killing center of murdering forced laborers from Allied nations but not of murdering German patients: "With a sovereign gesture, the court has refused to consider crimes committed against Germans. That only proves how degraded we have become. Now that no one is preventing us, don't we want to show that we have a conscience? There are employees of the institution who are still free because they 'only' murdered Germans. When will a prosecutor bring charges against them?"[71] Prosecutors did step forward, and from 1945 to 1993 there were thirty-one "euthanasia" trials involving one or more defendants in West Germany.[72] The verdicts in these trials show how the West German legal system approached the crime of "euthanasia" and also how the courts regarded this particular group of people with disabilities.

In all of these trials, the circumstances were quite similar, but they were marked by extremely varying sentences. In the verdicts handed down during the occupation period, the courts viewed the actions as murder and pronounced heavy sentences. In what was probably the first "euthanasia" trial, held in Berlin in March 1946, a nurse and a woman doctor were found guilty of murdering mentally ill patients. They received death sentences that were later commuted.[73] In the larger Frankfurt trial of 1947, along with other defendants who received varying sentences, two doctors from Hadamar were sentenced to death.

While the country was still under Allied occupation, it seems that the German courts wanted to demonstrate that they were willing to pronounce heavy sentences against Nazi criminals. After the Federal Republic was founded in 1949, however, the sentences became much lighter, and many defendants were acquitted. The two Hadamar doctors had their sentences reduced to life imprisonment and then were released early in 1953 and 1956. In the early 1950s, a kind of pardon fever broke out in the Federal Republic, as calls intensified for ending the efforts to bring Nazi perpetrators to justice. More and more judges who had been Nazi Party members were reinstated in their former positions, and this continuity undoubtedly contributed to the light sentences and acquittals in subsequent "euthanasia" trials into the 1960s (195).

In many of these trials, judges and lawyers continued to express eugenic views of disabled people. For example, in the Cologne trial of Dr. Alfred Leu, which proceeded through several appeals from 1951 to 1953, the court excused his actions by explaining that while killing disabled children was objectively murder the defendant was not guilty subjectively because he had believed he was releasing "low forms of existence with no perceptible emotional life" from their misery. Furthermore, in an unusually perverse argument, the court stated that Leu had not acted maliciously "because the children or the mentally ill were guileless or defenseless in the first place" (186). Similar arguments were made in 1951 in the trial of Hermann Pfannmüller, the former director of the Eglfing-Haar state hospital. He was not accused of murder but only of manslaughter and was sentenced to five years in prison. In 1972, Kurt Born, the doctor in charge of the killing centers in Sonnenstein and Bernburg, was acquitted in a Frankfurt trial, and the verdict was upheld by the Federal Supreme Court two years later. West German newspapers lambasted the court's decision, writing, for example, that it "puts our state back into the disgraceful position of being an accomplice to murder" (189). A number of prominent intellectuals, including the artist Joseph Beuys and the writers Heinrich Böll, Günter Grass, and Martin Walser, wrote an open letter to Federal President Gustav Heinemann protesting the verdict but to no avail. The last "euthanasia" trials in the 1980s resulted in short prison sentences or defendants being excused because they were too old and ill (193). In general, then, after the 1960s the courts tended to accept defendants' claims that they had not realized the criminal nature of their acts while the West German press often criticized the courts severely for accepting this argument. The exoneration of these perpetrators in postwar West Germany is summed up well on the memorial plaque for the victims of "euthanasia" at the site of the T4 headquarters in Berlin: "The perpetrators were scientists, doctors, nurses, members of the judiciary, the police, the health and labor offices. The victims were poor, desperate, rebellious, or in need of help. They came from psychiatric clinics and children's hospitals, from nursing homes and welfare institutions, from military hospitals and concentration camps. The number of victims is great; the number of convicted perpetrators is small."

Additional "euthanasia" trials were also conducted in the Soviet Occupation Zone (SBZ) and the German Democratic Republic. To date, extensive documentation has been published about the major one of these trials, which was held in Dresden in the summer of 1947. The Nuremberg Medical Trial and the Frankfurt "euthanasia" trial were taking place at this time, and the Soviet Military Administration in Germany (SMAD) wanted to conduct a similar trial in its zone in view of its goal of strict denazification. In Dresden, six doctors, three orderlies, and two nurses from the Sonnenstein killing center and other institutions were put on trial for murder and crimes against humanity. The most prominent doctor was Paul Nitsche, a head evaluator of patients in the T4 program and planner of the Nazi film *Dasein ohne Leben.* While the prosecution argued that the entire civilized world had been horrified to learn about the murders of the mentally ill committed in Germany, the "country of poets and philosophers," the defendants claimed either that they had mercifully released the sick from their misery or that their patients were hardly human to begin with.[74] The court sentenced Nitsche, another doctor, and two orderlies to death and handed down varying sentences to the other defendants. Nitsche was beheaded on March 25, 1948.

The documentation of the Dresden trial is especially interesting for what it reveals about how widely the trial was publicized all over Germany and about various attitudes among the population toward the disabled "euthanasia" victims. First, in the process of planning the trial in early 1947, newspapers all over Germany published notices calling for witnesses. Many Germans whose relatives had been murdered at Sonnenstein sent information to the court, volunteered to testify at the trial, and asked the court to investigate murders at other institutions (147ff.). Some called for the most severe punishments for the perpetrators, as did a woman in a letter regarding her murdered brother: "When Hitler took over the government in 1933, life in these state hospitals gradually became unbearable for these poor, ill people. . . . We, too, demand a just punishment for all those guilty of committing this enormous crime against these poor, helpless, ill people, because with good care many of them would have become healthy again. After all, that's what such an institution is for" (168). After the verdicts were handed down, some members of the public wrote letters either praising or criticizing the court's decision. The latter group used the typical eugenic argument that the mentally ill were useless eaters who had merely been released from their misery (429ff.). By contrast, the Dresden press—operating under SMAD censorship but undoubtedly also expressing the real opinion of many German antifascists—welcomed the four death sentences as a just punishment for "the murderers in white coats." As one editorial stated, "It is not pitiful, ill fellow human beings who have caused or will ever cause our misery. Rather, it is the fascist warmongers and enemies of the people who have brought about our misery" (480). These documents demonstrate that relatively widespread public discussions about "euthanasia" took place in Germany at least while the trial was being planned and conducted. They also bring out the complex attitudes in postwar Germany toward the group of disabled people previously stigmatized as "lives unworthy of life." While some Germans continued to think within the hostile eugenic paradigm, others expressed compassionate acceptance of these disabled people as fellow human beings.

A small number of victims of Nazi eugenic measures organized self-advocacy groups in the early years of the Federal Republic, including the Interest Group of the Sterilized (Interessengemeinschaft der Sterilisierten), founded on October 1, 1949,[75] and the Central Association of the Sterilized and Those with Damaged Health (Zentralverband der Sterilisierten und Gesundheitsgeschädigten), which existed in the early 1950s. The latter group published a newsletter called *Der Notschrei: Kampf- und Aufklärungsorgan der durch Naziterror Verstümmelten, Gesundheitsgeschädigten und Euthanasiehinterbliebenen* (The Cry of Distress: Action and Education Organ of Those Maimed by Nazi Terror, Those with Damaged Health, and the Surviving Relatives of Euthanasia Victims).[76] The activities of these groups occurred in the context of debates about federal legislation for compensating victims of national socialism. In their petitions to the Ministry of the Interior, these groups argued that the Law for the Prevention of Offspring with Hereditary Diseases had been an illegitimate law and those sterilized under its terms should have parity with the racial, religious, and political victims of national socialism. Accordingly, they demanded social rehabilitation and financial compensation for the wrongs that had been done to them.[77]

In spite of these efforts, those who had been sterilized involuntarily or whose relatives were murdered in the "euthanasia" program were long disregarded in public debates about coming to terms with the past in the Federal Republic. In the early 1950s, this group was not included in the federal laws passed to regulate compensation for victims of national socialism. Politicians used two main legal arguments to justify this decision. First, they claimed that since some other European countries, as well as the United States, had eugenic sterilization laws there was nothing specifically national socialist about the law passed in Germany in 1933. Furthermore, many West German politicians continued to argue using strongly eugenic terminology against giving federal money to the "insane and retarded," as did Finance Minister Franz Josef Strauß in the 1960s.[78] These standpoints would prevail in legal and political circles into the 1970s because of the continuity of the eugenic paradigm, because almost all the perpetrators from the medical profession had been restored to respected professional standing, because the surviving victims felt understandable shame and fear about speaking out, and because for a long time the victims hardly had any strong advocates to speak on their behalf.

In the last two decades, however, this situation has changed somewhat. In 1987, the Association of Victims of "Euthanasia" and Involuntary Sterilization (Bund der "Euthanasie"-Geschädigten und Zwangssterilisierten) was formed as a self-advocacy organization that also seeks to educate the public. In that year, victims of eugenic racism testified in the Bundestag for the first time. This small group has had some modest success at securing monetary compensation from the federal government although, to be sure, many victims died of old age without receiving any payments. The Sterilization Law had simply expired without comment in 1968 (204), but in 1998 the decisions of the Nazi Hereditary Health Courts (Erbgesundheitsgerichte) were finally annulled, which had been a central demand of those living under the shadow of this stigma.[79] With respect to broad questions of cultural representation, the shift entailed in these efforts is to recognize those people formerly labeled inferior as equal citizens today. Along with their allies, the activists in this area—many of them elderly people— have mustered up the courage to speak out and identify themselves or their relatives as belonging to this stigmatized group and to insist that their society has a responsibility to acknowledge the wrongs committed against them.

If the victims of Nazi eugenics still experienced much stigmatization in the postwar period, the same can be said for most cognitively disabled and mentally ill people of all ages who previously would have been labeled lives unworthy of life. With respect to the generation of cognitively disabled children born after the war, aside from a few remnants of efforts to educate them in church-run institutions, they were basically written off as uneducable (bildungsunfähig). Consequently, medical professionals generally pressured parents to institutionalize these children until the late 1950s. The turning point came in 1958, when a group of parents, friends, and experts founded the organization Life Help for the Mentally Handicapped Child (Lebenshilfe für das geistig behinderte Kind). Mothers were the driving force in this citizens' movement. They rejected the negative prognoses handed down by doctors and lobbied instead for better education and greater possibilities in life for their cognitively disabled children.[80] By 1968, Lebenshilfe had 312 local chapters and thirty-eight thousand members. As late as 1964, almost no cognitively disabled children were in school, but 71 percent were attending special schools by 1974.[81] Accompanying this progress was an effort to normalize terminology. These children were now called "mentally handicapped" rather than "feebleminded," and they were generally not referred to as "uneducable" anymore. Other vocabulary shifts also reflected a more affirmative perspective toward educating these children, who now attended a "school" (Schule) instead of a "training center" (Bildungsstätte) and were in a "class" (Klasse) rather than a "group" (Gruppe). They received a "report card" (Zeugnis) instead of a "report" (Bericht), and they had "teachers" (Lehrer) rather than "trainers" (Erzieher).[82] Since a large percentage of cognitively disabled adults had been murdered by the Nazis, Lebenshilfe was initially concerned mainly with educating children. Later the organization also began to focus on developing job training and services for adults.

In contrast to these efforts to improve the lives of cognitively disabled people, the process of reforming psychiatric treatment in institutions for mentally ill people was delayed longer and followed a different course. Rather than developing as a citizens' movement, psychiatry reform arose mainly from activities of young, critical psychiatrists supported by a few legislators. Certainly one important reason for these differences is the fact that a large percentage of cognitively disabled people were children, and disabled children have always been viewed with more sympathy and interest than disabled adults—especially mentally ill adults, who generally occupy the lowest rungs in the disability hierarchy. In the first half of the twentieth century, German psychiatrists had seen thousands of patients starve to death in institutions during World War I, had undertaken a brief period of reform in the relatively stable years from 1924 to 1929, had been deeply implicated in mass murders during the Nazi era, and had done little to prevent large numbers of their patients from starving after 1945. This history of brutality and hopelessness pervaded the atmosphere in state hospitals and nursing homes in the postwar period. As the historian Hans-Walter Schmuhl describes it, "The patients who had been spared from mass murder were packed together in confined spaces in crowded wards, working quarters, or barracks. Their labor power was totally exploited. Therapy . . . was generally discontinued. Caregiving, even at the lowest level, was hardly possible anymore."[83] Yet, because of the unwillingness of many psychiatrists to face up to their involvement in murdering their patients, little was done to improve these terrible conditions for many years.

This situation slowly began to change beginning in about 1958 when qualitatively new ways of dealing with the national socialist past began to develop in many spheres in the Federal Republic.[84] Historians from the so-called skeptical generation, such as Martin Broszat, began to publish their critical research. The Ulm Einsatzgruppe Trial of 1958 called public attention to mass murders committed by Germans in Eastern Europe. During 1959–60, a wave of anti-Semitic incidents forced more public debate about continuities with Nazi ideology. In the sphere of literature, Günter Grass published his spectacular first novel *Die Blechtrommel* (The Tin Drum) in 1959. The novel's opening sentence refers explicitly to institutions where Nazi medical crimes occurred when Oskar, the main character, declares, "Granted, I am an inmate of a mental hospital."[85] Perceptive readers such as Hans Magnus Enzensberger realized immediately that Grass had taken the radical step of creating a disabled character who barely escapes Nazi "euthanasia" and is confined to a state hospital in the 1950s and of privileging Oskar as the mouthpiece and mirror of German society in the first half of the twentieth century.[86] Also in 1959 the Heyde/Sawade scandal erupted into public consciousness. The physician Werner Heyde had been the head T4 evaluator before Paul Nitsche. After 1945, he changed his name to Fritz Sawade and continued to work as a doctor in Schleswig-Holstein, where many colleagues knew his real identity but protected him. In 1959, he was finally arrested and was to be tried for murdering at least one hundred thousand patients, but he committed suicide in prison.[87] This affair marked the beginning of more intense public debates about Nazi medical crimes.

In the late 1950s and early 1960s, a small number of activist psychiatrists began to critique Nazi eugenic ideology, including the concepts of mercy killing and "euthanasia"; to probe into continuities between Nazi practices and West German psychiatry; and to try to improve conditions in state hospitals.[88] A pioneering book in this regard was Manfred in der Beeck's *Praktische Psychiatrie* (Practical Psychiatry, 1957). These psychiatrists asserted that because of the failure of most of their colleagues to come to terms with their complicity in the murderous Nazi past Germany had fallen far behind international standards of psychiatric treatment, specifically those in the United States and Britain. As Professor Walter von Baeyer said in a lecture at the Berlin Free University in 1966, "In Germany we are still suffering today from the aftereffects of this setback. In contrast to most civilized countries, we unfortunately lag behind in the areas of psychiatry having to do with social, therapeutic methods and with social, occupational, and family rehabilitation. It will take great efforts to overcome these deficits. The lead that we could once claim here thanks to our internationally recognized accomplishments is long gone. In many instances, developments stopped where they were forcibly interrupted in 1933. . . . It is obvious that medicine, psychiatric medicine, must lose credibility and trust if it allows—and even recommends—the killing of large numbers of its patients, instead of providing them with the best possible treatment and rehabilitation" (77). Some of these West German psychiatrists took note of developments in the United States, such as President John Kennedy's speech to Congress on February 6, 1963, outlining his national program for mental health (one of Kennedy's sisters was mentally disabled), and they began to call for similar changes in their own country. Also during the 1960s the first West German television documentaries rejecting old prejudices and advocating more humane treatment for the mentally ill were aired, including one called *Bremens kranke Seelen* (Bremen's Sick Souls, 1967).[89]

It was the far-reaching, democratizing transformations of the late 1960s and early 1970s that created the social and cultural climate necessary for fundamental psychiatry reform in West Germany. In his first programmatic speech upon becoming chancellor in 1969, Willy Brandt had called for better care and treatment for the handicapped.[90] Subsequently some engaged psychiatrists, supported by the Bundestag representative and disabled veteran Walter Picard of the CDU, pushed for a parliamentary investigation into the conditions prevailing in state hospitals and the general approach to treating mentally ill people in the Federal Republic. The preliminary report in 1973 lambasted the treatment of the mentally ill in institutions as violating human dignity.[91] In 1975, the final report created the framework for a fundamental transformation in care for mentally ill people in the FRG. It called for less frequent institutionalization, expanded community and outpatient treatment, better psychiatric care for children and youths, improved treatment for alcoholism and drug addiction, and parity between the mentally and physically ill in financial, legal, and social terms.[92] Of course, not all of these goals have been realized in any country even today, but this West German investigation marked a fundamental turning point in the direction of treating mentally ill people in a more humane way, as fellow human beings, and as citizens with rights. After this date, many mental health professionals, patients' collectives, and other self-help groups have worked along these lines to improve the lives of people with mental illnesses, stressing community integration and insisting that all lives have inherent value and human dignity.[93]

CHAPTER 5 • Breaking the Spell of Metaphor: Three Examples from Film, Literature, and the Media

After the early 1970s, depictions of illness multiplied rapidly in West and East German, Austrian, and Swiss literature, autobiography, film, and art. Within the framework of this development, certain illnesses seemed particularly well suited for portraying complex struggles over normative discourses—whether about the psychic pressures of the contemporary world, the isolation of the individual and the fragility of the self, or sexuality in all its ramifications.[1] Consequently, the vast majority of these representations deal with schizophrenia, depression, cancer, or AIDS. While characters may have physical symptoms of such illnesses, physical disability as such is rarely a theme. It appears that the creators of these texts distinguish between illness, which runs its course over time and thus provides rich material for developing conflicts, and disability, which they view as stable and thus as less interesting.

Yet it is precisely the relative stability of disability, in contrast to illness, that has served to shore up the most reductive stereotypes of disabled people. There are few main characters in any national literature who have physical disabilities because disability has traditionally been so strongly stigmatized—that is, it has been viewed as a defining characteristic that negates all other individual qualities.[2] Accordingly, when physically disabled characters do appear, literary discourse tends to invest their disabilities with systems of meaning, make them a spectacle, and present them as metaphors with negative resonances. For example, the Austrian writer Thomas Bernhard used disability in this metaphorical way in his frequently performed first play, *Ein Fest für Boris* (A Celebration for Boris, 1970). Here legless, wheelchair-using, grotesque cripples stand for the atrophy of human relationships in the modern world. Similar examples from the literature of the German-speaking countries include Max Frisch's *Mein Name sei Gantenbein* (A Wilderness of Mirrors, 1964), Heinar Kipphardt's *März* (1974), Siegfried Lenz's *Der Verlust* (The Loss, 1981), Libuse Moníková's *Pavane für eine verstorbene Infantin* (Pavane for a Dead Infanta, 1982), and Anna Duden's *Übergang* (Transition, 1982). This type of reductive discourse, which flattens out the real, lived experiences of disabled people, prevailed into the 1980s. After that, disability rights and disability culture groups in the FRG finally began to make some headway in bringing different images into the public sphere that showed disabled people as multifaceted human beings.

In the following, I discuss three transitional representations of physical disability in West German film, literature, and media since the late 1960s. These illustrate how old representations of disability as nothing but negative metaphor began to be replaced by more complex ways of depicting it. The film director Rainer Werner Fassbinder set out to break taboos but ended up re-creating stereotypes of disability. The dramatist Franz Xaver Kroetz rejected metaphors of disability in favor of depicting disabled characters who are simply ordinary human beings searching for happiness. Finally, in the debates over whether Wolfgang Schäuble could be chancellor while using a wheelchair and Franklin D. Roosevelt should be shown as disabled, the old view of disability as standing for shameful incompetence and weakness clashed with a newer perception that visibly disabled people could also be competent and powerful in a positive sense.

The Scandal That Never Was: Disability in Fassbinder's *Chinese Roulette*

The disjuncture between the visibility of disabled people in daily life and the dearth of filmic representations of disability in the Federal Republic is striking. It is all the more remarkable, then, that a rare depiction of disability by Rainer Werner Fassbinder, arguably the most famous West German film director, has never drawn the attention of cultural historians. Fassbinder is known for his sometimes scandal-provoking films, which often revolve around female characters and minorities such as foreign workers, gay men, and Jews. A member of another minority group, a visibly disabled girl, is the central figure in his *Chinesisches Roulette* (Chinese Roulette, 1976). Fassbinder used this character to set in motion the film's reflections on the bourgeois marriage trap, the shadows of the German past, and the continuities between that past and the present. Since this is one of Fassbinder's lesser-known films, a brief outline of the minimalist plot is in order. In a short scene at the beginning, the well-to-do parents of Angela, a disabled young teenager who uses crutches and one leg brace, are saying goodbye to each other—ostensibly for the father to fly to Oslo on business and the mother to fly to Milan. However, they have secretly planned to meet their respective lovers for the weekend at the family's country estate. Angela and her governess, Traunitz, who can hear but does not speak, also travel to the estate, and it appears that Angela has brought about an embarrassing confrontation between the two couples. For the rest of the weekend, these six characters circle around each other in a claustrophobic atmosphere of repressed tensions and hatred, joined by the middle-aged housekeeper and her son. The film builds to a climax when Angela insists that the characters all play Chinese Roulette, a guessing and truth-telling game. At the game's violent climax, the mother briefly points a pistol at Angela but shoots Traunitz instead. As the film ends, a second gunshot is heard from within the mansion, but the spectator does not know who fired the pistol and can only imagine who the perpetrator and victim are. In this manner, the film's entanglement of hostilities is projected beyond the closing frames into the spectator's imagination.

The critics who have taken note of *Chinese Roulette* at all have generally assessed it as one of Fassbinder's "most perfectly realized art films."[3] Thus, both West German and foreign critics highlight the ways in which the virtuoso camera work creates an atmosphere of extreme artificiality. If everything in the film leads up to the game of Chinese Roulette, then the film itself is constructed as a puzzle, a "chessboard" on which the figures move, followed by the circling camera in tightly choreographed sequences.[4] While some critics viewed the film as "too coldly intellectual,"[5] others described it as characterized by "dazzling technique,"[6] "playfulness," "creative visual games,"[7] and "hysterical intensity and formal extravagance."[8] In any event, as Thomas Elsaesser noted, the film marked Fassbinder's "bid for a place as a European auteur" and, with its two Godard actresses (Anna Karina and Macha Méril), was his first international coproduction.[9]

Most critics have observed that the highly stylized cinematography of *Chinese Roulette* creates a claustrophobic atmosphere in which the repressed emotions, tensions, and especially hatreds among the characters come to the fore. Described by one critic as a "melodramatic chamber piece,"[10] it has been likened to Louis Buñuel's *Exterminating Angel* (1962) in that by the end all bourgeois pretenses of highly sophisticated manners break down, yielding to the violence seething underneath the façade of convention.[11] Critics have unanimously viewed Fassbinder's film as a tightly constructed evocation of intimate relationships in crisis—a theme common to many of his films. Here marriage and bourgeois family life are exposed as institutions rotten to the core, built on the shifting sands of lies, evasions, and half-truths. Whether between spouses, lovers, or parents and children, verbal communication among the characters remains indirect, misleading, or blocked. In fact, they often interact mainly on a wordless level, through meaningful looks that give a more straightforward indication of their mutual hostility and distrust. Consequently, considering the ambiguity of these interpersonal relationships and the final anarchic acts of violence, as well as the dearth of specific political content, critics have agreed that the film evades "a direct reference to contemporary sociohistorical reality." In fact, labeling *Chinese Roulette* a "high art melodrama," one critic has gone so far as to claim that "the film operates in a social vacuum."[12]

Critics have thus declared *Chinese Roulette* to be a well-made art film lacking in sociopolitical relevance, which is why the film has received so little attention in contrast to the intense interest in other films by Fassbinder that deal with women, gays, foreign workers, or Jews. However, it is possible to dismiss the film in this way only if its central figure, Angela, is not understood as a filmic representation of another significant minority group—people with disabilities. Disability is generally not yet on the radar screen of cultural historians, and so commentators on this film have ignored Angela's significance. For example, Thomas Elsaesser states that Fassbinder's *Ali: Angst essen Seele auf* (Ali: Fear Eats the Soul, 1973) deals with blacks and Arabs, while *Chinese Roulette* deals with moneyed professionals.[13] It is inconceivable that any critic would neglect the dimension of race and ethnicity in discussing the former film, but it has been standard to overlook the dimension of disability in discussing the latter. Furthermore, Elsaesser discusses the "inscription of 'awkward' bodies into the social symbolic" in Fassbinder's films and even mentions Fassbinder's own "fat body," but he does not refer to Angela.[14] The critics writing about *Chinese Roulette* seem to conceive of disability as an individual misfortune and a medical problem but not as a culturally constructed sociopolitical category. Therefore, they view the film as giving a true picture of a disabled girl, a picture it is unnecessary to unmask as deeply ideological and embodying significant power relationships.

This lack of attention to Angela, who actually has one of the most strikingly awkward bodies in all of Fassbinder's films, is most evident in the imprecise, negative language critics use to describe her. The facts that attentive spectators see and hear in the film are that Angela uses crutches, she wears a brace on her left leg, she became ill eleven years ago, and seven years ago doctors declared they could give her no more help. Reviews label her in wildly contradictory ways: a "crippled child," a "partially disadvantaged child," a "paraplegic," a teenager with "paralyzed legs," the victim of an "accident" or "injury," as having a "permanently crippled right leg," as wearing an "artificial leg," and as "polio-stricken." Of these, only the medical diagnosis of polio might possibly be accurate, whereas pejorative adjectives such as *crippled* merely reflect the social prejudices of the critics. Some reviews also describe Traunitz, Angela's governess, as deaf and mute, whereas in fact she does not speak but obviously can hear.

Similarly, when critics comment on Angela's personality, they generally employ the old cliché of deriving twisted, negative emotions from abnormal physical appearance. Thus, without reflecting on the cultural origins of these categories, they unthinkingly label her "vindictive," "relentless," "tyrannical" (in contrast to her "essentially innocent" parents), "helpless and all-destroying," "precocious and secretive," and as "singularly unpleasant, possessed of the hereditary gift to hate and destroy." One critic, Richard Combs, made the connection to the horror film most explicit when he said of Angela, "She can thereafter be heard, for the duration of the weekend, clumping about the chateau on her crutches, presiding over the misery of her elders with the satisfaction of a cherubic Bela Lugosi."[15] The point here is not that these critics always give mistaken assessments of how Angela appears in the film—many of these descriptions are quite apt. However, they take these negative, horrific qualities to be self-evident psychological accompaniments of physical disability rather than filmic representations that call for interpretation. But I do not want to be unfair to these critics. After all, except for Elsaesser and Shattuc, they were writing in the late 1970s, shortly after the film appeared, a time when almost no one had thought of interpreting disability in a way that went beyond old stereotypes. Today, however, such criticism is outdated.

Focusing on the overlooked factor of disability provides the key to understanding the sociopolitical statements this film makes about power relations and continuities between the German past and present. In this context, it is important to know what Fassbinder himself said about Angela's disability. In creating the alienated married couple, he imagined that they were motivated to take long-term lovers because of problems with their child. He stated, "For the child to be a real threat, she would have to be more intelligent than other children—and infirm (*gebrechlich*) children are more intelligent. That's how I got the idea." He also remarked that the child needed a partner who also has an "infirmity" (*Gebrechen*), and so he created the mute governess, Traunitz.[16]

Fassbinder's statement about Angela should be analyzed on two levels. First, he created a character who sees through many of the lies and hypocrisies around her, and she can do this because her physical difference places her in the position of an observing outsider. But, on the other hand, there is nothing natural about her precocity, as Fassbinder's statement seems to imply. Rather, as in most of his other films, Fassbinder is operating with massive cultural stereotypes, here ones of disability. Yet these stereotypes were so culturally ingrained that he does not display a consciousness of them, just as most spectators probably have not viewed the film as significantly about disability.

Fundamentally, Fassbinder's film is about modes of walking and talking, that is, about bodies moving through life in acceptable and unacceptable ways and about evading and telling the truth. This becomes evident by analyzing the sounds associated with Angela, her visual presence, her personality traits as she interacts with others, and two other characters with anomalous bodies. First, the sound track of the film emphasizes how Angela disturbs the others as they go about approaching and betraying each other. Throughout the weekend their even, measured footsteps constantly echo on the wood floors of the mansion's halls. But whenever Angela appears the sound track produces the uneven, unrealistically loud clanking of her crutches and brace, which announces her interruptions of the other characters' entanglements. Her body also appears disruptive in the visual field. Complicated camera shots and angles contrast her with the nondisabled characters, drawing the spectator's attention to her disabled leg or the lower half of her body. Two related images seem to point toward this directorial strategy. First, the advertising poster for the film shows a view of Angela from the back, crushing a flower underfoot with her expressionistically elongated disabled leg as she walks alone through a hallway with doors leaning at strange angles. Barely visible in the background, a ghostly image of Angela with nondisabled legs and no crutches hovers in the air. Second, in the mansion's dining room, where all the characters gather to play Chinese Roulette, there is a strange painting that shows two female figures against a black background. One is a nude, with beautiful, long, white legs, and the other is a ghostly blue figure cut off at the waist with no legs at all. Both the poster image and the painting hint that the spectator would do well to pay attention to the film's depiction of physical deviation from desirable norms.

Following these signals and focusing on the motif of walking provides a key to understanding many of the scenes that have been dubbed too enigmatic and thus to understanding some of the film's statements about power relationships. Numerous shots are constructed meticulously around the contrast between disabled and nondisabled legs. Early in the morning, after the two pairs of lovers have spent the night together in the mansion, Angela clanks down the hall, opening the bedroom doors to look at the couples. In one bedroom, her father's lover, Irene, is sitting on the windowsill with her lovely leg bent. It forms a studied rectangle with the naked leg of her father, who lies in bed. Angela looks at

Fig. 21. Publicity poster for Fassbinder's *Chinese Roulette,* 1976. (© Rainer Werner Fassbinder Foundation.)

the couple in a precociously knowing way and leaves to go to the next bedroom, where her mother, Ariane, has spent the night with her lover. Opening the door, Angela sees her mother naked in bed with her long, slender legs stretched out. The two exchange looks of hatred, and Angela says, "Yes, yes," in an amused and knowing way as she clumsily leaves.

Later there are other shots in which the camera is positioned behind legs, making them a frame for the image. A shot through Angela's legs, emphasizing the brace and crutches in the foreground, provides the frame for a view of the housekeeper's son eavesdropping on the two couples. A shot through Ariane's shapely legs provides the frame when Angela hobbles awkwardly into the dining room to play Chinese Roulette. Angela's limitations and clumsiness are brought out in other ways, too, such as when she makes her way laboriously down a staircase while the housekeeper's son slides quickly by her down the banister or when she drops her crutch trying to get her dolls out of the car and the housekeeper laughs maliciously at her. All of these scenes show Angela as an anomalous outsider rather than a smoothly functioning participant in social interactions.

Angela's exclusion from the games of life the other characters play is readily apparent in several other scenes, which become more comprehensible when we focus on her visual appearance and the motif of walking. When her father and Irene stop on the way to the mansion, Irene swings her long, shapely legs out of the car and hops on a hopscotch diagram. Irene, as a nondisabled adult woman, is physically able to express her elation at the thought of a weekend with her lover in this way, but this kind of girlish physical playfulness seems barred to Angela because of her impairment. Similarly, later in the film the housekeeper's son watches Traunitz hopping around playfully on Angela's crutches. Indifferent to Traunitz's high spirits, Angela leans passively against a wall. Again, Angela appears set apart from the games the others are playing.

Two longer scenes, which seem opaque if considered separately but are more comprehensible when juxtaposed, heighten the sense that Angela is a foreign body. With opera music playing in the background, the opening shots of the film show Angela's mother sitting on top of a radiator in their home with her bare legs outstretched on the windowsill. Across the room, Angela, who leans against another radiator, looks down uncomfortably at the record player, which blocks the spectator's view of her body from the waist down. Her mother walks over to her, says "Schön?" ("nice" or "beautiful"?) and wordlessly lays her head on Angela's shoulder. Since Angela does not respond, the feeling is one of loneliness, emptiness, and distance between mother and daughter. The difference between their bodies blocks communication between them. A contrasting scene occurs when Angela's mother meets her husband's lover. The two women look at each other directly, and the spectator sees the entire bodies of both women. Ariane acknowledges Irene by saying, "Sie sind schön" (You're beautiful). Irene replies, "Sie sind auch schön" (You're beautiful, too), and they kiss each other on the cheeks. A later scene shows Ariane laying her head on Irene's shoulder and saying, "I like you," and yet another shows Irene styling Ariane's hair while they exchange confidences, an intimate scene that might be expected between mother and daughter but not between wife and lover. Yet, viewed from the perspective of discourses about disability, these scenes become comprehensible. They show close interactions between nondisabled women based on a smoothly flowing whirl of sexual adventures.

Of course, Angela is an adolescent, but it is not only her age that precludes her participation in adult games. Rather, she seems to be excluded, or the film at least intimates that she will be excluded in the future, because of the disturbing sounds and sights her body presents. Angela is quite aware of this situation and talks about it bluntly with the housekeeper's son, Gabriel, while her parents are sleeping with their lovers. Lying alone in bed in the mansion with only her uncanny collection of dolls for company, Angela asks Gabriel in a serious but matter-of-fact way if he "would ever want to sleep with a cripple." When he only grimaces in reply, she declares, "I know the answer. I tell it to myself almost every day." Such scenes present Angela as the helpless victim of a cruel biological fate that causes others to reject her as a matter of course.

Yet, as is the case with all of Fassbinder's filmic portrayals of minority group members, there are other sides to Angela that prevent the viewer from sympathizing totally with her as a victim.[17] As the scene with Gabriel continues, Angela attributes her parents' love affairs to her illness, saying that her father began his affair eleven years ago when she became ill and her mother's affair began seven years ago when the doctors said they couldn't help her anymore. But the housekeeper, Kast, who seems to know all the family secrets, tells Gabriel soon thereafter that this is nonsense. This scene, along with others, relativizes Angela's status as a passive victim and steers the spectator toward viewing her more critically. Because she is not able to compete and interact with the other characters on some levels, she has learned to get what she wants by being secretive, manipulative, and stubborn—she is a spoiled brat. Knowing that her parents will give in to her, she insists that the entire group should eat together and play the discomfiting game of Chinese Roulette, which she directs like an evil little puppet master. Physically limited and weak, she has honed her verbal skills until she is quite the equal of the adults in this respect at least. Her resentments intensify into malevolence, and there are strong indications that she even enjoys her role as a victim in some ways. Another disabled figure in the film furnishes a parallel to Angela's instrumentalization of her victimhood. A blind beggar comes to the mansion, and Kast gives him money. After she goes inside, she looks out the window, only to see him remove his dark glasses and drive away in a car sporting a license plate that reads FUCK. This culturally familiar figure of the malingering cripple underscores the suspicion that to some extent Angela also chooses to be helpless. She exploits her status as a victim to get what she wants—the quintessential subaltern form of resistance.

Angela appears as much as a monstrous alien child from a horror film as a victim with frilly dresses and long curls who evokes sympathy.[18] Accordingly, although her father and Traunitz seem to sympathize with her, some of the other characters view her with repulsion and hatred and ultimately think of annihilating her. For example, when it dawns on Kast that Angela has probably engineered the entire gathering at the mansion, she blurts out, "This monster, this disgusting cripple." At several other points, however, there appears to be a certain understanding between Angela and Kast. This might be based on Kast's outsider position as a servant, which allows her, like Angela, to see through the pretenses of her well-to-do employers. Thus, during the game of Chinese Roulette Kast states that Angela has every right to hate the other characters.

The main person who returns Angela's hostility with an intense hatred of her own, however, is Angela's mother, Ariane. At one point, she suggests a game of target practice and points a pistol at Angela, who is hobbling awkwardly across the mansion's grounds, but Irene pulls down her arm. The hatred between mother and daughter reaches its apex at the end of the game of Chinese Roulette. Throughout the game, Angela interprets Traunitz's sign-language answers to the others, so she appears to be an apt pupil of her governess, and the spectator is led to view the two as a dyad. At this point, the film's discourse about disability intersects explicitly with the theme of fascism and the German past. For the game's final question, the players are supposed to say what they think their chosen person would have been during the Third Reich. Gabriel says a professor involved with euthanasia, Traunitz (through Angela) says a clerk at Gestapo headquarters, and Angela says a commandant in Bergen-Belsen. Ariane realizes that they mean her, and she hisses at the wickedly laughing Angela, "You're a monster. You're a revolting monster. A dirty, revolting monster." Enraged, Ariane first aims her pistol at Angela, then turns and shoots Traunitz in the throat. That is, she wounds the disabled teacher who has apparently forged a close bond with her disabled daughter.

With this mention of "euthanasia," Fassbinder broke a taboo in West German cinema by referring unusually explicitly to the murder of people with disabilities under national socialism. And, with his typically keen sense for the unfinished process of coming to terms with the past in the Federal Republic, he showed the persistence of an eliminationist mentality directed against Angela and Traunitz as representatives of a group still perceived by many to be fundamentally different and "other." In this sense, *Chinese Roulette* belongs to the group of Fassbinder's films that revolves around the theme of continuity between the overt violence of the fascist past and the subterranean, repressed violence of the present. Yet, as is always the case for Fassbinder, the film cannot be taken as a simple exposé of social wrongs in the Federal Republic. This is because he makes such seamless use of overbearing cultural stereotypes of disability that—as can be seen from the film critics' reactions—most spectators have not understood the film as making a statement about the varieties of violence directed against a group of outsiders.

All of Angela's physical and personality characteristics are contemporary manifestations of two of the oldest stereotypes in cultural discourses about disability, discourses that stretch back through the centuries in literature and visual art and were taken over unchanged into the twentieth-century medium of film. As David Mitchell and Sharon Snyder explain, "Physiognomy orders the film universe of psychic discordance through a recognizable portraiture of external deformities."[19] On the one hand, people with disabilities have traditionally been represented as weak and helpless, as passive victims needing help or charity, and, relatedly, often as the targets of other people's cruel impulses. In motion pictures, such figures are usually children or women who have been termed "sweet innocents." They appear in films as diverse as *City Lights* (1931), the many versions of *A Christmas Carol, Magnificent Obsession* (1954), *Pollyanna* (1960), and *A Patch of Blue* (1965).[20] Counterposed to this stereotype and rooted in premodern magical thinking, physical anomaly has also often been taken as the sign of a warped or evil spirit. This means that when disabled characters are depicted as powerful rather than weak they "virtually always represent a dangerous force unleashed on the social order."[21] More specifically, powerful disabled characters are often shown as malicious and revengeful, as full of resentment that appears to be motivated by their physical difference. Examples from films of such "disabled avengers" (generally men) include Richard III, the Hunchback of Notre Dame, Captain Hook, Dr. Strangelove (with his wheelchair and black prosthetic hand), and the mean, wheelchair-using tightwad Potter in *It's a Wonderful Life* (1946).[22]

Although the German film tradition does not have such an extensive repertoire of these stereotypes as does American cinema, Fassbinder seismographically registered these cultural images and used them to create his Angela, for she oscillates between these two poles. On the one hand, she is shown as a dependent, helpless outsider who is a potential target of cruelty, a victim. On the other hand, however, she is also an unusual example of a young female disabled avenger in that she uses her intelligence to set in motion a game of unmasking the hypocrisies of the adults.[23] The maliciousness of the other characters toward each other is free floating and unmotivated, simply part of their human intermingling of love and hatred. By contrast, since disability in a cultural text is almost always a call to interpret, Angela's physical difference appears as the motivation for her maliciousness. In order to bring into focus how heavily the film relies on these two stereotypes of disability, it is only necessary to imagine how both Angela's helplessness and her vengeful qualities would diminish in intensity if her body were not marked as conspicuously different. A "cherubic Bela Lugosi," indeed, there are no signals in the film's narrative or aesthetic structure that would lead spectators to a critical view of these stereotypes. Angela thus remains the object of a mystifying gaze that locates her as the other, as someone outside the realm of normal humanity with all its entanglements. By taking this approach, the film perpetuates the exclusion of difference that it seeks to critique with its reference to fascist "euthanasia." Ultimately, the stereotypes of disability in the film prevent its characters, as well as the film's spectators, from finding the truth they are being led to seek through the film's central game, Chinese Roulette.

Fassbinder's problematic use of stereotypes of disability here is similar to the way he used anti-Semitic stereotypes in his play *Der Müll, die Stadt, und der Tod* (Garbage, the City, and Death), which was published in 1976, the same year *Chinese Roulette* was released. Critics have shown that in this play, as well as in some of his films, Fassbinder's Jewish figures generally stand for absolute otherness. While he was certainly not consciously anti-Semitic, he nevertheless created Jewish characters who "remain bearers of symbols," who are "distanced observers," who are not "merged into the suffering cosmos of life where the other characters are located," and who are thus "dismissed from history." Accordingly, when the Frankfurt Schauspielhaus attempted in 1985 to stage this play, with its character the "Rich Jew," a huge controversy erupted.[24] Members of the Jewish community and their supporters demonstrated in front of the theater, preventing the premiere from taking place and asserting their right to have a say about how Jews would be represented in German culture. As one critic wrote, "They [the Jews] have begun to negotiate the meaning of their identity and are not simply letting their identity be defined as their otherness, even if it is an otherness that Fassbinder loved and in which he saw politically redemptive moments."[25]

But in 1976, when *Chinese Roulette* appeared, the disability rights movement was only in its infancy in the Federal Republic. A few culturally sensitive spectators may have felt uncomfortable upon seeing Fassbinder's stereotypical depiction of a physically disabled girl. However, there were not yet any well-organized, sizeable activist groups of people with disabilities who were engaged in resisting objectifying gazes and defining their own identities, and who might have protested against the outrageous, defamatory images of disability in this film.[26] And so Fassbinder's figure of the "Rich Jew" led to storms of controversy, but his figure of the physically helpless, malevolent "cripple" did not even register as problematic. Indeed, to judge by the reaction of critics and film scholars, the film seemed merely to reflect the widely held assumption that people with disabilities are naturally and legitimately dismissed from history. In contrast, then, to the protests against anti-Semitic stereotypes in Fassbinder's play, the scandal of *Chinese Roulette* is that it was never perceived as scandalous at all.

Disruptions of Daily Life: Disability in the Works of Franz Xaver Kroetz

One of the most striking things about the works of Franz Xaver Kroetz, who was born in 1946 in Munich and was counted among West Germany's most frequently performed playwrights in the 1970s and early 1980s, is that they often feature disability as a major theme. Whether in his first short plays, which provoked theater scandals and established his reputation, in his one major prose work, or in his adaptation of a play by the expressionist dramatist Ernst Toller, Kroetz explores the ramifications of disability in daily life with a depth and sensitivity that are unusual in postwar German literature. His naturalistic works are situated in small Bavarian towns, on farms, or in impoverished surroundings in Munich. As the best-known representative of the *Neues Volksstück* (new popular dialect play), Kroetz built on traditions from Weimar culture in his evocations of provincial, underclass misery and the false consciousness that pervades the language of his characters. Accordingly, he belongs in a literary tradition stretching back to Georg Büchner's *Woyzeck* (1837) and including writers such as Ödön von Horváth and Marieluise Fleißer. Along with a contemporary playwright, Martin Sperr, as well as the filmmaker Rainer Werner Fassbinder, Kroetz sought to expose the narrow-mindedness, conformism, religious bigotry, and downright ugliness of life in the provinces.[27]

Literary critics have stated that Kroetz was always interested in "cripples as victims"[28] as part of his broader concern with "'damaged' persons from the lowest social milieu."[29] Closer attention to the characters in Kroetz's works, however, reveals something much more complex and fascinating than a simplistic portrayal of disabled people as helpless victims of meanness and cruelty. One of the unique things about disability as a constituting factor in the construction of an outsider group is that—unlike other causes of social marginalization—disability is something that can happen to anyone at any time. That is, one's body may suddenly or gradually stop functioning in an accustomed way and begin to function in a new, unfamiliar way. Social and cultural discourses about disability often overlook this basic fact with the result that impenetrable boundaries are frequently drawn between the disabled and the normal. The aesthetic effect of this misconceived binarism is a stereotype. Kroetz's works, by contrast, do not fall into this common trap of essentializing disability. Rather, time and again he has created situations in which characters unexpectedly become disabled or are confronted with the effects of disability. In these new situations, both the disabled characters and those around them are forced to deal with the consequences in daily life of having their bodies function in a different way from what they have always assumed to be normal. Accordingly, disability for Kroetz is a means to set narration in motion, which is a common technique in all sorts of cultural texts. Yet he does not rely on the outworn aesthetic strategy of using disability as a ready metaphor for social ruin, evil, and so forth. Rather, he is concerned with subtly working out how characters respond to being placed in new situations that disrupt their accustomed patterns of daily life. Almost all his characters have few or no economic or intellectual resources, and so his portrayal of disability in this provincial milieu is all the more unique and thought provoking.

Kroetz uses disability as a catalyst for the dramatic tensions and conflicts among his characters in a group of his first short plays that made him famous. All of these plays take place in the present in a Bavarian village or farm milieu that seems almost premodern or at most early capitalist. The characters are generally uneducated and ignorant, they are deeply and fearfully Catholic, they value conformity and worry constantly about what others might think of them, they have hardly any conception of individual rights, and they are anxious about their economic security. In such a milieu, as Kroetz presents it, any sort of deviation from accustomed patterns of life is usually perceived as a potential threat to livelihood, reputation, and identity. Generally speaking, Kroetz uses the disruptiveness of disability to show how his characters in this social milieu react to change.

In the first of these plays, *Der Soldat* (The Soldier, written in 1968, premiered in 1987), a young veteran, Helmut, has had a foot amputated due to an army training accident and returns to his fiancée, Christine, and his family in his small hometown. Both Christine's father and Helmut's father own inns in the town, and before the accident Helmut and Christine had planned to marry and run the inns together. When Helmut returns, the town first celebrates him as a hero, but then other considerations take over. His father disinherits him and says that he will leave his inn to a younger, healthy son, Axl. Christine breaks off their engagement, gets an abortion rather than have Helmut's child, and will probably marry Axl. Driven to despair, Helmut hangs himself at the end of the play. In contrast to this harrowing plot, Kroetz employs a sober, matter-of-fact style in which the pauses and silences in the dialogue are often just as meaningful as what the characters say. The effect of this is that his early plays are a kind of learning laboratory for the audience in the Brechtian sense.

In *Der Soldat,* Helmut's sudden, unexpected disability forces the other characters to confront moral dilemmas revolving around how they are going to react to him now as someone they have always accepted unconditionally before. For a while Christine vacillates, and she views Helmut with a rather complex mixture of liking, pity, aesthetic considerations, and economic calculations. Finally, however, she decides to reject him, explaining, "Because I always wanted a husband who's normal. One who don't have nothing wrong with him before the wedding."[30] She upholds the traditional view of normality in her world by excluding Helmut from sexuality and marriage due to his physical appearance and perceived inability to be a breadwinner.

If Christine's reactions to Helmut are somewhat multifaceted, the reactions of the two fathers are much less ambiguous. Christine's father, Heinrich, tries to dissuade his daughter from marrying Helmut, saying that of all the disabled veterans he knows none was able to come to terms with his disability or make a good living. While Heinrich may pity Helmut, he cannot imagine how someone with such an injury could provide for his daughter. Claiming that "a cripple ain't nothing but a cripple" (169), Heinrich declares that Helmut's mutilation has deformed his character, too, for otherwise he would have been careful not to get Christine pregnant, and he urges Christine to get an abortion. Here he voices the age-old fallacy that physical disability necessarily causes character defects, thus absolutizing the difference that Helmut represents.

Since Willi, Helmut's father, cares more for his son, he is a somewhat more complex character. Yet even he seems to be driven mainly by economic considerations that are intertwined with worries about the opinions of others. He does not believe that Helmut is physically capable of running the inn, and even if he were Willi thinks his appearance is unacceptable for an innkeeper. Willi goes so far as to order his wife to bar Helmut from the restaurant, remarking, "Just look how he hobbles through the pub, what a sight he is. How the customers stare" (167). Stating that the customers can expect to be served properly, Willi declares that a "wooden leg" is a "disgrace" and Helmut cannot possibly be a headwaiter for "he ruins the atmosphere" (168). As is typical in all his works about disability, Kroetz is unusually perceptive in these passages about mechanisms of exclusion that have to do with appearance rather than capability. Willi cannot bear the fact that the customers stare at Helmut, thus marking him as aesthetically deficient and embodying suffering in the midst of a place meant for enjoyment. Consequently, in order to avoid being stigmatized by association, Willi excludes Helmut from the public sphere of work. He promises Helmut, however, that he will provide him with board and lodging for the rest of his life, thus upholding a traditional view of disabled people as only fit to be recipients of charity.

Helmut tries to convince the others that he can still participate in the realms of sexuality and work, even with his changed body. Having grown up in the same milieu as the nondisabled characters, however, he shares their insecurities. Repeatedly he asks Christine whether she really loves him or finds him repulsive, thus indicating his own doubts about himself. With respect to work, Helmut insists that as soon as he gets a better-functioning English prosthesis he will be able to work just as well as before. When Willi does not believe this and Axl urges Helmut to study at the university, Helmut complains that he is an innkeeper's son and can't possibly become a lawyer or minister. In such passages, Helmut's own limitations in how he thinks about disability become evident. He can imagine overcoming his disability in order to fit back into the familiar working world, but he cannot imagine accepting the different way his body now functions and beginning another, less physically demanding career that potentially could be quite satisfying. Consequently, there is a ring of truth to Axl's resentful accusation that Helmut is stubbornly refusing to begin a new life: "Because you're a martyr and a hero. And we have to lick your boots" (179). In the end, Helmut's suicide appears to be motivated just as much by his inflexible attachment to his previous plans as by the rejection of others.

It is precisely this stubbornness that Kroetz highlighted in the second version of *Der Soldat,* entitled *Hartnäckig* (Stubborn). Written in 1970, this play established his reputation as an important young playwright when it premiered, together with his *Heimarbeit* ("Home Work" or "Cottage Labor") in the Werkraumtheater of the Munich Kammerspiele in 1971. Tumultuous protests accompanied the performances of this pair of one-act plays due to their taboo-breaking scenes of sexual intercourse, masturbation, and an abortion attempt with a knitting needle. But critics recognized the aesthetic quality of the plays and the depth of their characterization, stating, for example, that "these crippled, hardened people with their pathetic efforts to survive are not exotic monsters, but creatures from daily life, Everyman figures."[31]

Disability is a minor but significant theme in *Heimarbeit,* for the illegitimate baby is born with "bumps" on his head that cause the betrayed husband to hate him even more as "deformed" and "abnormal." In *Hartnäckig,* however, Helmut's disability remains the central theme of the play. Compared to the earlier version, Kroetz made substantial revisions in the plot that result in changed perceptions of disability and daily life. There are more short scenes between Christine and Helmut in which they talk about or have sex, and Christine seems more committed to loving Helmut. He, on the other hand, seems more self-conscious and suspicious. As in the earlier version, Christine finally decides to reject Helmut, but here she emphasizes aesthetic considerations, telling her father, "His foot's something you can't get used to. . . . You ain't never seen the stump, makes you want to vomit."[32] The two fathers are somewhat more multidimensional in the later version. While Christine's father still pays for her to have an abortion, he also voices mild criticism of Helmut's father for disinheriting him. And, while Helmut's father is thinking primarily about his business and financial security, he offers to pay for Helmut to study at the university so he can have a new profession. In this version, Helmut's brother Axl is a young child, and so the theme of competition for Christine's love is omitted.

As in *Der Soldat,* all the characters are caught up to some extent in inflexible attitudes and habits, and they frequently have only proverbs or clichés at their disposal to try to come to grips with the new situation Helmut's disability presents. When Helmut's parents discuss Christine's pregnancy, for example, his mother remarks, "Cripples and crazies are oversexed, they say" (17). But, in general, the revisions shift the emphasis more toward Helmut's own stubbornness. He refuses to believe that Christine could still love him, he declares that he cannot be a student, and he places just as much emphasis on property as his father does. At the end of this play, Helmut does not commit suicide, but rather he plays a game that endangers his little brother and then watches angrily while his father burns his pornographic magazines. Here the disabled character appears less victimized and more responsible for his predicament, while the other characters seem somewhat more willing to adjust their concepts of normality. In this context, Helmut's father even makes a significant reference to children affected by thalidomide, stating that the situation would be easier to deal with if their younger son were disabled. He muses to his wife, "It'd be better if Axl was crippled and Helmut was healthy. Then I could fix things. Then I'd send Axl to the university because then it wouldn't matter if he'd be a teacher or doctor. Not a bit. Just look at everything the state does for the thalidomide kids" (14). In this short play, Kroetz imagined that possibilities might exist for a newly disabled man from this particular social milieu to lead a fulfilling life, even though his characters are still ensnared in fears of change.

Both of these plays belong in the context of German sociocultural debates about disabled veterans after World War II. In the heated controversies over rearmament that began in the 1950s, opponents in both East and West Germany constantly invoked the danger of becoming disabled as one of their main arguments against creating a new army.[33] Kroetz's two plays are rare depictions in postwar literature of a physically disabled veteran whose amputation results from an army accident in peacetime rather than in war but who nevertheless experiences rejection. Although statistics show that many disabled veterans in fact found employment and social integration, Kroetz wanted to bring out what he saw as continuities with fascism lurking underneath the surface of well-to-do West Germany. Consequently, he focused on mechanisms of social exclusion still directed against outsiders in daily life in his portrayal of this disabled veteran.

Kroetz's next play that revolves around disability takes place on a Bavarian farm. An even more notable theatrical success, his *Stallerhof* (Staller's Farm, written in 1971) premiered in 1972 at the Deutsches Schauspielhaus in Hamburg, enjoyed a two-year run there with over one hundred performances, and featured Eva Mattes as Beppi in the first major role for this subsequently famous actress. Later the Austrian composer Gerd Kühr made it into an opera, which premiered in Munich in 1988. In this play, the fourteen-year-old Beppi, who—possibly because of her extreme nearsightedness—appears to be cognitively disabled, becomes pregnant by a middle-aged, down-and-out farmhand named Sepp. Her father chases Sepp away from the farm, and her mother considers giving her an abortion. In the final scene, Beppi is going into labor. As in his plays about the disabled veteran, Kroetz does not use disability as a metaphor here. Rather, as was the case with Helmut, Kroetz simply explores the ramifications of Beppi's disability in daily life. The gender and class relationships in *Stallerhof* are different, however, for Beppi is a cognitively disabled girl from a religious, uneducated, rather poor farm family.

Described by the director of the Hamburg production as a "strange love story between two outsiders,"[34] the style of *Stallerhof* radicalizes the sparseness of Kroetz's other early plays in that here the characters are inarticulate almost to the point of muteness. With respect to how disability functions in the play, this means it is important to pay attention to the silences and stage directions as well as the dialogue. Beppi's parents waver between treating her roughly and showing hints of kindness. For example, at one point her father remarks that she is "retarded," and her mother says bluntly, "You're backward, listen to what papa says. You don't make us happy."[35] They are worried about what others might think of them for not preventing their young daughter's pregnancy. Her "retardation" rather than her age leads them even to consider murdering her, and her mother muses, "People say that nutcases don't feel death like us" (283). For religious reasons, they reject this way out of their predicament, but the mother still decides to give Beppi a home abortion. For a long pause, Beppi stands naked before her mother, who finally cannot bring herself to perform the abortion. She sends her daughter off to get dressed with the words, "You're freezing, dummy" (285), which is as close as she ever comes to expressing tenderness. Beppi's parents seem to want to protect her at times, but they are trapped within the limitations of their socioeconomic class.

Sepp both takes advantage of Beppi's ignorance and trustfulness and—in contrast to her parents—appears to accept her more for who she is. After Beppi's father orders him to leave the farm, he promises Beppi that he will come back to see the child and tells her, "You ain't got no rights, you ain't nothing, that's it" (282). Sepp thus displays a certain empathetic understanding for Beppi that emerges from his own experience of social marginalization. Beppi herself hardly speaks, and her difficulties with language strengthen the impression that she is a young teenager under the control of others. Nevertheless, at certain points it appears that she has more of an inner life than she can express in words. She tries to keep her parents from finding out what she is doing because she likes Sepp and enjoys having sex with him. And, when Sepp is packing to leave, Beppi cries and begs him not to go, saying, "Stick with you, me" (282). In such passages, together with Beppi's nude scene, Kroetz indicates the fundamental humanity of this girl with all her limitations.

Some of the critics who wrote about *Stallerhof* seem to have been so caught up in traditional discourses of disability that they were unable to see the subtleties in Kroetz's play. For this group of critics, Sepp and Beppi were nothing but "animals," and the play confirmed their opinion that Kroetz was a dramatist of "abnormalcy."[36] But other critics—while they did not deal explicitly with the theme of disability—perceived both the depth of characterization and the socially critical impetus of the play. Ulrich Heising, for example, who directed the play's premiere in Hamburg, explained that the main problem for the actors was how to avoid exoticizing and denouncing the figures. Accordingly, this production conceived of Beppi as a complicated character who is not just a "pitiful victim" and in general sought to bring out the problem of violence directed against outsiders.[37] Positive reviews of the play emphasized that all the characters are deformed by social norms and that with this "complaint about the world's miserable conditions" Kroetz had achieved an unusual poetic depth that went far beyond run-of-the-mill political theater.[38]

The continuation of *Stallerhof,* entitled *Geisterbahn* (House of Horrors), was written in 1971 but did not premiere until 1975 in Vienna. In this play, Beppi, Sepp, and their baby, Georg, live together in Munich until Sepp dies. Beppi's parents arrange for Georg to be institutionalized in a children's home, but Beppi kills her baby rather than be forced to give him up. At the end, Beppi is in prison. *Geisterbahn* was performed much less often than *Stallerhof,* probably because the subject matter was no longer so novel. The play brings up some thought-provoking perspectives on disability, however, which critics did not seem to notice. One review stated, for example, that the aesthetic weakness of the play lies in the fact that it seems reasonable to take the baby away from Beppi for "a living child in an institution is better than a strangled one in the hands of a feebleminded woman."[39] There is no indication that Beppi would have killed her baby, however, if her parents and the welfare officials had allowed her to keep him. While Kroetz shows Beppi as having serious limitations, he also includes scenes that show her taking good care of the baby. The sparse reception of this play could also reflect a lack of openness to its unfamiliar idea that a character such as Beppi might deserve a chance to live independently. It is easy to imagine productions of *Geisterbahn* that might be more successful today in view of current discussions in Germany about independent living for people with learning difficulties.[40]

Kroetz's concern for how West German society treated the poorest of the poor, as he put it, led him to join the German Communist Party (DKP) in 1972.[41] For the next several years, along with becoming established in the theater world, he was extremely active politically and even ran for office. By 1980, however, he had decided to resign from the DKP, citing his disagreements with party policy over political and ecological issues.[42] With respect to his writing, the years around 1980 also seem to have been a turning point. In notes written at this time, Kroetz reassessed his previous works as having been too negative and stated that now he wanted to depict real alternatives and positive utopian moments.[43] In other words, rather than focusing mainly on dead ends of oppression and suffering, he also wanted to show the points at which people on the bottom were moved to resist. Kroetz then spent several years writing his one major prose work, a two-volume novel. Its main character is a young Bavarian farm boy who contracts polio at the age of six in 1938, becomes disabled, is institutionalized, barely escapes Nazi "euthanasia," and grows up in a postwar West Germany that avoids coming to terms with its past. The novel is an exercise in imagining how even such a character, who is potentially among the most victimized figures imaginable, not only could have survived but could also try to live life to the fullest.

The two volumes of the novel, *Der Mondscheinknecht* (The Moonlight Farmhand, 1981) and *Der Mondscheinknecht: Fortsetzung* (The Moonlight Farmhand: Continuation, 1983), were part of a larger, uncompleted project. Kroetz wrote unpublished dramatic scenes for parts of the novel,[44] and he intended to publish a third volume.[45] As a result, there are certain gaps in the narration. On the whole, however, I know of no other postwar German literary work written before Kroetz's novels that portrays a disabled character so realistically and empathetically, above all in the passages about the childhood of the main character, Anton Kreuzberger. Significantly, the novel revolves around questions of memory, for Anton is working as a typesetter in the 1970s and has decided to write the story of his life.

As in Kroetz's plays, the novel explores what happens when disability unexpectedly appears in the daily life of a tradition-bound farm family. By situating Anton's childhood during the Third Reich, however, Kroetz raised the stakes much higher for his characters. Anton's family seems apolitical and largely preoccupied with farmwork. Yet what Kroetz develops so well in his portrayal of these rural people is their varying reactions to Anton after he becomes disabled and the political consequences of their behavior. Far from simply denouncing the characters as fascists, the novel subtly depicts attitudes toward excluding or including someone who is different in this milieu—here, uniquely so, a visibly disabled character—during and after the Third Reich.

Before contracting polio, Anton is a beloved son and heir to the family farm. His family, however, reconfigures their situation drastically as a result of his illness and subsequent disability. Kroetz's descriptions of polio as a viral disease that first mimics influenza, of Anton's weakness and collapse, of his confinement to an iron lung in a Munich hospital, and of his subsequent difficulties walking with crutches are notable for their accuracy. This realistic depiction of the illness and its aftereffects makes the novel's probe into the family's mentality all the more believable. Anton's father has two main concerns. First, he basically writes off Anton as useless, since he cannot perform heavy farmwork, and turns his attention more toward his nondisabled younger son. Second, uneducated and not understanding that polio is a contagious disease, he views it as somehow a hereditary defect that is a shameful blot on his good name. At various points, the novel shows the peasants as susceptible to Nazi eugenic ideology because of the importance they attach to good breeding in their farm animals. Viewing human stock in the same way, Anton's father sees his crippled son (in the Bavarian dialect *pressthaft*) as disgracing him in the community. At first, Anton's mother is more concerned about her son, insists on taking him to the doctor, visits him in the hospital, and tries to heal him with holy water from Lourdes. However, she stops visiting him when she realizes that he will remain a cripple. In 1939, his family abandons him, just as Nazi plans to kill certain disabled people in institutions are getting under way.

Anton remains alone, shuffled from one institution to another, until the end of the war. In the chapter entitled "Resurrection: He Was Lucky," Kroetz imagines in a unique way a child's survival and even small instances of self-assertion in the midst of the Nazi "euthanasia" wards in 1941. Of course, Nazi "euthanasia" was aimed at those considered to be hereditarily diseased and not at those who had contracted contagious diseases such as polio. But historians have shown how people who did not fall into Nazi categories for elimination were sometimes swept up in the killing process. In particular, this includes disabled and sick people of all ages in institutions whose families did not have the economic resources to care for them at home. It is thus quite realistic for Kroetz to depict his Anton as belonging to a heterogeneous group of institutionalized children. When Anton first arrives at the institution, he thinks he is better than the others because he is merely physically disabled and announces, "I ain't like you. You're all dummies."[46] He then becomes close to a "Mongoloid" boy and is crushed when uniformed men take his new friend away along with the other cognitively disabled children. Kroetz thus imagines cross-disability solidarity to be possible within this group of outcasts from the Nazi racial community. The personnel at the institution react in varying ways to the "selection" of the children. One nurse tells Anton to be glad he is still alive and forget what happened. Another hangs herself, however, because of her guilt over having unwittingly collaborated in sending the children to their deaths. This chapter thus anticipates the themes of guilt and memory that become so central after the end of the war.

In 1946, Anton's family suddenly receives a letter from the institution informing them that he is able to return home. When he arrives they are not enthusiastic about seeing him again, especially on discovering that he can only walk with difficulty using crutches. Just as when Anton first became ill, thoughts of hard physical labor and disgrace in the eyes of others shape their reactions to this unexpected turn of events. When it becomes clear that Anton is not able to do heavy work, his father orders him to stay away from the barn and the fields. At first, his family tries to include him in other activities, but Kroetz shows again, in an unusually perceptive way, how outside pressures mitigate against this. For example, Anton's parents take him to a local fair, but the negative reactions of others to his visible disability spoil their enjoyment. The narrator recalls, "But it isn't fun. It's like running the gauntlet because when people see the cripple they stare as if they had never seen anybody like that before, as if there were no war-disabled men, as if there were just one cripple like him in the whole world. And you can't move along with him, can't get away from the people, can't sit down and hide in a corner of the beer tent. You have to walk along with him, at his pace, so that you think you're growing roots or the gaping people will eat you up."[47] This passage captures realistically how these rural Germans direct the exclusionary practice of staring against a disabled person who is not a veteran.

The family members react in somewhat different ways to being stigmatized by association with Anton. His father declares that he no longer wants to be seen in public with Anton and so he has to stay at home. Anton's mother goes along with this, and gradually the family isolates him more and more. Finally, his father banishes him to an attic room and takes away his crutches. His kind grandmother, however, views this as imprisonment and buys him a radio for company, while his older sister secretly brings him his crutches at night so he can practice walking. Anton calls himself the "moonlight farmhand" because he sneaks out of the house and walks around the farmyard in the moonlight. Anton's exclusion from his family's daily life appears to be motivated mainly by the disciplinary effect of the shame his parents feel. Living in a premodern milieu that values unquestioning conformism over enlightened, independent judgment, they choose to uphold group norms of appearance, health, and function by distancing themselves from Anton rather than standing by him.[48]

Beyond this level of the plot, however, there is another way in which complex feelings of shame, disgrace, and guilt appear to motivate the exclusion of Anton. This physically disabled character also functions as the voice of memory about the Nazi past, a voice that no one in this postwar setting wants to hear. When Anton returns home, he not only tries as hard as he can to participate in daily life, but he also wants to talk about everything that happened to him in the institution: about the doctors, the nurses, and his narrow escape from "euthanasia." Not only do his parents refuse to listen, but they also want to prevent him from telling neighbors about his experiences. They think, "This has to stop, . . . he runs around like a crazy horsefly and takes all the disgrace everywhere, and tells everybody things that maybe they don't even want to know, and if they do want to know, that's even worse" (126). The parents feel disgraced because their son is speaking about Nazi crimes that they want to forget. Consequently, they distance themselves from Anton, who represents the disturbing factor of memory and guilt in their lives.

It is precisely in order tell his own story that Anton decides as an adult to write about his childhood as well as his present situation. He is working as a typesetter, and his colleagues respect him enough to have elected him as their trade union representative. Outside the workplace, though, he leads a frustrated, solitary life. These chapters, which take place in the present, are less convincing in that Anton sometimes serves too much as a didactic mouthpiece for Kroetz's theses about politics and sexuality in contemporary West Germany. Most significantly for the theme of disability, however, Anton examines how others have treated him and how his inner life has been affected by humiliation and rejection. In this context, he thinks, "You have to tell your own truth. That wounds you, but roots grow from these wounds, such strong roots that no one can pull them out again. A network of rooted identity" (91). With this validation of Anton's search for authentic self-expression, Kroetz moved into the orbit of the new subjectivity of the 1980s. He avoided the solipsistic moments of this literary trend, however, by portraying his Anton as continuing to hope—perhaps against hope—that eventually some connection can be made between his story and the broader world around him.

The two volumes of Kroetz's novel attracted relatively little critical interest. This was partly due to flaws in the work's structure but also, in my opinion, because in the early 1980s there was not yet a broad discussion in West Germany about the significance of Nazi crimes against disabled people and the persistence of exclusionary practices in the postwar period. At this time, the disability rights movement was in its infancy, and disabled West German activists were just beginning to insist publicly on the cultural and political importance of telling their stories. As a consequence, there were hardly any competing, let alone emancipatory, discourses about disability that were forceful enough to challenge most critics' comfortable assumption of an inevitable separation between the worlds of the "disabled" and the "normal." Accordingly, critics praised the "authenticity" of Kroetz's "ribald, earthy scenes from Bavarian peasant life,"[49] but they generally overlooked the novel's greatest strength: its convincing social criticism expressed through the realistic portrayal of a disabled man's life story.

Kroetz produced and directed one more play that revolves around a disabled character whose difficulties in standing by his own truth recall Anton's project of telling his story. In 1986, Kroetz's adaptation of Ernst Toller's *Hinkemann* (1924), entitled *Der Nusser* (The Gelding), premiered at the Munich Residenztheater. Kroetz made extensive changes in Toller's tragedy about a veteran whose genitals are mutilated in the war and who returns home to his wife. These revisions did not prevent him from taking over Toller's metaphorical approach to disability, which led to a confused backtracking from Kroetz's previous depictions of disabled characters simply as ordinary human beings searching for happiness. This is most evident in Kroetz's entirely new scene (act II, scene 3) between Hinkemann and a dwarf. Here disability stands for ruin and destruction, and the dwarf asserts in his inflammatory speeches that if all people would admit that they are inner cripples a transformed life might be possible. The expressionistic pathos of the scene seems outdated, while the cliché that everyone is somehow disabled deflects attention away from Hinkemann's specific situation and the reactions of the other characters to him.

More significant with respect to the place of disability in theater, however, is that the dwarf urges Hinkemann to "show his wounds" rather than shamefully trying to hide what happened to him. This exhortation becomes physically concrete, as described in the stage directions: "From the alleys brave people slowly emerge. They are visibly disabled. They position themselves on the ramp and look at the audience. This lasts a very long time."[50] The dwarf invites Hinkemann to leave his isolation and join this community of the disabled, which Hinkemann angrily and fearfully refuses to do. It was this scene featuring disabled actors that provoked the indignation of some critics. For example, Rudolf Helmstetter attacked the scene as a "blind, pointless provocation that both terrorizes the spectator and exploits the walk-ons in question."[51] The appearance of disabled actors onstage seems to have been so unusual that this reviewer could not imagine there might be something worth exploring both aesthetically and politically in a call to ally oneself with their particular forms of embodiment.

Kroetz had affirmed that genuinely disabled bodies had a place onstage even in the notes to his earliest play, *Der Soldat,* where he stated that ideally the main character should be played by an actor with an amputated foot.[52] This rare openness to employing disabled people as actors was noticed by Peter Radtke, founder of the Munich Crüppel Cabaret and director of the Project Group on Disabled People in the Media (Arbeitsgemeinschaft Behinderte in den Medien). Born in 1943 with brittle bone disease, Radtke had narrowly escaped Nazi "euthanasia" thanks to his supportive parents and a sympathetic doctor.[53] He had already acted in a Medea play directed by George Tabori at the Munich Kammerspiele, and now Radtke suggested that Kroetz should direct him in a one-man dramatization of Franz Kafka's "Ein Bericht für eine Akademie" (Report to an Academy). The two collaborated at the Kammerspiele in 1986 on the production of Kafka's story about an ape who becomes civilized by renouncing all his animal strengths, and Radtke's success has led to many subsequent performances and roles for him. Initially, his appearance onstage as a severely disabled actor was met with incomprehension from most critics, whose negative reaction was captured in a rhetorical headline in the *Bildzeitung:* "Darf ein Behinderter einen Affen spielen?" (May a Handicapped Man Play an Ape?) (137). In recent years, however, a more sophisticated critical approach is developing with regard to the aesthetic and political effects of including a wider range of bodily variation in the performing arts.[54] To return to Kroetz, one could say that the impressive efforts of this nondisabled writer to thematize disability have been partly superseded on the cultural scene by disabled writers, actors, and dancers who are inventing new ways to express their embodied truths.

In the works discussed here, Kroetz was concerned with the mechanisms of social exclusion that make a disabled person into an outsider. That is, he presented disability as socially constructed in a way that was quite unusual for the time in which he was writing. In his complex approach, the nondisabled characters are not uniformly indifferent or cruel but are shown either as trapped by the limitations of their circumstances or as even having certain glimmers of humaneness and understanding. The disabled characters are not only victims but are shown, on the one hand, as also entrapped in their milieu and thus not willing to take advantage of some of the real possibilities open to them. On the other hand, at times they demonstrate a certain potential for self-assertiveness even in their extremely constricted situations. Kroetz does not denounce his nondisabled characters only as perpetrators, and he does not exoticize his disabled characters. Rather, he draws attention to the poverty and backward social norms that constrict the lives of all his characters.

"A Cripple as Chancellor?" Wolfgang Schäuble and Franklin D. Roosevelt

On November 25, 1991, the German weekly newsmagazine *Der Spiegel* featured an article on the prominent Christian Democratic politician Wolfgang Schäuble, who was widely regarded as the most likely conservative successor to Chancellor Helmut Kohl. The cover photo, captioned "Will he hold up?" showed Schäuble seated in his wheelchair in a thoughtful pose, while another photo placed him in the awkwardly posed center of a group of his cabinet colleagues. Schäuble, the minister of the interior, had been shot in an assassination attempt in October 1990, shortly after German reunification, and as a result his legs were paralyzed. Now back on the job and using a wheelchair, he was about to assume the chairmanship of the Christian Democratic Union (CDU) in the German Bundestag. This position gave him a great deal of leverage in his attempt to convince his party to select him as its future candidate for chancellor. As *Der Spiegel* commented on this new situation, "After Kohl has finished off all his opponents within his party, it could seem as though he is making a mockery of Schäuble's possible rivals by setting up a paralytic as his potential successor to the chancellorship. Kohl talks about the example of U.S. President Franklin D. Roosevelt, who, Kohl says, also governed his country from a wheelchair. The important difference: Roosevelt, who contracted polio, could walk unaided (though with crutches). Schäuble is paralyzed from the third vertebra down, and the wheelchair is his irrevocable fate."[55]

Yet of course the wheelchair was also Roosevelt's irrevocable fate. The fact that the leading German newsmagazine could present such an erroneous description of the U.S. president more than forty-five years after his death testifies to the enduring legacy of Roosevelt's efforts to control his public image. While this strategy was entirely necessary during his lifetime in order for him to attain his goals, it has also perpetuated misconceptions about the true extent of his disability in popular memory. Roosevelt and Schäuble are not at all comparable in terms of political stature as Schäuble is basically a clever, conservative bureaucrat. However, from the instant when he set out to reenter the German political arena in a wheelchair, media depictions of his disability became central to all speculations about whether he was capable of filling the highest political office. Debates about Schäuble's qualifications have been enmeshed with the images that the German public sees of him. On this side of the Atlantic, another kind of controversy arose in recent years over the depiction of Roosevelt's disability at the new memorial to him in Washington, D.C. Therefore, juxtaposing

Fig. 22. Wolfgang Schäuble: "Will he hold up?" (From *Der Spiegel,* November 25, 1991. Courtesy of SPIEGEL-Verlag.)

the visual images of these two prominent politicians is a way to focus on the changing perceptions and symbolic meanings of disability in the United States and Germany.[56]

Historians have documented in detail the great lengths to which Roosevelt went, almost always with the cooperation of the press, to present himself to the public as nondisabled after he contracted polio in 1921 at the age of thirty-nine.[57] After that, he used a wheelchair and was only able to take a few precarious steps alone using braces and crutches. Yet Roosevelt was also a wealthy, well-established politician, which certainly made it easier for him to reenter politics in spite of speculation about his physical condition. He became governor of New York in 1928 and was elected to his first term as president in 1932. Shortly into his fourth term, he died on April 12, 1945, at the Little White House in Warm Springs, Georgia, close to the treatment center for polio that he had founded.

Roosevelt's first major public appearance after contracting polio was at the 1924 Democratic National Convention, when he nominated Al Smith for president. From the outset, he was determined to avoid the stigma of being seen in public using a wheelchair, and he was photographed using crutches at this convention for the first and only time. Later his physical therapist reported him saying, "I'll walk without crutches. I'll walk into a room without scaring everybody half to death. I'll stand easily enough in front of people so that they'll forget I'm a cripple."[58] From then on, Roosevelt employed two strategies to present himself to the public as nondisabled. He exuded an aura of self-confidence and authority, and he avoided disrupting visual expectations of bodily normality. Accordingly, probably the most familiar images of Roosevelt are his trademark big smile with the jaunty cigarette holder and the photographs of him seated between Stalin and Churchill at Yalta.

Any arbitrary selection of media images shows how Roosevelt avoided making his disability a distracting focal point. When standing, he usually either held onto a lectern or gripped the arm of a companion while using one gentlemanly cane. He wore pants cut extra long to hide his metal braces. When sitting, he appeared in ordinary poses: behind the wheel of his car, at his desk, or conversing with other politicians. There are only two photographs that show him using a wheelchair, including a very tender one with his beloved dog Fala and an employee's young daughter at his estate in Hyde Park.

With very few exceptions, which came from the ranks of his most adverse critics, there appears to have been a gentleman's agreement between Roosevelt and the press not to make an issue of his disability or focus on it visually. In contrast to a later politician such as Schäuble (or George Wallace in the United States), Roosevelt lived in the age before television at a time when visual images were much easier to control— and also during the heyday of radio, a medium in which the stigma of visible physical disability disappeared and one that Roosevelt used with great virtuosity. Since he was already a proven politician, perhaps the press granted him the benefit of the doubt when he reentered politics. And after he became president he created a generally cordial relationship with the Washington press corps. It is known that photographers voluntarily destroyed negatives that might have shown his disability too starkly. Even political cartoonists, who traditionally exaggerate the slightest deviations from the norm, never portrayed Roosevelt's disability but focused on other features, most notably his broad grin and the cigarette holder. Cartoons depicting his entire body portrayed him as nondisabled and active.

The representation of Roosevelt's disability is particularly complex. On the one hand, he knew that physical disability was an automatic disqualification for public life let alone for the highest political office. But he also believed that if he could conceal his disability and present a nondisabled image to the public he could attain his goals. In spheres outside the fishbowl of Washington politics, Roosevelt identified himself in certain ways as disabled and became an advocate for disabled people. He established the Georgia Warm Springs Foundation and socialized with other polio patients there; he helped create the National Foundation for Infantile Paralysis (the March of Dimes), which raised money for needy polio patients and supported the development of a polio vaccine; and on at least one occasion he visited a hospital ward for disabled veterans in his wheelchair to comfort and inspire these men.

Of course, Roosevelt's disability was caused by disease and was not hereditary. Nevertheless, it is remarkable that a president with a visibly disabled body was elected for four terms during a period when eugenic thinking was widespread in many countries, including the United States. Given the elevation of eugenics to national ideology in Nazi Germany, it might be logical to think that the Nazi press would have seized on Roosevelt's physical condition as convenient material for anti-American propaganda. Yet the pictorial images of Roosevelt in the Nazi press hardly ever showed his disability, although here a different dynamic was at work than in American visual images of him. A book published in Germany in 1941 called *Roosevelts Reden und Taten im Scheinwerfer der Presse und der Karikatur* (Roosevelt's Speeches and Actions in the Spotlight of the Press and of Political Cartoons) collected cartoons from the German and foreign press that often used hateful anti-Semitic images to depict Roosevelt as a puppet of the Jews, a warmonger, or a failure with his New Deal, but his disability is seldom evident.[59] For example, the book's front cover features Roosevelt admiring his mirror reflection as a Jew. Other cartoons show Roosevelt and Churchill as puppets of the Jews, a blind Roosevelt being led by a Jew (this from a U.S. pro-Nazi newspaper), and Roosevelt being ridden, and thus controlled, by Jews in a "Jewish kindergarten." Another group of cartoons combines anti-Semitic imagery with attacks on America's alleged desire for world domination. The back cover shows a standing Roosevelt placing Uncle Sam's hat over the entire globe, and another cartoon transforms his famous toothy grin into a mouthful of bombs. The satirical magazine *Kladderadatsch* published the only cartoon I know of that shows Roosevelt with two canes, headed down the "path of Wilson" into war. It appears that Nazi images of Roosevelt did not change significantly as the war continued.

Undoubtedly there was a certain amount of knowledge abroad, including in Nazi Germany, about Roosevelt's physical condition, although it is not clear whether foreign observers realized the extent of his impairment. Mussolini made at least one blunt statement in an attack on Roosevelt: "Never in the course of history has a nation been guided by a paralytic. There have been bald kings, fat kings, handsome and even stupid kings, but never kings who, in order to go to the bathroom and the dinner table, had to be supported by other men."[60] In Nazi Germany, commentators on Roosevelt's disability seem to have tried to link his physical illness to alleged mental instability. The Nazi editor of the book of political cartoons, for example, referred to Roosevelt's bout with polio by saying that it was probably possible to understand his mentality only by realizing that he was "a physically broken person who is constantly venting his hysteria."[61]

Hitler himself referred to Roosevelt as manipulated by the Jews, wealthy (in contrast to Hitler's supposedly impoverished origins), and insane. Yet even in his final monologues, which record his more informal conversations, he did not refer to Roosevelt's physical condition. Instead, he emphasized repeatedly his belief that Roosevelt was mentally unstable, as in a passage from March 23, 1942, where he attributed the mass hysteria over the "War of the Worlds" radio broadcast to Roosevelt's unsettling influence: "Roosevelt is insane, as a professor already explained years ago. He rushes chaotically from Washington to his estate out of fear of being bombed, rushes back, and so on. His press statements also show that the man is insane. He's making his whole country hysterical, the way he's going. How could it be possible otherwise that a panic could break out among reasonable people in Chicago because of a radio play about Martians landing there?"[62] Again, it is unclear what Hitler and other Nazi leaders knew about the extent of Roosevelt's disability. However, it is easy to imagine that if photographs of him using a wheelchair had been widely circulating, the Nazi press would have made use of these as an opportunity to portray their great adversary in a negative way.

More than half a century after the longest-serving president devised his strategy for success, the development of the mass media, and above all of television, has made it impossible for public figures to hide a visible disability in the same way. And, more positively put, modern civil rights movements have had some success in disentangling physical characteristics from automatic assignments of social status. Consequently, since Roosevelt's time, awareness has also grown that there should be no compelling reason to hide disability or try to pass in the able-bodied world. The case of Wolfgang Schäuble is particularly interesting in this regard. He is not only a prominent politician with a disability but also an object of media attention in the country that tried during the Nazi period to eliminate all manner of "deviants" from public life. Visual images of Schäuble and other people with disabilities in Germany today can thus be taken as one measure of more tolerant attitudes in the country, which underwent such extreme political and cultural ruptures in the twentieth century.

The visual images of Schäuble in press photographs, in political cartoons, and on German television differ from those of Roosevelt in that Schäuble is always shown using his wheelchair except in a few family shots. These images oscillate between two poles that are complemented by Schäuble's tactic of going on the offensive as a cripple. One group of images—consciously or unconsciously—shows him literally as a foreign body, a disturbance in the normative, well-ordered, physical world. These images provoke discomfort in the viewer, making Schäuble into the object of the stare by showing him sitting while others are standing, sitting alone, or sitting in unusual situations or by using captions that draw attention to his physical condition. One of the best illustrations of this is a photograph of Schäuble perched awkwardly at the top of the steps among the rest of Kohl's cabinet, which makes it seem impossible that such a person could ever fit into this political scene. A similar photograph appeared in the illustrated magazine *Stern* (Star, a kind of German *Life*) on August 20, 1992. Captioned "Unapproachable, Uncanny, Relentless," it shows Schäuble in a row of other people who are only visible from the waist down. This article stereotypically attributed Schäuble's hard-nosed brand of politics to his supposed bitterness over being excluded from the normal world. A second group of photographs, however, treats Schäuble's disability in a more matter-of-fact way by not making the wheelchair into a personal or political feature that overrides all his other traits. Numerous images show him sitting and conversing with Kohl and other politicians or addressing the Bundestag in his wheelchair from the podium.

Political cartoons featuring Schäuble always show his wheelchair, in contrast to those depicting Roosevelt, and also reflect these ambivalent perceptions of disability. In some, the wheelchair is simply a fact but is not central to the political point being made. In others, the perception of disability is inextricably entangled in the political statement. These all center around the fact that Kohl and the CDU had begun to have serious difficulties in the early 1990s due to the political and economic problems associated with reunification. One cartoon shows a diminutive Schäuble with his wheelchair hitched to a large wagon, labeled "CDU," containing Kohl and other politicians. Is it an impossible task for this disabled politician to save his party? Another, captioned "Getting Out of the Critical Zone," shows a clearly overburdened Schäuble zooming along in his wheelchair, almost crushed by Kohl, who is sitting on his lap. Yet another, captioned "The Miracle Weapon," shows Schäuble as an archer in his wheelchair, leading the CDU forces into battle. Is he hopelessly inadequate to the task, or is he a courageous fighter?[63]

These ambivalent views of disability also come through in the letters to the editor that reacted to *Der Spiegel*'s cover story on Schäuble. Some readers viewed his disability as an automatic disqualification for political office. One stated, "Now Kohl has picked somebody whom no one can compete with out of simple decency—even though it must be obvious to every clearly thinking person that a man with such a severe handicap as Schäuble's is physically not up to the stress of being chancellor." Others criticized *Der Spiegel* for emphasizing Schäuble's disability so strongly in the article and called for a more objective appraisal, as did one reader who wrote, "If Dr. Schäuble holds up, that will depend only on his politics and not on the wheelchair portrayed on your cover."[64] Such statements indicate the ongoing tension between older, negative stereotypes that equate disability with incompetence and more liberal, tolerant attitudes.

Until Helmut Kohl finally announced in April 1997 that he would run for a fifth term as chancellor, Schäuble was looked upon as the most likely Christian Democratic candidate. During these years, he was determined to bury the issue of the wheelchair once and for all by appropriating for himself the pejorative vocabulary that his opponents had sometimes directed against him. He went on the offensive in the January 9, 1997, issue of *Stern*, appearing seated in his hand cycle on the cover. The headline quoted him: "'A Cripple as Chancellor? Yes, the Question Must Be Asked': Wolfgang Schäuble on His Future and His Relationship to Kohl." The magazine interviewed him about his health, which was described as stable, and his close relationship with Kohl, noting that 57 percent of the respondents to a recent poll believed him qualified to be chancellor in spite of his disability. In the next week's issue, the editor reported that he had never received as much criticism as he had for this cover story and printed a sampling of indignant letters. Most readers had not noticed that the headline was a quote from Schäuble himself, and so they accused *Stern* of gross insensitivity for describing him as a cripple. A few others challenged his political qualifications, while only one characterized his disability as a metaphor for incompetence. That person stated, "Why shouldn't a cripple become chancellor? The German people are limping along in a bad way, anyhow. So a chancellor in a wheelchair fits into the picture really well."

The subsequent media discussion about the *Stern* article evaluated it as highly significant for Schäuble's efforts to break two taboos. First, he had publicly expressed his interest in becoming Kohl's successor. Second, by appropriating for himself the negative label "cripple," he had made it more difficult for his political adversaries to take a patronizing approach toward him. Along these lines, for example, *Der Spiegel* stated on February 10, 1997, "Only by constantly breaking taboos can he convince the Germans, who are always curious and torn back and forth between admiration and discomfiture, that his existence as a paraplegic is only marginally different from real life. . . . The leader of the CDU wants to prove that a politician needs little more than a head and arms to be successful." In spite of all these efforts, however, Schäuble became entangled in the financial scandals of the Kohl administration, and this made him no longer viable as a candidate for chancellor.

The bluntness with which both Schäuble and journalists visualized and described his disability has both positive and negative aspects. On the one hand, as a disability rights advocate noted, the *Stern* cover photograph could be taken as an emancipatory portrait, for it shows how Schäuble covers new terrain with his hand cycle.[65] Furthermore, by calling himself a cripple, Schäuble took control of this pejorative term for himself, although he has never associated himself with disability rights efforts. On the other hand, some journalists continued to characterize him as "nothing but a head" or photographed him in ways that called unnecessary attention to the wheelchair. For example, when there was talk in 2004 that the CDU might nominate Schäuble as its candidate for federal president, the magazine section of the *Süddeutsche Zeitung* featured a cover photograph on February 13 of an empty wheelchair, enlarged and distorted grotesquely by the low-angle shot. The caption read, "The President's Seat." The accompanying article complained that Schäuble would not be able to stand and chat at cocktail parties and whined, "When the wheelchair is empty, it almost looks like an electric chair."[66] In the end, due at least as much to inner-party wrangles as to his disability, Schäuble was not nominated.[67] Still, such recurring representations emphasize his freakishness as a disabled politician trying to function on the national and world stages.

The debate about whether to include a frank depiction of Franklin D. Roosevelt's disability at the new memorial dedicated to him in Washington, D.C., took quite a different form than the debates about Schäuble. Rather than an argument over the tactic of aggressive openness, this controversy revolved around whether the memorial should conceal Roosevelt's disability, given that he presented himself to the public as nondisabled, or whether it should show him sitting in his wheelchair. The Memorial Commission decided to build a sculpture that shows Roosevelt in a typical public pose: sitting in a chair with his long U.S. Navy cape draped around him and covering his lower body. In the original plans, the memorial refers to his disability with small wheels on the chair legs in back and the subtle way in which one of his legs is shown as somewhat withered (a detail that would probably be lost on most viewers), through a time-line inscription noting that after he had polio he "never again walked unaided," and with a museum replica of the kitchen chair on wheels that he sometimes used. As the chief architect of the memorial, Lawrence Halprin, explained, "Roosevelt was very desirous of keeping his disability out of the limelight. We're not trying to hide it, but it would be going against his desire to evidence it in a sculpture."[68]

As soon as the design of the memorial became public, disability rights activists and some historians began to protest the omission of a clear depiction of Roosevelt's disability and called for the memorial to include another statue showing him sitting in his wheelchair. From this standpoint, while it had been necessary half a century ago for Roosevelt to conceal his disability in order to continue his political career, times had now changed due to the efforts of the disability rights movement. For example, the Rhode Island secretary of state, James Langevin, who has used a wheelchair since 1980, wrote to the Memorial Commission that Roosevelt's decision to conceal his disability was more a testament to his times, when disability was viewed as a sign of weakness, than to a "strongly felt personal desire to hide this basic fact about his life from future generations." Langevin and others suggested that if Roosevelt had been president at a later time he probably would have actively supported civil rights legislation such as the Americans with Disabilities Act rather than "remaining a silent voice."[69]

As the protests mounted, the Memorial Commission was pressured into releasing a statement on March 1, 1995, addressing issues brought up by those whom it termed "individuals in the handicapped community."[70] This response presented two main justifications for refusing to depict Roosevelt in a wheelchair. First, Senator Daniel Inouye, cochair of the commission, emphasized how important it had been for the U.S. president to project a strong image during the war, stating, "I for one would not want to redo history. FDR was Commander-in-Chief of the greatest fighting force in the world and he wanted to be viewed as a strong leader. I would hate to see the man exploited after he was dead." Second, Curtis Roosevelt recalled his grandfather's stoicism, writing,

"He was a very private person and went to great lengths to avoid any discussion or comment on any illness that might be plaguing him." Such statements did not consider how attitudes toward disability have changed in the past half century and did not reflect on the fact that memorials speak to the present and future as well as about the past.

As the day of the dedication of the memorial approached in the spring of 1997, protests by disability rights organizations against the design intensified. During one demonstration at the construction site on February 27, for example, I. King Jordan, the first deaf president of Gallaudet University, stated, "If this memorial has no depiction of Roosevelt in a wheelchair, then instead of a memorial to a great American, I honestly believe that it becomes a memorial to hypocrisy."[71] Finally, when disability activists threatened a potentially embarrassing protest at the official dedication of the memorial on May 2, President Clinton agreed to submit legislation to Congress asking that the memorial be modified to include a sculpture of Roosevelt sitting in his wheelchair. Supported by sixteen of Roosevelt's grandchildren, as well as by former presidents Bush, Carter, and Ford, Clinton's announcement was welcomed by those who had criticized the commission's original design.

After a successful fund-raising campaign by the National Organization on Disability and other groups, a statue depicting Roosevelt in his self-designed wheelchair was unveiled at the memorial on January 10, 2001. Located at the entrance to the memorial, the statue is at ground level and accessible to visitors who use wheelchairs. While there were still some who criticized the statue as too politically correct, many others praised this positive public depiction of Roosevelt as disabled. For example, Taylor Hines, a young man with muscular dystrophy, wrote on January 17, 2001, in the *Washington Post,* "FDR did what he did while in a wheelchair. Shouldn't future generations know about it? Too many people think that life comes to an end when you have a disability, and that people with disabilities are destined to live pathetic and useless lives. This sculpture will show everyone that is not the case." For those who automatically associate disability with incompetence and weakness, this memorial exposes the inappropriateness of pity and condescension. For all the employers and gatekeepers to social institutions who have excluded people with disabilities from full participation, this memorial bears witness to their untenable position. And, in historical terms, this memorial is an important reminder that a man who could not walk served as president for longer than any other and that this man led the fight to defeat fascism, a movement that sought to eliminate the unfit from the healthy body of the German nation.

CHAPTER 6 • Disability and Socialist Images of the Human Being in the Culture of the German Democratic Republic

Disability and Illness as Challenges to Socialist Realism

The relationship of socialist theory and practice to the body, and specifically to the disabled body, is fraught with contradictions. It is a complex story both of seeing and blocking from view; of susceptibility to eugenic, biologistic tendencies; and of compassionate, supportive perspectives rooted in a commitment to human equality. In telling this story of many layers, it is crucial to keep in mind that socialism, as it arose in Germany in the nineteenth century, intended to liberate the industrial working class from the slavery of wage labor by abolishing private property and the division of labor. Socialists dreamed of creating a classless society in which all people would share equally in the duties of production and would thus have enough time to develop all their capabilities and talents. From the outset, in attacking the gross socioeconomic inequalities associated with the unfolding of capitalist industrial production, German socialists (along with other social reformers) took two approaches to representing the body. On the one hand, beginning in the 1840s, they wrote repeatedly about working-class men, women, and children living in misery, which members of the property-owning classes generally disregarded, in order to expose social injustices.[1] One thinks here, for example, of Wilhelm Wolff's *Das Elend und der Aufruhr in Schlesien* (Misery and Revolt in Silesia, 1844), Georg Weerth's *Skizzen aus dem socialen und politischen Leben der Briten* (Sketches from the Social and Political Life of the British, 1843–44), Friedrich Engels's *The Condition of the Working-Class in England* (1845), Ernst Dronke's *Berlin* (1846), and a host of similar writings that include long descriptions of illnesses and disabilities caused by poverty, malnourishment, and lack of medical care: tuberculosis, rickets, spinal curvatures, untreated injuries, and so forth. On the other hand, also beginning in the 1840s, the first uplifting portrayals of industrial workers appeared in German literature.[2] As in Ferdinand Freiligrath's poem

"Von unten auf" (Up from Below, 1846), the male figures here have strong bodies and resolute wills. They are titans with hard, calloused fists, giants with broad shoulders, the creators of all wealth, the active subjects of history. In this vein, Georg Herwegh exhorted in his famous "Bundeslied für den Allgemeinen deutschen Arbeiterverein" (Anthem for the General German Workers' Association, 1864), "Man of labor, awake! / And recognize your power! / All the wheels will stand still / If this is the will of your strong arm."[3] Healthy and whole of body, such figures were intended to be inspiring allegorical figurations of the rising working class.

These two tendencies—to expose disability and illness as indicative of class-based misery or to create shining visions of healthy, nondisabled workers—underwent many permutations throughout the history of socialist and communist cultural production. In the so-called naturalism debate of the early 1890s, for example, leading German social democrats criticized bourgeois modern art as decadent and pessimistic in contrast to the optimistic outlook of the proletariat. Along these lines, Karl Kautsky, who later became the most prominent social democrat who favored eugenics, criticized Gerhart Hauptmann's drama *Vor Sonnenaufgang* (Before Dawn, 1889) for only portraying degeneracy among the lower classes—specifically, the hereditary defects attributed to alcoholism—rather than depicting the idealism of the proletarian struggle to create a new society.[4] In general, however, for many years neither social democrats nor communists tried to control in any consistent way how literature should serve their party programs. Accordingly, portrayals of disabled or ill workers, as well as of strong, healthy, model proletarians, long coexisted within their literature and art. During the Weimar Republic, leftist artists and writers frequently created drastic depictions of disabled veterans and workers in order to attack the injustices of capitalism and militarism. By contrast, in the waning years of the Republic, several communist authors wrote a series of "Red-One-Mark-Novels" that centered on protagonists meant as positive heroes with whom readers were to identify. Like much literature aimed at a mass audience, these novels featured physiognomic touches whereby the communist workers were shown as young, strong, manly, and healthy, while their opponents were portrayed as tired and weak, and thus veered dangerously into the stigmatized realm of disability and illness.[5]

It was only in the early 1930s in the Soviet Union, however, parallel to the comprehensive program of socialist construction in economics and politics, that a view of literature—and thus of specific representations of the body—as serving particular functions within socialist society became obligatory. Andrei Zhdanov gave the program of socialist realism its classic formulation in 1934 at the first All-Union Congress of Soviet Writers, sharply differentiating it from what he termed bourgeois, decadent literature. The artist was to depict objective reality in its revolutionary development with the goal of educating working people in the optimistic spirit of socialism. Preferred subject matter was the working world of socialist production, and works were to feature positive heroes as models for readers to emulate.[6] Speaking at the same congress, Maxim Gorky characterized the image of the human being in prerevolutionary literature as alienated, suffering, alcoholic, or suicidal. By contrast, he apotheosized the image of the human being in socialist realism as a victorious hero of labor who was healthy, long-lived, happy, tireless, and industrious.[7] This program was loosened in the Soviet Union during World War II and was increasingly called into question there during the cold war thaw of the 1950s.

After four years of occupation by the four Allied powers, the capitalist Federal Republic of Germany (FRG) and the socialist German Democratic Republic (GDR) were both founded in 1949 in the context of the cold war. Marx and Engels had proclaimed that the true emancipation of the working class had to be accomplished by workers themselves, but tragically the GDR did not arise from a German socialist revolution. Rather, socialism was imposed from outside by the victorious Soviet Union. Many Germans in the newly founded GDR had been Nazi Party members or sympathizers, and many others were also antisocialists of various persuasions. On the other hand, until 1933 Germany had been at the center of the strongest left-wing workers' movement in the world outside the Soviet Union. Consequently, after 1945 there were also many Germans who wanted to build a new antifascist, socialist society in the GDR, a society that would have no place for anti-Semitism or racism, would be committed to proletarian internationalism, and would break the power of monopoly capitalism and achieve economic justice for all. Many older, leftist artists, writers, and intellectuals returned to the GDR from exile and tried to contribute to this project, including Ernst Bloch, Bertolt Brecht, Anna Seghers, and Arnold Zweig. Many younger intellectuals, too, wanted to participate in constructing socialism and complied voluntarily with calls from the ruling Socialist Unity Party (SED) in the late 1950s to take the working world as their subject matter.[8] In the works they created, these intellectuals were not only complying with SED censorship requirements but were also trying to realize an ideology in which they genuinely believed.

In its early years, the GDR faced an almost impossible situation that threatened its very existence: the war's economic devastation and the lack of funds for rebuilding; the ever present, tempting alternative of the

FRG with its rapidly rising standard of living supported by the U.S. Marshall Plan; and a population in which sizable sectors were antisocialist. Consequently, both SED leaders and many writers, artists, and others deemed it necessary to create easily comprehensible representations of what the new socialist society could offer, generally through urging identification with positive heroes. In the GDR, socialist realism was still the officially sanctioned program in the early 1950s. It achieved even more force by being paired with Georg Lukács's theory of realism, which praised "closed" art forms that depicted the "totality" of society while criticizing "open," fragmentary forms that employed techniques such as montage and alienation.[9] In 1951, the Central Committee of the SED attacked authors such as Kafka, Joyce, and Proust, along with GDR artists, writers, and musicians who were employing aesthetically innovative techniques, labeling them formalists and accusing them of being negative and pessimistic, that is, decadent and antisocialist. Similarly, a debate occurred between Bertolt Brecht, who maintained that his audience could learn more from thinking about the negative example of his Mother Courage, and the dramatist Friedrich Wolf, who insisted on the need to create positive heroes as models for audience identification, as he did in his play *Bürgermeister Anna* (Mayor Anna, 1950). This was also the period in which the SED began to hold up Goethe's Faust, with his insatiable thirst for knowledge and his tireless striving, as a model for the new human being in socialism. Iconic images from this period portray strong, healthy workers as positive heroes of socialist production. The sculptor Fritz Cremer, for example, did this with two statues of male and female workers, which recall such representations going back to the 1840s, that were placed in a prominent position in the center of East Berlin. As far as depictions of poverty, disability, or illness among working people or the lower classes were concerned, these occurred only as projections onto the exploitative, inhumane capitalist West. In this vein, Karl Erich Müller's painting *Blinder Neger* (Blind Negro, 1964) shows a ragged beggar wearing a sign that reads in English, "I am blind. Please one penny. Thank you."[10]

The relevance of this entire complex of socialist aesthetic theory and practice to representations of disability and illness is that socialist realism sought to assert a unity of interests between the collective and the individual. It often did this, however, by portraying the human being mainly in terms of productivity and by blotting out representations of bodies that did not conform to rigid standards of performance, behavior, and appearance. The norms propagated were often not emancipatory or revolutionary at all but were drawn frequently from the Protestant work ethic or narrow-minded, conformist provincialism. As Bertolt Brecht wrote in a letter to the GDR head of state Walter Ulbricht after the workers' revolt of June 17, 1953, "The workers were pressured to increase production, and the artists were pressured to make this palatable. . . . The production of the artists, like that of the workers, had the character of a means to an end and was not viewed as gratifying or free in itself."[11] When GDR writers began to discern contradictions between avowed collective goals and individual diversity, they gradually stopped creating positive images of workers that were intended to spur the populace on to greater feats of production. Rather, they turned increasingly to other topics. They wrote about young people who had difficulty finding a place in socialist society, problems and contradictions in the lives of women who tried to combine work and family, the destruction of the environment through unrestrained industrial production, and what happens when the body stops functioning in normative ways due to disability or illness.

It would not be useful to try to distinguish too sharply between representations of disability and illness in GDR literature when analyzing their significance as challenges to socialist realism's assertion that collective and individual interests are identical. Of course, one can say that illness is usually more of a process than disability and that many disabled people are not ill, but these distinctions are not so relevant here. Rather, the important thing is that in really existing socialism—after the nationalization of large sectors of the economy and the establishment of one-party rule—many GDR writers became concerned with the ways in which the body could be a disturbing factor within planned socialist production. Consequently, on the one hand, they portrayed disability and illness as universal human conditions that were unjustifiably neglected by socialist realism, as individualizing experiences that could not be totally sublated (*aufgehoben*) to use Hegelian and Marxist terminology. On the other hand, by employing these themes to critique an overemphasis on performance, they also often upheld stereotypes of inadequacy that had little to do with the lived experiences of many disabled or ill people. The turn to these topics also had aesthetic consequences, especially in works that deal in some way with mental impairments. To express this aspect of reality as effectively as possible, authors drew on stylistic techniques such as different levels of language, interruptions in chronology, fragmentation, montage, or dream sequences, which had all been labeled formalistic and decadent. That is, these writers drew on the entire complex of disability, illness, and mental impairments in order to challenge the one-sided image of the socialist human being within socialist realism.

In a very small number of short texts written during the early years of the GDR, disabled men are depicted as positive heroes in the sense of socialist realism. The first is a reportage about a tractor driver named Paul Arndt contained in the collection *Helden der Arbeit* (Heroes of Labor, 1951).[12] In his enthusiasm for building up the new socialist society, Arndt had risked his life to plow fields that had been mined by the retreating German army. After his tractor set off a land mine, his leg had to be amputated. In line with the tenets of socialist realism, the reportage dismisses Arndt's newly acquired disability as a trivial matter and presents him as longing only for the day when he would become accustomed to his new prosthesis and able to go back to plowing. The reporter states, "This is what real heroes are like. Nothing keeps them from reaching their goal" (211). By ignoring the individual, psychological experience of disability in favor of emphasizing performance in the realm of production, this reportage repeats familiar patterns found throughout rehabilitation narratives since World War I. It differs from the most reactionary of these, however, in its proposal that a physically disabled man could lead a useful life in peacetime rather than as a rehabilitated soldier returned to the battlefield.

The story of Paul Arndt was well known, and it was reworked by two GDR writers in very different ways. Anna Seghers, who returned to the GDR from Mexican exile, is the only German writer I know of from the immediate postwar period who created disabled figures reminiscent of Brecht's Kattrin and Zweig's Tom Barfey, that is, figures who overcome their disabilities to carry out positive, constructive actions. She did this in two short stories.[13] The first, "Der Traktorist" (1950), recounts the Arndt story in fictional form, telling of a young tractor driver who runs over a land mine and whose leg has to be amputated. Deeply depressed at first, his spirits are raised when he discovers that a prosthesis will enable him to go back to work. Similar to the reportage, the story is a rehabilitation narrative of overcoming disability to serve the greater community. The second, "Der Kesselflicker" (The Tinker, 1950), is a rare GDR cultural representation of a disabled veteran and explicitly connects the experience of disability to antiwar sentiments. Here a veteran whose leg was amputated travels through the countryside in a small cart pulled by his dog, repairing pots and pans for villagers. He is an emissary of peace amid the devastation left after the war. In both stories, Seghers imagined physically disabled men as capable of contributing to the new socialist society. After Seghers, however, whenever GDR writers turned to these themes, they did not do so in order to show the real capabilities of some disabled people but rather to critique socialist norms of performance.

Drawing on material from the Arndt reportage and Seghers's story,

Heiner Müller's play *Traktor* (written in 1955–61) centers on the tractor driver "P. A."[14] Unlike his sources, however, Müller did not create a linear narrative that tells a straightforward story of overcoming disability in order to contribute to social transformation through work and performance. Rather, he created a montage of scenes that explore the entanglements and contradictions between collective and individual and performance and disability. The reportage invests Arndt's disability with transcendent, metaphorical meaning by portraying it as a worthwhile, heroic sacrifice for the greater collective good. On the one hand, Müller's play is also not entirely free of traditional metaphorical associations of disability. Certainly his maimed tractor driver stands in a sense for the deformed, crippled beginnings of the GDR. What makes Müller's play such an unusual representation of disability, however, is that it also voices a consciousness that disability does not have any inherent meaning in itself but has traditionally been invested with meanings that are highly ideological. Here disability is not only a worthwhile sacrifice or a negative metaphor but rather something arbitrary that happens to an individual human being. This is shown by the tractor driver's explicit resistance to having his disability made into a source of meaning for others. He does not want to be called a hero of labor in the newspaper or have schoolchildren compose essays about following his example. He says, "I am not a hero. I want to have my leg back" (16). He is horrified at having to wear an artificial leg and points out to a well-meaning but ideologically rigid visitor in the hospital that the German skill in making such excellent prostheses was perfected in wartime. In opposition to all such efforts to keep him functioning in the realm of production by combining his body with mechanical parts, he declares, recalling similar perspectives in Weimar culture, "The human being is not a machine" (21). He laughs at the visitor's clichéd efforts to place his "heroic sacrifice" in the service of a political cause, ironically telling him to "keep on singing. Amputees of the world" (a reference to Marx and Engels's "Workers of the world, unite") and saying "I'm a bone-lending station" (a reference to the lending stations for farm machinery in the GDR). The visitor is finally reduced to silence by the tractor driver's insistence that his "leg stump is the center of the world"—in other words, by his insistence on mourning rather than repressing his most individual loss.

In a short commentary that he wrote and incorporated into the play's montage in 1974, Müller described his "story of the amputated hero" as something "that can happen to anyone, that has no meaning" (14). Considering the outcome of the heroic, self-sacrificial efforts to create a new and qualitatively different society in the early GDR, such a statement certainly has tragic overtones. With respect to traditional discourses about disability, however, Müller's play stands out for the artistic integrity of its refusal to invest its disabled character with metaphorical significance. This text recognizes the violence that can be done to the human being through a denial of individual experience, a repression of mourning, and an unmitigated insistence on overcoming. In short, even though Müller's tractor driver does return to work and invents a safer way to plow, he still resists the violence of being reduced to nothing but ideology. As Müller said later about his approach to theater, "Bodies and their conflict with ideas are thrown onto the stage. As long as there are ideas, there are wounds. Ideas inflict wounds on bodies."[15] Müller's play was the first work of GDR literature to portray disability as an irreducibly disturbing factor in calls for uninterrupted function and performance, thus challenging the socialist realist aesthetic of the positive hero.

Müller, who became the best-known GDR dramatist internationally, employed themes and images of disability and illness in many of his subsequent plays. His *Philoktet* (written in 1958–64) is a reworking of Sophocles's tragedy about the war hero Philoctetes, whose foot has been bitten by a poisonous snake. In the Greek drama, the infected wound is a religious pollution that prevents the hero's comrades from sacrificing to the gods, and when they cannot bear the stench from his wound or his screams of pain, they abandon him on the island of Lemnos.[16] After nine years, the Greeks learn that they will never be able to vanquish Troy without the bow and arrows of Heracles, which Philoctetes possesses. They fetch Philoctetes and his weapons, Troy falls, and healers cure his wound. Müller's play, written in elevated iambic pentameter, is darker than his source. Here Philoctetes is the disabled war hero, the disabled worker, but also the writer himself. There is no place for him in the world of totally instrumentalized rationality represented by Odysseus, who comes to fetch the weapons of Heracles. When Philoctetes, described as "wounded in the service" of the Greeks and "no longer serviceable to them with such a wound," refuses to hand over the bow, Odysseus kills him. The final stage directions suggest that the play could end with projected images from many wars. In Müller's multilayered view of history, Philoctetes's wound—also called "my sex/the wound" and thus associated with original sin—stands for the suffering body that resists being instrumentalized. But it also stands for the unending cycles of war and violence that recur throughout human history. This wound can be compared with Oedipus's transgressions, and, indeed, Müller also wrote an adaptation of Friedrich Hölderlin's version of Sophocles's *Ödipus Tyrann* (Oedipus the Tyrant), which premiered in East Berlin in

1967. In his commentary on this play, Müller highlighted the issue of "blind" instrumental rationality, comparing Ödipus's self-blinding to the blindness of modern scientists who continue to build atomic weapons even though they know the terrible consequences.[17] Disability functions aesthetically in a more traditional way in these plays as an unending chain of metaphors.

In other plays, Müller continued to use images of disability to signify weakness, impotence, and deformity, but at times these representations also evoked an as yet unimagined liberation. His *Germania Tod in Berlin* (Germania Death in Berlin, written in 1956–71), replete with representations of disability and illness, is a panorama of violent German history from the Nibelungs to the GDR. The play furnishes a bitterly ironic commentary on the bankrupt cultural tradition of the disabled war hero. In the scene entitled "Hommage à Stalin I," injured warriors from the Nibelungs to Wehrmacht soldiers trapped at Stalingrad cut off each other's limbs in a never-ending slaughter. In the surrealistic scene in Hitler's bunker entitled "The Holy Family," a "thalidomide wolf," which emerges from the womb of a pregnant Goebbels, is intended to symbolize the birth of the deformed Federal Republic (West Germany). In the final scene, a GDR worker who still hopes that socialism will prevail in all of Germany is dying of cancer in the hospital; the metaphor of his cancer resonates with both the destructiveness of German history and the deformities within socialism. Many of Müller's plays include scenes featuring body parts or self-mutilations in the tradition of Antonin Artaud's theater of cruelty in order to bombard his audience with overwhelming images of corporeal disintegration that explode the strictures of instrumental rationality. Along these lines, his play *Hamletmachine* (1977), which proclaims the death of the (male) author, concludes with a scene of Ophelia in a wheelchair. Two doctors are tying her up with gauze bandages (what an image of the "wheelchair bound!"), and in her closing speech she cries out, "Long live hatred, contempt, rebellion, death."[18] Here Müller drew on the familiar cultural figure of the helpless but vengeful cripple in this image of resistance to the "machine" of European history and cultural production. By thus linking disability with the female principle, the revolt invoked by Ophelia appears all the more forceful because of its seeming impossibility.

In prose fiction, Christa Wolf, the GDR's best-known novelist and arguably the best-known postwar German woman writer, also turned increasingly toward themes of illness taken in the broadest sense as a breakdown in physical or mental functioning. Rita, the protagonist in her first novel, *Der geteilte Himmel* (Divided Heaven, 1963), is a young woman who tries earnestly to identify with the proletariat by going to work in a factory. When her lover decides to leave the GDR for the West shortly before the Berlin Wall is built, Rita is distraught and collapses on the tracks between two moving railroad cars in a thinly veiled suicide attempt. Saved, she awakens crying in the hospital and relives the moment when she felt like the helpless target of the two "well-functioning" cars. This novel brought up many topics that were previously taboo in GDR literature, but it still ends with a forced harmony rooted in the aesthetic of socialist realism. Rita recovers her emotional stability, represses her desire for love, and is still intent on becoming a well-functioning contributor to socialism. Wolf's next novel, *Nachdenken über Christa T.* (The Quest for Christa T., 1968), however, left all such compromises behind. Here the woman narrator remembers her friend, Christa T., who was impatient, intense, and forthright and sought the same unconditional qualities in others. Yet she finds that GDR society does not want individuals like her; rather, it encourages the development of people who perform like well-oiled cogs in the socialist system. As an acquaintance who is a doctor living a comfortable life advises her, "The essence of health is conformity."[19] Christa T. becomes more and more fatigued and finally dies of leukemia. This disease is the metaphor for the psychic exhaustion and emptiness that she feels in her thwarted attempts to live without making self-destructive compromises—whether in her work as a teacher or in her personal relationships. Christa T.'s illness and death signify that there is no place within really existing socialism where a person like her can live authentically.

Wolf's novel about Christa T. was a milestone in GDR culture, but it was also an early expression of a general trend in the literature of the German-speaking countries since about 1970 to take disability and illness—especially mental disorders and emotional crises—as a major theme.[20] When GDR writers turned to these subjects, however, this always implied a challenge to official proclamations that socialism was creating a new type of human being who found unambiguous fulfillment in working hard for the socialist community. In some works, disability or illness causes characters to question their previous positions in society or drop out altogether. For example, in Jurek Becker's novel *Schlaflose Tage* (Sleepless Days, 1978), published in the FRG, a teacher who believes he is in danger of having a heart attack quits his profession, in which he feels compelled to be dishonest, and takes a less stressful job driving a bread delivery truck. Similarly, in Stefan Heym's novel *Collin* (1979, FRG) the protagonist has a heart attack brought on by stress, and when he decides to be honest and stop conforming his health improves. Or in Rolf Schneider's novel *November* (1979, FRG) a teenage boy is partially paralyzed in a bicycle accident. The narrator portrays his disability as an individualizing factor, stating that before the accident "there was nothing different about him, but afterward he was suddenly no longer like all the others. He was just himself."[21] The boy becomes a sensitive outsider who is more aware and critical of the contradictions in his surroundings. Furthermore, there are numerous GDR works in which characters attempt suicide because of depression, isolation, or unbearable emotional stress—one of the most significant examples being Volker Braun's "Unvollendete Geschichte" (Unfinished Story/History, 1975).[22] Also, many works portray women characters who experience mental breakdowns because of unresolved conflicts between society's demands for performance and their emotional needs, including Brigitte Martin's *Nach Freude anstehen* (Lining up for Joy, 1981), Monika Helmecke's *Klopfzeichen* (The Knock, 1981), and Manfred Völlger's *Das Windhahnsyndrom* (The Weathervane Syndrome, 1983).[23]

Christa Wolf brought most of these themes into her subsequent works in ways that challenged socialist realism's reliance on Goethe's dictum that "the classical is healthy; the romantic is ill."[24] In her novel *Kein Ort: Nirgends* (No Place on Earth, 1979), she portrayed the suicide pact between the romantic writers Heinrich von Kleist and Karoline von Günderrode in the early nineteenth century. Other GDR writers were also fascinated with mentally fragile or mentally ill outsider figures from the German cultural heritage, such as Kleist, Jakob Michael Reinhold Lenz, or Friedrich Hölderlin. In this context, Wolf's identification with such figures served to claim the heritage of literary modernism and to reject doctrinaire prescriptions of classical or realist aesthetics. For example, in her novel *Kassandra* (1983) Wolf used the concept of "holy madness" from antiquity in her depiction of the seer; similarly, the circles of antipsychiatry in West Germany enhanced the status of insanity. In this novel, the ascending patriarchy declares Cassandra to be insane as a means of disciplining her and repudiating her insights, which deviate from rational, patriarchal norms.[25] Thus, the focus of an author such as Wolf on both physical illness and mental instability implied a repudiation of socialist realism on the level of content (health, Faustian striving). And her use of modernistic forms such as different points of view and levels of language rather than an omniscient narrator also implied a repudiation of socialist realism on the level of form (aesthetics derived from the nineteenth-century novel).

A number of other well-known GDR authors portrayed atypical mental states using modernist literary techniques to create complex representations that expressed solidarity with people who were disabled or ill. Two works, for example, deal with traumas rooted in the national socialist past. Jurek Becker's novel *Bronsteins Kinder* (Bronstein's Children, 1988, FRG; 1989, GDR) tells of a young Jewish man in East Berlin whose older sister, Elle, is confined to a mental institution. Their father had paid strangers to hide her during the war, and afterward she had to be institutionalized because she unpredictably attacks people whom she perhaps associates with Nazi persecutors. Becker portrays her brother and father—who are outsiders themselves because of their Jewishness—as not abandoning her but continuing to love and respect her. Her brother visits her, asks her advice, and takes her seriously even though it is often difficult for him to follow her train of thought. With respect to form, the passages that are told from Elle's point of view introduce a level of poetic, dreamlike language into the more prosaic narration about her brother's everyday life. This implies that her associative, irrational perspective is also a valid part of reality.

In a similar fashion, Christoph Hein's novel *Horns Ende* (Horn's End, 1985) includes a cognitively disabled character and is the only work of GDR literature I know of that explicitly thematizes Nazi "euthanasia."[26] It is situated in a small GDR town in the 1950s where time seems to have stood still even though, of course, the town is nominally socialist. The novel revolves around a man named Horn who has been expelled from the SED and relegated to a job as a museum curator. He is then unjustly denounced and accused of subversion, and after the State Security Police (Stasi) interrogates him he hangs himself. By telling Horn's story from the perspectives of several townspeople, the novel's structure demonstrates that there is no one truth about these events. Hein explored the continuity between the treatment of Horn and fascist actions by introducing the figure of Gohl, an isolated artist who is taking care of his "feebleminded" daughter. The Gohls had tried to hide their daughter from Nazi officials, but someone from the town denounced her, and she was supposedly taken away in 1943. (Here, in order to create his parallel, Hein made the "euthanasia" program more drastic than it actually was because historians do not know of instances in which disabled people were taken away from their homes against the wishes of their relatives.) Her ashes were returned, and Gohl buried them under a gravestone with no name or date. Soon afterward, however, townspeople saw his daughter again and realized that Gohl's wife had tricked the Nazi authorities into taking her away and murdering her instead of her daughter. After the war, Gohl puts his wife's name on the gravestone and hardly speaks to any of the townspeople. His only friends are the gypsies, also targets of Nazi elimination, who begin returning to the town shortly after the end of the war and whom the townspeople still dislike intensely. As for Gohl's daughter, Hein gives her a voice in the novel that is just as valid as any other character's. Her passages intermingle illusions and facts and show how helpless and trusting she is. In the end, a nameless man comes to the house and rapes her; the victimization of the weak continues. Hein used the theme of cognitive disability to expose continuing patterns of excluding outsiders. He presented this behavior as encouraged in some ways by socialist norms that elided individual differences, but he also showed it as having a much longer history rooted in petit bourgeois and even premodern conformism. Hein's portrayal of East German provincial life is quite similar to Franz Xaver Kroetz's portrayal of West German provincial life in his novel *Der Mondscheinknecht,* which also thematizes Nazi "euthanasia" and postwar reactions to disability as difference. By remembering past persecutions and illuminating continuing patterns of injustice, both authors expressed solidarity with those individuals and groups that continued to suffer from exclusion.

Perhaps the most radical work in content and form that features a disabled character is the short story "kein runter kein fern," which the GDR author Ulrich Plenzdorf wrote in 1973, published in the FRG in 1978, and could only produce in the GDR as a play in January 1990.[27] The title of the story is almost untranslatable but could be rendered as "no downstairs no t," which is how the learning-disabled ten-year-old protagonist expresses the fact that his authoritarian father has grounded him and forbidden him to watch television until his grades improve. The boy's learning disability shapes the form of the story, which is narrated from his point of view. His difficulties in spelling, forming complete sentences, and thinking in a coherent way are reflected in the three levels of language that Plenzdorf shaped using interior monologue and montage. These levels are the pathos of official slogans; fragments of conversations, parental admonitions, and school material; and the boy's own thoughts. Taking place in 1969, when the GDR state was celebrating the twentieth anniversary of its founding, loudspeaker voices are constantly blaring out slogans such as "The socialist community is our greatest success."[28] Yet this propaganda appears totally false when juxtaposed with the boy's difficult life and his confused attempts to express himself. He watches the anniversary parade on television to find out whether any "special ed pupils" (Hilfser) are allowed to march along with the radiant, exemplary Free German Youth and does not see any of his schoolmates. The official speeches promoting performance and cheerful resolve complement his father's authoritarianism. His father, a party functionary, does not want to admit that his own son could be "feebleminded" and only finds out after his wife flees to the West that she has placed the boy in a special school (Hilfsschule) for the "educable feebleminded." Enraged at this discovery, he sputters to the school principal, as the boy remembers overhearing it: "But feeblemindedness is just a result of capita wait a minute uh capita where's the cause of feeblemindedness in socialism! Where's the cause of cancer in socialism? Cancer is a sick. Feeblemindedness is a sick, too."[29] The boy cannot perform as required by the political and educational system or by his father and policeman brother, and so he is isolated and harassed. In the story's ironic presentation of class hierarchies that still exist in socialist society, the boy has a real talent for becoming a skilled carpenter, but his father looks down on manual labor and does not want to allow this. The boy's problems are shown as not due primarily to his own inadequacies but rather to narrow, inflexible social norms. Plenzdorf thus chose to write sympathetically about a learning-disabled child and to structure the story around this character's use of language in order to question the normality of official ideology.

How did GDR censors react to such a controversial depiction of disability? In 1971, the new SED general secretary, Erich Honecker, had declared that there should be no more taboos in literature as long as authors proceeded from a "socialist standpoint."[30] Believing that times had changed, Plenzdorf, along with Klaus Schlesinger and Martin Stade, decided to invite a number of writers to contribute to a volume of Berlin stories in 1973. As they explained later, they did not consider themselves to be opponents of socialism but wanted to find a place within it. They had been influenced both by the antiauthoritarian Western student movement and by efforts to democratize socialism in Czechoslovakia.[31] Accordingly, they explained that they wanted to burst the bounds of convention, to break with the norms of the older generation. In spite of Honecker's maxim, however, by 1976 they had encountered such massive resistance to publishing their anthology that they gave up. Documents about this case published in 1995 show that Stasi agents viewed Plenzdorf's story as the most problematic of all the submissions (264). Writing under the code name "Renate" in 1976, one Stasi informant attacked Plenzdorf's use of montage and stream of consciousness as a "nightmare," saying that his story was similar to works by Western authors who showed the world as "insane" and the "mentally abnormal" person as the only one who is in fact "normal." Consequently, "Renate" labeled Plenzdorf's story "incredibly disgusting" (290) due to its "idiotic attacks against our so-called achievement-oriented society" (292). And so Plenzdorf's story could only be published in the FRG. But a reviewer struck quite a different note in January 1990 when a dramatic version of the story was performed at the Deutsches Theater in East Berlin during the tumultuous period immediately after the opening of the Berlin Wall. The reviewer stated, "The boy could be portrayed as feebleminded . . . but the actor shows us a humiliated creature, a child in need of affection, a boy who would be normal if he were treated normally."[32] That is, this reviewer reflected thoughtfully on how the story shows the boy's disability as socially constructed by the harsh way he is treated in the GDR.

Some of these writers used medical metaphors of disability in a problematic way for they often simply assumed that disability and illness obviously stood for nothing but the inability to perform according to the norms of socialist production. Only rarely were they interested in portraying the actual everyday lives of disabled people in the GDR as, for example, Siegfried Maaß did in his more middlebrow novel, *Keine Flügel für Reggi* (No Wings for Reggi, 1984), which centers on a man who uses a wheelchair and deals rather concretely with prejudices and problems of accessibility. On the other hand, however, these writers were appropriately skeptical about socialist realist pronouncements against "decadence." This was a notable insight, for whenever this term is used in a prescriptive sense, as it was in the early years of the GDR, one needs to probe into its implications for representations of people who are disabled or ill. The writer Franz Fühmann saw this problem especially clearly. In the same vein as Christa Wolf, he opposed the verdicts of socialist cultural politics against illness and decadence in his long essay on the expressionist writer Georg Trakl, "Der Sturz des Engels" (The Fall of the Angel, 1982). Here Fühmann evaluated decadence positively as the "decline of questionable values." In his opinion, decadence could be viewed as "the decline of alliances with the strong; the decline of an order dominated by the respectable, the healthy, the industrious, the productive. Whoever belongs to this order does not like to form alliances with anyone outside it. For that would mean that he stops being what he most wants to be: respectable, strong, healthy, in short: normal. But this decline releases humane qualities and brings them into literature as something new."[33] By turning to themes of disability and illness, then, GDR writers such as Fühmann expressed solidarity with those who had been stigmatized as unrespectable, weak, unhealthy—in short, abnormal.

Fühmann is the only GDR writer I know of who cultivated contacts with disabled people and incorporated the insights he gained from these experiences into his writing, including his Trakl essay. For several years in the early 1980s before his death in 1984, he regularly visited the Protestant Samariter institution in Fürstenwalde in the GDR and the Stetten institution close to Stuttgart in the FRG, where he gave readings, told fairy tales, and discussed an exhibition of woodcuts by the leftist West German artist HAP Grieshaber with the cognitively disabled patients. At the request of one patient, he wrote his own fairy tale about a little witch with one short leg and one long leg: "Anna, genannt Humpelhexe" (Anna, called Hobblewitch, 1981). Stasi informants were highly suspicious of these activities, reporting that Fühmann was spending time with the feebleminded, that he intended to write "about and for the mentally disturbed," and that perhaps he needed to be committed to a psychiatric institution himself.[34] Fühmann's writings about these institutions were published as accompanying texts to Dietmar Riemann's series of photographs of patients entitled *Was für eine Insel in was für einem Meer: Leben mit geistig Behinderten* (What Kind of Island in What Kind of Sea: Life with the Mentally Disabled, 1985). These photographs are sensitive portraits that present their cognitively disabled subjects as human beings with an aura of dignity (in contrast to the photographs of Diane Arbus, who relied on a freak show aesthetic).[35] Nor did Riemann shy away from showing the failings of the GDR institution such as overcrowding, the use of restraints, inadequate equipment, general shabbiness, and so forth. In his essays, Fühmann described how his initial discomfort on seeing these patients was transformed as he got to know them better. He reminded the reader that the physically and mentally disabled were the first to be murdered by the Nazis and that this had been more or less forgotten. And he stated that even today disabled people still had to bear heavier burdens than most "so-called normal people": "How many of them had to learn to endure the fact that their parents disown them, that their sexual longings usually remain unfulfilled? In an environment that is not created for them and that they can hardly use, how many of them experience insults and even hostility in dealing with the authorities, on public transportation, on the street, in stores? A year of hypocritical willingness to help [referring to the United Nations (UN) Year for People with Disabilities in 1981] doesn't change much in this regard."[36] Fühmann was open to being changed by these cognitively disabled people, and he gradually began to feel more solidarity with them. He described them as also having something to give and came to think of some as his friends. He summed up what he had learned by declaring that disabled people are like us and we are like them and by invoking Marx and Engels's vision from the *Communist Manifesto* that the "free development of each is the condition for the free development of all." Rather than writing these disabled people off as pariahs on the margins of the socialist community based on performance, Fühmann thus made an unusual move toward including them as equals in the discourse of Marxism.

Fig. 23. Boy at a pottery wheel in an East German institution for cognitively disabled people. (From Franz Fühmann and Dietmar Riemann, *Was für eine Insel in was für einem Meer: Leben mit geistig Behinderten* [Rostock: Hinstorff, 1988], 82. Photo by Dietmar Riemann.)

Locations of Disability in the Socialist State, 1945–1990

Literature in the GDR often functioned as a substitute for a public sphere. The censorship authorities judged the readership of most literary works to be relatively limited and thus were much stricter about preventing critical discussions of social problems in media that reached a broader audience and had a greater potential to provoke dissatisfaction. This means that literary works—whether fictional or biographical—were more revealing about issues related to disability than either mass media reporting or scholarship in fields such as sociology, education, rehabilitation, or medicine. Of course, frank debates took place in closed circles, and these sometimes had significant policy ramifications. Furthermore, like other social groups, disabled people were almost never allowed to organize their own associations to promote their own conceptions of their interests. Accordingly, when attempting to write about the lives of disabled people in the GDR—both the positions others thought appropriate for them and the positions they wanted for themselves—cultural historians face major methodological problems. The main difficulty is finding sources about these topics in a country where disabled people could not express their views publicly without being subjected to the vagaries of censorship. Therefore, many of the theses presented here are necessarily only a tentative beginning. This entire field awaits extensive research whereby it will be especially useful to interview disabled people who lived in the GDR before 1989.

Performance and the Socialist Personality

As a working-class movement, socialism had a long history, stretching back into the nineteenth century, of supporting the right of the individual to health. Based on their materialist viewpoint, socialists believed that all human beings were fundamentally equal and largely shaped by their environment although early social democratic advocates of eugenics were not at all averse to supporting measures that would prevent births of the hereditarily diseased.[37] From the beginning, socialists advocated preventive medicine, occupational and social hygiene, and universal health insurance. Social democratic and communist physicians made enormous efforts to treat the physical, mental, and emotional problems of poor and working people.[38] This solidarity with the disabled and ill was largely destroyed under national socialism, when many left-wing medical professionals were forbidden to practice, forced into exile, imprisoned, or killed. One could say that the humane vision of socialism, "all for one," was displaced during the Third Reich by the nationalistic, racially determined slogan "one for all." After 1945, the GDR tried to revive progressive traditions from before 1933, when Germany had been widely regarded as having the best rehabilitation system in the world. The GDR had fewer economic resources than West Germany, and this always prevented well-meaning people there from realizing many improvements. Consequently, when comparative international statistics were published during the UN Year for People with Disabilities in 1981, the GDR was found to have significant deficits but also impressive achievements. Official government statements described the "impaired" (Geschädigte, the term generally used in the GDR rather than the West German Behinderte [disabled]) as "citizens" (Bürger) rather than the patronizing "fellow citizens" (Mitbürger) often heard in the FRG. As such, like all GDR citizens, they were constitutionally guaranteed the rights to work and education. Yet, when masses of GDR citizens took to the streets in 1989, demonstrating for a greater say in their government under the slogan "We are the people," many disabled people also immediately began protesting and organizing self-advocacy groups. They issued public statements declaring that they were tired of being ignored and marginalized, and that they, too, were "the people." What had gone wrong in the forty years of the socialist project that led to the alienation of many disabled East Germans from their state?

Two concepts from socialist theory are important background for discussing policies and attitudes toward disabled people in the GDR, as well as for understanding statements about the place of disabled people in the socialist community: "performance" (Leistung) and the "socialist personality." The concept of performance was derived from Marx's reflections in *The Critique of the Gotha Program* (1875) on how the proceeds of labor could be distributed fairly in the future cooperative society. Assuming that all members of socialist society had an equal relationship to the means of production and also assuming a synchronicity of interests between the individual and the collective, GDR policymakers held that it was still necessary to compensate workers according to their performance in order to motivate them to work hard and conscientiously. This "performance principle," which was codified in the 1968 GDR constitution, can be expressed succinctly as "From each according to his ability, to each according to his performance." It would only be in a future communist society, when the division of labor had vanished, that the "needs principle" of distribution could prevail, formulated by Marx as "From each according to his ability, to each according to his needs."[39] It was one of the greatest tragedies in the course of efforts to create more humane socialist societies that, although performance had to be increased in order to raise the standard of living, workers often felt that their individual interests did not coincide with those of the state. Throughout the history of the GDR, workers frequently resisted the performance principle in various ways, almost bringing down the government with their revolt of June 17, 1953, against state-decreed increases in production norms. With respect to disabled people, the constant emphasis on performance had contradictory tendencies. On the one hand, it served to support efforts to rehabilitate them and get them into the work-place. But on the other hand the pressure to perform also had an exclu-sionary effect on many disabled people who needed extra support or were truly not able to work. As one young man with cerebral palsy explained in 1987, "I'm a cripple. But what I don't get is why I'm always put on the spot, why I always have to prove that I'm good for something, that I'm a useful part of society. I try hard, I really make an effort, but obviously that's not enough."[40] That is, the performance principle made such disabled people feel marginalized and stigmatized as hardly capa-ble of adding anything valuable to the socialist community.[41]

The second important concept that played a central, recurring role in policies toward disabled people in the GDR is that of the "well-rounded, educated, harmoniously developed socialist personality." This was both a norm that all teachers were to cultivate in their pupils and a general social goal for all GDR citizens. This ideal was derived from Marx's proposal that there was no such thing as anthropological human nature and that humans (in contrast to animals) made their own living conditions and their own history. Marxist-Leninist theory and GDR pedagogy, however, often applied this viewpoint in reductive, oversimplified ways.[42] In order to become socialist personalities, GDR citizens were supposed to be active, industrious, honest, rational, well educated, and proficient. They were urged to perform socially useful work, take responsibility for the collective, lead a healthy lifestyle, and participate in sports.[43] Along these lines, the SED urged the population at the end of the 1960s, "You should raise your children to be well-rounded, educated people with strong characters and tough bodies!"[44] But the problem of disability was a kind of Achilles heel for such views that assumed the uniformity of all people.

The goal of socialism was to eliminate class inequalities arising out of the unequal distribution of resources by abolishing private property. The hope was that if all people had a more equal starting point, they would have a greater chance to develop equally in all ways. But after the socialist state was established the question became how to deal with the many human differences that still existed. Specifically, what would be the place of disabled people in a society that attached the highest value to performance for the collective good and to the development of rigidly specified personality characteristics? Some disabled people were able to perform, but often they did not conform in other ways to norms of human uniformity having to do with appearance or behavior. Others could perform only in limited ways; some could not perform at all in an economically productive sense. Could socialism uphold the principle of equality and yet make room for these differences or was this an impossible demand? The problem of reconciling equality (based in economics) with freedom (based in human variation) is a specific problem of disability within socialism.

Representations of Disability in Law and Official Policy before 1989

After the defeat of fascism, which had either rehabilitated disabled people to work and fight for the nation or killed them outright as lives unworthy of life, what happened to disabled people in the Soviet Occupation Zone (SBZ) and then in the GDR? What happened under socialism to disabled veterans, disabled people considered capable of rehabilitation, and disabled people who had been the objects of Nazi eugenic policies? How did the new state try to control representations of disability and the locations assigned to disabled people? What types of bodies qualified as full members of the socialist community, and what sorts of struggles occurred over this? How did policymakers and experts view disabled people? As in all countries, disabled people made up a numerically significant group within the population as a whole. By 1980, out of a total population of about 17 million, approximately 1.3 million GDR citizens above the age of fourteen had government identification cards classifying them as impaired. Of these, about 1,163,000 were physically impaired, 44,000 mentally impaired, 58,000 blind or visually impaired, and 29,000 deaf or hearing impaired. Additionally, about 540,000 children were identified as impaired.[45] Policies and attitudes toward disabled people in the GDR were often strikingly similar to the West German situation, but there were also fundamental differences, and this entire subject awaits much more comparative historical research.

Policies toward disabled veterans in the SBZ and GDR were unlike those in West Germany as a result of both the more consistent antifascist policies in the East and the limited economic resources there.[46] In the SBZ, war-disability pensions as such were abolished because of the determination to end German militarism once and for all. It was only in 1948 that a decree allowed disabled veterans to receive pensions from state social insurance if they were evaluated as having at least a two-thirds reduction in earning capacity. This meant that veterans with less severe disabilities received no benefits. This coalescing of policies for disabled veterans with social welfare policies for civilian victims of accidents and illnesses meant that there were hardly any more policy debates in the GDR about disabled veterans as a specific group. Consequently, in the GDR there was a permanent discontinuity in the treatment of disabled veterans in contrast to West Germany, where war-disability pensions were eventually reestablished and organizations of war victims became quite active. Since all such organizations were forbidden in the GDR, disabled veterans did not appear in public in any recognizable groups, although certainly disabled individuals were just as visible in daily life there as in the West. There were only a few cultural representations of this group of men in the immediate postwar period in works by artists such as Theo Balden, Oskar Nerlinger, and Wilhelm Rudolph, as well as in some prominently displayed political posters featuring the classic figure of the amputee as a warning against militarism and rearmament.[47]

Policies toward the disabled people who had been the objects of Nazi sterilization and "euthanasia" were more complex, evidencing both breaks and continuities with pre-1945 practices as well as similarities and dissimilarities with West Germany. From the mid-1930s to the late 1950s, Soviet biology was under the sway of Trofim Denisovich Lysenko, who rejected the concept of genes and claimed that only the environment influenced the development of organisms. Lysenko's ideas, which Stalin supported, blocked research in genetics and were later discredited. The emphasis on environmental factors in biology meant, however, that eugenics never gained a foothold in the Soviet Union, and so there was never any sterilization law directed against disabled people there. Coming from this perspective, the Soviet Military Administration in Germany (SMAD) revoked the Law for the Prevention of Offspring with Hereditary Diseases in the SBZ with its Command No. 6 of January 8, 1946. This document characterized involuntary sterilization as a "Nazi law" that was untenable "because of its antidemocratic character and its fascist, tendentious presentation of theories about hereditary diseases."[48] There was some interest in the SBZ in determining whether the Nazis had carried out any sterilizations for political reasons. But there were never any debates about individual cases or financially compensating victims in either the SBZ or the GDR in contrast to West Germany, where groups of disabled people and their allies were finally able to publicize these issues and receive some small government benefits.[49]

As in the three Western zones, the treatment and care of severely disabled people— especially those who were still institutionalized after 1945—was extremely precarious in the immediate postwar years. In May 1948 in East Berlin, a conference of psychiatrists and neurologists issued a self-critical statement, which had no equal in the West at this early date, rejecting sterilization and "euthanasia" and emphasizing that medical professionals should work in a social spirit of sacrifice to help ill people.[50] But this was an isolated occurrence, and no similar statements were issued for many years. After the Nazi murders of institutionalized patients, many state hospitals had empty wards or were turned into military hospitals after the war. Psychiatric hospitals and treatment centers were only gradually created again. As in the Western zones, many institutionalized patients died of starvation in the immediate postwar years, but problems with the food supply lasted longer in the East due to the precarious economic situation. Even though the SMAD had a stated policy of trying to purge Nazi personnel from the medical and health care system, in practice this could hardly be carried out, and, as in the West, few physicians in the East were affected by denazification (239ff.). The churches, especially the Protestant Church, took care of the majority of severely disabled people who needed institutional care in their hospitals and nursing homes. Historians now working on this time period generally conclude that from 1945 to 1965 the similarities in treatment and care of severely disabled people, and particularly of mentally disabled people, in East and West Germany were greater than the differences.[51]

Due to the influence of Lysenkoism and because the Nazis had so misused concepts of heredity, genetics was taboo in certain ways in the first years after the defeat of fascism.[52] Because of this, the view that hereditary factors could cause developmental disabilities was repressed, and, especially in pedagogy, only environmental influences were acknowledged as important for human development. This perspective made it difficult to deal with many complex issues related to disability. Experts who advocated this one-sided view tended to maintain that illness and disability would gradually disappear in socialism since they no longer had any material basis.[53] For example, a Soviet advocate of Lysenkoism enthused in a lecture at East Berlin's Humboldt University in 1960 that in socialist-communist society "people must be young, strong, and healthy until they are two hundred years old."[54] In the same year, the Central Committee of the SED stated in a report that the task of socialism was to create "health, productivity, and joy in life" and only mentioned disabled people by saying that more institutions were needed for them.[55] Although such ideas were criticized later in the GDR, health and performance still continued to be strongly emphasized as crucial for realizing the economic goals of socialism. As a result, it was difficult to integrate disabled and ill people into a society conceived in such a manner, in which the ideal of the socialist personality prevailed.[56]

According to Dr. Gerda Jun, a neurologist and child psychiatrist who was a leader in improving treatment for children with psychiatric and cognitive disabilities in the GDR and in establishing extensive day programs for them, this official approach of more or less ignoring the needs of such people in the state's early years had two main effects.[57] On the one hand, of course, it delayed improvements in their care, treatment, and education in many ways. On the other hand, however, since these disabled people were so marginalized that they were not even supposed to exist within an optimistic socialist society, medical professionals and special education teachers sometimes felt that they had a paradoxical freedom to try out new approaches because bureaucrats were paying so little attention to what they were doing. For example, in 1987 one teacher remembered beginning to work in 1950 when Nazi "euthanasia" had only recently ended, when there was little knowledge about the disabled and still much rejection of them, and when many people were still afraid of contagious diseases such as spinal tuberculosis. She told about wanting her "spastic" pupils to be seen in public rather than hidden away. The first time she took her pupils out in the city, she prepared them for the ignorance and mistreatment they might encounter by having them repeat the sentence "We are the nicest children in the world." She described the excursion as successful and "something unusual at that time. For some children this was the first contact they had ever had with the broader public."[58] From the beginning, then, there were differences of opinion among GDR professionals and policymakers concerned with these issues, although these debates did not begin to appear in published research until the 1980s.

In 1963, some reform-minded GDR psychiatrists formulated the so-called Rodewisch Theses in an effort to bring about more humane approaches to treating people with mental illnesses. These theses, whose thrust is comparable to the government psychiatry report of 1975 in the FRG, emphasized that doctors should not focus solely on medical treatment but should also help rehabilitate and reintegrate mentally ill people into society. The theses proposed that the mentally and the physically ill should receive equally good care, that there were no hopeless cases, that inpatient treatment and locked hospital wards should be replaced as much as possible with outpatient treatment and open wards, that young and elderly patients should be separated, and that institutions, methods, and equipment should be modernized and brought up to the highest international standards. Furthermore, rejecting the ideological promotion of human uniformity, the theses argued that socialist physicians should educate the public in developing tolerance toward the mentally ill and stated, "The fundamentally humane character of the socialist way of life must be demonstrated by avoiding everything that defames the mentally ill in public and excludes them from society."[59] Continuing this initiative, a number of GDR psychiatrists formulated the so-called Brandenburg Theses in 1974–76, which sought to focus more on ill individuals in all their social circumstances rather than only on restoring their ability to work.[60] These theses continued to serve as important guidelines for many GDR medical professionals and were a real accomplishment, having stated many essential goals that have not yet been fully realized anywhere in the world. In practice, however, due to economic, political, and social constraints, improvements in this entire area remained more limited in the GDR than in the FRG, where reform efforts intensified after the mid-1960s.

As in all industrialized countries, the GDR gradually developed an extensive system of laws dealing with the identification, treatment, rehabilitation, and education of people with all types of disabilities. These laws continued and expanded the progressive traditions that had been in existence before 1933.[61] Here are a few highlights. From the beginning, emphasis was placed on early intervention, and a regulation passed in 1954 required medical professionals to report young people under the age of eighteen who had physical, mental, hearing, and visual impairments to the health care authorities (174ff.). In 1961, the first guidelines were issued for the tasks of rehabilitation commissions (58ff.). And in 1976 the most detailed regulation to date was passed regarding social support for disabled people. Its preamble stated programmatically, "By means of purposeful social measures, the socialist state aims to enable impaired and severely impaired citizens and their families to participate more and more in society" (53). This decree set the goals of improving rehabilitation (and specifically vocational rehabilitation), living conditions, various financial benefits, and medical care and equipment. As in many other countries, the earliest GDR laws assumed that a significant number of disabled people would be institutionalized, while the later laws placed greater emphasis on social integration, especially in the workplace.

Many of the benefits and services available to disabled people in the GDR were similar in theory to those available to West German citizens, although the lack of money often limited their realization in practice.[62] The more striking difference, of course, is that between countries such as the two German states, which had a strong tradition of social welfare extending back to the nineteenth century, and a country such as the United States, which provides a much weaker safety net for its citizens. One major difference between the GDR and the FRG, however, was the GDR system of invalid pensions established in 1973. This policy awarded a pension beginning at age eighteen to disabled people whose earning capacity was judged to be diminished by at least two-thirds. It also entailed benefits such as rent control, which limited rent payments for pensioners to no more than 5 percent of a family's gross income. Like retired pensioners, the state allowed disabled pensioners of all ages to travel to the FRG for the cynically pragmatic reason that if they decided to stay in the West their pension payments would cease, thus lessening the drain on the GDR economy. This policy reinforced the view that old and severely disabled people had little of value to contribute to socialist society. Some GDR citizens did in fact decide to go to the West for disability-related reasons. These were the so-called assistance refugees (Assistenzflüchtlinge), who felt they would have a better life in the West because they needed power wheelchairs and other modern equipment unavailable in the GDR. Others, however, visited the West and returned home, finding that they preferred the GDR to capitalist West Germany with its "cold" competitiveness.[63] Most, if not all, GDR invalid pensions were abolished after reunification in 1990 to the dismay of many former recipients.

The churches—primarily the Protestant Church—played a major role in providing services to disabled people, especially the cognitively disabled. Even though the state gradually became more active in this area, in 1987 the churches were still caring for about 50 percent of all severely mentally disabled people in institutions.[64] In 1976, the Protestant Church ran 51 hospitals, 89 institutions for the physically and mentally disabled, 226 nursing homes, and 19 day programs for the disabled, and the Catholic Church ran a smaller number of such institutions.[65] These church institutions were financed mainly by the state and donations from the FRG; in this manner, collaboration between church and state in health and social services reached a level in the GDR that was unprecedented in the socialist countries. In many ways, especially for cognitively disabled people and their relatives, the churches often served as refuges for expressing and practicing tolerance.[66] For example, a parents' group active within the Protestant Church during the 1980s petitioned the GDR parliament (Volkskammer), asking that the special education system be made more flexible and for the problems of disabled people to be discussed in schools. It received no response.[67] Furthermore, a GDR Protestant study group published a critique of the performance principle in 1981 in the FRG, which noted, "The anticipated socialist personality . . . frequently represses and hinders perception of the imperfect human being in really existing socialist society. . . . One must simply realize that human nature is not constructed for perfect, continual performance. Therefore, even in the best planned economy, human nature will remain a 'disruptive factor.'"[68] Such a perspective emphasized respecting and supporting all people equally as unique human beings rather than judging them only according to their productivity.

The GDR Society for Rehabilitation, founded in 1957, was eventually represented in relevant international commissions, and so its member professionals were aware of worldwide trends toward integrating rather than segregating disabled people. A society publication of 1981 gives a good idea of how the thinking among GDR experts about the proper place for disabled people in socialist society had evolved over the years and shows a certain diversity of opinion in these matters.[69] The authors defined the development of socialist society as the "objective process" in which "the humanistic ideal of the all-around personality is increasingly realized" (6). They pointed out, however, that socialist humanism had hardly ever concerned itself with trying to define the place of "impaired life." The authors thus proposed that the goal of socialist rehabilitation was full integration of disabled people into all aspects of society. Some of the authors still declared that severely disabled people incapable of performance could not become socialist personalities but proposed that they should be respected nevertheless as members of the human race. While such statements were advances over earlier one-sided pronouncements, they still carried the disparaging implication that disabled people were not as valuable as the nondisabled. Other authors, such as Gerda Jun, found it imperative to develop a new image of the human being, which she summed up by stating, "A human being is someone who is born of a human being" (95). From this perspective, it was a mistake to judge the value of a human being according to performance or economic criteria. Rather, taking the place of the most severely mentally disabled in society as a litmus test, she proposed that it was the duty of a humane society to try to satisfy not only their material needs but also their needs for communication, validation, and love (96).

The GDR guaranteed all its citizens, including disabled citizens, the right to education. As in West Germany, it was thought necessary to segregate most disabled people in special schools, training facilities, and vocational schools. As a result, a system of special education was gradually established that relied on segregated grouping for disabled young people of all ages.[70] This included day care and preschool centers, special schools for children of normal intelligence with various types of physical and sensory disabilities (Sonderschulen), special schools for the learning disabled (Hilfsschulen), training schools for children with mental disabilities, institutions for children labeled uneducable and untrainable, and special vocational schools. When disabled children reached school age, a commission from the Health and Social Welfare Department tested them to determine which type of school they would attend; parents frequently tried to protest these decisions but with little success.[71] While the Hilfsschulen offered only eight grades (another cause of parents' protests), the Sonderschulen had the usual ten grades, and some offered twelve grades leading to the university qualifying examination (Abitur). Many of these special schools existed only in certain places in the GDR, meaning that children and young people attending them had to leave their families and board there. For example, few regular schools were accessible to those with mobility impairments. As a result, for severely physically disabled young people who were categorized as needing special education but intellectually capable of university study, the Abitur was only offered in one special boarding school, which was combined with a hospital in Birkenwerder just north of Berlin. The young people there were often separated from their families for the entire twelve-year duration of their schooling. The perpetual lack of state financial resources often strengthened tendencies to marginalize the most severely disabled people, especially those with cognitive disabilities. In one instance, a mother managed to secure a place for her son, who had cerebral palsy, in a regular kindergarten only by agreeing to do the cleaning there.[72] And in another instance a child with Down syndrome was doing quite well in a kindergarten attached to a Hilfsschule but was expelled by a neurologist who insisted that this place should be reserved for a child with greater intellectual ability.[73]

Because of the lack of a public sphere in which disabled people and their allies could protest discriminatory treatment and put forth their own self-concepts, pejorative labels continued to be used longer in the GDR than in West Germany, especially in connection with the education of cognitively disabled people. By the 1980s in West Germany, the term *cognitively disabled* or *mentally handicapped* (geistig behindert) was in general use. But terms still current in the 1980s within the medicalized classifications of the GDR special education system included *morons* (Debile), *imbeciles* (Imbezille),[74] the *uneducable but trainable feebleminded* (schulbildungsunfähige förderungsfähige Schwachsinnige), and the *uneducable, untrainable feebleminded* (schulbildungsunfähige förderungsunfähige Schwachsinnige).[75] There was little or no public reflection about how disabled people, their relatives, and their friends might feel about such harsh labels that gave a false impression of scientific exactness. And these labels had dire consequences. Children classified as uneducable and untrainable, for example, were frequently placed for their entire lives into nursing homes or psychiatric hospitals where they received little stimulation and only custodial care; for example, there were 6,990 such children in Saxony alone in 1989. Reform-minded psychiatrists tried to advocate community placement for this group, but this could hardly be realized due to lack of personnel and money.[76]

The main difference between the two German states with respect to special education, aside from the ever-present economic difficulties in the GDR, was that, in spite of individual parents' protests about placement of their children, no supporters of integrated education were allowed to organize in the GDR. In the FRG, on the other hand, parents did organize around this issue. They have succeeded in achieving a limited amount of school integration of disabled and nondisabled children, although international studies still fault Germany for lagging far behind many other European countries in this area.[77] In the GDR, however, the abilities of the nondisabled almost always remained the unquestioned norm. For example, in 1984 I visited the East Berlin center of the Pioneer Youth Organization (the socialist mass organization for children). This was a large, modern building with facilities for arts and crafts, reading rooms and movies, club meetings, sports and games, and so forth. The director told us that disabled young people were allowed to use the building one day per week. When I asked whether they were allowed to come on any other day, he said that if they did not need assistance and were able to do everything that the nondisabled children could do, they could participate at other times. This was the prevailing attitude among policymakers and educators in the GDR. By contrast, however, my disabled GDR acquaintances have also told me about individual cases in which engaged teachers, friends, and relatives enabled young people with disabilities to attend regular but inaccessible schools by helping them go up the stairs or to the toilet. This seems to have happened more frequently in rural areas where there were no other alternatives because the special school system was not so extensive. In sum, people with physical and mental disabilities were included in the GDR unified educational system, but they were rigidly assigned to special places that were often inferior from an educational as well as a human standpoint. Many special education experts were well intentioned and felt that they were protecting disabled young people by keeping them separate. However, since the time of the Weimar rehabilitation experts, segregated special education has generally upheld an image of disabled people as incapable of taking responsibility for their own lives and as needing the constant supervision of nondisabled experts.[78] This patronizing treatment fed into the discontent that many disabled GDR citizens were finally able to express in 1989.

As a socialist society, the GDR also guaranteed all its citizens, including disabled citizens, the right to work, and this was fundamentally different from capitalist West Germany. In the planned economy, choices of trades and professions were steered and limited for all people and even more so for disabled people. Nevertheless, socialist ideology stressed both that work gave meaning to life and that the state needed its citizens to be as productive as possible. Especially for those disabled citizens who needed little or no extra assistance, an active working life was possible and indeed expected. One elderly woman I interviewed in 2000, for example, who had always used a wheelchair as a result of childhood polio, remembered the early years of the GDR as a wonderful, idealistic time with many opportunities. She joined the SED in 1946, was encouraged to study political economy even though she had not attended high school, and worked in the administration of the Agriculture Department at the Wilhelm Pieck University in Rostock.[79] Another elderly man from a communist family, who had had polio in 1914 and used crutches, had worked in administrative positions, founded holiday camps for disabled children, and served on rehabilitation commissions.[80] Max Schöffler, a blind communist activist during the Weimar Republic, became the director of the German Central Library for the Blind in Leipzig after 1945, which had been largely destroyed during the war and which he rebuilt with great energy.[81] Certainly other researchers will be able to uncover many more such stories.

While some young disabled people could pursue the same career paths as the nondisabled, for others there was an extensive system of special vocational schools that led to specific trades and professions. The more severely disabled, including cognitively disabled people classified as trainable, received job training in vocational rehabilitation centers. The goal was to teach them to do useful work either in sheltered workshops or at sheltered workplaces within enterprises. The number of sheltered workplaces rose from 3,774 in 1972 to 36,996 in 1982.[82] The directors of state-owned enterprises were obliged to make suitable apprenticeships and jobs available to disabled people, in contrast to West Germany (and reunified Germany), where employers could (and still can) avoid employing their assigned quota of disabled people by paying a small fine.[83] Some of these jobs involved meaningless busywork, as, for example, instances in which products assembled by cognitively disabled people would be taken apart for them to put back together again.[84] In general, however, there was a real effort to bring all disabled people, including as many of the severely disabled as possible, into the workplace in one way or another.

With respect to how laws, the education system, and labor policies developed over the years, the most striking contrast to West Germany is that in the GDR disabled people themselves (as well as parents of disabled children) were almost never allowed to participate in making the decisions that affected them. Writing in 1981, for example, Wolfgang Presber of the GDR Society for Rehabilitation brushed aside requests from "the impaired" to represent themselves. From his patronizing perspective, there was "nothing wrong with including the impaired in relevant discussions if possible," but "one must not fail to recognize that the impaired person does not speak and can never speak . . . for the impaired, but only for his particular group: the spastics, the paraplegics, the cystic fibrosis cases."[85] Such nondisabled experts and policymakers kept a tight grip on their power to decide what was best for disabled people. For example, Ilja Seifert, who uses a wheelchair and became one of the most tireless disability rights advocates after reunification, reported being received with icy silence when he once tried to give a somewhat critical talk at a conference of the GDR Society for Rehabilitation.[86] The only organizations of disabled people allowed to exist in the GDR were the Disabled Sports Association (Versehrtensportverband), with 8,500 members, and two others that had a long history from before 1933: the Association for the Blind and Visually Impaired (Blinden- und Sehschwachenverband or BSV), with 25,000 members; and the Association for the Deaf and Hard of Hearing (Gehörlosen- und Schwerhörigenverband or GSV), with 16,200 members.[87] These two organizations participated in international associations and had a certain right to participate in decision making that affected their members. The BSV organized music groups, sports clubs, counseling for parents, and special support for older members. The GSV had a pantomime group and even its own television program in the 1980s called *Im Bilde* (In the Picture). Other groups of disabled people frequently tried to form cross-disability self-advocacy groups, but the authorities never allowed this.[88] The lack of public forums where disabled people could advocate their interests constantly played out in detrimental ways to realizing their equality and contributed to their growing alienation from the socialist state.

As the economic crisis intensified during the 1980s, the deficits in the quality of life of many disabled people in the GDR compared to the FRG became more glaring. By then, the greatest hindrance to social integration seemed to be primarily the state's lack of financial resources rather than any rhetoric about norms of performance and the socialist personality, which had been largely jettisoned as the country struggled to survive. Citizens of the GDR had access to West German media; many had personal contacts with West Germans and had visited the FRG. As a result, they knew that disabled West Germans generally did not have to endure conditions such as the following, which were unfortunately typical in the GDR. Both disabled and elderly people often had to wait for years to be placed in a nursing home if they needed this type of care, and in 1989 there were 160,000 people on waiting lists. Because of the lack of facilities, various types of inappropriate placement were not uncommon: physically disabled people, including young people, were placed in nursing homes; people who were not mentally ill (usually cognitively disabled people) were placed in psychiatric institutions; adults and elderly people were placed together with children; and some people who were not ill were placed in hospitals.[89] Many of the nursing homes were in old buildings, such as former manor houses and barracks, that lacked elevators, accessible toilets and bathrooms, and so forth. Better nursing homes and medical facilities were built for SED functionaries, activists, and people classified as victims of fascism, and this favoritism fed popular resentment. There were enormous shortages of modern equipment and medical supplies such as wheelchairs, crutches, hearing aids, converted automobiles, and hospital beds (which were only manufactured for export). In particular, the lack of wheelchairs, and especially of power wheelchairs, which could be imported only occasionally from the West, was a major cause of citizens' petitions (Eingaben) to the government.[90] In many cases, people with mobility impairments had to wait years to get a wheelchair and were effectively trapped in their apartments.[91] Beginning in the 1970s, a few curb cuts were created, and there was an effort to create some accessible housing, but in East Berlin in 1989 there were only about eight hundred wheelchair-accessible apartments for about five thousand potential users. In other cities, conditions were even worse.[92] Little was done to make facilities for leisure and culture accessible. For example, in 1989 there were only twelve wheelchair-accessible restaurants in central East Berlin, and of these only one had an accessible toilet.[93] And as late as 1994 only 39 out of 272 public libraries in Saxony were wheelchair accessible.[94] The disabled activist Ilja Seifert described having to fight the bureaucracy for every small improvement: "It was really wearing to see that whenever we wanted to do something new, we had to 'educate' the authorities all over again."[95] The following situation dramatically illustrates the effects of the financial crisis on a specific group of disabled and ill people. Incontinence supplies were not manufactured in the GDR, so adults with these needs had to use washable diapers, which was very difficult and unhygienic. In 1987, the Ministry of Health reported buying a small supply of disposable pads from nonsocialist countries for extremely severe cases, but in 1988 there was no hard currency anymore even for this purchase.[96]

Of course, rehabilitation experts and government officials were acutely aware of these problems and discussed them internally, within the Ministry of Health, the state federation of trade unions, and the SED.[97] The state-controlled media never reported on any of these issues, however, continuing to proclaim instead that the needs of disabled (and elderly) people were being met satisfactorily and that socialism had great achievements and no deficits in these areas. Consequently, when disabled people took to the streets in 1989, one major cause was certainly their sense that their real problems were not being addressed, as well as their conviction that they had not been taken seriously as partners in public discourse.

Representations of Disability in Biographies, Reports, and Autobiographies

There was one way, however, in which a kind of partial public sphere developed during the 1980s where more open discussions about disability took place. A significant number of biographies, reports, and autobiographies were published that provide unique insights into how some disabled people and their relatives viewed their lives and problems in contrast to official perspectives. This relatively frank discourse was a corrective both to the hegemony of the experts and the whitewashing tactics of the media. These texts showed disabled people either as capable of performance and wanting to be recognized for it or—like some of the literary works discussed earlier—as deserving of respect and equal treatment as human beings even if they were not able to be economically productive.[98] The following is a chronological list of these books. The first was Roswitha Geppert's autobiographical novel *Die Last, die du nicht trägst* (The Burden You Do Not Bear, 1978), which was reprinted many times in response to the pent-up demand for critical discussion of these topics. Geppert recounted her experiences bringing up her cognitively disabled son from 1966 to 1977. Another frequently reprinted book was Wilhelm and Elfriede Thom's *Rückkehr ins Leben* (Return to Life, 1979). In this first GDR autobiography by a physically disabled person, Thom and his wife told about his rehabilitation after becoming paraplegic from an injury. While some disabled readers envied him for the superior care he received as a former police officer, some health care professionals were horrified at his relatively frank portrayal of the bad conditions he endured in clinics.[99] As a contribution to the UN Year for People with Disabilities, the physician Gerda Jun published *Kinder, die anders sind: Ein Elternreport* (Children Who Are Different: A Parents' Report, 1981). Jun explained that in the 1950s socialism had not planned for the mentally ill and cognitively disabled. Later, however, this one-sided image of the human being began to change, and there was a growing desire to learn about disability. To address this lacuna, her book presented eleven interviews with parents of disabled children along with medical information and practical advice. Sibylle

Muthesius wrote about her mentally ill daughter in *Flucht in die Wolken* (Escape to the Clouds, 1981) and reflected more generally on the problems of outsiders in socialist society. Also in 1981, Volker Kessling published his *Tagebuch eines Erziehers* (Diary of an Educator), which he had kept while working in a day program for developmentally disabled young people. The journalist Heinz-Joachim Petzold wrote a report about physically disabled people for the UN year entitled *Anerkennung statt Mitleid* (Respect, Not Pity, 1981). Petzold compiled another report about cognitively disabled people in 1984 called *Verstehen und fördern* (To Understand and Support). That same year, Klaus Möckel published *Hoffnung für Dan* (Hope for Dan), a report about his son, who was deaf and had brain damage. Irene Oberthür's *Mein fremdes Gesicht* (My Strange/Alien Face, 1984), in which she recounted her experiences after her face was badly disfigured in an automobile accident, reached a large readership when it also appeared in the GDR women's magazine *Für Dich* (For You).[100] In 1987, Manfred Wolter published a report called *Frank: Umweg ins Leben* (Frank: Detour into Life) about a young man who had cerebral palsy. Wolter spoke to Frank's mother, brother, colleagues, teacher, and Frank himself for this collection of interviews that give an in-depth look at the life of a person with this type of disability. While Wolter's book was allowed to be published, his DEFA film about a girl with cerebral palsy entitled *Rückwärtslaufen kann ich auch* (I Can Walk Backwards, Too) was suppressed for ten years. Upon its release in January 1990, a reviewer surmised that the film had been censored because it "did not present a picture of industrious, successful people."[101] Wilhelm and Elfriede Thom continued their earlier rehabilitation narrative with *Mitten im Leben* (In the Middle of Life, 1988), which also included many letters from readers. Another book that should be mentioned is Matthias Vernaldi's autobiographical novel *Dezemberfahrt* (December Journey, 1995). Here the author (who was born in 1966) told about growing up as a wheelchair user with muscular dystrophy, living in special boarding schools and institutions, and creating the first (and probably only) commune of disabled and nondisabled people in the GDR in a village close to Leipzig. Finally, Ulrike Gottschalk has compiled an as yet unpublished collection of interviews with physically disabled people, mostly her schoolmates from the Birkenwerder boarding school for the physically disabled.

The majority of these texts are about people with cognitive or developmental disabilities, and of course the books have somewhat different emphases depending on the type of disability involved. Nevertheless, it is possible to make some generalizations about how these works present the positive and negative aspects of living with a disability in the GDR.

The disabled people who spoke out in these works frequently mentioned parental love and encouragement; parents (especially mothers) often recounted standing by their disabled children. Supportive networks of friends and relatives were crucial; engaged teachers and medical professionals often provided guidance, advice, and good treatment. Those with physical impairments, in particular, sometimes told stories of overcoming their disabilities through persistent efforts and becoming relatively integrated into their communities and workplaces. That said, however, the reason for writing these books was to expose serious problems that disabled people and those close to them, especially parents, frequently encountered. The problems began with the birth of a disabled child. Parents told about difficulties in getting information and diagnoses, marriages falling apart, and suicidal despair. These writers described feeling intense stress, isolation, and hopelessness. They documented the detrimental effects of the lack of medical equipment and supplies, and they wrote extensively about difficulties in daily life such as inaccessible buildings and transportation problems.

These texts express extremely strong criticisms in the area of interpersonal relations, that is, in describing the reactions disabled people frequently encountered whether from authority figures or strangers in public situations. As one young man with cerebral palsy declared, "The nondisabled always know exactly what I'm allowed and not allowed to do."[102] The books frequently characterize bureaucrats and medical professionals as authoritarian, unfeeling, and tactless. They express the view that all too often these experts wrote off disabled people as deficient and ignored their real abilities and human needs. Both parents and disabled people often took issue with the system of total school segregation, pointing out that it neither prepared disabled young people for life in the nondisabled world nor promoted tolerance for diversity among normal schoolchildren. The authors reported on varying types of discrimination; in this context, some wrote about a "compulsion to be sad" and suggested that some members of the nondisabled public were unwilling to mingle with disabled people who were happy and enjoying life.[103] At times, disabled people were excluded from public places; some wheelchair users, for example, reported being barred from restaurants. And a young woman who had had polio told about an instance when a group of wheelchair users were not allowed to attend a Dresden soccer game. As she recalled, organizers claimed they "would disturb the athletic event because the healthy could not be expected to put up with the sight of us, and we had to leave." She went on to explain, "It's very painful to us to be devalued like this because we work hard at our jobs and would like to be respected and accepted like other people."[104]

The logic behind this argument was that at least some disabled people are able to overcome their impairments and contribute to society through work, and they should be valued for this.

The texts about people with visible disabilities all mention the feelings of pain and isolation caused by inappropriate, even hostile reactions from strangers in public situations, primarily in the forms of intense staring and tactless remarks. Many writers stated that it was only after having a disabled family member or becoming disabled themselves that they noticed this ugly side of daily life. For example, a father praised a sensitive teacher who helped his developmentally disabled daughter and her schoolmates deal with the public as follows: "It was easier for them to bear the piercing, curious stares of our fellow citizens when they took field trips together to local attractions, the post office, the museum, and the department store than it was when they went out only with their parents. . . . It was only when I saw how the public treated our daughter while she was growing up that I noticed what harsh judgments some people make."[105] The educator Volker Kessling reported that it was almost impossible to change negative public attitudes toward his cognitively disabled pupils and recounted, "In our part of town we still cause a sensation when we go for walks. When we go out with baby carriages, strollers, with the big and little children who walk clumsily and whose speech is incomprehensible to strangers, people turn around and stare at us. After we've gone past them, they put their heads together and talk about us." He stressed that his pupils' parents experienced this exclusionary behavior every day and that out of shame they still tended to hide their children away.[106] Tactless remarks were common. The worst one was reported by a mother who took her cognitively disabled son to the supermarket and was horrified when another customer said, "Oh, another one they forgot to gas."[107] By contrast, a married couple that had served as diplomats in African and Latin American countries reported that people there were much more accepting of their cognitively disabled daughter than their fellow GDR citizens were (116). In sum, many of these writers often seemed to find it easier to cope with practical problems related to impairment than with the thoughtless, cruel ways in which nondisabled citizens sometimes treated disabled people who did not conform to rigid norms of appearance, behavior, or intelligence.

The most striking thing about these texts in the context of socialist images of the human being is that they show many ways in which disability was socially constructed under socialism. The experiences narrated here conclusively rebut all undialectical views that creating socialist relations of production would automatically create social equality and ending capitalist exploitation would necessarily create kinder, more humane interpersonal relationships. Rather, these writers and interviewees frequently recalled the historical burden of national socialism's hierarchical distinction between valuable and valueless lives. They asserted the obligation to break with old patterns of intolerance and instead practice acceptance of difference. As the mother of a disabled child declared in this regard, "We need a revolution within ourselves" (129). These writers and interviewees hardly experienced a supportive socialist community characterized by solidarity among all its members. Rather, they suffered from an environment in which conformism, evasion of responsibility, and rudeness prevailed all too frequently. Indeed, except for the effects of economic shortages, almost everything described in these books about issues related to disability is also found in West German texts of the 1970s and 1980s. Writers in both German states reported on comparable problems with authoritarian medical professionals and bureaucrats, feelings of isolation and hopelessness, and prejudices against disabled people. These similarities to the West German situation are the most provocative thing about these GDR texts, for they brought up serious problems that were not supposed to exist any longer in socialist society according to official claims.

Yet there was one essential difference between the locations of disabled people in the two German states. In contrast to texts that disabled activists began to publish in the FRG as disability rights efforts emerged there in the 1970s, the most striking thing about these critical GDR works is that almost all of them are by parents or experts rather than disabled people themselves. In the FRG, the UN Year for People with Disabilities in 1981 was the occasion for the first large disability rights protests and the first countrywide organizing efforts *of* disabled people, whereas in the GDR it was only an occasion for publishing some sympathetic books *about* disabled people. Like all other groups that were potentially disruptive to officially proclaimed harmony and uniformity,[108] the SED state systematically silenced disabled GDR citizens until they began to claim their right to speak out in the winter of 1989–90.

Disabled GDR Citizens and the Turning Point of 1989–90

The contradictions between the promises of the state and the real conditions disabled people experienced led many of them to feel increasingly alienated and ready to take to the streets when the opportunity came. As Ilja Seifert wrote, "The state's policies toward people with disabilities

were mainly oriented toward using welfare measures to cover up everything that didn't fit into the picture of an 'ideal world.' . . . In this manner, we were prevented for years from having a voice about the things
that concerned us. But also, with regard to policies affecting the disabled, it became clear that it doesn't work in the long run to make policies *for* a social group. Those concerned are always the best experts
about their own lives. In the end, we turned out to be 'ungrateful.' We
didn't want to be 'taken care of!' We wanted to take care of ourselves!"[109]
Therefore, when political upheaval began to occur in 1989, many disabled GDR citizens immediately started to organize. Others joined them
who had also developed a critical perspective on these issues, including
personnel from state institutions, who were frequently relatives of disabled people, dropouts from performance-oriented workplaces, or citizens who had applied to leave the GDR. Furthermore, individuals who
were dissatisfied with low wages and bad working conditions in the
health care system also supported the initial disability rights efforts.
Others taking part in these activities included caregivers, doctors, and
special education teachers who had become acutely aware of the contradictions between official claims that all was well and actual practices
toward disabled people. Finally, members of Protestant church groups
who wished to facilitate better social integration of disabled people also
joined to further this cause. In contrast to West Germany, where disability rights activists had generally insisted on autonomy, there were
stronger alliances in the GDR among disabled people, their relatives,
and critical professionals who were familiar with international developments and wanted reforms but had not been able to prevail against the
political bureaucracy.[110]

Many disabled GDR citizens and their allies were ready to mobilize
immediately when the opportunity came in 1989. They insisted that disability was a product of social conditions that needed to be transformed.
They criticized the official, medicalized approach to disability as above
all an individual and family problem, as well as the common view of
disabled people as defective and unproductive. They attacked the belief
that strictly segregating disabled people in special schools, institutions,
and living quarters was necessary in order to integrate them eventually.
They also faulted the GDR practice of emphasizing integration into the
workplace but paying little attention to other areas of life (3). Instead,
they demanded practical improvements such as improved accessibility,
medical equipment, care, services, and benefits. But they also wanted
more fundamental transformations, including integrated education,
independent living, self-determination, and education of the public
about issues related to disability.[111]

In order to work toward all these goals, disabled people and their supporters immediately began to form cross-disability and self-help organizations, which had long been forbidden in the GDR. Ironically, because disabled people had been segregated so strictly, many had gotten to know each other well and had formed an informal network of social clubs.[112] These clubs seized the moment and became the nuclei for planning the first large disability rights meetings in the winter of 1989–90.[113] On November 25, 1989, a Berlin initiative was launched with the goal of founding a cross-disability organization as part of the democratizing process. This group wanted to make the public aware of "the real situation of the disabled and their almost total exclusion from all truly important decision-making realms of state and political power as well as from society in general."[114] Accordingly, one of the first forums of disabled people met on December 2, 1989, in East Berlin under the slogan "The forgotten ones of society."[115] The Berlin group began publishing a newspaper called *Die Stütze* (The Support/Crutch) in early 1990 and organized the founding conference of the GDR Association of the Disabled (Behindertenverband der DDR) on April 12–14 in East Berlin. Shortly before reunification on October 3, 1990, this group changed its name to the General Association of the Disabled in Germany (Allgemeiner Behindertenverband in Deutschland or ABiD). Its president, Ilja Seifert, a member of the Party of Democratic Socialism (PDS, the successor to the SED), was elected to the Bundestag in 1990 and thus acquired a national podium for advocating disabled people's interests. The ABiD advocates the international principles of the independent living movement and stresses self-determination while also emphasizing social solidarity. Although the ABiD is relatively small, with about eight thousand members in 1995, its significance is that it still strives to represent specific East German interests. Many more disabled East German citizens have joined previously existing West German organizations, and by 1994 about six hundred self-help groups for people with specific disabilities had also been founded in East Germany.[116]

Although these forums and organizations spoke of including people with all types of disabilities, they were in fact largely dominated by physically disabled people. The parents and relatives of cognitively disabled people also organized immediately in the winter of 1989–90 but felt that they had somewhat different concerns. A parents' group issued the following statement of grievances in January 1990: "We feel that doctors do not accept us as partners, and in many instances experts underestimate our competence to care for our children. In principle, impaired citizens and children are cared for in special institutions in the GDR. This means that true integration into daily life and society is impossible."[117] Like the new organizations of mainly physically disabled citizens, these parents demanded better material conditions, as well as more fundamental transformations such as integrated schools, group homes in the community rather than institutional placement, and integrated play and leisure activities (229). After reunification, many joined Lebenshilfe, the West German advocacy organization for cognitively disabled citizens. The speed with which physically disabled people and relatives of cognitively disabled people founded and joined self-advocacy organizations testifies to their urgent need for a real voice in shaping their lives.

As was the case for many other GDR citizens in the winter of 1989–90, the disabled people and their allies who became active were not calling at first for the abolishment of socialism but for improving their state. Events overtook them, however, and by the spring of 1990 it was clear that reunification with the capitalist FRG was inevitable. In May, the first united East-West demonstration of disabled people and their supporters took place in Berlin. Eastern speakers expressed apprehension over what capitalism and the West German health care system would mean for them. Slogans on their banners demanded "work for all," questioned whether disabled people would be left behind economically after the imminent currency reform, and called for policies that supported independent living. Disabled people had been restricted in many ways in the GDR, but they also feared that their basic, everyday needs would no longer be met.[118] Yet also, as the group rolled and walked by the East German Parliament (Volkskammer), there was a sense of exhilaration over finally being able to speak out in public. Other banners demanded "mobility for the disabled," "no exclusion," and "self-determination, not charity" and proclaimed, "Whoever excludes us violates human rights." One man's poster declared "The state lets us live, but doesn't let us participate in life" while another picked up on the slogan from 1989 to assert "We are also the people." In this demonstration, disabled East and West Germans represented themselves with images of diversity and constructive action that evoked dreams of a more open and inclusive world.

What has happened, then, to disabled East Germans in reunified Germany, a country that, to be sure, has a long tradition of providing for social welfare but is also a capitalist society oriented toward profit and competitive individualism? In Germany in 1991, out of a population of about 85 million, there were about 1,325,000 disabled East Germans and 5,400,000 disabled West Germans. These statistics refer to people whose earning capacity was judged to be diminished by at least 50 percent and who had a government identification card classifying them as disabled.[119] Of course, this is an extremely heterogeneous group in terms of self-concepts and life experiences. Nevertheless, some tentative generalizations can be made, even though they await much more research. The GDR rehabilitation system had some notable accomplishments that were generally abolished after reunification. Above all, these were the comprehensive early identification and treatment of disabled children, programs in occupational therapy, and the effort to employ as many disabled people as possible (334–35). When the market economy was imposed and enterprises were privatized after 1990, all disabled employees receiving pensions as invalids were fired for reasons of cost efficiency, including cognitively disabled people employed in sheltered workplaces within enterprises.[120] Disabled East Germans sometimes sum up their situation today by saying that their living conditions have improved but their work status has worsened. As has always been the case in West Germany, most disabled East Germans are now unemployed, underemployed, or only working part time.[121] In one comparative study, for example, some disabled East German women stated that they had felt a stronger sense of belonging to their society through their workplaces than disabled West German women did, and one East German woman declared that her greatest problem since reunification was not her disability but the fact that she had become unemployed.[122]

Some of the deficits related to issues of disability in the GDR have not been overcome and are still serious problems today. Personnel shortages are worse in many areas because about three million East Germans have moved to West Germany since 1990. In particular, about two thousand physicians left the East for the West, and there are similar shortages of nurses and other professionals. Because of reunified Germany's economic problems, it has not been possible yet to improve buildings, facilities, and equipment adequately in the East. Accessibility is gradually improving, but much remains to be accomplished.[123] On the other hand, however, the international disability rights agenda of self-determination and integration is now firmly established in East Germany in many ways. As in West Germany, the trend in the East is increasingly toward deinstitutionalization, community placement, and even integrated schools, although tremendous deficits still exist in this area.[124] Working to achieve these goals implies developing a concept of the human being in which the norm becomes respect for differences rather than pressure to conform. For example, disabled and nondisabled people created a center in Magdeburg where they could get to know each other better and stated that they did not aim to "make those concerned conform to social norms or ideals but rather to uncover their capabilities and abilities by means of self-realization and self-development."[125] In the best instances, then, a prescriptive understanding of the human being is being replaced gradually by a concept of accepting human diversity.[126] Yet such freedom often means little without a comprehensive social welfare network. In reunified Germany today, the economic security of many disabled people, along with that of the so-called bottom third of society, is becoming more precarious. One can only hope that European countries such as Germany will be able to maintain their strong traditions of social security and resist becoming Americanized in this sense.

Viewed from the perspective of disability studies, socialism manifested two contradictory utopian tendencies. On the one hand, going back to the late nineteenth century, there were socialists whose visions of improving the human being took health and efficiency as the measure of all things. As a result, it was often difficult to integrate disabled people into socialist societies such as the GDR, which held up uniform standards of performance and the development of the socialist personality as ideals. Biologistic tendencies were strong within really existing socialism but were often denied and simply projected onto the imperialist enemy.[127] On the other hand, socialism was also a utopia of accessibility. Working people were to break their chains and gain access to the fruits of their labor. Poor people were to have access to the joys and pleasures of life. As the *Communist Manifesto* declared, "We shall have an association, in which the free development of each is the condition for the free development of all."[128] Of course, Marx and Engels were referring to the class struggle, but many groups suffering from unjust restrictions, including disabled people, have expressed similar visions of liberation. After the end of the GDR, the effort to understand and learn from these tensions within socialism has continued. Along these lines, at a conference in 1990 about the living situations of cognitively disabled people in East Germany, participants stated that they wanted to develop a new kind of culture of dialogue between the disabled and the nondisabled. In their words, this would be a culture "that rejects custodial care, therapeutic arrogance, distanced neglect, and a stress on economic efficiency. It is our task today to reappraise critically what 'socialist humanism' meant for those directly and indirectly concerned. It is our task to take up the missed opportunities of the encounter between culture and disability in order to continue these in the present and future."[129] The humane ideal of socialism—that, independent of their origins, all people should have the chance to develop according to their capabilities supported by the solidarity of others—is yet to be realized.

CHAPTER 7 • Disability Rights, Disability Culture, Disability Studies

Since the 1970s in the Federal Republic, and then in reunified Germany, many disabled people have increasingly insisted on self-determination and have achieved some notable successes in many areas. The disability rights movement has rejected the outdated view of disabled people as only needy and helpless, and it has worked toward empowering them to live as citizens with full civil rights. Growing out of this political movement, practitioners of disability culture have rejected stereotypical images of disability and created a multitude of new self-representations. And, as the scholarly counterpart to these developments, the new disability studies carries on research in many fields from the perspectives of disabled people.

The Disability Rights Movement: From Problem Children to Citizens

On December 9, 1975, the General Assembly of the United Nations adopted a Declaration on the Rights of Disabled Persons, which stated that prejudice and discrimination were preventing millions of physically and mentally disabled people around the world from participating appropriately in their communities. The assembly emphasized that disabled people were entitled to civil rights and social integration in all areas of life and that their human dignity should be respected.[1] This declaration served as a basis for national and international activities undertaken during the UN Year for People with Disabilities in 1981. As in many countries, government agencies and other organizations in the FRG planned a series of events in conjunction with this UN year. But at the opening ceremony, held in Dortmund on January 24, 1981, a coalition of disabled activists occupied the stage and read a resolution attacking the UN year, and this ceremony in particular, as against their interests. Who were these activists, where did they come from, and what did they want?

During the 1950s it was primarily the organizations of the war disabled that achieved the first postwar improvements for disabled people. In the late 1950s and early 1960s, several advocacy organizations, such as Life Help for the Mentally Handicapped Child (Lebenshilfe für das geistig behinderte Kind) and the Spastics' Association (Spastikerverein), were formed. These were run mostly by parents and professionals. In connection with the far-reaching, democratic, social transformations of the late 1960s, however, some younger disabled and nondisabled people became dissatisfied with this arrangement. They began to critique these organizations for advocating the segregation of disabled people in many types of special institutions and for pressuring disabled people to conform to unquestioned standards of normality in many ways.

The founding of Club 68 of Hamburg is generally taken to be the beginning of the disability rights movement in the FRG.[2] Its members were young disabled people who split off from the Spastics' Association and planned social events together with nondisabled people. For many, this was the first time they had participated in leisure activities in such mixed groups. Soon similar clubs were founded all around the FRG, and in the early 1970s they formed the National Coalition of Clubs of the Handicapped and their Friends (Bundesarbeitsgemeinschaft der Clubs Behinderter und ihrer Freunde or CeBeeF). In the course of trying to go out and enjoy cultural and recreational activities in their communities, the members of these clubs encountered both prejudiced attitudes and practical problems such as inaccessible public buildings, restaurants, theaters, restrooms, transportation, and so forth. These barriers were nothing new, but, because these disabled people and their allies were facing them together, they could strategize among themselves about how to resist exclusion in daily life and claim their civil rights.

Parallel to the growth of the CeBeefs, a course called "Coping with the Environment" had begun at the Adult Education Center in Frankfurt in 1973. Led by the nondisabled journalist Ernst Klee and the disabled activist Gusti Steiner, the participants in this course wanted to improve the living situations of disabled people in Frankfurt. At first, this group asked city officials to make specific buildings and services accessible, but they were ignored. Consequently, influenced by the student movement and the U.S. civil rights movement, they proceeded to direct, nonviolent confrontation. Their most widely publicized action was to blockade the streetcars during a rush hour in 1974 in order to make the public aware that people with mobility impairments could not use this means of transportation. As a crowd gathered around the blocked streetcars, heated discussions took place. While a few voices were heard saying that "such people" would have been gassed under Hitler, many more passersby and streetcar riders supported the protesters.[3] Among other projects, participants in the Frankfurt courses also protested the inaccessibility of trains (still a huge problem today) and the fact that wheelchair users had to travel in unheated baggage wagons without toilets while paying full fares.[4] They demonstrated against the inaccessibility of the main post office in Frankfurt, and a ramp was built as a result. Disabled West Germans in other cities learned from the example of the Frankfurt group and began to carry out similar actions protesting exclusion and prejudice.[5]

From the beginning, participants in the Frankfurt course had sought to challenge widespread negative perceptions of disabled people as passive, pitiable recipients of welfare or charity. They declared, "We didn't want to keep on being grateful, nice, a little bit stupid, and easy to manage. We wanted to confront the everyday hostility toward disabled people."[6] Accordingly, they decided to create an antiprize to be awarded annually on the Day of Prayer and Atonement for conduct they deemed especially hostile to their interests.[7] In 1978, they presented the first Golden Crutch award to the Association of Automobile Insurance Companies for their advertising campaign promoting seat belt use that employed the slogan, "To be crippled for the rest of your life is a fate worse than death." The award ceremony in Frankfurt was partly a festival of alternative culture, featuring music by the popular Left-Radical Brass Orchestra. But it also had a serious message to deliver. The citation critiqued the advertising slogan as reminiscent of the Nazi idea that disabled people were "lives unworthy of life." Furthermore, presenters re-created various scenes from the lives of disabled people in the FRG such as an incident in Lüneburg in which a judge had divorced a woman on the street because she could not get into the court in her wheelchair. In 1979, the second Golden Crutch award focused on abuses in institutions and was given to the Alsterdorf Institutions and the Munich Spastics' Center. During the skits at this ceremony, disabled organizers asked the audience to remain silent for "one minute of pity." Some nondisabled audience members took offense at this part of the program, apparently finding such ridicule of their desire to "help" the disabled too much to bear.

These early disability rights efforts in the FRG focused on challenging traditional rehabilitation practices. As Ernst Klee wrote, since the 1920s ingrained ideas within rehabilitation psychology about the abnormal "cripple soul" had been used to justify segregating disabled people for they were generally viewed as dependent on the care, treatment, and training of experts.[8] During the 1970s, however, critical voices began to be heard from within the medical and applied medical fields that sometimes overlapped with the goals of the fledgling disability rights movement. For example, the widely read book *Kopfkorrektur oder der Zwang gesund zu sein: Ein behindertes Kind zwischen Therapie und Alltag* (Head Correction or the Compulsion to Be Healthy: A Disabled Child between Therapy and Daily Life, 1980) told the story of a child who had cerebral palsy from the perspective of her parents and therapists. The parents criticized medical professionals who viewed their daughter only as defective and who seemed obsessed with molding her into less conspicuous and "disturbing" patterns of appearance and behavior. By contrast, they wanted to love and accept their daughter for who she was and to encourage her spontaneous enjoyment of life. This difficult experience with the rehabilitation system led them to include a chapter in their book about Nazi "euthanasia" and to reflect on continuing, if repressed aggressions against disabled people that were still expressed sometimes in therapy and various exclusionary practices.[9]

Disability rights activists, along with some professionals, also began to critique how these normalizing rehabilitation practices had supported the segregation of disabled people in the broadest sense. For example, the authors of *An den Rand gedrängt: Was Behinderte daran hindert, normal zu leben* (Pushed to the Margins: What Prevents the Disabled from Living Normal Lives, 1980), who were all medical professionals working at the Spastics' Center in West Berlin, wrote about successful models of inclusion in Italy, Sweden, and the United States. They advocated such practices for the FRG, too, and declared, "Integration is the prerequisite for a normal life."[10] This statement marked a Copernican revolution with regard to views about the proper place for disabled people in the FRG. In this connection, Ernst Klee ridiculed the definition of a physically handicapped person given in the Federal Social Welfare Law: "People whose ability to become integrated into society is seriously impaired as a result of a physical irregularity."[11] He pointed out that this definition turned the facts upside down for disabled people actually wanted and tried to be a part of society but found that society constantly rejected and excluded them. Disability rights activists thus began to demand total integration in personal interactions, residence, education, and work. With respect to personal interactions, they urged disabled people not to remain isolated at home but to insist on going out in public and trying to do whatever they wanted. With respect to residence, they argued against institutionalization and advocated accessible housing in the community, that is, the right to a family life of one's choosing. With respect to education, they argued that the extensive system of special schools should be abolished and that children with disabilities should have the right to attend regular schools.

And, with respect to work, they noted the staggeringly high unemployment rate among disabled people (72 percent as a whole in 1981 and 85 percent among disabled women), which they viewed as rooted in prejudiced attitudes equating disability with incompetence.[12]

These more individually or locally oriented protests and activities soon grew into several disability rights campaigns organized on the national level. On February 25, 1980, the Frankfurt district court handed down a verdict that many disabled people and their allies found to be outrageously discriminatory. A West German woman had sued the travel agency that arranged her trip to Greece because a number of Swedes who supposedly had cognitive disabilities were staying at her hotel. She alleged that the sight of these people had made it impossible for her to enjoy her vacation. The court, headed by Judge Otto Tempel, concurred and awarded her a refund of half her expenses in damages. The court's decision read in part, "It is undeniable that the presence of a group of the severely disabled can reduce the enjoyment of a vacation for sensitive people. In any event, this is the case when it is a matter of deformed, mentally disturbed people who are not in command of language, who sometimes emit inarticulate screams in an irregular rhythm, and who occasionally have seizures. . . . There is suffering in the world, and this cannot be changed. However, the plaintiff is justified in not wanting to see it during her vacation."[13] As so often throughout history, the court upheld a view of visibly disabled people as "affronts to the healthy eye" and thus as appropriately kept out of sight where they would not disturb normal citizens.

Of course, this was not the first instance in postwar West Germany in which some citizens had carried out acts aimed at excluding disabled people and some officials had tacitly or overtly supported such tactics. Notoriously, when a doctor proposed in 1969 to turn an old mill building near the Bavarian town of Passau into a home for cognitively disabled and wayward children, local residents had burned down the building, saying that they wanted "a national park, not a park for idiots." Nothing was done to find the arsonists.[14] But the difference between the responses to this incident and the Frankfurt verdict was a decade of consciousness-raising and political organizing. Accordingly, when news of the verdict was made public, groups of activists organized their first national protest, which drew five thousand disabled and nondisabled people to Frankfurt on May 8, 1980, and turned out to be the largest demonstration for disability rights that had ever taken place in Europe.[15] On this occasion, Gusti Steiner declared, "We won't let ourselves be equated with defective toilet seats or be made into a vacation problem."[16] Participants pointed out how ironic it was that the court deliv-

Fig. 24. Banner reading "Don't pity the disabled person; pity the society that rejects him" displayed at the demonstration protesting the discriminatory verdict of the Frankfurt court at the Fountain of Justice in Frankfurt, May 8, 1980. (Photo © Walter H. Pehle, Frankfurt am Main.)

ered this decision shortly before the upcoming UN Year for People with Disabilities. They called for abolishing the segregation and isolation of disabled people and for creating a tolerant society in which such a verdict would be impossible. Large segments of the press and media supported the demonstrators and condemned the court's decision as inhumane and disgraceful.

Fig. 25. A disabled demonstrator wears the yellow star to protest the discriminatory verdict of the Frankfurt court, May 8, 1980. (Photo © Walter H. Pehle, Frankfurt am Main.)

Shortly after this demonstration, a number of disability rights organizations formed the Action Group against the UN Year (Aktionsgruppe gegen das UNO-Jahr). Members of this group carried out three spectacular actions during 1981 that attracted a great deal of media attention. First, they disrupted the opening ceremony of the UN year on January 24 in Dortmund by entering the hall in a "Parade of Cripples and Do-Gooders," occupying the stage, and forcing Federal President Karl Carstens to withdraw to a locked room to deliver his keynote address. The resolution that the group read deserves quoting at length as one of the most important early West German statements of disability rights.

> We are a coalition of initiatives of the disabled from the entire Federal Republic and West Berlin. We declare that the "International Year of the Disabled," as well as this opening ceremony, are being put on without our input and against our interests. This event is nothing but an expensive integration operetta that is intended to cover up the deplorable situation of disabled people. We reject the congratulatory speeches of politicians and experts that only serve "helpers" and prominent people who are craving to be admired. With their pity and insistence on helping us, they will destroy our hard-won efforts to represent ourselves. We also reject the speeches of those disabled people who claim that integration has been achieved. Today and tomorrow we are allowed to pee in accessible toilets that have been brought here for this occasion. The day after tomorrow we will have to stand in the corner like dogs again. Today and tomorrow we are allowed to use the special transportation that has been brought here with so much fanfare. The day after tomorrow we will be sitting at home again. The policy of special institutions, special equipment, special treatment, etc., has led to nothing but ghettoization, isolation, dependence, and mistreatment. Today, too, on January 24, the disabled are housed and mistreated in institutions. Today, too, the disabled are subjected to bureaucratic arbitrariness, unemployment, and inhumane conditions. We demand: no speeches, no segregation, no violations of human rights.[17]

In their statement, these activists rejected the prevailing medical model that conceived of disabled people as defective individuals who need to be helped, treated, and normalized by nondisabled experts. By contrast, they declared that disability was socially constructed and caused by exclusionary policies directed against them as an oppressed minority group and that their demands were a question of human rights.

The second action against the UN year occurred at the opening ceremony of the Rehabilitation Fair in Düsseldorf on June 18, 1981, and once again Federal President Karl Carstens was the target. This time a member of the Bremen "Cripple Group," Franz Christoph, ascended the stage and hit Carstens with his crutch, shouting that the president was again sponsoring an event in which, as always, "people were talking about us but not with us."[18] With this sensational action, Christoph

Fig. 26. "No speeches, no segregation, no violations of human rights." Disabled demonstrators occupy the stage at the opening ceremony of the UN Year for People with Disabilities, Dortmund, January 24, 1981. Gusti Steiner is in the center with the beard. (Photo by Frajo Krick, courtesy of Birgit Rothenberg.)

challenged not only the image of the grateful cripple but also that of the noble helper. He and his group issued a statement attacking the entire "rehabilitation circus" as leading only to more segregation and declared that the "Year of the Disabled is in fact directed against us disabled people."[19] During the confusion onstage, two outraged women in the audience shouted aggressively, "Be thankful that something like this is being done for you!" and "Too bad he can still walk!"[20] A photograph of Christoph about to strike Carstens appeared on the front pages of West German newspapers with accompanying articles ranging from sensationalistic accounts to thoughtful reflections on why "cripples" were so desperate. As for Christoph, he framed his goal as follows: "We have to manage to confuse our benefactors so much that when they see one of us on the street they don't know whether they're seeing a problem child or a terrorist cripple."[21] Christoph kept disability rights in the headlines and applied (unsuccessfully) for political asylum in Holland in 1983 because of what he termed "the persecution of the disabled in the FRG" (64). In the meantime, in several other cities a number of Cripple Groups had formed that also advocated a politics of separatist confrontation with the nondisabled world.

Building on the momentum generated by these events, fifteen disability rights groups decided to hold a Cripple Tribunal in Dortmund on December 12–13, 1981. Analogous to the Russell Tribunal, it accused

Fig. 27. Disability rights activist Franz Christoph about to strike Federal President Karl Carstens with his crutch, Düsseldorf, June 18, 1981. (Photo: dpa/Landov.)

the Federal Republic of violating the human rights of disabled people. It published its findings in a document entitled *Krüppel-Tribunal: Menschenrechtsverletzungen im Sozialstaat* (Cripple Tribunal: Human Rights Violations in the Social Welfare State, 1983). The organizers asserted that the Frankfurt court decision of 1980 had not been an isolated case for the "power of normality" enforced discriminatory policies of segregating disabled people in all areas of life. They noted that, even though after 1945 the more humane-sounding term *disabled* had replaced *cripple,* they were still subject to discrimination, oppression, and deprivation of rights.[22] Accordingly, the goal of the tribunal was to bring abuses to light and empower disabled people to resist. Participants researched and discussed conditions in institutions, arbitrary government policies, inaccessible public transportation, unemployment, sheltered workshops that paid very low or no wages, women's issues (abortion, rape, prejudiced treatment by gynecologists), the pharmaceutical industry (thalidomide and other drugs), the rehabilitation system, and psychiatric issues. This was the first comprehensive effort by disabled people to formulate their own perspectives on such a wide range of issues that were central to their civil rights and quality of life. As an article in *Die Welt* stated on December 14, 1981, the Cripple Tribunal transformed the "Year of the Disabled" into the "Year of the Disablers."

These widely publicized actions against the UN year brought issues of disability rights to broad public consciousness for the first time in the FRG, but in practical terms they had relatively little effect. Consequently, since the early 1980s disabled people have organized a multitude of self-help groups and political initiatives aimed at making concrete improvements in their lives while continuing to develop their ideological critiques. Broadly speaking, these initiatives include disabled women's groups, the independent living movement, and the push to pass a comprehensive antidiscrimination law.

Disabled women had been active in disability rights efforts from the beginning, focusing at first on the oppression experienced by all disabled people rather than issues specifically related to gender. Along these lines, for example, Christa Schlett wrote in 1974, "The severely disabled person . . . must find the strength to rebel. He must rebel against his parents, the know-it-alls, the well-intentioned people. . . . Only self-awareness makes it possible to take the first steps toward emancipation."[23] Very soon, however, some began to reflect on what this increasing self-awareness could mean for women who were disabled. Furthermore, they started to make connections with nondisabled activists in the growing women's movement. Perhaps the most influential expression of this perspective was *Herz im Korsett: Tagebuch einer Behinderten* (Heart in a Corset: Diary of a Disabled Woman, 1977) in which a thirty-year-old Swiss activist, writer, and wheelchair user, Ursula Eggli, recounted her efforts to resist isolation and live life to the fullest. Not only did she finally leave her parents' home and move into an apartment together with disabled and nondisabled friends, but she also wrote openly about her problems finding love and sex as a disabled woman. The significance of her book for its time is that Eggli and her disabled friends are portrayed as multifaceted, increasingly self-confident women who were no longer willing to accept marginalization and became active in disability rights efforts.

Eggli's book inspired a few nondisabled West German women to discuss disability within the framework of women's liberation. Accordingly, the two leading magazines of the West German women's movement published special issues on the topic of disability around the time of the UN year: *Courage* in January 1980 and *Emma* in May 1981. The nondisabled editors noted that since they hardly ever encountered disabled people in their daily lives they had to search out disabled women to write for these issues.[24] The editorial in *Emma* stated, with rather brutal naïveté, that it was easier for disabled women to emancipate themselves because they were physically unattractive and could not possibly compete with nondisabled women for men's attention.[25] Other contributors, however, were more aware of the complexities of being both disabled and female. Both issues featured insightful autobiographical and theoretical texts by disabled women born in the 1950s and early 1960s. These authors wrote about the dual discrimination they experienced as women but especially because of their disabilities. They described often being dismissed as neuter and sexless because they did not conform to expected female roles and beauty ideals. Some felt they had found a home in the women's movement, as did Theresia Degener, who stated, "If I'm already stared at less in a leftist, alternative pub than in a middle-class pub, then I'm even more accepted by women."[26] Other contributors reflected similarly on the satisfactions of making personal and political connections with women who were striving for emancipation in many areas.

Solidarity between disabled and nondisabled women was always difficult to achieve for many reasons. Accordingly, arising out of the Cripple Tribunal, a Cripple Group that limited its membership to disabled women was formed in 1982 with its center in Bremen. Disabled women from Marburg, Kassel, and Frankfurt wrote *Geschlecht: behindert; Besonderes Merkmal: Frau* (Sex: Disabled; Special Characteristic: Woman, 1985), which was the first book in the FRG to combine both a disability rights and a feminist perspective. Stating that society viewed them as "inferior, useless beings," these activists proclaimed that they were no longer willing to live in a "ghetto" and were going to write about themselves rather than being written about by the nondisabled.[27] Contributors told their life stories, reflected on oppressive norms, and proposed possible strategies of resistance. Throughout, they explored the differences and commonalities between themselves and nondisabled women in many areas. With respect to education and job training, they highlighted the limited expectations for women but also their experiences of occasionally being pushed to find jobs because it was assumed that no man would be willing to marry and support them. They began to write more openly about the taboo subject of disability and sexuality, telling how they were perceived in many contexts as not being "real women." This included difficulties with finding partners as well as the perception that disabled women are unfit mothers. They told about doctors who urged them to be sterilized or tried to convince them to have abortions and about encounters with strangers who made hateful remarks on seeing them with their children (72, 184). They also critiqued the rehabilitation system for its fixation on traditional norms of appearance. In this connection, some of the women described being forced as children to wear uncomfortable, nonfunctional prostheses and wrote movingly about their feelings of liberation when they grew up, decided to accept their bodies, and threw away their prostheses.

Fig. 28. Disabled women critique the beauty ideal and its consequences in 1985: "Wearing a tank top without arms is like wearing a mini-skirt with braces." (Photo by Martin Glück, courtesy of Gisela Hermes.)

Since the early 1980s, many disabled women's groups have been organized and many publications by disabled women have appeared in the FRG and reunified Germany. In 1998, most disabled women's organizations formed a national Women's Network (Weibernetz), which explicitly includes disabled lesbians and girls. The network also reaches out to women with cognitive disabilities by publishing a version of its newspaper, *WeiberZeit* (Women's Times), in what is termed easy language. This network seeks to improve the lives of disabled women in the areas of political and social policy, health care, employment, and sexual abuse, and it brings critical, disability-oriented perspectives into debates about bioethics and beauty ideals.[28] Many of these disabled women's organizations provided feedback for the first comprehensive government report on disabled women in Germany in 1999.[29] This report found striking differences between the experiences of older and younger disabled women, which it attributed to the gradual process of individualization in postwar society. Women above the age of forty-five had generally experienced a high degree of exclusion and isolation and often expressed feelings of resignation and helplessness. They were much less frequently married or living with a partner than were nondisabled women of the same age. Younger disabled women, however, had both more positive self-concepts and better experiences of at least partial integration with their families and peers. In conclusion, the study recommended improvements in employment and benefits, education of medical professionals, counseling and services for sexual abuse victims, and public education about disability and disabled women.

In the early 1980s, a number of West German disability rights activists, including Ottmar Miles-Paul, spent time in Berkeley, California, which was the center of the American independent living movement of disabled people. They returned to the FRG to establish the first Center for Independent Living in Bremen in 1986, and since then many such centers have been established all around Germany. As Miles-Paul explained, the goals of the German independent living movement are peer support, an end to institutionalization and all forms of segregation, personal assistance to enable disabled people to live in their communities, rejection of the medical model of disability, and control by disabled people of their own organizations and services.[30] In 1991, these activists formed the umbrella organization for independent living called Interessenvertretung Selbstbestimmt Leben (ISL), which is run solely by disabled people and has become an important voice in debates about policies and rights.[31] Throughout this process, it is striking that many disabled people have become articulate in formulating their own goals and adept at carrying out their own projects.

After German reunification in 1990, as violent attacks escalated against foreigners, there was a brief flurry of articles in the press between about 1992 and 1994 that noted several such attacks against visibly disabled Germans and attempted to explain them in the context of general right-wing violence.[32] For those concerned with the civil rights of disabled people, these attacks—though few in number—seemed symptomatic of broader problems of discrimination. In this connection, statistics are frequently cited on education and employment, two of the most crucial areas for measuring integration. Thus, 93 percent of children identified as needing special education in Germany in 2003 were still segregated in special schools.[33] And, according to the microcensus of 2003, only 24 percent of disabled men and 18 percent of disabled women were supporting themselves entirely by working.[34]

In view of such persistent patterns of exclusion, the main goal of the disability rights movement on the national level since reunification has been to push the Bundestag to pass a comprehensive antidiscrimination law. German activists drew much of their inspiration in this regard from U.S. civil rights legislation, especially the 1990 Americans with Disabilities Act (ADA). These activists and their allies have had notable successes. In 1994, the Bundestag added a clause to the federal constitution that prohibits discrimination on the basis of disability, and the Federal Equal Rights Law for Disabled People went into effect in 2002. However, these laws did not apply to civil contract law, meaning that public accommodations, owners of rental housing, and so forth, could still legally discriminate against disabled people and, indeed, against whomever they wanted.

Several years ago, the European Union passed guidelines stating that all its member countries must prohibit discrimination in such situations on the basis of race and ethnicity. In Germany, activists convinced the ruling SPD–Green Party coalition in 2005 to propose a more extensive law that would also prohibit discrimination on the basis of disability, age, sex, sexual orientation, religion, and worldview.[35] This proposed law applied to what is termed the right to enter into mass contracts, that is, contracts that are typically concluded without taking personal characteristics into account. An example would be the right to eat in a restaurant: it could be expected that any customer would be served regardless of the personal characteristics listed in the legislation. It has been fascinating to follow the debate about this law in the Bundestag, which is reminiscent of the one that took place in the United States before the ADA was passed.[36] As in the United States, the main opponents of the proposed law in Germany came from the CDU and the Free Democratic Party (FDP), which represented various sectors of the business community. They argued that they should be free to refuse to enter into such contracts with whomever they please, and they conjured up the threat of a huge flood of lawsuits if the legislation were enacted. Although the Bundestag passed the antidiscrimination law in 2005, the CDU and FDP blocked its approval in the Bundesrat (the upper house of Parliament), and so supporters of the law had to begin at square one again.[37] Since the national elections in 2006, when a "grand coalition" between the SPD and CDU was formed, the political climate became more receptive to this legislation. In a great advance for civil rights in Germany, the antidiscrimination law, now called the General Law on Equal Treatment (Allgemeines Gleichbehandlungsgesetz), was passed in June 2006 and went into effect on August 18, 2006.

Disability Culture: From Objects of the Stare to Self-Representation

Running like a red thread through the autobiographies of Germans with visible disabilities are distressing accounts of how strangers frequently stare at them. These writers tell how being stared at provokes feelings ranging from shame and fear to anger. Along these lines, a twelve year old who had no arms because of thalidomide wrote in the early 1970s, "It's mainly the older people who stare at me. They look at me not just because I don't have arms but as if I had lost my mind. . . . For a while, people treated me so badly that I didn't dare to go out on the street anymore. Then my mother sewed me a cape to wear so that I could hide under it."[38] A woman described the reaction of strangers to her and her blind daughter: "Everybody looks, or at least that's how I felt. . . . It seemed so strange to me. As if you don't belong, such a bad feeling. We're different, we're stared at, it's so peculiar."[39] And another mother whose daughter had cerebral palsy described how strange it felt to go to town without her daughter, saying that she always thought, "Now no one is looking at you! Today you're a human being just like everyone else!"[40] A young woman whose leg had been amputated due to a street-car accident wrote in her diary in 1972, "People look at my prosthesis as if I were some kind of freak. That makes me feel so aggressive that I almost become confrontational."[41] Another woman affected by thalidomide reported in 1992, after a trip to South America, that she felt more accepted there than in Germany, stating, "Here everybody really gapes at you. Their eyes are popping so far out of their heads that if you had a knife, you could cut them off."[42] As these quotes illustrate, staring is a largely unconscious action that marks the starer as normal and the staree as an abnormal outsider in terms of behavior or appearance. Disabled Germans have reflected on how being the object of the stare impacts their self-concepts. According to the wheelchair user Ulrike Gottschalk, who grew up in the GDR, the looks she encountered expressed "pity, sorrow, disgust, horror, or admiration that also implied distance and ruled out equality. . . . The gaze made something out of me that I didn't want to be. But what was I? For how many years did I hear the voice that declared me to be someone who should have been prevented from exist-ing?"[43] Gottschalk's insightful statement places the nonphysical vio-lence of staring at one end of a continuum whose most extreme mani-festation occurs in acts of physical annihilation.

Of course, as early as the Weimar Republic some disabled individu-als and self-advocacy groups in Germany resisted objectification and violence of all sorts. These disability rights pioneers spoke out for self-determination and advocated egalitarian, rights-based concepts of their place in society. In contrast to these early emancipatory efforts, which national socialism almost totally crushed, the disability rights activities of recent decades have been able to formulate more substantial critiques and thus to register significant, hopefully enduring accomplishments in transforming representations of disabled people. Taken in the broadest sense, current worldwide disability culture production has been engaged in refusing to be the object of the stare and in expressing more autonomous self-concepts and identities.[44]

In Germany, one of the best illustrations of this reversed perspec-tive, which can set the parameters for presenting the new disability cul-ture, is Didi Danquart's film *Der Pannwitzblick: Wie Gewalt gegen Behinderte entsteht* (The Pannwitz Gaze: How Violence against Disabled People Originates, 1991). The film's title is taken from a Holocaust sur-vivor, Primo Levi, who wished he could fathom the dehumanizing look with which a Nazi named Dr. Pannwitz regarded him in Auschwitz.[45] The film thematizes structural violence against disabled people in the old eugenics of the past and the new euthanasia debate, including views of disabled people as costing society too much and as symbols for suf-fering and unhappiness. As Danquart explained, the film interrogates the gaze that expresses the power of normality.[46] First, it critiques eugenic images by juxtaposing clips from Nazi films with segments fea-turing Germans who speak from a disability rights perspective. For example, a clip from the sterilization film *Opfer der Vergangenheit* and a clip from the Nazi medical film *Eine 4 1/2-jährige Mikrocephalin* are interspersed with reflections by Theresia Degener, who was born with-out arms, on how she suffered from being forced to wear nonfunctional prostheses as a child. She states, "For me this was really almost the worst time in my life, when I was told, 'You have to have arms—you have to get accustomed to them now.'" Degener describes how thera-pists made her wear laced-up boots to prevent her from using her feet, even though it was much easier for her to do most things with her toes. In clips from a medical film made of Degener as a little girl, it is obvious that she hated the prostheses and resisted using them. She characterizes the normalizing, medicalized gaze to which she was subjected as follows: "So there was always this . . . gaze of the cameraman or of the therapists and doctors. It was always the same gaze, which said, *You* are different. *You* are alien. *You* don't belong to us. We'll change *you*. . . . You are being made into an object, . . . and that is a way of killing a human being" (106–7). Second, the film includes statements by contemporary advocates of euthanasia, such as Hans-Henning Atrott and Peter Singer, and refutes their point of view with critiques by disabled people that reflect on continuities and dissimilarities between the old eugenics and new debates in bioethics. Far from being a heavy-handed documentary, the film features poetic texts, thoughtfully composed music, and provocative editing. One reviewer observed that after viewing the film, spectators understand that their own problems with looking at the disabled are not the problems of disabled people (140). This is surely one of the main goals of disability culture.

Since the late 1960s in the FRG, activists, writers, filmmakers, artists, dancers, and actors have been engaged in creating alternative representations of disability within the context of the worldwide struggle for disability rights. Broadly speaking, these activities have critiqued negative images of disabled people and begun to replace them with alternative representations that question many assumptions about normality. These new texts often explore the differences of disability without resorting to outdated, simplistic metaphors. In the FRG, these efforts have been concentrated in three main areas: (1) debates about the language of disability, (2) repudiation of Nazi eugenic images and the introduction of disability rights perspectives into current bioethical debates, and (3) new experimental approaches to representing disability.

Disabled Germans and their allies have created new kinds of representations by questioning the language traditionally used to speak about disability. One crucial part of this struggle has been to reject older negative terms. The successful effort discussed in chapter 4 to change the name of Campaign Problem Child to Campaign Human Being can stand as an important example here. Conversely, another approach, common to most civil rights movements, was that some disabled people began to reappropriate the most negative label and claim an identity as "cripples." The first Cripple Groups, which formed in the FRG in the late 1970s, declared that "by calling ourselves cripples we simply say out loud what the nondisabled think about us" and insisted on remaining autonomous in order to define their own needs and separate themselves from well-meaning but overbearing nondisabled people.[47] The stigmatizing term *cripple* was thus used to assert strength and independence whether in the Bremen *Krüppelzeitung* (Cripple Newspaper), the Cripple

Tribunal, or the Munich theater group Crüppel Cabaret, which recently nonplussed an audience in Passau with its ironic play *Rollennium*.

These approaches to critiquing and transforming the language of disability are part of the far-reaching efforts to move from a medicalized definition to a modern definition of disability as socially constructed. Such a definition recognizes that disability is not merely an individual flaw but rather is above all a social attribution. This reversed perspective is captured well in the title of a book published in connection with the effort to pass antidiscrimination legislation: *Die Gesellschaft der Behinderer* (The Society of the Disablers, 1997). Drawing on suggestions from the World Health Organization, the authors distinguish between *impairment* (Beeinträchtigung), which refers to a medical condition, and *disability* (Behinderung). They cite the definition proposed by the Forum of Disabled Lawyers (Forum behinderter Juristinnen und Juristen) in 1995: "A disability is every measure, structure, or behavior that removes, limits, or impedes opportunities for people with impairments."[48] So, for example, applying this definition means that public transportation should be made accessible to people with mobility impairments rather than meaning that these people should resign themselves to staying at home. This reconceptualization of disability as a civil rights issue recognizes, as one German activist put it, that there is a "broad spectrum of forms of human existence, but none of these should be a cause for segregation or exclusion." Rather, with the consistent application of such a perspective, "the integration and support of all people in all areas of life would become the normal thing."[49] With respect to cultural representations of disability, this definition eliminates negative labels and no longer views disabled people solely as the carriers of abnormalities that need to be cured or fixed. Rather, it insists on transforming a discriminatory society.

Second, challenging negative representations of disabled people has entailed breaking through silences and intentional cover-ups in the postwar period to speak out on a number of levels about Nazi crimes against people with disabilities. During the 1980s, disabled activists, medical professionals such as Dr. Klaus Dörner, and members of the Green Party and Alternative List pushed for the federal government to recognize disabled survivors as victims of fascism and thus as entitled to monetary compensation.[50] The Association of Victims of "Euthanasia" and Involuntary Sterilization, which was formed in 1987 as a self-advocacy organization, was finally successful in securing some payments, although, of course, many victims had passed away by then. Furthermore, a small number of disabled people who had been involuntarily sterilized or were witnesses to "euthanasia," including Elisabeth Claasen (a pseudonym), Josef Demetz, and Klara Nowak, published autobiographical accounts of how they experienced this violence.[51] The Nazi eugenic propaganda directed against them was never far from their minds. This can be seen in a compilation of survivors' memoirs entitled *Ich klage an* (I Accuse, 1989), which speaks out against the murderous gaze trained on certain disabled people in the Nazi "euthanasia" film of the same name.

Another highly significant way in which negative representations of disability from the Nazi past have been rejected since the early 1980s is the development of critical scholarship and public education about this topic. A new generation of activists, historians, physicians, and other professionals has produced an enormous amount of scholarship about the medical crimes committed during the Third Reich, including historical accounts of almost all the hospitals and nursing homes in which crimes took place. Memorials have been placed at important sites, including the T4 headquarters, located at Tiergartenstraße 4 in Berlin, where a plaque explains what happened there. The first national memorial service for the disabled victims of national socialism was held in 2000 at the Sonnenstein asylum in Saxony, where about fifteen thousand people were gassed in 1940 and 1941.[52] Also memorials and informational exhibits have been created at hospitals and asylums that were centers for the sterilization and killing of disabled people. For example, a monument to twenty-one children murdered in Nazi medical experiments has been placed at the entrance to the Heidelberg University Psychiatric Clinic.[53] And, as one of its creators explained, the historical memorial at the psychiatric hospital in Hadamar, where more than ten thousand patients were gassed in 1941, seeks to illustrate the "subtle beginnings and horrible effects of mechanisms of segregation, repression, persecution, and annihilation" directed against disabled people in the Third Reich.[54]

To my mind, there is no better illustration of the enormous changes in attitudes toward disabled people over the past sixty years in Germany than the fact that People First, a self-advocacy organization of people with cognitive disabilities, was involved in designing the historical exhibit at the Hadamar hospital. In 2003, members of People First participated in a conference at Hadamar to provide input on how the memorial could be made more accessible to people with learning difficulties (*Lernschwierigkeiten,* the term that the German branch of People First prefers). As a result, a new catalog about the historical site was published in what is termed "easy language" using short words and sentences.[55] In general, because Germans involved in disability rights, disability culture, and disability studies are so aware that people with cognitive and mental disabilities were the prime targets of Nazi eugenics, there are beginning to be a number of such efforts to include people with learning difficulties in public events having to do with disability and to create easy-language versions of disability-related texts.

Disabled people and their allies have not only critiqued past crimes and abuses but have also intervened in the new euthanasia debate and other bioethical debates related to disability. Many of these issues relate to questions of reproduction, and since the 1980s disabled women have been participating in political and scientific discussions about such matters as gene technology, reproductive medicine, the so-called eugenic indication for abortion, and sterilization practice and law. Of course, these are enormously complex issues, but all of these scholars and activists challenge the automatic linking of disability and suffering. Proceeding from the perspective of social construction, they point out that many disabled people suffer much more because of discrimination than because of their impairments.[56] In this conflict-laden area, positions and alliances are constantly shifting, but in general many German intellectuals now take standpoints that differ from those of their counterparts in other European countries and the United States. This is because of their knowledge of Nazi crimes and because of the success of the German disability rights movement in bringing the perspectives of disabled people into these debates. A good statement of these positions is the "Grafenecker Erklärung zur Bioethik" (Grafeneck Declaration on Bioethics, 1996), published by the Working Group on Researching the History of "Euthanasia" and signed by many leading physicians, philosophers, historians, and others.[57] It insists on the universality of human rights, including the right to life and human dignity for all people, and rejects any sort of devaluation of people with disabilities.

Disability is a very fluid, imprecise category that is a site of struggle rather than a clearly delimited set of characteristics. This means that it is difficult to arrive at precise statistics about disabled people. Today both government officials and disability rights activists usually say that approximately eight million people in Germany have some kind of disability.[58] Until recently, most mainstream cultural representations of this significant minority group have been created by nondisabled people and have upheld damaging stereotypes. Influenced by the disability rights movement, however, many newer cultural texts now depict disability and disabled people in ways that are more realistic, positive, and even avant-garde.

An excellent example of a text by nondisabled authors that advocates activism in order to secure civil rights for disabled people is the play by Roy Kift and Volker Ludwig entitled *Stärker als Superman* (Stronger than Superman). This has been the most frequently performed play of the Grips Theater in Berlin, which is known for its progressive children's plays. The 1993 version takes up the issue of integrating children with disabilities into regular schools, which is not yet a legal right in Germany. As the play begins, Micha, a boy who uses a wheelchair and likes to pretend he is Superman, claims, "I can do everything in the world! I don't need help from anybody."[59] He soon finds out that this is not true, however, when his neighborhood school refuses to accept him because it is inaccessible. Help comes in the person of Krüppelkalle (Crippled Carl), an adult neighbor who also uses a wheelchair, dresses like a punk rocker, and calls himself the "avenger of the oppressed." Krüppelkalle urges Micha to resist being segregated in a special school and declares that the real disabled people are the "marching farts," the "ice-cold zombies," the "dummies who think they're better than us just because they can walk and who don't even let us get on the bus" (8). He encourages Micha and his friends to fight for their rights and solves problems so that Micha can finally attend the school. In the end, the characters are stronger than the individualistic Superman because they cooperate with each other. The audience at such Grips Theater productions is largely composed of schoolchildren, teenagers, and even entire school classes, which discuss the controversial issues later. After seeing this play, for example, the older sister of a disabled girl mused, "Of course, it's bad that Karline is disabled, but somehow it's good, too, because now we can do the right thing, and we can show how much we love her."[60] This statement shows the influence of positive cultural models in fostering new norms of inclusion and acceptance.

As is typical of many liberation movements, the first texts created by disabled people who were coming to a new consciousness of their civil rights were mostly autobiographical accounts of searching for more positive self-concepts. Examples include Ernst Klee, *Behindert sein ist schön* (Disability Is Beautiful, 1974), Ursula Eggli, *Herz im Korsett* (Heart in a Corset, 1977), Franz Christoph, *Krüppelschläge: Gegen die Gewalt der Menschlichkeit* (Cripple Bashes: Against the Violence of Being Humane, 1983), Ortrun Schott and Erhard Schott, *Verspottet als Liliputaner, Zwerge, Clowns* (Mocked as Lilliputians, Dwarfs, Clowns, 1983), Carola Ewinkel, *Geschlecht: behindert; Besonderes Merkmal: Frau* (Sex: Disabled; Special Characteristic: Woman, 1985), Fredi Saal, *Warum sollte ich jemand anders sein wollen? Erfahrungen eines Behinderten* (Why Should I Want to Be Someone Else? Experiences of a Disabled Man, 1992), Sigrid Arnade, *Weder Küsse noch Karriere: Erfahrungen behinderter Frauen* (Neither Kisses nor a Career: Experiences of

Disabled Women, 1992), and Gerlinde Barwig and Christiane Busch, *"Unbeschreiblich weiblich!?" Frauen unterwegs zu einem selbstbewussten Leben mit Behinderung* ("Indescribably Female!?" Women on the Way to a Self-Confident Life with a Disability, 1993). More recently, efforts to assist cognitively disabled people in telling their stories have resulted in books such as Christa Reuther-Dommer's *"Ich will Dir erzählen . . .": Geistig behinderte Menschen zwischen Selbst- und Fremdbestimmung* ("I Want to Tell You a Story . . .": Cognitively Disabled People between Self-Determination and Control by Others, 1997) and Ulrich Hähner's *Vom Betreuer zum Begleiter: Eine Neuorientierung unter dem Paradigma der Selbstbestimmung* (From Caregiver to Companion: A Reorientation according to the Paradigm of Self-Determination, 2003). All of these firsthand accounts break through silences and distortions to tell life stories that are often distressing but nevertheless illustrate an irrepressible striving for self-determination, usually together with other disabled people in similar situations.

As Lothar Sandfort wrote in his "Medien-Manifest" (Media Manifesto, 1982), it is crucial for disabled people to create their own media outlets and spaces for public discussions in order to have more control over how they are represented in the public sphere.[61] Such projects in self-representation have taken many forms in the FRG, and then in reunified Germany, since the 1970s. Magazines from *Die Randschau: Zeitschrift für Behindertenpolitik* (View from the Margins: The Magazine for Disability Politics, published 1985–2000) to *Ohrenkuss* (Kiss on the Ear, which features writing by people who have Down syndrome) are forums where disabled people express their own interests and perspectives. *Die Randschau,* for example, focused on topics such as eugenics and euthanasia, bioethics, disability rights and culture, disabled women and men, work, children with disabilities, the Left and disability, disabled immigrants, aging and disability, disabled gays and lesbians, and people with cognitive disabilities. Increasingly, the print media have been augmented by an explosion of Web sites with a disability focus. The most useful one for keeping up-to-date on disability rights and culture in Germany is www.kobinet-nachrichten.org, which features a daily summary of press articles on disability, media tips, and a nationwide calendar of meetings, cultural events, and protest demonstrations. In recent years, conferences have been held all over Germany that take an emancipatory rather than a medicalized approach to disability, exploring topics such as employment opportunities, disability and sexuality, and lesbians and gay men with disabilities. In June 2000, a national conference in Bremen called "Enthinderungen" (Undoing Disability) focused on integrating disabled people as equally as possible into all areas of life.[62] And in May 2005 a conference in Berlin sponsored by the European Institute for Design and Disability, called "Kultur für Alle" (Culture for Everyone), dealt with broad questions of accessibility, including access to the cultural heritage, the city environment, and public transportation.[63] Independent living festivals, film festivals, and photography exhibits with a disability focus are frequently held throughout Germany. For example, in the spring of 2005 an exhibition of photographs entitled "Berlin durch die Hintertür" (Berlin through the Back Door) showed the city from the perspectives of people who have various types of impairments.[64]

In the realm of artistic experimentation, individuals and a number of small groups are extending the possibilities for self-expression and sometimes even asserting that they are creating a new disability culture. These include theater groups such as Theater Thikwa, RambaZamba, the Visuelles Theater Hamburg, and the Munich Crüppel Cabaret and dance groups such as the Tanztheater HandiCapace in Ludwigsburg, the Tanzprojekt Telos, and DIN A 13 (the name of this group refers to the ubiquitous "German industrial norms"). One of the best statements about the goals of such groups is found on the Web site of andersARTig (Different/ART), a coalition of disabled cultural activists. These writers, painters, photographers, actors, and dancers reject a limiting focus on integrating disabled people into the "normal cultural scene." Instead, they assert that most socially marginalized groups must develop their own independent culture in order to "express their own personalities, to become autonomous, and simply to survive."[65]

What does it mean to set aside aesthetic standards based on corporeal perfection while foregrounding a consciousness of disability liberation? Several projects may serve as illustrations. Many examples of such cultural experimentation may be found in the field of photography. Heino Ehlers's photography exhibitions, entitled "Körperbilder: Wider die normale Ästhetik" (Body Images: Against an Aesthetics of Normalcy, 1998) and "'Behindert' durch andere" ("Disabled" by Others, 1999), seek to critique "prevailing norms and aesthetic ideals" and to affirm that a "crippled body is desirable and lovable."[66] His nude photography of disabled men and women explores their bodies without voyeurism or sensationalism. With a similar goal but a different emphasis, Tanja Muster's photographs and collages entitled "EntARTungen" (Degenerations/ART) show affirmatively conceived images of disabled people who are assertive and active.[67] What a long way these contemporary depictions have come from all the negative images of disability that were their forerunners! Now, as Ehlers states, the goal of such artistic projects is the "mutual acceptance of physical, cultural, and behavioral

Fig. 29. The dance company HandiCapache performing *Tablestories,* January 2000. (Photo from www.clauslanger.de.)

differences as a basis for the development of common ground and common interests."[68]

Another project is Dance-Ability, a form of dance developed in the United States during the 1990s. Based on contact improvisation between dancers without any type of prescribed steps or movements, it can be performed by people who have even the most severe disabilities. Heino Ehlers, who initiated the first Disability Culture Week in the FRG in 1981, holds workshops on Dance-Ability in Germany. He explained that the positive resonance of this type of dance lies in the fact that "here something can and must be realized which people can always avoid in everyday life: the unconditional acceptance of the crippled body" by both disabled and nondisabled dancers. The expressive power of this dance does not derive from the movements that the nondisabled dancers are able to perform but rather from the involvement of all the dancers with each other as equal partners in creating meaning.[69] Similarly, the Austrian performance group Bilderwerfer (Image Throwers) also disrupts traditional interpretations of the disabled body as ugly, passive, or tragic. In its "Einblicke" (Insights, 1995), a wheelchair user, Elisabeth Löffler, is stylishly dressed and performs inside a display window of a Viennese department store. As the cultural critic and community dance artist Petra Kuppers explained, this performance is too complex for easy narration and thus does not allow the viewer to apply any of the stereotypical guiding metaphors of disability.[70]

Actors with cognitive disabilities make up the theater troupe RambaZamba, founded in 1991 by the East Berlin actors and directors Gisela Höhne and Klaus Erforth, whose son was born with Down syndrome in 1976.[71] The goal of this theater is not therapy or social work, but rather it offers its members a place for creativity and artistic expression. As Erforth stated, "There is no distinction between art by the nondisabled and art by the disabled. Either it's art or it's not."[72] RambaZamba has become recognized as Germany's most important integrative theater on the strength of the fourteen productions it has mounted to date. Some deal specifically with a disability theme, such as *Mongopolis,* about a city in the future on another planet where parents only want perfect children. Others are adaptations of classical themes: Medea, Orpheus, and Woyzeck. The production style combines seriousness and depth with festive, circuslike elements and tragedy with joy according to Volksbühne director Frank Castorf, who has collaborated with RambaZamba.

To be sure, these disability culture groups are small and only reach a limited audience, but on the whole, images of disabled people in the public sphere in Germany have changed significantly for the better. Perhaps the most active organization in this regard is the Project Group on Disabled People in the Media (Arbeitsgemeinschaft Behinderte in den Medien or ABM).[73] Founded in Munich in 1983, the ABM is directed by the actor, writer, and disability rights activist Peter Radtke. Currently this organization has several regular series about disability on cable television, maintains a rental catalog of several hundred films, sponsors a biannual international film festival, and makes films available for school use. In addition to presenting feature films from many countries, the ABM's documentary films focus on the political, cultural, and social aspects of disability such as realistic life stories, practical questions of accessibility, women and disability, disability culture, foreigners with disabilities, and disabled people in other countries. Working together with People First, the ABM has also produced films in easy language. For example, in a film from 2004, people with learning difficulties interviewed leading politicians, including Chancellor Gerhard Schröder and Christian Democrat Angela Merkel, about important political topics.[74]

The ABM strives to "critique clichéd, prejudiced depictions of disabled people in the media and replace these with authentic, realistic images." Along these lines, the ABM notes that earlier media representations of disabled people generally employed two opposing stereotypes: pitiful problem children who need help or exceptional supercrips who courageously overcome disability in order to conform to the norms of the nondisabled world. With regard to the latter group, by highlighting a few unusual individuals, the media long avoided debates about how society needs to be changed so that all people with disabilities can lead richer, more fulfilling lives. By contrast, a number of films available through the ABM reveal an alternative perspective that deemphasizes overcoming disability and validates acceptance of difference such as the short film *Alice und der Aurifactor* (Alice and the Aurifactor, 1995). Included in the ABM's school catalog, this film is an expressionistic silent film, a fairy tale in sign language. Its heroine, the deaf girl Alice, liberates the world from an evil, hearing magician who wants to attach huge ears to deaf people and turn them into hearing mutants. Featuring deaf actors from the Hamburg Visual Theater, the film shows Alice fighting successfully against the hearing world for the right to use sign, her native language. Here members of the Deaf minority group assert proud self-acceptance rather than internalizing negative standards from outside that lead to feelings of inferiority. A casual survey of German television reveals a large number of programs—whether features with disabled characters or documentaries about disabled people's lives—that are in accord with the perspectives developed by the ABM. Of course, much still remains to be done in the ongoing effort to represent disabled people in nonstigmatizing ways, but, nevertheless, disabled producers of culture and their allies have achieved noteworthy successes. A review of one of RambaZamba's plays from 2000 captures this transformation well: "This is no longer theater as a protected zone in which normal spectators marvel at the presence of disabled actors who are enjoying themselves. This theater, like any other, is nothing less than an experiment." That is, in such cultural productions disabled people no longer appear as objects of the stare, but present themselves as belonging to the continuum of humanity.[75]

Disability Studies: The Researched Become the Researchers

Linked to the political movement for disability rights, disability studies has emerged in recent years as a new interdisciplinary field in the humanities and social sciences. While not trivializing the facts of impairment, disability studies does not focus on medical definitions of disability. Instead, it views disability in terms of all its historical and cultural ramifications as a socially constructed category that yields many new insights into the history and functions of concepts of normality. This new direction in research and teaching about disability has been developed mostly by disabled scholars in the United States and Great Britain rather than in a country such as Germany where disabled people have been excluded much more strictly from the regular educational system. In the past few years, however, disability studies is also starting to gain a foothold in Germany. This new field was initiated there with a unique, major exhibition tracing the history of disabled people over the centuries that was presented at the Deutsches Hygiene-Museum in Dresden in 2000–2001 and the Gropius Museum in Berlin in 2002 along with two international conferences held in both cities. While the German events and debates draw on the extensive U.S. and British scholarship that already exists in this field, they also foreground significantly different perspectives arising out of the history of disabled people in Germany and the present situation there.

The exhibition, entitled "Der (im)perfekte Mensch: Vom Recht auf Unvollkommenheit" (The [Im]Perfect Human Being: On the Right to be Imperfect), was sponsored by two institutions in a unique cooperation between a major museum and a social advocacy group.[76] The first, the Deutsches Hygiene-Museum in Dresden, was founded in 1912 on the initiative of Karl August Lingner, the Odol mouthwash manufacturer. During the Weimar Republic, the museum mounted innovative exhibitions that contributed to developing a more democratic public health system. After 1933, it quickly became one of the most significant propagators of Nazi eugenic ideology with exhibitions that advocated eliminating the hereditarily diseased. During the forty years of the German Democratic Republic, the Hygiene-Museum functioned as a national museum of health. Since 1990, it has defined itself as a universal scientific museum about the human being. The exhibition on disability was one in a series that sought to critique various exclusionary practices toward groups often held to be different or inferior, including: "Old and Young: The Generation Adventure" (1998), "Gene Worlds: Workshop Man?" (1998), and "Foreign Body—Foreign Bodies: On Unavoidable Contact and Conflicting Feelings" (2000). The second sponsor of the exhibition was the largest, best-known German charitable organization, Aktion Mensch (Campaign Human Being), now a social advocacy organization. Thus, both the Hygiene-Museum and Aktion Mensch have reassessed and revised their past treatment of people with disabilities. Curated by Gisela Staupe, deputy director of the museum, and Heike Zirden, head of public relations for Aktion Mensch, the "(Im)Perfect Human Being" exhibition reflected this shift in conceptualizations of disability.

When the exhibition opened in Berlin, the two curators discussed its broad social relevance. Staupe noted that a central concern of the Hygiene-Museum was "the consequences of scientific developments for our concept of the human being."[77] She pointed out that the exhibition opened in Dresden a year after Peter Sloterdijk gave his notorious Elmau speech, "Rules for the Human Zoo," which unleashed a heated debate about the end of humanism and the future of "anthropotechnology." Yet Sloterdijk's speech was only one intervention in the increasingly complex discussion about bioethical questions. Accordingly, Staupe characterized the exhibition's goals as follows: "The exhibition asks extremely relevant, explosive questions. How do we construct our concepts of normality? What meaning do dreams of perfection have in our everyday lives? What historical situations have led to the creation and shifting of boundaries between normality and deviancy? Where does the gaze come from that turns human beings into the 'disabled'? Against this background, we are presenting the cultural history of disabled people."

Sensitive to the issue of inclusion, the exhibition's organizers made sure that disabled scholars, advisers, and activists had input in most phases of these events. The exhibition was made accessible to those with mobility impairments (physical access), visual impairments (Braille, raised signage, and a compact disc version of the catalog), hearing impairments (print descriptions), and learning difficulties (text version in easy language). Also disabled volunteers were trained as docents. An unusual effort in the German cultural landscape, these practices attracted interest from other museum directors around the country who wanted to make their own events more accessible.

Described by some as a combination of interactive experiences and infotainment, the most impressive thing about the exhibition was its creative presentation of a great breadth of material. In images grouped around the Hygiene-Museum's famous life-size model "The Transparent Man," the ironic prologue presented social ideals of normalcy and perfection such as beauty, health, competence, autonomy, and rationality. These were surrounded by drawers containing an "archive of flaws" shared by everyone such as fearfulness and forgetfulness, to demonstrate that perfection would mean the end of the human being. In the second section, the visitor moved through "worlds" in which people with various kinds of disabilities live: seeing (Braille and other tactile systems), hearing (sign language), understanding (various documents about cognitive disabilities and mental illness), moving (physical disabilities, featuring Franklin D. Roosevelt's homemade wheelchair), and touching (an interactive installation).

The next sections traced the history of disabled people along a trajectory from being controlled and abused by others to recent emancipatory efforts. This part examined the often violent efforts to normalize disabled people, beginning with an impressive demonstration of staring that featured the medical, pitying, excluding, annihilating, fascinated, astonished, and admiring gazes. From straitjackets to unnecessary prostheses, realia illustrated the recurring tensions between useful, life-enhancing methods of treatment and repressive methods of normalizing appearance or behavior. The section about conditions in institutions showed how people with certain types of bodies and minds have been segregated in certain types of physical spaces and concluded with the modern deinstitutionalization movement, which aims to return disabled people to their communities. Next came a darkened room labeled "Selection," which documented the Nazis' efforts to eliminate disabled people from the "healthy body of the German nation" through involuntary sterilization and "euthanasia." By contrast, the following section, "Normalizing," focused on recent emancipatory movements of disabled people, taking as its motto the famous statement by Federal President Richard von Weizsäcker in 1993 that "it is normal to be different." Set up as a construction site to indicate that this is an unfinished process, the room was encircled with medicine cabinets containing information from all sorts of self-advocacy groups, and it featured film clips of theater, music, and dance performed by disabled people. The final section, "The Clearing," offered an opportunity to learn about current negotiations over human existence. Museumgoers could listen to taped statements by well-known politicians and scholars on bioethical issues such as pre-implantation and prenatal testing for disabilities, abortion of disabled fetuses, active and passive euthanasia, assisted suicide, and so forth. Also a number of film clips showed disabled people expressing their opinions about these questions. The metaphor of the clearing was meant to recall the clarity associated with the Enlightenment. But, through the clashing opinions presented there, this concluding section was also intended to make visitors ponder whether new scientific possibilities are creating a dream or a nightmare of perfecting the human being and whether these might better be opposed by advocating a culture of diversity.

As the first major exhibition I know of anywhere in the world that attempted to give a comprehensive overview of the history of disabled people, "The (Im)Perfect Human Being" drew large crowds in both cities, and with 170,000 visitors in Dresden it attracted more people than any other exhibition at the Hygiene-Museum. Yet the exhibition generally did not motivate media commentators to revise their stereotypes of disability. I believe this was due to a problematic lack of clarity in the overall conception. Neither the exhibition nor the publications connected with it tried to define who was included in the category of disabled people. Rather, even though the exhibition did include some examples of acquired disabilities, its main thrust was to emphasize issues surrounding hereditary and congenital disabilities. While this approach is understandable in view of German history, it gives a distorted presentation of disabled people as a minority group, for about 90 percent of all disabilities are acquired after birth through illnesses or accidents.

The exhibition did not stress the basic point that anyone can become disabled at any time, and so it missed a high-profile chance to critique unquestioned concepts of normalcy and to ask what true inclusion of disabled people might really mean. This led to the unfortunate consequence that the media coverage had little incentive to focus on barriers to inclusion or to look at German society from the perspectives of disabled people themselves. Rather, the media discussions tended to proceed in two outdated directions. Most reports on the exhibition focused on disability as more or less synonymous with irreducible genetic or congenital difference and also continued to insist that "suffering" is the defining characteristic of disabled people.[78] For example, in an article entitled "Auf dem Behindertenspielplatz" (On the Disabled Playground) in a leading Berlin newspaper, Jens Bisky wrote that the exhibition "opens up experiences from the world of the blind, deaf, the cripples, the deformed, and the idiots." He argued for the essential difference of the disabled, saying that they were simply not able to use the institutions and techniques that the "healthy" employ in everyday life.[79] Yet the exhibition did not motivate him or most other journalists to wonder why this is so. For example, the new subway station at Potsdamer Platz, one of the showpieces of reunified Berlin, was constructed without elevators or escalators. (Only after ongoing protests from disabled Germans and tourists was the station finally retrofitted and made accessible in 2006.) Whether someone has a mobility impairment due to a genetic condition or an acquired disability is irrelevant: that person could not use this subway stop. So the most useful question in this and countless other situations would be what concept of normalcy made architects and Berlin city planners feel that it was acceptable to exclude this particular group of citizens from one of the most heavily used public transportation stops in the city? The exhibition did not force such questions into public debate, though it would have been easy to do so.

The case was different with the two large international conferences that accompanied the exhibition. The Dresden conference was called "The (Im)Perfect Human Being: Between Anthropology, Aesthetics, and Therapy," and the Berlin conference was called "Phantom Pain: Debates about the (Im)Perfect Human Being in the Twentieth Century."[80] At both conferences, scholars from Germany and the United States problematized the equation of disability with suffering and presented approaches to cultural history that validated the perspectives of disabled people themselves. As Christian Holtorf, of the Hygiene-Museum, explained, the conferences investigated how norms are established, how concepts of the human being become fixed, and what the alternatives are to normalization.[81] Other participants, such as Anja Tervooren, of the Free University in Berlin, emphasized that disability studies in the United States was bringing more disabled people into scholarly research and thus changing this field from "research about objects into research by subjects."[82] Accordingly, as one journalist explained, "There was quite a lot of dynamite in this debate about the social power of norms, which is only just beginning here in Germany and is importing its utopian visions from the United States at the moment."[83]

The Berlin conference concluded with a meeting organized by Anne Waldschmidt, of Cologne University, and Anja Tervooren with the intention of establishing a network of disability studies scholars. At this gathering, Waldschmidt also introduced the Working Group for Disability Studies in Germany: We Do Research Ourselves! (Arbeitsgemeinschaft Disability Studies in Deutschland: Wir forschen selbst!). This working group had been organized two months earlier at Dortmund University by Waldschmidt and Theresia Degener of the Protestant University of Applied Sciences in Bochum. Waldschmidt posed the following questions as central to disability studies in Germany. How should disability be defined? Is disability studies applied research or theoretically oriented research in cultural studies and the humanities? What is its relation to the traditional applied fields (medicine, rehabilitation, special education, social work, and so on)? Is it sufficient to conceptualize disability as socially constructed?

Here disciplinary distinctions between Germany and the United States became evident. In the United States, scholars in cultural studies, especially in English and history departments, are doing much of the most important research in disability studies. In Germany, in spite of the enormous interest in body theory among cultural studies scholars, almost no one in the humanities has focused on disability yet. That is, the impetus for disability studies in Germany is still coming primarily from scholars in the social sciences and applied medical fields, who are trying to persuade humanities scholars to expand their perspectives. Waldschmidt also explained that, although nondisabled scholars were welcome to join the larger network, the members of the working group were to be people who identified themselves as disabled. Based on the peer principle of insiders doing research about insiders, she stated that it was politically important at the moment to form an organization of disabled scholars in Germany. This insistence on separation as necessary for developing scholarship by disabled people indicated the intensity of the exclusion to which they had been subjected in Germany. An American disability studies scholar, Rosemarie Garland-Thomson, stated at the Berlin conference that the situation in the United States was somewhat different, that disability was being introduced as a category into humanities fields in many ways there, and that it was unlikely that professional groups would exclude nondisabled scholars. Yet Waldschmidt's justification for the structure of the German working group, as well as for the creation of disability studies in Germany, was one to which disabled scholars in many countries could surely subscribe: "There has been a monopoly against us for far too long." Disability studies continues to expand in the German-speaking countries, where it now features many types of collaboration among disabled and nondisabled researchers.

In contrast to the patronizing UN year in 1981, which catalyzed early disability rights protests in the FRG, the European Year of People with Disabilities took place in 2003 under the motto "Nothing about us without us," and disabled people were involved in all phases of planning it. As part of this European year, the Education and Research Institute for Independent Living in Bremen organized a two-week Summer University on disability featuring panels and workshops conducted primarily by disabled scholars and activists.[84] After the two conferences discussed earlier, the highlight was the third major German disability studies event: an international conference called "Disability Studies in Germany: Reconceiving Disability."[85] Since then, a number of such meetings have taken place, including one in Berlin called "Ethics and Disability: A Change in Perspective."[86] Organizers of these disability studies conferences occasionally try to make them accessible to at least some people with cognitive disabilities either by inviting them to speak or by giving presentations in easy language. For example, at the Bremen conference, Theresia Degener, a professor of law, delivered the keynote address on the planned UN Declaration of Rights for People with Disabilities in easy language, and the members of People First in the audience praised this act of solidarity. As of 2005, an International Research Institute of Disability Studies at Cologne University, directed by Anne Waldschmidt, had been established, and research and teaching in this field were also under way at universities in Berlin, Bochum, Bremen, Dortmund, Düsseldorf, Marburg, Innsbruck, and Zürich.[87] The process of developing this new field is slow, but, as the title of Ottmar Miles-

Paul's influential book about independent living declares, "We won't be held back any longer."[88] Disability studies scholars in Germany and around the world are engaged in critiquing the strategies of power that have traditionally constructed and enforced the categories of "normal" and "disabled." In other words, the researched are becoming the researchers.

CHAPTER 8 • German/American Bodies Politic: A Look at Some Current Biocultural Debates

During the week of September 18–24, 2003, Berlin became the "City of 1,000 Questions." A visitor at that time might have been surprised to see large projections on the city's most prominent buildings with questions such as: "Where is the gene going?" "What if my child wants optimized parents?" "Does disability begin with the wrong hair color?" "Is there 'valueless' life?"[1] That week the curious visitor would have discovered an extensive program of lectures, discussions, theater performances, film screenings, and television specials about current bioethical issues arranged by Aktion Mensch (Campaign Human Being), the largest German advocacy organization for people with disabilities. This event marked the culmination of the organization's year-long "1,000 Questions Project," which sought to encourage broad citizen participation in bioethical debates by creating a Web site where the public could ask questions, make comments, engage in dialogue, and find information about these issues. During the year more than 500,000 people visited the site, which is still in operation, and 8,500 questions were posted along with 35,000 comments. The project is documented in a book entitled *Was wollen wir, wenn alles möglich ist? Fragen zur Bioethik* (What Do We Want if Everything Is Possible? Questions about Bioethics, 2003). Categories of questions include pre-implantation and prenatal diagnosis, eugenics and selection, disability, cloning, gene technology and economic issues, experimentation on human subjects, embryonic stem cell research, the promises and pitfalls of modern medicine, euthanasia, and physician-assisted suicide. As by far the largest documentation of a citizens' forum on bioethical issues in Germany, the book offers unique insights into some of the public's opinions, hopes, and fears about these developments in medicine and biotechnology. And in 2005 a play based on these questions, entitled *Wohin Gen?* (Where Is the Gene Going?), was performed at a dozen theaters, including the Maxim Gorky Theater in Berlin.

The broad resonance this project has found in Germany testifies to a widespread desire for serious and substantial public reflection on these

London erlaubt die Embryo-Selektion.*

Fragwürdig?

Wir brauchen Ihre Frage: **www.1000fragen.de**

Eine Initiative der AKTION MENSCH   *Generalanzeiger, 26.02.02.

Fig. 30. "London allows the selection of embryos. Questionable?" Poster from the 1,000 Questions Project. (Courtesy of Aktion Mensch.)

bioethical questions. This is not surprising, of course, for at the most basic level these are issues of life and death that touch the lives of everyone in one way or another. The national scope of this debate and the amount of resources invested in it are quite striking, however, to this American observer. In the United States, public interest in these questions is undoubtedly just as high, but there is no comparable effort to encourage serious reflection on them among broad groups within the population. Rather, debates in the United States tend to remain confined within particular groups—the intellectuals, the policymakers, the activists, and so forth—or to be sensationalized in the mass media, as in the recent Terry Schiavo case.

Be all that as it may, the large amount of public interest in these matters corresponds to a significant interdisciplinary intellectual development, which at the moment is being more explicitly formulated in the United States and Great Britain than in Germany: the turn toward the "biocultural." Recently posited by a U.S. scholar, Lennard Davis, as a "prime area of cultural and theoretical analysis," the biocultural can be understood as comprising all the fields that are concerned with "the body in its social, political, cultural, and scientific aspects" and specifically study what happens when the "human intersects with the technological" in the twenty-first century.[2] Notable in this area are the intensifying dialogues among scientists, medical practitioners, and intellectuals from such humanities fields as literature, philosophy, disability studies, and cultural studies.

Within these biocultural debates, ethical questions have assumed a particularly central place as medical technology becomes ever more powerful and the far-reaching, even species-transforming implications of new scientific discoveries become more apparent. Scholars in disability studies are bringing out the centrality of sociocultural attitudes toward disability and disabled people with regard to these bioethical issues. Indeed, one of the organizers of the 1,000 Questions Project asserted that *all* bioethical debates revolve around concepts of "illness," "disability," and "suffering" that are contrasted with concepts of "health," "normalcy," and "happiness."[3] The many cultural expressions of unease over bioethical issues arise in large part from the new possibilities created by science for mitigating or abolishing the former in favor of the latter. As the U.S. legal philosopher Ronald Dworkin explained in *Die Zeit* in 1999 with respect to new developments in gene technology: "The clear boundary between chance and freely made decisions is the backbone of our morality, and every substantial shift in this boundary brings about a serious disruption."[4]

Scholars in German studies are in a position to bring some important comparative perspectives to bear on these biocultural and bioethical debates. Namely, there are significant ways in which concepts of the "German" and the "American" appear as national subtexts in these controversies, particularly with regard to discourses about disability. These comparisons should not be confined to facts of law, although this would be a worthwhile undertaking in itself, as the following, somewhat arbitrary list indicates. Pre-implantation genetic screening for disabling traits in embryos created by in vitro fertilization is routine in the United States but illegal in Germany (although this may soon change). Abortion because prenatal testing reveals a disabled fetus is legal in the United States but illegal since 1995 in Germany (although this appears to be meaningless in practice since abortion is allowed there at any time if birth will cause distress to the mother).[5] Physician-assisted suicide has been legal in Oregon since 1997; it is illegal in Germany. Embryonic stem cell research (which requires the destruction of human embryos) was pioneered in the United States, although it has since been restricted in laboratories that receive federal funding. In Germany, it was illegal until 2002 and can now be carried out only on imported stem cells created before January 1, 2002. In 1990, the U.S. Congress passed the Americans with Disabilities Act, a far-reaching civil rights law for disabled people. In Germany, legal progress in this area has been steady but quite a bit slower. In the United States, 96 percent of children identified as needing special education attend regular schools; in Germany, 93 percent of such children are segregated in special schools.[6] There is no national health insurance in the United States; in Germany everyone has access to affordable health care.

Many scholars in various fields study the reasons for such national differences. My intention here, however, is to explore several cultural discourses around bioethical and biocultural issues related to disability in each country that invoke the other country in specific contexts. I will set the stage by discussing briefly how these debates in the United States refer to Germany almost solely through the negative example of the Nazi past. To illustrate the different ways in which knowledge about this past shapes these discussions, I will then contrast the reactions in each country to the controversial philosopher and bioethicist Peter Singer. In German debates about bioethics, the United States frequently appears as a source of technological and scientific innovation, which some view as desirable and others criticize for neglecting ethical issues in favor of economic profit. These conflicting views came out quite pointedly in the so-called Philosophers' Debate of 1999–2000 over Peter Sloterdijk's "Regeln für den Menschenpark" (Rules for the Human Zoo), a lecture about the ethical limits of gene technology. Finally, in contrast to these mostly negative or ambivalent views of the United States, I will discuss efforts in Germany to pass an antidiscrimination law as a biocultural debate that draws on a positive conception of the United States as a model for civil rights. In conclusion, I will reflect on some of the lessons that concerned Germans and Americans might learn from each other's histories.

On July 16, 2001, *Der Spiegel* published an installment in its series of articles about the "presence of the past" entitled "A Pure Race." The introduction states, "Genetic testing, cloning, physician-assisted suicide: Whenever scientists celebrate progress, they also provoke strong resistance. For memory of the Nazis' murderous euthanasia campaigns is still alive."[7] If the newsmagazine observed that knowledge about Nazi crimes against people with disabilities significantly influences current bioethical debates in Germany, this can also be discerned in the United States. Indeed, when American intellectuals, politicians, and concerned citizens speak out about these bioethical issues, no matter what their standpoints are, Nazi Germany is an omnipresent, more or less explicit subtext. As the historian Martin Pernick has pointed out, the ethicists, scientists, and historians who advocate the new biotechnologies view the Nazi past as fundamentally different from the present. They see the past eugenic abuses that took their most extreme form in Germany as caused by "compulsory measures for the collective good, defined and imposed by the state," and they view this problem as having been largely solved by the contemporary commitment to individual free choice and informed consent.[8] A related distinction often made is that between the value-laden mix of science and ideology in the past and more rigorous efforts to be objective in the present. Others, however, are more disturbed by perceived continuities. They point out, as Pernick does, that "the absence of government coercion does not guarantee real individual choice" (174) for individual freedom in these matters is still limited by economic and cultural constraints. Furthermore, they assert that judgments about the quality of human lives always reflect cultural values and can never be totally objective or value free.

A particularly clear illustration of how Germany always appears in these debates with reference to Nazi eugenics is to be found in the opposing positions taken by scientists, philosophers, cultural critics, and activists on human germ line engineering. This technique would not only change the genetic makeup of the individual but of all future offspring. Probably the best-known advocate of this procedure is Nobel laureate James Watson, who co-discovered the structure of DNA. Having no fundamental objections to "making better human beings," Watson proclaimed to German molecular biologists at a Berlin conference in 1997 that "it is time to leave Hitler behind us."[9] Many others, however, are deeply suspicious of perceived continuities between Nazi eugenics and contemporary genetics, to the point of advocating a ban on germ line engineering. In the United States these groups include many social and religious conservatives, but also progressives such as some feminists, some environmental activists, some disabled people, and some members of the scientific and medical community. Interviewed in *Die Zeit* on September 21, 2000, for example, the U.S. physician who developed pre-implantation diagnosis rejected germ line engineering as "unthinkable" eugenics, thus implicitly equating it with the immoral policies of Nazi Germany.[10] Similar arguments could be quoted from controversies over most other bioethical issues in the United States. From every standpoint, then, Germany appears in these debates in the United States as the country where these eugenic practices took their most extreme form, the negative example that must be rejected in one way or another.

Nazi crimes cast a long shadow over contemporary bioethical debates in both Germany and the United States, but, as one would expect, there are significant differences in how knowledge about this past enters into these controversies. Over the past fifteen years, one of the most striking examples of the contrasting discourses about these topics is the reactions in each country to the controversial philosopher and bioethicist Peter Singer. Born in 1946, Singer had three grandparents who were murdered in the Holocaust. He emigrated with his family from Austria to Australia and became a professor of philosophy in Melbourne. Best known for his books about animal liberation, Singer has also published widely about many issues in bioethics. Most relevant here is the fact that he advocates active euthanasia for severely disabled infants and for older people in certain instances. In the summer of 1989, Singer was invited to speak at a European symposium entitled "Bioengineering, Ethics, and Mental Disability" in Marburg and to lecture in Dortmund on the topic "Do severely disabled newborn infants have a right to life?" For my present purposes, the exact grounding of his arguments—which I would characterize as a utilitarian approach remarkably lacking in sensitivity to the complexities of life—is less important than the reactions his scheduled appearances provoked in the Federal Republic. Condemning Singer's standpoints as basically a revival of Nazi eugenics, various organizations, disabled activists, and coalitions against genetic engineering mounted strong protests against him. As a result, his lectures were canceled, and one of the conferences where he was scheduled to speak was moved to Holland. Afterward Singer wrote an essay for the *New York Review of Books* entitled "On Being Silenced in Germany" in which he accused the FRG of restricting freedom of speech and expressed his surprise at being opposed most strongly there by progressives and leftists rather than right-wing conservatives.[11] In December 2004, Singer finally spoke in Germany for the first time on the topic "Human Dignity and Research" at the invitation of the German-American Institute in Heidelberg, although disability rights and church groups still protested against him.[12]

Those who opposed Singer in Germany took the position that, in view of the Nazi past, discussing bioethical questions such as euthanasia should be prevented at all costs because this is always the first step along the proverbial slippery slope that leads to judging some lives to be more valuable than others. In other words, the most vocal opponents of Singer, particularly groups of disabled Germans, appear to have conceived of bioethics as quite simply an illegitimate field of inquiry. Along these lines, for example, an article in *Der Spiegel* declared, "In order not to be bothered with philosophical misgivings, the biologists in the USA have chosen their own philosophers. Within the past twenty-five years, the discipline of bioethics has developed."[13] According to this point of view, bioethics is an import from Anglo-Saxon countries, and particularly from the United States, that seeks to justify questionable practices rather than a discipline concerned with the ethical quandaries posed by new scientific and medical developments.

Many German intellectuals criticized such views as narrow-minded and intolerant and sought to bring out the ways in which memory of Nazi crimes continues to shape these confrontations. Writing in *Die Zeit* on October 25, 1991, for example, the philosopher Ernst Tugendhat made a plea for an open debate about bioethical issues such as euthanasia, maintained that it was "only in the German-speaking regions that the disabled were reacting in such a way," and criticized the irrationality and lack of differentiation on both sides of the confrontation over Singer.[14] He attributed this inability to carry on rational debate to repressed guilt feelings over the Nazi past that still have not been worked through, criticizing both those who tried to prevent Singer from speaking and those who withdrew their invitations to him. In any event, probably the main result of the controversies about Singer in 1989–1990 is that since then there has been a flood of publications in Germany about all sorts of bioethical issues. In particular, countless books and articles have been published about the question of euthanasia both in the present and from a historical perspective. This body of publications is generally referred to now as comprising the "new euthanasia debate."[15] Some Germans continue to find it deeply problematic that these discussions are occurring at all, as an organization called the Forum Bioethik stated, "If it was still unthinkable a few years ago to talk seriously about killing the disabled, about euthanasia, and about active physician-assisted suicide, it is now becoming possible again."[16] It seems to have become a more generally prevailing opinion, however, that avoiding these problems will not make them go away and that open discussion is the best way to deal with them, as the 1,000 Questions Project demonstrates.

In 1999, Peter Singer was appointed to a chaired professorship in bioethics at Princeton University's Center for Human Values. Organizations from the National Council on Disability to Princeton Students against Infanticide issued statements against his hiring, which university spokespersons defended by saying they had appointed him because of his qualifications and not because he advocates any particular point of view.[17] When his first semester on campus began, he was met with about two hundred protesters representing various groups, most notably the disability rights and antieuthanasia organization Not Dead Yet, who carried signs comparing him to Hitler and Princeton to Auschwitz.[18] These protests were a smaller version of the much larger and more vehement demonstrations against Singer in Germany.

It has been more characteristic of reactions against Singer in the United States, however, that scholars and activists have critiqued him and even debated with him from the perspective of the new disability studies, which focuses on disability in its social, cultural, economic, and political contexts rather than as narrowly defined medical impairment. Those who are critiquing Singer's ideas in this manner generally point out that he makes little distinction between disability and impairment; that he fails to address how devaluation of particular bodily characteristics is reinforced in public life; and that he "ignores the large body of work on disability from a social-model perspective."[19] Along these lines, for example, Adrienne Asch of Wellesley College, an international authority on disability and bioethics, debated Singer at Princeton in 1999 in an event that was broadcast on National Public Radio, and the South Carolina lawyer and disability rights activist Harriet McBryde Johnson spoke at Princeton in 2002 about how to judge quality of life. Of course, these radically diverging outlooks cannot be reconciled. In a cover story for the *New York Times Magazine* about her encounter with Singer, Johnson referred to the genocide that happened in Germany, "in what was considered the most progressive medical community in the world," and left open the question of whether Singer's ideas might lead in the future to a much more thorough elimination of so-called imperfect lives.[20]

In discussions about bioethics, a central concern in Germany, and to a lesser extent in the United States, is to call attention to similarities or continuities between the Nazi past and contemporary developments. In Germany, however, one also finds another very different perspective on the meaning of this past for the present. This is the view that many Germans have learned important lessons from the Nazi past and thus are more aware of new types of dangers, in contrast to the citizens of some other countries, particularly the United States. A *Der Spiegel* article expressed this casually in 1999, describing Germans traumatized by fascism as understanding themselves to be "guardians of human nature" in contrast to U.S. bioethicists, who are supposedly guided only by pragmatic principles in which the profits to be made from the new biotechnologies play a decisive role.[21] Consequently, it was only fitting, according to another *Der Spiegel* article from 2001, that a U.S. elite university would hire Peter Singer, whom the magazine characterized as a "cold-hearted prophet of a world in which human beings become the objects of a growing biomedical industry and their dignity counts for less and less."[22]

This approach to contrasting Germany with the United States is not only the province of journalism; it is also an important tendency in intellectual debates. One of the most articulate advocates of this point of view is the psychiatrist and historian Klaus Dörner, who has long been a leader in the West German movement to deinstitutionalize people with mental illnesses and cognitive disabilities as well as in efforts to secure government financial compensation for victims of Nazi involuntary sterilization and "euthanasia." Viewing Singer's philosophy as updated social Darwinism, Dörner has critiqued utilitarian perspectives on eliminating people who do not fit easily into social norms or systems of production.[23] He has stated ironically that with respect to these questions most other Western countries, including the United States, "are much more 'reasonable' and 'progressive' than we are because perhaps we have learned a little bit from our history."[24] In contrast to a country such as the United States, with its ahistorical emphasis on technological progress, Dörner enumerated four lessons that, in his opinion, have been learned in Germany from efforts to come to terms with the role of medicine in national socialism.[25] First, engaged researchers have delved into the history of almost all German psychiatric hospitals and institutions that existed under Nazism. This movement of lay historians, inspired by a kind of ethics from below, prompted professional historians to research the heretofore neglected area of Nazi crimes against disabled people. Second, historians began researching eugenics and other exclusionary attitudes and practices before 1933 that culminated in the Nazis' categorization of people according to their utility to the national community. Third, Dörner postulated that a worldwide process of learning from Nazi crimes has been an important factor in the human rights movement to deinstitutionalize disabled people over recent decades. This movement is rooted in the conviction that all people have human dignity in contrast to a philosopher such as Singer, who denies some disabled human beings the status of personhood. Finally, Dörner concluded that, as a result of these lessons learned from the Nazi past, "bioethics is pursued in a more restrained manner and has to engage more with an ethics from below in Germany than is the case in most other European countries [and, by extension, also in the United States]."[26] The prominent disability rights activist Gusti Steiner expressed a similar sentiment in 2001 when he stated that in view of the success of disabled Germans in bringing their perspectives into bioethical debates there, he could finally say that he was almost proud to be a German.[27]

It has frequently been observed that because of the moral imperative to prevent any recurrence of Nazi crimes, debates about human genetics, biotechnology, and bioethical issues of human reproduction often take different forms in Germany than in other countries. These differences came out especially starkly in the so-called Philosophers' Debate of 1999–2000 over Peter Sloterdijk's Elmau lecture entitled "Regeln für den Menschenpark: Ein Antwortschreiben zum Brief über den Humanismus" (Rules for the Human Zoo: An Answer to the Letter on Humanism, 1999).[28] Maintaining that the traditional civilizing project of humanistic education was long outdated in view of increasing tendencies toward illiteracy and violence, Sloterdijk proposed that an elite group of the "wise" should pursue genetic engineering and develop what he called "anthropotechniques" aimed at the "selection" of particularly valuable characteristics to improve the human race.

A storm of indignation broke out over Sloterdijk's speech in Germany, and for several months the press was filled both with critical reactions to it and with articles in which well-known intellectuals—both German and American—weighed in with their opinions about gene technology.[29] On September 27, 1999, *Der Spiegel* focused on the debate in its cover story entitled "Zucht und deutsche Ordnung" (Breeding and German Order). Here the magazine asserted that there was something very "German" about the controversy for, after all, intellectuals in other countries—and specifically in the United States—had already advocated similar things without provoking such heated opposition. The Princeton molecular biologist Lee Silver, for example, had greeted the birth of Dolly, the first cloned sheep, in 1997 by enthusing, "Now we can do everything." The prominent biophysicist Gregory Stock from the University of California at Los Angeles (UCLA) had long urged scientists to seize control of human evolution.[30] As the article went on to state, what provoked the scandal was that a well-known *German* philosopher was advocating these things, along with the fact that Sloterdijk had gone further than any other German intellectual—at least in his choice of words—in breaking taboos heretofore thought of as inviolable in Germany.

The controversy about Sloterdijk's speech was the most recent in a series of heated intellectual debates that have centered around questions of reinterpreting German identity in view of the Nazi past: the Historians' Debate (1986), Botho Strauß's essay "Anschwellender Bocksgesang" (The Rising Goat's Song/Tragedy, 1993), Daniel Goldhagen's book *Hitler's Willing Executioners* (1996), Martin Walser's "Frankfurter Rede" (Frankfurt Lecture, 1998), the new euthanasia debate of the 1990s, and the controversy over the Berlin Holocaust memorial. The point I want to focus on here, however, is how contradictory concepts of what it means to be German or American informed both Sloterdijk's speech and the reactions to it with respect to the bioethical and political issues it raised. On the one hand, Sloterdijk seemed to take a sweepingly anti-American position. He created a chain of associations that juxtapose a positively viewed German antidemocratic elitism and tradition of philosophical depth with resentments against the superficial yet omnipresent Western mass media culture that originated in the United States. Sloterdijk gave only two concrete examples of the contemporary "tendencies toward barbarism" that he criticized: one from U.S. popular culture (the *Texas Chainsaw Massacre* film) and the other from crime reports (the Columbine school murders).[31] Yet, paradoxically, Sloterdijk complemented this negative view of the United States subsequently with a more positive view that seemed just as one-sided. In his Elmau lecture he did not specifically associate genetic engineering with the United States. A year later, however, on May 21, 2000, he appeared at a conference cosponsored by the Goethe Institute and UCLA entitled "Enhancing the Human: Genomics, Science Fiction, and Ethics Collide." There Sloterdijk delivered a lecture entitled "The Operable Human: On the Ethical State of Gene Technology," which can be viewed as a continuation of his Elmau speech. His main point was to call for humans to transform themselves "autotechnologically," and his statements seemed to meet with the approval of most of the participating U.S. scientists and bioethicists.[32] In this setting, Sloterdijk appeared to view the United States in a positive way, as the country where the biotechnology he advocated is the most advanced.

Sloterdijk's contradictory positions can be summarized as follows. On the one hand, he presented the United States as a source of barbaric violence perpetuated through the mass media, which he rejected—identifying himself as a member of the German intellectual elite. Some German critics of Sloterdijk were quick to zero in on the conservative political implications of this position. In this regard, for example, Reinhard Mohr grouped him among a number of formerly leftist intellectuals who had given up all pretensions to social criticism and were now advocating a "national rebirth of Germany" to counteract the "harmful influences of global Americanism."[33] On the other hand, however, Sloterdijk also promoted the biotechnology in which the United States is a leader and toward which many Germans remain skeptical due to their awareness of Nazi crimes. Consequently, Sloterdijk's advocacy of gene technology, identified in this way with America, was also a call for Germans to get beyond their supposedly outdated moral inhibitions rooted in the trauma of fascism. Furthermore, it was an attack on the postwar generation of intellectuals—represented most prominently by Jürgen Habermas and Günter Grass—who shaped the course of debates for so long by insisting on the centrality of efforts to come to terms with the Nazi past. Thomas Assheuer made this point most succinctly by stating that the Philosophers' Debate was not merely about gene technology but about what it means to be German in the new Berlin republic.[34]

Both in the United States and Germany, the similarities between Sloterdijk and some prominent U.S. advocates of genetic engineering gave rise to pointed criticisms that often revolved around the implications of these new technologies for social justice. The historian of science Diane Paul, for example, noted that the "new eugenics" promoted by "enthusiasts such as Lee Silver and Peter Sloterdijk" is premised on a belief in the absolute freedom of individual choice that might lead eventually to the division of humanity into different biological castes, the genetic "haves" and "have-nots."[35] In Germany, some press reports on the UCLA conference specifically associated this uncritical acceptance of the newest technology with the "American trust in the regulatory forces of the free market economy," in contrast to Germans, who were still concerned with moral questions about "exploitation."[36]

Jürgen Habermas made the most substantial intervention in this debate with his book *Die Zukunft der menschlichen Natur: Auf dem Weg zu einer liberalen Eugenik?* (The Future of Human Nature: On the Path to a Liberal Eugenics? 2001). He dismissed Sloterdijk and others of his ilk as merely a "handful of flipped-out intellectuals" who were propagating an all too familiar "German ideology."[37] But he also pointed out the dangers of a "liberal eugenics" that could arise if only the individual preferences of participants in the so-called free market were allowed to prevail (38). He critiqued various intellectuals in the United States who support this process, including Peter Singer, as not thinking through the ethical implications for human equality and social justice if new biotechnological developments enable one group of humans to become the creators of another group's genetic makeup (78). Realizing how fast science is developing, however, he also mused: "Today in the USA and elsewhere, don't these old European ethical orientations seem to be merely endearing, outmoded quirks?" (32). Such a philosophical position is similar to that taken by the psychiatrist Klaus Dörner with regard to bioethics, for Habermas also associated an uncritical, ahistorical belief in technological progress most strongly with the United States. By contrast, he presented his insistence on upholding the human dignity of all people as rooted in his European identity and specifically in his identity as a German who has not forgotten the results of the old eugenics.

Many cultural critics, including Habermas, have characterized new developments in biotechnology as seeming to come straight from science fiction, and, indeed, recent critical texts from this area of popular culture express quite vividly some of the fears and anxieties about the potential shape of a coming Brave New World. For example, Andrew Niccol's film *Gattaca* (United States, 1997), depicts a frightening future in which embryos are selected for their desired qualities, genetic destiny is known at birth, and abilities or disabilities determine the life's course. One of the most imaginative recent German texts to thematize the unease over such developments is the novel *Der Letzte seiner Art* (The Last of His Kind, 2003) by the best-selling science fiction author Andreas Eschbach. This work tells the story of a secret U.S. military program to create invincible soldiers by surgically enhancing the bodies of a select group of men in all sorts of ways: through implanting computer chips, titanium bones, powerful artificial eyes, superhumanly strong muscles, and so forth. But the soldiers do not function properly, and so they never see action in the field. Instead of defending U.S. interests around the globe as unconquerable Terminators, they are nothing but disabled cyborgs eking out a pitiful existence as invalid pensioners while one artificial body part after another fails. Tension is maintained as the Central Intelligence Agency attempts to exterminate the cyborgs before their plight comes to light for the military has developed yet another secret program to create the perfect soldier—this time through the use of gene technology to create chimeric combinations of humans and animals. Through the exaggerations of fantasy, Eschbach portrays the United States as a superpower that has no moral qualms about employing any available technology to serve its economic and military interests. In contrast to Sloterdijk's glib advocacy of biotechnology, this dystopian view of the future questions what it really means to improve human nature and highlights the dangers inherent in treating human beings as a means to an end.

As in this example from critical science fiction, Habermas voiced the unease occasioned by the blurring of boundaries between nature and technology, chance and planning, everything that he called "das Gewachsene und das Gemachte" (that which grows without human intervention and that which is created by humans). He characterized these developments as a technologizing of human nature that is provoking a transformed self-understanding of the human species and thus giving rise to never before encountered ethical dilemmas (75). Today one only has to be a sensitive cultural and political observer to realize that such feelings of anxiety, along with welcome stirrings of resistance to some of these trends, are spreading not only in Germany and the United States but throughout the world—as more questions arise about the implications of new practices in areas from human reproduction to genetically engineered agriculture. It goes without saying that wherever profits are to be made it is global corporations that are generally pressing these interests.

To this point, my discussion of the German and American subtexts in current bioethical and biocultural debates has focused on the ways in which each country serves mainly as a negative example for the other.

Yet, just as Germany is more and better than its Nazi past, the United States is not only a country of entrepreneurs pursuing the latest technological advances with little regard for their ethical consequences. Most bioethical and biocultural controversies revolve in some way around the question of whether certain kinds of bodies should have greater civil rights than others.[38] Accordingly, it is just as significant in the present context that the United States is also a country with a long tradition of civil rights efforts by minority groups that have experienced discrimination. The civil rights movement of African Americans has been a great gift emerging from the twentieth-century United States to countless similar struggles around the world. Wherever excluded groups have sought to cast off stigma, assert their worth as human beings, and claim their rights as citizens, they have often drawn on the powerful African American model. This is also true for the disability rights movements of recent decades in many countries, including Germany.

From the 1970s to the ongoing struggles in Germany today over including disabled people in federal antidiscrimination legislation, activists there have been inspired by U.S. civil rights strategies. In the first phase of these efforts, West German disability rights activists studied the writings of Martin Luther King Jr. and adapted the slogans of the black power movement to develop a more positive self-image. The clearest illustration of this influence is Ernst Klee's book *Behindert sein ist schön* (Being Disabled Is Beautiful, 1974), which employs analogies between the positions of African Americans and West German disabled people to argue that the latter should learn to assert their rights as citizens. Just as African Americans had to learn to reject self-hatred, believe in their self-worth, and become active on their own behalf, the book's contributors explained how disabled people needed to overcome feelings of inferiority, develop a new consciousness of themselves as an oppressed minority, and learn strategies of self-organization. As Klee and his collaborator, Gusti Steiner, wrote on another occasion, "We learned from the American civil rights movement. We studied how the American Negro leaders assessed their situation and what their experiences were when they demanded the most normal thing that could be demanded: human equality. We learned that privileged groups do not voluntarily renounce their privileges out of generosity or insight."[39] Putting these ideas into practice, Klee and his collaborators initiated disability rights consciousness-raising groups in 1974 in Frankfurt and then moved on to nonviolent direct actions.

The first phase of West German disability rights efforts invoked African American civil rights models to call for both a new disability pride and total integration of the disabled into society. Subsequently the second phase—beginning around 1980—often drew on the more advanced U.S. disability rights movement as a model both for creating independent living centers and proposing antidiscrimination legislation. West German disabled activists were impressed by the enormous improvements in the everyday lives of people with disabilities brought about by a number of major civil rights laws. These were section 504 of the Rehabilitation Act of 1973, which prohibited programs receiving federal money from discriminating against disabled people; the Education for All Handicapped Children Act of 1975, which guaranteed all disabled children the right to attend public school and in most cases to be mainstreamed into regular schools; and the Americans with Disabilities Act of 1990 (ADA), a sweeping civil rights law that banned discrimination and required reasonable accommodations in areas including government services, employment, public accommodations such as restaurants and hotels, and telecommunications.

These U.S. laws have given a great impetus to disability rights activists around the world who want to create similar legal protections in their own countries. As discussed earlier in chapter seven, after much opposition and many setbacks, German disability rights activists along with many other groups achieved a great success when the General Law on Equal Treatment went into effect on August 18, 2006. Those working to have disabled people protected by this antidiscrimination law often contrasted the vulnerable position of disabled Germans to that of disabled Americans, who have had many more enforceable legal rights for a longer time. To support their arguments, German activists documented cases of discrimination against people with disabilities that were still legal in Germany but illegal in the United States such as property owners who refused to rent them apartments or garden plots, restaurants and concert halls that denied them admittance, or public places that excluded people with guide dogs.[40] As the many activists agreed who formulated the Bremen Declaration for a Civil Antidiscrimination Law in the summer of 2003, "Racial discrimination and discrimination against disabled people must be confronted in the same way. Both must be abolished."[41] This controversy has been a struggle over which kinds of bodies are going to be recognized as having equal rights as citizens, and German disabled activists have been determined that people should not be excluded from full participation in society merely because they are disabled, as the law professor Theresia Degener put it.[42]

American civil rights struggles and antidiscrimination laws have served as positive models for German disability rights efforts, but what about the more subjective sides of these national differences? Since the early 1990s, a number of fascinating statements have been made by disabled German activists who traveled to the United States to experience daily life there for themselves. Without exception, these activists enthusiastically praised the greater accessibility and openness of U.S. society and the more accepting attitudes they encountered there, describing Germany as still a "developing country" in these respects.[43] Several noted that it was a "major culture shock" to be treated with respect, as persons with rights, rather than as charity cases.[44] For example, one woman recounted, "Many things that I had previously taken to be self-evident and inevitable for someone in my situation seemed totally different in the USA. I was able to move around freely there for the most part. My mobility was not limited by stairs, narrow aisles, or a lack of accessible toilets. Also people reacted to me as a wheelchair user in a different way from what I had experienced in Germany up to this point. Nobody stopped and stared at me with an open mouth. Nobody whispered or put on a face full of pity when I went into a store or restaurant. It was obvious that in the USA people took the sight of disabled people more as a matter of course than in Germany."[45] Another woman declared, "You can simply hold your head higher there than here in Germany, where everything is so terribly difficult."[46] And one woman summed up her experiences by saying that being treated matter-of-factly in Berkeley as a disabled person who had a right to be a student like anyone else "totally changed her life."[47]

Yet these disabled Germans did not view the United States as a desirable model in every respect. Their perspective is best expressed in the title of an anthology of their travel reports, *Traumland USA? Zwischen Antidiskriminierung und sozialer Armut* (Dream Country USA? Between Antidiscrimination and Social Poverty, 1998). These activists recognized the enormous accomplishments made in the United States in securing civil rights for disabled people, but they also criticized the inadequate medical and social welfare systems, which have extremely deleterious financial consequences and thus dilute these legal rights. On the one hand, then, one woman wrote that "after disabled people have tasted freedom [in the USA], it is difficult for almost all of them to continue to accept the discriminatory living conditions in Germany."[48] However, the main conclusion she and other activists drew from their experiences in the United States was that, while they remained committed to working toward the passage of a German antidiscrimination law like the ADA, they also wanted to preserve their social safeguards.

Looking back over the national subtexts in these bioethical and biocultural debates, it is obvious that there is a broader spectrum of views about the United States in Germany than the other way around. There are at least three things, however, that those of us in the United States who are concerned with these issues might learn from Germany. First, as exemplified in the 1,000 Questions Project, disabled people and their allies—who are often the most directly affected by bioethical and biocultural policies—have been more successful in Germany at organizing imaginative forms of wide-ranging debates about these questions. The goal of such activities is for the public to become as well informed as possible since almost everyone is faced at some point in life with making decisions about these issues. Second, the labor movement, and thus the social welfare net, has historically been much stronger in Germany than in the United States. This means that both disabled and nondisabled Germans have better access to a system of economic and healthcare benefits that are also needed in the United States to secure our civil rights.[49] Third, growing out of the extensive efforts in Germany to come to terms with the legacy of Nazi medical crimes, Germans have often been incisive advocates of "bioethics from below." As Klaus Dörner explained, the categorical imperative of such an approach to bioethics would be to "act in such a manner in your area of responsibility . . . that you always begin where it seems to be the least worthwhile rather than the most worthwhile. Always begin with the weakest person. . . . Everyone should live in society with just as much security as I do."[50] In opposition to utilitarian approaches that promote unquestioned norms of ability, health, and perfection, such a statement voices a far-reaching commitment to democracy and inclusiveness with which many Americans would surely agree.

CHAPTER 9 • We Shall Overcome Overcoming: An American Professor's Reflections on Disability in Germany and the United States

I am a professor of German studies at Brown University in Providence, Rhode Island. Because I contracted polio at the age of three in the epidemic of 1952, I use crutches and wear leg braces. Over thirty-five years ago I traveled to the Federal Republic of Germany for the first time, spending fifteen months there in 1970–71. Given my family background, becoming a university professor was an unlikely career path. My father's parents had been small Georgia cotton farmers, and he was a nurseryman of great aesthetic sensibility who knew all about plants and flowers but never earned much money. My mother, from a Nebraska farm family, became schizophrenic and was committed to the Georgia state mental institution in Milledgeville at about the same time I became ill with polio. My relatives worked mostly at jobs that demanded hard physical labor. They were resourceful and created useful and beautiful things in daily life, but they generally had not had the privilege of being able to develop many intellectual interests. In addition to coming from this socioeconomic class, I was, of course, a disabled girl and grew up exposed to mostly traditional models of gender roles. But I benefited from the advantages of being white in the segregated South. With respect to health care, this meant I had access to treatment paid for by the March of Dimes charitable organization at the best polio rehabilitation center in the country, the Georgia Warm Springs Foundation established by President Franklin D. Roosevelt. This institution refused to treat African American patients until forced to do so by civil rights laws in the 1960s.[1] With respect to education, being white meant that I had access to good public schools. In high school, I took German because I had heard it was an important language for scientists to know. I was sure I wanted to be a physicist or an astronomer and make important discoveries about the universe.

Fortunately for me as a young person from such a socioeconomic background, I was applying to college at a time when scholarship money from the federal government was much more readily available than it is today. Receiving four years of financial support to attend Vanderbilt

University in Nashville, Tennessee, I declared a major in mathematics and a minor in physics, continuing to take German and other humanities courses on the side. By the end of my sophomore year in 1968, I had decided that great literature and high culture were where my heart lay and changed my major to German and my minor to philosophy. I had always wanted to teach, and my long-term goal was to get my doctorate and become a university professor. By the time I graduated two years later, I had read Thomas Mann's *Der Zauberberg* (The Magic Mountain) and was planning to go to the FRG for a year. First, I attended a language institute for two months in the little Bavarian village of Grafing close to Munich; then I worked for four months in Munich alphabetizing yellow-page entries for the Bayerischer Adressbuchverlag, a company that published all the Bavarian telephone books. Subsequently, having received a Fulbright fellowship, I spent two semesters studying German literature at the university in Tübingen. In 1971, I returned to the United States to attend Indiana University, where I completed my master's degree in 1972, and then I went to the University of Wisconsin-Madison, receiving my doctorate in 1979. I have taught at Brown University since 1982 and have returned to the FRG, the GDR, and reunified Germany many times.

It is uncommon to find substantial statements by disabled people in any country about how they experienced daily life before the disability rights movement began in the late 1960s.[2] In recent years in both Germany and the United States, however, disabled people have been increasingly interpreting their own lives through autobiographies and memoirs, and U.S. disability studies scholars are reflecting on the theoretical implications of this type of self-representation.[3] As David Mitchell has noted, however, perhaps the main pitfall of this type of life writing is the temptation to confirm the "tradition's devotion to narcissistic self-revelation" rather than attempting to work out larger historical, social, and cultural connections with the suppressed history of disabled people as a minority group.[4] The most thought-provoking recent autobiographical writings by disabled people from many countries reflect on the oppressive practices of the past in order to expose and disrupt continuities with the present and work toward imagining more democratic, inclusive ways of living.

Within the general field of autobiography, travel writing recounts a special type of life experience. Of course, one of the greatest benefits of travel abroad is that it can cause travelers to view their own countries in a new light. By directly experiencing other cultures, the traveler may learn to appreciate life at home better or, on the other hand, may discover desirable alternatives to familiar conditions heretofore accepted as natural and unchangeable. For obvious reasons—whether financial, attitudinal, or medical—people with disabilities generally have been less able than others to take advantage of the life-expanding experiences of travel. Consequently, until quite recently there have been few pieces of travel writing by disabled people. The latest examples, however, such as the journalist John Hockenberry's *Moving Violations: War Zones, Wheelchairs, and Declarations of Independence* (1995), give valuable insights into how different societies respond to the unexpected disabled traveler in their midst.[5]

Just as consciousness of disability as a minority identity has grown within disability rights circles and has been expressed increasingly in autobiography in both the FRG and the United States since the 1970s, a similar process has been going on within the academy—though still to a greater extent in the multicultural United States than in Germany. In the past few decades, there have been many autobiographical, historical, and theoretical reflections on what it means to become a professor as someone from the working class, as a woman, as a person of color—that is, as a member of groups previously excluded from intellectual life at a university. Scholars engaged in developing disability studies in the United States have begun to reflect in similar ways on their paths into the academy as well as the personal and epistemological meanings of their presence there.[6]

Yet why are these life stories of disabled individuals potentially of more general interest to cultural historians? Speaking in the broadest sense, narratives about disability have the potential to illuminate the strength of norms within particular societies. For, if told in the right way, they must always reflect on both the individual and the societal response to someone who does not quite fit smoothly into daily life, who disrupts assumptions about how the human body should function, and thus about what it means to be a human being. Accordingly, keeping this entire framework in mind, the story that I will tell here has two main emphases. The first part recounts how I experienced the FRG during my first extended stay there in 1970–71 as a visibly disabled young American woman who had an intense interest in German culture and knew the language. I know of no other autobiographical text by a disabled American traveler in Germany. In the second part, I reflect on what it has been like for me as a disabled person to become a professor of German studies in the United States and to return to Germany over the years. In writing about my experiences in Germany, I am reflecting for the most part on anonymous encounters with strangers and contrasting this to similar situations in daily life in the United States. In writing about the United States, I focus on how my first experiences in the FRG affected my subsequent path of study, on my employment situation at the university, and on my growing interest as a German cultural historian in disability studies. This approach can hopefully connect my personal story to much larger developments. One of these is the enormous transformation in Germany since 1945 from the Nazi view of many disabled people as "lives unworthy of life" to the recent, successful efforts to pass antidiscrimination legislation. Another is the ongoing debate over the meanings of access and diversity in the United States. The story I tell here is thus a small building block in a yet to be written comparative cultural history of normalcy in Germany and the United States.

I often wish that I had kept a diary of the fifteen months I spent in the FRG in 1970–71, filled as they were with many positive and enriching things but also with many negative experiences that I could not have anticipated. Certainly such a diary would give a more complete and exact record for, of course, memory is always selective and unreliable in many ways. But one thing I am very sure of is that when I arrived exhausted in the Bavarian village of Grafing on April 3, 1970, after a two-day trip on Icelandic Airlines from New York via Reykjavik to Luxembourg and then by train to Munich, I was an extremely naive twenty year old. When I try to remember now what I thought I was going to do in the FRG, only vague things come to mind: I was going to speak German, read modern drama, go to great theater and concerts, perhaps see castles, and certainly travel a lot. I had never been very interested in history, and the professors I had encountered up until then had rarely related culture to social or political issues, let alone spoken about the Nazi period. I had developed a certain liberal commitment to the civil rights movement of African Americans and had been involved on the fringes with the Vietnam War protests in Nashville. But great literature seemed to me then like a timeless realm of beauty that would raise me up and away from my working-class, rural origins. Yes, I think I was looking forward to finding a refined, contemplative sphere of high culture in the FRG. I certainly had no theoretical or ideological framework for understanding what was about to happen to me there.

My life experience in the United States had been one of feeling relatively integrated into the world around me. Although I had significant physical limitations, I had always been included in more things than I was excluded from. Considering that I grew up before the legal accessibility requirements of the Americans with Disabilities Act, this experience was partly due to the fact that I was able to walk and eventually go up stairs with crutches rather than having to use a wheelchair. It was also due to the inclusive attitudes of those around me. I always lived at home (my father rejected suggestions to place me in an institution for "crippled children" after my mother became mentally ill). I always attended regular public school (in the first few years, the white teachers and the African American maids helped me go up the stairs and to the bathroom). I had friends, participated in many appropriate activities for my age, and learned to drive my own car with hand controls when I was nineteen, a great liberation. I graduated from one of the best universities in the South and had many experiences typical of students in the late 1960s. I experienced some first ups and down in love. In short, having been supported and accepted so often by others, I had a basically positive attitude toward myself in many ways and eagerly anticipated what the future might bring. Of course, there were times when I felt intensely that I was excluded, that I was on the outside looking in, but more often than not I think I generally felt comfortable with other people in many different contexts.

This was not to be the case in the FRG. Now that many specific incidents have faded from my memory, it requires a process of intellectual and emotional excavation to recall what was so shocking to me about my experiences there and to put this into coherent form as an autoethnography.[7] It all revolved around the way many West Germans reacted to me as a young woman with a visible physical disability. What I immediately began to experience was so unexpected and foreign to me that I could not really take it in for quite a while. At first, I was so disoriented that I wondered whether I was in touch with reality, and so I developed a plan to find out whether someone else would validate what was happening to me. After I had been in the FRG for about five months, my best friend from college, a nondisabled woman my own age, visited me in Munich. Her boyfriend had enlisted in the army in order to avoid being drafted and sent to Vietnam, and they had gotten married so she could be with him while he was stationed in Darmstadt. I was looking forward to being the expert and showing her around, and I decided I would not say anything to her about how some West Germans were reacting to me. I wanted to see if she noticed the same things I had been noticing. I took her everywhere in Munich—to all the typical tourist attractions. But after a few days, when we came back to my room one evening, she burst into tears and said, "I don't know how you can stand the way people treat you here."

So my friend confirmed the reality of what was happening. But what was it? What was so different about the FRG in contrast to the United States? And were the two countries really so dissimilar? Today, thirty-five years later, I would group my memories into two types of incidents that I had not experienced so intensely in the United States. The first was frequent acts of nonverbal and verbal harassment by strangers in daily life. I felt these to be violations of my private sphere that contradicted everything I had ever learned about good manners and the golden rule to "do unto others as you would have them do unto you." The second was repeated efforts to assign me physically to particular places that were occasionally removed from and even inferior to those meant for nondisabled citizens. I experienced this as disorienting, too. For in this strange land it seemed as though my time-honored American approach of "overcoming" my disability in order to fit as smoothly as possible into the nondisabled world was not working any more.

Certainly in the United States I had sometimes been stared at or asked personal questions by strangers along the lines of "Whatever happened to you?" But in my home country, it seemed to me, such behavior was generally limited to the occasional ignorant adult or above all to children who had not yet learned good manners ("Don't stare, it's not polite!" being a frequent parental admonition). In the FRG, however, from the first day I found that many people of all ages, social classes, and educational levels engaged in staring and seemed to consider this perfectly acceptable rather than rude behavior. The only group distinction I noticed was that more old people than young ones stared, which was very strange to me since I expected older people to be more polite. Experiences such as the following were new to me. I walked past a construction site, and all the workers laid down their tools and stared at me while I passed by. I walked past a sidewalk café in Bohemian Schwabing, and most of the patrons stopped drinking their coffee to stare. I sat on one side of the streetcar in Munich or the subway in West Berlin, and the eyes of everyone sitting on the opposite bench remained fixed intently on my feet for the duration of the ride. Almost daily adults I passed on the street would stop, turn around, and keep on staring at me as I walked past. Perhaps most disconcertingly, occasionally parents pointed me out and told their little children to look at me. These people aimed their long, absent-minded stares at my crutches, brace, and feet and generally did not make eye contact with me. I had also never experienced the frequent, intrusive, personal questioning that I encountered in the FRG from strangers of all ages and backgrounds, though again somewhat more from older people. Adults often asked loudly in public places some version of the question "What's the matter with you?" An example of a more pointed question came from a woman on the street in Munich who wanted to know what my mother had done to cause me to be born "like that." It was also new to me that strangers tried now and then, sometimes almost aggressively, to give me money (ten pfennigs or so). Strangely, they seemed not to register at all the fact that I was wearing nice clothes and often carrying a student's book bag—that is, I did not look like an indigent person.

The second type of extreme, unfamiliar reaction from some Germans was their efforts to assign me rigidly to particular places. Often these efforts seemed to reflect their consternation that a disabled person was appearing in their surroundings and their desire to control the situation. I was frequently singled out and told (not asked politely) where to stand or sit by strangers who seemed to assume as a matter of course that they had every right to order me around. Occasionally, however, these efforts were clearly aimed at removing me from places reserved for "normal" citizens. One day in West Berlin, for example, not having a telephone in my room, I went to the post office, where there were several telephone booths, to make some calls. I settled down in a booth with a notebook and my phone numbers and started to dial. Immediately a postal official came to the booth. He told me that I shouldn't use the phone and had to go to another booth, which was designated for handicapped persons. No matter how much I insisted that I was fine and argued that it was more difficult and inconvenient for me to get up and move than to stay where I was, he insisted that I did not belong in the normal telephone booth. I finally moved because otherwise he would not have let me make my calls. This scenario has remained in my memory as bringing out unusually explicitly what I perceived as persistent efforts to consign me to particular physical places and moral categories during the fifteen months I spent in the FRG.

Another new experience (fortunately only a one-time occurrence) was being denied admission to a public place. Loving music and excited about going to the opera for the first time, I immediately discovered the National Theater in Munich and wanted to take advantage of the inexpensive student tickets. One evening when I went with a German acquaintance, the cashier at the box office first refused to sell me a ticket, saying that I would disturb (stören) the people seated around me. I argued with him, and he finally sold me the ticket. My German acquaintance thanked him for being so accommodating, and I was angry with her for acting in what I considered to be a servile way. She tried to explain by saying to me, "You think you have rights, and people don't expect that from the handicapped." In sum, I remember feeling that almost every day I was in the FRG something unpleasant happened to me related to the fact that West Germans could see I had a disability— whether a minor irritation or a major confrontation. All this strange behavior was even more difficult for me to understand because disability was omnipresent in daily life in the FRG in a way I had never seen before. Wherever I went I noticed the disabled veterans: men of a certain age who were blind, had amputated legs or arms, or used old-fashioned, lever-operated wheelchairs. But I was obviously not one of them, and sometimes I wondered whether this affected the way people were treating me.

So how did this naive young American woman react? At first, I responded on an emotional level, with surprise and disbelief, then with hurt and anger. In daily life, I developed various strategies of response. Sometimes I tried to stare back, which was very difficult since this violated my concept of polite behavior. This approach was usually ineffective for the economy of gazes was disconcertingly different from what I was accustomed to. In the United States, to maintain hostile eye contact with strangers for longer than a second or two was asking for trouble. In the FRG, however, if I returned the stare, the West German staring at me would almost never look away, and the cold, appraising eye contact between us would continue for what seemed like an eternity until I often looked away myself. Sometimes I tried to argue or educate, thereby improving my German in ways I couldn't have imagined: "That's none of your business!" "Leave me alone!" "What bad manners you have!" Most frequently, I tried to ignore it all, not lose my composure, and continue doing what I wanted to do.

But most important, under the pressure of these unexpected encounters, I was forced to begin thinking more historically and theoretically. Having grown up in the segregated South, the paradigm I reached for to try to make sense out of my experiences was that of the civil rights movement. After all, the first political thought I remembered having as a child connected disability and race. In 1961, Charlayne Hunter and Hamilton Holmes had been the first African American students admitted to the University of Georgia in my hometown of Athens, and white mobs had demonstrated against them.[8] I remember thinking then that I wouldn't want anyone to prevent me from going to college because of the way I looked, that is, because I was handicapped. Now, in the FRG, I was experiencing exclusion that of course did not compare with the much greater discrimination and hostility directed against black people back home, but I still began to think that my choice was to be either an Uncle Tom or a Black Panther. I could believe the negative messages many West Germans were giving me that I really was some kind of inferior person. I could give in to the anxiety I felt sometimes about going out in public and simply stay in my room and read, away from all the unpleasantness. Or I could continue to do what I wanted, be angry and aggressive, fantasize about violent revenge, and ask the next older West German who harassed me what he or she had done during the Third Reich. My interest in history was awakening.

At the time, however, it never occurred to me to seek out other disabled people for their potential support or friendship. Furthermore, I did not think about my culture shock as reflecting something important about differing societal concepts of normality that had to do specifically with disability—that is, with the ways bodies function in the world— rather than with race or ethnicity. The roots of my behavior are indicative of the position of disabled people in both countries at that time. Since the age of three, my life had been shaped around the individualistic paradigm of overcoming my disability in order to fit into the realm of the normal. On the one hand, this approach had taken me a long way, and until people with disabilities achieve full acceptance and equality it would be self-defeating to reject it entirely. On the other hand, the desperate tenacity with which I sometimes clung to this strategy also shows that I had internalized the stigma attached to being disabled in the United States as well as the FRG. For, after all, this type of overcoming, which is based on a medical model of disability, tries to bring the individual disabled person more into line with unquestioned social norms. Accordingly, this approach begs the question of how society needs to be changed in order to become more inclusive of all types of human variation. And so, wanting to have a normal, full life, I actively avoided other disabled people, thinking that such associations would only call attention to something abnormal about myself—a kind of internalized self-hatred as I see it now. Disability still seemed to me to be an individual fate to be denied rather than a political identity that might lead to other types of emancipatory efforts. Consequently, during those fifteen months I never tried to meet any disabled Germans.

Of course, the time I spent in the FRG had many of the positive sides that anyone would expect from studying abroad: learning, travel, new perspectives. And, of course, I had good experiences with West Germans, too, with people who reacted to me at least neutrally and often in a friendly way. After all, many people did not stare, ask inappropriate questions, or try to control what I did. The women I worked with at the Bayerischer Adressbuchverlag in the summer of 1970 were salt-of-the-earth Bavarians. As soon as our supervisor would leave the room, they would stop their boring work of alphabetizing index cards, pass around the hidden cognac bottle, and talk about their families or the headlines in the *Bildzeitung.* We came to like each other, and my spoken German improved more in those gossip sessions than at the university in Tübingen, where there was always a temptation to spend time with other foreign students. But I also made a few friendly contacts among West German students. We worked in groups on Lukács, Brecht, and the political theater of the 1960s, ate meals together, and went to cultural events. So in all these ways my time in the FRG was positive and rewarding.

Yet, when I arrived back in the United States in July of 1971, I felt an overwhelming sense of liberation, as if I had been released from prison. I could walk down the street without being stared at or harassed with intrusive questions out of the blue. I could go grocery shopping and not be bothered with aggressively persistent efforts to "help." I could go into a restaurant and not encounter frantic confusion from the staff over where I was going to put my crutches. I remember thinking that I didn't want to go back to Germany again, at least not alone, but at the same time knowing that I was going to have to go back if I wanted to pursue this career and feeling afraid. So, if I also had some good interactions with West Germans, why did the negative experiences seem so overwhelming? As I remember, I felt the exclusionary practices to be statements popping up in the most unpredictable places that there was something wrong with me. This constant pressure caused me to become hypervigilant, wondering where the next insult would come from and how I could respond. In short, I was being repeatedly startled by negative perceptions from others that were quite at odds with how I felt about myself. No wonder it was such a relief to escape from this disorienting, frustrating situation.

Once back in the United States, it seemed to me that as long as I continued to overcome my disability I was not going to be prevented from pursuing my dreams. In the FRG, however, this hadn't seemed to be the case for much more rigid notions seemed to prevail there about where disabled people belonged. I wondered: if I had grown up in the FRG, would I have been allowed to lead such a good, full, normal life? Or wasn't it much more likely that I would have been shunted aside into the dead end of a special school and prevented from achieving what I was capable of? And, having such fundamental doubts, wasn't it strange that I was still studying German literature? But in graduate school I found that I loved teaching students the German language, and when I went to the University of Wisconsin in Madison, the professors and other graduate students there opened up for me a compelling new world of literary history and cultural politics. The intellectual atmosphere was intense, political, and congenial—I felt as though it was almost like living in the FRG without all the bad parts. So I plunged into the whirl of 1970s Marxist reading groups, joined the teaching assistants' union and discovered the labor movement, became fascinated with GDR literature, and began to write my dissertation on the workers' literature written by German social democratic exiles and immigrants to the United States in the late nineteenth century. Of course, I was interested in the topic, but there was always a small thought in the back of my mind that this was a way to avoid having to spend a long time in Germany doing research since all the material I needed was in U.S. library archives.

The historical approach to understanding culture that my professors advocated seemed to me an intellectual liberation: a kind of thinking with implications that went far beyond ivory tower academic topics. For the first time, the structure of the world around me began to make more sense in many ways because I began to see that there were larger economic, social, historical, and cultural factors at work that shaped the lives and behaviors of individuals. Above all, the class relationships that were such a significant, formative part of my life started to seem clearer rather than veiled in confusion. I believe that I became friendlier and less arrogant toward my relatives as a result. But this materialist approach to culture had a frightening implication as well. For, if everything could be analyzed in this way, then it would only be logical to subject the phenomenon of disability to this type of intellectual scrutiny. This thought entered my mind soon after I began studying in Madison, and I immediately pushed it aside—the idea of identifying myself with disability in any way was too disturbing. And yet, as we continued in the following years to extend our critiques in more and more directions—exploring the cultural politics of class, race, ethnicity, gender, and sexual orientation—the thought that I should try to approach disability in this way, too, was always something consigned to the corner of my mind reserved for things too difficult, painful, and isolating to deal with.

I also wanted to distance myself from disability because of a discovery I made at this time, when I was about twenty-five years old. Once, while visiting my father, I accidentally found letters in his house from the Georgia State Board of Eugenics written to him shortly after my mother had been committed to the state hospital in 1952. The letters informed him that unless he objected my mother was scheduled to be sterilized. The reason given was that she was likely to "procreate a child who, by reason of inheritance, would have a tendency to serious physical, mental, or nervous disease or deficiency."[9] My father had never told me about this, and it seemed like such a taboo subject that I photocopied the letters and put them back in the drawer without asking him about them. Many years later, during one of my visits, the television program we were watching showed clips from a Nazi sterilization film as part of a feature about the mistreatment of disabled people during the Third

Reich. At that moment, I felt that I could finally say to my father: "Mama was sterilized, too." I could see how much it hurt him to be reminded of that. He had always felt guilty that he couldn't afford to place her in a private hospital where she would have received better care than in the dreadful state hospital. And so he asked me if I thought it was wrong that he had agreed for her to be sterilized. He didn't know anything at all about eugenics so such considerations had never entered his mind. Rather, he said friends had told him that my young, pretty mother was sure to be raped by male patients and staff at the state hospital and that he had wanted to protect her at least from getting pregnant. Of course, I told him that I thought he had done the right thing, and we never spoke about it again.

As my graduate studies neared an end and the time was approaching to apply for university teaching positions, the contradiction between being fascinated with what I was studying and being reluctant to go back to the FRG became much too glaring. After much hesitation, I finally got up the courage to talk for the first time about how I had experienced the FRG. The person with whom I dared broach the subject was my dissertation adviser, Jost Hermand. I believed he would understand what I was saying for two reasons. First, the entire thrust of his research and teaching revolved around placing particular cultural phenomena into larger historical and political contexts. But also he had had a severe speech impediment, and because of this, along with his leftist views, universities in the FRG had been unwilling to hire him in the late 1950s. When he was hired as an assistant professor of German at the University of Wisconsin in 1958, his colleagues did not make an issue of his difficulties with speaking.[10] By the time I met him in the early 1970s, he was a distinguished research professor and had largely overcome his speech impediment. So when I blurted out to him my fears about returning to the FRG because of how I had been treated there I almost felt that it was a relief to him, too, to talk about this subject. He immediately asked me if I thought things were different there, and when I replied in the affirmative, he said that unfortunately he thought I was right. We traded some stories, and then he talked about the nineteenth-century radical German Jewish writer Heinrich Heine and his years in exile. I think I appreciated this swerve into cultural history for the point was that one could love and hate Germany at the same time and that many people had felt these conflicting emotions over the years.[11] Having broken through the silence I had kept for seven or eight years, I left this conversation with my German professor feeling uplifted and thinking that perhaps, after all, I could be brave enough to go back to the FRG, and to the GDR, which I was quite curious about, and to try to have a future as a professor of German literature.

After the expansion of higher education in the 1960s, the late 1970s and early 1980s were difficult times for young scholars who were looking for university teaching positions. Especially in the humanities, departments were being reduced in size, and many students who finished their doctorates in those years did not get jobs in their fields and sometimes had to make drastic career changes. In 1979, I began applying for positions, and, like many others at my career stage, was unsuccessful for quite a while. Along with the scarcity of positions, I had several other disadvantages, not the least being my dissertation topic, which was about as far away from the literary canon as one could get. But I had done very well in graduate school in the best German department in the country, and so I hoped for good luck. Over the next four years, I had about thirty-five interviews at the annual Modern Language Association convention and received as many rejection letters. Of course, I wondered whether my disability was a factor in my failure. After all, these brief, preliminary convention interviews relied so much on first impressions, and it seemed to me that sometimes people needed longer in order to feel comfortable around me. Only once did an interviewer—an American professor in a major German department at a large midwestern state university—tell me bluntly, as if it were self-evident, that his department would not hire me because "we would not want to have a colleague who looks the way you do." But in every other instance an American concept of good manners, that is, of appearing to ignore the disability, made it impossible to know for sure what was going on. So, even though all my professors throughout graduate school had always treated me correctly and been extremely encouraging to me as a good student, it seemed as though finding appropriate work and being accepted on an equal basis as a colleague at the university was going to be an entirely different matter. I began to wonder: perhaps when someone with a disability reached this stage, that of wanting to have an impact on the world through working in a highly qualified profession, the United States was not that different from Germany after all.

So time was passing. I was working at temporary secretarial jobs and continuing to do research and writing, revising my dissertation for publication. I got married and, as the rejection letters piled up, started looking a little more seriously into possibilities for alternative careers. My former professors noticed, of course, that I had not found a teaching position, and they tried to support me in any way they could. One day, while talking about my situation with Professor David Bathrick, I mentioned something about what it had been like to live in the FRG as a disabled person. He was one of the founders and editors of the New Left journal *New German Critique* and, just as importantly for our conversation, had a brother who was cognitively disabled. He immediately urged me to write about my experiences, and when I asked rather cynically who would ever want to publish such an essay, he promised to bring it out in his journal. This prospect gave me an enormous incentive to begin investigating the history of how disabled people had been treated in Germany and how they had tried to resist exclusion. And also I felt that if my disability was perhaps one reason that German departments in U.S. universities were unwilling to hire me I could at least get a little bit of vengeful personal satisfaction by beginning to write about these prejudices, resistance to discrimination, and disability as an important part of German cultural history.

At the same time, in 1981, I made up my mind to return to the FRG and received a Fulbright Fellowship to spend the summer there at a seminar for college German teachers in Bonn and West Berlin. Participants in this federal program had to have a medical examination, and, since I was so healthy, I thought of this as a rather pro forma matter. Not having a family physician, I made an appointment at a local clinic in Madison with a doctor whom I had never seen previously. Before even beginning to examine me, seeing my crutches and brace, he exclaimed: "You can't possibly go to Europe by yourself!" But when I replied that it was a good thing he hadn't told me that before I lived in Germany for over a year on my own, he gave me an extremely irritated look, took my temperature, and signed the form I needed for the fellowship. Now I was on my way back to the FRG for the first time in ten years.

The Fulbright lectures and seminars were outstanding, and I also used those months to collect as much material as possible about the history of disability in Germany and about the growing disability rights movement in the FRG. It was the UN Year for People with Disabilities, and in 1981 there were many controversies, including pathbreaking protests by disabled West Germans against being treated as second-class citizens and for self-determination. I was thrilled to pick up a leaflet written by the disabled activist Franz Christoph explaining why he had hit Federal President Karl Carstens with his crutch at the opening ceremony of the Düsseldorf Rehabilitation Fair. In the leaflet, Christoph declared, "People won't understand why a disabled man 'resorts to violence.' But as disabled people we are permanently subjected to both structural violence and violence directed against us as individuals. Therefore, it is logical that in spite of our physical limitations, some of us arrive at the idea of resisting violence with 'violence.'"[12] Discovering this resistance to oppression was a great affirmation to me that my research was worth doing. It was also a relief to find that in the ten years since I had been in the FRG the general climate with regard to disability and everyday life seemed to have changed for the better. There were not as many stares and intrusive questions as I had experienced the first time, though still more than in the United States. To be sure, it struck me that frequently West Germans became unnecessarily nervous and disturbed in situations in which I did not function quite in ways they thought of as normal: when I was slow going up steps, when I preferred to take a taxi rather than walk, and so on. But on the whole the summer was a positive experience, certainly made more congenial by being part of a group of U.S. professors intent on learning about contemporary West German culture and politics. I returned to the United States glad that I had taken the trip and with a large amount of new material for an article, entitled "Disability as Disobedience? An Essay on Germany in the Aftermath of the United Nations Year for People with Disabilities," which *New German Critique* published in 1982.

In that same year, I also finally struck gold on the academic job market, having been offered a position as an assistant professor in the German department at Brown University. With regard to the factor of disability, I believe I was hired there for two reasons in addition to whatever my qualifications were. First, my colleagues to be in that department were a unique group of liberal, flexible, open-minded intellectuals who, because of their own life stories, had an unusual commitment to fairness and equality. I was extremely fortunate to encounter that constellation of people in my job search. Second, though, is a factor about which I feel more uncertain. The night before I arrived for my interview, ten inches of snow had fallen in Providence. This was not the type of weather in which I would have chosen to take a hike, especially since it is a tradition in Rhode Island not to shovel sidewalks when it snows. But when one interviewer said that the two of us would go for a long walking tour of campus I knew that if I wanted this job I had better kick into the "overcoming" mode and act as if it were the most normal thing in the world for me to walk through deep snow. What this incident highlights is the difficult communicative dynamic between disabled and nondisabled people as well as some prevalent assumptions. Of course, the interviewer's purpose was to find out how I would function in the workplace environment, specifically, how I would move around campus. After all, I would need to go to the library, to meetings, to classes and events in various buildings. Yet the assumption was that in order to do this I would have to cope with the university environment as it then existed—with stairs, missing railings, deep snow and thick ice on sidewalks, classes scheduled in widely separated buildings, inadequate parking, and so on. At that time, almost ten years before the ADA was passed, there was little or no consciousness—at Brown or most other universities—that perhaps the workplace environment should be modified to enable the best-qualified candidate to do the job. So the interviewer was being polite in a certain way by not asking directly about whether my disability might affect my work, and my entire life experience up to that point made me certain it would be a big mistake to say that I would have preferred a driving rather than walking tour of campus on that particular day.

Once on the faculty at Brown, I felt that my colleagues in my own department, as well as many others I met, were extremely congenial and respected my work. However, unmistakable messages sometimes came from other sectors of the university that identifying myself as disabled would not be good for my career. For example, shortly after I came to Brown, colleagues in my department wanted to invite Jürgen Habermas to campus, as he was then a visiting professor at Cornell University. A colleague in another department who controlled the funds of the university lectureship committee intervened, saying that someone like Habermas, who had a speech impediment, was not worth inviting to Brown.[13] And so we were prevented from hearing West Germany's foremost political philosopher. But, just as in my job interviews, such open, unselfconscious discrimination was rare.

A much more obvious problem was the lack of any procedures for making the campus more accessible. This state of affairs was typical of most U.S. universities in the 1980s and seemed to reflect a prevailing attitude that people whose bodies did not function in normal ways did not belong there in the first place. Consequently, concerned more with survival and keeping my job than with being an activist in these matters, I continued to maneuver carefully and to work mainly on topics besides disability that interested me. That is, I avoided associating myself too obviously or exclusively with disability issues. I was able to pursue this strategy because I could go up stairs and walk across campus, even in bad weather, although I often became quite tired from doing so. If my impairment had been more severe, I would have been forced to insist more loudly on changes.[14] In any event, the pressure I felt not to make an issue of my disability at work was strong enough that I never identified myself as disabled on any official university form, such as those compiled for statistical purposes by the Equal Opportunity/ Affirmative Action Office, until after I received tenure in 1988.

In the meantime, however, I wanted to try to "claim disability" in some other way outside the workplace, and so I became a mentor to a young girl through an organization that links children from difficult family situations with interested adults.[15] "Linda," as I'll call her here, is affected by cerebral palsy, meaning in her case that she wears leg braces, is cognitively disabled, and has a speech impediment. Her disability is severe enough that she was always in special education classes located within the regular schools she attended. Being with Linda in many situations has given me new perspectives—positive and negative—on the world around us. Over the more than fifteen years we have known each other, I have learned many things from her about the relationships between people with physical and cognitive disabilities, the interweavings of social class and disability, and the meaning of courage. As someone with a physical disability, I had had the experience of people looking at me and assuming that something was wrong with my mind, too. This, together with memories of my mother's mental illness, had usually led me to distance myself unthinkingly or fearfully from any association with mental disability. Consequently, it was a very new and unfamiliar experience for me to make a commitment to try to build a close relationship with a young person who has a cognitive disability.

When I first met Linda, I saw immediately that she had the same desires as any other nine year old for security, friends, and fun and, as she grew older, for satisfying activities and close relationships with her peers. Furthermore, I saw what serious, extensive efforts were made by her school system and various state agencies to conform to the law and enable her to be integrated as much as possible into school and community life. I also found out, though, how Linda's socioeconomic class background (father absent, mother unemployed and uneducated, very low income, drugs and alcohol in the home) often placed enormous obstacles in her path. Coming from this chaotic family situation and going to public schools in the Providence, Rhode Island, area that are notoriously bad and thus attended almost solely by children from low-income families, Linda has been surrounded all her life by an atmosphere of thoughtlessness, roughness, and sometimes downright meanness very different from the way I grew up. Children and teenagers her own age frequently teased her, called her terrible names, and knocked her down, to the point that she hated going to school and became rather withdrawn. Her tormentors had a keen sense of the fact that her cognitive disability and speech impediment made it almost impossible for her to fight back verbally, and so this often made them all the more eager to be cruel to her. The adults in her life sometimes meant well, but more frequently they neglected her and got away with it easily because of her inability to protest. This aspect of reality in the United States would have remained mostly hidden from me if I had not been friends with a cognitively and physically disabled person from a very poor background. Various forms of embodiment provoke various responses, but to see these realities it is usually necessary to be allied in some way with those whose presence challenges standards of normality.

Through knowing Linda, the meaning of courage—a quality unthinkingly attributed so often to disabled people—has been confirmed to me. For both of us—two people of such different ages and backgrounds—courage has almost never meant overcoming our physical or cognitive impairments. We both want to live and enjoy our lives to the fullest—how could it be otherwise? Often we need varying degrees of assistance, and sometimes we don't realize our dreams, but the desire is still there. It is absurd to say that there is something brave about a desire that everyone has. Rather, courage for us has meant pulling ourselves together, sometimes alone and sometimes with support, to face the ignorance or hostility of other people. Because of her environment and her particular type of disabilities, Linda is confronted with more rejection than I ever experienced, and so I think she has had to be more courageous than I.

Since 1981, I have returned regularly to the FRG, West Berlin, the GDR before 1989, and reunified Germany. It has been quite striking to me how the harassment in daily life in the form of staring, questioning, and efforts at physical control has gradually diminished over this long period of time. Occasionally I still notice it more than in the United States, but in general it has become much more possible for me as a visibly disabled person to move comfortably through daily life in Germany. In other words, with respect to attitudes toward disability as a type of human variation, I experience Germany as having become increasingly similar to the United States over this period in an extremely positive way, which, however, I also want to interrogate. In order to extend and refine the theses I propose here, it would be crucial for a future project to develop cross-cultural perspectives that would compare disability experiences to the experiences of other groups such as racial and ethnic minorities or gays and lesbians.[16]

The following anecdote crystallizes important comparative aspects with respect to the kinds of situations I have encountered as a disabled person and can be helpful in getting at some of the reasons for the positive transformation of attitudes that I have experienced in Germany. In 1992, an East German acquaintance visited me in Providence. She was a well-educated woman in her fifties who had been born in Dresden and spent her entire adult life in East Berlin, and this was her first trip to the United States. One afternoon, while we were sitting at a sidewalk café in Harvard Square, a man and woman walked by who were both rather overweight and sloppily dressed. I did not notice them until my companion exclaimed: "That couple—impossible! And nobody is staring at them!" My spontaneous reply was to say: "It doesn't harm me if they look strange." My companion thoughtfully repeated what I had said and then commented, "That is American democratic self-understanding." I interpreted this situation as follows to myself. The couple was not obviously disabled, but their physical appearance was unusual enough to my companion that she remarked on it.[17] What my perceptive companion noticed just as much, however, was the unfamiliar reaction of other people: they were not staring at the couple, who—implicit in my companion's remark—would have been stared at in Germany. She then labeled this behavior and my reply an example of American democracy. What cultural differences are evident in this exchange? What kind of concept of democracy is at work here, and is it totally positive or does it have problematic sides as well?

As the philosopher Isaiah Berlin once noted, "To be normal means that one does not feel oneself to be observed."[18] Following this insight, it is possible to characterize staring as a type of behavior that has the effect of ritually upholding rigid, unquestioned norms of appearance or behavior.[19] Staring sends a nonverbal message that someone who does not conform to these norms is out of place, out of line, or even not quite human. For the starer, it is a way of affirming morality and normality—that is, group cohesiveness of the majority over and against a negatively viewed individual or minority. Anyone can experience being stared at by putting himself or herself into a situation where his or her difference from a normative group attracts attention. To understand the dynamic at work here, the difference between intentional and involuntary conspicuousness is significant. In the former case, for example, someone might choose to become an object of curiosity by walking down the street wearing an outrageous costume. This attracts stares that are wanted attention. On the other hand, bodily deviations from the norm over which one has no control also attract curiosity in the form of stares that are unwanted attention. Therefore, staring at disabled people, and indeed, at anyone who is involuntarily conspicuous, is a form of behavior which upholds the belief that outward conformity to group norms is the highest social value and any noticeable deviation from these norms is threatening to group cohesiveness.

The admonition against staring as bad manners enacts the modern conviction that people should be valued as individual human beings rather than categorized according to outward characteristics beyond their control. Over the past decades, the number of older Germans exposed to the Nazi ideology of the national racial community has gradually diminished; far-reaching democratizing changes emerging from the student movement in the FRG have occurred; and public debates about multiculturalism and what it means to be German have come to the fore. Consequently, a more modern concept of individual rights has taken hold in Germany that manifests itself in many different permutations with regard to different social groups. With respect to behavior toward disabled people, all of these factors, together with the important civil rights gains of the disability rights movement, have led to a noticeable decrease in the practice of staring.

Commenting in negative ways or asking intimate questions about involuntary characteristics that make a stranger conspicuously different from the unquestioned norm extends the ritual exclusion enacted by staring from the nonverbal into the verbal realm. As scholars in disability studies have noted, just as disability is often used in literature as a plot device to set narration in motion, the physical presence of a disabled person in daily life frequently provokes demands that the person narrate his or her story.[20] This desire for narration is often so strong that if disabled people resist being compelled to narrate in this way we often meet with disconcerted surprise and occasionally even with an aggressive response. Such questions or remarks indicate the force of disability as stigma.[21] That is, in such situations disability is viewed as the marked category that overrides any sense of the disabled person as an individual with a private sphere. By verbalizing the dynamic involved in staring, such questioning voices the moral assumptions that disabled people should not be what they are or where they are, that their variation from the norm is unwanted and disruptive in a community defined by outward aesthetic markers, and that they should be on call at all times to answer for their difference. Consequently, my experience that this type of questioning has lessened in Germany over the past decades also indicates the development of a more stable, modern sense of individual privacy as not necessarily threatening to society as a whole. This transformation in consciousness has been formulated at the highest levels of government. Federal President Richard von Weizsäcker's comment in 1993 that it is "normal to be different" validated increasingly flexible, tolerant attitudes toward a wider range of human bodily variation.[22]

Segregation of disabled people structures the physical environment in accordance with the nonverbal exclusion enacted by staring and the verbal exclusion voiced in questions that violate individual privacy. All three aspects of exclusion exemplify residual forms of discourse which hold that disability automatically makes a person helpless, immature, repellent, or even nonhuman and thus that it is sufficient cause for assigning a person to inferior roles and places in society.[23] In all three behaviors, the rigidity of preconceived notions generally prevents those enforcing exclusion from seeing the disabled person as a multifaceted individual, as a human being with rights. The power of these residual discourses with respect to disability was much stronger in Germany than in the United States thirty-five years ago, and this is why my strategy of overcoming my disability did not work so well there. In many countries over recent decades, however, including the United States and Germany, the disability rights movement has drawn on other civil rights struggles to insist on improved access to all realms of society and has finally achieved many notable successes.

Of course, the physical environment is still much more inaccessible in Germany than in the United States even though many improvements have been made. To be sure, this has to do partly with the fact that there are so many more older buildings in Europe. (In 2002, I met a French scholar who said he had moved to Berlin from Paris because the German capital was so much more accessible to him as a wheelchair user.) Sometimes I also sense an approach of self-defeating thoroughness, however, which is well illustrated by the reasons for the lack of accessible restrooms in public places. According to German industrial norms, an accessible restroom must be quite large and outfitted with complicated technology to accommodate all imaginable eventualities. As a result, there are very few accessible restrooms because few businesses can afford them—for example, it is rare to find one in public places such as restaurants, cafés, or movie theaters. Accordingly, Germans who use wheelchairs have remarked on how much easier it is to do what they want in daily life in the United States because so many more restrooms are accessible here, which usually means simply enlarging a toilet stall and attaching a couple of grab bars.

In both countries, however, as is the case around the world, disabled people disproportionally occupy the lowest rungs of the socioeconomic ladder no matter what differences there may be in manners and customs. Varying methods of defining disability and compiling statistics make cross-cultural comparisons difficult, but education and work are two of the most important areas where the fullest possible integration of disabled people must be achieved if we are to take our place as citizens with equal rights. Segregation of disabled children in special schools necessarily leads to second-class education and fuels intolerance. In the United States as of 1996, only about 5 percent of children with disabilities were still educated in separate, special schools; approximately 20 percent were educated for the entire school day in special classrooms within regular schools, like my friend Linda; and the remaining 75 percent were partially or totally integrated into the regular classroom.[24] In 2003 in Germany, 93 percent of children with disabilities still attended separate, special schools. This contrasts with the Scandinavian countries and Italy, where almost 100 percent of disabled children attend regular schools; to Portugal with 70 percent integration; to Spain with 50 percent; and to England and Austria with 30 percent. A recent Pisa study of schools in the European Union criticized Germany for lagging behind in its commitment to integrative education for children with disabilities.[25]

The striking differences in educational opportunities for children and young people with disabilities in the United States and Germany do not yet appear, however, to have had very much effect on employment opportunities and income. In this respect, it is almost impossible to compare statistics from the two countries. One U.S. survey conducted in 2000 found, for example, that only 56 percent of disabled people were working who said they were able to work, in contrast to 81 percent of nondisabled people.[26] German government statistics from 1996 claim that of 6.6 million officially recognized disabled people 5.5 million were not (or were no longer) looking for work, and 940,000 were working in the regular labor force (not in sheltered workshops).[27] It is undoubtedly true that in both countries disabled people have a much higher unemployment rate and lower income than nondisabled people. Because health insurance, disability benefits, and the social welfare net in general are much more comprehensive in Germany, however, it is safe to say that many of the basic financial needs of disabled people are covered better there than in the United States. Even in Germany, though, given the current world economic situation, there is now serious talk about reducing these benefits. Various activist organizations are working intensively to prevent this, as they also continue to advocate better educational and employment opportunities for disabled people.

Two experiences from 2001 illustrate from my foreign perspective some of the changes that have taken place in Germany over the past decades. In that year, I visited some German colleagues in Dortmund and Bochum who had long been active in the West German disability rights movement. One day I went to lunch at an elegant restaurant in a small castle outside Dortmund with a couple: a man who was quadriplegic and used a wheelchair and his nondisabled partner. Before entering the restaurant, knowing that there was no accessible restroom, the man used a urinal they had brought along. Then we went up the ramp, were seated politely by the staff, who matter-of-factly moved a chair aside to make room for his wheelchair, were waited on attentively while his partner helped him eat, and had a long conversation over the delicious asparagus dishes. The man mentioned at one point how he had been greatly influenced by Martin Luther King Jr. and the Black Panther leader Eldridge Cleaver. After lunch, we walked and rolled around the park outside, all the while being stared at most obtrusively by a middle-aged woman sitting on a bench, whose worn-out clothing probably reflected her lower socioeconomic status. I was ignoring her because I was having such a good time, but my nondisabled colleague finally went over and had a sharp exchange of words with her. Afterward we talked about our enjoyable outing and how there was such a great world of difference between our pleasant day and what might have happened thirty years ago. For then it probably would have been physically impossible for the three of us to have entered the restaurant. And, even if we had managed to get in, we would certainly have been stared at constantly, and it was unlikely that we would have been treated so politely by the restaurant staff—that is, simply as customers with money to spend. Now, however, the three of us had been able to enjoy the everyday activity of eating out with only a couple of minor untoward incidents.

On that same trip to Germany, I also visited a colleague who is a law professor and disability rights activist and has no arms as a result of thalidomide. After I gave a lecture at her university about cultural representations of disability in Germany and the United States, I asked her how we were going to get to her home thirty kilometers away, assuming we would take the train or bus. When she said her car was parked close by, I had to drop instantly—and I hope, not too obviously—one of *my* preconceived notions about embodiment: that arms and hands were necessary for driving. After a speedy trip on the autobahn, the two of us went out to eat, sitting outside since it was a pleasant evening. My friend often went to this restaurant since it was close to her house and the food was excellent. The pleasant waitress, who knew her, asked politely if she should cut up her meat as usual before serving it. My friend eats by holding the silverware with her toes, and two boys, about eight or nine years old, immediately positioned themselves on the sidewalk about twenty feet behind her, so that she could not see them, in order to stare at her while she ate. But no one else in this familiar environment paid us any attention, and we enjoyed our dinner and conversation. My friend recounted how she had frequently been thrown out of restaurants in Germany because of what people saw as the abnormal, repelling way she ate, and we talked about how necessary it was for countries to have strong equal rights laws, such as the ADA, that would forbid such discrimination.

Over the past decade, I have tried to identify myself more openly and consistently with disability issues, including working with others on practical questions of accessibility, as well as doing scholarly research and teaching disability studies courses. An essential source of intellectual support has been the growth of disability studies in the humanities in the United States, which is now beginning to gain a foothold as an emerging interdisciplinary field in Germany as well. With respect to both scholarship and teaching, when I break through the reluctance I still have sometimes to speak about disability, I often find that my partners in dialogue are touched by these issues in ways that I did not imagine: the colleagues with invisible disabilities, the colleague with a blind sister or whose son is autistic, the older French colleague who also had polio and found coming to the United States to be a liberation, students who are grappling with issues of race and disability, the newly disabled student trying to cope with strangers who invade his privacy, the engineering student who wants to design better-functioning wheelchairs, students who have disabled relatives, students who want to become more sensitive medical professionals, disabled students who know that 70 percent of disabled people are unemployed in spite of the ADA and worry about finding satisfying work, and so on. Becoming more aware of the threads connecting such disparate people and experiences has made it easier for me to accept disability as a universal phenomenon that touches most people's lives at one time or another.

As one of the last groups to claim the promises of the Enlightenment for themselves, disabled people are now insisting on their right to freedom and equality, that is, the right to live as individuals in a modern sense. And they have finally been successful in significant ways in creating new discourses about disability, in being recognized, to some extent at least, as citizens with equal rights. This process in Germany is what I have experienced as an increasing similarity to my daily life as a white, disabled, now middle-class American in the United States. But does this transformation really go far enough? After all, in the increasingly globalized capitalist world economy, achieving formal civil rights generally also means gaining a more atomized existence—that is, securing the freedom to become modern individuals in the sense of equalized consumers whose main social obligation is to spend money. This is a problematic aspect of the more flexible attitudes that are emerging toward minority groups, including disabled people, who formerly were excluded more rigorously on the basis of characteristics irrelevant to the market economy.[28] After all, as the German sociologist and disability studies scholar Anne Waldschmidt has noted, disabled people's struggles for self-determination are occurring now in a precarious economic situation in which privatization, meaning more individual assumption of risks, is increasing and in which any broader social consensus is crumbling.[29] To perceive clearly the grave dangers of this development for disabled people, it is important to realize, as the women's group WinVisible states, that "much of disability and ill-health is caused by poverty, pollution, war and the arms trade, industrial accidents and job injuries, and other deadly effects of a world economy which prioritizes profit over people's needs."[30]

At its best, the disability rights movement has been about the "revaluation of an ethos of community and care, as opposed to the cutthroat individualism of the dominant culture," according to Robert McRuer and Abby Wilkerson.[31] Therefore, a cultural and political focus on formulating in the broadest possible terms what it means to create access, that central demand of disability rights, might be a way of moving beyond limited, individualistic goals toward potentially more far-reaching social transformations. If access only means access to a top position within the globalized market economy, it is not enough. Rather, it will be crucial to ask hard questions about accessibility issues in terms of the socioeconomic inequalities that not only cause so much disability, especially in poor countries, but also provide the foundation for the utilitarian perspective that the most desirable human beings are those who conform most readily to the values of a consumer society. What kind of changes would have to occur, for example, for all human beings, disabled or not, to have access to the needs of daily life, to satisfying work or activities, to forms of culture that express and speak to all their faculties, and to a world where nature and biodiversity are preserved and cherished rather than destroyed? Access understood in this way would go far beyond achieving certain rights within existing systems of power for it would mean access to global social justice for all.

Notes

PREFACE

1. Sander Gilman's numerous publications related to disability in German culture include *Difference and Pathology: Stereotypes of Sexuality, Race, and Madness* (Ithaca: Cornell University Press, 1985); *Disease and Representation* (Ithaca: Cornell University Press, 1988); *Picturing Health and Illness: Images of Identity and Difference* (Baltimore: Johns Hopkins University Press, 1995); and *Seeing the Insane* (Lincoln: University of Nebraska Press, 1996). Elizabeth Hamilton wrote a pioneering Ph.D. dissertation: "Disabling Discourses in German Literature from Lessing to Grass" (Ohio State University, 1998). The first major German disability studies publication was Petra Lutz et al., eds., *Der (im)perfekte Mensch: Metamorphosen von Normalität und Abweichung* (Cologne: Böhlau, 2003). The best social history of disabled people in Germany remains Walter Fandrey, *Krüppel, Idioten, Irre: Zur Sozialgeschichte behinderter Menschen in Deutschland* (Stuttgart: Silberburg, 1990). For more specific references, see the notes to the following chapters.

2. A number of references can be mined for useful material about the cultural history of disability and disabled people in Germany before World War I. These include Pilar Baumeister, *Die literarische Gestalt des Blinden im 19. und 20. Jahrhundert* (New York: Lang, 1991); Helmut Bernsmeier, *Das Bild des Behinderten in der deutschsprachigen Literatur des 19. und 20. Jahrhunderts* (Bern: Lang, 1980); Michael Hagner, *Der falsche Körper: Beiträge zu einer Geschichte der Monstrositäten* (Göttingen: Wallstein, 1995); Achim Hölter, *Die Invaliden: Die vergessene Geschichte der Kriegskrüppel in der europäischen Literatur bis zum 19. Jahrhundert* (Stuttgart: Metzler, 1995); Irmela Krüger-Fürhoff, *Der versehrte Körper* (Göttingen: Wallstein, 2001); Georg Reuchlein, *Bürgerliche Gesellschaft, Psychiatrie, und Literatur: Zur Entwicklung der Wahnsinnsthematik in der deutschen Literatur des späten 18. und frühen 19. Jahrhunderts* (Munich: Fink, 1986); Stephan Sas, *Der Hinkende als Symbol* (Zürich: Rascher, 1964); Elisabeth Sudeck, *Bettlerdarstellungen vom Ende des XV. Jahrhunderts bis zu Rembrandt* (Strassburg: Heitz, 1931); and Hans-Jorg Uther, *Behinderte in populären Erzählungen* (New York: De Gruyter, 1981).

CHAPTER 1

1. Heinz Faulstich, *Hungersterben in der Psychiatrie, 1914–1949* (Freiburg: Lambertus, 1998), 63–67.

2. Tobin Siebers, "What Can Disability Studies Learn from the Culture Wars?" *Cultural Critique* 5 (2003): 182–216.

3. For an excellent history of care for physically disabled children in Germany and the relationship between children's institutions and care for disabled veterans, see Klaus-Dieter Thomann, *Das behinderte Kind: "Krüppelfürsorge" und Orthopädie in Deutschland, 1886–1920* (Stuttgart: Gustav Fischer, 1995).

4. Michael Hau, *The Cult of Health and Beauty in Germany: A Social History, 1890–1930* (Chicago: University of Chicago Press, 2003).

5. Deborah Cohen, *The War Come Home: Disabled Veterans in Britain and Germany, 1914–1939* (Berkeley: University of California Press, 2001), 64.

6. Hau, *Cult of Health and Beauty,* 135.

7. Sabine Kienitz, "'Fleischgewordenes Elend': Kriegsinvalidität und Körperbilder als Teil einer Erfahrungsgeschichte des Ersten Weltkrieges," in *Die Erfahrung des Krieges: Erfahrungsgeschichtliche Perspektiven von der Französischen Revolution bis zum Zweiten Weltkrieg,* ed. Nikolaus Buschmann and Horst Carl (Paderborn: Schöningh, 2001), 234.

8. Quoted in Christoph Zuschlag, *"Entartete Kunst": Ausstellungsstrategien in Nazi-Deutschland* (Worms: Wernersche Verlagsgesellschaft, 1995), 25.

9. Irma Dresdner, "Über Körperbehinderung und seelische Entwicklung," *Zeitschrift für angewandte Psychologie* 44:5–6 (April 1933): 399–437.

10. On the figure of 2.7 million and the difficulties in arriving at precise statistics on disabled veterans, see Robert Whalen, *Bitter Wounds: German Victims of the Great War, 1914–1939* (Ithaca: Cornell University Press, 1984), 9.

11. Klaus-Dieter Thomann, "Die medizinische und soziale Fürsorge für die Kriegsversehrten in der ersten Phase des Krieges, 1914–1915," in *Die Medizin und der Erste Weltkrieg,* ed. Wolfgang Eckart and Christoph Gradmann (Pfaffenweiler: Centaurus, 1996), 185.

12. Sabine Kienitz, "Der Krieg der Invaliden: Helden-Bilder und Männlichkeitskonstruktionen nach dem Ersten Weltkrieg," *Militärgeschichtliche Zeitschrift* 60 (2001): 375.

13. See Elisabeth Sudeck, *Bettlerdarstellungen vom Ende des XV. Jahrhunderts bis zu Rembrandt* (Strassburg: Heitz, 1931), for many examples of crippled beggars in art. For a social history that gives many insights into connections among disability, poverty, and begging, see Christoph Sachße and Florian Tennstedt, eds., *Bettler, Gauner und Proleten. Armut und Armenfürsorge in der deutschen Geschichte: Ein Bild-Lesebuch* (Reinbek: Rowohlt, 1983).

14. Walter Fandrey, *Krüppel, Idioten, Irre: Zur Sozialgeschichte behinderter Menschen in Deutschland* (Stuttgart: Silberburg, 1990), 108.

15. Cohen, *The War Come Home;* James Diehl, "Victors or Victims? Disabled Veterans in the Third Reich," *Journal of Modern History* 59:4 (December 1987): 705–36.

16. Fandrey, *Krüppel, Idioten, Irre,* 160.

17. Konrad Biesalski, *Kriegskrüppelfürsorge: Ein Aufklärungswort zum Troste und zur Mahnung* (Leipzig: Voss, 1915), 34. Subsequent page references are given in the body of the text. On the history of the Oskar-Helene

Home, see Philipp Osten, *Die Modellanstalt: Über den Aufbau einer "modernen Krüppelfürsorge,"* *1905–1933* (Frankfurt: Mabuse, 2004).

18. Dora Apel, "Cultural Battlegrounds: Weimar Photographic Narratives of War," *New German Critique* 76 (winter 1999): 62.

19. For good examples of this perspective, see Fandrey, *Krüppel, Idioten, Irre;* Thomann, *Das behinderte Kind;* and Heather Perry, "Re-arming the Disabled Veteran: Artificially Rebuilding State and Society in World War One Germany," in *Artificial Parts, Practical Lives: Modern Histories of Prosthetics,* ed. Katherine Ott et al. (New York: New York University Press, 2002), 75–101.

20. Peter Sloterdijk, *Critique of Cynical Reason,* trans. Michael Eldred (Minneapolis: University of Minnesota Press, 1987), 444.

21. Thomann, *Das behinderte Kind,* 331.

22. Ibid., 318.

23. Fandrey, *Krüppel, Idioten, Irre,* 161.

24. Thomann, *Das behinderte Kind,* chap. 7.

25. Thomann, "Die medizinische und soziale Fürsorge für die Kriegsversehrten," 183.

26. Apel, "Cultural Battlegrounds," 62; Bernd Ulrich, "'. . . als wenn nichts geschehen wäre': Anmerkungen zur Behandlung der Kriegsopfer während des Ersten Weltkriegs," in *"Keiner fühlt sich hier mehr als Mensch . . .": Erlebnis und Wirkung des Ersten Weltkriegs,* ed. Gerhard Hirschfeld and Gerd Krumeich (Essen: Klartext, 1993), 120.

27. Fandrey, *Krüppel, Idioten, Irre,* 163; Cohen, *The War Come Home,* 161.

28. Fandrey, *Krüppel, Idioten, Irre,* 169–70.

29. Thomann, *Das behinderte Kind,* 282.

30. Ibid., 317.

31. Cohen, *The War Come Home,* explores the role of charitable organizations in connection with disabled veterans.

32. Quoted in Christine Beil, "Zwischen Hoffnung und Verbitterung: Selbstbild und Erfahrungen von Kriegsbeschädigten in den ersten Jahren der Weimarer Republik," *Zeitschrift für Geschichtswissenschaft* 46 (1998): 144.

33. Quoted in Kienitz, "Fleischgewordenes Elend," 234.

34. Carl Herrmann Unthan, *Das Pediskript: Aufzeichnungen aus dem Leben eines Armlosen* (Stuttgart: Robert Lutz Verlag, 1925), 276.

35. Cohen, *The War Come Home,* 151.

36. Whalen, *Bitter Wounds,* 98.

37. Quoted in Kienitz, "Krieg der Invaliden," 378.

38. Whalen, *Bitter Wounds,* 187.

39. Paul Lerner, "An Economy of Memory: Psychiatrists, Veterans, and Traumatic Narratives in Weimar Germany," in *The Work of Memory: New Directions in the Study of German Society and Culture,* ed. Alon Confino and Peter Fritzsche (Urbana: University of Illinois Press, 2002), 173–95; Paul Lerner, *Hysterical Men: War, Psychiatry, and the Politics of Trauma in Germany, 1890–1930* (Ithaca: Cornell University Press, 2003).

40. Kienitz, "Fleischgewordenes Elend," 235.

41. For descriptions of these war victims' demonstrations, see Whalen, *Bitter Wounds,* 116–24.

42. Quoted in ibid., 55.

43. Beil, "Zwischen Hoffnung und Verbitterung," 150.

44. Quoted in Whalen, *Bitter Wounds,* 49.

45. Quoted in Kienitz, "Fleischgewordenes Elend," 46.

46. Cohen, *The War Come Home,* 97.

47. See Wolfgang Rothe, *Tänzer und Täter: Gestalten des Expressionismus* (Frankfurt: Vittorio Klostermann, 1979), for a discussion of images of illness and disability in expressionist art and literature. See also Jost Hermand and Richard Hamann, *Expressionismus* (Berlin: Akademie Verlag, 1975), 36ff.

48. Hermand and Hamann, *Expressionismus,* 194–95, gives numerous examples of portrayals of illness in expressionist art.

49. Georg Heym's poems on insanity include "Die Irren" (1:91), "Die Irren" (1:253–54), "Die Irren im Garten" (1:428), and "Die Irren" (1:449), all in his *Dichtungen und Schriften: Gesamtausgabe. Lyrik,* 2 vols. (Hamburg: Ellermann, 1964).

50. Georg Heym, "Der Irre," in ibid., 2:19–34.

51. These poems are all included in ibid., vol. 1.

52. See Rothe, *Tänzer und Täter,* for specific references.

53. Maria Tatar, *Lustmord: Sexual Murder in Weimar Germany* (Princeton: Princeton University Press, 1995).

54. George Grosz, *A Little Yes and a Big No: The Autobiography of George Grosz* (New York: Dial, 1946), 146–47.

55. Mathias Eberle, *Der Weltkrieg und die Künstler der Weimarer Republik: Dix, Grosz, Beckmann, Schlemmer* (Stuttgart: Belser, 1989), 102.

56. Beth Irwin Lewis, *George Grosz: Art and Politics in the Weimar Republic* (Princeton: Princeton University Press, 1991), 143.

57. Willi Schuster, *Der Dank des Vaterlandes* (Berlin: Franke, 1921), 3.

58. Quoted in Fritz Löffler, *Otto Dix: Leben und Werk* (Dresden: VEB Verlag der Kunst, 1977), 72.

59. Quoted in Michael Hagner, "Verwundete Gesichter, verletzte Gehirne: Zur Deformation des Kopfes im Ersten Weltkrieg," in *Gesichter der Weimarer Republik: Eine physiognomische Kulturgeschichte,* ed. Claudia Schmölders and Sander Gilman (Cologne: DuMont, 2000), 86.

60. Kienitz, "Fleischgewordenes Elend," 226.

61. Quoted in Apel, "Cultural Battlegrounds," 69.

62. Quoted in Löffler, *Otto Dix,* 71.

63. Ibid., 96.

64. Fritz Lang's film *Spione* (Spies, 1928), based on a novel by his wife, Thea von Harbou, and known as the first modern spy film, also takes up the subject of malingering in connection with a portrayal of disability. The evil mastermind Haghi, shown in a wheelchair, is a bank owner out to rule the world. After many twists in the plot, he is about to kill Sonia, the good secret agent. He tells her that first she will find out his secret, whereupon he rises from the wheelchair and walks—a plot device that enables him to escape from the bank. Haghi is evil, revengeful, and sexually frustrated—all qualities traditionally associated with the figure of the cripple. Yet in the end he is not disabled at all.

65. Bertolt Brecht, *Die Dreigroschenoper,* in *Gesammelte Werke* (Frankfurt: Suhrkamp, 1967), 2:402. Subsequent page references are given in the body of the text.

66. Mia Fineman, "Ecce Homo Prostheticus," *New German Critique* 76 (winter 1999): 85–114.

67. Karoline Hille, "'. . . über den Grenzen, mitten in Nüchternheit': Prothesenkörper, Maschinenherzen, Automatenhirne," in *Puppen Körper Automaten: Phantasmen der Moderne,* ed. Pia Müller-Tamm and Katharina Sykora (Cologne: Oktagon, 1999), 145. The order in which Dix created these four paintings is impossible to determine.

68. Fineman, "Ecce Homo Prostheticus," 95.

69. Hille, ". . . über den Grenzen," 146.

70. Löffler, *Otto Dix,* 40.

71. Fineman, "Ecce Homo Prostheticus," 93.

72. Dix's contemporary, Conrad Felixmüller, stated that this was the subtitle of the painting (Eberle, *Der Weltkrieg,* 46).

73. Raoul Hausmann, "Prothesenwirtschaft," in *Bilanz der Feierlichkeit: Texte bis 1933* (Munich: edition text und kritik, 1982), 1:137–38.

74. Fineman, "Ecce Homo Prostheticus," 105–7.

75. Sigmund Freud's essay on "Das Unheimliche" (The Uncanny) probes the boundary crossings between living bodies and inanimate matter. In particular, German romantic authors such as E. T. A. Hoffmann frequently depicted uncanny marionettes and machine people in this sense.

76. Franz Seiwert, "Krupp-Krüppel," in *Heinrich Hoerle: Leben und Werk, 1895–1936,* ed. Dirk Backes (Cologne: Rheinland-Verlag, 1981), 100.

77. Dirk Backes, "Heinrich Hoerle: Ein Realist zwischen Ironie und Metaphysik," in *Heinrich Hoerle: Leben und Werk, 1895–1936,* ed. Dirk Backes (Cologne: Rheinland-Verlag, 1981), 34.

78. Fineman, "Ecce Homo Prostheticus," 108.

79. All of these works are reproduced in Backes, *Heinrich Hoerle.*

80. Stefan Rieger, "Arbeitshand und Ausdruckshand: Zur Prothetik des Menschen," in *Der (Im-)Perfekte Mensch: Metamorphosen von Normalität und Abweichung,* ed. Petra Lutz et al. (Cologne: Böhlau, 2003), 162–183.

81. Rosemarie Garland-Thomson, *Extraordinary Bodies: Figuring Physical Disability in American Culture and Literature* (New York: Columbia University Press, 1997), 10.

82. On the portrayal of insanity and abnormal mental states in expressionist literature, see Rothe, *Tänzer und Täter.* For an analysis of the expressionist film *The Cabinet of Dr. Caligari* with respect to traumatized disabled veterans, see Anton Kaes, "Shell Shock: Krieg und Trauma im expressionistischen Film," in *Der (Im-)Perfekte Mensch: Metamorphosen von Normalität und Abweichung,* ed. Petra Lutz et al. (Cologne: Böhlau, 2003), 128–41.

83. Leonhard Frank, *Der Mensch ist gut* (Leipzig: Reclam, 1985), 126. Subsequent page references are given in the body of the text.

84. Erich Maria Remarque, *Der Weg zurück* (Frankfurt: Ullstein, 1986), 147ff.

85. Ernst Toller, "Eine Jugend in Deutschland," in *Prosa Briefe Dramen Gedichte* (Reinbek: Rowohlt, 1961), 94ff.

86. Ernst Toller, *Die Wandlung,* in *Prosa Briefe Dramen Gedichte* (Reinbek: Rowohlt, 1961), 256. Subsequent page references are given in the body of the text.

87. Wolfgang Rothe, *Ernst Toller in Selbstzeugnissen und Bilddokumenten* (Reinbek: Rowohlt, 1983), 46.

88. Klaus Dörner, *Die Gesundheitsfalle: Woran unsere Medizin krankt—Zwölf Thesen zu ihrer Heilung* (Munich: Econ, 2003), 91ff.

89. Rothe, *Tänzer und Täter,* 173, 178ff.

90. Ernst Toller, *Hoppla, wir leben!* (Stuttgart: Reclam, 1980), 106.

91. Here I am following Sabine Kienitz, "Die Kastrierten des Krieges: Körperbilder und Männlichkeitskonstruktionen im und nach dem Ersten Weltkrieg," *Zeitschrift für Volkskunde* 95:1 (1999): 63–82.

92. Toller, "Eine Jugend in Deutschland," 177.

93. Ernst Toller, *Hinkemann* (Stuttgart: Reclam, 1993), 18. Subsequent page references are given in the body of the text.

94. Wolfgang Frühwald and John M. Spalek, eds., *Der Fall Toller: Kommentar und Materialien* (Munich: Hanser, 1979), 144, 146. Subsequent page references are given in the body of the text.

95. Richard Weikart, *From Darwin to Hitler: Evolutionary Ethics, Eugenics, and Racism in Germany* (New York: Palgrave Macmillan, 2004); Paul Weindling, *Health, Race, and German Politics between National Unification and Nazism, 1870–1945* (Cambridge: Cambridge University Press, 1989); Peter Weingart et al., *Rasse, Blut, und Gene: Geschichte der Eugenik und Rassenhygiene in Deutschland* (Frankfurt: Suhrkamp, 1988).

96. Quoted in Henry Friedlander, *The Origins of Nazi Genocide: From Euthanasia to the Final Solution* (Chapel Hill: University of North Carolina Press, 1995), 4.

97. Hau, *Cult of Health and Beauty,* 120. See also Udo Benzenhöfer, *Der gute Tod? Euthanasie und Sterbehilfe in Geschichte und Gegenwart* (Munich: Beck, 1999). For a comparison between Germany and the United States, see Martin Pernick, *The Black Stork: Eugenics and the Death of "Defective" Babies in American Medicine and Motion Pictures since 1915* (New York: Oxford University Press, 1996).

98. Philip Reilly, *The Surgical Solution: A History of Involuntary Sterilization in the United States* (Baltimore: Johns Hopkins University Press, 1991).

99. Friedlander, *Origins of Nazi Genocide,* 10.

100. Patricia Heberer, "Targeting the 'Unfit' and Radical Public Health Strategies in Nazi Germany," in *Deaf People in Hitler's Europe,* ed. Donna Ryan and John Schuchman (Washington, DC: Gallaudet University Press, 2002), 52.

101. Quoted in Petra Fuchs, *"Körperbehinderte" zwischen Selbstaufgabe und Emanzipation* (Neuwied: Luchterhand, 2001), 35.

102. All information here is taken from Statistisches Reichsamt, ed., *Die Gebrechlichen im Deutschen Reich nach der Zählung von 1925–26: Statistik des Deutschen Reichs,* vol. 419 (Berlin: Verlag von Reimar Hobbing, 1931).

103. Michael Burleigh, *Death and Deliverance: "Euthanasia" in Germany, 1900–1945* (Cambridge: Cambridge University Press, 1994), 29.

104. Fandrey, *Krüppel, Idioten, Irre,* 177. Subsequent references are given in the body of the text.

105. On parents' resistance to placing their children in cripples' homes, see Klaus-Dieter Thomann, "Der 'Krüppel': Entstehen und Verschwinden eines Kampfbegriffs," *Medizinhistorisches Journal* 27:3–4 (1992): 246ff.

106. Konrad Biesalski, *Grundriss der Krüppelfürsorge* (Leipzig: Voss, 1926), 15.

107. Oliver Musenberg, *Der Körperbehindertenpädagoge Hans Würtz (1875–1958): Eine kritische Würdigung des psychologischen und pädagogischen Konzeptes vor dem Hintergrund seiner Biographie* (Hamburg: Verlag Dr. Kovac, 2003). In 1933, Würtz, a freemason and social democrat, emigrated to Czechoslovakia and then lived unobtrusively in a working-class area of Vienna. In January 1946, he returned to Berlin and helped rebuild the Oskar-Helene Home.

108. Thomann, in *Das behinderte Kind*, 323–24, notes the importance of church-run homes for disabled people and especially children. The staff at these homes often resisted cost-benefit calculations, asserting that even invalids could often perform some simple work, and insisted on the human dignity of all people.

109. Hans Würtz, *Zerbrecht die Krücken* (Leipzig: Voss, 1932), 64.

110. On the discussion in Germany among psychiatrists after World War II about mental "dystrophy" among returning prisoners of war in comparison to psychiatric discussions of shell shock after World War I, see Frank Biess, "The Protracted War: Returning POWs and the Making of East and West German Citizens, 1945–1955," *German Historical Institute Bulletin* 28 (spring 2001): 155–69.

111. Lerner, "An Economy of Memory," 185–87.

112. Thomann, "Der 'Krüppel,'" 251. Subsequent references are given in the body of the text.

113. Thomas Anz, *Gesund oder krank? Medizin, Moral, und Ästhetik in der deutschen Gegenwartsliteratur* (Stuttgart: Metzler, 1989), 38. Subsequent references are given in the body of the text.

114. See Hau, *Cult of Health and Beauty*, on Nordau and the life reform movement.

115. Hau, *Cult of Health and Beauty*, 161.

116. Paul Schultze-Naumburg, *Kunst und Rasse*, 1st ed. (Munich: Lehmann, 1928), 92.

117. Ibid., 89.

118. Preface to second edition of *Kunst und Rasse* (1934), in Paul Schultze-Naumburg, *Kunst und Rasse*, 3rd ed. (Munich: Lehmann, 1938), 6.

119. Schultze-Naumburg, *Kunst und Rasse*, 1st ed., 87–88.

120. Peter Gorsen, *Kunst und Krankheit: Metamorphosen der ästhetischen Einbildungskraft* (Stuttgart: Europäische Verlagsanstalt, 1980), 19–20.

121. Schultze-Naumburg, *Kunst und Rasse*, 3rd ed., 5.

122. Whalen, *Bitter Wounds;* "World War I, Veterans, and the Weimar Republic," chap. 1 in James Diehl, *The Thanks of the Fatherland: German Veterans after the Second World War* (Chapel Hill: University of North Carolina Press, 1993).

123. Fandrey, *Krüppel, Idioten, Irre*, 166.

124. Here I follow Jochen Muhs, "Deaf People as Eyewitnesses of National Socialism," in *Deaf People in Hitler's Europe*, ed. Donna Ryan and John Schuchman (Washington, DC: Gallaudet University Press, 2002), 70–98.

125. My discussion of this film follows John Schuchman, "Misjudged People: The German Deaf Community in 1932," in *Deaf People in Hitler's*

Europe, ed. Donna Ryan and John Schuchman (Washington, DC: Gallaudet University Press, 2002), 98–113.

126. Petra Fuchs, *Otto Perl (1882–1951): Das Recht auf Selbstbestimmung für "den geistig normalen Krüppel,"* http://bidok.uibk .ac.at/texte/fuchs-perl.html; Hans-Günter Heiden et al., *Otto Perl und die Entwicklung von Selbstbestimmung und Selbstkontrolle in der Körperbehinderten-Selbsthilfe-Bewegung* (Krautheim: Bundesverband Selbsthilfe Körperbehinderter, 1993).

127. Quoted in Fuchs, *Otto Perl.*

128. Otto Perl, *Krüppeltum und Gesellschaft im Wandel der Zeit* (Gotha: Klotz, 1926), 27.

129. Thomann, "Der 'Krüppel,'" 254. In this article, Thomann explains the complicated reasons why the rehabilitation experts insisted on using the term *cripple.*

130. Heiden, *Otto Perl,* 20.

131. Perl, *Krüppeltum und Gesellschaft,* 41.

132. Quoted in Fuchs, *"Körperbehinderte,"* 78.

133. Information on Gruhl is based on Petra Fuchs, *Marie Gruhl (1881–1929): Engagement für die gemeinsame Erziehung "gesunder" und "krüppelhafter" Kinder und Jugendlicher in der Weimarer Republik,* http://bidok.uibk.ac.at/texte/fuchs-gruhl.html. On another woman member of the SBK with similar goals, see Petra Fuchs, *Hilde Wulff (1898–1972): Leben und Wirken für die Emanzipation körperbehinderter Menschen in der Weimarer Republik und in der Zeit des Nationalsozialismus,* http://bidok.uibk.ac.at/texte/fuchs-wulff.html.

134. Information about Dresdner is based on Petra Fuchs, "Irma Dresdners Untersuchung 'Über Körperbehinderung und seelische Entwicklung,' Leipzig 1933," *Die neue Sonderschule* 46:2 (April 2001): 84–95.

135. Irma Dresdner, "Über Körperbehinderung und seelische Entwicklung," *Zeitschrift für angewandte Psychologie* 44:5–6 (April 1933): 403. Subsequent page references are given in the body of the text.

136. Fuchs, "Irma Dresdners Untersuchung," reproduces Dresdner's questions (93–94).

137. Klaus Völker, *Max Herrmann-Neiße: Künstler, Kneipen, Kabaretts—Schlesien, Berlin, im Exil* (Berlin: Edition Hentrich, 1991), 22. The biographical information provided here is based on Völker's book.

138. Untitled essay in Max Herrmann-Neiße, *Im Stern des Schmerzes: Gedichte* (Frankfurt: Zweitausendeins, 1986), 1:433–34.

139. Max Herrmann-Neiße, "Groteske," in *Der Todeskandidat: Prosa* (Frankfurt: Zweitausendeins, 1987), 2:7–10.

140. Herrmann-Neiße, *Im Stern des Schmerzes,* 436.

141. Quoted in Völker, *Max Herrmann-Neiße,* 63–64.

142. Max Herrmann-Neiße, *Cajetan Schaltermann. Die Bernert-Paula: Prosa* (Frankfurt: Zweitausendeins, 1986), 1:171.

143. Völker, *Max Herrmann-Neiße,* 171. Subsequent page references are given in the body of the text.

CHAPTER 2

1. See for example: Reichsführer SS—SS Hauptamt, ed., *Der Untermensch* (Berlin: Nordland, [1942]).

2. James Diehl, "Victors or Victims? Disabled Veterans in the Third Reich," *Journal of Modern History* 59:4 (December 1987): 716.

3. Christoph Beck, *Sozialdarwinismus, Rassenhygiene, Zwangssterilisation, und Vernichtung "lebensunwerten" Lebens: Eine Bibliographie zum Umgang mit behinderten Menschen im "Dritten Reich"— und heute* (Bonn: Psychiatrie-Verlag, 1995).

4. Paul Weindling, *Health, Race, and German Politics between National Unification and Nazism, 1870–1945* (Cambridge: Cambridge University Press, 1989); Peter Weingart et al., *Rasse, Blut, und Gene: Geschichte der Eugenik und Rassenhygiene in Deutschland* (Frankfurt: Suhrkamp, 1992); Robert Proctor, *Racial Hygiene: Medicine under the Nazis* (Cambridge: Harvard University Press, 1998); Stefan Kühl, *The Nazi Connection: Eugenics, American Racism, and German National Socialism* (New York: Oxford University Press, 1994); Philip Reilly, *The Surgical Solution: A History of Involuntary Sterilization in the United States* (Baltimore: Johns Hopkins University Press, 1991).

5. James Diehl, *The Thanks of the Fatherland: German Veterans after the Second World War* (Chapel Hill: University of North Carolina Press, 1993), 45. Subsequent references are given in the body of the text.

6. Diehl, "Victors or Victims?" 729–30.

7. David A. Gerber, ed., *Disabled Veterans in History* (Ann Arbor: University of Michigan Press, 2000).

8. Diehl, "Victors or Victims?" 726; Deborah Cohen, *The War Come Home: Disabled Veterans in Britain and Germany, 1914–1939* (Berkeley: University of California Press, 2001), 97.

9. Stefan Busch, *"Und gestern, da hörte uns Deutschland": NS-Autoren in der Bundesrepublik* (Würzburg: Königshausen und Neumann, 1998), 218.

10. Otto Schmeil, *Der Mensch,* revised by Paul Eichler, 97th ed. (Leipzig: Quelle und Meyer, 1938), 141.

11. See, for example, "Soll der Schwerkriegsbeschädigte arbeiten?" *Deutsche Kriegsopferversorgung* 3:3 (December 1934): 14ff.

12. Peter Sloterdijk, *Critique of Cynical Reason,* trans. Michael Eldred (Minneapolis: University of Minnesota Press, 1987), 445.

13. *Waltharius* and *Ruodlieb,* ed. and trans. Dennis Kratz (New York: Garland, 1984), 67ff. Of course, modern scholarship views Waltharius as an ironic representation of heroic ideology, written as it is in Latin hexameter by a monastic author.

14. Carlo von Kügelgen, *Aus eigener Kraft: Gedanken und Erfahrungen eines Einarmigen* (Nuremberg: Willmy, 1943), 19.

15. On disability in *Minna von Barnhelm,* see Elizabeth Hamilton, "Disabling Discourses in German Literature from Lessing to Grass," PhD diss., Ohio State University, 1998.

16. Kügelgen, *Aus eigener Kraft,* 59–60.

17. For Wilhelm Frick's speech of June 28, 1933, see Axel Friedrichs, comp., *Die nationalsozialistische Revolution 1933: Dokumente der deutschen Politik* (Berlin: Junker und Dünnhaupt, 1938), 1:169–77.

18. The best source on involuntary sterilization during the Nazi era is Gisela Bock, *Zwangssterilisation im Nationalsozialismus: Studien zur Rassenpolitik und Frauenpolitik* (Opladen: Westdeutscher Verlag, 1986).

19. Arthur Gütt, Ernst Rüdin, and Falk Ruttke, *Gesetz zur Verhütung*

erbkranken Nachwuchses vom 14. Juli 1933 nebst Ausführungsverord-nungen (Munich: J. F. Lehmann, 1936), 161.

20. *Der Erbarzt* 5:11 (1938): 139–40.

21. Victor Klemperer, *Ich will Zeugnis ablegen bis zum letzten: Tagebücher, 1933–1945* (Berlin: Aufbau, 1995), 1:176.

22. For a selection of relevant quotes from *Mein Kampf,* see Martin Rudnick, *Behinderte im Nationalsozialismus: Von der Ausgrenzung und Zwangssterilisation zur "Euthanasie"* (Weinheim: Beltz, 1985), 42ff.

23. Quoted in Bock, *Zwangssterilisation,* 79.

24. Claudia Koonz, *The Nazi Conscience* (Cambridge: Harvard University Press, 2003), 122.

25. Bock, *Zwangssterilisation,* 114. Subsequent page references are given in the body of the text.

26. Garland E. Allen, "The Ideology of Elimination: American and German Eugenics, 1900–1945," in *Medicine and Medical Ethics in Nazi Germany,* ed. Francis Nicosia and Jonathan Huener (New York: Berghahn, 2002), 13–39; Reilly, *Surgical Solution.*

27. Henry Friedlander, *The Origins of Nazi Genocide: From Euthanasia to the Final Solution* (Chapel Hill: University of North Carolina Press, 1995), 27.

28. Quoted in Klaus Dörner, " 'Ich darf nicht denken': Das medizinische Selbstverständnis der Angeklagten," in *Vernichten und Heilen: Der Nürnberger Ärzteprozess und seine Folgen,* ed. Angelika Ebbinghaus and Klaus Dörner (Berlin: Aufbau, 2001), 337.

29. Friedlander, *Origins,* 29.

30. For many more examples of sterilization cases, see Bock, *Zwangssterilisation.*

31. *Der Erbarzt* 2:9 (1935): 144. Josef Mengele did his doctoral research on cleft palate with Verschuer.

32. *Der Erbarzt* 2:12 (1935): 192.

33. *Der Erbarzt* 4:5 (1937): 72.

34. *Der Erbarzt* 2:3 (1935): 46.

35. *Der Erbarzt* 9:8 (1941): 188–89.

36. Bock, *Zwangssterilisation,* 175. Subsequent page references are given in the body of the text.

37. Quoted in *Volk und Rasse* 11 (1936): 313.

38. For the text of the law, see Axel Friedrichs, comp., *Deutschlands Weg zur Freiheit: Dokumente der deutschen Politik* (Berlin: Junker und Dünnhaupt, 1937), 3:155–56.

39. Bock, *Zwangssterilisation,* 147.

40. "Gesundheitsverhältnisse der Bewerber um Ehestandsdarlehen," *Neues Volk* 3:9 (September 1935): 30.

41. *Der Erbarzt* 3:7 (1936): 111.

42. *Der Erbarzt* 1:4 (1934): 64.

43. *Der Erbarzt* 2:10 (1935): 160.

44. *Der Erbarzt* 3:1 (1936): 16.

45. *Der Erbarzt* 5:4 (1938): 56.

46. Bock, *Zwangssterilisation,* 225.

47. *Der Erbarzt* 2:9 (1935): 144.

48. *Der Erbarzt* 5:4 (1938): 56.

49. *Der Erbarzt* 3:5 (1936): 80.

50. Reichsnährstand, *Führer durch die 1. Reichsnährstands-Ausstellung zu Erfurt* (Berlin: Reichsnährstand Verlagsgesellschaft, 1934), 46.

51. Claudia Frank, "Der 'Reichsnährstand' und seine Ursprünge." PhD diss., Hamburg University, 1988.

52. "Die amtsärztlichen Untersuchungen von bäuerlichen Siedlern auf ihre erbbiologische Eignung in Preußen im Jahre 1934," *Der Erbarzt* 3:6 (1936): 93ff.

53. *Volk und Rasse* 13 (1938): 381.

54. Martin Staemmler, *Die Auslese im Erbstrom des deutschen Volkes: Nationalsozialistische Schulungsschriften Heft 4* (Berlin: Eher Nachf., 1939), 35.

55. Hellmut Neubert, "Die Schülerauslese an den höheren Schulen," *Der Körperbehinderte* 5:6 (June 1935): 67.

56. "Auslese der höheren Schüler," *Unsere HJ: Nachrichten der körperbehinderten Hitler-Jugend* 3 (April 1936): 13.

57. Walter Fandrey, *Krüppel, Idioten, Irre: Zur Sozialgeschichte behinderter Menschen in Deutschland* (Stuttgart: Silberburg, 1990), 187–88.

58. Karl Tornow, "Rassenhygiene, Volksaufartung und Hilfsschule," *Volk und Rasse* 9 (1934): 111.

59. Petra Fuchs, *"Körperbehinderte" zwischen Selbstaufgabe und Emanzipation* (Neuwied: Luchterhand, 2001), 130ff. Subsequent page references are given in the body of the text.

60. Fandrey, *Krüppel, Idioten, Irre,* 187–88.

61. Susanne Hahn, "Entwicklungstrends der Betreuung chronish Kranker im Rahmen der faschistischen Gesundheitspolitik in Deutschland," in *Medizin unterm Hakenkreuz,* ed. Achim Thom (Berlin: Volk und Gesundheit, 1989), 117.

62. Fandrey, *Krüppel, Idioten, Irre,* 188; Christine Makowski, *Eugenik, Sterilisationspolitik, "Euthanasie," und Bevölkerungspolitik in der nationalsozialistischen Parteipresse* (Husum: Matthiesen, 1996), 144; Martin Rudnick, ed., *Aussondern—Sterilisieren—Liquidieren: Die Verfolgung Behinderter im Nationalsozialismus* (Berlin: Marhold, 1990).

63. Karl Tornow and Herbert Weinert, *Erbe und Schicksal: Von geschädigten Menschen, Erbkrankheiten, und deren Bekämpfung* (Berlin: Metzner, 1942), 53, 69.

64. Horst Biesold, *Klagende Hände: Betroffenheit und Spätfolgen in bezug auf das Gesetz zur Verhütung erbkranken Nachwuchses, dargestellt am Beispiel der "Taubstummen"* (Solms: Oberbiel, 1988). English translation by William Sayers: *Crying Hands: Eugenics and Deaf People in Nazi Germany* (Washington, DC: Gallaudet University Press, 1999).

65. Gabriel Richter, "Blindheit und Eugenik: Zwischen Widerstand und Integration," in *Blinde unterm Hakenkreuz: Erkennen, Trauern, Begegnen,* ed. Martin Jaedicke and Wolfgang Schmidt-Block (Marburg: Deutscher Verein der Blinden und Sehbehinderten, 1991), 31.

66. Manfred Höck, *Die Hilfsschule im Dritten Reich* (Berlin: Marhold, 1979).

67. These figures were cited in *Der Spiegel,* January 26, 1981, 171.

68. *Verhandlungen der deutschen Orthopädischen Gesellschaft* 31 (1936): 62, citing paragraph 19, section 2 of the *Reichsärzteordnung.* On orthopedics during the Third Reich, see Carol Poore, "Disability as

Disobedience? An Essay on Germany in the Aftermath of the United Nations Year for People with Disabilities," *New German Critique* 27 (fall 1982): 161–95.

69. Christopher Browning, *The Origins of the Final Solution* (Lincoln: University of Nebraska Press, 2004), 185.

70. Quoted in Klaus Dörner, "Nationalsozialismus und Lebensvernichtung," *Vierteljahreshefte für Zeitgeschichte* 15 (1967): 128.

71. Browning, *Origins,* 185.

72. Friedlander, *Origins,* 45.

73. Browning, *Origins,* 186. Subsequent references are given in the body of the text.

74. Friedlander, *Origins,* 82ff.

75. Hans-Walter Schmuhl, "Die Patientenmorde," in *Vernichten und Heilen: Der Nürnberger Ärzteprozess und seine Folgen,* ed. Angelika Ebbinghaus and Klaus Dörner (Berlin: Aufbau, 2001), 308.

76. Dieter Kuntz, ed., *Deadly Medicine: Creating the Master Race* (Washington, DC: U.S. Holocaust Memorial Museum, 2004), 150.

77. Friedlander, *Origins,* 111–13.

78. "Der Bischof von Limburg an den Reichsminister der Justiz," in *Dokumente zur "Euthanasie,"* ed. Ernst Klee (Frankfurt: Fischer, 1985), 231.

79. Christhard Schrenk, *Rudolf Kraemer: Ein Leben für die Blinden (1885–1945)* (Heilbronn: Stadtarchiv Heilbronn, 2002), 242.

80. Klemperer, *Ich will Zeugnis ablegen,* 1:660.

81. Joachim Fest, "Glückliche Jahre," in *Meine Schulzeit im Dritten Reich: Erinnerungen deutscher Schriftsteller,* ed. Marcel Reich-Ranicki (Cologne: Kiepenheuer und Witsch, 1982), 187.

82. For the text of Galen's sermon, see Klee, *Dokumente,* 193–99; this book also documents many other statements by church leaders against "euthanasia."

83. Makowski, *Eugenik,* 234.

84. Friedlander, *Origins,* 188.

85. Browning, *Origins,* 264.

86. Franz Büchner, *Der Eid des Hippokrates: Die Grundgesetze der ärztlichen Ethik—Vortrag gehalten in der Universität Freiburg i. Br. am 18. November 1941* (Freiburg: Verlag Herder, 1945), 27.

87. Schmuhl, "Die Patientenmorde," 315.

88. Heinz Faulstich, *Hungersterben in der Psychiatrie, 1914–1949, mit einer Topographie der NS-Psychiatrie* (Freiburg: Lambertus, 1998), 581ff.; Max Lafont, *L'extermination douce: La mort de 40 000 malades mentaux dans les hôpitaux psychiatriques en France sous le Régime de Vichy* (Ligné: L'Arefppi, 1987).

89. Fritz Heinsius and Georg Ebert, *Sonne und Schatten im Erbe des Volkes: Angewandte Erb- und Rassenpflege im Dritten Reich—Eine Bildfolge* (Berlin: Verlag der Deutschen Ärzteschaft, 1935), 43.

90. Quoted in Stephanie Barron, ed., *"Degenerate Art": The Fate of the Avant-Garde in Nazi Germany* (New York: Abrams, 1991), 19.

91. On the Erlangen Degenerate Art exhibition of 1933, the first one that juxtaposed paintings by contemporary artists with works by children and mentally ill people, see ibid., 12ff. On the forerunner and successor exhibitions to the Degenerate Art exhibition of 1937, see Christoph Zuschlag,

"Entartete Kunst": Ausstellungsstrategien im Nazi-Deutschland (Worms: Wernersche Verlagsgesellschaft, 1995).

92. Christian Mürner, *Gebrandmarkte Gesichter: "Entartete Kunst"— Die Denunzierung der Bilder von psychisch Kranken, Behinderten, und Künstlern* (Herzogenrath: Murken-Altrogge, 1997), 33. Subsequent references are given in the body of the text.

93. The guide to the Degenerate Art exhibition is reproduced in Barron, *"Degenerate Art."* The reference here is to pages 383–89.

94. Ibid., 22.

95. Exhibition guide reproduced in ibid., 376. Subsequent references are given in the body of the text.

96. Quoted in Joseph Wulf, *Die Bildenden Künste im Dritten Reich: Eine Dokumentation* (Gütersloh: Sigbert Mohn, 1963), 327.

97. Exhibition guide in Barron, *"Degenerate Art,"* 374. Subsequent references are given in the body of the text.

98. Mortimer G. Davidson, *Kunst in Deutschland, 1933–1945: Eine wissenschaftliche Enzyklopädie der Kunst im Dritten Reich. Malerei* (Tübingen: Grabert, 1991), 1:206. Subsequent references are given in the body of the text.

99. Deutsches Historisches Museum, *Bilder und Zeugnisse der deutschen Geschichte* (Berlin: Deutsches Historisches Museum, 1997), 2:658.

100. Gerd Albrecht, "Medizin und Mediziner im Film des Dritten Reiches," in *Medizin im Spielfilm des Nationalsozialismus,* ed. Udo Benzenhöfer and Wolfgang Eckart (Tecklenburg: Burgverlag, 1990), 10.

101. Wolfgang Willrich, "Eine hohe Aufgabe Deutscher Kunst: die Darstellung des vollwertigen Germanischen Menschen," *Volk und Rasse* 9 (1934): 286, 280.

102. For a list of all the works in this exhibition, see Haus der Deutschen Kunst, *Große Deutsche Kunstausstellung, 1937* (Munich: Knorr und Hirth, 1937). According to newspaper accounts, five times as many people saw the "Degenerate Art" exhibition as saw the First Great German Art exhibition.

103. "Hitlers Rede zur Eröffnung der 'Großen Deutschen Kunstausstellung 1937,'" in *Die "Kunststadt" München 1937: Nationalsozialismus und "Entartete Kunst,"* ed. Peter-Klaus Schuster (Munich: Prestl, 1987), 250–52.

104. Brian Ladd, *The Ghosts of Berlin: Confronting German History in the Urban Landscape* (Chicago: University of Chicago Press, 1997), 122.

105. Jost Hermand, *Old Dreams of a New Reich: Volkish Utopias and National Socialism,* trans. Paul Levesque (Bloomington: Indiana University Press, 1992), 230–33. Subsequent references are given in the body of the text.

106. Mürner, *Gebrandmarkte Gesichter,* 65.

107. Quoted in ibid., 63–64. On Himmler, see *Volk und Rasse* 13 (1938): 92.

108. Rosemarie Garland-Thomson, ed., *Freakery: Cultural Spectacles of the Extraordinary Body* (New York: New York University Press, 1996); Rosemarie Garland-Thomson, *Extraordinary Bodies: Figuring Physical Disability in American Culture and Literature* (New York: Columbia University Press, 1997).

109. Albert Friehe, *Was muss der Nationalsozialist von der Vererbung wissen? Volks- und Schulausgabe,* 6th ed. (Frankfurt: Diesterweg, 1938), 53.

110. Michael Burleigh, *Death and Deliverance: "Euthanasia" in Germany, 1900–1945* (New York: Cambridge University Press, 1994), 43.

111. Bock, *Zwangssterilisation,* 195.

112. Ernst Klee, *"Euthanasie" im NS-Staat: Die "Vernichtung lebensunwerten Lebens"* (Frankfurt: Fischer, 1985), 76ff.

113. Burleigh, *Death and Deliverance,* 44.

114. Bock, *Zwangssterilisation,* 195.

115. Burleigh, *Death and Deliverance,* 44ff.

116. Gusti Steiner, "Warum mich meine Mutter versteckte," in *Behindertsein ist schön,* ed. Ernst Klee (Düsseldorf: Patmos, 1974), 42–43.

117. Kuntz, *Deadly Medicine,* is a particularly interesting collection of visual images about eugenics from Germany and other countries.

118. Quoted in Koonz, *Nazi Conscience,* 116. Subsequent references are given in the body of the text.

119. Ludwig Rost, *Sterilisation und Euthanasie im Film des "Dritten Reiches"* (Husum: Matthiesen, 1987), 45.

120. Walter Gross, "Drei Jahre rassenpolitische Aufklärungsarbeit," *Volk und Rasse* 11 (1936): 333.

121. For example, Konrad Dürre's "drama about population policy" entitled *Erbstrom* (The Stream of Heredity) was presented fifteen hundred times to hundreds of thousands of spectators, including fifty-five thousand Berlin students and school pupils in 1934. It called for supporting hereditarily healthy families and eliminating the hereditarily unfit. See Bock, *Zwangssterilisation,* 92.

122. For a list of the most important medical journals and popular magazines that dealt with eugenics see ibid., 470–72.

123. Koonz, *Nazi Conscience,* 123.

124. Otto Helmut, *Volk in Gefahr: Der Geburtenrückgang und seine Folgen für Deutschlands Zukunft,* 8th ed. (Munich: Lehmann, 1936), 27.

125. Rost, *Sterilisation und Euthanasie,* 41. For more information about Unger, see also Karl Heinz Roth, "Filmpropaganda für die Vernichtung der Geisteskranken und Behinderten im 'Dritten Reich,'" in *Reform und Gewissen: "Euthanasie" im Dienst des Fortschritts,* ed. Götz Aly et al. (Berlin: Rotbuch, 1985), 129.

126. Koonz, *Nazi Conscience,* 117–19.

127. *Neues Volk* 1:5 (November 1, 1933): 6–7.

128. Ibid., 14–15.

129. *Neues Volk* 2:1 (January 1, 1934): 8.

130. *Neues Volk* 1:5 (November 1, 1933): 30–31.

131. Koonz, *Nazi Conscience,* 125.

132. For a list of some of these slide series and posters, see the advertisement from J. F. Lehmanns Verlag on the end page of Helmut, *Volk in Gefahr.*

133. Hans Bender, "Willst du nicht beitreten?" in *Meine Schulzeit im Dritten Reich: Erinnerungen deutscher Schriftsteller,* ed. Marcel Reich-Ranicki (Cologne: Kiepenheuer und Witsch, 1982), 38.

134. Reproduced in Koonz, *Nazi Conscience,* 155.

135. Rudolf Frercks and Arthur Hoffmann, *Erbnot und Aufartung: Bild und Gegenbild aus dem Leben* (Erfurt: Verlag Kurt Stenger, 1934). For an

advertisement of a slide show of these images, see the inside cover of *Neues Volk*, 2:5 (May 1, 1934).

136. Rost, *Sterilisation und Euthanasie*, 43ff.

137. See, for example, "Kulturaufbau im Dorf," *Neues Volk* 3:9 (September 1, 1935), which includes a photograph of a village exhibition about eugenics.

138. Bock, *Zwangssterilisation*, 92.

139. *Volk und Rasse* 11 (1936): 322.

140. *Volk und Rasse* 12:1 (1937): 5. See also: Ruth Marko, "Die Rolle des Deutschen Hygiene-Museums in der Zeit des Faschismus," in *Medizin im Faschismus*, ed. Achim Thom and Horst Spaar (Berlin: Volk und Gesundheit, 1985), 118–21.

141. *Volk und Rasse* 13 (1938): 294.

142. Quoted in Bock, *Zwangssterilisation*, 92.

143. Gross, "Drei Jahre rassenpolitische Aufklärungsarbeit," 331.

144. Frank, *Der "Reichsnährstand,"* 141.

145. Hermand, *Old Dreams*, 109–10; see also pages 208ff. on "Continuing Forms of Peasant Mythology."

146. On "better baby contests" in the United States in the early twentieth century, which were modeled on livestock shows at rural state fairs, see Martin S. Pernick, *The Black Stork: Eugenics and the Death of "Defective" Babies in American Medicine and Motion Pictures since 1915* (New York: Oxford University Press, 1996), 22.

147. Reichsnährstand, *Führer durch die 1. Reichsnährstands-Ausstellung zu Erfurt*, 46. On the third exhibition, which was held in Frankfurt am Main in 1936, see Eberhard Wiegand, "Bluterbe verpflichtet: Zur Dritten Reichsnährstandsausstellung in Frankfurt/Main," *Neues Volk* 4:7 (July 1936): 36ff.

148. Eberhard Wiegand, "Rassenpolitisches Ausstellungswesen des Reichsnährstandes," *Volk und Rasse* 12:6 (1937): 263ff.

149. *Volk und Rasse* 11 (1936): 326. Subsequent references are given in the body of the text.

150. Albrecht, "Medizin und Mediziner," 10.

151. Ulf Schmidt, *Medical Films, Ethics, and Euthanasia in Nazi Germany: The History of Medical Research and Teaching Films of the Reich Office for Educational Films/Reich Institute for Films in Science and Education, 1933–1945* (Husum: Matthiesen, 2002), 41–48.

152. Quoted in Roth, "Filmpropaganda," 127–28; which does not give the title of this film.

153. Ulf Schmidt, "Der medizinische Forschungsfilm im 'Dritten Reich': Institutionalisierung, politische Funktion und ethische Dimension," *Zwischen Dokumentation und Propaganda: "Euthanasie" im NS-Film*, special issue of *Zeitgeschichte* 28:4 (July-August 2001): 200–201. See also Ulrich Hägele, "Optische Internierung des Menschen: Patientenphotos aus der Tübinger Nervenklinik 1920 bis 1950," in *"Euthanasie": Krankenmorde in Südwestdeutschland*," ed. Hermann Pretsch (Zwiefalten: Verlag Psychiatrie und Geschichte, 1996), 135–42.

154. Schmidt, *Medical Films*, 219–28, contains many more examples and stills from films of patients.

155. Quoted in Schmidt, "Der medizinische Forschungsfilm," 205.

156. Schmidt, *Medical Films*, 263. This film was included in German

television documentaries about the "euthanasia" program in the 1990s and also in the film *Der Pannwitzblick* directed by Didi Danquart.

157. My discussion of this film follows ibid., 249ff.

158. Quoted in Koonz, *Nazi Conscience*, 125.

159. Quoted in Rost, *Sterilisation und Euthanasie*, 43.

160. Jochen Muhs, "Deaf People as Eyewitnesses of National Socialism," in *Deaf People in Hitler's Europe*, ed. Donna Ryan and John Schuchman (Washington, DC: Gallaudet University Press, 2002), 89. Subsequent references are given in the body of the text.

161. Rost, *Sterilisation und Euthanasie*, 61.

162. Roth, "Filmpropaganda," 131.

163. Rost, *Sterilisation und Euthanasie*, 77ff.

164. Ludwig Rost, "Propaganda zur Vernichtung 'unwerten Lebens' durch das Rassenpolitische Amt der NSDAP," *1999: Zeitschrift für Sozialgeschichte des 20. und 21. Jahrhunderts* 3:3 (July 1988): 48.

165. Burleigh, *Death and Deliverance*, 195.

166. Koonz, *Nazi Conscience*, 126.

167. Rost, *Sterilisation und Euthanasie*, 74. Subsequent references are given in the body of the text.

168. Gertrud Koch, "Der phobische Blick: Zur Körper- und Stimminszenierung im 'Euthanasie'-Propagandafilm," *Zwischen Dokumentation und Propaganda: "Euthanasie" im NS-Film, Zeitgeschichte* 28:4 (July–August 2001): 230.

169. See Rost, *Sterilisation und Euthanasie*, 83, on the difficulties in ascertaining the actual reactions of spectators to these films. Subsequent references are given in the body of the text.

170. Burleigh, *Death and Deliverance*, 202. Subsequent references are given in the body of the text.

171. Karl Ludwig Rost, "'Euthanasie'-Filme im NS-Staat: Sozial- und filmhistorische Hintergründe einer Verführung zum Töten," *Zwischen Dokumentation und Propaganda: "Euthanasie" im NS-Film, Zeitgeschichte* 28:4 (July–August 2001): 219.

172. Roth, "Filmpropaganda," 178.

173. Burleigh, *Death and Deliverance*, 200ff.

174. Koch, "Der phobische Blick," 233.

175. Roth, "Filmpropaganda," 125. Subsequent references are given in the body of the text.

176. On three written treatments of this type, see Burleigh, *Death and Deliverance*, 202ff. Subsequent references are given in the body of the text.

177. Quoted in Karl Ludwig Rost, "*Ich klage an*, ein historischer Film?" in *Medizin im Spielfilm des Nationalsozialismus*, ed. Udo Benzenhöfer and Wolfgang Eckart (Tecklenburg: Burgverlag, 1990), 39.

178. On Hitler's plans for an assisted suicide law (Sterbehilfegesetz), see Roth, "Filmpropaganda," 147.

179. Rost, *Sterilisation und Euthanasie*, 208ff. On the Propaganda Ministry guidelines for reviewing *Ich klage an*, see Roth, "Filmpropaganda," 168.

180. Sylke Hachmeister, *Kinopropaganda gegen Kranke: Die Instrumentalisierung des Spielfilms "Ich klage an" für das nationalsozialistische "Euthanasieprogramm"* (Baden-Baden: Nomos, 1992), 142.

181. Burleigh, *Death and Deliverance,* 216ff. For more detailed information on the report of the Security Service, see Rost, *Sterilisation und Euthanasie,* 211ff.

182. Rost, *Sterilisation und Euthanasie,* 217. For an interview with an unrepentant Wolfgang Liebeneiner in 1983, see Rost, *"Ich klage an, ein historischer Film?"* 218.

183. Biesold, *Crying Hands,* 57. For a few other firsthand accounts, see Elisabeth Claasen [pseud.], *Ich, die Steri* (Rehburg: Psychiatrie-Verlag, 1985); Klara Nowak, "Verweigerte Anerkennung als NS-Verfolgte: Zwangssterilisierte und 'Euthanasie'-Geschädigte," in *Medizin und Gewissen: 50 Jahre nach dem Nürnberger Ärzteprozess,* ed. Stephan Kolb and Horst Seithe (Frankfurt: Mabuse, 1998), 163–68; and "Erinnerungen von Josef Demetz," in *"Euthanasie": Krankenmorde in Südwestdeutschland,* ed. Hermann Pretsch (Zwiefalten: Verlag Psychiatrie und Geschichte, 1996), 110–14.

184. "Gespräch mit Zeitzeugen," in *Blinde unterm Hakenkreuz: Erkennen, Trauern, Begegnen,* ed. Martin Jaedicke and Wolfgang Schmidt-Block (Marburg: Deutscher Verein der Blinden und Sehbehinderten, 1991), 76.

185. Bock, *Zwangssterilisation,* 280. Bock's book contains numerous summaries of sterilization cases. Subsequent references are given in the body of the text. See also Burleigh, *Death and Deliverance,* 57ff., for more examples of cases.

186. Biesold, *Crying Hands,* 109ff. Subsequent references are given in the body of the text.

187. Bock, *Zwangssterilisation,* 280. Subsequent references are given in the body of the text.

188. "Beleidigungsvergehen gegenüber Sterilisierten," *Der Erbarzt* 3:2 (1936): 32.

189. "Beleidigung Erbkranker ist Versündigung gegen die Volksgemeinschaft," *Volk und Rasse* 12:1 (1937): 44.

190. Bock, *Zwangssterilisation,* 140. Subsequent references are given in the body of the text.

191. See Friedlander, *Origins,* 164ff. In addition to the references in note 183, see Elvira Manthey, *Die Hempelsche: Das Schicksal eines deutschen Kindes, das 1940 vor der Gaskammer umkehren durfte* (Lübeck: Hempel Verlag Heinz Manthey, 1997); and the statements by survivors in Klee, *"Euthanasie,"* 143ff.

192. In addition to the references in note 191, see Peter Delius, *Das Ende von Strecknitz: Die Lübecker Heilanstalt und ihre Auflösung 1941* (Kiel: Neuer Malik Verlag, 1988); Johannes Neuhauser et al., eds., *Hartheim, wohin unbekannt: Briefe und Dokumente* (Friestadt: Plöchl-Druck, 1992); and summaries in Burleigh, *Death and Deliverance.*

193. Klee, *"Euthanasie,"* 143. Subsequent references are given in the body of the text. For more examples see Burleigh, *Death and Deliverance,* 142ff.

194. Burleigh, *Death and Deliverance,* 21ff. Subsequent references are given in the body of the text.

195. Klee, *"Euthanasie,"* 307. Subsequent references are given in the body of the text.

196. Klemperer, *Ich will Zeugnis ablegen,* 660.

197. Biesold, *Crying Hands,* 120.

198. Klee, *"Euthanasie,"* 309. Subsequent references are given in the body of the text.

199. Neuhauser, *Hartheim,* 12. Subsequent references are given in the body of the text.

200. Klee, *"Euthanasie,"* 308.

201. Neuhauser, *Hartheim,* 46. Subsequent references are given in the body of the text.

202. Klee, *"Euthanasie,"* 313. Subsequent references are given in the body of the text.

203. Klee, *Dokumente,* 195.

204. Friedlander, *Origins,* 119. Subsequent references are given in the body of the text. See also Susanne Willems, *Lothar Kreyssig: Vom eigenen verantwortlichen Handeln* (Göttingen: Steidl, n.d.).

205. Richter, "Blindheit und Eugenik," in *Blinde unterm Hakenkreuz: Erkennen, Trauern, Begegnen,* ed. Martin Jaedicke and Wolfgang Schmidt-Block (Marburg: Deutscher Verein der Blinden und Sehbehinderten, 1991), 28ff. Subsequent references are given in the body of the text.

206. "Blinde im Widerstand," in *Blinde unterm Hakenkreuz: Erkennen, Trauern, Begegnen,* ed. Martin Jaedicke and Wolfgang Schmidt-Block (Marburg: Deutscher Verein der Blinden und Sehbehinderten, 1991) 149ff. Subsequent references are given in the body of the text.

207. Jochen Muhs, "Deaf People as Eyewitnesses of National Socialism," in *Deaf People in Hitler's Europe,* ed. Donna Ryan and John Schuchman (Washington, DC: Gallaudet University Press, 2002), 89. Subsequent references are given in the body of the text.

208. Ibid., 75.

209. Biesold, *Crying Hands,* 100. Subsequent references are given in the body of the text.

210. "Das neue Deutschland und der RBK," *Der Körperbehinderte* 3:6 (June 1933): 1; *Der Körperbehinderte* 3:7 (July 1933): 49.

211. "Wer ist Körperbehinderter?" *Der Körperbehinderte* 5:3 (March 1935): title page; "Richtlinien für die Arbeit des RBK," *Der Körperbehinderte* 6:5 (May 1936): 2.

212. "Jahresbericht des RBK für 1939," *Der Körperbehinderte* 10:2 (February 1940): 3.

213. *Der Körperbehinderte* 14:3–4 (March-April 1944): 2. This is apparently the last issue of the journal.

214. Fuchs, *"Körperbehinderte,"* 188ff.

215. "Die Eingliederung der Körperbehinderten in die Volksgemeinschaft," *Der Körperbehinderte* 3:9 (September 1933): 69–70.

216. Fuchs, *"Körperbehinderte,"* 170.

217. "Richtlinien für die Arbeit des RBK," *Der Körperbehinderte* 6:5 (May 1936): 2.

218. "Das Rassenpolitische Amt der NSDAP über die Aufgaben des Reichsbundes der Körperbehinderten," *Der Körperbehinderte* 5:11 (November 1935): 134ff. Films shown at this RBK conference included *Die Sünden der Väter, Arbeitsfähige Jugend,* a film about the preparations for the Olympics, and one about the Hitler Youth (138).

219. *Der Körperbehinderte* 5:7 (July 1935): 82.

220. August Richard, "Frauenfragen im RBK," *Der Körperbehinderte* 6:6 (June 1936): 3–4; "Einarmige Frau im Haushalt und Beruf," *Der Körperbehinderte* 12:7 (July 1942): 1.

221. "Die Behinderung hindert nicht," *Der Körperbehinderte* 9:1 (January 1939): 3.

222. "Der Genesungs- und Arbeitswille: Ein neuer Film und ein neues Buch," *Der Körperbehinderte* 11:5 (May 1941): 1.

223. Peter Demmel, "Ein wehrhafter Mann: Frontbericht," *Der Körperbehinderte* 10:3 (March 1940): 7.

224. "Sonderfälle unserer Fürsorgearbeit: Schwieriger Arbeitseinsatz," *Der Körperbehinderte* 10:4 (April 1940): 2; and "Erfolge in schwierigen Fällen unserer Fürsorge," *Der Körperbehinderte* 10:9 (September 1940): 6.

225. "Lebensmöglichkeiten für Körperbehinderte: Rundfunkvortrag gehalten über den Deutschlandsender am 7. November 1935 von Dr. Hellmut Eckhardt," *Der Körperbehinderte* 5:12 (December 1935): 147; and "Er leidet nicht unter seiner Behinderung," *Der Körperbehinderte* 10:10 (October 1940): 8.

226. Fuchs, *"Körperbehinderte,"* 225.

227. "Warum so ängstlich? Ein Wort an noch Fernstehende," *Der Körperbehinderte* 5:12 (December 1935): 148.

228. Otto Perl, "Auswählende Krüppelfürsorge," *Ethik* 12:6 (July-August 1936): 247–52.

229. Quoted in Fuchs, *"Körperbehinderte,"* 228.

230. Petra Fuchs, "Hilde Wulff (1898–1972): Leben und Wirken für die Emanzipation körperbehinderter Menschen in der Weimarer Republik und in der Zeit des Nationalsozialismus," *Die neue Sonderschule* 44:6 (1999): 460–65.

231. "Aufruf an die körperbehinderte Jugend und deren Eltern!" *Der Körperbehinderte* 5:9 (September 1935): 110; Klaus-Dieter Thomann, "Der 'Krüppel': Entstehen und Verschwinden eines Kampfbegriffs," *Medizinhistorisches Journal* 27:3–4 (1992): 262.

232. "Aufruf an die körperbehinderte Jugend und deren Eltern!" *Der Körperbehinderte* 5:9 (September 1935): 111; *Unsere HJ: Nachrichten der körperbehinderten Hitler-Jugend* 3 (April 1936): 13.

233. "Aufruf an die körperbehinderte Jugend und deren Eltern!" *Der Körperbehinderte* 5:9 (September 1935): 110. Subsequent references are given in the body of the text.

234. "Das körperbehinderte Kind im neuen Deutschland," *Unsere HJ: Amtliches Organ der Reichsführung der Körperbehinderten HJ* 1 (October 1935): 3.

235. Fuchs, *"Körperbehinderte,"* 218ff.

236. "Mitarbeit im Bann K der HJ," *Unsere HJ* 2 (November 1935): 7.

237. Thomann, "Der 'Krüppel,'" 262.

238. Jost Hermand, *A Hitler Youth in Poland: The Nazis' Program for Evacuating Children during World War II*, trans. Margot Bettauer Dembo (Chicago: Northwestern University Press, 1997), 93.

239. Bock, *Zwangssterilisation*, 279.

240. Schrenk, *Ein Leben für die Blinden*, 55. Subsequent references are given in the body of the text.

CHAPTER 3

1. Gisela Bock, *Zwangssterilisation im Nationalsozialismus: Studien zur Rassenpolitik und Frauenpolitik* (Opladen: Westdeutscher Verlag, 1986), 295.

2. Ernst Bloch, *Das Prinzip Hoffnung* (Frankfurt: Suhrkamp, 1973), 1:531. Subsequent page references are given in the body of the text.

3. Barbara Bromberger et al., eds., *Medizin, Faschismus und Widerstand* (Frankfurt: Mabuse, 1990). See also Kurt Kühn, ed., *Ärzte an der Seite der Arbeiterklasse* (Berlin: Volk und Gesundheit, 1977); and Achim Thom and Horst Spaar, eds., *Medizin im Faschismus* (Berlin: Volk und Gesundheit, 1985).

4. Since the standard English translation by Eric Bentley, *Mother Courage and Her Children* (New York: Grove, 1966), omits several important passages, I am quoting from the German original, Bertolt Brecht, *Mutter Courage und ihre Kinder* (Frankfurt: Suhrkamp, 1968), 86. Subsequent page references are given in the body of the text.

5. Quoted in Klaus-Detlef Müller, ed., *Brechts Mutter Courage und ihre Kinder* (Frankfurt: Suhrkamp, 1982), 79.

6. Ibid., 163.

7. On Maria Leitner, see Carol Poore, *The Bonds of Labor: German Journeys to the Working World, 1890–1990* (Detroit: Wayne State University Press, 2000), 139ff.

8. Maria Leitner, *Elisabeth, ein Hitlermädchen: Erzählende Prosa, Reportagen und Berichte* (Berlin: Aufbau, 1985).

9. For a brief report in an exile publication on Nazi sterilization practices, see Hanna Schmitt, "Die Entrechtung der Frauen," in *Deutsche Frauenschicksale,* ed. Union für Recht und Freiheit (London: Malik, 1937), 23.

10. Carol Poore, "'No Friend of the Third Reich': Disability as the Basis for Antifascist Resistance in Arnold Zweig's *Das Beil von Wandsbek*," in *Disability Studies: Enabling the Humanities,* ed. Sharon Snyder et al. (New York: Modern Language Association, 2002), 260–70.

11. Jost Hermand, *Engagement als Lebensform: Über Arnold Zweig* (Berlin: Sigma, 1992), 173–91.

12. Jost Hermand, *Arnold Zweig* (Reinbek: Rowohlt, 1990), 96.

13. Arnold Zweig, *Das Beil von Wandsbek* (Berlin: Aufbau, 1996), 600. Subsequent page references are given in the body of the text.

14. For misinterpretations of Tom Barfey, see Heinrich Vormweg, "Gerechtigkeit über sich fühlend: Arnold Zweigs Roman *Das Beil von Wandsbek*," in *Deutsche Exilliteratur, 1933–1945,* ed. Manfred Durzak (Stuttgart: Reclam, 1973); and Hans-Albert Walter, "Die Geschäfte des Herrn Albert Teetjen: Das faschistische Deutschland in Arnold Zweigs Exilroman *Das Beil von Wandsbek*," *Frankfurter Hefte* 36:4 (1981): 49–62.

15. The English translation of Zweig's novel, Arnold Zweig, *The Axe of Wandsbek,* trans. Eric Sutton (New York: Hutchinson, 1948), contains many inaccuracies and omissions. All the translations here are my own.

16. Birgit Lönne explains that Zweig planned to write a novel entitled *Die Hemmung* (The Inhibition/Hindrance), which he said would "tell the story of my eyes." See Zweig, *Beil von Wandsbek,* 642.

17. Christopher Browning, *Ordinary Men: Reserve Police Battalion 101 and the Final Solution in Poland* (New York: Asher, 1992), draws on

archival sources to trace the steps by which a group of "ordinary men" from Hamburg became mass murderers.

18. A DEFA film version of *Das Beil von Wandsbek,* directed by Falk Harnack, was made in the German Democratic Republic in 1951. The film concentrates the novel's complex plot around the antifascist struggle. Tom Barfey appears as less disabled and more of a communist in the film than in the novel. He walks with two canes rather than using a wheeled platform, and he is shown producing antifascist leaflets with a communist resistance group.

CHAPTER 4

1. Wolfgang Albert, *Lösung des Schwerbeschädigtenproblems durch Arbeit* (Berlin: Duncker und Humblot, 1956), 16.

2. Wolf Donner, *Die sozial- und staatspolitische Tätigkeit der Kriegsopferverbände* (Berlin: Duncker und Humblot, 1960), 94.

3. Quoted in Karl Ernst and Michael Svoboda et al., eds., *Schicksal Kriegsopfer: Die Geschichte der Kriegsopfer nach 1945* (Vienna: Verlag des österreichischen Gewerkschaftsbundes, 1995), 107.

4. Quoted in David J. Levin, "Taking Liberties with Liberties Taken: On the Politics of Helke Sander's *BeFreier und Befreite,*" *October* 72 (spring 1995): 76.

5. Inge Müller, "Weiße Hyazinthen," in *Irgendwo: Noch einmal möcht ich sehn* (Berlin: Aufbau, 1996), 86. Subsequent page numbers are given in the body of the text.

6. Bertolt Brecht, "Der Einarmige im Gehölz," in *Werkausgabe* (Frankfurt: Suhrkamp, 1967), 10:1013.

7. Wolfgang Borchert, *Draußen vor der Tür* (Reinbek: Rowohlt, 1956), 12. Subsequent page references are given in the body of the text.

8. Wolfgang Borchert, "Schischyphusch oder der Kellner meines Onkels," in *Gesamtwerk* (Reinbek: Rowohlt, 1959), 289. Subsequent page references are given in the body of the text.

9. Albert, *Lösung des Schwerbeschädigtenproblems,* 13.

10. Martin Norden, *The Cinema of Isolation: A History of Physical Disability in the Movies* (New Brunswick, NJ: Rutgers University Press, 1994), 160ff.

11. Peter Pleyer, *Deutscher Nachkriegsfilm, 1946–1948* (Münster: Fahle, 1965); Robert Shandley, *Rubble Films: German Cinema in the Shadow of the Third Reich* (Philadelphia: Temple University Press, 2001).

12. David Gerber, "Anger and Affability: The Rise and Representation of a Repertory of Self-Presentation Skills in a Disabled Veteran of World War II," *Journal of Social History* 27 (fall 1993): 1–21; David Gerber, "Heroes and Misfits: The Troubled Social Reintegration of Disabled Veterans in *The Best Years of Our Lives,*" *American Quarterly* 46:4 (December 1994): 545–74.

13. David Serlin, *Replaceable You: Engineering the Body in Postwar America* (Chicago: University of Chicago Press, 2003).

14. Wilfried von Bredow, "Filmpropaganda für Wehrbereitschaft: Kriegsfilme in der Bundesrepublik," in *Film und Gesellschaft in Deutschland,* ed. Wilfried von Bredow and Rolf Zurek (Hamburg: Hoffmann

und Campe, 1975), 316–26. Obviously these films contain no depictions of disability.

15. Kirsten Burghardt, *Werk, Skandal, Exempel: Tabudurchbrechung durch fiktionale Modelle. Willi Forsts "Die Sünderin"* (Munich: Diskurs-Film-Verlag Schaudig und Ledig, 1996).

16. Heide Fehrenbach, *Cinema in Democratizing Germany: Reconstructing National Identity after Hitler* (Chapel Hill: University of North Carolina Press, 1995).

17. Peter Stettner, *Vom Trümmerfilm zur Traumfabrik. Die "Junge Film-Union," 1947–1952: Eine Fallstudie zur westdeutschen Filmproduktion* (New York: Olms, 1992), 128.

18. On the ways in which attention to disability reconfigures older ideological categories, see Tobin Siebers, "Disability in Theory: From Social Constructionism to the New Realism of the Body," *American Literary History* 13:4 (2001): 737–54.

19. Fehrenbach, *Cinema*, 117.

20. Burghardt, *Werk, Skandal, Exempel*, 17. Subsequent page reference is given in the body of the text.

21. Fehrenbach, *Cinema*, 111.

22. Burghardt, *Werk, Skandal, Exempel*, 265.

23. This is referred to, though often inaccurately, in Sylke Hachmeister, *Kinopropaganda gegen Kranke: Die Instrumentalisierung des Spielfilms "Ich klage an" für das nationalsozialistische "Euthanasieprogramm"* (Baden-Baden: Nomos, 1992). The series appeared in *Kristall* 5:6, 10, 11 (1950). Subsequent page references to *Kristall* are given in the body of the text.

24. Helmut Ziem, *Der Beschädigte und Körperbehinderte im Daseinskampf einst und jetzt* (Berlin: Duncker und Humblot, 1956), 61.

25. Albert, *Lösung des Schwerbeschädigtenproblems*, 17.

26. Vera Neumann, *Nicht der Rede wert: Die Privatisierung der Kriegsfolgen in der frühen Bundesrepublik—lebensgeschichtliche Erinnerungen* (Münster: Westfälisches Dampfboot, 1999), 16, 137.

27. Donner, *Die sozial- und staatspolitische Tätigkeit der Kriegsopferverbände*, 14.

28. Alice Förster and Birgit Beck, "Post-traumatic Stress Disorder and World War II: Can a Psychiatric Concept Help Us Understand Postwar Society?" in *Life after Death: Approaches to a Cultural and Social History of Europe during the 1940s and 1950s*, ed. Richard Bessel and Dirk Schumann (Washington, DC: German Historical Institute, 2003), 19–31.

29. Svenja Goltermann, "Verletzte Körper oder 'Building National Bodies': Kriegsheimkehrer, 'Krankheit,' und Psychiatrie in der westdeutschen Nachkriegsgesellschaft, 1945–1955," *Werkstatt Geschichte* 24 (1999): 85. Subsequent page reference is given in the body of the text.

30. For a comparative overview, see David Gerber, *Disabled Veterans in History* (Ann Arbor: University of Michigan Press, 2000).

31. James Diehl, *The Thanks of the Fatherland: German Veterans after the Second World War* (Chapel Hill: University of North Carolina Press, 1993), 73. Subsequent page references are given in the body of the text.

32. Heinrich Braun, "Zur geschichtlichen Entwicklung der Rehabilitation Behinderter in Deutschland," in *Rehabilitation von Behinderten in Deutschland*, ed. Valentin Siebrecht (Frankfurt: Deutscher Verein für öffentliche und private Fürsorge, 1966), 14.

33. Walter Fandrey, *Krüppel, Idioten, Irre: Zur Sozialgeschichte behinderter Menschen in Deutschland* (Stuttgart: Silberburg, 1990), 200, 205.

34. Donner, *Die sozial- und staatspolitische Tätigkeit der Kriegsopferverbände,* 87.

35. Albert, *Lösung des Schwerbeschädigtenproblems,* 99.

36. Quoted in Dagmar Barnouw, *Germany 1945: Views of War and Violence* (Bloomington: Indiana University Press, 1996), 172.

37. Christoph Hein, *Landnahme* (Frankfurt: Suhrkamp, 2004), 23.

38. Frank Biess, "Survivors of Totalitarianism: Returning POWs and the Reconstruction of Masculine Citizenship in West Germany, 1945–1955," in *The Miracle Years: A Cultural History of West Germany, 1949–1968,* ed. Hanna Schissler (Princeton: Princeton University Press, 2001), 62.

39. Goltermann, "Verletzte Körper," 90–94.

40. Biess, "Survivors of Totalitarianism," 61–62. Subsequent page references are given in the body of the text.

41. Neumann, *Nicht der Rede wert,* 118.

42. Wolfgang Kraushaar, *Die Protest-Chronik, 1949–1959: Eine illustrierte Geschichte von Bewegung, Widerstand und Utopie* (Hamburg: Rogner und Bernhard bei Zweitausendeins, 1996), 3:2118, 2175, 2206. Subsequent page references are given in the body of the text.

43. Albrecht Tietze and Paul Kühne, eds., *Die Poliomyelitis: Bearbeitet nach den Erfahrungen bei den Berliner Epidemien, 1947/1949* (Berlin: De Gruyter, 1949); "Kinderlähmung: Später Sieg," *Der Spiegel,* February 12, 1964, 83–84.

44. Braun, "Zur geschichtlichen Entwicklung," 13.

45. On these name changes, see Klaus-Dieter Thomann, "Der 'Krüppel': Entstehen und Verschwinden eines Kampfbegriffs," *Medizinhistorisches Journal* 27:3–4 (1992), 221–71. Subsequent page references are given in the body of the text.

46. Ziem, *Der Beschädigte,* 5.

47. Albert, *Lösung des Schwerbeschädigtenproblems,* 17.

48. Ziem, *Der Beschädigte,* 67.

49. Fandrey, *Krüppel, Idioten, Irre,* 200, 205.

50. Albert, *Lösung des Schwerbeschädigtenproblems,* 26. Subsequent page references are given in the body of the text.

51. Günther Cloerkes, *Einstellung und Verhalten gegenüber Körperbehinderten* (Berlin: Marhold, 1979), 434.

52. G. Hauck, "Die Einstellung der Bevölkerung zur Epilepsie in USA und Deutschland," *Nervenarzt* 39 (1968): 181–83.

53. G. W. Jansen, "Einstellungen, Meinungen, und Vorurteile gegenüber Körperbehinderten in der Bundesrepublik Deutschland," *Fortschritte der Medizin* 88 (1970): 631–32; K. H. Seifert, "Einstellungen von Berufstätigen zur beruflich-sozialen Integration von Körperbehinderten," *Rehabilitation* 18 (August 1979): 163.

54. Andrea Buch et al., eds., *An den Rand gedrängt: Was Behinderte daran hindert, normal zu leben* (Reinbek: Rowohlt, 1980), 31.

55. Eugen Glombig, "Berufliche Rehabilitation, international gesehen," in *Rehabilitation von Behinderten in Deutschland,* ed. Valentin Siebrecht (Frankfurt: Deutscher Verein für öffentliche und private Fürsorge, 1966), 231–35.

56. Monika Aly and Götz Aly, *Kopfkorrektur oder der Zwang gesund zu*

sein (Berlin: Rotbuch, 1981); Buch, *An den Rand gedrängt;* Ernst Klee, *Behindert: Ein kritisches Handbuch* (Frankfurt: Fischer, 1980); Ernst Klee, ed., *Behinderten-Kalender, 1980* and *1981* (Frankfurt: Fischer, [1979] 1980); Ernst Klee, *Behinderten-Report I* and *II* (Frankfurt: Fischer, [1974] 1980).

57. Donner, *Die sozial- und staatspolitische Tätigkeit der Kriegsopferverbände,* 203.

58. Fandrey, *Krüppel, Idioten, Irre,* 263–64.

59. *Forum, das Online-Magazin für Behinderte,* November 12, 1999, http://www.cebeef.com/1999/04/f3383.html.

60. Heide Fehrenbach, *Race after Hitler: Black Occupation Children in Postwar Germany and America* (Princeton: Princeton University Press, 2005).

61. Wilfried Rudloff, "Sozialstaat, Randgruppen, und bundesrepublikanische Gesellschaft: Umbrüche und Entwicklungen in den sechziger und frühen siebziger Jahren," in *Psychiatriereform als Gesellschaftsreform: Die Hypothek des Nationalsozialismus und der Aufbruch der sechziger Jahre,* ed. Franz-Werner Kersting (Paderborn: Schöningh, 2003), 200. See also Axel Murken, *Joseph Beuys und die Medizin* (Münster: Coppenrath, 1979), which includes an artwork by Beuys entitled *Das Contergankind* (The Thalidomide Child, 1963), 73.

62. Franz Schönberger, *Die sogenannten Contergankinder* (Munich: Kösel, 1971).

63. See Theresia Degener, "Die Emanzipation ist leichter für mich," *Emma* 5 (1981): 16; and her contributions in Carola Ewinkel et al., eds., *Geschlecht: behindert; Besonderes Merkmal: Frau—Ein Buch von behinderten Frauen* (Munich: AG SPAK, 1985).

64. Paul Longmore, "Conspicuous Contribution and American Cultural Dilemmas: Telethon Rituals of Cleansing and Renewal," in *The Body and Physical Difference: Discourses of Disability,* ed. David Mitchell and Sharon Snyder (Ann Arbor: University of Michigan Press, 1997), 134–60.

65. Web site of Arbeitsgemeinschaft Behinderte in den Medien: http://www.abm-medien.de.

66. Quoted in *Forum: Online-Magazin für Behinderte,* October 15, 1999, http://www.cebeef.com.

67. Quoted in Franz-Werner Kersting, "Vor Ernst Klee: Die Hypothek der NS-Medizinverbrechen als Reformimpuls," in *Psychiatriereform als Gesellschaftsreform: Die Hypothek des Nationalsozialismus und der Aufbruch der sechziger Jahre,* ed. Franz-Werner Kersting (Paderborn: Schöningh, 2003), 63.

68. Ernst Klee, *Was sie taten, was sie wurden: Ärzte, Juristen und andere Beteiligten am Kranken- oder Judenmord* (Frankfurt: Fischer, 1986); Thomas Gerst, "Catel und die Kinder: Versuche an Menschen—ein Fallbeispiel, 1947–1948," *1999* 15:2 (2000): 100–109; Norbert Frei, *Vergangenheitspolitik: Die Anfänge der Bundesrepublik und die NS-Vergangenheit* (Munich: Beck, 1999).

69. Heinz Faulstich, *Hungersterben in der Psychiatrie, 1914–1949: Mit einer Topographie der NS-Psychiatrie* (Freiburg: Lambertus, 1998), 71. Subsequent page references are given in the body of the text.

70. Angelika Ebbinghaus and Klaus Dörner, eds., *Vernichten und Heilen: Der Nürnberger Ärzteprozess und seine Folgen* (Berlin: Aufbau, 2001), 10ff., 414ff.

71. Quoted in Landeswohlfahrtsverband Hessen, ed., *"Verlegt nach Hadamar": Die Geschichte einer NS-"Euthanasie"-Anstalt* (Kassel: Eigenverlag des LWV Hessen, 1991), 173.

72. Dick de Mildt, *In the Name of the People: Perpetrators of Genocide in the Reflection of Their Postwar Prosecution in West Germany—the "Euthanasia" and "Aktion Reinhard" Trial Cases* (Boston: Martinus Nijhoff, 1996).

73. Friedrich K. Kaul, *Nazimordaktion T4: Ein Bericht über die erste industriemäßig durchgeführte Mordaktion des Naziregimes* (Berlin: Volk und Gesundheit, 1973), 182. See also Willi Dreßen, "Mord, Totschlag, Verbotsirrtum: Zum Wandel der bundesrepublikanischen Rechtsprechung in NS-"Euthanasie"-Prozessen," in *Halbierte Vernunft und totale Medizin: Zu Grundlagen, Realgeschichte und Fortwirkungen der Psychiatrie im Nationalsozialismus,* ed. Matthias Hamann and Hans Asbek (Berlin: Schwarze Risse, 1997), 181. Subsequent page references to Dreßen's article are given in the body of the text.

74. Joachim Hohmann, *Der "Euthanasie"-Prozess Dresden 1947: Eine zeitgeschichtliche Dokumentation* (New York: Lang, 1993), 176, 317. Subsequent page references are given in the body of the text.

75. Sabine Hanrath, *Zwischen "Euthanasie" und Psychiatriereform: Anstaltspsychiatrie in Westfalen und Brandenburg, ein deutsch-deutscher Vergleich, 1945–1964* (Paderborn: Schöningh, 2002), 104.

76. Constantin Goschler, *Wiedergutmachung: Westdeutschland und die Verfolgten des Nationalsozialismus, 1950–1954* (Munich: Oldenbourg, 1992), 158, 194.

77. Hanrath, *Zwischen "Euthanasie" und Psychiatriereform,* 104.

78. Katja Neppert, "Warum sind die NS-Zwangssterilisierten nicht entschädigt worden? Argumentationen der fünfziger und sechziger Jahre," in *Halbierte Vernunft und totale Medizin: Zu Grundlagen, Realgeschichte und Fortwirkungen der Psychiatrie im Nationalsozialismus,* ed. Matthias Hamann and Hans Asbek (Berlin: Schwarze Risse, 1997), 215. Subsequent page reference is given in the body of the text.

79. For a summary of the legal status of the victims of involuntary sterilization and "euthanasia," see "PDS fordert Wiedergutmachung für die NS-Opfer der Zwangssterilisation und der 'Euthanasie,'" *Forum: Das Online-Magazin für Behinderte,* December 7, 1999.

80. Monika Schumann, "Zur (Eltern-)Bewegung gegen die Aussonderung von Kindern mit Behinderungen 'Gemeinsam leben—gemeinsam lernen,'" *Behindertenpädagogik* 35:1 (1996): 37–55; Heinz Bach, "Von den Ansätzen der pädagogischen Förderung geistig behinderter Menschen in der Bundesrepublik Deutschland in den fünfziger, sechziger und siebziger Jahren," *Behindertenpädagogik* 39:3 (2000): 304–12.

81. Rudloff, "Sozialstaat," in *Psychiatriereform als Gesellschaftsreform: Die Hypothek des Nationalsozialismus und der Aufbruch der sechziger Jahre,* ed. Franz-Werner Kersting (Paderborn: Schöningh, 2003), 199.

82. Bach, "Von den Ansätzen," 310.

83. Hans-Walter Schmuhl, "Einführung," in *Psychiatriereform als Gesellschaftsreform: Die Hypothek des Nationalsozialismus und der Aufbruch der sechziger Jahre,* ed. Franz-Werner Kersting (Paderborn: Schöningh, 2003), 16.

84. Franz-Werner Kersting, "Vor Ernst Klee," in *Psychiatriereform als*

Gesellschaftsreform: Die Hypothek des Nationalsozialismus und der Aufbruch der sechziger Jahre, ed. Franz-Werner Kersting (Paderborn: Schöningh, 2003), 69.

85. Günter Grass, *Die Blechtrommel* (Neuwied: Luchterhand, 1971), 9.

86. Hans Magnus Enzensberger, "Wilhelm Meister auf der Blechtrommel," in *Die Blechtrommel: Attraktion und Ärgernis. Ein Kapitel deutscher Literaturkritik,* ed. Franz Josef Görtz (Neuwied: Luchterhand, 1984), 64. See also Peter Arnds, *Representation, Subversion, and Eugenics in Günter Grass's "The Tin Drum"* (Rochester, NY: Camden House, 2004).

87. Hohmann, *Der "Euthanasie-Prozess Dresden" 1947,* 124.

88. Kersting, "Vor Ernst Klee," 72ff. Subsequent page reference is given in the body of the text.

89. Volker Jakob, "Wartesaal mit Hoffnung: Psychiatrie und Reform im Spiegel zeitgenössischer Filme aus Gütersloh, Bremen und Eickelborn, 1963–1967," in *Psychiatriereform als Gesellschaftsreform: Die Hypothek des Nationalsozialismus und der Aufbruch der sechziger Jahre,* ed. Franz-Werner Kersting (Paderborn: Schöningh, 2003), 144.

90. Rudloff, "Sozialstaat," 187.

91. Franz-Werner Kersting, "Einführung," in *Psychiatriereform als Gesellschaftsreform: Die Hypothek des Nationalsozialismus und der Aufbruch der sechziger Jahre,* ed. Franz-Werner Kersting (Paderborn: Schöningh, 2003), 4. For a discussion of a literary work that reflects the issues brought up in the Psychiatry Enquete, see Tilman Fischer, *"Gesund ist, wer andere zermalmt." Heinar Kipphardts "März" im Kontext der Anti-Psychiatrie Debatte* (Bielefeld: Aisthesis, 1999); and Carol Poore, "'Reportagen der Innenwelt': The Example of Heinar Kipphardt's *März,"* *German Quarterly* 60:2 (spring 1987): 193–204.

92. Heinz Häfner, "Die Inquisition der psychisch Kranken geht ihrem Ende entgegen: Die Geschichte der Psychiatrie-Enquete und Psychiatriereform in Deutschland," in *Psychiatriereform als Gesellschaftsreform: Die Hypothek des Nationalsozialismus und der Aufbruch der sechziger Jahre,* ed. Franz-Werner Kersting (Paderborn: Schöningh, 2003), 113–40. The Psychiatry Enquete documentation was published as *Bericht über die Lage der Psychiatrie in der Bundesrepublik Deutschland: Zur psychiatrischen und psychotherapeutisch/psychosomatischen Versorgung der Bevölkerung* (Bonn: Bundesdrucksache 7:4200 and 7:4201, 1975).

93. Cornelia Brink, "Radikale Psychiatriekritik in der Bundesrepublik: Zum Sozialistischen Patientenkollektiv in Heidelberg," in *Psychiatriereform als Gesellschaftsreform: Die Hypothek des Nationalsozialismus und der Aufbruch der sechziger Jahre,* ed. Franz-Werner Kersting (Paderborn: Schöningh, 2003), 165–80.

CHAPTER 5

1. Thomas Anz, *Gesund oder krank? Medizin, Moral, und Ästhetik in der deutschen Gegenwartsliteratur* (Stuttgart: Metzler, 1989), 55ff.

2. Rosemarie Garland-Thomson, *Extraordinary Bodies: Figuring Physical Disability in American Culture and Literature* (New York: Columbia University Press, 1997), 9.

3. Jane Shattuc, *Television, Tabloids, and Tears: Fassbinder and Popular Culture* (Minneapolis: University of Minnesota Press, 1995), 127.

4. *Filmfacts,* 20:8 (1977): 180.

5. This was how the film was generally received in the FRG according to Wallace Watson, *Understanding Rainer Werner Fassbinder* (Columbia: University of South Carolina Press, 1996), 171.

6. *Filmfacts,* 179.

7. Shattuc, *Television,* 131, 138.

8. Richard Combs, "*Chinese Roulette* and *Despair,*" *Sight and Sound* 48 (autumn 1978): 259.

9. Thomas Elsaesser, *Fassbinder's Germany: History Identity Subject* (Amsterdam: Amsterdam University Press, 1996), 286.

10. Combs, "*Chinese Roulette* and *Despair,*" 259.

11. Herbert Spaich, *Rainer Werner Fassbinder: Leben und Werk* (Weinheim: Beltz Quadriga, 1992), 202.

12. Shattuc, *Television,* 132–33.

13. Thomas Elsaesser, "Historicizing the Subject: A Body of Work?" *New German Critique* 63 (fall 1994): 17.

14. Ibid., 32–33.

15. Combs, "*Chinese Roulette* and *Despair,*" 259.

16. Peter Berling, *Die 13 Jahre des Rainer Werner Fassbinder* (Bergisch Gladbach: Gustav Lübbe, 1992), 293.

17. Elsaesser, *Fassbinder's Germany,* 30ff., discusses Fassbinder's portrayals of other types of victims as just as mean, inhuman, and evil as anyone else. He quotes Fassbinder as saying, "I have always maintained that one can learn most about the majority by looking at the behavior of the minorities. I can understand more about the oppressors, when I show the actions of the oppressed, or rather, how the oppressed try to survive in the face of oppression. At first I made films where I made the oppressors evil and the victims unfortunate. But in the end, that is not how it is."

18. See Paul Longmore, "Screening Stereotypes: Images of Disabled People," *Social Policy* (summer 1985): 33, which states that "the subtext of many horror films is fear and loathing of people with disabilities."

19. David Mitchell and Sharon Snyder, *Narrative Prosthesis: Disability and the Dependencies of Discourse* (Ann Arbor: University of Michigan Press, 2000), 97.

20. See Martin Norden, *The Cinema of Isolation: A History of Physical Disability in the Movies* (New Brunswick, NJ: Rutgers University Press, 1994).

21. Thomson, *Extraordinary Bodies,* 36.

22. Mitchell and Snyder, *Narrative Prosthesis,* 99.

23. Here Angela should also be seen in the context of the New German Cinema's fascination with child figures, who become a projection screen for adult yearnings for freedom or fears of victimization. I am indebted to Marc Silberman for this insight.

24. Gertrud Koch, "Torments of the Flesh, Coldness of the Spirit: Jewish Figures in the Films of Rainer Werner Fassbinder," *New German Critique* 38 (spring-summer 1986): 36, 38.

25. Seyla Benhabib, "Rainer Werner Fassbinder's *Garbage, the City, and Death,*" *New German Critique* 38 (spring-summer 1986): 20.

26. An example of how times have changed in Germany in this regard

is a controversy over defamatory remarks about disabled people made by a television moderator on the RTL network. On April 10, 2000, Birgit Schrowange had described disabled people as "hopelessly ugly people" and "natural catastrophes." Protests from various groups and individuals pressured her into issuing an on-air apology. See *Forum: Online-Magazin für Behinderte,* April 17, 2000, and May 8, 2000.

27. One could add here Jo Baier's outstanding film *Hölleisengretl* (1996), which is an adaptation of Oskar Maria Graf's "Die Geschichte von der buckligen Hölleisengretl" (The Story of the Hunchback Hölleisengretl, 1931). These works tell the story of a young woman who owns a farm in Bavaria and is ostracized by her neighbors because of her hunchback. Baier added a deeper historical dimension to the story by situating it in the early 1950s and showing the villagers as quite aware of the Nazis' "euthanasia" program.

28. Hellmuth Karasek, "Vom Hinkemann zum Nusser," *Der Spiegel,* March 17, 1986, 230.

29. Karl Ude, writing in the *Süddeutsche Zeitung,* April 3–4, 1971, quoted in *Franz Xaver Kroetz,* ed. Otto Riewoldt (Frankfurt: Suhrkamp, 1985), 75.

30. Franz Xaver Kroetz, *Der Soldat,* in *Stücke* (Frankfurt: Suhrkamp, 1989), 1:172. Subsequent page references are given in the body of the text.

31. Ernst Wendt, "Dramen über Zerstörung, Leiden, Sprachlosigkeiten im Alltag—auf der Flucht vor den großen politischen Stoffen?" *Theater heute* 5 (May 1971): 34.

32. Franz Xaver Kroetz, *Hartnäckig,* in *Stücke* (Frankfurt: Suhrkamp, 1989), 2:19. Subsequent page references are given in the body of the text.

33. See Hans Edgar Jahn, *Für und gegen den Wehrbeitrag: Argumente und Dokumente* (Cologne: Greven, 1957); and Wolfgang Kraushaar, *Die Protest-Chronik, 1949–1959: Eine illustrierte Geschichte von Bewegung, Widerstand, und Utopie,* 4 vols. (Hamburg: Rogner und Bernhard bei Zweitausendeins, 1996).

34. Ulrich Heising, "Der radikale Realismus von Kroetz," in *Franz Xaver Kroetz,* ed. Otto Riewoldt (Frankfurt: Suhrkamp, 1985), 202.

35. Franz Xaver Kroetz, *Stallerhof,* in *Stücke* (Frankfurt: Suhrkamp, 1989), 1:270. Subsequent page references are given in the body of the text.

36. Joachim Kaiser, quoted in Heising, "Der radikale Realismus von Kroetz," in *Franz Xaver Kroetz,* ed. Otto Riewoldt (Frankfurt: Suhrkamp, 1985), 210.

37. Ibid., 203.

38. Rolf Michaelis, "*Stallerhof:* Deutsches Schauspielhaus Hamburg," *Theater heute* 8 (August 1971): 11–12.

39. Paul Kruntorad, "Späte Uraufführung: *Die Geisterbahn* von Kroetz in Wien," *Theater heute* 12 (December 1975): 50.

40. People First, the self-advocacy organization of people with cognitive disabilities that was founded in the United States, is now active in Germany. The members' preferred term for themselves is now "Menschen mit Lernschwierigkeiten" (people with learning difficulties). A theater group in Munich, Phoenix aus der Asche (Phoenix from the Ashes), whose members are mostly young people with autism, recently performed one of Kroetz's early plays, *Wildwechsel* (Game Crossing) (see http://www.kjr-muenchen-stadt.de/projekte/phoenix_wildwechsel_artikel.php.4).

41. Quoted in Heising, "Der radikale Realismus von Kroetz," 209.

42. Franz Xaver Kroetz, "Erklärung," in *Franz Xaver Kroetz,* ed. Otto Riewoldt (Frankfurt: Suhrkamp, 1985), 178–79.

43. Franz Xaver Kroetz, "Kirchberger Notizen," in *Franz Xaver Kroetz,* ed. Otto Riewoldt (Frankfurt: Suhrkamp, 1985), 172.

44. Otto Riewoldt, "Der ganze Kroetz," in *Franz Xaver Kroetz,* ed. Otto Riewoldt (Frankfurt: Suhrkamp, 1985), 16.

45. Franz Xaver Kroetz, "Interview," in *Franz Xaver Kroetz, "Bauern sterben": Materialien zum Stück,* ed. Antje Ellermann (Reinbek: Rowohlt, 1985), 162.

46. Franz Xaver Kroetz, *Der Mondscheinknecht* (Frankfurt: Suhrkamp, 1981), 144.

47. Franz Xaver Kroetz, *Der Mondscheinknecht: Fortsetzung* (Frankfurt: Suhrkamp, 1983), 126. Subsequent page references are given in the body of the text.

48. Dieter Kafitz, "Die Problematisierung des individualistischen Menschenbildes im deutschsprachigen Drama der Gegenwart (Franz Xaver Kroetz, Thomas Bernhard, Botho Strauß)," *Basis* 10 (1980): 93–126. On conformity shame, see Deborah Greenwald and David Harder, "Domains of Shame: Evolutionary, Cultural, and Psychotherapeutic Aspects," in *Shame: Interpersonal Behavior, Psychopathology, and Culture,* ed. Paul Gilbert and Bernice Andrews (New York: Oxford University Press, 1998), 225–44.

49. Stephan Reinhardt in *Nürnberger Nachrichten,* December 5–6, 1981, quoted in *Franz Xaver Kroetz,* ed. Otto Riewoldt (Frankfurt: Suhrkamp, 1985), 187.

50. Franz Xaver Kroetz, *Der Nusser,* in *Stücke* (Frankfurt: Suhrkamp, 1989), 4:341.

51. Rudolf Helmstetter, "Politische Wirkung im Theater ist eine Frage der Ästhetik," *Theater heute* 7 (July 1986): 53.

52. Kroetz, *Der Soldat,* 1:162. It is still almost impossible for disabled actors to break into the theater world and find appropriate roles.

53. Peter Radtke, *Karriere mit 99 Brüchen: Vom Rollstuhl auf die Bühne* (Munich: Allitera Verlag, 2001), 16. Subsequent page reference is given in the body of the text.

54. Petra Kuppers, *Disability and Contemporary Performance: Bodies on Edge* (New York: Routledge, 2003). See also the discussion of the 1997 Berne Dance Festival, which featured performances with disabled and nondisabled dancers and referred specifically to Peter Radtke. See http://www.tanznetz.ch/tanzding/td38/TD3810.PDF.

55. "Ein Test für den Kanzler," *Der Spiegel,* November 25, 1991, 31.

56. For a more extensive discussion of these images, see Carol Poore, "'But Roosevelt Could Walk': Envisioning Disability in Germany and the United States," in *Points of Contact: Disability, Art, and Culture,* ed. Susan Crutchfield and Marcy Epstein (Ann Arbor: University of Michigan Press, 2000), 63–92.

57. Hugh Gallagher, *FDR's Splendid Deception* (New York: Dodd–Mead, 1985); Betty Winfield, *FDR and the News Media* (Urbana: University of Illinois Press, 1990).

58. Gallagher, *FDR's Splendid Deception,* 63.

59. Martin Pase [Ernst Pasemann], *Roosevelts Reden und Taten im Scheinwerfer der Presse und der Karikatur* (Berlin: Lühe, 1941).

60. Nicholas Halasz, *Roosevelt through Foreign Eyes* (Princeton: Van Nostrand, 1961), 228.

61. Pase, *Roosevelts Reden,* 108.

62. Henry Picker, ed., *Hitlers Tischgespräche im Führerhauptquartier, 1941–1942* (Stuttgart: Seewald, 1963), 201.

63. These three cartoons appeared in *Der Spiegel* on September 23, 1991, 20; November 25, 1991, 35; and December 16, 1991, 9.

64. Letters to *Der Spiegel,* December 16, 1991, 9.

65. Letter to the editor, *Stern,* January 16, 1997, 8–9.

66. Herbert Prantl, "Wolfgang, nimm dich nicht so wichtig!" *Süddeutsche Zeitung Magazin,* February 13, 2004.

67. Michael Naumann, "Politik ohne Würde," *Die Zeit,* March 11, 2004, 1.

68. "Roosevelt's Disability an Issue at Memorial," *New York Times,* April 10, 1995, A10.

69. Letter of James K. Langevin to Dorann Gunderson, Executive Director of the Franklin Delano Roosevelt Memorial Commission, January 9, 1995.

70. "FDR Memorial Commission Statement on March 1, 1995 Commission Meeting." 1.

71. "Disabled Protest Memorial to FDR," *Providence Journal-Bulletin,* February 28, 1997.

CHAPTER 6

1. Carol Poore, *The Bonds of Labor: German Journeys to the Working World, 1890–1990* (Detroit: Wayne State University Press, 2000), 24ff.

2. Jost Hermand, *Der deutsche Vormärz: Texte und Dokumente* (Stuttgart: Reclam, 1997), 195–242.

3. Franz Diederich, comp., *Von unten auf: Ein neues Buch der Freiheit* (Berlin: Buchhandlung Vorwärts, 1911), 2:73.

4. Karl Kautsky, "Der Alkoholismus und seine Bekämpfung," in *Naturalismus-Debatte 1891–1896,* ed. Norbert Rothe (Berlin: Akademie-Verlag, 1986), 34–38; Michael Schwartz, *Sozialistische Eugenik: Eugenische Sozialtechnologien in Debatten und Politik der deutschen Sozialdemokratie, 1890–1933* (Bonn: Dietz, 1995), 44. See also Reinhard Mocek, *Biologie und soziale Befreiung: Zur Geschichte des Biologismus und der Rassenhygiene in der Arbeiterbewegung* (Frankfurt: Lang, 2002); and Richard Weikart, *Socialist Darwinism: Evolution in German Social Thought from Marx to Bernstein* (San Francisco: International Scholars Publications, 1999).

5. Michael Rohrwasser, *Saubere Mädel, starke Genossen: Proletarische Massenliteratur?* (Frankfurt: Roter Stern, 1975).

6. Andrei Zhdanov, "Rede auf dem I. Unionskongress der Sowjetschriftsteller," in *Marxismus und Literatur,* ed. Fritz Raddatz (Reinbek: Rowohlt, 1969), 1:347–53.

7. Maxim Gorki, "Rede auf dem I. Unionskongress der Sowjetschriftsteller," in *Marxismus und Literatur,* ed. Fritz Raddatz (Reinbek: Rowohlt, 1969), 1:335–46.

8. Poore, *Bonds of Labor,* 161–210.

9. Wolfgang Emmerich, *Kleine Literaturgeschichte der DDR: Erweiterte Neuausgabe* (Leipzig: Kiepenheuer, 1996), 120.

10. Ernst Ullmann, "Das Bild des sozialistischen Menschen in der bildenden Kunst," in *Das sozialistische Menschenbild: Weg und Wirklichkeit,* ed. Elmar Faber and Erhard John (Leipzig: VEB Bibliographisches Institut, 1967), 378.

11. Quoted in Wolfgang Emmerich, *Kleine Literaturgeschichte der DDR* (Darmstadt: Luchterhand, 1981), 78.

12. Paul Körner-Schrader, "Paul Arndt: Traktorist auf der MAS Sachsendorf, Kreis Seelow," in *Helden der Arbeit,* ed. Karl Grünberg et al. (Berlin: Kultur und Fortschritt, 1951), 201–14. Subsequent page reference is given in the body of the text. The shifts in GDR censorship policies are too complex to be explained here. Dates in parentheses refer to the GDR unless noted as FRG, meaning that a work was published only in West Germany.

13. Anna Seghers, *Der Bienenstock* (Berlin: Aufbau, 1963), contains both "Der Traktorist" (13–15) and "Der Kesselflicker" (15–20).

14. Heiner Müller, *Traktor,* in *Geschichten aus der Produktion 2* (Berlin: Rotbuch, 1974), 9–26. Subsequent page references are given in the body of the text.

15. Quoted in Patrick Primavesi, "Traktor," in *Heiner Müller Handbuch,* ed. Hans-Thies Lehmann and Patrick Primavesi (Stuttgart: Metzler, 2003), 279.

16. Martha Edwards, "Philoctetes in Historical Context," in *Disabled Veterans in History,* ed. David Gerber (Ann Arbor: University of Michigan Press, 2000), 55–69.

17. Emmerich, *Kleine Literaturgeschichte* (1996), 275–76.

18. Heiner Müller, *Hamletmaschine,* in *Mauser* (Berlin: Rotbuch, 1978), 97.

19. Christa Wolf, *Nachdenken über Christa T.* (Neuwied: Luchterhand, 1970), 141.

20. Thomas Anz, *Gesund oder krank? Medizin, Moral, und Ästhetik in der deutschen Gegenwartsliteratur* (Stuttgart: Metzler, 1989).

21. Rolf Schneider, *November* (Hamburg: Knaus, 1979), 7.

22. Michael Rohrwasser, "Das Selbstmordmotiv in der DDR-Literatur," in *Probleme deutscher Identität,* ed. Paul Klussmann and Heinrich Mohr (Bonn: Bouvier, 1983), 209–31.

23. Carol Poore, "Illness and the Socialist Personality: Philosophical Debates and Literary Images in the GDR," in *Studies in GDR Culture and Society,* ed. Margy Gerber (Lanham, MD: University Press of America, 1986), 6:123–35.

24. Georg Lukàcs, "Gesunde oder kranke Kunst?" in *Schicksalswende* (Berlin: Aufbau, 1956), 155–61.

25. Anz, *Gesund oder krank?* 182, 189.

26. On the struggle with GDR censors to publish Christoph Hein's *Horns Ende,* see Manfred Jäger, *Kultur und Politik in der DDR, 1945–1990* (Cologne: Deutschland Archiv, 1994), 214–16.

27. Plenzdorf returned to the theme of disability in a much less radical manner in his novel *Die Legende vom Glück ohne Ende* (The Legend of Unending Happiness, 1979), in which the protagonist uses a wheelchair.

28. Ute Brandes, "Toward Socialist Modernism: Ulrich Plenzdorf's

'kein runter kein fern,'" in *Studies in GDR Culture and Society,* ed. Margy Gerber (Lanham, MD: University Press of America, 1984), 4:107–24.

29. Ulrich Plenzdorf, "kein runter kein fern," in *Geschichten aus der Geschichte der DDR,* ed. Manfred Behn (Darmstadt: Luchterhand, 1981), 168.

30. Jäger, *Kultur und Politik in der DDR,* 140.

31. Ulrich Plenzdorf et al., eds., *Berliner Geschichten: "Operativer Schwerpunkt Selbstverlag." Eine Autoren-Anthologie: wie sie entstand und von der Stasi verhindert wurde* (Frankfurt: Suhrkamp, 1995), 7. Subsequent page references are given in the body of the text.

32. Gerhard Ebert, "Tragisches Kinderschicksal als Spiegel einer unheilen Welt," *Neues Deutschland,* January 16, 1990, 46.

33. Franz Fühmann, *Der Sturz des Engels: Erfahrungen mit Dichtung* (Hamburg: Hoffmann und Campe, 1982), 148.

34. Barbara Heinze, ed., *Franz Fühmann: Eine Biographie in Bildern, Dokumenten, und Briefen* (Rostock: Hinstorff, 1998), 315.

35. See also the photo essay by Karin Wieckhorst, "Siegmar Schulze—querschnittgelähmt," in the special issue on GDR photography of the journal *Niemandsland* 2:7 (1988): 36–39.

36. Franz Fühmann, "Canto ami et non mourier," in *Was für eine Insel in was für einem Meer: Leben mit geistig Behinderten,* Franz Fühmann and Dietmar Riemann (Rostock: Hinstorff, 1988), 150.

37. Schwartz, *Sozialistische Eugenik.*

38. Kurt Kühn, ed., *Ärzte an der Seite der Arbeiterklasse* (Berlin: Volk und Gesundheit, 1977).

39. Karl Marx, "Critique of the Gotha Program," in *The Marx-Engels Reader,* ed. Robert Tucker (New York: Norton, 1978), 531. See also the entries on "Leistung" (1:828) and "materielle Interessiertheit" (2:878) in Bundesministerium für innerdeutsche Beziehungen, ed., *DDR Handbuch* (Cologne: Wissenschaft und Politik, 1985).

40. Manfred Wolter, *Frank: Umweg ins Leben* (Berlin: Buchverlag Der Morgen, 1987), 172.

41. See the section "Menschlichkeit oder Leistung" in Parteihochschule "Karl Marx" beim ZK der SED, ed., *Worauf vertrauen wir? Humanistische Werte in der DDR* (Berlin: Dietz, 1986), 100ff.

42. Ute Angerhoefer, "Gedanken zum pädagogisch wirksamen Menschenbild in der DDR und sein Einfluss auf die Sonderpädagogik: Reflexionen und Ausblicke," in *Behindertenpädagogik im vereinten Deutschland: Über die Schwierigkeiten eines Zwiegesprächs zwischen Ost und West,* ed. Ulrich Bleidick and Sieglind Ellger-Rüttgardt (Weinheim: Deutscher Studien Verlag, 1994), 13.

43. See Bundesministerium für innerdeutsche Beziehungen, *DDR Handbuch,* entries on "sozialistische Lebensweise" (1:817) and "sozialistische Persönlichkeit" (2:982).

44. Quoted in Angerhoefer, "Gedanken," 14.

45. Bundesministerium für innerdeutsche Beziehungen, *DDR Handbuch,* entry on "Rehabilitation" (2:1115); Gisela Helwig, "Handicapped People in the GDR: Cooperation between Church and State," in *Studies in GDR Culture and Society,* ed. Margy Gerber (Lanham, MD: University Press of America, 1987), 7:43.

46. James Diehl, *The Thanks of the Fatherland: German Veterans after*

the Second World War (Chapel Hill: University of North Carolina Press, 1993), 75. It would also be important to learn about policies toward members of the GDR's Nationale Volksarmee who became disabled in military service.

47. Karin Thomas, ed., *Menschenbilder: Kunst aus der DDR* (Cologne: Dumont, 1986); Hermann Raum, *Bildende Kunst in der DDR* (Berlin: edition ost, 2000); Hans Edgar Jahn, *Für und gegen den Wehrbeitrag: Argumente und Dokumente* (Cologne: Greven, 1957).

48. Quoted in Sabine Hanrath, *Zwischen Euthanasie und Psychiatriereform. Anstaltspsychiatrie in Westfalen und Brandenburg: Ein deutsch-deutscher Vergleich, 1945–1964* (Paderborn: Schöningh, 2002), 202.

49. Two important GDR publications on Nazi "euthanasia" are Friedrich Karl Kaul, *Nazimordaktion T4: Ein Bericht über die erste industriemäßig durchgeführte Mordaktion des Naziregimes* (Berlin: Volk und Gesundheit, 1973); and Kurt Nowak, *"Euthanasie" und Sterilisierung im "Dritten Reich"* (Halle: Niemeyer, 1977).

50. Hanrath, *Zwischen Euthanasie und Psychiatriereform,* 215. Subsequent page references are given in the body of the text.

51. Ibid., 462; Georg Theunissen, *Wege aus der Hospitalisierung* (Bonn: Psychiatrie-Verlag, 1999), 36ff.

52. Gerda Jun, "Probleme geistig Behinderter im Kindesalter," in *Sozialistischer Humanismus und Betreuung Geschädigter,* ed. Wolfgang Presber and Rolf Löther (Jena: VEB Gustav Fischer Verlag, 1981), 86.

53. Angerhoefer, "Gedanken," 21.

54. Quoted in Susanne Hahn, "'Man muss bis zu 200 Jahren jung, kräftig und stark sein . . .': Das sozialistische Menschenbild und seine problematischen Wechselbeziehungen zur genetischen Forschung und Praxis in der DDR," *Menschenbilder in der Medizin—Medizin in den Menschenbildern,* ed. Günter Dörner et al. (Bielefeld: Kleine, 1999), 444.

55. Sozialistische Einheitspartei Deutschlands, Zentralkomitee, ed., *Gesundheit, Leistungsfähigkeit, Lebensfreude* (Berlin: Volk und Gesundheit, 1960).

56. Susanne Hahn, "Nun wächst zusammen, was zusammengehört . . . Biologistische Tendenzen im real existierenden Sozialismus," *1999* 7:2 (April 1992): 47–48.

57. Dr. Gerda Jun, interview with the author, Berlin, May 20, 2000.

58. Wolter, *Frank,* 142, 150.

59. The Rodewisch Theses were first published in the *Zeitschrift für die gesamte Hygiene und ihre Grenzgebiete* 11 (1965): 61–63. They are quoted here from "Die Rodewischer Thesen von 1963," in *Psychiatriereform als Gesellschaftsreform: Die Hypothek des Nationalsozialismus und der Aufbruch der sechziger Jahre,* ed. Franz-Werner Kersting (Paderborn: Schöningh, 2003), 97–100.

60. Sabine Hanrath, "Strukturkrise und Reformbeginn: Die Anstaltspsychiatrie in der DDR und der Bundesrepublik bis zu den 60er Jahren," in *Psychiatriereform als Gesellschaftsreform: Die Hypothek des Nationalsozialismus und der Aufbruch der sechziger Jahre,* ed. Franz-Werner Kersting (Paderborn: Schöningh, 2003), 61.

61. These laws are all listed in Ministerium für Gesundheitswesen, ed., *Schwerbeschädigtenbetreuung und Rehabilitation: Rechtliche Bestim-*

mungen und Arbeitsmaterialien (Berlin: Staatsverlag der DDR, 1981). Subsequent page references are given in the body of the text.

62. Information on these benefits and services is given in Joachim Mandel, *Schwerbeschädigte—betreut und gefördert* (Berlin: Staatsverlag der DDR, 1984).

63. Matthias Vernaldi, interview with the author, Berlin, May 23, 2000; Nicole Eiermann et al., *LIVE: Leben und Interessen Vertreten—Frauen mit Behinderung* (Stuttgart: Kohlhammer, 1999), 210.

64. Helwig, "Handicapped People in the GDR," 47.

65. Gisela Helwig, *Am Rande der Gesellschaft: Alte und Behinderte in beiden deutschen Staaten* (Cologne: Wissenschaft und Politik, 1980), 57.

66. André Zimpel and Manfred Jödecke, "Zur Lebenssituation geistig behinderter Menschen in der DDR bzw. den 'Neuen Bundesländern,'" in *Ende der Verwahrung?! Perspektiven geistig behinderter Menschen zum selbständigen Leben,* ed. fib e.V. (Munich: AG-SPAK, 1991), 227.

67. Marianne Schulz, "'Für Selbstbestimmung und Würde': Die Metamorphose des Behindertenverbandes der DDR zum Allgemeinen Behindertenverband in Deutschland" (Berlin: Max-Planck-Gesellschaft, March 1995), 6 (manuscript in the author's possession).

68. Theologische Studienabteilung beim DDR-Kirchenbund, "Kritik der Leistung: Die allseitig reduzierte Persönlichkeit—Ursachen und Auswege," in *Beton ist Beton: Zivilisationskritik aus der DDR,* ed. Peter Wensierski and Wolfgang Büscher (Hattingen: Scandica-Verlag, 1981), 166–67.

69. Presber, *Sozialistischer Humanismus.* Subsequent page references are given in the body of the text.

70. For a list of the types of special schools, see the entry "Sonderschulen und sonderpädagogische Einrichtungen," in Bundesministerium für innerdeutsche Beziehungen, *DDR Handbuch,* 1:326. See also K.-P. Becker and R.A. Greenberg, eds., *Educational Rehabilitation of the Handicapped in the German Democratic Republic and in the United States of America: An Overview* (New York: Pergamon, 1985).

71. Mandel, *Schwerbeschädigte,* 44–54; Angerhoefer, "Gedanken," 17.

72. Wolter, *Frank,* 24.

73. Zimpel and Jödecke, "Zur Lebenssituation," 224.

74. Mandel, *Schwerbeschädigte,* 47.

75. Zimpel and Jödecke, "Zur Lebenssituation," 222.

76. Horst Harych and Katrin Gerbatsch, "Zur Situation von Behinderten und Pflegebedürftigen in Ostdeutschland," in *Soziale Sicherheit für alle,* ed. Richard Hauser and Thomas Olk (Opladen: Leske und Budrich, 1997), 346.

77. Justin J. W. Powell, "Hochbegabt, behindert oder normal? Klassifikationssysteme des sonderpädagogischen Förderbedarfs in Deutschland und den Vereinigten Staaten," in *Wie man behindert wird: Texte zur Konstruktion einer sozialen Rolle und zur Lebenssituation betroffener Menschen,* ed. Günther Cloerkes (Heidelberg: Winter, 2003), 116ff.

78. Angerhoefer, "Gedanken," 15–16.

79. Erika Richter, interview with the author, Berlin, May 28, 2000.

80. "Erich R," unpublished collection of interviews with disabled GDR citizens compiled by Ulrike Gottschalk; manuscript in the author's possession.

81. Martin Jaedicke, "Max Schöffler," in *Blinde unterm Hakenkreuz—Erkennen, Trauern, Begegnen,* ed. Martin Jaedicke and Wolfgang Schmidt-

Block (Marburg: Deutscher Verein der Blinden und Sehbehinderten in Studium und Beruf e.V., 1991), 152–64.

82. Mandel, *Schwerbeschädigte,* 95.

83. Harych and Gerbatsch, "Zur Situation von Behinderten," 348–50.

84. Ilja Seifert, ". . . 'versorgt' bis zur Unmündigkeit oder Fachleute für das eigene Leben," in *Aufbruch im Warteland: Ostdeutsche soziale Bewegungen im Wandel,* ed. Michael Hofmann (Bamberg: Palette, 1991), 50.

85. Presber, *Sozialistischer Humanismus,* 52.

86. Ilja Seifert, *Schonzeit gab es nicht: Eine Dokumentation zur Entstehung des Allgemeinen Behindertenverbandes in Deutschland e.V. "Für Selbstbestimmung und Würde" (ABiD)* (Berlin: Kolog-Verlag, 1990), 11.

87. The entry "Geschädigte," in Bundesministerium für innerdeutsche Beziehungen, *DDR Handbuch* 1:534–35.

88. Ilja Seifert, ". . . 'versorgt' bis zur Unmündigkeit," 58.

89. Harych and Gerbatsch, "Zur Situation von Behinderten," 351.

90. Beatrix Bouvier, *Die DDR—ein Sozialstaat? Sozialpolitik in der Ära Honecker* (Bonn: Dietz, 2002), 205; Monika Kohnert, "Pflege und Umgang mit Behinderten in der DDR," in *Materialien der Enquete-Kommission "Überwindung der Folgen der SED-Diktatur im Prozess der deutschen Einheit,"* ed. Deutscher Bundestag (Baden-Baden: Nomos, 1999), III/2: 1733, 1752.

91. Horst Seifert, ed., *Alle Könige sind gleich: Eine Dokumentation zur Entstehung des Allgemeinen Behindertenverbandes in Deutschland e.V. "Für Selbstbestimmung und Würde"* (Berlin: Kolog-Verlag, 1991), 10.

92. Ilja Seifert, ". . . 'versorgt' bis zur Unmündigkeit," 56.

93. Klaus-Peter Schwitzer, "Behinderte in der DDR," in *Minderheiten in und Übersiedler aus der DDR,* ed. Dieter Voigt and Lothar Mertens (Berlin: Duncker und Humblot, 1992), 137.

94. Harych and Gerbatsch, "Zur Situation von Behinderten," 369.

95. Ilja Seifert, ". . . 'versorgt' bis zur Unmündigkeit," 56.

96. Kohnert, "Pflege und Umgang mit Behinderten," 1752.

97. Ibid., 1727. For a good example of how some GDR rehabilitation experts discussed these issues in the late 1980s, see Reinhold Herrfurth and Autorenkollektiv, *Sozialintegration intellektuell geschädigter Jugendlicher und Erwachsener* (Berlin: Volk und Gesundheit, 1988).

98. There were also a number of autobiographical accounts of illness published during the 1980s, notably Maxie Wander's account of having cancer, *Leben wär eine prima Alternative* (1987). Other writers dealt with themes of euthanasia and assisted suicide such as Charlotte Worgitzky, *Heute sterben immer nur die andern* (1986).

99. Ilja Seifert, ". . . 'versorgt' bis zur Unmündigkeit," 65.

100. Ibid.

101. "Rückwärtslaufen kann ich auch," *Neues Deutschland,* January 19, 1990.

102. Wolter, *Frank,* 129.

103. Gerda Jun, *Kinder, die anders sind: Ein Elternreport* (Berlin: Volk und Gesundheit, 1981), 47ff.

104. Heinz-Joachim Petzold, *Anerkennung statt Mitleid: Report über Körperbehinderte* (Rudolstadt: Greifenverlag, 1981), 10.

105. Jun, *Kinder, die anders sind,* 71.

106. Volker Kessling, *Tagebuch eines Erziehers* (Berlin: Neues Leben, 1981), 102–3.

107. Jun, *Kinder, die anders sind,* 16. Subsequent page references are given in the body of the text.

108. Jan Behrends et al., eds., *Fremde und Fremd-Sein in der DDR: Zu historischen Ursachen der Fremdenfeindlichkeit in Ostdeutschland* (Berlin: Metropol, 2003).

109. Ilja Seifert, ". . . 'versorgt' bis zur Unmündigkeit," 69.

110. Schulz, "'Für Selbstbestimmung und Würde,'" 5, 8. Subsequent page reference is given in the body of the text.

111. Ilja Seifert, ". . . 'versorgt' bis zur Unmündigkeit," 47.

112. Schulz, "'Für Selbstbestimmung und Würde,'" 3.

113. Ilja Seifert, ". . . 'versorgt' bis zur Unmündigkeit," 60.

114. Quoted in Schulz, "'Für Selbstbestimmung und Würde,'" 1.

115. Horst Seifert, *Alle Könige sind gleich,* 10.

116. Schulz, "'Für Selbstbestimmung und Würde,'" 26; Harych and Gerbatsch, "Zur Situation von Behinderten," 356.

117. Quoted in Zimpel and Jödecke, "Zur Lebenssituation," 222. Subsequent page references are given in the body of the text.

118. Ilja Seifert, *Schonzeit gab es nicht,* 66.

119. Harych and Gerbatsch, "Zur Situation von Behinderten," 357. Subsequent page reference is given in the body of the text.

120. Helga Hackenberg and Katja Tillmann, "Zur Entwicklung der Lebenslage von behinderten und gesundheitlich eingeschränkten Personen in den neuen Bundesländern," in *Soziale Sicherheit für alle,* ed. Richard Hauser and Thomas Olk (Opladen: Leske und Budrich, 1997), 380; Zimpel and Jödecke, "Zur Lebenssituation," 229.

121. Harych and Gerbatsch, "Zur Situation von Behinderten," 364.

122. Eiermann, *LIVE,* 170.

123. Schwitzer, "Behinderte in der DDR," 134.

124. Harych and Gerbatsch, "Zur Situation von Behinderten," 355; Hans-Dieter Hoyer, "Intra- und interpersonale Bedingungen zu einem selbstbestimmten Leben für Jugendliche mit Behinderungen in den ostdeutschen Bundesländern," *Behindertenpädagogik* 30:4 (1991): 437.

125. Zimpel and Jödecke, "Zur Lebenssituation," 232.

126. Angerhoefer, "Gedanken," 13.

127. Hahn, "Nun wächst zusammen, was zusammengehört," 47–52.

128. Karl Marx and Friedrich Engels, "Manifesto of the Communist Party," in *The Marx-Engels Reader,* ed. Robert Tucker (New York: Norton, 1978), 491.

129. Zimpel and Jödecke, "Zur Lebenssituation," 234.

CHAPTER 7

1. *Yearbook of the United Nations* (New York: Office of Public Information, United Nations, 1975), 29: 691. See also Carol Poore, "Disability as Disobedience? An Essay on Germany in the Aftermath of the United Nations Year for People with Disabilities," *New German Critique* 27 (fall 1982): 161–95.

2. Anneliese Mayer, "Behinderteninitiativen in der Bundesrepublik,"

in *Hand- und Fußbuch für Behinderte,* ed. Gusti Steiner (Frankfurt: Fischer, 1988), 165.

3. Ernst Klee, *Behindert. Über die Enteignung von Körper und Bewusstsein: Ein kritisches Handbuch* (Frankfurt: Fischer, 1980), 242.

4. Antje Henninger and Gusti Steiner, eds., *Schwarzbuch "Deutsche Bahn AG": Handbuch der Ignoranz* (Neu-Ulm: AG-SPAK, 2003).

5. On the Frankfurt courses, see Ernst Klee, *Behinderten-Report II: "Wir lassen uns nicht abschieben"* (Frankfurt: Fischer, 1976), 22ff.

6. Quoted in Ottmar Miles-Paul, *"Wir sind nicht mehr aufzuhalten." Behinderte auf dem Weg zur Selbstbestimmung. Beratung von Behinderten durch Behinderte. Peer Support: Vergleich zwischen den USA und der BRD* (Munich: AG-SPAK, 1992), 117.

7. Klee, *Behindert,* 260ff.

8. Ibid., 98ff.

9. Today the child's father, Götz Aly, is one of the leading historians writing about Nazi eugenics and population policies.

10. Andrea Buch et al., *An den Rand gedrängt: Was Behinderte daran hindert, normal zu leben* (Reinbek: Rowohlt, 1980), 13.

11. Klee, *Behindert,* 11.

12. *Päd. extra Sozialarbeit* 5 (March 1981): 33.

13. Ernst Klee, *Behinderte im Urlaub? Das Frankfurter Urteil—Eine Dokumentation* (Frankfurt: Fischer, 1980), 33.

14. For a discussion of this incident and a list of similar incidents see ibid., 9ff.

15. Klee, *Behindert,* 275.

16. Mayer, "Behinderteninitiativen," 166.

17. Ibid., 167.

18. "Doppelte Wut nach dem Krückenschlag auf den Präsidenten," *Kölner Stadtanzeiger,* June 19, 1981.

19. Franz Christoph, "Warum schlägt ein Krüppel den Bundespräsidenten?" Leaflet distributed in Berlin, Bonn, and various other cities, archive of the author.

20. "Doppelte Wut."

21. Franz Christoph, *Krüppelschläge: Gegen die Gewalt der Menschlichkeit* (Reinbek: Rowohlt, 1983), 71. Subsequent page reference is given in the body of the text.

22. Susanne von Daniels et al., eds., *Krüppel-Tribunal: Menschenrechtsverletzungen im Sozialstaat* (Cologne: Pahl-Rugenstein, 1983), 10.

23. Christa Schlett, "Rebellion als Sinn des schwerbehinderten Lebens," in *Behindertsein ist schön: Unterlagen zur Arbeit mit Behinderten,* ed. Ernst Klee (Düsseldorf: Patmos, 1974), 85.

24. "behindert leben," *Courage* 5 (January 1980): 15.

25. *Emma,* May 1981, 7.

26. Theresia Degener, "Die Emanzipation ist leichter für mich," *Emma,* May 1981, 17.

27. Carola Ewinkel et al., eds., *Geschlecht: behindert; Besonderes Merkmal: Frau—Ein Buch von behinderten Frauen* (Munich: AG-SPAK, 1985), 7, 184. Subsequent page reference is given in the body of the text.

28. http://www.weibernetz.de/ also includes its online newspaper in regular and easy language versions.

29. Nicole Eiermann et al., *LIVE: Leben und Interessen vertreten—Frauen mit Behinderung* (Stuttgart: Kohlhammer, 1999).

30. Miles-Paul, *"Wir sind nicht mehr aufzuhalten,"* 122.

31. http://www.isl-ev.org.

32. Martin Schwarz, "Gewalt gegen Behinderte oder: Was ist noch übrig vom Sozialstaat?" in *Angegriffen und bedroht in Deutschland,* ed. Herbert Beckmann (Weinheim: Deutscher Studien Verlag, 1993), 141–52.

33. Justin J. W. Powell, "Hochbegabt, behindert oder normal? Klassifikationssysteme des sonderpädagogischen Förderbedarfs in Deutschland und den Vereinigten Staaten," in *Wie man behindert wird: Texte zur Konstruktion einer sozialen Rolle und zur Lebenssituation betroffener Menschen,* ed. Günther Cloerkes (Heidelberg: Winter, 2003), 116, 119.

34. http://www.weibernetz.de/2005/html.

35. http://www.kobinet-nachrichten.org, June 6, 2005.

36. http://www.kobinet-nachrichten.org is the best source for following the debate on the antidiscrimination law.

37. http://www.kobinet-nachrichten.org, September 7, 2005.

38. Klee, *Behinderten-Report II,* 176–77.

39. Dietke Sanders, "Ich seh ja nie welche: Über das Verhältnis von nichtbehinderten zu behinderten Frauen," in *Behindertenfeindlichkeit: Ausgrenzungen und Vereinnahmungen,* ed. Birgit Rommelspacher (Göttingen: Lamuv, 1999), 80.

40. Gerda Jun, *Kinder, die anders sind: Ein Elternreport* (Berlin: Volk und Gesundheit, 1981), 91.

41. Dagmar Büssow, "Aus einem Tagebuch," *Courage* 5 (January 1980): 22.

42. Sigrid Arnade, *Weder Küsse noch Karriere: Erfahrungen behinderter Frauen* (Frankfurt: Fischer, 1992), 73.

43. Ulrike Gottschalk, "'Sie haben Probleme mit Macht': Therapieerfahrungen aus 40 Jahren," in *Behindertenfeindlichkeit: Ausgrenzungen und Vereinnahmungen,* ed. Birgit Rommelspacher (Göttingen: Lamuv, 1999), 104.

44. For a U.S. anthology that focuses on staring, see Kenny Fries, ed., *Staring Back: The Disability Experience from the Inside Out* (New York: Plume, 1997).

45. Primo Levi, *Survival in Auschwitz* (New York: Touchstone, 1996), 105–6.

46. Udo Sierck and Didi Danquart, eds., *Der Pannwitzblick: Wie Gewalt gegen Behinderte entsteht* (Hamburg: Verlag Libertäre Assoziation, 1993), 7. Subsequent page references are given in the body of the text.

47. Nati Radtke and Udo Sierck, "Lieber lebendig als normal!" in *Sie nennen es Fürsorge: Behinderte zwischen Vernichtung und Widerstand,* ed. Michael Wunder and Udo Sierck (Berlin: Verlagsgesellschaft Gesundheit, 1982), 149. See also the article in this book by Udo Sierck, "Die Entwicklung der Krüppelgruppen," 151ff.; and Horst Frehe, "Konfrontation oder Integration," *Forum für Medizin und Gesundheitspolitik* 18 (February 1982): 7–21.

48. Sigrid Arnade et al., eds., *Die Gesellschaft der Behinderer: Das Buch zur Aktion Grundgesetz* (Reinbek: Rowohlt, 1997), 15.

49. Hans-Günter Heiden, ed., *"Niemand darf wegen seiner Behinderung*

benachteiligt werden": Grundrecht und Alltag—eine Bestandsaufnahme (Reinbek: Rowohlt, 1996), 49–50.

50. Klaus Dörner, ed., *Gestern minderwertig—heute gleichwertig?* (Gütersloh: Jakob van Hoddis, 1985); Die Grünen im Bundestag/Fraktion der Alternativen Liste Berlin, ed., *Anerkennung und Versorgung aller Opfer nationalsozialistischer Verfolgung* (Berlin: agit druck, 1986). The Green Party also strongly advocated inclusion of disabled people in all aspects of society in their first national program. See Die Grünen, *Bundesprogramm* (Bonn: Die Grünen, 1982).

51. Klara Nowak, "Verweigerte Anerkennung als NS-Verfolgte: Zwangssterilisierte und 'Euthanasie'-Geschädigte," in *Medizin und Gewissen: 50 Jahre nach dem Nürnberger Ärzteprozess,* ed. Stephan Kolb and Horst Seithe (Frankfurt: Mabuse, 1998), 163–68; Elisabeth Claasen [pseud.], *Ich, die Steri* (Rehburg: Psychiatrie-Verlag, 1985); "Erinnerungen von Josef Demetz," in *"Euthanasie": Krankenmorde in Südwestdeutschland,* ed. Hermann Pretsch (Zwiefalten: Verlag Psychiatrie und Geschichte, 1996), 110–14; *Ich klage an: Tatsachen- und Erlebnisberichte* (Detmold: Bund der "Euthanasie"-Geschädigten und Zwangssterilisierten, 1989).

52. Sabine Rieser, "Nationale Gedenkfeier für die Opfer der 'Aktion T4,'" *Deutsches Ärzteblatt,* March 2000.

53. Christoph Zuschlag, "Das Mahnmal als künstlerische Herausforderung," in *Psychiatrische Forschung und NS-"Euthanasie": Beiträge zu einer Gedenkveranstaltung an der Psychiatrischen Universitätsklinik Heidelberg,* ed. Christoph Mundt et al. (Heidelberg: Wunderhorn, 2001).

54. Bettina Winter, "Gedenkstätte Hadamar: Ort des Gedenkens und der historisch-politischen Bildung," in *"Verlegt nach Hadamar": Die Geschichte einer NS-"Euthanasie"-Anstalt,* ed. Landeswohlfahrtsverband Hessen (Kassel: Eigenverlag des LWV Hessen, 1991), 195.

55. On People First in Germany, see http://www.people1.de. On the Hadamar memorial, see http://www.gedenkstaette-hadamar.de.

56. Theresia Degener and Swantje Köbsell, *"Hauptsache, es ist gesund?" Weibliche Selbstbestimmung unter humangenetischer Kontrolle* (Hamburg: Konkret Literatur Verlag, 1992).

57. "Grafenecker Erklärung zur Bioethik," http://www.theo-physik.unikiel.de/~starrost/akens/texte/info/31/77.html.

58. The statistic of eight million disabled Germans is used by the Federal Commissioner for Disability Affairs (Behindertenbeauftragter).

59. Volker Ludwig and Roy Kift, *Stärker als Superman,* unpublished theater script, 1. Subsequent page reference is given in the body of the text.

60. Monika Aly et al., *Kopfkorrektur oder der Zwang gesund zu sein: Ein behindertes Kind zwischen Therapie und Alltag* (Berlin: Rotbuch, 1981), 150.

61. Lothar Sandfort, "Medien-Manifest: Forderungen Behinderter an die Medien," in *Massenmedien und Behinderte: Im besten Falle Mitleid?* ed. H. Jürgen Kagelmann and Rosmarie Zimmermann (Weinheim: Beltz, 1982), 207ff.

62. http://www.enthinderungen.de.

63. A report on the "Kultur für Alle" conference was accessed on the Web site www.kobinet-nachrichten.org on May 12, 2005.

64. A report on the "Berlin durch die Hintertür" exhibition can be found at www.fdst.de.

65. http://www.selbsthilfe-online.de/laediert/andersartig/.

66. http://www.selbsthilfe-online.de/laediert/foto.

67. http://members.aol.com/tanuschka/entART/.

68. http://www.selbsthilfe-online.de/laediert/foto.

69. http://www.selbsthilfe-online.de/laediert/andersartig/heino/dance.htm.

70. Petra Kuppers, *Disability and Contemporary Performance: Bodies on Edge* (New York: Routledge, 2003), 61.

71. The information in this paragraph is taken from: http://www.theater-rambazamba.org.

72. Klaus Erforth, "Wir sind da. Wir sind immer da: 'Die Freiheit, ein Fehler zu sein,'" in *In einem reichen Land: Zeugnisse alltäglichen Leidens an der Gesellschaft,* ed. Günter Grass et al. (Göttingen: Steidl, 2002), 330.

73. Information here about the Arbeitsgemeinschaft Behinderte in den Medien is from: http://www.abm-medien.de.

74. http://www.kobinet-nachrichten.org, accessed June 7, 2005.

75. *Berliner Zeitung,* January 31, 2000, quoted on the RambaZamba Web site: http://www.theater-rambazamba.org.

76. http://www.imperfekt.de is the Web site of the exhibition. The exhibition was preceded by a photography exhibition compiled in the book *Bilder, die noch fehlten: Zeitgenössische Fotografie* (Ostfilden-Ruit: Hatje Cantz, 2000). The exhibition catalog is *Der (im)perfekte Mensch: Vom Recht auf Unvollkommenheit* (Ostfilden-Ruit: Hatje Cantz, 2001). See also Carol Poore, "'The (Im)Perfect Human Being' and the Beginning of Disability Studies in Germany: A Report," *New German Critique* 86 (spring-summer 2002): 179–90.

77. *Der Tagesspiegel,* March 10, 2002.

78. Thomas Macho, "Freaks in den Zeiten von Baywatch," *Frankfurter Rundschau,* July 6, 2001; Miriam Lau, "Terror der Normalität: Ist ein Leben ohne Arme armes Leben?" *Die Welt,* July 9, 2001; Andreas Schäfer, "Leiden und Lebenssinn," *Berliner Zeitung,* March 15, 2002.

79. Jens Bisky, "Auf dem Behindertenspielplatz," *Berliner Zeitung,* December 27, 2000.

80. Most of the lectures given at these two conferences were published in Petra Lutz et al., eds., *Der (Im-)Perfekte Mensch: Metamorphosen von Normalität und Abweichung* (Cologne: Böhlau, 2003).

81. Christian Holtorf, "'Der (im)perfekte Mensch': Behinderung als Thema der amerikanischen Kulturwissenschaften," *Die Zeit,* June 21, 2001.

82. Anja Tervooren, "Den Diskurs anreizen," *Tagesspiegel,* March 10, 2002.

83. Martina Meister, "Der Terror der Normalität," *Frankfurter Rundschau,* July 9, 2001.

84. Gisela Hermes and Swantje Köbsell, eds., *Disability Studies in Deutschland: Behinderung neu denken! Dokumentation der Sommeruni 2003* (Kassel: bifos, 2003).

85. For the proceedings of this conference, see Anne Waldschmidt, ed., *Kulturwissenschaftliche Perspektiven der Disability Studies* (Kassel: bifos, 2003). See also Gisela Hermes and Eckhard Rohrmann, eds. *"Nichts über uns—ohne uns!" Disability Studies als neuer Ansatz emanzipatorischer*

und interdisziplinärer Forschung über Behinderung (Neu-Ulm: AG-SPAK, 2006); and "Focus on Disability Studies in German-Speaking Countries," *Disability Studies Quarterly* 26:2 (spring 2006).

86. Sigrid Graumann et al., eds., *Ethik und Behinderung: Ein Perspektivenwechsel* (New York: Campus, 2004).

87. http://www.hrf.uni-koeln.de/de/sozbeh/content/540.htm is the Web site of the Cologne International Research Institute of Disability Studies in Germany; it contains links to other disability studies Web sites in Germany.

88. Miles-Paul, *"Wir sind nicht mehr aufzuhalten."*

CHAPTER 8

1. http://www.1000fragen.de.

2. http://www.uic.edu/orgs/uicsymrg/uicsymrg/Biocenter.

3. Heike Zirden, ed., *Was wollen wir, wenn alles möglich ist? Fragen zur Bioethik* (Munich: Deutsche Verlags-Anstalt, 2003), 12.

4. Ronald Dworkin, "Die falsche Angst, Gott zu spielen," *Zeit dokument* 2 (1999): 39.

5. Michael Wunder explains these changes in German abortion law in "Bioethik: Eine Philosophie ohne Menschlichkeit," in *Medizin und Gewissen: 50 Jahre nach dem Nürnberger Ärzteprozess,* ed. Stephan Kolb and Horst Seithe (Frankfurt: Mabuse, 1998), 313–19. See also Hans Schuh, "Streit ums frühe Leben: Abtreibungspraxis und Embryonenschutz stehen in eklatantem Widerspruch zueinander," *Die Zeit,* January 7, 1990, 23–25.

6. Justin J. W. Powell, "Hochbegabt, behindert oder normal? Klassifikationssysteme des sonderpädagogischen Förderbedarfs in Deutschland und den Vereinigten Staaten," in *Wie man behindert wird: Texte zur Konstruktion einer sozialen Rolle und zur Lebenssituation betroffener Menschen,* ed. Günther Cloerkes (Heidelberg: Winter, 2003), 116, 119.

7. "Reine Rasse," *Der Spiegel,* July 16, 2001, 128.

8. Martin Pernick, *The Black Stork: Eugenics and the Death of "Defective" Babies in American Medicine and Motion Pictures since 1915* (New York: Oxford University Press, 1996), 172. Subsequent page references are given in the body of the text.

9. "Zucht und deutsche Ordnung," *Der Spiegel,* September 27, 1999, 316.

10. Ulrich Bahnsen, "'Wunderbare Kräfte': Mark Hughes hat ein Retortenbaby erzeugt—es soll dem kranken Bruder Knochenmark spenden," *Die Zeit,* September 21, 2000, 42.

11. Peter Singer, "On Being Silenced in Germany," *New York Review of Books,* August 15, 1991, 36–52. For a more recent statement about Germany by Singer, see Peter Singer, "Euthanasia: Emerging from Hitler's Shadow," in *Writings on an Ethical Life* (New York: Ecco Press, 2000), 201–8. For a collection of documents about the protests against Singer, see Christoph Anstötz et al., eds., *Peter Singer in Deutschland: Zur Gefährdung der Diskussionsfreiheit in der Wissenschaft. Eine kommentierte Dokumentation* (New York: Lang, 1995).

12. http://www.kobinet-nachrichten.org, accessed December 13, 2004.

13. "Zucht und deutsche Ordnung," 314.

14. Ernst Tugendhat, "Auch ein Recht zum Sterben: In der Debatte um

die Thesen Peter Singers spiegeln sich immer noch verdrängte Schuldgefühle," *Die Zeit,* October 25, 1991, 17.

15. Some of the most important books about this debate are Till Bastian, ed., *Denken—schreiben—töten: Zur neuen "Euthanasie"-Diskussion und zur Philosophie Peter Singers* (Stuttgart: Hirzel, 1990); Udo Benzenhöfer, *Der gute Tod? Euthanasie und Sterbehilfe in Geschichte und Gegenwart* (Munich: Beck, 1999); Werner Brill, *Pädagogik im Spannungsfeld von Eugenik und Euthanasie. Die "Euthanasie"-Diskussion in der Weimarer Republik und zu Beginn der neunziger Jahre: Ein Beitrag zur Faschismusforschung und zur Historiographie der Behindertenpädagogik* (St. Ingbert: Röhrig, 1994); Alexander Bogner, *Bioethik und Rassismus: Neugeborene und Koma-Patienten in der deutschen Euthanasie-Debatte* (Hamburg: Argument, 2000); Franz Christoph, *Tödlicher Zeitgeist: Notwehr gegen Euthanasie* (Cologne: Kiepenheuer und Witsch, 1990); Klaus Dörner, *Tödliches Mitleid: Zur Frage der Unerträglichkeit des Lebens* (Gütersloh: Verlag Jakob van Hoddis, 1988); Rainer Hegselmann and Reinhard Merkel, eds., *Zur Debatte über Euthanasie: Beiträge und Stellungnahmen* (Frankfurt: Suhrkamp, 1991); and Oliver Tolmein, *Geschätztes Leben: Die neue Euthanasie-Debatte* (Hamburg: Konkret, 1990).

16. http://www.forum-bioethik.de/BioethikN1_3.html.

17. For the statement of the National Council on Disability, see http://www.ncd.gov/newsroom/testimony/ncd_4–17–99.html. For the statement of Princeton Students against Infanticide, see http://www.geocities.com/Athens/Agora/2900/psai3.html. For the statement of the Princeton administration, see http://www.euthanasia.com/prince.html.

18. Richard Just and Emma Soichet, "Protests Mark First Class Day for Princeton Bioethics Prof," *Daily Princetonian,* September 23, 1999.

19. Disability Rights Education and Defense Fund (DREDF), "Against the Philosophy of Peter Singer," http://www.thearclink.org/news/article.asp?ID=426.

20. Harriet McBryde Johnson, "Unspeakable Conversations; or, How I Spent One Day as a Token Cripple at Princeton University," *New York Times Magazine,* February 16, 2003, 79.

21. "Zucht und deutsche Ordnung," 316.

22. "Nicht alles Leben ist heilig," *Der Spiegel,* November 26, 2001, 237.

23. See the following writings by Klaus Dörner: "Zur Professionalisierung der sozialen Frage," in *Denken—schreiben—töten: Zur neuen "Euthanasie"-Diskussion und zur Philosophie Peter Singers,* ed. Till Bastian (Stuttgart: Hirzel, 1990), 23–36; "Geschichte und Kritik des Tötens als 'Erlösen,'" *Behindertenpädagogik* 29:1 (1990): 51–55; and *Tödliches Mitleid.* For Singer's Darwinian views, see Peter Singer, *A Darwinian Left* (New Haven: Yale University Press, 2000).

24. Dörner, "Zur Professionalisierung der sozialen Frage," 33.

25. Klaus Dörner, "Nationalsozialismus und Medizin—wurden die Lehren gezogen?" in *NS-Euthanasie in Wien,* ed. Eberhard Gabriel and Wolfgang Neugebauer (Vienna: Böhlau, 2000), 131–36.

26. Ibid., 134.

27. Gusti Steiner, interview with the author, Dortmund, summer 2001.

28. Peter Sloterdijk, "Regeln für den Menschenpark: Ein Antwortschreiben zum Brief über den Humanismus—die Elmauer Rede," *Zeit dokument* 2 (1999): 4–15.

29. A selection of responses to Sloterdijk from the German press is reprinted in *Zeit dokument* 2 (1999). See also Andrew Piper, "Projekt Übermensch: German Intellectuals Confront Genetic Engineering," *Lingua Franca,* December-January 2000, 74–77. For more comprehensive discussions of these issues, see Christian Geyer, ed., *Biopolitik. Die Positionen* (Frankfurt: Suhrkamp, 2001); and Ellen Kuhlmann and Regine Kollek, eds., *Konfigurationen des Menschen: Biowissenschaften als Arena der Geschlechterpolitik* (Opladen: Leske und Budrich, 2002). For a good summary of the opinions of various self-advocacy organizations of disabled people, see Anita Hönninger, "Die Bedeutung der humangenetischen Beratung und Pränataldiagnostik für Behindertenverbände und die Behindertenbewegung," *Behindertenpädagogik* 39:4 (2000): 390–405.

30. See also "Klon der Angst: Der Segen der Gen-Technik—Ein Gespräch mit dem Wissenschaftler Gregory Stock," *Süddeutsche Zeitung,* April 4, 1998.

31. Sloterdijk, "Regeln für den Menschenpark," 14–15.

32. For the text of Sloterdijk's speech, see the conference Web site http://www.goethe.de/uk/los/symp/enabout.htm.

33. Reinhard Mohr, "Züchter des Übermenschen," *Zeit dokument* 2 (1999): 20.

34. Thomas Assheuer, "Was ist deutsch? Sloterdijk und die geistigen Grundlagen der Republik," *Zeit dokument* 2 (1999): 58–59.

35. Diane Paul, "Genetic Engineering and Eugenics: The Uses of History," *Proceedings of the Pittsburgh Workshop in History and Philosophy of Biology,* available at http://philsci-archive.pitt.edu/archive/00000852/00Chapter_1.pdf.

36. Christiane Peitz, "Eine Plastikrose für Marilyn Monroe: Künstliche Welten, fröhliche Wissenschaft, und ein deutscher Philosoph. Peter Sloterdijk auf einem Symposium über Gentechnik in Los Angeles," *Berliner Tagesspiegel,* May 28, 2000.

37. Jürgen Habermas, *Die Zukunft der menschlichen Natur: Auf dem Weg zu einer liberalen Eugenik?* (Frankfurt: Suhrkamp, 2001), 43. Subsequent page references are given in the body of the text.

38. See Tobin Siebers, "What Can Disability Studies Learn from the Culture Wars?" *Cultural Critique* 5 (2003): 182–216.

39. Ernst Klee, *Behindert: Ein kritisches Handbuch* (Frankfurt: Fischer, 1980), 239.

40. Netzwerk Artikel 3, *Dokumentation von Diskriminierungsfällen für ein zivilrechtliches Antidiskriminierungsgesetz* (Kassel: Netzwerk Artikel 3, 2003). Available through the Web site of Netzwerk Artikel 3, the organization that is coordinating the campaign to have disabled people included in the antidiscrimination law: http://www.nw3.de/zag.

41. "Bremer Erklärung für Antidiskriminierungsgesetz," *Kobinet-Nachrichten,* July 28, 2003, available at http://kobinet-nachrichten.org/2003/07/2110.php.

42. "Theresia Degener mahnt Antidiskriminierungsgesetz an," *Kobinet-Nachrichten,* July 22, 2003, available at http://kobinet-nachrichten.org/2003/07/2063.php.

43. Statement made in the film *Gleich, frei und selbstbewusst: Was eine USA-Reise für Behinderte verändert hat,* directed by Oliver Tolmein and shown on the German television network NDR on June 19, 1994.

44. Oliver Tolmein, "Empowerment oder warum stärken wir uns nicht selbst," in *Traumland USA? Zwischen Antidiskriminierung und sozialer Armut,* ed. Gisela Hermes (Kassel: bifos, 1998), 13. Similar statements may be found in the film *Gleich, frei und selbstbewusst.*

45. Katja Dettmering, "Behinderung und Anerkennung," in *Behindertenfeindlichkeit,* ed. Birgit Rommelspacher (Göttingen: Lamuv, 1999), 179.

46. Ulrike Rittner, "Freizeit und Erholung für ALLE Menschen," in *Traumland USA? Zwischen Antidiskriminierung und sozialer Armut,* ed. Gisela Hermes (Kassel: bifos, 1998), 82.

47. Theresia Degener in the film *Gleich, frei und selbstbewusst.*

48. Gisela Hermes, "Vorwort," in *Traumland USA? Zwischen Antidiskriminierung und sozialer Armut,* ed. Gisela Hermes (Kassel: bifos, 1998), 5.

49. See Garland E. Allen, "Genetics, Eugenics, and the Medicalization of Social Behavior: Lessons from the Past," *Endeavour* 23:1 (1999): 10–19.

50. Dörner, "Nationalsozialismus und Medizin," 135–36.

CHAPTER 9

1. Tony Gould, *A Summer Plague: Polio and Its Survivors* (New Haven: Yale University Press, 1995), 77–81, 189–91.

2. Petra Fuchs, *"Körperbehinderte" zwischen Selbstaufgabe und Emanzipation* (Neuwied: Luchterhand, 2001), 14; Douglas C. Baynton, "Disability and the Justification of Inequality in American History," in *The New Disability History: American Perspectives,* ed. Paul Longmore and Lauri Umansky (New York: New York University Press, 2001), 133–57.

3. See Karen Hirsch, "Culture and Disability: The Role of Oral History," *Journal of the Oral History Association* 22:1 (1995): 1–27; G. Thomas Couser, *Recovering Bodies: Illness, Disability, and Life-Writing* (Madison: University of Wisconsin Press, 1997); G. Thomas Couser, "The Empire of the 'Normal': A Forum on Disability and Self-Representation— Introduction," *American Quarterly* 52:2 (2000): 305–10, as well as the other articles on this topic in this issue; and all the articles under the heading "Autobiographical Subjects" in Sharon L. Snyder et al., eds., *Disability Studies: Enabling the Humanities* (New York: Modern Language Association, 2002), 109–72.

4. David Mitchell, "Body Solitaire: The Singular Subject of Disability Autobiography," *American Quarterly* 52:2 (2000): 3–11.

5. Of course, there are now many travel agencies in Germany, the United States, and many other countries that specialize in offering accessible travel opportunities to people with disabilities. It is becoming much more common for disabled people to travel, and their reflections on their experiences would be a valuable source of material for cross-cultural comparisons.

6. As examples of such reflections by disabled scholars on their presence within the university, see Irving Zola, *Missing Pieces: A Chronicle of Living with a Disability* (Philadelphia: Temple University Press, 1982); Robert Murphy, *The Body Silent* (New York: Holt, 1989); Georgina Kleege, *Sight Unseen* (New Haven: Yale University Press, 1999); David T. Mitchell

and Sharon L. Snyder, *Narrative Prosthesis: Disability and the Dependencies of Discourse* (Ann Arbor: University of Michigan Press, 2000), ix–xvii; Mary G. Mason, *Life Prints: A Memoir of Healing and Discovery* (New York: Feminist Press, 2000); all the articles under the heading "Enabling Pedagogy" in *Disability Studies: Enabling the Humanities,* ed. Sharon L. Snyder et al. (New York: Modern Language Association, 2002), 283–336; Tanya Titchkosky, *Disability, Self, and Society* (Toronto: University of Toronto Press, 2003); and Simi Linton, *My Body Politic* (Ann Arbor: University of Michigan Press, 2006). For more recent discussions of this topic in Germany, which took place at the Bremer Sommeruniversität "Disability Studies," see www.sommeruni2003.de.

7. Murphy's *The Body Silent* is a particularly interesting case of an autoethnography written by a disabled person for Murphy was an anthropology professor at Columbia University who became disabled as a middle-aged man. Noticing that many people treated him differently after he became disabled, he used his knowledge of anthropological field research to analyze their reactions to him.

8. Calvin Trillin, *An Education in Georgia: Charlayne Hunter, Hamilton Holmes, and the Integration of the University of Georgia* (Athens: University of Georgia Press: 1991); Charlayne Hunter-Gault, *In My Place* (New York: Farrar Straus, 1992).

9. Letters from Dr. T. G. Peacock, Superintendent of the Milledgeville State Hospital and Chairman of the Georgia State Board of Eugenics, to Charles L. Poore, November 7 and 18, 1952, archive of the author. On conditions in this hospital in the early 1950s, see Peter Cranford, *But for the Grace of God: The Story of the World's Largest Insane Asylum, Milledgeville* (Augusta, GA: Great Pyramid Press, 1981).

10. Jost Hermand recounts his experiences in the Hitler Youth as a highly intelligent yet delicate boy with a speech impediment in *Als Pimpf in Polen: Die erweiterte Kinderlandverschickung, 1940–1945* (Frankfurt: Fischer, 1993), translated as *A Hitler Youth in Poland: The Nazis' Program for Evacuating Children during World War II* (Evanston, IL: Northwestern University Press, 1997). For his experiences after coming to the United States in 1958, see his *Zuhause und anderswo: Erfahrungen im Kalten Krieg* (Cologne: Böhlau, 2001).

11. Jost Hermand, *Sieben Arten an Deutschland zu leiden* (Königstein/Ts.: Athenäum, 1979).

12. "Warum schlägt ein Krüppel den Bundespräsidenten?" Leaflet, archive of the author.

13. Jürgen Habermas has written movingly about the significance of his cleft palate and speech impediment for his life and work in the essay "Öffentlicher Raum und politische Öffentlichkeit: Lebensgeschichtliche Wurzeln von zwei Gedankenmotiven," published in his *Zwischen Naturalismus und Religion* (Frankfurt: Suhrkamp, 2005), 15–26.

14. Within the disability rights movement in both the United States and the FRG, it is striking that often the most effective, outspoken activists have been people with quite severe disabilities.

15. Simi Linton, *Claiming Disability: Knowledge and Identity* (New York: New York University Press, 1998).

16. For an essay that reflects on some of the mechanisms of exclusion I

have been describing from the perspectives of race, gender, and sexual orientation, see Ngozi O. Ola, "A Yoruba American in Germany," in *MultiAmerica: Essays on Cultural Wars and Cultural Peace,* ed. Ishmael Reed (New York: Viking, 1997), 25–30. Ola describes how she was stared at in Berlin because of her race: "I am in Berlin, where after five years it still appalls me to receive rude, penetrating stares from strangers. In New York, where I was not born but raised, a stare is simply asking for trouble. . . . A typical day in Berlin for me means being constantly subject to intrusive stares" (26). Yet in other respects she experiences Berlin as more democratic than New York, and she concludes, "I like Berlin. . . . I can see an interracial couple, a homosexual couple, an interracial homosexual couple and smile because they can walk the streets, hold hands, and exchange a kiss without receiving derisive remarks or cringes from the rest of the world. Yes, I like Berlin. And even with its minuses I'm grateful that it's not New York" (30).

17. On the intersections of discourses about obesity and disability, see Sander Gilman, "The Fat Detective: Obesity and Disability," in *Disability Studies: Enabling the Humanities,* ed. Sharon L. Snyder et al. (New York: Modern Language Association, 2002), 271–82.

18. Quoted in C. K. Williams, "Das symbolische Volk der Täter," *Die Zeit,* November 7, 2002, 37.

19. On staring, see Rosemarie Garland-Thomson, "Seeing the Disabled: Visual Rhetorics of Disability in Popular Photography," in *The New Disability History: American Perspectives,* ed. Paul Longmore and Lauri Umansky (New York: New York University Press, 2001), 335–74. Thomson is currently writing a book about staring.

20. Mitchell and Snyder, *Narrative Prosthesis.*

21. Erving Goffman, *Stigma: Notes on the Management of Spoiled Identity* (Englewood Cliffs, NJ: Prentice-Hall, 1963).

22. Weiszäcker's statement was published in the *Frankfurter Rundschau,* July 20, 1993.

23. See Anne Waldschmidt, *Selbstbestimmung als Konstruktion: Alltagstheorien behinderter Männer und Frauen* (Opladen: Leske und Budrich, 1999); and Anne Waldschmidt, "Selbstbestimmung als behindertenpolitisches Paradigma: Perspektiven der Disability Studies," *Aus Politik und Zeitgeschichte* B8 (February 17, 2003): 13–20.

24. "Who's Teaching Our Children with Disabilities?" http://www.kidsource.com/kidsourcecontent4/Spec_Ed/Spec_Ed5.html.

25. Hans Eberwein, "Es ist normal, verschieden zu sein: Was ist aus dem Ziel des gemeinsamen Lernens geworden?" *Der Tagesspiegel* (Berlin), February 27, 2003. Quoted on http://www.netzwerk-artikel-3.de/netzinfo02–03/032.php.

26. *National Organization on Disability/Harris 2000 Survey of Americans with Disabilities,* quoted on http://www.nod.org/content.cfm?id=134.

27. Bundesministerium für Arbeit und Sozialordnung, *Vierter Bericht der Bundesregierung über die Lage der Behinderten und die Entwicklung der Rehabilitation* (Bonn: Bonner Universitäts-Buchdruckerei, 1998), 69.

28. Emily Martin, *Flexible Bodies: Tracking Immunity in American Culture from the Days of Polio to the Age of AIDS* (Boston: Beacon, 1994).

29. Waldschmidt, *Selbstbestimmung als Konstruktion,* 43–44.

30. Quoted in Robert McRuer, "Critical Investments: AIDS, Christopher Reeve, and Queer/Disability Studies," in *Thinking the Limits of the Body,* ed. Jeffrey Jerome Cohen and Gail Weiss (Albany: State University of New York Press, 2003), 160.

31. Robert McRuer and Abby L. Wilkerson, "Introduction," *GLQ: Desiring Disability: Queer Theory Meets Disability Studies* 9:1–2 (2003): 4.

Selected Bibliography

This list contains some of the most important references about disability in twentieth-century German culture as suggestions for further reading. For more specific sources, see the notes to the individual chapters.

Albert, Wolfgang. *Lösung des Schwerbeschädigtenproblems durch Arbeit.* Berlin: Duncker und Humblot, 1956.

Aly, Götz, et al., eds. *Reform und Gewissen: "Euthanasie" im Dienst des Fortschritts.* Berlin: Rotbuch, 1985.

Aly, Monika, and Götz Aly. *Kopfkorrektur oder der Zwang gesund zu sein.* Berlin: Rotbuch, 1981.

Anz, Thomas. *Gesund oder krank? Medizin, Moral, und Ästhetik in der deutschen Gegenwartsliteratur.* Stuttgart: Metzler, 1989.

Arnade, Sigrid. *Weder Küsse noch Karriere: Erfahrungen behinderter Frauen.* Frankfurt: Fischer, 1992.

Arnade, Sigrid, et al., eds. *Die Gesellschaft der Behinderer: Das Buch zur Aktion Grundgesetz.* Reinbek: Rowohlt, 1997.

Barron, Stephanie, ed. *"Degenerate Art": The Fate of the Avant-Garde in Nazi Germany.* New York: Abrams, 1991.

Beck, Christoph. *Sozialdarwinismus, Rassenhygiene, Zwangssterilisation, und Vernichtung "lebensunwerten" Lebens: Eine Bibliographie zum Umgang mit behinderten Menschen im "Dritten Reich"—und heute.* Bonn: Psychiatrie-Verlag, 1995.

Benzenhöfer, Udo. *Der gute Tod? Euthanasie und Sterbehilfe in Geschichte und Gegenwart.* Munich: Beck, 1999.

Benzenhöfer, Udo, and Wolfgang Eckart, eds. *Medizin im Spielfilm des Nationalsozialismus.* Tecklenburg: Burgverlag, 1990.

Bernsmeier, Helmut. *Das Bild des Behinderten in der deutschsprachigen Literatur des 19. und 20. Jahrhunderts.* Bern: Lang, 1980.

Biesold, Horst. *Crying Hands: Eugenics and Deaf People in Nazi Germany.* Trans. William Sayers. Washington, DC: Gallaudet University Press, 1999.

Bleidick, Ulrich, and Sieglind Ellger-Rüttgardt, eds. *Behindertenpädagogik im vereinten Deutschland: Über die Schwierigkeiten eines Zwiegesprächs zwischen Ost und West.* Weinheim: Deutscher Studien Verlag, 1994.

Bock, Gisela. *Zwangssterilisation im Nationalsozialismus: Studien zur Rassenpolitik und Frauenpolitik.* Opladen: Westdeutscher Verlag, 1986.

Buch, Andrea, et al., eds. *An den Rand gedrängt: Was Behinderte daran hindert, normal zu leben.* Reinbek: Rowohlt, 1980.

Burleigh, Michael. *Death and Deliverance: "Euthanasia" in Germany, 1900–1945.* Cambridge: Cambridge University Press, 1994.

Christoph, Franz. *Krüppelschläge: Gegen die Gewalt der Menschlichkeit.* Reinbek: Rowohlt, 1983.

Cloerkes, Günther. *Einstellung und Verhalten gegenüber Körperbehinderten.* Berlin: Marhold, 1979.

Cloerkes, Günther, ed. *Wie man behindert wird: Texte zur Konstruktion einer sozialen Rolle und zur Lebenssituation betroffener Menschen.* Heidelberg: Winter, 2003.

Daniels, Susanne von, et al., eds. *Krüppel-Tribunal: Menschenrechtsverletzungen im Sozialstaat.* Cologne: Pahl-Rugenstein, 1983.

Degener, Theresia, and Swantje Köbsell. *"Hauptsache, es ist gesund?" Weibliche Selbstbestimmung unter humangenetischer Kontrolle.* Hamburg: Konkret Literatur Verlag, 1992.

Deutsches Hygiene-Museum and Aktion Mensch, eds. *Der (im)perfekte Mensch: Vom Recht auf Unvollkommenheit.* Ostfildern-Ruit: Hatje Cantz, 2001.

Diehl, James. *The Thanks of the Fatherland: German Veterans after the Second World War.* Chapel Hill: University of North Carolina Press, 1993.

Disability Studies Quarterly 26:2 (spring 2006). Special issue, "Focus on Disability Studies in the German-Speaking Countries."

Dörner, Klaus. *Gestern minderwertig—heute gleichwertig?* Gütersloh: Jakob van Hoddis, 1985.

Dörner, Klaus. *Tödliches Mitleid: Zur Frage der Unerträglichkeit des Lebens.* Gütersloh: Jakob van Hoddis, 1988.

Ebbinghaus, Angelika, and Klaus Dörner, eds. *Vernichten und Heilen: Der Nürnberger Ärzteprozess und seine Folgen.* Berlin: Aufbau, 2001.

Eiermann, Nicole, et al. *LIVE: Leben und Interessen Vertreten—Frauen mit Behinderung.* Stuttgart: Kohlhammer, 1999.

Ewinkel, Carola, et al., eds. *Geschlecht: behindert, Besonderes Merkmal: Frau—Ein Buch von behinderten Frauen.* Munich: AG SPAK, 1985.

Fandrey, Walter. *Krüppel, Idioten, Irre: Zur Sozialgeschichte behinderter Menschen in Deutschland.* Stuttgart: Silberburg, 1990.

Faulstich, Heinz. *Hungersterben in der Psychiatrie, 1914–1949.* Freiburg: Lambertus, 1998.

fib. e.V., ed. *Ende der Verwahrung?! Perspektiven geistig behinderter Menschen zum selbständigen Leben.* Munich: AG SPAK, 1991.

Fineman, Mia. "Ecce Homo Prostheticus." *New German Critique* 76 (winter 1999): 85–114.

Friedlander, Henry. *The Origins of Nazi Genocide: From Euthanasia to the Final Solution.* Chapel Hill: University of North Carolina Press, 1995.

Fuchs, Petra. *"Körperbehinderte" zwischen Selbstaufgabe und Emanzipation.* Neuwied: Luchterhand, 2001.

Fühmann, Franz, and Dietmar Riemann. *Was für eine Insel in was für einem Meer: Leben mit geistig Behinderten.* Rostock: Hinstorff, 1988.

Gerber, David, ed. *Disabled Veterans in History.* Ann Arbor: University of Michigan Press, 2000.

Geyer, Christian, ed. *Biopolitik: Die Positionen.* Frankfurt: Suhrkamp, 2001.

Gilman, Sander. *Seeing the Insane.* Lincoln: University of Nebraska Press, 1996.

Graumann, Sigrid, et al., eds. *Ethik und Behinderung: Ein Perspektiven-wechsel.* New York: Campus, 2004.

Habermas, Jürgen. *Die Zukunft der menschlichen Natur: Auf dem Weg zu einer liberalen Eugenik?* Frankfurt: Suhrkamp, 2001.

Hamann, Matthias, and Hans Asbek, eds. *Halbierte Vernunft und totale Medizin: Zu Grundlagen, Realgeschichte und Fortwirkungen der Psychiatrie im Nationalsozialismus.* Berlin: Schwarze Risse, 1997.

Hamilton, Elizabeth. "Disabling Discourses in German Literature from Lessing to Grass." PhD diss., Ohio State University, 1998.

Hanrath, Sabine. *Zwischen "Euthanasie" und Psychiatriereform: Anstalts-psychiatrie in Westfalen und Brandenburg—Ein deutsch-deutscher Vergleich, 1945–1964.* Paderborn: Schöningh, 2002.

Hegselmann, Rainer, and Reinhard Merkel, eds. *Zur Debatte über Euthanasie: Beiträge und Stellungnahmen.* Frankfurt: Suhrkamp, 1991.

Heiden, Hans-Günter, ed. *"Niemand darf wegen seiner Behinderung benachteiligt werden": Grundrecht und Alltag—eine Bestandsaufnahme.* Reinbek: Rowohlt, 1996.

Hermes, Gisela, ed. *Traumland USA? Zwischen Antidiskriminierung und sozialer Armut.* Kassel: bifos, 1998.

Hermes, Gisela, and Swantje Köbsell, eds. *Disability Studies in Deutschland: Behinderung neu denken! Dokumentation der Sommeruni, 2003.* Kassel: bifos, 2003.

Hermes, Gisela, and Eckhard Rohrmann, eds. *"Nichts über uns—ohne uns!" Disability Studies als neuer Ansatz emanzipatorischer und interdisziplinärer Forschung über Behinderung.* Neu-Ulm: AG SPAK, 2006.

Herrfurth, Reinhold, and Autorenkollektiv. *Sozialintegration intellektuell geschädigter Jugendlicher und Erwachsener.* Berlin: Volk und Gesundheit, 1988.

Höck, Manfred. *Die Hilfsschule im Dritten Reich.* Berlin: Marhold, 1979.

Hohmann, Joachim. *Der "Euthanasie"-Prozess Dresden 1947: Eine zeitgeschichtliche Dokumentation.* New York: Lang, 1993.

Jaedicke, Martin, and Wolfgang Schmidt-Block, eds. *Blinde unterm Hakenkreuz.* Marburg: Deutscher Verein der Blinden und Sehbehinderten, 1991.

Jun, Gerda. *Kinder, die anders sind: Ein Elternreport.* Berlin: Volk und Gesundheit, 1981.

Kersting, Franz-Werner, ed. *Psychiatriereform als Gesellschaftsreform: Die Hypothek des Nationalsozialismus und der Aufbruch der sechziger Jahre.* Paderborn: Schöningh, 2003.

Klee, Ernst. *Behindert: Ein kritisches Handbuch.* Frankfurt: Fischer, 1980.

Klee, Ernst. *Behinderte im Urlaub? Das Frankfurter Urteil: Eine Dokumentation.* Frankfurt: Fischer, 1980.

Klee, Ernst. *Behinderten-Report.* 2 vols. Frankfurt: Fischer, 1974–80.

Klee, Ernst. *"Euthanasie" im NS-Staat.* Frankfurt: Fischer, 1985.

Klee, Ernst. *Was sie taten, was sie wurden: Ärzte, Juristen und andere Beteiligten am Kranken- oder Judenmord.* Frankfurt: Fischer, 1986.

Klee, Ernst, ed. *Behindertsein ist schön.* Düsseldorf: Patmos, 1974.

Klee, Ernst, ed. *Dokumente zur "Euthanasie."* Frankfurt: Fischer, 1985.

Kolb, Stephan, and Horst Seithe, eds. *Medizin und Gewissen: 50 Jahre nach dem Nürnberger Ärzteprozess.* Frankfurt: Mabuse, 1998.

Koonz, Claudia. *The Nazi Conscience.* Cambridge: Harvard University Press, 2003.

Kühl, Stefan. *The Nazi Connection: Eugenics, American Racism, and German National Socialism.* New York: Oxford, 1994.

Kuhlmann, Ellen, and Regine Kollek, eds. *Konfigurationen des Menschen: Biowissenschaften als Arena der Geschlechterpolitik.* Opladen: Leske und Budrich, 2002.

Lutz, Petra, et al., eds. *Der (im)perfekte Mensch: Metamorphosen von Normalität und Abweichung.* Cologne: Böhlau, 2003.

Mandel, Joachim. *Schwerbeschädigte: Betreut und gefördert.* Berlin: Staatsverlag der DDR, 1984.

Miles-Paul, Ottmar. *"Wir sind nicht mehr aufzuhalten": Behinderte auf dem Weg zur Selbstbestimmung.* Munich: AG SPAK, 1992.

Osten, Philipp. *Die Modellanstalt: Über den Aufbau einer "modernen Krüppelfürsorge," 1905–1933.* Frankfurt: Mabuse, 2004.

Perl, Otto. *Krüppeltum und Gesellschaft im Wandel der Zeit.* Gotha: Klotz, 1926.

Petzold, Heinz-Joachim. *Anerkennung statt Mitleid: Report über Körperbehinderte.* Rudolstadt: Greifenverlag, 1981.

Poore, Carol. "'But Roosevelt Could Walk': Envisioning Disability in Germany and the United States." In *Points of Contact: Disability, Art, and Culture,* ed. Susan Crutchfield and Marcy Epstein, 63–92. Ann Arbor: University of Michigan Press, 2000.

Poore, Carol. "Recovering Disability Rights in the Weimar Republic." *Radical History Review* 94 (winter 2006): 38–58.

Proctor, Robert. *Racial Hygiene: Medicine under the Nazis.* Cambridge: Harvard University Press, 1998.

Radtke, Peter. *Karriere mit 99 Brüchen: Vom Rollstuhl auf die Bühne.* Munich: Allitera Verlag, 2001.

Rommelspacher, Birgit, ed. *Behindertenfeindlichkeit: Ausgrenzungen und Vereinnahmungen.* Göttingen: Lamuv, 1999.

Rost, Ludwig. *Sterilisation und Euthanasie im Film des "Dritten Reiches."* Husum: Matthiesen, 1987.

Rudnick, Martin. *Aussondern—Sterilisieren—Liquidieren: Die Verfolgung Behinderter im Nationalsozialismus.* Berlin: Marhold, 1990.

Rudnick, Martin. *Behinderte im Nationalsozialismus.* Weinheim: Beltz, 1985.

Ryan, Donna, and John Schuchman. *Deaf People in Hitler's Europe.* Washington, DC: Gallaudet University Press, 2002.

Schmidt, Ulf. *Medical Films, Ethics, and Euthanasia in Nazi Germany.* Husum: Matthiesen, 2002.

Schrenk, Christhard. *Rudolf Kraemer: Ein Leben für die Blinden (1885–1945).* Heilbronn: Stadtarchiv Heilbronn, 2002.

Schwartz, Michael. *Sozialistische Eugenik: Eugenische Sozialtechnologien in Debatten und Politik der deutschen Sozialdemokratie, 1890–1933.* Bonn: Dietz, 1995.

Sierck, Udo, and Didi Danquart, eds. *Der Pannwitzblick: Wie Gewalt gegen Behinderte entsteht.* Hamburg: Verlag Libertäre Assoziation, 1993.

Steiner, Gusti, ed. *Hand- und Fußbuch für Behinderte.* Frankfurt; Fischer, 1988.

Süß, Winfried. *Der "Volkskörper" im Krieg: Gesundheitspolitik, Gesund-*

heitsverhältnisse, und Krankenmord im nationalsozialistischen Deutsch-land, 1939–1945. Munich: Oldenbourg, 2003.

Thomann, Klaus-Dieter. *Das behinderte Kind: "Krüppelfürsorge" und Orthopädie in Deutschland, 1886–1920.* Stuttgart: Gustav Fischer, 1995.

Thomann, Klaus-Dieter. "Der 'Krüppel': Entstehen und Verschwinden eines Kampfbegriffs," *Medizinhistorisches Journal* 27:3–4 (1992), 221–71.

Tolmein, Oliver. *Geschätztes Leben: Die neue Euthanasie-Debatte.* Hamburg: Konkret, 1990.

Unthan, Carl Herrmann. *Das Pediskript: Aufzeichnungen aus dem Leben eines Armlosen.* Stuttgart: Robert Lutz Verlag, 1925.

Waldschmidt, Anne. *Selbstbestimmung als Konstruktion: Alltagstheorien behinderter Männer und Frauen.* Opladen: Leske und Budrich, 1999.

Weindling, Paul. *Health, Race, and German Politics between National Unification and Nazism, 1870–1945.* Cambridge: Cambridge University Press, 1989.

Weingart, Peter, et al., *Rasse, Blut, und Gene: Geschichte der Eugenik und Rassenhygiene in Deutschland.* Frankfurt: Suhrkamp, 1988.

Whalen, Robert. *Bitter Wounds: German Victims of the Great War, 1914–1939.* Ithaca: Cornell University Press, 1984.

Wunder, Michael, and Udo Sierck, eds. *Sie nennen es Fürsorge: Behinderte zwischen Vernichtung und Widerstand.* Berlin: Verlagsgesellschaft Gesundheit, 1982.

Ziem, Helmut. *Der Beschädigte und Körperbehinderte im Daseinskampf einst und jetzt.* Berlin: Duncker und Humblot, 1956.

Zirden, Heike, ed. *Was wollen wir, wenn alles möglich ist? Fragen zur Bioethik.* Munich: Deutsche Verlags-Anstalt, 2003.

Index of Names